ease remember that this is a library book,
nd that it belongs only temporarily to each
person who uses it. Be considerate. Do
not write in this, or a WITHDRAWN

Psychology
An Introduction

Bruce K. Crockett

O.P.

Please remember that this is a library book,
and that it belongs only temporarily to each
person who uses it. Be considerate. Do
not write in this, or any, library book.

WITHDRAWN

Second Edition

Prentice-Hall, Inc., Englewood Cliffs, New Jersey

Bruce K. Crockett

Psychology
An Introduction

VERCOLL COLLEGE MONTREAL UNIV MEMORIAL LIBRARY

Charles G. Morris
University of Michigan

Library of Congress Cataloging in Publication Data

Morris, Charles G.
    Psychology: An Introduction.

    Bibliography: p. 633
    Includes indexes.
    1. Psychology. I. Title. [DNLM: 1. Psychology.
BF139 M875p]
BF121.M598   1976   150   75-32534
ISBN 0-13-733881-3

© 1976 by Prentice-Hall, Inc.
Englewood Cliffs, New Jersey

All rights reserved.
No part of this book may be reproduced
in any form or by any means
without permission in writing from the publisher.

Printed in the United States of America

10 9 8 7 6 5 4 3 2 1

PRENTICE-HALL INTERNATIONAL, INC., *London*
PRENTICE-HALL OF AUSTRALIA, PTY. LTD., *Sydney*
PRENTICE-HALL OF CANADA, LTD., *Toronto*
PRENTICE-HALL OF INDIA PRIVATE LIMITED, *New Delhi*
PRENTICE-HALL OF JAPAN, INC., *Tokyo*

Photo Research: Rosemary Eakins and Ann Novotny, Research Reports
Cover Photo: Richard Frieman, Rapho/Photo Researchers, Inc.

Text Acknowledgments

Grateful acknowledgment is made to the following sources for permission to reprint: Box, page 128: Excerpt abridged from pp. 20–23 in *Brave New World* by Aldous Huxley. © 1932, 1960, by Aldous Huxley. Reprinted by permission of Harper & Row, Publishers, Inc. Box, page 481: J. H. Masserman. *Principles of Dynamic Psychiatry.* Philadelphia: W. B. Saunders, 1946, p. 35. Box, page 483: H. P. Laughlin, *Mental Mechanisms.* New York: Appleton-Century-Crofts, 1963, p. 98. Box, page 484: H. P. Laughlin, *The Ego and Its Defenses.* New York: Appleton-Century-Crofts, 1970, p. 227. Courtesy of Appleton-Century-Crofts, Publishing Division of Prentice-Hall, Inc. Box, page 533: L. Hersher, Ed., *Four Psychotherapies.* New York: Appleton-Century-Crofts, 1970, pp. 64–66. Courtesy of Appleton-Century-Crofts, Publishing Division of Prentice-Hall, Inc. Box, page 541: From F. S. Perls, *Gestalt Therapy Verbatim.* Copyright 1969, Real People Press, Moab, Utah.

Photo Acknowledgments for Part and Chapter Openers

pp. xiv–1—Jan Lukas, Rapho/Photo Researchers; p. 3—Movie Star News; p. 31—Jim Jowers, Nancy Palmer Photo Agency; p. 73—John Oldenkamp; pp. 120–121—Joel Gordon; p. 123—Wayne Miller, Magnum Photos; p. 173—United Press International; p. 205—Burk Uzzle, Magnum Photos; p. 235—Wide World Photos; pp. 274–275—Bernard P. Wolff, Photo Researchers; p. 277—Mary M. Thacher, Photo Researchers; p. 311—Arthur Tress, Photo Researchers; pp. 354–355—Rhoda Galyn, Photo Researchers; p. 357—Culver Pictures; p. 389—Joel Gordon; pp. 420–421—Joel Gordon; p. 423—William J. Hampton, Photo Researchers; p. 465—Ylla, Rapho/Photo Researchers; p. 491—Ken Heyman; p. 527—Alex Webb, Magnum Photos; pp. 556–557—Robert E. Knopes, Nancy Palmer Photo Agency; p. 559—Sahm Doherty/Camera 5.

Contents

43184

150
M875p

ONE
Psychology: An Introduction   1

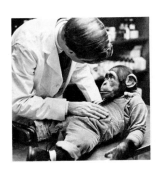

1 The Science of Psychology   2
The Goals of Psychology 4   The Growth of
Psychology 6   *Wundt and Titchener: Structuralism 6*
Sir Francis Galton: Individual Differences 8   William James:
Functionalism 9   John B. Watson: Behaviorism 10   Gestalt
Psychology 11   B. F. Skinner: S-R Psychology 12
Sigmund Freud: Psychoanalytic Psychology 13   Some New
Schools 14   Areas within Psychology Today 15
Methods of Psychology 18   *The Naturalistic-Observation*
Method 18   The Experimental Method 20   The Correlational
Method 21   Ethics in Psychology 23   The Social
Relevance of Psychology 24   *Pure versus Applied*
Psychology 24   Using Animals in Psychological Research 25
New Directions in Psychology 26   Summary 26
Suggested Readings 29

2 Biology and Behavior   30
Genetics 32   *Cell Mechanisms in Heredity 32   Biochemical*
Genetics 34   Behavior Genetics 35   *Sex-Linked*
Characteristics 36   Genetic Abnormalities 37   Polygenic
Inheritance 40   Genetics and Development 41   Social
Implications of Behavior Genetics 43   The Endocrine
System 44   The Nervous System 50   *The Neuron 50*
The Neural Impulse 51   The Synapse 52   Divisions of the
Nervous System 54   The Autonomic Nervous System 55
The Central Nervous System 56   Psychosurgery and Electrical
Stimulation of the Brain 65   Summary 67   Suggested
Readings 70

3 Development 72

The Newborn Baby 74 *Individual Differences 76*
Physical Growth 76 *Maturation 77 Developmental
Norms for Children 78 Physical Changes in
Adolescence 78* Motor Abilities 80 Perceptual
Development 83 *Visual Discrimination 83 Depth
Perception 84 Object Perception 85 Perceptual Set and
Whole-Part Perception 86 The Role of Experience 87*
Language Development 88 *A Brief Chronology 88
Theories of Language Development 89* Cognitive
Development 91 *Piaget's Approach 91 Bruner's
Approach 95* Personality Development 96
*Attachment 98 Autonomy 98 Imitation and
Identification 100 Peer Groups 103 Development of
Identity 103* The Transition to Adulthood 104 *Young
Adulthood 105* Adulthood 106 *Personality
Development 106 Milestones of Adult Development 107*
Old Age 111 *Physical Changes 111 Cognitive
Changes 112 "Successful" Aging 113* Death and
Dying 114 *Preparation for Dying 114 Dying 115*
Summary 115 Suggested Readings 118

TWO
Psychology and Cognitive Processes 120

4 Learning 122

Classical Conditioning 124 *Pavlov's Conditioning
Experiments 125 Classical Conditioning in Human
Beings 126 Necessary Factors in Classical
Conditioning 127 Extinction and Spontaneous
Recovery 129 Generalization 132 Discrimination 133
Higher-Order Conditioning 133* Operant
Conditioning 134 *Acquisition of the Response 136
Reinforcement 137 Generalization 143
Discrimination 143 Extinction and Spontaneous
Recovery 144 Shaping 146 Behavior Chains 147
Learning to Learn 147* New Viewpoints on
Learning 150 *The Cognitive Revolution 150 Social
Learning Theory 151 Biological Factors in Learning 154*
Applications of Learning Principles 156 *Autonomic
Conditioning and Biofeedback 156 Behavior Modification in
Education 158 Self-modification of Behavior 164*
Summary 166 Suggested Readings 170

5 Memory 172

Measuring Retention 174 *Recall 175*

Recognition *176*   Savings *176*   The Three Levels of
Memory   *178*   *The Sensory Store 180*   *Short-Term*
Memory 180   *Long-Term Memory 183*   Biological Bases of
Memory   *189*   *The Location of Memory 189*   *The Unit of*
Storage 190   Forgetting *192*   *Decay of the Memory*
Trace 193   *Interference 194*   *Motivated Forgetting 198*
Organic Amnesia 200   Summary *201*   Suggested
Readings *203*

6   Thinking   204
The Units of Thought *206*   *Images 206*   *Concepts 209*
Language 211   *Language Learning in Chimpanzees 216*
Directed Thinking *219*   *Logic and Reasoning 219*   *Steps*
in Problem Solving 220   *Factors Affecting Problem*
Solving 221   *Insight and Creative Problem Solving 224*
Associative Thinking *225*   *Daydreaming 226*
Dreams 227   *Creativity 228*   Summary *231*   Suggested
Readings *232*

7   Intelligence and Creativity   234
The Nature of Intelligence *236*   *Spearman's g*
Factor 237   *Thurstone's Primary Mental Abilities 237*
Guilford's Structure of the Intellect 238   The Nature of
Creativity *239*   *The Creative Process 240*   *Intelligence and*
Creativity 241   Measuring Intelligence and
Creativity *242*   *Aptitude and Achievement Tests 244*
What Makes A Good Test? *245*   *Reliability 245*
Validity 246   *Standardization 247*   Intelligence
Tests *247*   *The Stanford-Binet Scales 247*   *Performance*
Tests 250   *The Wechsler Adult Intelligence Scale 254*
Culture-Fair Intelligence Tests 256   *Group Tests 258*   Types
of Creativity Tests *259*   Determinants of
Intelligence *260*   *Heredity 260*   *Environment 263*   *Race*
Differences: Jensen and His Critics 266   *Sex Differences 269*
Summary *271*   Suggested Readings *272*

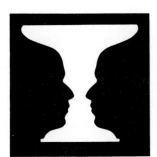

**THREE
Psychology and Awareness   274**

8   Sensation   276
The Nature of Sensation *278*   *General Characteristics of*
Sensation 278   *Measurement of Sensation 279*   *Sensory*
Adaptation 281   Vision *281*   *The Eye 282*   *Rods and*
Cones 283   *Neural Connections 284*   *Adaptation 286*
Color Vision 287   Hearing *290*   *Sound 290*   *The*
Ear 291   *Neural Connections 293*   *Theories of*

Hearing 293 The Chemical Senses 295 *Smell 295*
Taste 296 The Body Senses 299 *Kinesthesis 299*
The Vestibular Sense 299 The Skin Senses 302
Receptors and Neural Connections 302 Pressure 304
Temperature 304 Pain 304 Summary 306
Suggested Readings 309

9 Perception 310

Attention 312 *The Focus of Attention 312 Marginal*
Attention 313 Selective Attention 314 The
Information-Processing Model of Perception 315
Organization of Perception 317 Perception of Distance
and Depth 322 *Monocular Cues 322 Binocular*
Cues 325 Perception of Movement 327 Perceptual
Constancy 329 Factors Affecting Perception 335
Motivation 335 Expectations 336 Personality and
Perception 336 Cultural Differences 337 Altered States
of Consciousness 338 *Sensory Deprivation 339*
Sleeping and Dreaming 340 Hypnosis and Meditation 343
Drug-Induced Experiences 345 Summary 350
Suggested Readings 353

FOUR
Psychology of Motivation and Emotion 354

10 Motivation 356

Physiological Motives 359 *Hunger 359 Thirst 361*
Sleep and Dreaming 363 Pain 364 Sex 365 The
Maternal Drive 366 Stimulus Motives 367
Activity 367 Exploration and Curiosity 369
Manipulation 370 Contact 371 Learned Motives 372
Fear 372 Aggression 373 Social Motives 374
Consistency 380 Unconscious Motives 381
A Hierarchy of Motives 382 Summary 384
Suggested Readings 386

11 Emotion 388

The Nature of Emotion 390 *The Physiology of*
Emotion 390 The Psychology of Emotion 395 Basic
Emotional Experiences 402 The Function of
Emotion 407 *Emotions and Attitudes 407 Emotions:*
Disruptive or Adaptive? 408 Emotions as Motives 409
The Communication of Emotion 410 *Verbal*
Communication 411 Nonverbal Communication 412
Summary 416 Suggested Readings 418

FIVE
Psychology and the Individual   420

12 **Personality**   **422**

Constitutional Theory 424   Psychoanalytic
Theory 425   *Sigmund Freud 425*   *Carl Jung 431*
Alfred Adler 432   *Karen Horney 434*   *Erich Fromm 435*
Erik Erikson 435   Self Theory 438   *Origin of
Personality 438*   *Development of the Self 439*   Trait
Theory 439   *Development and Classification of Traits 441*
Measurement of Traits 442   *Alternate Views of Trait
Theory 443*   Personality Assessment 448   *The
Interview 449*   *Observation 450*   *Objective Tests 451*
Measuring Values 453   *Projective Tests 454*
Summary 458   Suggested Readings 462

13 **Adjustment**   **464**

What Do We Have to Adjust To? 466   *Stress 466*
Pressure 470   *Anxiety 471*   *Frustration 471*
Conflict 473   Ways of Adjusting 476   *Direct
Coping 476*   *Defensive Coping 478*   The Well-Adjusted
Individual 486   Summary 487   Suggested
Readings 489

14 **Normal and Abnormal Behavior**   **490**

What Is Abnormal? 491   *Historical Views of Abnormal
Behavior 493*   *Current Views of Abnormal Behavior 496*
Neuroses 497   *Anxiety Neurosis 498*   *Phobias 498*
Dissociative Neurosis 500   *Conversion Reaction 501*
Obsessive-Compulsive Neurosis 502   *Neurotic
Depression 504*   *Individual Differences and Neurotic
Behavior 506*   Character Disorders 506   *Sexual
Deviation 507*   *Alcoholism and Addiction 510*   *Sociopathic
Behavior 512*   Psychoses 513   *Affective Psychosis 514*
Schizophrenia 515   *Organic Psychosis 518*   *The Causes of
Psychosis 519*   Summary 522   Suggested Readings 525

15 **Therapies**   **526**

Individual Psychotherapies 528   *Psychoanalysis 528*
Client-Centered Therapy 531   *Existential Therapy 532*
Rational Therapy 532   *Reality Therapy 534*   Behavior
Therapies 535   *Operant Conditioning 535*   *Aversive
Conditioning 535*   *Desensitization 537*   *Reciprocal
Inhibition 537*   Group Therapies 539   Physical
Treatment 544   *Shock Treatments 544*
Psychosurgery 545   *Drug Therapy 546*
Institutionalization 546   *Token Economies 548*

Community Psychology 550   Summary 551   Suggested Readings 555

SIX
Psychology and Society   556

16 Social Psychology   558

Interpersonal Relations 560   *Person Perception 560*
Attribution Theory 562   Attraction and Liking 564
Interpersonal Influence 566   Group Dynamics 574
Leadership 574   Patterns of Communication 575   Problem
Solving 576   Attitudes and Attitude Change 577   *The*
Development of Attitudes 579   Attitude Change 581
Postscript: Environmental Psychology 587   *Effects of the*
Social Structure on the Individual 587   Personal Space and
Crowding 588   Conclusion 590   Summary 590
Suggested Readings 593

Appendix: Measurement and Statistical Methods   **594**

Glossary   **609**

References   **633**

Name Index   **647**

Subject Index   **649**

Preface

Prefaces often attempt to persuade students that they will enjoy the subject they are about to study. Psychology does not need such a sales pitch. Students, like all people, are curious about themselves and their friends, about their dreams and anxieties, about how the nervous system works, and how drugs affect thinking and perception. They come to an introductory course in psychology with a hundred difficult questions—and an equal number of common-sense assumptions. This book aims to satisfy the student's curiosity and to provide him with an understanding of psychological methods so that he can evaluate his own and other people's assumptions about behavior.

The second edition of *Psychology: An Introduction* is designed for the introductory course. It surveys the essentials of psychology, from physiological facts and classical theories to current trends. After studying this book, the student will have a grasp of the scope and content of psychology, a working knowledge of its vocabulary, and an understanding of its research methods. He will also have met some of the personalities who made psychology what it is today. It is hoped that this book will be interesting and useful both to the student who plans to major in psychology and to the biology or French major who desires a true liberal arts education.

Because this is an introductory book, it encompasses a wide range of theoretical viewpoints. This inclusive approach was chosen for several reasons. First, it would be misleading to suggest that psychologists are all of one mind. Much of the vitality of contemporary psychology derives from continuing controversies over approaches and methods. Second, it is important for students to develop the ability to recognize different theoretical stances. Understanding the viewpoints of the various researchers discussed in the text is essential to evaluating their studies and experiments, and in later years to reading a newspaper article on educational policies or choosing a psychiatrist for oneself or one's child. Finally, and perhaps most important, both student and instructor need to have room to think.

Psychology: An Introduction is firmly grounded in research as well as theory, but it is more than a survey of the literature. Learning that psychology is a science is often a shock for students. We have tried to lessen that shock by showing the relevance of experiments and data, and by choosing examples that fall within a student's experience. In addition, the text confronts such controversial questions as: Are there racial differences in intelligence? Is there a "maternal instinct"?

Organization

In revising this book we were in the fortunate position of having had a very successful first edition. So, when the time came to prepare the second edition, we had a pretty good idea of what worked and what didn't. For this reason, we tried to be better rather than different the second time around. New topics and recent research have been incorporated throughout in response to the present state of psychological research and the comments and reviews we received, but the overall structure of the book is the same.

The book is divided into six parts. Part One defines psychology, introduces physiological psychology, and ends with a detailed chapter on development. New topics in Chapter 1 include the naturalistic-observation method, ethics in psychological research, pure research versus applied psychology, the relevance of animal studies to human behavior, and a brief discussion of environmental psychology as a new trend. Chapter 2 has been somewhat streamlined to include discussions of behavior genetics, the social implications of applying eugenic principles to humans, and a look at psychosurgery and electrical stimulation of the brain and the assumptions behind them. In response to strong demand, Chapter 3 now covers development over the whole life span.

The subject of Part Two is cognition. Chapter 4 presents classical and operant conditioning, as well as new material on other viewpoints on learning including cognitive theory, social learning theory, and the ideas of the comparative psychologists. Applications of learning principles such as autonomic conditioning and biofeedback, behavior modification in education, and the self-modification of behavior are also discussed. Chapters 5, 6, and 7 have been revised to reflect recent developments in information processing, language learning in chimpanzees, and the controversy over the heritability of intelligence.

Part Three returns to physiology with a chapter on sensation. This material is related to the cognitive processes in a chapter on perception, which has been revised to include the information-processing approach to perception and a look at altered states of consciousness.

Part Four covers motivation and emotion. The discussions of aggression, achievement motivation, and women's "fear of success" have been expanded in Chapter 10. Chapter 11 has been substantially reorganized and expanded to include work by Olds, Milner, Delgado, Aronfreed, Valins, Arnold, and Lazarus. In addition, verbal and nonverbal communication of emotion are covered in more detail.

Part Five is the section many students will have been waiting for because it covers personality theory and testing, adjustment, normal and abnormal behavior, and therapies. New topics in Chapter 12 include Erikson's theory of personality development and the alternate views of trait theory, particularly the ideas of Skinner and Mischel.

A discussion of pressure as a form of stress has been added to Chapter 13. In Chapter 14, learning and personality theory approaches to neurosis and psychosis have been given more attention. The chapter on therapies has been revised to include reality therapy, transactional analysis, and family therapy, and the discussions of institutionalization and community psychology have been updated.

Part Six deals with social psychology, focusing on interpersonal relations, group dynamics, and attitudes. New topics include attribution theory, obedience to authority, types of social conflict, and a brief postscript on environmental psychology. An appendix on measurement and statistics completes the text.

The chapters in this book are designed to stand on their own, so that the instructor can deal with the topics in whatever order suits his plan. No chapter depends on other chapters, but in order to show students how integrated psychology is, we have more cross references to other chapters in this edition, particularly in the last third of the book. Psychological terms have been set in bold type and are defined in context; italics have been used for emphasis and for secondary terms. There is an extensive glossary at the end of the book. There are nearly 200 new photographs; some were taken especially for this book and others have never before appeared in print.

Other study aids include an outline at the beginning of each chapter, a summary at the end, and annotated suggestions for further reading. In addition, we have retained the boxed inserts on special topics and have included many new ones in the second edition. These inserts range from in-depth treatments of issues raised in the text, to recent research and applications, to new theories and controversies, to clinical case histories. A student workbook is available to help the student understand and integrate the material presented in the text. Our hope is that all these—new material, supplements, photographs, boxed inserts, chapter outlines, and summaries—will make the second edition of *Psychology: An Introduction* as well received as the first edition was and as easy to study, enjoyable, and thought-provoking.

Acknowledgments

Revising this book has been made easier because of the many comments and suggestions we received from instructors, students, and colleagues. I particularly want to thank Eastwood Atwater, Jack Badaracco, Tom Bourbon, Neil A. Carrier, Patricia Crane, Bruce D. Downing, Vernon P. Estes, Jr., Jay M. Finkleman, Ralph W. Heine, Robert J. Porter, Jr., David F. Ricks, Marvin Schwartz, Alden E. Wessman, and Thomas Zentall for their helpful reviews of the text. My editors at Prentice-Hall, Sandra Bloomfield and Eleanor Perz, were invaluable. Their expertise, good spirits, and tireless efforts helped to make the book better. They also helped me to realize that publishing a book can be fun.

C. G. M.

one

Psychology:
An Introduction

outline

THE GOALS OF PSYCHOLOGY 4

THE GROWTH OF PSYCHOLOGY 6

Wundt and Titchener: Structuralism
Sir Francis Galton: Individual Differences
William James: Functionalism
John B. Watson: Behaviorism
Gestalt Psychology
B. F. Skinner: S-R Psychology
Sigmund Freud: Psychoanalytic Psychology
Some New Schools

AREAS WITHIN PSYCHOLOGY TODAY 15

METHODS OF PSYCHOLOGY 18

The Naturalistic-Observation Method
The Experimental Method
The Correlational Method
Ethics in Psychology

THE SOCIAL RELEVANCE OF PSYCHOLOGY 24

Pure versus Applied Psychology
Using Animals in Psychological Research
New Directions in Psychology

SUMMARY 26

SUGGESTED READINGS 29

The Science of Psychology

"Whenever I'm working with a writer who's never been on a Hitchcock project before," Alfred Hitchcock, the famous director of suspense movies, relates, "he invariably becomes obsessed with the MacGuffin. And though I keep on explaining that it's not important, the most elaborate schemes are mapped out. For instance, in *The Thirty-Nine Steps*, what are the spies after? The man with the missing finger? And that woman at the beginning, was she on to some big secret? Is it because she was getting close to the truth that it became necessary to stab her in the back?" (cited in Truffaut, 1967, p. 99).

What's a MacGuffin? It's Alfred Hitchcock's term for a necessary but essentially irrelevant plot element. As he explained in a different interview, "The MacGuffin is the thing that the spies are after but the audience don't care."

What we do care about in such movies is, of course, the people. We want to know "what will happen next" because we have been caught up in the thoughts and fears of the characters. The typical Hitchcock hero is a perfectly average, unexceptional person who could well be you or someone you know. In Hitchcock films, the situations are bizarre, not the people.

In a sense, we are all like characters in a movie. We move from situation to situation, armed, for better or worse, with our own individual tendencies, strivings, confusions, obsessions, and anxieties. Psychology tries to help us to see the movie we are in by focusing on our behavior and the reasons for it. It provides a method for understanding ourselves and, more important, for bettering ourselves mentally, emotionally, and socially. It challenges us to go beyond the superficial "MacGuffins" in our lives and to confront what really lies behind and around our most basic actions.

Because almost all of us have natural desires to understand ourselves and others better, we don't need a hard sell on the virtues of studying psychology. We are all proper subjects of psychological investigation—we are as average as a Hitchcock hero or as potentially odd or antisocial as one of his villains. Each of us is unique from birth; and even if our actions in life are not unique, the perceptions, personality, and development that lead to those actions are. Our heredity has definite effects on our general personalities. But we are also affected by the ever-changing factor of our social—and sometimes unsociable—environment. Psychology can accommodate our curiosity not only about "what made this person that way?" but about "what will he do next?" and "has this experience changed her at all?"

There are no heroes or villains in the science of mental, emotional, and behavioral processes. There are only people. Yet we should not forget the metaphor of the "MacGuffin." There are numerous MacGuffins in modern psychology. There are the MacGuffins of what the experimental subject thinks he is being tested on; of what the observer thinks he perceives or remembers; of what a simple dream appears to have been about; of what the maladjusted individual thinks is annoying or frightening him. In all these cases and more, what we think is the answer may be a MacGuffin that throws us off the track from finding the real answer.

Psychology is not just common sense about people. It is a field calling for quite uncommon insights, experimental methods, and formulations. And, we trust, it holds enduring rewards for us in the better understanding of ourselves and our fellow human beings.

The Goals of Psychology

Like other sciences, psychology seeks to *explain, predict,* and *control* what it studies. Take, for example, sex differences. Intuition or common sense may tell us that women are naturally maternal and unaggressive; but some women argue that this is male propaganda. In trying to

(© 1960 United Feature
Syndicate, Inc.)

explain sex differences, some psychologists might begin with anatomy and body chemistry. Other psychologists might select a number of women for study, first exploring their biographies, then examining their present attitudes and abilities. Perhaps their mothers taught them that it was right to protect helpless people (like babies) and that it was wrong to fight.

Suppose one researcher feels that women are unaggressive only when they are around men (because they think men expect them to be passive). His first step would be to test the idea by seeing whether it enables him to *predict* behavior. The researcher might place an ad in the paper offering $35 for participation in an experiment, women only. When the applicants arrived, half would be sent to a male interviewer, half to a female interviewer. Both would give the applicants a hard time, insulting them in not so subtle ways. If the women argued with the female interviewer but not with the male, the researcher might conclude that his original idea was correct.

Control in psychology is generally directed toward therapeutic ends. A child is terrified of dogs, so his parents consult a psychologist. In the hope of overcoming the child's fears, the psychologist might create pleasant situations for him that included nice dogs. Similarly, a therapist might help an unhappy female patient to overcome her feeling that it is wrong for her to compete in business by showing her he approves of her ambitions. In both cases, the psychologists are attempting to change behavior and feelings.

The behavioral sciences—anthropology, sociology, political science, and psychology—are so closely related that it is often difficult to tell where one ends and the next begins. For example, all of them would consider a campus demonstration a good subject for study. But how would their approaches differ?

An anthropologist would see the day's activities in terms of cultural patterns and rituals. He would note that making speeches from a soapbox has a long and honored tradition in American culture; that linking arms to form a human barricade resembles the snake dance of Japanese students; that in political movements, as in primitive societies, people often call people who are not related to them "brother" and "sister."

A sociologist would be most interested in the interactions of the groups that were formed and in the bonds formed between individuals. Crowds, he would note, behave differently from individuals and small groups. The crowd develops an organizational structure and a status system; it establishes and enforces codes of correct and incorrect behavior.

A political scientist would focus on the distribution of power and authority among leaders and groups. An economist, being concerned mainly with the distribution of goods, would note that the students have a different attitude toward property than most Americans have. A historian would try to compare this event to others in the past and would look for its causes.

A psychologist surveying the same scene would be most interested in the individuals and how they behaved. He would wonder why some apparently conservative students had been attracted to the scene. Listening to the speeches, he would hear innuendos and references that might provide clues as to what kind of people were leading the crowd and what their motives were. He might follow up with interviews and case studies.

Psychology is unique among the behavioral sciences in its emphasis on the individual. We turn now to a brief history of this relatively young science.

The Growth of Psychology

Wundt and Titchener: Structuralism

In 1879 Wilhelm Wundt, physiologist and philosopher, left Zurich for Leipzig, where university officials had kindly consented to his request for a psychological laboratory—the first in Europe. Wundt had stated his intentions quite plainly 5 years earlier in *Principles of Physiological Psychology:* the mind, he argued, must be studied objectively and scientifically. Apparently no one took him too seriously at this point— Leipzig had no plans to establish a department of psychology, and students who attended Wundt's lectures would not even be given credit. Still, he was a sound philosopher, and they decided to be indulgent.

The birth of scientific psychology in Leipzig had none of the outward signs of a revolution. No one called Wundt a heretic; no one campaigned on an anti-Wundt platform, conjuring up pictures of children being subjected to terrifying experiments. In fact, hardly anyone seemed to notice: four students attended Wundt's first lecture.

This was more than a little surprising. Man has always regarded his mental processes—his thoughts and dreams—with considerable awe. Centuries before, Plato had divided the world into two realms, one pure and abstract, the other physical and mundane. Without question, Plato preferred the former. Thomas Aquinas revised this scheme in the Middle Ages, arguing that man had the body of an animal but the soul of an angel (to simplify somewhat). Meanwhile, on the streets, people turned for advice to oracles, fortune-tellers, astrologers, soothsayers, and inspired old women (who were sometimes burned for their efforts). The glorification of Reason and discoveries in the natural sciences in the seventeenth century did little to dispel the idea that mind and matter, spirit and body, are separate.

Even today we think of personality, intelligence, genius, creativity, and charisma in abstract terms. We consult astrology columns in the newspapers, offer our palms to fortune-tellers for a reading, believe

Wilhelm Wundt
(*The Bettmann Archive*)

that some people can read minds and predict the future. The Zodiac, Tarot cards, and ESP are growing more popular every day. In the late eighteenth century mystical powers were taken even more seriously than they are now.

Wundt rejected all this. Thinking, he argued, is a natural event like wind in a storm or the beating of the heart. Why did this frontal attack on the mystery of man go unchallenged? First, a number of British philosophers had made a good case for the idea that physical sensations are the basis of thought. The only world we know, said Hobbes and Locke, is the one we experience through our senses. Second, by 1879 the scientific method commanded a great deal of respect. The wedding of philosophy and science proposed by Wundt might have seemed bizarre to his father, a simple Lutheran pastor, but not to the academic community. Finally—and perhaps most important—the Establishment of the time had its hands full with Charles Darwin. Man, Darwin argued, was the top of a hierarchy of animals, the pinnacle of evolution—but an animal nonetheless. Compared with the theory of evolution, scientific psychology seemed tame.

By the mid-1880s the new psychological lab was attracting large numbers of students. Wundt's main concern at this point was with techniques for uncovering the natural laws of the human mind. He began by looking at the processes of perception to find the basic units of thought. When we look at an object like a banana, for example, we immediately think, here is a fruit, something to peel and eat. But these are associations: all we actually *see* is a long yellow object. Wundt and his co-workers wanted to strip perception of its associations, to discover the very *atoms* of thought.

To accomplish this, they trained themselves in the art of objective introspection, observing and recording their perceptions and feelings. Some days, for example, were spent listening to the ticking of a metronome. Which rhythms are most pleasant? they asked themselves. Does a fast tempo cause excitement, a slow beat relaxation? They recorded their reactions in minute detail, supplementing them with measures of their heartbeats and respiration. However crude and irrelevant these activities may seem today, they did introduce measurement and experiment into psychology, which until this time had been a branch of philosophy.

Edward Bradford Titchener
(*The Granger Collection*)

But perhaps the most important product of the Leipzig lab was its students, the enthusiasts who took the gospel of the new science to universities around the world. Among them was Edward Bradford Titchener.

British by birth but German in training and temperament, Titchener established himself as the dean of American psychology soon after he became professor of psychology at Cornell University. He maintained this position until his death in 1927. A typical day in Titchener's life began with a lecture to beginning students. Donning a cap and gown and surrounding himself with attentive graduate students and assistants, Titchener descended on the lecture hall in a ceremony bound to impress young minds with the seriousness of psychology. A discussion hour with his staff followed, after which he retired to his private study to write. Here, while his colleagues busied themselves with Wundtian experiments, Titchener worked on a series of books stating the techniques and rules of psychology.

Psychology, he wrote, is the science of consciousness—physics with the observer kept in. In physics an hour or a mile is an exact measure; to the observer, however, an hour may seem to pass in a matter of seconds, a mile may seem endless. Psychology is the study of this phenomenon, the study of experience. Titchener broke experience down into what he saw as its three basic elements: physical sensations (including sights and sounds), affections or feelings (which are like sensations, but less clear), and images (such as memories and dreams). When we recognize a banana, according to Titchener's scheme, we are combining a physical sensation (what we see) with feelings (liking or disliking bananas) and with images (memories of other bananas). Even the most complex thoughts and feelings, Titchener argued, can be reduced to these simple elements. Psychology's role is to identify the elements and show how they are combined. Because of its emphasis on the basic units of experience and the combinations in which they occur, this school of psychology is called **structuralism.**

Sir Francis Galton: Individual Differences

While Wundt and Titchener were working to prove the serious and scientific nature of psychology, Francis Galton—Darwin's half-cousin—was dabbling in medicine,* experimenting with electricity, exploring the Sudan and Southwest Africa, charting weather, and poring over the biographies of famous men. Born into a wealthy and illustrious family, Galton never had to work for a living; nor did he

Sir Francis Galton
(*The Bettmann Archive*)

have to seek university approval for his projects (which included studies of gregariousness in cattle, the Australian marriage system, and diving goggles). Throughout his life Galton remained an intellectual adventurer—to the enormous profit of psychology.

Impressed by the number of exceptional men in his own family, Galton studied the histories of other families. He found that great men tended to have great ancestors and great sons. It began to look as if genius was hereditary. Intrigued, Galton invented tests to measure individual capabilities and went on to work out methods of comparing

---

*Galton and the faculty at Trinity College did not see eye to eye on methods of studying medicine. Galton thought his idea of sampling each potion in the pharmacy, starting with the *A*'s, was quite ingenious; they did not!

scores and analyzing data. He found a wide range of abilities and began to correlate these with other factors. Later he became interested in mental imagery and word associations. Using himself as a subject, he recorded his first two associations for each of 75 words and tried to explain them in terms of his past experiences. Madness also fascinated Galton. He decided the best way to study madness was to become mad oneself. Accordingly, he began pretending to himself that everyone he saw on his walks through the park was out to get him—including the dogs.

Galton thus fathered mental tests and the study of individual differences, allied psychology with statistics and mathematics, and published a number of articles on mental imagery based on subjective (untrained) introspection, something that Wundt and Titchener had rejected.

William James: Functionalism

William James, the first native American psychologist, was as versatile and innovative as Galton—and a bit more disciplined. At 19 James abandoned his dreams of becoming a painter and enrolled in Harvard, where he studied first chemistry, then physiology, anatomy, biology, and medicine. Unhappy with university life, he left it in 1865 and joined an expedition to the Amazon. Collecting biological specimens did little to lift his spirits. Physically ill and depressed to the point of considering suicide, James returned to America and obtained his medical degree in 1869. For the next few years he wandered about America and Europe, trying to decide on a career. Finally, in 1872, he accepted an offer to teach physiology at Harvard. Still restless, James started reading philosophy in his off hours, hoping to find the answer to his malaise. By 1875 he had begun to see connections between his two vocations, physiology and philosophy—the two seemed to converge in psychology.

William James
(The Bettmann Archive)

In that year James started a class in psychology (commenting that the first lecture he ever heard on the subject was his own), set aside part of his laboratory for psychological experiments, and began work on a text. *The Principles of Psychology* did not appear until 1890. By this time James's interest had shifted to philosophy, and he was already at work on two new books, *Pragmatism* and *The Meaning of Truth*.

In preparing his lectures and his textbook, James studied structuralist publications quite thoroughly. The idea of psychological experiments appealed to him, but something in Wundt's and Titchener's approach was wrong. Looking into himself, James came to the conclusion that the atoms of experience—sensations without associations—simply do not exist in real life. Our minds are constantly weaving associations, revising experience, starting, stopping, jumping back and forth in time. Consciousness, he argued, is a continuous flow, not an assemblage of bits of sensation and pieces of imagery. Perceptions and associations, sensations and emotions, cannot be separated: what we see is a banana, not a long yellow object.

Still focusing on everyday experience, James turned to the question of habit. Much of what we do is automatic: we do not have to think about how to get dressed, open a door, or walk down the street. James suggested that when we repeat an activity a number of times, our nervous systems are altered so that the next time we encounter a door, opening it is easier.

This was the clue he needed. The biologist in him firmly believed that all activity—from the beating of the heart to the perception of a banana—is functional. If we could not recognize a banana, we would have to figure out what it was each time we saw one. Mental associations allow us to benefit from previous experience. Once we have solved a problem, the solution becomes automatic. This, James argued, is the essence of adaptation.

With *The Principles of Psychology* James thus forged a new link between psychology and natural science. Applying biological principles to the mind, he arrived at a **functionalist** theory of mental life and behavior. In addition, James argued for the value of subjective introspection and insisted that psychology focus on everyday, true-to-life experience.

In 1894 one of James's students, James R. Angell, became the director of the new Department of Psychology at the University of Chicago. John Dewey, who had studied structuralist psychology at Johns Hopkins, became professor of philosophy at Chicago that same year. Together, they made Chicago the center of the functionalist school of psychology. Building on James, they began to look for parallels between animal and human behavior and for ways of applying psychological knowledge in education.

John B. Watson
(*Underwood & Underwood*)

John B. Watson: Behaviorism

John Broadus Watson was the first student to receive a doctorate in psychology from the University of Chicago. Watson's dissertation was concerned with learning in rats. One of the department's requirements was that he speculate on the kind of consciousness that produced the behavior he observed in his experiments. Watson found this downright absurd. What evidence is there that rats have any consciousness at all? he asked. Nevertheless, he complied with the regulations, received his degree, and returned to his laboratory, brooding over consciousness.

Ten years and many experiments later, Watson was ready to confront both the structuralist and functionalist schools. In "Psychology As the Behaviorist Views It" (1913), he stated flatly that the whole idea of consciousness, of mental life, is superstitious, a leftover from the Middle Ages. You cannot define consciousness any more than you can define a soul, Watson argued; nor can you locate it or measure it. Basing a

Max Wertheimer
(*Omikron*)

Wolfgang Köhler
(*The Granger Collection*)

Kurt Koffka
(*Underwood & Underwood*)

science on something so vague is plainly ridiculous. Psychology should concern itself with observable, measurable behavior—and nothing more.

Watson's position was based largely on Ivan Pavlov's famous experiments. Some years earlier, this Russian scientist had noticed that the dogs in his laboratory began to drool as soon as they heard their feeder coming—even before they could see their dinner. Pavlov had always thought salivation was a natural response to food and found the dogs' anticipation a bit odd. He decided to see whether he could teach them to associate the sound of a tuning fork with food. Before long Pavlov had his dogs salivating at the sound of a tuning fork, even when there was no food in the room. He explained this as follows: All behavior is a response to some stimulus in the environment. In ordinary life, food (the **stimulus**) makes dogs salivate (the **response**). All Pavlov did was to train his animals to expect food when they heard a certain sound. He called this training **conditioning.**

Watson showed, in a famous experiment with an 11-month-old child, that people can be conditioned. Little Albert was a secure, happy baby who had absolutely no reason to fear soft, furry, white rats. Watson gave him a reason: each time Albert reached out to pet the rat, Watson banged a hammer against a metal bar. Soon Albert was afraid not only of rats but also of white rabbits, dogs, fur coats—and even a Santa Claus mask (Watson & Rayner, 1920). Thus, conditioning changed the child's behavior radically.*

Watson saw no reason to refer to consciousness or mental life in explaining this change. An 11-month-old child does not reason, he simply responds to his environment—in this case the coincidence of loud noises and white, furry things. Watson felt the same was true for adults. Words, he argued, are simply a verbal response; when we think, we are actually talking to ourselves. Emotions are a glandular response, he said, and all behavior can be explained with the stimulus-response formula. Psychology, he felt, must be purged of "mentalism."

In the 1920s, when Watson's **behaviorist theory** was first published, American psychologists had all but exhausted the structuralist approach; Wundtian experiments had lost their novelty and attraction. So, Watson's orthodox scientific approach (if you cannot see it and measure it, forget it) found a warm audience. In addition, Watson suggested two new areas for study: learning and child development.

Gestalt Psychology

Meanwhile, in Germany, a group of psychologists was attacking structuralism from another angle. Wertheimer, Köhler, and Koffka were all

---

*Watson had planned to work further with Albert—to take away the fears he had caused the boy to develop—but, unfortunately, Albert's mother took the boy away before Watson had the chance (Watson & Rayner, 1920).

interested in perception, particularly in certain tricks the mind plays on itself. Why, they asked, when we see a series of still pictures flashed at a constant rate (movies or "moving" neon signs), do they seem to move? The eye sees only a series of still pictures; what intervenes to make us perceive motion?

The structuralists, as you will recall, wanted to strip perception to its elements. In the figure at the left a trained Wundtian introspectionist would see nothing but six dots. This is unreal, Wertheimer and his colleagues argued. Anybody looking at this would see a triangle and a line.

Phenomena like these were the impetus for a new school of thought, **Gestalt psychology.** Roughly translated from German, *gestalt* means "whole" or "form." Applied to perception, it refers to our tendency to see patterns, to distinguish an object from its background, to complete pictures from a few cues. Like James, the Gestalt psychologists thought the attempt to break perception and thought down into their elements was misguided: when we look at a tree we see just that, a tree.

A simple experiment with chickens demonstrates the implications of this view. Köhler put hens in a cage with two cardboard squares—one white, the other gray, both covered with seed. When the hens pecked at the gray square, they were left alone. When they pecked at the white square, they were shooed away. Soon the birds learned where they could eat without interference. Then Köhler switched the squares, replacing the white one with a dark gray one. Watson's theory would lead us to expect that the hens would continue pecking at the light gray square, but the opposite was true: Köhler's hens went for the darker square. The Gestalt psychologists' explanation is that the hens solved the problem of where to eat by comprehending relationships (the darker of two squares was permitted), not by focusing on a single characteristic (one particular shade of gray). In this they disagree with Watson, who felt that people and animals learn to respond to specific stimuli—not to situations or the *gestalt.*

In the 1930s the Gestalt school broke up, primarily because Nazism was on the rise. Wertheimer, Köhler, and Koffka all eventually settled in America.

B. F. Skinner
(Ken Heyman)

B. F. Skinner: S-R Psychology

Behaviorism was thriving when the Gestalt psychologists reached America. Watson himself had deserted the academic world, retiring to New York, where he devoted himself to writing popular articles on conditioning and child rearing. However, a number of other psychologists were waiting to take his place as spokesmen for behaviorism, among them B. F. Skinner.

Like Watson, Skinner believes that psychology should restrict itself to the study of observable and measurable behavior. Also like Watson,

Skinner explains behavior in terms of the stimulus-response formula.* He too is primarily interested in changing behavior through conditioning—and discovering natural laws of behavior in the process. But his approach is subtly different from that of his predecessor.

Watson changed Albert's behavior by changing the stimulus. As far as Albert knew, white rats made loud, scary noises. In order for Albert to learn this, Watson had to repeat the experience over and over, sounding a loud noise every time Albert saw the rat. Skinner adds a new element—**reinforcement.** He rewards his subjects for behaving the way he wants them to. For example, an animal (rats and pigeons are Skinner's favorite subjects) is put in a special cage (called a **Skinner box**) and allowed to explore. Eventually the animal will reach up and press a lever or peck at a disk on the wall. A food pellet drops into the box. Gradually the animal learns that pressing the bar or pecking at the disk always brings food. Why does the animal learn this? Because it has been reinforced, or rewarded. Skinner thus makes the animal an active agent in its own conditioning.

Sigmund Freud: Psychoanalytic Psychology

Psychoanalysis was the dark horse of psychology. When James was setting down his principles of mental life and Watson was building his case against them, Dr. Freud was largely unknown in America. He had visited this country in 1909; in fact, James had attended one of his lectures. But Freud was a doctor, a practitioner; the other psychologists were scientists. Only in the late 1920s did psychoanalytic theory begin to attract attention. By then Freud had worked his clinical discoveries into a comprehensive theory of mental life that was radically different from those of his American colleagues.

Sigmund Freud
(The Bettmann Archive)

Much of our behavior, said Freud, is governed by hidden motives and unconscious wishes. It is as if a part of each of us never grows up. The adult in us struggles to keep the infant in control, but with only partial success. Childish desires and wishes surface in the kind of mistakes called "Freudian slips" and in our dreams. We feel that many of our impulses are forbidden or sinful; therefore, we do not want to admit them to consciousness. Often this conflict leads to vague feelings of anxiety, sometimes to exaggerated fears.

Freud invariably found that adult problems could be traced back to childhood experiences. Always, he maintained, the repressed feelings were sexual. A little boy desires his mother and wants to destroy his rival, her husband and his father. Of all Freud's concepts, this—the idea of infant sexuality—was the most shocking. Many of Freud's own

---

*In their writings, psychologists usually abbreviate the terms "stimulus" and "response" as S and R. This shorthand, appropriately enough, gave this school of psychology its name.

Jean Piaget
(*Yves DeBraine, Black Star*)

colleagues rejected his emphasis on sex—among them Alfred Adler, who felt the child's sense of inferiority in relation to "big people" was central to personality, and Carl Jung, who emphasized self-realization in the context of man's racial history and his religious impulse.

Nonetheless, Freudian theory had a tremendous impact on academic psychology (particularly the study of personality) and remains controversial today. Some psychologists consider the theories of the unconscious, infantile sexuality, and dream interpretation sacred; others find them ridiculous. But few are indifferent to Freud. In addition, Freud the doctor laid the foundation for psychotherapy, with his famous "talking cure," **psychoanalysis.**

Some New Schools

In the past 40 years the different views of psychology we have discussed here have been challenged and revised, as discoveries in one area have suggested new possibilities in another. Nowhere is this more evident than in the development of cognitive psychology.

Cognitive psychology is basically a combination of S-R and Gestalt approaches. S-R psychology teaches that learning depends on reinforcement: if a particular action always brings rewards, the person or animal makes it a permanent part of his behavioral repertoire. Gestalt theory suggests that learning depends on insight, on the perception of relationships. Putting the two together, E. C. Tolman and others came to the conclusion that once we learn that a particular response to a situation or stimulus works, we begin to see the stimulus in a new way. For example, a student has always been told to respect teachers. He gets to college and finds one young instructor is very displeased with his polite, restrained style. Be honest, be open, the instructor demands. The student begins to see teachers in a new way. Cognitive psychology is the study of the way perception influences behavior and the way experience influences perception; it is the study of thought processes in the broadest sense. One of the leading members of the cognitive school is Jean Piaget, whose research on the cognitive processes of children will be described in Chapter 3.

Existential psychology, as the name suggests, draws on both personality theory and the existential philosophy made famous in the 1940s by Jean-Paul Sartre and others. Modern Americans, argues psychoanalyst Rollo May, are lost souls. We no longer believe in the myths of the frontier and progress, in stories of poor boys who make it in the big time. Patriotism, hard work, and freedom have lost their magical appeal; we are a people without myths and heroes. This sense of meaninglessness and alienation, existential psychologists believe, is the source of apathy and psychological problems, of alcoholism and drug addiction. R. D. Laing, another existential psychologist, feels that we must reevaluate our attitude toward psychotic behavior. Laing says that

Rollo May
(*Jill Krementz*)

Abraham Maslow
(*Brandeis University—
Ralph Norman*)

such behavior is not abnormal; it is a reasonable response to an abnormal world. The goal of existential psychology is to lead individuals to an inner sense of identity so that they are able to care, to commit themselves, to love.

Humanistic psychology and existential psychology are closely related. Both argue that individuals must learn ways of realizing their potential. But where existential psychology emphasizes an inner sense of identity and will power, humanistic psychology focuses on nonverbal experience, the unity of mind and body, communication through touch, altered states of consciousness, and letting go. Only by opening ourselves to sensations—touching others and listening to our own bodies—can we achieve self-actualization and joy in others, said psychologist Abraham Maslow. The most famous offspring of this movement is the Esalen Institute in Big Sur, California, which celebrates nonverbal experience and communication in the here and now.

Areas within Psychology Today

Like so many other professionals in society these days—from doctors to professional football players—psychologists have become specialists. As psychologists study problems, they come across new questions that require examination, which raises further questions, and on and on. And so new areas of research continually emerge, and psychologists are continually becoming more specialized. Some new areas of research—environmental psychology, for example—are bringing these specialties together again to focus on broader issues. Psychology is, we should remember, a relatively young science, and there is much to learn.

The days when psychologists were found only in universities or hospitals or private offices are long gone. In schools, there are **educational psychologists** who deal with learning and reading problems and administer psychological and vocational tests. In businesses and factories, **industrial psychologists** address themselves to the problems of training personnel, improving working conditions, and the effects of automation on humans.

One area that has expanded greatly is **social psychology,** in which the focus is directly on people in their interrelationships with other people. How are individuals influenced by the people around them? Why do we like some people and dislike others? Do opposites really attract? Do people behave differently in groups than they do when they are alone?

Developmental psychologists investigate mental and physical growth in humans from infancy to old age. **Physiological psychologists** investigate the extent to which behavior is caused by physical changes in the body and give particular attention to the brain, nervous system, and the body's biochemistry.

This man is an industrial psychologist who works at a large department store in New York City. He and the woman could be discussing the woman's problems as an employee or as a supervisor, or the effect of staggered working hours.
(Sepp Seitz, Magnum Photos)

A clinical psychologist giving a personality test. By analyzing the person's response to the picture, the clinical psychologist may get valuable insights into the person's personality, thus enabling him to better help the person with his problems.
(Van Bucher, courtesy Wagner College Department of Psychology. This photo has been slightly retouched.)

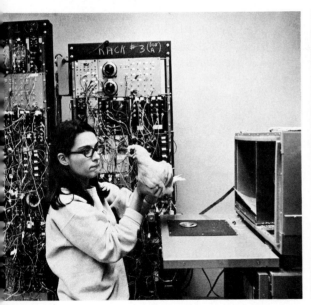

An experimental psychology laboratory. That mass of electronic equipment in the background is connected to the chicken's cage. It monitors the chicken's activity and rewards it with food when it makes the proper response.
(Van Bucher, Photo Researchers)

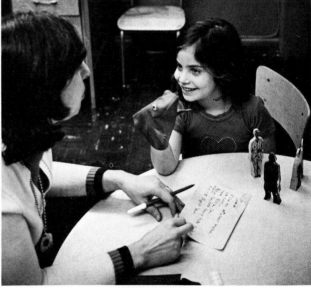

This woman, an educational psychologist, works with children in the school environment. The hand puppet and the dolls on the table are part of the standard testing equipment used to evaluate the children's verbal and cognitive abilities, as well as providing information about their personalities.
(Alex Webb, Magnum Photos)

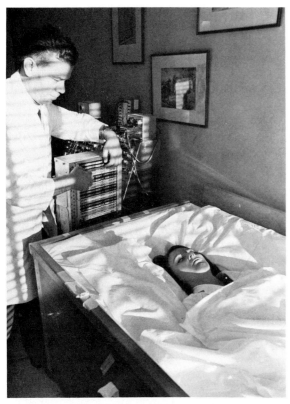

This girl is not dead; she is asleep. Her strange-looking bed is actually a large tub of water; the sheets keep her from getting wet. The man is a physiological psychologist who is studying the effects of weightlessness on sleep.
(*Van Bucher, courtesy University of Florida Clinical Psychology Department*)

By careful observation of children at play, this developmental psychologist can get a better understanding of children's thinking, feeling, and motor abilities. Other developmental psychologists study babies, older children, adolescents, adults, and the elderly, thus compiling a picture of our growth and development over the entire life span.
(*Abigail Heyman, Magnum Photos*)

The **clinical psychologist** studies, diagnoses, and treats problems of adjustment. This is the person we often hear referred to as a "shrink." Clinical psychologists treat groups as well as individuals and may be in private practice or may work for public agencies.

A good way to appreciate the concerns of the various specialties of psychology is to take a single issue and see what questions each specialist might ask about it. For example, do sex differences relate to behavior, and if they do, what causes those differences?

A developmental psychologist might ask, At what age do boys and girls start behaving differently, and why does this happen? The educational psychologist might investigate whether one sex is better in certain school subjects than the other and why. The physiological psychologist might want to know, To what extent is the generally more aggressive nature of males linked to the sex hormone known as testosterone? The clinical psychologist might ask, Do men become depressed more often than women do, and if they do, why? The social psychologist might wonder, To what extent are differences in behavior the result of traditional social roles that we are expected to act out? And the industrial psychologist might be curious about whether female bosses behave differently than male bosses. Clearly, each of these specialists has something to contribute to our total understanding of sex differences and, more generally, to our understanding of all behavior.

Methods of Psychology

All of us know something about human behavior. We observe ourselves and others; we exchange experiences, philosophies, and gossip with friends; we speculate on why people act as they do. How does the psychologist's knowledge differ from common sense?

Psychologists are scientists, and like all scientists they are skeptics. If you met a friend on your way across campus and you told him you were depressed because you had an exam, he would probably believe you. But maybe you are always depressed; maybe you feel bad because you were up all night studying or because you did not eat any breakfast. Before a psychologist would accept your simple statement, "I am depressed because I have an exam," he would have to rule out all other possible explanations. This is the essence of the scientific method.

Obviously a psychologist cannot put your depression under a microscope or dissect your anxiety. But he can study you scientifically in a variety of ways. Any of the specialists we discussed earlier may use any or all of the following methods.

The Naturalistic-Observation Method

We have all heard about the virtue of "telling it like it is." **Naturalistic observation** is essentially a way of "seeing it like it is." Psychologists use this method to study animal or human behavior in its natural context instead of in the laboratory under imposed conditions. We all probably practice this method in everyday life without realizing it. When you watch dogs play in the park, or observe how your various professors conduct their classes, you are using a form of naturalistic observation. A psychologist with this real-life orientation might observe behavior in a school or a factory. Another might actually become a part of a family to better study the behavior of the family members. Still another would observe animals in nature, not in cages. The primary advantage of this method is that behavior will be more natural, spontaneous, and varied than it would be in a laboratory.

For example, W. H. Whyte (1956) wanted to see how people living in a suburban community chose their friends. He kept tabs on his subjects by reading the local newspaper. The social column told him when parties were given and who was invited. After collecting such data for some time, Whyte noticed that there were definite friendship patterns in the community. *Proximity*—people's nearness to other people—turned out to be the critical factor in determining which people became friends. Whyte concluded that, all other things being equal, people are more likely to make friends with people who live nearby. He might have been able to find this out by asking the people, but he could not have found it out in a laboratory.

Whyte restricted his observations to one specific behavior—going to parties. One of the difficulties with naturalistic observation is that it is not always possible to make such restrictions. Because the point about naturalistic observation is not to interfere with people's behavior in any way, you have to take their behavior as it comes. You can't suddenly yell, "Freeze!" when you want to study what is going on in more detail. You can't tell people to stop what they are doing because it's not what you want to study.

Because people's behavior is so unpredictable, psychologists depend on careful, detailed notes to organize their observations. From these notes, they can discover patterns that may have been blurred by behavior that later turned out to be irrelevant. There is also the problem of observer bias. Any policeman will tell you how unreliable eyewitnesses can be. Even psychologists, who are trained observers, may subtly distort what they see to conform to what they hope to see or may not record some behavior they personally judge to be irrelevant. Having a team of trained observers who pool their notes often results in a more complete picture than one observer could draw on his own.

Another problem with naturalistic observation is that the behavior observed is dependent on the particular time and place and on the particular group of people involved. Unlike laboratory experiments that can be repeated again and again, each natural situation is a one-time-only occurrence. Because of this, scientific psychologists do not like to make general statements based on information from naturalistic studies. They will first test the information under controlled conditions in the laboratory before they apply it to situations other than the original one.

In spite of these disadvantages, naturalistic observation is a valuable tool for psychologists. After all, real-life behavior is what psychology is really about. So, although the complexity of behavior may be a drawback to the naturalistic observer who is trying to interpret that behavior, naturalistic observation is a boon to experimental psychologists: It provides them with new ideas and suggestions for research. Experimental researchers then study these ideas more systematically and in much greater detail in their laboratories than researchers in the field are able to. It also helps researchers keep their perspective by reminding them of the larger world outside the lab.

The Experimental Method

The psychologist, like the biologist and the chemist, is a kind of detective. He wants to know "who done it"—that is, who or what is making you feel lousy today. He begins with a hunch: You did not get enough sleep, so you cannot think straight. The psychologist may choose this **hypothesis** for a variety of reasons. Perhaps he has noticed that students in his Saturday morning class are unusually dull and suspects this is because they stay up late Friday nights. But this is just a common-sense explanation. The psychologist wants proof—he wants facts that are unbiased, and he wants to know that all other possible explanations have been ruled out. So he decides to conduct an experiment on the relationship between sleep and learning.

His first step is to pick **subjects,** people he can observe to see whether his hypothesis is right or wrong. He decides to use student volunteers and, so that his results will not be influenced by sex or intelligence, he chooses a group made up of equal numbers of male and female subjects who scored between 520 and 540 on their College Boards.

Next he designs a learning task. He needs something that none of his subjects will know in advance. If he chooses a chapter in a history book, for example, he runs the risk that some of his subjects may be history buffs. Considering various possibilities, he decides to print a page of geometric forms, each labeled with a nonsense word. Circles are "glucks," triangles "pogs," and so on. He will give the students a half-hour to learn the names, then take away the study sheets and ask them to label a new page of geometric forms.

Now the psychologist is ready to consider procedures. Asking people if they have slept well is not a reliable measure. Some may say no so that they will have an excuse if they do poorly in the test; others will say yes because they do not want a psychologist to think they are unstable and cannot sleep; two people who both say they slept poorly may not mean the same thing. So the researcher decides to intervene—to control the situation a little more closely. Everyone in the experiment, he decides, will spend the night in the same dormitory. They will be kept awake until 4:00 A.M., and then they will be awakened at 7:00 sharp. He and his colleagues will patrol the halls to make sure no one falls asleep ahead of schedule, and they will check to see who is sleeping soundly between 4:00 and 7:00. By determining the amount of sleep the subjects get, the psychologist is introducing and controlling an essential element of the experimental method—an **independent variable.** The psychologist believes that the students' ability to learn his labels for geometric forms will depend on their having had a good night's sleep; the ability to perform well on the learning task thus becomes the **dependent variable.** If the independent variable (the amount of sleep) is altered, the dependent variable (performance on the learning task) should also be changed, according to his hypothesis.

At this point the experimenter begins looking for loopholes. Maybe sleeping in a strange room and knowing they are participating in an experiment—not lack of sleep—will influence students' performance on the learning test. He wants to be sure his experiment measures only the effects of inadequate sleep, so he divides the subjects into two groups. He checks to make sure that the two groups contain equal numbers of males and females, that the ages of members of both groups are the same, and that the College Board scores of the two groups are the same. One of the groups, the **experimental group,** will be kept awake until 4:00 in the morning. The other, the **control group,** will be allowed to go to sleep whenever they want to. Because the only consistent difference between the two groups is the amount of sleep they get, the difference in the way the two groups perform in the morning will allow the experimenter to determine if sleep has any effect on their ability to learn.

Finally, the psychologist questions his own objectivity. He knows he is inclined to think that lack of sleep makes students dull, and he does not want to prejudice the results. That is, he wants to avoid **experimenter bias.** He decides to ask a third person, who does not know who slept all night and who did not, to score the tests.

To review, the experimenter begins with a hunch, or hypothesis, about the relationship between two variables, in this case sleep and performance on a learning task. To determine whether the two are related, he manipulates one (the independent variable) and observes how it affects the other (the dependent variable). To make sure that he is observing only the effects of sleep, he takes a number of precautions: his two groups are alike in age, sex, and intelligence; none had any prior knowledge of the test; he manipulates the amount of sleep. If the students who slept as much as they wanted score higher than the experimental group, the psychologist can probably conclude that his hypothesis was correct.

This psychologist may only want to prove to the head of his department that Saturday morning classes are a bad idea. In most cases though, the results have greater implications. Only after other researchers in other laboratories with other subjects have repeated the experiment and found the same results does the psychologist really consider his conclusions reliable. (Psychology, like all sciences, is a communal enterprise.)

The Correlational Method

An experiment is one of the most reliable ways to investigate questions about behavior, but it is not always the most practical way. Suppose a psychologist wants to find out what makes a good pilot. Perhaps the Air Force has asked him to study this question because it costs thousands of dollars to train a single pilot, and every year a number of trainees drop out. The psychologist could conduct an experiment—he might raise 10 children in playrooms filled with toy planes and maps and compare their performance as adults in the training program to that of 10 children raised with planes, cars, baseballs, and stuffed animals. This method, called the **longitudinal method,** would probably tell the psychologist what he wanted to know, but both he and the Air Force would have to wait years for the results. The **correlational method** provides a shortcut.

The psychologist would begin by choosing 100 proven pilots and 100 unsuccessful ones. To gather information, he could give his pilots a variety of aptitude and personality tests. Suppose he found that all the successful pilots score higher than the unsuccessful pilots on mechanical aptitude tests, and that all the successful pilots are cautious individuals who do not like to take chances. Obviously there is some correlation between these characteristics and success as a pilot. He could then recommend that the Air Force use certain specific tests in choosing the next group of trainees. Suppose he also found that all the pilots played golf, came from the Midwest, and liked watermelon. There is no logical reason why these facts should go with piloting a plane; they just do. Puzzled, the psychologist might test another group of pilots for these characteristics. If he found that these men, too, played golf, came from the Midwest, and liked watermelon, he could conclude that a correlation existed, even though he could not explain it.

Correlational studies thus enable psychologists to identify relationships between two or more variables, without necessarily explaining why these relationships exist. This method has proved extremely useful in making up standardized tests. Intelligence tests, College Boards, tests for clerical and mechanical aptitude, are all based on extensive correlational studies—a person's performance on a test of clerical aptitude, for example, is compared to success or failure in an office job.

Stanley Milgram and one of his shock machines.
(*David Gahr, Time Magazine,*
© *Time Inc.*)

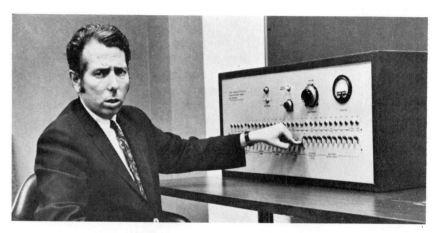

Most psychologists use a variety of methods to study a single problem. For example, a researcher interested in creativity might begin by giving a group of college students a creativity test invented by one of his colleagues. He will compare individuals' scores with their scores on intelligence tests and with their grades to see if there is any correlation between them. Then he might arrange to spend several weeks observing a college class and interviewing teachers, students, and parents to correlate classroom behavior and the adults' evaluations with the students' scores on the test of creativity. He decides to test some of his ideas with an experiment and chooses a group of the students to serve as subjects. His findings might give his colleague ideas for revising his test, or they might give the teachers and parents new insight about a particular student, a student like you.

Ethics in Psychology

The chances are not remote that you will have the opportunity to be a subject in some experiment in your psychology department. You will probably be offered a nominal sum of money or class credit for your participation. But it is possible that your participation may cause you some puzzlement and that you will learn the true purpose of the experiment only when it is over. Is this deception necessary in psychology experiments? And what if the experiment should cause you some discomfort?

All psychologists agree that these questions raise ethical issues. And so, more than 20 years ago the American Psychological Association (APA) drew up a code for treatment of experimental subjects (American Psychological Association, 1953). But in 1963, the issue of ethics was raised again when Stanley Milgram published the results of several experiments.

Milgram hired people to help him with a learning experiment and told them that they were to teach other people, the "learners," by giving them electric shocks when they gave wrong answers. The shocks could be given in various intensities from "Slight Shock" to "Severe Shock." The people were told to increase the intensity of the shock each time the learner made a mistake. As the shocks increased in intensity, the learners began to protest that they were being hurt. They cried out in pain and became increasingly upset as the shocking continued. The people giving the shocks often became concerned and frightened and asked if they could stop. But the experimenter politely but firmly pointed out that they were expected to continue.

This was the crux of the experiment. Milgram was not doing a learning experiment—he was investigating obedience. He wanted to find out whether anyone in the situation just described would actually go all the way and give the highest level of shock. Would they follow their consciences, or would they obey the experimenter? Incredibly,

65 percent of Milgram's subjects did go all the way, even though the learner stopped answering toward the end, and many subjects worried that the shocks might have done serious damage.

So Milgram found out what he wanted to know. But, in order to do it, he had to deceive his subjects. The stated purpose of the experiment—the testing of learning—was a lie. The shock machines were fakes—the learners received no shocks at all. And the learners themselves were Milgram's accomplices who had been trained to act as though they were being hurt (Milgram, 1963).

Although the design of this experiment is not typical of the vast majority of psychological experiments, it caused such a public uproar that the profession began to reevaluate its ethical health. In the wake of the controversy, a new code of ethics governing psychological experimentation has now been approved (Committee on Ethical Standards, 1971, 1972).

Temperatures run high on the issue. Those favoring stringent ethical controls feel that the rights of the subject are of prime importance, that procedures should never be emotionally or physically distressing, and that the experimenter should first explain to the potential subject what can be expected to happen.

But quite a few psychologists argue that strict ethical rules could damage the scientific validity of an experiment and could cripple future research. "Absolute moral values corrupt absolutely" (Gergen, 1973, p. 908). These psychologists also point out that few subjects—by their own admission—have been appreciably harmed. Even in Milgram's manipulative experiment, only 1.3 percent of the subjects reported negative feelings about their experience (Milgram, 1964).

Between these two extremes are the researchers who admit that abuses might occur, but who feel that research should be done to disclose exactly what effects experimental procedures have on subjects. They say that if psychology is really the science it claims to be, it should demonstrate and not just assert the need for a strict experimental code.

In the long run, psychology can only benefit from the ethical-standards controversy. Although unanimous adherence to a formal code of ethics is a long way off, very few experimenters conduct research studies that in any way raise serious ethical questions. If there is a serious ethical question, it is investigated, and the offenders are expected to change their methods.

The Social Relevance of Psychology

Pure versus Applied Psychology

We all, psychologists included, have basic curiosities about what makes Bill tick and Barbara tock. In all sciences, there are two basic approaches to satisfying those curiosities. One is **pure research**—that is,

(Dan Bernstein, Photo Researchers)

research for its own sake. Usually pure research grows out of a theory or other research and is only rarely a response to a pressing practical problem. Some pure research findings may then be utilized in concrete practical ways in society, thus becoming part of what is known as **applied psychology,** which is the second basic approach to psychological research. The pure psychologist does a lot of work that may not have immediate practical application to social problems. The applied psychologist, on the other hand, is directly involved in studying the problems of the teacher, the worker, the spouse, or perhaps the wider social effects of racism or militarism. But no one can tell in advance whether a study will have social relevance or whether a piece of applied research will turn out to have major theoretical significance.

This distinction between scholarly theorist and practical implementer is long-standing. Psychologists themselves have mixed views about it. In a recent survey of some 2,500 graduate students and faculty in the psychology departments of over 100 American universities, nearly half of those polled chose social relevance as "the most important issue confronting contemporary psychology" (Lipsey, 1974, p. 542). However, when asked where they would like to work, many of the respondents rated institutions stressing "help with social problems" as their least favorite choice. Most preferred scholarly, pure-research-oriented universities (Lipsey, 1974).

This rather contradictory finding reminds us that the harmony between pure psychological research and applied psychology is not yet perfect. However, theory without testing and application tends to become sterile. As one psychologist has put it, "Theory for theory's sake is scientism, not science" (Bass, 1974, p. 871). The reverse is also true. Practice without theory to support it tends to become merely technology. As you read this book, you will find examples of both theory and application, since most psychologists draw from both pure and applied research in their attempts to understand behavior.

(Bruce Buchenholz, Photo Researchers)

Using Animals in Psychological Research

One interesting aspect of the breach between pure and applied science is the question of using animal subjects in research that is basically designed to help us learn more about human behavior. Some psychologists believe that, since psychology is the science of behavior, animal behavior is just as important as human behavior. But however interesting animal behavior may be, what possible relevance does the life style of a 7-inch-long laboratory rat have to everyday human problems? Immediately, none perhaps. But many experiments—systematic brain surgery, for example—simply cannot be performed on human beings and so must be done with animals if anything at all is to be learned. Psychologists also use animal subjects because their behavior is simpler and their genetic history and immediate environment can be better

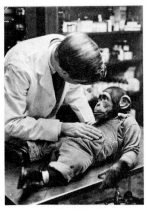

controlled. Animals' shorter life spans make it possible to study behavior over many generations, which would be highly impractical or impossible with humans. In addition, with animals there are no "social" complications between experimenter and subject.

The trained psychologist is able to observe behavioral similarities between animals and human beings without making oversimplified, one-to-one comparisons. Certainly, "mental illness" in a rat is of a different order from that in a human. But, if we are careful not to translate animal behavior too readily into human equivalents, then animal research does in fact contribute significantly to our understanding of behavior, including human behavior.

(Burk Uzzle, Magnum Photos)

New Directions in Psychology

Psychology, despite these problems and others we shall get into as we go along, is emphatically alive and well. Exciting things are happening, and they are happening in some previously unexplored areas. For example, there is the rapidly expanding field of environmental psychology, which looks at how our environment affects our behavior. It is not a separate specialty area as much as it is a combination of several specialties, all addressing themselves to the interaction of people and their environment. How does the layout of a park relate to its frequency of use? What do the contents of a living room tell us about its occupants? What cultural factors influence a person's perceptions of his own city? What are the psychological effects of traffic noise? How do physical surroundings mold personality and attitudes? Answers to questions such as these will help define the human factor in the man-environment relationship, which will, in turn, help to increase our chances of creating a more pleasant and supportive environment. In the coming years, you will be hearing new terms: psychogeography, ecological psychology, architectural psychology, and others not even thought of yet.

(Leonard Freed, Magnum Photos)

There is a hopeful note in this new direction. The integration of several specialties to form a new specialty, environmental psychology, is a good omen for the integration of other separate areas within psychology. By pooling their knowledge, psychologists will be able to make a bigger contribution to the effort to make life in our time more beneficial and rewarding for us all.

Summary

1. Psychology is the science that studies behavior and the unseen processes that shape behavior. Psychologists seek to *explain, predict,* and *control* behavior. Psychology is one of the behavioral sciences, but it is unique among this family of disciplines in that it emphasizes the individual.
2. Wilhelm Wundt established Europe's first psychological laboratory at the

University of Leipzig in 1879, where he intended to study the mind in an objective and scientific manner. He introduced measurement and experiment into psychology, which until then had been a branch of philosophy.

3. One of Wundt's students, Edward Bradford Titchener, became professor of psychology at Cornell University and established himself as the dean of American psychology. Wundt and Titchener both believed that psychology's role is to identify the basic elements of experience and to show how they are combined. Because of its emphasis on the basic units of experience and the combinations in which they occur, this school of psychology is known as *structuralism*.

4. While Wundt and Titchener were doing their work, Sir Francis Galton began dabbling in medicine and eventually became the father of mental tests. Galton pioneered the study of individual differences and the use of statistics and mathematics in psychological research. He also published several articles on mental imagery based on subjective introspection—an approach rejected by Wundt and Titchener.

5. William James, the first native American psychologist, believed that sensations cannot be separated from associations. Mental associations, he claimed, allow us to benefit from previous experience. James firmly believed that all activity is functional, and by applying biological principles to the mind, he arrived at the *functionalist* theory of mental life and behavior.

6. John B. Watson confronted both the structuralist and functionalist schools, stating that we can no more define "consciousness" than we can define the "soul." Psychology, he maintained, should only concern itself with observable, measurable behavior. Watson's theory is part of the *behaviorist school* of psychology. Watson based much of his work on Pavlov's conditioning experiments and thought that all behavior could be explained in terms of stimulus and response. He also suggested two new areas for study—learning and child development.

7. While Watson was working in America, a new school of thought, *Gestalt psychology*, was being developed in Germany. Roughly translated, *gestalt* means "whole" or "form." Gestalt psychologists suggested that learning depends on insight and on the perception of relationships; they concentrated on our tendency to see patterns, to distinguish an object from its background, to complete pictures from a few cues. They felt that attempts to break perception and thought down into its elements were misguided, since people and animals respond not to specific stimuli but to whole situations.

8. Behaviorism was thriving in America when B. F. Skinner replaced Watson as its leader. Skinner's beliefs were similar to Watson's, but he made the animal an active agent in the conditioning process by adding reinforcement, or reward, to stimulate learning. Skinner's work led to a school of psychology known as *S-R psychology*, which has made significant contributions to applied psychology by proposing effective methods of changing behavior.

9. *Psychoanalysis* was not recognized as a part of psychology until the late 1920s, after Freud had worked out his theories on the conflict between unconscious desires and the demands of society. This conflict, he felt, often leads to anxiety or exaggerated fears. His theories of the unconscious, of

infantile sexuality, and of dreams remain controversial today. Nevertheless, Freud laid the groundwork for psychotherapy with his famous "talking cure."

10. In the past 40 years different views of psychology have emerged. *Cognitive psychology* combines behaviorism and Gestalt psychology by studying how perception influences behavior and, conversely, how experience influences perception.

11. *Existential psychology* views modern man's alienation as the cause of his apathy and psychological problems. The goal of the existential psychologist is to lead people to an inner sense of identity so that they can care, commit themselves, and love.

12. *Humanistic psychology,* similar to existential psychology in arguing that people must learn to realize their potential, emphasizes communication through the senses in order to achieve self-actualization and joy through other people.

13. Today psychology is divided more according to specialties than according to theories. Some of the areas of specialization are *educational psychology, industrial psychology, social psychology, developmental psychology, physiological psychology,* and *clinical psychology.*

14. Psychologists use scientific methods to study behavior. The *naturalistic-observation method* is used to study animal and human behavior in natural settings, instead of in the laboratory under artificial conditions.

15. The *experimental method* begins with an idea or hypothesis about the relationship between two or more variables. To determine whether they are related, the experimenter manipulates one—the *independent variable*—to see how it affects the other—the *dependent variable.* The experimenter uses a number of precautionary *controls* to help ensure that he is observing only the effects of the one independent variable.

16. The *correlational method* provides a means of investigating the relationships between certain characteristics and behavior variables without necessarily manipulating or controlling those variables. As a result, it is often difficult to explain with any certainty why the correlation exists.

17. More than 20 years ago the American Psychological Association drew up a code of ethics for the treatment of subjects in psychological experiments. Although not all psychologists are convinced that such a code is needed, very few do work that raises serious ethical questions.

18. Psychologists have two basic approaches to satisfying their curiosity. *Pure research* is research done for its own sake rather than to respond to a specific practical problem. In *applied research,* the psychologist is directly involved in studying real-life social problems. Most psychologists draw from both approaches in their attempts to understand behavior.

19. Psychologists use animals in research because some types of experiments cannot be done on humans; animals have shorter life spans, which allows a researcher to study behavior over several generations; and animals' genetic history and immediate environment can be better controlled. Although psychologists are careful about generalizing from animal to human behavior, they find that animal research does make a significant contribution to their understanding of behavior in general.

20. An important new area in psychology is *environmental psychology,* which looks at how our environment affects our behavior. Because several spe-

cialties in psychology have combined to investigate a single issue, environmental psychology represents a break in the trend toward increasingly narrow specialization that has characterized psychology in recent years.

Suggested Readings

Bachrach, A. J., *Psychological Research: An Introduction,* 3rd ed. (New York: Random House, 1972). A philosophical overview of the goals and methods of science that also discusses ethics and the role of the scientist in society.

Doherty, M. E., and Shemberg, K. M., *Asking Questions about Behavior: An Introduction to What Psychologists Do* (Englewood Cliffs, N.J.: Prentice-Hall, 1970). Starting with the topic of stress, the authors illustrate the principles of research by describing approaches taken by a wide variety of psychologists.

Hyman, R., *The Nature of Psychological Inquiry* (Englewood Cliffs, N.J.: Prentice-Hall, 1964). A concise description of the process of psychological research, from getting the ideas through communicating the results.

Krawiec, T. S., *The Psychologists: What They Do and How They Came to Do It,* vols. I and II (New York: Oxford University Press, 1972, 1974). Brief biographies of contemporary psychologists that describe how they got interested in psychology, what their careers were like, and so on.

McCain, G., and Segal, E. M., *The Game of Science,* 2nd ed. (Belmont, Calif.: Brooks/Cole, 1973). A very clever and light introduction to scientific investigation.

Moursund, J. P., *Evaluation: An Introduction to Research Design* (Belmont, Calif.: Brooks/Cole, 1973). A very good, if traditional, overview of research design and data collection.

Murphy, G., and Kowack, J. K., *Historical Introduction to Modern Psychology,* 4th ed. (New York: Harcourt Brace Jovanovich, 1975). A good standard history of psychology, going all the way back to the philosophical roots.

Pfungst, O., *Clever Hans* (New York: Holt, Rinehart & Winston, 1965). Hans was a horse who appeared to know how to add and subtract, multiply and divide, read and spell. Pfungst's book, especially the introduction by Robert Rosenthal, is a fascinating case history of the scientific methods used to discover that Hans was really responding to his owner's unintentional cues.

outline

GENETICS 32

Cell Mechanisms in Heredity
Biochemical Genetics

BEHAVIOR GENETICS 35

Sex-Linked Characteristics
Genetic Abnormalities
Polygenic Inheritance
Genetics and Development
Social Implications of Behavior Genetics

THE ENDOCRINE SYSTEM 44

THE NERVOUS SYSTEM 50

The Neuron
The Neural Impulse
The Synapse
Divisions of the Nervous System
The Autonomic Nervous System
The Central Nervous System
Psychosurgery and Electrical Stimulation of the Brain

SUMMARY 67

SUGGESTED READINGS 70

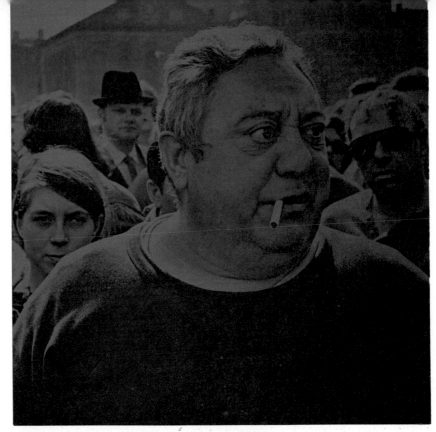

Biology and Behavior

The famous inventor Thomas Alva Edison once remarked that "the chief function of the body is to carry the brain around." We can all see his point. Yet, actually your body does much more than transport your thoughts and feelings from place to place. The activities in your body are as tied to your individuality as what goes on in the proverbial gray matter of your brain is. Every cell in your body, not just your thinking apparatus, determines the kind of person you are.

You are born with your body, and it is the most familiar thing in the world to you, but do you really know how it works? In this chapter—without trying to become medical experts—we turn our attention to the genetic and biological underpinnings of psychology, the flesh-and-blood side of behavior. As students of psychology, we owe it to ourselves to know something about genetics and about how our physical systems—such as the endocrine system and the nervous system—work, because these have important effects on the way we think, feel, and behave. Also, the study of the physiological side of psychology, as we shall see, raises some important social and ethical issues.

Our initial focus in this chapter is a microscopic one, that of genetics—the study of the elemental biological alphabet that accounts for our individual natures.

Genetics

Genetics is the study of how traits are passed from one generation to the next—in plants, animals, people. A trait in this context means whatever characteristic is being discussed—curly hair, a crooked little finger, the inability of the blood to clot, or an allergy to poison ivy.

A Moravian monk named Gregor Mendel gave modern genetics its beginning in 1867, when he reported the results of many long years of systematically breeding garden peas (Mendel, 1867). Mendel had devised a set of laws that he believed applied to all inherited characteristics, both in plants and in animals.

Every trait, Mendel believed, was controlled by elements that were transmitted unchanged from one generation to the next. He called these elements **genes.** According to Mendel's laws, offspring inherited one tendency for a particular attribute—toward tallness or shortness, for example—from one parent and a second tendency from the other parent. Sometimes the two tendencies were the same; sometimes they were different. If the two tendencies were contradictory, one would dominate the other. The particular combination of genes an offspring received would determine the course of its development.

Figure 2-1

Magnified millions of times, this single gene was the first ever to be isolated and photographed. Its actual length is only 50 millionths of an inch. (From J. Shapiro et al. "The Isolation of Pure *Lac* Operon DNA," *Nature* (London), 1969, *224,* 768. Electron micrograph by Lorne MacHattie; reprinted by permission of Dr. James Shapiro and *Nature* magazine.)

Cell Mechanisms in Heredity

Genes were hypothetical entities to Mendel—ideas he invented to account for the facts he observed. We know a great deal more about the mechanisms of heredity today. We know, for example, that genes exist in the nucleus of every living cell. We know that genes are lined up on tiny threadlike bodies called **chromosomes,** which can be seen under a microscope. The chromosomes are arranged in pairs inside the cell nucleus, and each species has a particular number of pairs. Mice have 20 pairs, monkeys 27, garden peas 7. Human beings have 23 pairs of chromosomes in every normal body cell (see Figure 2-2).

When one of these ordinary human cells divides, each of the 46 chromosomes in the cell nucleus splits in two. The cell matter that surrounds the nucleus separates too, and the two new cells are exact copies of the parent cell. Each contains a full set of 46 chromosomes, or 23 pairs.

However, when sex cells, called **gametes,** are formed, the chromosomes do not divide. One member of each pair of chromosomes goes to each of the two new cells. Gametes thus have only 23 chromosomes,

Figure 2-2
The 46 human
chromosomes, separated
into 23 pairs.
(*Leonard Lessin, Photo
Researchers*)

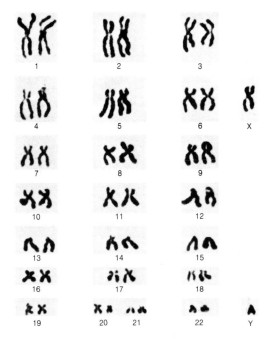

not 46. Moreover, each gamete formed has received a different random collection of 23 chromosomes from the original 46. When a female sex cell, an **ovum,** is fertilized by a male sex cell, a **sperm,** a one-celled **zygote** is formed. The zygote thus has 46 chromosomes—the 23 chromosomes from the mother's ovum plus the 23 chromosomes from the father's sperm.

Each set of chromosomes carries a complete set of genes. Any given gene may exist in two or more alternate forms. We can think of a gene for eye color, for example, as having one form, *B,* that will result in brown eyes and another form, *b,* that will result in blue eyes. If a child receives *B* genes from both parents, his eyes will be brown. If he receives *b* genes from both parents, his eyes will be blue. But if he inherits a *B* gene from one parent and a *b* gene from the other, his eyes will be brown (see Figure 2-3). The *B* form is thus said to be a **dominant** gene, the *b* form is **recessive.** Although the person with one *B* gene and one *b* gene has brown eyes himself, the recessive *b* gene is still present and can be passed on to an offspring, who will have blue eyes if he receives a *b* gene from his other parent.

The existence of dominant and recessive genes helps to explain why a person's underlying genetic makeup, his genotype, can differ from the characteristics that can be seen or measured, his **phenotype.** As the eye-color example illustrates, a phenotype may not always be a reliable guide to the genotype underlying it. The person with one *B* gene and one *b* gene for eye color has the same phenotype as the person whose

Figure 2-3
Transmission of eye color by dominant (*B*) and recessive (*b*) genes. This figure represents the parents' probable offspring. If the parents have only two children, the odds are that both children will have brown eyes.

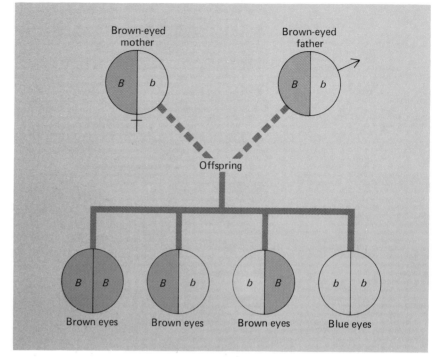

genetic inheritance is two *B* genes for eye color—both have brown eyes. But their underlying genotypes are different, and therefore the odds that they will pass their own eye color on to their children will also be different.

Biochemical Genetics

The last 20 years have brought a tremendous increase in our understanding of just how genetic information is transmitted. The biochemical basis of the gene is now understood to be **deoxyribonucleic acid—DNA.** DNA makes up about 40 percent of the chromosomal matter. Every cell contains billions of coils of DNA—enough genetic information, or "words," to direct the development of a single cell, the zygote, into a fully grown adult with billions of cells. It is DNA that enables a cell to reproduce exact copies of itself.

DNA never leaves the nucleus of the cell. Everything it needs to duplicate itself is already present within the nucleus. But DNA has a second function—it controls the production of proteins by the cell. These proteins, the fundamental elements of all bodily substances and the chemical middlemen that control all the basic life processes, are manufactured in every cell in the cytoplasm, the part of the cell that surrounds the nucleus. In order to control the production of proteins without leaving the nucleus, DNA manufactures molecules of **ribonucleic acid—RNA.** Two main kinds of RNA—*messenger-RNA* and *transfer-RNA*—are involved in the manufacture of proteins. The functions of these two kinds of RNA are exactly what their names indicate: messenger-RNA travels out of the cell nucleus into the cytoplasm, carrying a coded message that specifies which particular protein is to be produced. Transfer-RNA, meanwhile, picks up the necessary components and transfers them to the place in the cytoplasm where the protein is to be manufactured. Together, the messenger-RNA and the transfer-RNA carry out the instructions given to them by the DNA in the nucleus of the cell.

These discoveries go a long way toward providing a picture of how the genetic processes operate, but there is still much to be learned. Quite often, we do not even know which genes and chromosomes govern certain characteristics that clearly are inherited. But there are some situations where we do have specific knowledge about the effects of individual genes and chromosomes.

Behavior Genetics

While Mendel was studying plants and formulating his genetic laws, Charles Darwin was conducting his world-shaking research on the evolution of animal species. Darwin gradually came to recognize the importance of biological inheritance in behavioral traits, such as basic intelligence and athletic skills. However, it was his half-cousin, Francis Galton, who first attempted to explain the transmission of behavioral traits and who devised tests to measure these traits. His work laid the foundations of what is known today as **behavior genetics.**

The central concern in behavior genetics is to determine the influence of heredity on behavior. How much influence heredity has on behavior forms the basis of the long-standing argument called the "nature-nurture controversy." In other words, are you the way you are because of your genes or because of your environment?

The basic method for measuring the effects of heredity is to keep the effects of the environment constant. Psychologists then create genetic variations to see what happens. For example, will a rat from a laboratory-bred strain perform better in a maze than a rat picked at random, if both are raised in the same environment? Behavioral geneticists do considerable research to compare the behavioral traits of different breeds and strains of animals. Using animals other than humans, they have detected hereditary influence in such characteristics as general activity, willingness to explore strange environments, aggressiveness, eating habits, and territoriality. Researchers have discovered definite genetic factors in the hygienic behavior of bees, for example, by observing whether different bee colonies eject dead larvae (immature bees) from the hive (Rothenbuhler, 1958, 1964*a*, 1964*b*, 1967).

A so-called yellow gene has been shown to reduce the quantity of courtship activity in a species of wasp (Bastock, 1956).

But the demonstration of hereditary influence does not mean that it is the only determinant of behavior. We should remember that environment also plays a role in most behavior. For example, two psychologists raised rats chosen at random in enriched (or challenging) environments and found that the rats did just as well in mazes as those rats selectively bred for brightness (Cooper & Zubek, 1958).

In the area of human behavior, psychologists have related genetics to intelligence and to disorders such as schizophrenia.* But, generally speaking, we still know relatively little about the actual mechanisms of genetic inheritance in human beings, and here the goals of the behavior geneticists are more ambitious. They seek not only to measure the extent of heredity's effects on behavior but also to develop bio-chemical analysis of chromosomes to discover how so-called good traits (notably, intelligence) are genetically determined. Most research in this area has had to be done with animals. The causes of human behavior are complex, and, therefore, comparisons between animal and human behavior are not easily made. For example, can a rat's quickness in learning to perform in a maze be compared to a student's performance on tests? Keep this in mind as we look at some examples of genetic determination of behavior.

Sex-Linked Characteristics

Whether a person is male or female is one of the clearest examples of genetic determination. Twenty-two of the 23 pairs of chromosomes in human cells are structurally similar and contain equal amounts of genetic information. The members of the twenty-third pair, the sex chromosomes, are not alike (look again at Figure 2-2). Females have two equivalent X chromosomes, named for the fact that they look like the letter X. Males, however, have one X chromosome and one smaller Y chromosome, named for its resemblance to the letter Y. Therefore, the genetic makeup of the father's sperm determines the sex of the offspring. The mother can only offer X chromosomes. So, if the father contributes an X chromosome, the child will be a girl. If the father contributes a Y chromosome, the child will be a boy (see Figure 2-4). The Y chromosome appears to contain some kind of genetic information that directs certain cells in the unborn child to become testes. The hormones produced by the testes then take over and cause the other male characteristics to develop (see the discussion of the gonads later in this chapter).

However, the Y chromosome is smaller than the X chromosome and thus cannot carry as much information. This explains why several

---

*Schizophrenia, a serious behavior disorder, is discussed more fully in Chapter 14.

Figure 2-4
Sex is determined by the X
and Y chromosomes.
Females inherit two X
chromosomes; males inherit
one X and one Y.

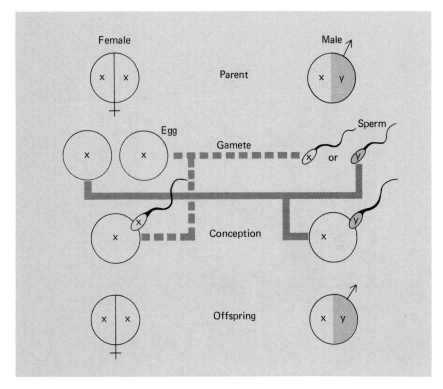

Figure 2-4
Sex is determined by the X and Y chromosomes. Females inherit two X chromosomes; males inherit one X and one Y.

inherited conditions occur far more frequently in males than in females. Hemophilia, for example, a disease that prevents the blood from clotting, may be carried as a recessive gene on one of a woman's X chromosomes. She herself will not suffer from the disease, because her other X chromosome will carry a dominant gene that will mask the recessive one and cause her blood to clot normally. But if she passes the X chromosome with the recessive gene for hemophilia on to a son, the Y chromosome he inherits from his father will not carry the dominant gene. The boy will inherit hemophilia (see Figure 2-5). Since the disease has been traced to the sex chromosomes, it is called a **sex-linked characteristic.** Other sex-linked characteristics are red-green color blindness and certain forms of muscular dystrophy. The recessive genes that cause these conditions are always carried by one of the mother's X chromosomes, even though she herself may have perfect color vision and normal coordination. The father's Y chromosome, being smaller, cannot protect his son from developing these handicaps.

Genetic Abnormalities

Since the sequence of events that governs genetic transmission is so enormously complex, it is amazing that more mistakes do not occur. A few do. Sometimes when a gamete is formed—long before fertiliza-

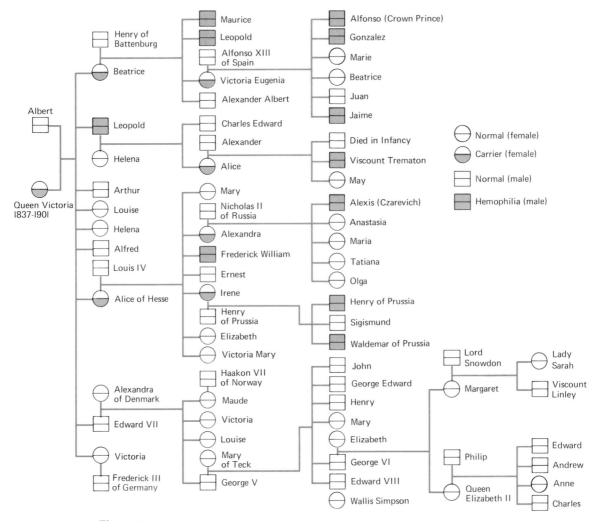

Figure 2-5

Queen Victoria of England carried a recessive gene for hemophilia and passed it on to many of her descendants. One of her sons and several of her grandsons and great-grandsons inherited the disorder. (Adapted from J. H. Otto and A. Towle, *Modern Biology.* New York: Holt, Rinehart & Winston, 1969.)

tion occurs—one or more of the chromosome pairs fail to separate normally. One of the ovum or sperm cells will get both members of the chromosome pair, while the other new gamete is missing it entirely. Or a chromosome may break. The part that is broken off may migrate mistakenly to one of the new cells, where it will be extra genetic material. The other cell formed at the same time will lack this crucial chromosomal material. If one of these abnormal gametes is later involved in fertilization, the resulting organism will be defective, if it survives at all. These genetic abnormalities act to disrupt the biochemical processes in the organism; this in turn affects the organism's behavior.

One such abnormality is *Down's syndrome,* or mongolism. Persons with this condition are severely retarded; IQs usually range from 20

Figure 2-6
The chromosome pattern
characteristic of Down's
syndrome, or mongolism.
Note that there are three
number-21 chromosomes
instead of the normal two.
*(Leonard Lessin, Photo
Researchers)*

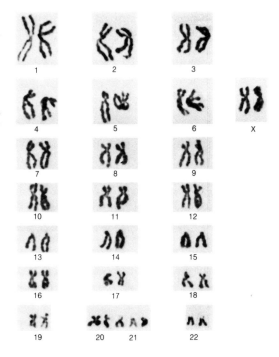

to 60.* The distinctive physical features—slanted eyes, flattened facial contours, a thick tongue—are the reason for the term mongolism. The condition has been traced to the chromosome pair that is usually numbered 21. The victim of Down's syndrome has inherited more than the two normal members of this chromosome pair—sometimes a complete third chromosome (as in Figure 2-6), sometimes just an extra fragment of chromosome-21 material.

A second genetic abnormality, *Turner's syndrome*, found mostly in females, causes retarded sexual development, shortness of stature, and a webbed neck. Many patients with this condition possess only 45 chromosomes. The missing one is an X, a sex chromosome. These people are called X0 females. Another characteristic of this condition is that although their intellectual abilities may fall within the normal range, these people often have serious deficiencies in perceptual abilities (for example, in perceiving three-dimensional relationships).

Another abnormality of the sex chromosomes can lead to *Klinefelter's syndrome*, which causes breast development, small testes, and lack of sperm production in males, along with slight mental retardation (in about half of the cases). The genetic makeup associated with this condition is XXY—two X chromosomes instead of the normal one.

---

*The average IQ for normal people is around 100. For more details about IQ, see Chapter 7.

It is also possible to find the genetic makeup XYY. For a while, the work of several investigators suggested that higher percentages of males with an extra Y chromosome could be found in maximum-security institutions than in the population at large, and that they were often not only very tall, but also unusually aggressive and subnormal in intelligence. This led, of course, to speculation that criminal tendencies might be inherited. Many psychologists question the relationship between the XYY genetic makeup and antisocial behavior, mainly because of the small number of people studied so far. The social consequences are such that these psychologists want to wait for more extensive research before they draw conclusions about the effects that an XYY genetic makeup may have on behavior. For example, more recent research has established that only a small number of serious criminals have an extra Y chromosome, and that neither tallness nor criminal habits invariably accompany an XYY configuration (McClearns & DeFries, 1973). Many XYY males lead ordinary lives, it would seem, like one fairly typical individual—a man with average height and build and an IQ of 97, who had been law-abiding all his life (Wiener & Sutherland, 1968).

The person with one extra X or Y chromosome may well have normal intelligence or be only mildly retarded. Multiple duplications, however—like XXX, XXXY, XXXX, or XXXXY—usually result in serious mental deficiency. The reasons for these gross abnormalities are not clear. Certain environmental agents have been suggested—radiation, perhaps, or viral infections—but no single answer explains all the cases that have been identified.

Polygenic Inheritance

Brother Mendel's laws were worked out to describe the transmission of simple, qualitative, either/or traits. They explain perfectly adequately the inheritance of characteristics governed by single genes—like blood type, for example. An individual has either A or B or O or AB type blood. But attempts to apply Mendel's rules to traits that are quantitatively distributed—traits that a person has more or less of—have failed. Intelligence, for example, is not an either/or trait that people have none of or all of; some people are plainly more intelligent than others. The same is true for height—most people are neither dwarfs nor giants, but somewhere in between and within a certain range. This seems in fact to be true of most human traits, particularly the ones that interest psychologists.

To describe the genetic transmission of quantitatively distributed characteristics, we must introduce the concept of **polygenic inheritance.** Most human traits are determined by the interaction of a number of separate genes. The reverse is also true—one gene can sometimes affect many traits. The genes that contribute to a particular polygenic trait may all be located on the same chromosome, or they may be spread over several chromosomes. Each gene in a polygenic system appears to act independently, as do the genes that "single-handedly" control a specific trait. But instead of having an all-or-none effect, each of the genes in a polygenic system makes a small contribution to the trait in question. Like the instruments in a symphony orchestra, each contributing a separate note to the sound that reaches the audience, the genes in a polygenic system have a cumulative effect.

It is thus more difficult to study polygenic inheritance than it is to trace the origins of traits that are determined by single genes. Complicated statistical techniques have been developed to analyze the effects of large numbers of genes acting together in a polygenic system. But the difficulties do not stop there—we also have to account for the effects of the environment on the way a particular trait will develop.

Genetics and Development

Many inborn traits or characteristics become manifest only at a later stage of the individual's development. One example of such a developmental interval is the grave hereditary disease known as *Huntington's chorea*. Men and women who have this disease are born with it, but its symptoms generally do not appear until the person is around 35 years old. The disease is caused by premature decay of nerve cells in the cerebrum and is characterized by involuntary jerky movements of the body and progressive intellectual deterioration. There are also unpleasant personality changes—irritable and hostile behavior, sloppiness, and loss of self-control. Since the disease is transmitted by a dominant gene, half the victim's children will be likely to inherit the disease. Unfortunately, many afflicted people have already had children before their condition is discovered.

Some genetic traits may be latent; that is, having the proper genes provides an individual with the *potential* for a trait, but that trait may not necessarily show up unless the environment cooperates. Thus, in many cases, both "nature" and "nurture" influence the realization of your genetic potential. For example, a white Himalayan rabbit has a genetic predisposition to black paws, but they will become black only if the rabbit is raised in a cold environment. Raising the rabbit in a warm environment causes its paws to stay white (Sinnott, Dunn, & Dobzhansky, 1958).

One way to approach the problem of the heritability of a trait in humans is through the study of twins. All identical twins, so called because they develop from a single fertilized ovum, are identical in genetic makeup. Any differences between them should, therefore, be due to environmental differences. Fraternal twins, on the other hand, develop from two separate fertilized egg cells and have no more in common genetically than any other brothers and sisters. The differences

(Courtesy Francis P. Riffle, American Himalayan Rabbit Association)

(*Charles Harbutt, Magnum Photos*)

between fraternal twins are thus due both to genetic and environmental differences.

The most significant studies involving comparisons of twins have concerned the heritability of schizophrenia. In a classic American study of 1,000 pairs of twins (Kallman, 1953), it was found that where one fraternal twin was schizophrenic, the other was schizophrenic in only 10 percent of the cases. But for identical twins, when one twin was schizophrenic, the other was schizophrenic in 69 percent of the cases. Thus, there is good reason to conclude that schizophrenia is highly heritable.

Another way to study trait heritability is through whole family groups. Here again there is strong evidence for a genetic basis for schizophrenia. In cases where both parents of a schizophrenic are schizophrenic, between 45 and 68 percent of their children are also schizophrenic. Where neither parent is schizophrenic, the figure is only 5 to 10 percent. Such findings (as opposed to those involving identical twins) do not rule out the possibility that environment is a contributing factor, because growing up in a household in which both parents are schizophrenic could cause a child to become schizophrenic even if he doesn't have a genetic predisposition for that disorder.

How can we more clearly isolate the influence of household atmosphere in studies of schizophrenia? One way is to study adopted children. If a child of a schizophrenic parent is given up for adoption at birth and raised thereafter in a normal home, is he more or less likely to become schizophrenic than an adopted child whose natural parents are not schizophrenic? One recent study located 47 people who had schizophrenic mothers but who had been adopted at birth. Of these

(*From the collection of Catherine Noren*)

(*Marvin Lichtner, Time-Life Picture Agency, © Time Inc.*)

47, five had become schizophrenic. In another group of people who had been adopted at birth but who did not have schizophrenic parents, there was no schizophrenia at all (Heston, 1966). Thus, although schizophrenia is highly heritable, both heredity and environment determine whether this trait will be displayed.

Clearly, the complex interaction of genetics and environment makes it difficult—if not inadvisable—to seek cut-and-dried conclusions about the effects of one or the other. The ultimate issue is not how much is contributed by heredity and how much by environment but how the two interact and how each one affects the other.

Social Implications of Behavior Genetics

Science, far from thriving in a vacuum, has definite effects on society at large. The implications of research in behavior genetics are perhaps greater than those of most other areas of the social sciences, because the findings may affect our evolution as a species. If a scientist were to demonstrate that a particular mental or physical deficiency is largely hereditary, should society take steps to avert "more of the same"? And if that scientist could also demonstrate a genetic influence for genius, should society try to breed only geniuses?

Even before the word "genetics" was introduced, Francis Galton had coined the term **eugenics** to refer to the science of improving a species through restrictive or selective breeding. This is a common practice among animal breeders all over the world. For example, a dairy farmer who lets only his best cows have calves is seeking to improve the overall quality of his herd by using selective breeding, or eugenics. Eugenics measures relating to human breeding have long been a reality in the United States. The first law for the sterilization of the feeble-minded was passed in Indiana in 1907. Other eugenics measures taken both in Europe and the United States include isolation of retarded people, immigration restrictions, and marriage proscriptions.

Ellis Island, 1913. The man on the right is an immigrant who is being given a test for feeble-mindedness. The man in the middle is a doctor for the U.S. Public Health Service, and the man on the left is an interpreter. The decorations on the wall were also used as part of the test. Although not very well publicized, such screening still goes on today, though it takes place in the immigrant's country of origin.
(*National Archives, Public Health Service Files, Photo 90-G-22D-10*)

Justice Oliver Wendell Holmes defended the sterilization law following its first application in Virginia in 1924 by saying: "It is better for the world, if instead of waiting to execute degenerate offspring for crime, or to let them starve for their imbecility, society can prevent those who are manifestly unfit from continuing their kind. The principle that sustains compulsory vaccination is broad enough to cover cutting the Fallopian tubes. . . . Three generations of imbeciles are enough" (Buck v. Bell, 274 U.S. 200, p. 207, cited in McClearns & DeFries, 1973, pp. 267–268).

We can all see that Justice Holmes had a point, but a consistent program of genetic control applied to humans has invariably been affected by political and racial considerations. The crucial words in Justice Holmes's opinion are "manifestly unfit." Who decides what traits make a person manifestly unfit? The moral dilemma and the example of the genetically determined genocide practiced by Nazi Germany have combined to make "eugenics" a dirty word for most people.

There is a positive side to genetic engineering. In only the past decade, the progress made in biochemistry and medicine—in birth control, artificial insemination, organ transplants, prenatal sex determination—have been breathtaking. By informing them of the risks, genetic counselors help parents who are concerned about passing undesirable traits on to their children. But are such advances, which proclaim a new scientific age of "donors," "screening," and "test-tube babies," really positive? Although some scientists anticipate the advantages of sperm banks of "superior" genes, others are wary of the dangers of manipulation of basic evolutionary processes. Sociologist Amatai Etzioni (1973), for example, warns that the ability to pre-select the sex of one's child might result in male-dominated societies, which could lead to class alienation, increasing violence, and cultural decline. Etzioni is not the only scientist calling for vigilant controls on such biological research. An international conference of biologists working on genetic engineering recently advised restrictions on some kinds of genetic research (McElheny, 1975).

Certainly there is a potential for misapplication in any scientific research. But the issues of behavior genetics are being brought to the attention of the government and the general public at a time when most research is still at the one-celled-animal level. The issues raised by behavior genetics are moral, legal, and political, as well as scientific. And if these moral, legal, and political aspects receive attention at the same time that scientific research is progressing, the chances are greater that we will use the knowledge effectively and wisely.

The Endocrine System

Billions of cells make up each adult human body, and these cells are obviously not all alike. Very early in the life of an unborn child, certain groups of cells differentiate to perform specialized functions—to form all the different organs and tissues that make up the human body. But when a group of cells begins to specialize in one job, it loses the potential ability to do many other jobs. It comes to depend on other groups of cells to perform those functions—the lungs depend on the heart to circulate blood, the heart depends on the stomach to digest food, and so on. The more complex the organism, the more crucial the need for organization, for the activities of one part of the body to be integrated with the activities of all the other parts.

As the human baby develops in its mother's womb, two distinct coordinating mechanisms evolve. One is organized to receive information, integrate it, and send instructions to various parts of the body by means of *electrical* messages; this is the **nervous system.** The other coordinating mechanism, the **endocrine system,** is attuned to receiving and sending *chemical* messages to regulate the activity of cells in various parts of the body. Each of these systems plays a part in coordinating the activities of the various parts of the body. And each of these systems helps to maintain **homeostasis**—to keep conditions inside the body in balance so the specialized cells can continue to function.

The endocrine system works automatically by means of internal organs called **glands.** Some of the endocrine glands are controlled by the nervous system; others respond directly to conditions inside the body.

The glands that make up the endocrine system control changes all over the body by secreting chemical substances called **hormones.** Hormones, either acting singly or together, are responsible for individual differences in vitality; for the readiness of nerves and muscles to react; for the rate of metabolism, growth, and sexual development; for the body's preparations for pregnancy and childbirth; for emotional balance in general. The endocrine glands release hormones directly into the bloodstream, which then carries them to whatever body tissue they act upon—their "target" tissue. This is what distinguishes the endocrine glands from the rest of the glands in the human body. The other glands, like the salivary glands or the tear glands, are called *exocrine glands.* Instead of using the bloodstream as a highway, the exocrine glands come equipped with ducts that carry their secretions directly to the tissues they serve. Some hormones affect organs directly; others act on other hormones, either increasing or canceling out their effects. Some hormones regulate the activity of many organs; others affect only one.

The locations of the endocrine glands are shown in Figure 2-7. Some of the glands occur in pairs, like the ovaries and testes. Sometimes, as in the case of the anterior and posterior pituitary, two parts of the same structure act quite independently. Some of the glands secrete only one hormone; others produce several. At present we know of at least 27 different hormones, all of which are important to behavior. Our discussion of the individual glands will focus on those whose functions are best understood and those whose effects are most closely related to the way we behave.

Figure 2-7
The glands of the endocrine
system.

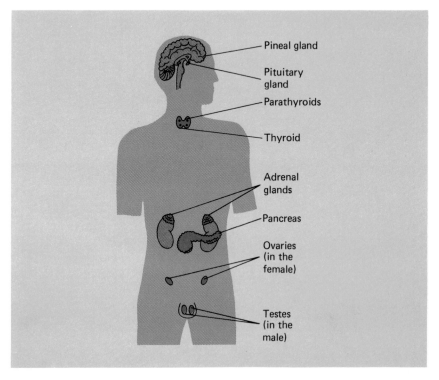

Pineal gland

Pituitary gland

Parathyroids

Thyroid

Adrenal glands

Pancreas

Ovaries (in the female)

Testes (in the male)

The thyroid gland. The thyroid gland is located just below the larynx, or voice box. It produces one primary hormone—*thyroxin,* which regulates the body's rate of **metabolism;** that is, it determines how fast or how slowly the foods we eat are transformed into the energy we need to function normally. Differences in the metabolic rate determine how alert and energetic people are, how fat or thin they tend to be.

If a person's thyroid gland produces too much thyroxin, his appetite will be huge, he will eat everything in sight, and he may still stay very much underweight. His reactions may also be speeded up and extremely intense—especially his reactions to stress.

Too little thyroxin leads to the other extreme—an eternally exhausted person who sleeps and sleeps and still cannot seem to stop being tired. His body is unable to maintain normal temperature; his muscle tone is reduced; his system is sluggish. If undersecretion of thyroxin happens in childhood, it can lead to a condition called *cretinism,* which is characterized mainly by mental retardation. If the condition is spotted in time, doses of thyroxin can correct it.

The parathyroid glands. Embedded in the thyroid gland are the **parathyroids**—four tiny pea-shaped organs. They secrete *parathormone,* which controls and balances the level of calcium and phosphate in the blood and tissue fluids. The level of calcium in the blood has a direct effect on the excitability of the nervous system. A person with too little parathormone will be hypersensitive and may suffer from twitches or muscle spasms. Too much parathormone, on the other hand, may lead to lethargy and poor physical coordination.

The pancreas. The pancreas lies in a curve between the stomach and the small intestine. The pancreas controls the level of sugar in the blood by secreting two hormones—*insulin* and *glucagon*. The two hormones work against each other to keep the blood-sugar level properly balanced.

When the pancreas secretes too little insulin so that there is too much sugar in the blood, the kidneys attempt to get rid of the excess sugar by excreting a great deal more water than usual. The tissues get dehydrated and poisonous wastes accumulate in the blood. The person has *diabetes mellitus* and needs insulin and a special diet to keep his blood-sugar level normal. Oversecretion of insulin, on the other hand, leads to too little sugar in the blood and the chronic fatigue of *hypoglycemia*.

The pituitary gland. The endocrine gland that produces the largest number of different hormones and thus has the widest range of effects on the body's functions is the pituitary gland. This gland is located on the underside of the brain, connected to a part of the brain called the hypothalamus. The pituitary gland, as we mentioned earlier, has two parts that function quite separately.

The tallest living man in the world, one of the smallest, and one who's just about average. Don Koehler is 8 feet 2 inches tall and lives in Chicago. Mihaly Mezaros, whose nickname is "Michu," is 33 inches short and is a clown with the Ringling Brothers Circus. The just about average man is television host David Frost, who arranged for the two extremes to meet. (*Wide World Photos*)

The *posterior pituitary* (toward the back) is controlled by the nervous system. It secretes two hormones—*oxytocin,* which signals the uterus to contract during childbirth and alerts the mammary glands to start producing milk, and *vasopressin,* which causes the blood pressure to rise and regulates the amount of water in the body's cells.

The *anterior pituitary* (toward the front) is controlled by chemical messages from the bloodstream and is often called the "master gland." It produces five hormones that trigger the action of other endocrine glands—*thyrotrophic hormone* (TTH), which activates the thyroid gland; *andrenocorticotrophic hormone* (ACTH), which triggers the reactions of the adrenal cortex; and three other hormones that control the gonads, the sex glands. The anterior pituitary also controls the timing and amount of body growth by producing *somatotrophic hormone* (STH). Too little STH creates a 3- or 4-foot-tall pituitary dwarf; too much STH creates a pituitary giant 8 or 9 feet tall.

The gonads. The gonads—the **testes** in males and the **ovaries** in females—work with the adrenal glands to stimulate the reproductive organs to become mature. They also account for the appearance of what are called *secondary sex characteristics*—breasts, beards, pubic hair, change of voice, and distribution of body fat appropriate to males or females.

These enormously influential glands produce several hormones—often called sex hormones—that fall into three types. These three types of hormones overlap and interlock in some very complex ways, but in broad outline this is the way they usually work: The **androgens** promote and maintain the male's secondary sex characteristics; they cause his genitals to develop, his beard to grow, and his voice to change and maintain its adult pitch. Recent research indicates that androgens also play a role in the level of sex drive in females. The **estrogens** promote the development of secondary sex characteristics in the female by stimulating her breasts to develop and her genitals to mature. The third group, the **progestins**, prepare the female's body for pregnancy, birth, and nursing the infant.

The adrenal glands. The two adrenal glands contribute enormously to the functioning of nerves and muscles and to the ability of the whole body to cope with stress. These influential glands are located just above the kidneys. Each adrenal gland has two parts—an outer covering called the *adrenal cortex* and an inner core called the *adrenal medulla*.

The adrenal cortex is one of the glands that is under the control of the anterior pituitary, the "master gland." When the anterior pituitary produces ACTH, the adrenal cortex manufactures a number of chemical substances that work together to speed up the metabolism of carbohydrates and to regulate the sodium-potassium balance in the body.

The adrenal cortex also works with the gonads to promote the development and maintenance of secondary sex characteristics and to control sexual functioning. In this role, the hormone that is most important is *androgen*, a male sex hormone produced by the gonads and the adrenal cortex in both males and females.

Both the adrenal cortex and the adrenal medulla are involved in the body's reactions to stress. Alerted by the nervous system that a speeding car or a surly acquaintance is approaching, the adrenal medulla secretes two hormones: *epinephrine* and *norepinephrine.** Epinephrine makes the heart beat faster and seems to be released mainly when the person is afraid. Norepinephrine raises the blood pressure by causing the blood vessels to become constricted; it seems to be released primarily when a person feels angry. Norepinephrine is carried by the bloodstream to the anterior pituitary, where it triggers the release of ACTH. This hormone then stimulates the adrenal cortex to increase the rate of metabolism of carbohydrates, making the body's tissues generally more tense. Digestion stops; the pupils of the eyes enlarge; more sugar flows into the bloodstream; and the blood is prepared to clot fast if necessary.

---

*These two hormones are also called **adrenalin** and **noradrenalin**.

SEX HORMONES: HOW'S YOUR TESTOSTERONE LEVEL?

Is your sex-role behavior the result of your upbringing and the role playing forced on you by society? Or was Freud right when he said, "Anatomy is destiny"? Recent endocrine research suggests that your maleness or femaleness is crucially influenced by the chemistry of your body—and your mother's.

Because both men and women produce both male and female sex hormones, we should all be considered at least potentially unisexual. What makes a man "masculine," then, is not an absence of female hormones, but his relatively higher level of the male hormone, testosterone, which counteracts the effects of his female hormones. Homosexual males have been found to have significantly lower testosterone levels than bisexual or heterosexual males, though one researcher suggests that this may be a result, rather than a cause, of homosexuality (Kolodny, 1972).

The most important role of sex hormones may be played before we are even born. As the fetus develops, its genes indicate what its sex ought to be, and if it is left alone, it will develop in line with that genetic predisposition. But if for some reason the prenatal sex hormones are not at the right levels during a critical period, sexual differentiation will not occur as genetically planned. In the 1940s, Alfred Jost, a French physiologist, surgically castrated a male rabbit while it was still inside its mother. Without its testes to secrete the testosterone necessary for sexual differentiation to occur, the rabbit, even though its genetic makeup was XY, was born with the external sex organs of a female. But removal of the ovaries of female rabbit fetuses had no effect at all on their physical characteristics at birth (Scarf, 1972). Thus, the female form appears to be the basic one, and even with an XY genetic makeup, it takes the addition of testosterone to change it into a male.

Prenatal hormone levels may also influence relative maleness or femaleness in the individual after puberty. Studies have found that some lower animals do have "male" or "female" areas in their brains. These areas, which are located in the hypothalamus, regulate the animal's sexual development and behavior at puberty and are preprogrammed to emphasize maleness or femaleness by the prenatal hormone levels. One study closely examined the behavior of young girls (from age 4 through age 15) whose mothers had been given the synthetic hormone progestin to prevent miscarriage. At birth the girls' sex organs were somewhat malformed, but this was surgically corrected when they were very young. Their behavior, however, was notably tomboyish and masculine (Ehrhardt & Money, 1967).

These findings suggest that our sexual natures may be pre-set by the levels of our prenatal hormones, particularly the presence or absence of testosterone. How these pre-set natures manifest themselves depends on our experience with the world. Much more research needs to be done, but this understanding may mean that our social environment could become the stage instead of the script for our sexual lives.

All these reactions prepare the person or animal to respond to something in the outside world that makes him angry or afraid.

The Nervous System

The second major coordinating and integrating mechanism of the body is the nervous system. The more we learn about the nervous system, the more certain we are that all of its parts work together, all the time, to integrate the extraordinarily intricate activities of the body. Yet its parts are so many, so various, so complex, and, to a large extent, still so mysterious that it is easier to approach the nervous system by looking first at its various parts. We will start with the smallest part, the individual neuron. Multiplied many billions of times, this single cell underlies the activity of the entire nervous system.

The Neuron

Ten to twelve billion nerve cells, or **neurons,** make up the nervous system. Neurons come in many different sizes and shapes, but they are all specialized to receive and transmit information. Figure 2-8 shows you what a typical neuron looks like.

What a neuron has in common with all other cells is a *nucleus,* which contains 23 pairs of chromosomes and the DNA that determines what kind of cell it is and what specific job it does; *cytoplasm,* which surrounds the nucleus and forms the cell body, where metabolism and respiration take place; and a *cell membrane,* which encloses the whole cell.

What makes a neuron different from other cells are the tiny fibers that extend out from the cell body. These extensions are what enable the neuron to perform its special job—to receive messages from surrounding cells, carry them a certain distance, and then pass them on to other cells.

Figure 2-8
A typical neuron.

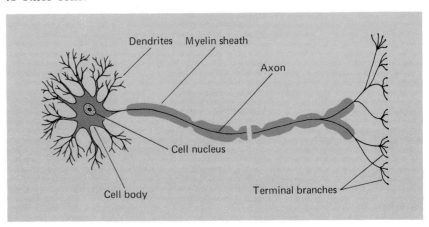

Look again at the neuron in Figure 2-8. The short fibers branching out around the cell body are called **dendrites.** Their role is to pick up incoming messages from their surroundings and carry them to the cell body. The single long fiber extending from the cell body is called an **axon.** The axon fiber is very thin and usually much longer than the dendrites. In adults the axons that run from the brain to the base of the spinal cord can sometimes be as long as 3 feet, but most axons are only an inch or two in length. The axon's job is to carry outgoing messages—either to pass them on to the next neuron in a series or to direct a muscle or gland to take action. When we talk about a **nerve,** we are referring not to a single fiber but to a group of axons bundled together like parallel wires in an electrical cable.

The axon shown in Figure 2-8 is surrounded by a fatty covering called a *myelin sheath.* The sheath is not continuous, but is pinched in at intervals, which makes the axon look somewhat like a string of microscopic sausages. Not all axons are covered by myelin sheaths, but myelinated axons can be found in all parts of the body. The sheath seems to act as an insulator, but just how it performs is not well understood. We do know, however, that nerve cells with myelin sheaths carry messages faster than nerve cells without this covering and that many axons seem to grow myelin sheaths as the body develops during childhood.

Neurons that collect messages from inside and outside the body and carry them to the spinal cord or to the brain are called **afferent** (or **sensory) neurons.** Messages are carried in the other direction—from the spinal cord or the brain to the muscles and glands—by **efferent** (or **motor) neurons.** Smaller neurons, usually in the brain or spinal cord, connect incoming and outgoing messages; these are known as **association neurons** (or **interneurons).**

The Neural Impulse

Just what are these messages that the neurons carry? What kind of code does a neuron use to help the parts of the body communicate with one another? The nervous system speaks a language that all the body's cells can understand—simple yes-or-no, on-or-off electrochemical impulses.

When an individual neuron is resting, its cell membrane forms a barrier between two semi-liquid solutions—one inside the neuron, the other outside it. Both solutions contain electrically charged particles, or *ions.* Outside the neuron the particles are mostly sodium and chloride ions, and the electrical charge is positive. Most of the ions on the inside of the neuron are potassium; the electrical charge inside the neuron is negative. Positive and negative ions, like the positive and negative poles of a magnet, are attracted to one another. Without the cell membrane to separate them, the positively charged ions outside the neuron and the negatively charged ions on the inside would flow together and neutralize one another. The membrane keeps them apart and maintains the neuron in a state of **polarization**—a sort of electrical equilibrium.

But the cell membrane is a very selective gatekeeper—while the neuron is in a resting state, the membrane lets many substances pass freely. It refuses, however, to allow sodium ions to slip into the neuron from the outside. When the neuron picks up a message from its surroundings—that is, when a point on the cell membrane is electrically stimulated—it suddenly opens up at that point and allows the sodium ions to rush inside. The neuron is no longer polarized at that point. This causes the next point on the membrane to open up. More sodium ions flow into the neuron at that point and depolarize that part of the neuron. This process is repeated down the whole length of the neuron, and we say that the neuron has "fired."

This whole process takes place in a split second. There is a wide range in the speed with which individual neurons conduct electrochemical impulses. In some of the largest myelinated axons, impulses travel at speeds of nearly 400 feet per second. These are the fastest impulses; the slowest, in small axons that have no myelin sheaths, can poke along at little better than 6 to 8 feet per second.

The neuron does not fire in response to every impulse it receives. If the incoming message is not strong enough, the cell membrane will continue to block the sodium ions, and nothing will happen. The incoming message must be above a certain *threshold* of intensity if it is to cause a nervous impulse, just as you must pull the trigger hard enough if a gun is to fire. But pulling even harder on the trigger of a gun will not cause the bullet to travel any faster or any further—it either fires because you pulled hard enough, or it does not fire because you did not pull hard enough.

After a nerve cell fires, it goes through an **absolute refractory period** for about a thousandth of a second. During this time, the neuron will not fire, no matter how strong the incoming messages may be. This is not too surprising if we remember that the neural impulse has caused the neuron to be depolarized. It takes a little time for the neuron to expel all the sodium ions and return to its resting state. After this initial period of total unresponsiveness, the neuron enters a **relative refractory phase.** During this phase, which lasts for a few hundredths of a second, the neuron will fire, but only if the incoming message is considerably stronger than is normally necessary.

The Synapse

Up to this point we have been considering the operation of a single neuron. But the billions of neurons in the nervous system work together to coordinate the body's activities. How do neurons interact? How does a message get from one neuron to another?

Let us retrace the path of a neural impulse. This one starts, let us say, when one of the dendrites of a neuron picks up a message. The dendrite carries the impulse to the cell body, and from there it travels down the axon. Near its end, the axon begins to branch out into numerous small fibers. At the end of each fiber is a tiny knob, or **axon terminal.** A minute gap separates the end of each terminal from the dendrites or cell body of another neuron. This tiny space is called a **synapse.** If the neural impulse is to travel on to the next neuron, it must somehow travel across this gap.

Until quite recently, there was a lively controversy about what actually happened at this point. The electrical impulse, some said, simply jumps across the gap. No, argued others, the transfer is chemical. Recent discoveries seem to have confirmed the chemical-transfer notion. What happens is this: some axon terminals contain a number of tiny oval sacs called **synaptic vesicles** (see Figure 2-9). When the neural impulse reaches the end of the axon, it causes these vesicles to release a chemical substance. This chemical transmitter substance is what actually travels across the gap between the two neurons and causes the second neuron to fire.

One question still to be answered is how many different kinds of chemical transmitter substances there are. One we are sure of is *acetylcholine.* Some others are *norepinephrine* (the same hormone produced by adrenal glands), *serotonin,* and *dopamine.* Not all the chemicals that are released cause the next neuron to fire. Some vesicles release *inhibitory* substances, which counteract the effects of the excitatory chemicals. When an inhibitory substance is present, more of the excitatory chemical is needed to cause the next neuron to fire. The inhibitory substances act as a filter, letting only the strongest neural impulses get through.

The second main question that is yet to be answered is what happens to the chemical transmitter substance after the "receiving" neuron has

Figure 2-9
A highly simplified drawing of the synapse, showing the synaptic vesicles and the tiny space that separates one neuron from another.

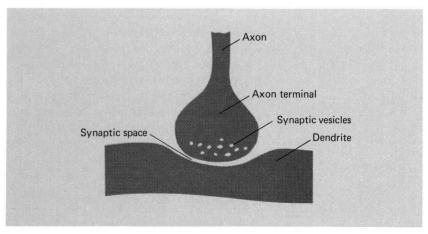

fired. If it remained loose in the synaptic gap, the neuron would continue to fire over and over again every time it completed its refractory period. One of the chemicals, acetylcholine, seems to be destroyed by other chemicals that are found in the fluids around the synapse. Norepinephrine and dopamine, however, are recycled—they are taken back into the vesicles to be used over again. The drugs we know as amphetamines (like Benzedrine and Dexedrine) produce a state of high arousal in the nervous system. One of the things amphetamines do is to prevent norepinephrine and dopamine from being reabsorbed into the synaptic vesicles, which can cause neurons to fire over and over again, erratically. In addition, current research suggests that malfunctions in synaptic transmission are involved in some psychological disorders, like depression and schizophrenia.*

The situation we have been describing so far is highly simplified here. If one neuron were connected to only two other neurons—one at each end—the nervous system would be incapable of performing all its interlocking functions. What actually happens is much more complicated. The axon terminals of a single neuron can reach the dendrites of many other neurons; the dendrites and cell bodies have synapses to the axons of other neurons over their entire surface. Thus each neuron practically can affect the activity of thousands of other neurons and can be affected by thousands. Each neuron is indirectly linked to every other neuron in the entire nervous system.

Divisions of the Nervous System

Try to imagine all the billions of cells in the human nervous system—all communicating with each other in the same code and at fantastic speed, all connected through an incredibly complex series of interlocking circuits, carrying a multitude of messages all at the same time. Then add all the cells that are directly exposed to external conditions—all the sense receptors that respond to heat and cold, light and dark, sound and silence, and so on and then send messages along the neural pathways. The complexity is staggering—by contrast, managing an airport begins to look like child's play!

How does the nervous system keep all its messages straight? One reason the communication lines do not get jammed is that each type of receptor cell communicates to higher nerve centers through its own private set of neural pathways. These separate routes provide one way of dividing up the nervous system for study.

When the nervous system is being thought of in a structural way—that is, *where* its parts are—it is seen as having two divisions, the **central nervous system** and the **peripheral nervous system.**

The whole nervous system consists of the brain, the spinal cord, and

---

*These conditions will be discussed in detail in Chapter 10.

the nerves that connect these two structures to the *receptors* (cells in the sense organs) and the *effectors* (cells in the muscles and glands). The brain and spinal cord make up the central nervous system. The bundles of nerve cells and fibers that are not in the brain and spinal cord make up the peripheral nervous system. The peripheral nervous system contains two kinds of nerves—*sensory nerves*, which carry messages from the sense organs to the central nervous system, and *motor nerves,* which carry messages from the central nervous system out to the muscles and glands.

The peripheral nervous system can be further divided, according to which parts of the body it serves. The nerves that travel from the sensory receptors and to the skeletal muscles form the **somatic nervous system**—the part of the peripheral nervous system that is concerned with body movements and reactions to changes in the external environment. The **autonomic nervous system,** on the other hand, serves the muscles and glands inside the body. Since its effects are so important to the understanding of behavior, the autonomic nervous system will be treated in greater detail.

The Autonomic Nervous System

To understand the autonomic nervous system it is necessary to make one more division. The autonomic nervous system consists of two branches—the **sympathetic** and **parasympathetic** divisions. These two divisions act in almost total opposition to each other, but both are directly involved in controlling and integrating the actions of the glands and blood vessels within the body.

The sympathetic division. The nerve fibers of the sympathetic division pathways are busiest when you are frightened or angry. They carry messages that tell the body to prepare for an emergency, to get ready to act quickly and strenuously. In response to messages from the sympathetic division, your heart pounds, you breathe faster, your pupils enlarge, digestion stops. The sympathetic nervous system also tells the adrenal glands to start producing epinephrine, which further intensifies these reactions. Sympathetic nerve fibers connect to every internal organ in the body, which explains why the body's reaction to sudden stress is so widespread.

The parasympathetic division. Parasympathetic nerve fibers connect to all the same organs as the sympathetic nerve fibers, but the messages they carry tell the organs to do just the opposite of what the sympathetic division has directed. The parasympathetic division says, in effect, "Okay, the heat's off. Let's get back to normal." So the heart goes back to beating at its normal rate, the stomach muscles relax, digestion begins again, breathing slows down, and the pupils of the eyes get smaller.

Thus the parasympathetic division compensates for the sympathetic division and lets the body take a rest after a period of stress.

Usually these two systems work together—after the sympathetic division has aroused the body, the parasympathetic division follows with messages to relax. In most people, one division or the other tends to dominate slightly. In ulcer patients, for example, the parasympathetic division tends to dominate—they salivate heavily, their hearts beat rather slowly, and their digestive systems are too active much of the time. People whose sympathetic division dominates show the opposite symptoms—their mouths are dry and their palms are moist, their hearts beat quickly even when they are resting.

The autonomic nervous system has traditionally been regarded as the "automatic" part of the body's response mechanisms. No one, it was believed, could tell his own autonomic nervous system when to speed up or slow down the heart's beating or to stop and start the digestive processes. These things were thought to be as automatic as the activity of a thermostat that controls the temperature of a room. The latest evidence, however, suggests that we have more control over the autonomic nervous system than we may realize. Several recent studies (reported in Chapter 4) have shown that people (and animals) do indeed seem capable of purposely manipulating the activities of this no longer "automatic" part of the nervous system.

The Central Nervous System

The central nervous system, as we said earlier, is composed of the brain and the spinal cord. The brain is undoubtedly the most fascinating part of the whole nervous system. Containing nearly 90 percent of the system's neurons, it is believed to be the seat of awareness and reason, the place where learning, remembering, hating, loving, fearing are centered, the part of us that decides what to do and later whether that decision was right or wrong and imagines how things might have turned out otherwise. The spinal cord tends to be less fully appreciated, but without it the brain could not function.

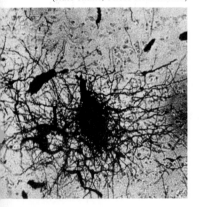

Enlarged photograph of human brain cells.
(*Russ Kinne, Photo Researchers*)

The spinal cord. The complex cable of nerves that connects the brain to most of the rest of the body is known as the **spinal cord.** The spinal cord is made up of bundles of long, nearly cylindrical nerve fibers. The outside part of the cable consists of *white matter,* axons with myelin sheaths that give them a whitish color. The inside is made up of *gray matter*—it contains both cell bodies and fibers without myelin sheaths. The cell nuclei are what give it a grayish color. If you look at a cross section of the spinal cord, like that shown in Figure 2-10, you can see that the gray matter forms a letter "H" with the white matter surrounding it. The nerve fibers in the white matter carry messages to and from the brain; but this is only one of the spinal cord's two jobs. The

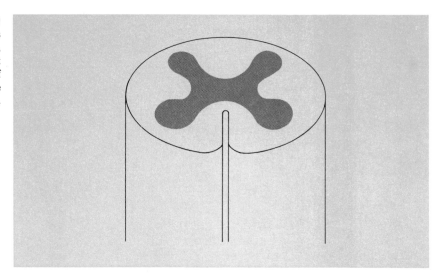

Figure 2-10
A highly simplified cross section of the spinal cord, showing the gray matter at the center in the shape of an "H" surrounded by white matter.

Figure 2-11
Simple reflexes, such as jerking your leg when someone hits your knee, are controlled by the spinal cord. The message travels from the sense receptors near the skin through the afferent nerve fibers to the spinal cord. In the gray matter of the spinal cord the messages are relayed through association neurons to the efferent nerve fibers, which carry them to the muscle cells that cause the reflex movement.
(Photo courtesy of American Museum of Natural History)

gray matter produces some *reflex movements*—a message, signaling pain from touching the thorn on a rose, for example, comes into your spinal cord from the sense receptors of your hand. The message is processed in the spinal cord, and an impulse is sent out to cause the almost instantaneous response of pulling your hand away (see Figure 2-11). Because of the way the neural circuits are arranged, the same incoming message produces the same response every time. The message does travel to the brain, but by the time it gets there you have probably already reacted. Most of these spinal reflexes are protective; they enable you to avoid damage to the body. Some other reflexes, which are not protective ones, do pass through circuits in the brain before action is taken. One reflex that involves the brain is a sneeze—you generally know when you are about to sneeze and sometimes you can control it.

We talk of the brain and the spinal cord as two distinct structures, but there really is no definite point of division between them. At its upper end, the spinal cord enlarges and merges into the lower part of

Figure 2-12
If the brain were divided in half down the middle, it would look something like this. The hindbrain, including the medulla, pons, and cerebellum, is at the rear. Then comes the midbrain, and finally the forebrain, which includes the thalamus, hypothalamus, and the cerebral hemispheres.

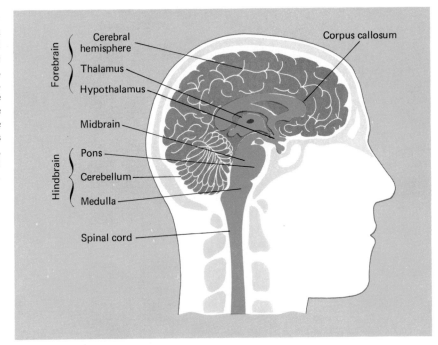

the brain, called the **brainstem.*** In an evolutionary sense, the brainstem contains many of the brain's oldest structures. In humans the brainstem is rather like a stalk that supports the other parts of the brain.

The brain. The nervous system develops quite early in the human embryo. As soon as the brain begins to take shape, we can detect three distinct cores—the hindbrain, the midbrain, and the forebrain. In the fully developed adult brain, they are not so easily distinguished from one another, but we can still use these three basic divisions to describe the parts of the brain, what they do, and how they interact to influence our behavior.

The **hindbrain,** since it is found in even the most primitive vertebrates, is believed to have been the earliest part of the brain to evolve. The part of the hindbrain nearest to the spinal cord is the *medulla,* a narrow structure about an inch and a half long. The medulla controls breathing and many important reflexes, such as those that help us maintain our upright posture. The medulla is also the point where many of the nerves from the higher parts of the brain are crossed—the nerves from the left part of the brain travel to the right side of the body, and vice versa.

Above the medulla lies the *pons,* a slightly wider structure that serves

---

*The brainstem includes all of the brain's parts except the cerebrum and the cerebellum. Many of these parts will be treated separately in the following discussion.

as a pathway for the nerves that connect the cortex at the top of the brain to the topmost section of the hindbrain, the *cerebellum.*

The cerebellum is composed of two circular hemispheres, whose outer surface, or cortex, is made up of gray matter. The cerebellum performs quite a number of chores—it handles certain reflexes, especially those that have to do with balance. In addition, it coordinates the body's actions to make sure that movements go together in efficient sequences.

Above the pons and cerebellum the brainstem widens even more to form the **midbrain**—in the middle, as the name implies, between the hindbrain at the base and the forebrain at the top. The midbrain is especially important to hearing and sight, and it is one of several places in the brain where pain is registered.

Supported by the brainstem, bulging out above it, and drooping over somewhat in order to fit into the skull is the **forebrain.** Some of the forebrain's most influential areas are the thalamus, the hypothalamus, and the cerebral cortex.

Inside the two cerebral hemispheres, in the central core of the forebrain and more or less directly over the brainstem, are the two egg-shaped structures that make up the **thalamus.** The thalamus is a relay station for incoming messages from the sense receptors all over the body. In addition, many of the messages that travel from one part of the cortex to another pass through the thalamus. Some of the neurons in the thalamus seem to be important in regulating the electrical activity of the cortex; other neurons in the thalamus control the activities of the autonomic nervous system.

Below the thalamus is a smaller structure called the **hypothalamus.** This part of the forebrain exerts an enormous influence on many different kinds of motivation. Centers in the hypothalamus govern eating, drinking, sexual behavior, sleeping, and temperature control. In addition, the hypothalamus is directly involved in all kinds of emotional behavior, in both pleasant and unpleasant situations. Centers in the hypothalamus direct the body to produce the organized and integrated patterns of behavior we recognize as rage, terror, and pleasure. In times of stress, the hypothalamus appears to perform a crucial integrating function. It acts directly, by determining what messages are sent out over the autonomic nervous system, both the sympathetic and parasympathetic divisions. And it acts indirectly, by controlling the activities of the anterior pituitary, which is located just below it, and by stimulating several other endocrine glands as well.

Ballooning out over the brainstem are the two hemispheres that form the **cerebral cortex.** They fold down over the brainstem and hide most of it. A great mass of white matter (myelinated axon fibers) called the *corpus callosum* connects the two hemispheres to each other and to the other parts of the nervous system. The cerebral cortex itself is made of gray matter—unmyelinated axons and cell bodies. The cerebral

CLOSING THE GATE ON PAIN

To most of us, pain seems a simple enough fact of life, and its relief a matter of prescriptions, surgery, or some form of physical therapy. Physiologists, neurosurgeons, and psychologists know otherwise. To them, the causes and cures of pain defy easy explanation. Pain really has two main determinants: a physiological component and a psychological one. The physiological component generally determines what we feel, and the psychological one determines how we feel about it. For example, two people have just burned their fingers on a stove. Pain messages are transmitted, and their hands are quickly drawn away; these actions represent the physiological side of pain. But we notice that one person calmly shakes his hand and then runs some cold water over it. The other person does the same thing, but screams his head off at the same time. Obviously, these two people *perceive* their pain differently; this is the psychological component of pain.

You would probably expect people to have unique psychological responses to pain, but you may be surprised to learn that people also have different physiological responses to painful stimuli. For example, there is the case of a Canadian girl who felt nothing when she inadvertently bit off part of her tongue and who got third-degree burns on her knees from kneeling on a hot radiator (McMurray, 1950; Baxter & Olszewski, 1960). On the other hand, some people feel extreme "spontaneous pain" when there is no apparent reason for it.

Physiological psychologists have developed several theories to account for the physical mechanisms of pain. Which organ sends out the pain message? Which organ receives it? How is the message transmitted? The *specificity theory* of pain, traditionally supported by Western medicine, holds that pain receptors at the site of an injury have a one-to-one signaling system with the brain. Some credence has also been given to *pattern theories*, which suggest that the central nervous system or the peripheral nervous system somehow totals up all incoming nerve impulses, and when the total is high enough, a pain message is sent out to the brain.

Lately, great interest has been generated by the *gate-control theory* of pain advanced by Ronald Melzack and Patrick Wall in 1965, which appears to explain more pain phenomena than any other theory. According to this theory, a neural "gate" mechanism in the spinal cord controls the transmission of nerve impulses to the central nervous system. Whether the gate is open or not depends on the relative activity of the small-diameter sensory fibers that conduct pain impulses on the one hand and of the large-diameter fibers that can inhibit those pain-sensitive fibers on the other. Thus, pain may be "blocked" by stimulating these large fibers, in the same way that we temper hot water with cold by turning on both faucets on a sink. Pain may also be moderated by blocking signals that descend on the spinal cord from the brainstem. Melzack and Wall's theory has had an immediate impact in that it "was quickly translated into a therapeutic reality for the relief of pain through stimulation of nerves through the skin or the central nervous system using highly sophisticated electronic devices" (Nashold, 1973, p. v).

cortex is the most recent part of the nervous system to evolve and is more highly developed in man than in any other animal. It accounts for about 80 percent of the human brain's weight. Its surface area is actually vast—if it were spread out, it would cover nearly 61 square feet. But to fit inside the skull, the cerebral cortex has developed an intricate pattern of folds—hills and valleys called *convolutions*. These convolutions form an individual pattern in every brain—as unique as a fingerprint.

Different areas of the cortex have been found to be responsible for different functions. The sensory messages from the right side of the body generally travel to the left hemisphere of the cerebral cortex, crossing in the medulla. Those from the left side of the body travel to the right hemisphere. Likewise, the motor messages that control the muscles and glands on the right side of the body originate in the left hemisphere, and vice versa.

The areas of the cortex where messages from the sense receptors register are called *sensory projection areas*. The areas of the cortex where response messages start their trip down the brainstem to tell the muscles and glands what to do are called *motor projection areas*.

There are also large areas throughout the cortex that are neither directly sensory nor directly motor. These are called *association areas;* they make up over three quarters of the area of the cortex. It is in the association areas that messages coming in from separate senses are combined into meaningful impressions and motor messages going out are integrated so the body can make coordinated movements. The association areas are involved in all of the activities we commonly attribute to the brain—learning, thinking, remembering, talking. The largest of the association areas is located in the frontal lobe of the brain, just under the forehead. The frontal lobe appears to be the location of the higher mental processes—abstract thinking and problem solving. The activities of the association areas are very highly integrated. The different areas seem to work together to a large extent, which becomes most obvious when an individual suffers damage to one of the association areas. The association areas seem to be able to take over for one another, unlike the projection areas, where brain damage to a particular area usually results in loss of all or part of the specific sensory or motor capability localized in that area. The amount and kind of malfunction seems to depend not on where the association areas are damaged but on how extensive the injury is. To get an idea where all these areas are located, look at Figure 2-13.

The reticular activating system. We have divided the brain into three separate sections as a way of simplifying our discussion. But the brain itself frequently ignores the distinctions made in textbooks and sets up systems that jump across the boundaries, using parts of the hind-

Figure 2-13
A side view of the human
brain, showing the location
of the four lobes. Motor
activities and higher mental
processes are localized in
the frontal lobe; the sensory
projection areas for the
body senses, vision, and
hearing are found in the
parietal, occipital, and
temporal lobes, respectively.

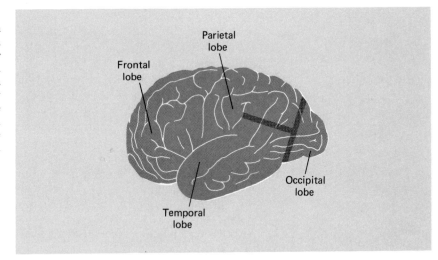

Figure 2-14
The shaded area indicates
the location of the reticular
activating system.

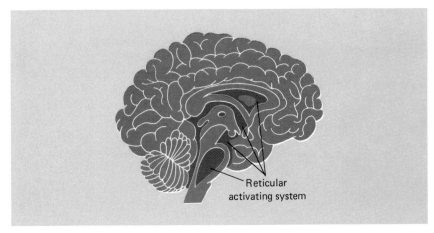

brain, midbrain, and forebrain together to perform certain functions.
One such circuit is the reticular activating system (see Figure 2-14).

The **reticular activating system,** or **RAS,** is made up of a netlike
bundle of neurons running through the hindbrain, the midbrain, and
a part of the forebrain called the hypothalamus. Its main job seems
to be to send "Wake up!" signals to the higher parts of the brain if an
incoming message is important. When two or more messages come in
at the same time, which happens continuously, the RAS apparently
decides which is most urgent. Some messages seem to be toned down
by the RAS; others never reach the higher centers at all. Because the
RAS is selective, it is possible for us to concentrate our attention and
ignore distracting messages from the sense receptors—to read an interesting book while the TV is blaring, telephones are ringing, and con-

THINK RIGHT, YOUNG MAN—OR LEFT?

The cerebral cortex of the human brain is composed of two distinct hemispheres, which are linked by a cablelike section called the *corpus callosum*. All communication between the two hemispheres goes through the corpus callosum. The two hemispheres operate *contralaterally*: the left hemisphere controls the right side of your body and the right half of your visual field, and the right hemisphere does the same job for the left side of your body. However, the two hemispheres are not equal partners; one of them will always dominate the other. The most obvious effect of this is your being right-handed or left-handed. In general, if you are right-handed, your left cerebral hemisphere is dominant.

If the hemispheres only controlled your physical dexterity, the domination of one side of your brain over the other wouldn't matter very much. Most of us probably don't care which hand we do things with. But each hemisphere also has control over our uniquely human faculties, and, moreover, each is responsible for different abilities. For example, the left hemisphere does our analytical thinking and talks for us. The right side is illiterate, artistic, and silent.

We know all this from studying people whose cerebral hemispheres have been surgically split by cutting the corpus callosum. This operation is done because the people were suffering from frequent massive seizures due to epilepsy or injury. After the operation their seizures usually stop, but they generally experience some bizarre side effects. When the corpus callosum is cut, all communication between the two hemispheres stops. "The left side of the brain no longer knows what the right side is doing, yet the speaking half of the patient, controlled by the left hemisphere, still insists on finding excuses for whatever the mute half has done, and still operates under the illusion that they are one person" (Pines, 1973, p. 32).

For its part, although it cannot speak, the right hemisphere can make emotional responses to what the left hemisphere is doing. According to Roger Sperry, who pioneered split-brain studies, "This is evidenced in frowning, wincing, negative head shaking, and the like, in test situations where the minor hemisphere [the right] hears the major [the left] making stupid verbal mistakes—in other words, where the correct answer is known only to the minor hemisphere" (cited in Pines, 1973, p. 122). The blundering left hemisphere will have no idea why "its" face is moving. The most extreme example of hemispheric rivalry is the man whose right brain didn't like his wife (Pines, 1973). The man's left hand would make obscene gestures at her and once tried to strangle her, but was wrestled away by the man's right hand!

In normal people, this rivalry is under better control. One hemisphere or the other will "shut itself off" when it is not needed. Because of hemispheric dominance, however, we all favor one side over the other and will prefer to do things that the favored side is better at. You thought *you* liked to read, didn't you? Well, your left hemisphere likes to read, too. Your friend who likes painting and seems to have trouble articulating his feelings has a dominant right hemisphere. How can you tell for sure? Ask your friend to stare off into space and tell you the number of letters in the word "Minnesota." Which way did he look while he was thinking? If he looked to the right, his left hemisphere is dominant; if he looked to the left, he is "right-brained" (Pines, 1973).

If you examine the subjects and skills you are required to learn in school and those considered important for success in your work you can see that society at large is left-hemisphere dominant. This is probably a reflection of the fact that the majority of us are right-handed and thus "left-brained," and we all like to do what we do best. But up to now, this has meant that we know very little about the special abilities of the silent right hemisphere, that "other person" who lives inside all of us.

Figure 2-15
Some of the brain structures
involved in the limbic
system.

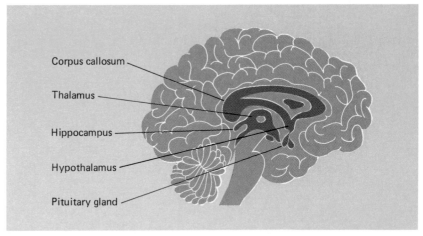

Corpus callosum

Thalamus

Hippocampus

Hypothalamus

Pituitary gland

versations are being carried on in other parts of the room. The best-documented effects of the RAS are on sleep. (See Chapter 9 for a fuller discussion.)

The limbic system. Another demonstration of the interconnected operations of the central nervous system is provided by the **limbic system,** a ring of structures in the center of each cerebral hemisphere (see Figure 2-15). The limbic system includes the hypothalamus, part of the thalamus, and several other forebrain structures that lie inside the cortex. It also contains nerve fibers that connect it to the cerebral cortex and to the brainstem.

The limbic system is believed to be important in learning, but just how it affects this process is not yet understood. One of its parts, the *hippocampus,* plays an important role in memory. Damage to the hippocampus in humans makes them unable to form new memories—patients can remember things that happened years ago, but forget the recent death of a close relative in an hour or so.

The limbic system also seems to be involved in a wide variety of emotional behaviors. We saw earlier that one of its parts, the hypothalamus, plays a role in such states as fear, anger, and pleasure. Other parts of the limbic system seem to yield some degree of pleasure, for animals will work to turn on a mild electrical current to electrodes implanted in these areas. The limbic system also seems to control a wide variety of autonomic responses—breathing, heart rate, intestinal activity, and so on—that are important components of emotional behavior.

Using laboratory animals, experimenters have attempted to probe the workings of the limbic system—what its parts do and how they work together—by removing or damaging or stimulating different parts of the system or different combinations of parts. What emerges from all of these studies is a picture of a very complicated set of interactions, with each part of the system depending on the actions of all the other parts to keep the individual functioning normally.

In the case of rage, for example, the cortical parts of the limbic system (the structures that are located within the cortex itself) seem to inhibit the effects of the subcortical parts. Animals who have had one or more of the cortical parts of their limbic systems removed become enraged at the slightest provocation. But their reaction does not last nearly as long as the rage reaction of normal animals, indicating that the cortical parts of the limbic system not only inhibit emotional reactions, but tend to smooth out emotional fluctuations in general.

There is little overall agreement about what the various parts of the limbic system do, but the fact of their interaction is plain. Emotional behavior is both activated and inhibited in the limbic system, and the separate components of emotional behavior are integrated there.

Psychosurgery and Electrical Stimulation of the Brain

Two areas in which there is a conspicuous overlap between psychology and physiology are psychosurgery and electrical stimulation of the brain. These techniques are related because both procedures presume that determinants of your behavior have precise locations in your brain.

Psychosurgery, operating on the brain to change a person's behavior, was introduced at the close of the nineteenth century. At that time, doctors thought that a diseased brain caused abnormal behavior. Removing the "sick" part of the brain ought, therefore, to stop the behavior. The best-known example of such radical measures is the prefrontal lobotomy, which was typically performed on uncontrollably violent people. This operation does pacify psychotic patients, but it also leaves them apathetic and irresponsible and impairs both their creativity and their intelligence. The operation cannot be undone, and, therefore, the damage is permanent.

There is a feeling among some advocates of psychosurgery that these undesirable side effects were due to crude techniques. Today psychosurgeons can use brain "atlases" and electrodes to perform more precise surgery with less unintentional destruction of brain tissue. Moreover, new areas of the brain, primarily in the limbic system, are being discussed as more appropriate targets for psychosurgery. Some highly dramatic cures do result from psychosurgery, but there have also been some dramatic failures. The functions of the brain are extremely well integrated, and our knowledge of the mechanisms of that integration is still so rudimentary that some researchers are skeptical about the wisdom of even limited use of psychosurgery (Chorover, 1974). Because of these concerns, psychosurgery is used today only as a last resort.*

*The therapeutic uses of psychosurgery will be discussed more fully in Chapter 15.

Electrical stimulation of the brain, or **ESB,** is a nondestructive means of tapping the brain to see how it controls—or impairs—actions and emotions. Stimulating part of the brain with electrical current produces a "counterfeit" nerve impulse. The brain is fooled into thinking that it has received a real nerve impulse from one of its sensory receptors. It thinks something is really going on "out there" and behaves, and makes *you* behave, accordingly.

Experimenters have used ESB to cause aggressive behavior in cats (Flynn et al., 1970) and in monkeys (Hofstatter & Girgis, 1972), and to inhibit aggressive behavior as well (Delgado, 1969). In his highly publicized demonstration, José Delgado implanted a radio-controlled electrode in the brain of a "brave bull." (These bulls are bred especially for bullfighting and will charge any human being.) He went into the arena with the bull, carrying only a radio transmitter. When the bull charged him, Delgado pressed a button on the transmitter, sending an impulse to the electrode in the bull's brain, and the bull abruptly broke off his charge. The experiment suggests that the stimulation had direct effect on the bull's aggressive tendencies, or, according to Delgado, "the result seemed to be a combination of motor effect . . . plus behavioral inhibition of the aggressive drive." The social implications for the future are provocative: Should we be concerned with such "behavioral inhibition" when projected in human terms?

Although intracerebral electrodes are now being used for therapeutic purposes in many parts of the world, visions of a Big Brother controlling our behavior seem to be premature. According to neuropsychologist Elliot Valenstein (1973), we are a long way from practical manipulation of human behavior through brain control. Success in this area has often been exaggerated. Delgado himself emphasizes the limitations of ESB. Many animal subjects have shown strong resistance to being electrically stimulated—monkeys, for example, have on occasion pulled out their electrodes (Hofstatter & Girgis, 1972). Unlike rats, human subjects do not seem to find pleasurable brain stimulation irresistible. Attempts to induce feelings of aggression, sexual desire, or hunger in humans by stimulating the hypothalamus have been far from completely successful.

For instance, consider Delgado's dramatic experiment with the bull. Did Delgado really find the precise location in the bull's brain that controls aggression? Valenstein contends that the electric shock to the bull's brain was like hitting it on the side of the head, and, as the bull turned its head away from the "blow," its body followed. Valenstein suggests that, rather than being pacified after repeated applications of the shock, as Delgado claimed, the bull was simply confused and frustrated and just gave up (Valenstein, 1973).

This criticism raises an important point. No single area of the brain is likely to be *the* single source of any given emotion. This is the main reason many psychologists are skeptical about the effectiveness of both ESB and psychosurgery. As Valenstein puts it, "Unfortunately, the nervous system is not organized in a way that makes it possible to separate functions in terms of their social implications" (Valenstein, 1973, p. 352).

The social implications of psychosurgery and ESB research are much the same as those we noted for behavior genetics. There are obvious dangers in seeing such options as tidy solutions to social problems, in confusing patient "management" with patient betterment, or in equating pleasure with happiness. Despite some successes in ESB inhibition of aggression, such psychotechnology has yet to make significant contributions to behavioral therapy. The failures may actually tell us more than the successes about the complex balancing, filtering, counterbalancing, and coordinating functions that go on all the time in the nervous system. This complex integration of activity enables the nervous system to perform the massive task assigned to it—to control and coordinate all the activities of the body's billions of cells so that the whole person can function normally and well.

Summary

1. *Genetics* is the study of how traits are passed from one generation to the next. *Genes* are the basic elements of heredity. They exist in the nucleus of every living cell and are lined up on tiny threadlike bodies called *chromosomes*, which are arranged in pairs inside the nucleus of every cell.

2. Each gene may exist in two or more alternate forms and may be *dominant* or *recessive*. Because of dominant and recessive genes, a person's *genotype*, his underlying genetic makeup, can differ from his *phenotype*, the characteristics that can be seen or measured.

3. *Deoxyribonucleic acid—DNA*—forms the biochemical basis of the gene. DNA controls the cell's production of proteins by manufacturing molecules of *ribonucleic acid—RNA*—which carry the DNA's instructions out of the cell nucleus to the cytoplasm, where proteins are manufactured.

4. *Behavior genetics* explores the relationships between heredity and behavior. Some human issues looked at by behavior geneticists are the heritability of sex characteristics, intelligence, and schizophrenia.

5. Sex is determined by the X and Y chromosomes. A female receives an X chromosome from each parent; a male receives one X (from his mother) and one Y (from his father). *Sex-linked characteristics*, such as hemophilia, red-green color blindness, and certain forms of muscular dystrophy, occur far more frequently in males than in females because males' smaller Y chromosome does not contain the dominant gene needed to mask the X chromosome's recessive gene for the characteristic.

6. *Genetic abnormalities*, such as Down's syndrome, Turner's syndrome, and Klinefelter's syndrome, occur when one or more of the chromosomes fail to separate normally.

7. Most traits, like intelligence and height, are transmitted by *polygenic inheritance*. Several genes interact to produce the trait, each making a small contribution.

8. In an effort to separate the relative contributions of heredity and environment in humans, behavior geneticists study twins, family groups, and adopted children, each of which allows the psychologist to explore different aspects of heredity. In identical twins, who have the same genetic makeup, the same trait does not appear in both twins 100 percent of the time. Thus, heredity and environment do act together to determine behavior.

9. *Eugenics*, the science of improving species through selective breeding, raises important social issues. Although animals have been bred eugenically for centuries, there is no systematic eugenics program applied to humans because of the racial and political overtones involved and the moral dilemma of who decides which traits are good and which are bad. Raising these questions while scientific research progresses is a hopeful sign that we will be able to use our new knowledge wisely and well.

10. The body's two major coordinating mechanisms are the *nervous system*, which uses electrical messages, and the *endocrine system*, which uses chemical messages. Both of these systems contribute to *homeostasis*, keeping conditions inside the body in balance so other cells can continue to function.

11. The endocrine system is made up of internal organs called *glands*, which secrete chemical substances called *hormones* directly into the bloodstream.

12. The *thyroid gland* produces a hormone known as *thyroxin* that regulates the body's rate of metabolism. The *parathyroid glands* secrete *parathormone*, which controls the level of calcium and phosphate in the blood. The *pancreas* secretes *insulin* and *glucagon*, which regulate the level of sugar in the blood.

13. The *pituitary gland* has two parts that function separately. The *posterior pituitary* secretes *oxytocin*, which stimulates the contractions of the uterus in labor and alerts the mammary glands to start producing milk, and *vasopressin*, which elevates the blood pressure and controls the level of water in the body's cells. The *anterior pituitary* produces *somatotrophic hormone* (STH), which controls the timing and amount of the body's growth, and five other hormones that control other endocrine glands.

14. The *gonads*—the *testes* and the *ovaries*—produce the sex hormones—*progestins*, *androgens*, and *estrogens*—that stimulate the maturation of the reproductive organs and the development of secondary sex characteristics.

15. The two *adrenal glands* contribute to the function of nerves and muscles and to the ability of the body to cope with stress. The inner core, called the *adrenal medulla*, secretes *epinephrine* and *norepinephrine*, which control the body's responses to such emotions as fear and anger. The outer covering, called the *adrenal cortex*, controls the body's sodium-potassium balance and increases carbohydrate metabolism.

16. The nervous system is made up of ten to twelve billion cells called *neurons* that are specialized to receive and transmit information. Neurons have tiny fibers called *dendrites* and a single long fiber called an *axon* extending out from the cell body. The dendrites pick up incoming messages and carry

them to the cell body; the axons carry outgoing messages. A *nerve* is a group of axons bundled together.

17. *Afferent* (or *sensory*) neurons carry information to the spinal cord or to the brain. *Efferent* (or *motor*) neurons carry messages from the spinal cord or the brain to the muscles and glands. *Association* neurons make the connection between incoming and outgoing messages.

18. Neurons conduct electrochemical impulses. When a neuron is resting, its cell membrane keeps it in a state of *polarization,* with positive ions on the outside and negative ions on the inside. When a point on the cell membrane is electrically stimulated, the positive ions rush in and cause the neuron to fire. The incoming message must be above a certain *threshold* to cause a nerve impulse. A neuron will fire at maximum intensity no matter how far over the threshold the incoming message is. After firing, the neuron goes through an *absolute refractory period*—it will not fire at all no matter how strong the incoming message; and then a *relative refractory phase*—it will fire only if the incoming message is stronger than is normally necessary.

19. Near its end, the axon branches out into numerous fibers, each of which has a tiny *axon terminal* at its end. A minute gap, called a *synapse,* separates the end of each terminal from the next neuron. When the neural impulse reaches the end of an axon, it causes tiny sacs called *synaptic vesicles* to burst and release a chemical substance, which then travels across the gap and causes the next neuron to fire.

20. The *peripheral nervous system* contains two kinds of nerves—*sensory nerves,* which carry messages from the sense organs to the central nervous system, and *motor nerves,* which carry messages from the central nervous system to the muscles and glands. The peripheral nervous system can be further divided into the *somatic nervous system* and the *autonomic nervous system.*

21. The autonomic nervous system is composed of the *sympathetic* and *parasympathetic* divisions. The sympathetic division activates the body to respond to stress. The parasympathetic division directs the body to settle down after a period of stress.

22. The *central nervous system* is made up of the brain and spinal cord. The *spinal cord,* the complex cable of nerves that connect the brain to most of the rest of the body, consists of an outer section of *white matter,* which carries messages to and from the brain, and an inner core of *gray matter,* which controls certain reflex movements.

23. At its upper end the spinal cord enlarges and merges into the *brainstem,* which supports the other parts of the brain above it.

24. The *hindbrain* consists of the *medulla,* which controls breathing and many other reflexes, and which is the place where many of the nerves from the higher parts of the brain cross; the *pons,* a pathway for the nerves that connect the cortex at the top of the brain to the cerebellum; and the *cerebellum,* which handles certain reflexes and coordinates the body's movements.

25. The *midbrain* is especially important to hearing and sight and is also one of several places in the brain where pain registers.

26. The *forebrain* is composed of the *thalamus,* which acts as a relay station for messages from the sense receptors and messages from one part of the

cortex to another and controls the activities of the autonomic nervous system; the *hypothalamus,* which influences many kinds of motivation and emotional behavior; and the *cerebral cortex.*

27. The different functions of the cerebral cortex are performed in the *sensory projection areas,* where messages from the sense receptors are registered; *motor projection areas,* where messages to the muscles and glands originate; and *association areas,* which are involved in the higher mental processes like abstract thinking, problem solving, remembering, and learning. The cerebral cortex can be divided into four lobes—the *temporal lobe,* the *occipital lobe,* the *parietal lobe,* and the *frontal lobe.*

28. The *reticular activating system* is a circuit of nerves that run through the hindbrain, midbrain, and part of the forebrain. Its primary function is to filter incoming messages and alert higher parts of the brain.

29. The *limbic system,* a ring of structures in the center of each cerebral hemisphere, plays an important role in learning, memory, and emotional behavior.

30. The techniques of *psychosurgery* and *electrical stimulation of the brain (ESB)* illustrate the overlap between the physiology of the brain and the psychology of behavior. Both techniques attempt to change behavior through direct physical manipulation of the brain. Although psychosurgery's destructive side effects have limited its use, ESB, which is a precise, nondestructive technique, has potential for helping us understand how the brain really works. ESB can be used to explore brain regions other than the cerebral cortex, and it thus highlights the interdependence of the various brain structures that work together to affect behavior.

Suggested Readings

Kaplan, A. R. (Ed.), *Human Behavior Genetics* (Springfield, Ill.: Thomas, 1974). A comprehensive set of materials covering all aspects of research on human behavior genetics.

Katz, B., *Nerve, Muscle, and Synapse* (New York: McGraw-Hill, 1966). A concise description of the neural impulse and how it is transmitted.

Lewin, R., *The Nervous System* (Garden City, N.Y.: Anchor, 1974). A good, easy-to-read discussion of the nervous system, intended for the layman.

Lubar, J. F., *A First Reader in Psychological Psychology* (New York: Harper & Row, 1972). Articles and brief introductory essays that cover the major areas of traditional physiological psychology.

Mazur, A., and Robertson, L., *Biology and Social Behavior* (New York: Free Press, 1972). A very general overview of physiological psychology in a variety of areas, including language, population genetics, animal behavior, and genetics and IQ.

Milner, P. M., *Physiological Psychology* (New York: Holt, Rinehart & Winston, 1970). A good general textbook in physiological psychology.

Pines, M., *The Brain Changers: Scientists and the New Mind Control* (New York: Harcourt Brace Jovanovich, 1973). An excellent, very well-written book on brain research; reviews recent work on localization of function, alpha rhythms, memory transfer, and split-brain studies.

Robinson, D. N., *The Enlightened Machine* (Encino, Calif.: Dickenson, 1973). A good introduction to physiological psychology, including the historical background and the classic philosophical problems involved in the study of our dual nature as spiritual and physical beings.

Valenstein, E. S., *Brain Control* (New York: Wiley, 1973). Besides detailing the historical and scientific aspects of psychosurgery and electrical stimulation of the brain, Valenstein presents a critique of the present capabilities of both techniques in a clear and readable way.

outline

THE NEWBORN BABY 74

Individual Differences

PHYSICAL GROWTH 76

Maturation
Developmental Norms for Children
Physical Changes in Adolescence

MOTOR ABILITIES 80

PERCEPTUAL DEVELOPMENT 83

LANGUAGE DEVELOPMENT 88

COGNITIVE DEVELOPMENT 91

Piaget's Approach
Bruner's Approach

PERSONALITY DEVELOPMENT 96

Attachment
Autonomy
Imitation and Identification
Peer Groups
Development of Identity

THE TRANSITION TO ADULTHOOD 104

Young Adulthood

ADULTHOOD 106

Personality Development
Milestones of Adult Development

OLD AGE 111

Physical Changes
Cognitive Changes
"Successful" Aging

DEATH AND DYING 114

SUMMARY 115

SUGGESTED READINGS 118

3

Development

The Sphinx of Greek legend, far from being a hulk of noseless stone in the desert, was a genuine, practicing monster. She amused herself by devouring people who could not answer her riddle: What walks on four legs in the morning, on two legs at noon, and is three-legged in the evening?

The answer to her life-or-death riddle was Man, who crawls on all fours as a child, walks on two legs when he grows up, and ends in old age by hobbling with a cane. When the correct answer was finally given by Oedipus—whose name will come up again later in this book—the Sphinx was left without a leg to stand on and killed herself.

The Sphinx's riddle reminds us that every human goes through changes and stages in the course of life. Human development, the subject of this chapter, is not exactly a riddle to modern-day psychologists, although some periods of development have been studied more and thus are understood better. At one time, the old proverb, "As the twig is bent, so grows the tree," could have been used to describe the focus of much of developmental psychology. In other words, if you study the child, you will know the adult. In this view, once you got through adolescence, you were set (literally, like Jell-O) for life. But psychologists now know that adulthood has stages of growth and periods of crisis, just as childhood and adolescence do, and that the adjustment to old age and approaching death can sometimes be as difficult as the adjustment to a new body and a new life that we face during adolescence. In this chapter, we look at the stages of life from birth to the "three-legged" period that awaits all of us.

The Newborn Baby

Figure 3-1

A newborn infant, photographed by his mother immediately after delivery. (*Tom Myers, Photo Researchers*)

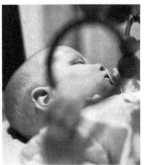

(*Raimondo Borea, Photo Researchers*)

For the first few weeks the newborn baby sleeps as much as 20 hours a day, waking only when he is hungry, uncomfortable, or startled. His body gives all the signs of dreaming: rapid eye movements, tremors, and sudden jerks. Within a few days, he begins to follow moving objects with his eyes and even shows a preference for looking at brightly colored and patterned objects.

Relatively insensitive to external pain, such as the prick of a diaper pin, the newborn baby is acutely aware of internal discomfort, such as hunger. He reacts negatively to strong smells, but does not find some odors pleasant and others disgusting as adults do. He may ignore loud, threatening noises, such as a fire engine, but find the sound of a paper being crumpled nearby terrifying. When startled, the newborn baby reacts immediately, but usually quiets down when he is picked up.

Lying in a crib, the newborn is completely helpless. He can neither lift his head nor turn over by himself and shows no inclination to reach out for pretty things dangled in front of him. However, when someone picks him up, he immediately begins searching for a nipple, grasping the adult with surprising strength. **Rooting behavior,** as this is called, is a reflex that directs the baby toward the food he needs.

Another crucial reflex for the infant is **sucking.** Shortly after birth he will suck on anything that touches his face—a bottle, a pacifier, a finger. Within a few days he seems to adjust to his mother's feeding style and begins to suck rhythmically. At first he shuts his eyes and concentrates fiercely. Later he begins to look around while he nurses and stops when anything catches his attention. Apparently the infant is not able to do more than one thing at a time.

Nevertheless, Jerome Bruner and his colleagues at Harvard's Center for Cognitive Studies have shown that babies can and do control their sucking. In one experiment, these researchers gave infants a "front-row seat" in a laboratory movie theater and gave them a pacifier that was connected to the projector. If the babies sucked hard enough, the picture came into focus. Surprisingly, even 3-week-old babies were able to focus the picture. They sucked extra hard, looked up quickly until the picture faded, and then began sucking again. This was surprising, not only because the infants were able to coordinate sucking and look-ing, but also because they were "smart" enough to realize that they controlled the movie—and interested enough to do so (Pines, 1970).

INFANTS' RIGHTS: A GENTLE WELCOME TO THE WORLD

There are countless books on natural, "painless," or fulfilling childbirth for mothers. But what about the baby? How traumatic is the experience of birth for the infant?

Very traumatic, according to French obstetrician Frederick Leboyer, who has proposed a gentle, soothing, and child-oriented method of delivery in his book *Birth without Violence* (1975). Leboyer's system is perhaps less a method than an atmosphere. Leboyer deplores the typical circumstances of delivery in a modern hospital: the glaring lights, the sudden harsh voices, the swift cutting of the umbilical cord, the doctor's traditional slap on the bottom.

In the Leboyer method, the delivery room is kept dimly lit, and all people present remain silent, to avoid shocking the baby, who has heard nothing but his mother's heartbeat in the quiet dark of the womb. When the baby is born, he is placed on his mother's stomach and gently massaged (by the mother as well as the doctor) for 4 or 5 minutes. Only then is the umbilical cord severed. The baby is then bathed in a basin of warm water where, Leboyer says, he is "free as in the distant good old days of pregnancy when he could play, move around in a boundless ocean. What might have remained of fear, stiffness, tension now melts away like snow in the sunshine" (p. 113).

These few minutes after delivery are all that distinguish Leboyer's method from standard obstetrical practice. All the resources of modern medicine are available should an emergency arise, and the mother's care during pregnancy and after delivery follows conventional guidelines.

In spite of this, the French medical community has been markedly unsympathetic to Leboyer's idea. Other obstetricians have charged Leboyer with everything from mystical and unmedical foolishness to plain quackery. Others claim his ideas are even medically dangerous. For example, undue delay in cutting the umbilical cord could invite infection, and a "good hearty scream" helps to assure proper breathing. Leboyer recently toured this country and spoke to various medical groups about his method, and American doctors seem to be equally skeptical.

Leboyer has delivered over 1,000 babies by his method. The preliminary results of one study of 50 Leboyer babies have shown them to be more content and more socially adaptive than other babies. They have fewer problems with eating and sleeping and have excellent relationships with their parents (Rapoport, cited in Englund, 1974). This may give some substance to Leboyer's argument that babies should be treated like "persons," not "mere squalling digestive tracts." And the Leboyer mothers? They find the birth experience "as safe and as secure as any other, and far more beautiful."

Still, the newborn baby is extremely limited. The only emotion he expresses is general excitement—usually shown by tearless crying and thrashing about. Hunger, pain, and fear all bring on the same response. Infant crying varies in intensity, but not in content or style. When warm and full, the newborn baby smiles with pleasure. He may also smile because of gas pains, but he does not smile in a social way, in response to other people, for a while yet. He recognizes neither his mother, his father, nor his own feet. He is completely at the mercy of his own body and those who care for him.

Individual Differences

Right from the start infants show **individual differences** that can be attributed to genetic makeup (what they inherit from their parents) and prenatal conditions (chiefly nutrition, their mother's diet). One baby curls quietly in an adult's arms; another squirms and kicks with remarkable energy. One sleeps through a rock concert in the next room; another wails when a dog barks two houses away. One baby feels almost limp when you pick him up; another is always tense and rigid.

What do these differences mean? One study of 141 children over 14 years suggested that these individual characteristics are an expression of the child's inborn temperament (Thomas, Chess, & Birch, 1970). "Easy" children, the authors found, are relaxed and adaptable from birth. In later life such children find school quite agreeable, learning how to make friends and play by the rules quite easily. "Difficult" children are moody and intense. They react violently to new people and new situations, sometimes withdrawing, other times protesting until the well-meaning adult gives up. Easily frustrated, they often find it hard to get along in school and in other demanding situations. "Slow to warm up" children, the authors' third type, are relatively inactive, withdrawn, and slow to react. Unlike the tantrum-prone "difficult" babies, they seem reluctant to express themselves. In later life these children often have difficulty with competitive and social encounters.

Many psychologists would disagree that temperament is inborn or predetermined. True, some children who were grumpy at birth are nasty at age 8 and impossible at age 12, but not, these psychologists say, because they were "born that way." Rather, the way an infant behaves affects his mother's reaction to him. Suppose, for example, the infant has digestive troubles and cries constantly. An inexperienced mother may rush him to the doctor in panic every other day. Another mother might react quite calmly. Similarly, a placid mother will find a quiet, rather unresponsive baby quite natural, while an energetic, extroverted mother might find the same infant disappointing.

Figure 3-2
Individual differences between babies show up very soon after birth. Such differences are caused by genetic factors, prenatal environment, and the circumstances at birth. One baby is placid and relaxed, the other fusses and cries.
(Top: Barbara Young, Photo Researchers; bottom: Fritz Henle, Photo Researchers)

Physical Growth

The newborn baby, as we have seen, is physiologically complete, but the simple act of picking up a toy requires abilities he does not have: judging how far away it is, crawling or walking to it, and coordinating his arm and hand to pick it up. A baby must go through various stages to get to the point where he is able to go across a room and grab hold of something he wants.

Figure 3-3
Body proportions at various ages. As the child grows older the head becomes relatively smaller and the legs longer in proportion to the rest of the body. (From Nancy Bayley, "Individual Patterns of Development." *Child Development,* 1956, 27, 45–74.)

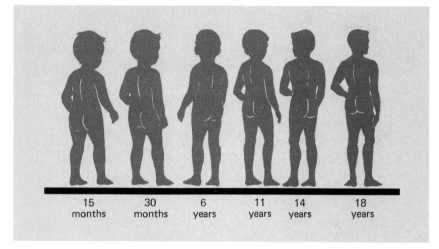

| 15 months | 30 months | 6 years | 11 years | 14 years | 18 years |

Maturation

Maturation is the continuation of a process that begins with conception, the fulfillment of genetic potential. It is as if the body had certain goals—say, a height of 5′9″. Nutrition may alter growth somewhat, but only an extremely poor diet will prevent the body from reaching its goal. Maturation is not, however, simply growth or increase in size; it involves dramatic changes in the *physical character* of the body. Most obviously, proportions change (see Figure 3-3). Puberty causes distinct changes in body chemistry that have a definite effect on behavior. These and other changes are "preprogrammed" genetically.

Maturation makes new behavior possible. The average 6-month-old is not able to walk; his legs simply cannot support his weight. But at about 13 to 14 months, he will be ready to walk. Even if his parents have not encouraged him, the readiness is there. Hopi Indian babies who are strapped to a stiff, confining cradleboard from birth learn to walk just as easily as Hopi babies who have been allowed to scramble around as they liked (Dennis & Dennis, 1940). Interestingly, there seem to be critical periods when a child is most able to start particular activities. Children who are bed-ridden from the age of 13 to 18 months (the average "walking readiness" period) find learning to walk much more difficult.

Some maturational changes, such as walking and sexual development, occur spontaneously. Others depend on the child's experiences: a child raised in isolation with a mute parent will not learn to talk, although he will make noises. Still other changes require previous development: a child cannot run until he has some confidence about walking. Maturation thus seems to follow a fairly predictable timetable, one step leading to another, until the body's physical goals are realized.

Developmental Norms for Children

Studies of the growth and maturation of many children have enabled psychologists to establish **developmental norms.**

Norms have several uses. While they do not predict the day on which a particular child will utter his first gratifying "Mama," they do alert parents and doctors to extremes. Brain damage may not be discovered until a mother notices her baby has not tried to lift his head at the age of 4 months. At the opposite extreme, the child who walks at 11 months, starts talking at 14 months, and is throwing a ball at 3 years may be happier if he starts school a year early. However, the child who develops more slowly than the norm will not necessarily always lag behind. Einstein, the story goes, did not begin to talk until he was 3 years old, a year and a half late according to most norms!

Norms have also been useful in suggesting patterns of child development. During his first month the infant's head must be supported when he is lifted. By the fifth week, however, he is able to lift his head, and in another month his chest. He does not begin to sit up for 3 to 5 months after that, and only starts to reach for things at the age of 6 months. Learning to walk takes even longer: the average baby cannot stand up until he is $10\frac{1}{2}$ months old.

Researchers have also discovered variations in the rate of maturation of different parts of the body. The brain and neural system develop rapidly, reaching nearly adult proportions by the time a child is 6 or 7 years old. The body grows quickly (though not as quickly as the neural system) for the first 6 years, and then seems to slow down until the child reaches adolescence. Sexual characteristics, of course, do not begin to develop until puberty and then proceed quite rapidly (see Figure 3-4).

Physical Changes in Adolescence

The period between the ages of 12 and 17 is marked by the most dramatic physiological change since the first 2 years of life. Even after 17, however, individuals continue to grow and develop, and it is not until the mid-twenties that the body is fully mature. The rapid growth and maturation that characterize adolescence affect almost every part of the body. While the rate of growth at any given age varies considerably from individual to individual, the sequence for each sex is fairly universal. The average girl has a 2-year head start on the average boy.

For girls, the first visible evidence of puberty appears between the ages of 8 and 13, with the development of breast buds. The next major change, growth in height, occurs about 18 months later, and by age 15 or 16, the average girl has reached 98 percent of her mature height. A corresponding weight gain comes about 6 months after the height spurt. Pubic hair may begin to appear at the same time as the breast

Figure 3-4

Patterns of growth of
various parts of the body.
The neural system develops
relatively early, while sexual
characteristics do not
appear until puberty.
(Adapted from C. W.
Jackson, "Some Aspects of
Form and Growth." In W. J.
Robbins et al., *Growth.* New
Haven, Conn.: Yale
University Press, 1928.)

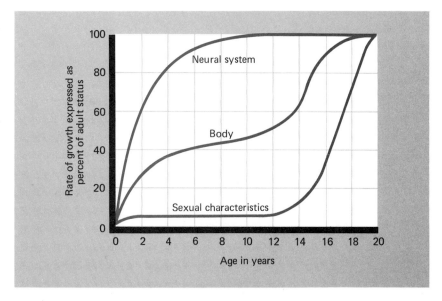

buds, but its major growth usually accompanies the height spurt.
Underarm hair begins to grow 2 years later. *Menarche,* or the onset
of menstruation, begins between the ages of 10 and 17—generally 2
years after breast development but rarely before the height spurt.

For boys the first evidence of puberty—growth of the testes and
scrotum—comes between the ages of 10 and 15. Penis growth begins
about a year later. The male height spurt can start at any time between
the ages of 10 and 16 and ends somewhere between the ages of 13 and
19. The average boy reaches 98 percent of his mature height by the
age of 17 or 18. Peak muscular growth comes about 3 months after the
height spurt, and maximum weight gain follows in another 3 months.
Physical strength and motor coordination do not begin to increase until
some 8 months after that and will not peak until sometime between
25 and 35. Pubic hair first appears between the ages of 10 and 14 and
is fully grown between 15 and 18, its maximum growth accompanying
the height spurt. Underarm hair and the long-awaited beard do not
come in until about 2 years after the appearance of pubic hair.

All these physiological changes can be extremely difficult for the
adolescent. Even the girl or boy who develops at the average age may
suffer from clumsiness, acne, or any number of other temporary afflic-
tions. But, more important, not everyone develops at just the "right"
age. During adolescence there is more disparity among individuals of
the same age than at any other time of life. Yet adolescent society places
great importance on physical appearance and on not being different,
so that the girl who matures earlier than her classmates and the boy
who lags behind them may have particularly difficult problems in
adjusting. If a 10-year-old girl has large breasts, or stands half a head
taller than the boys in her class, she is likely to be the object of ridicule.

Figure 3-5
During adolescence the differences in physical development among people of the same age are greater than at any other time in the life span. All these boys are nearly 15 years old, and all the girls are nearly 13. (Adapted from L. I. Gardner, *Endocrine and Genetic Diseases in Childhood.* Philadelphia: Saunders, 1969.)

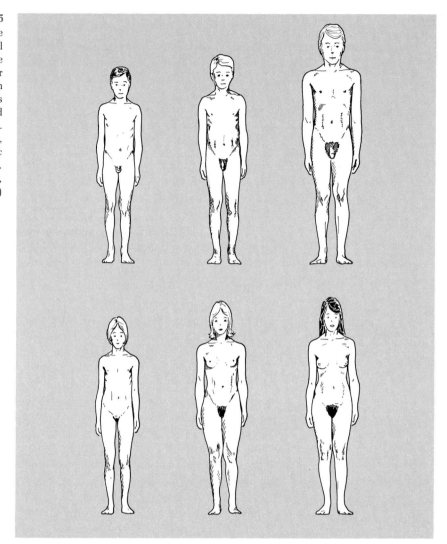

A "late-blooming" girl may fake monthly periods or resort to a padded bra for the sake of social acceptance. Life can be harder for a late-maturing boy, who cannot resort to such fakery to conceal his physical "inadequacies." Being teased for having a smaller penis than his friends can leave lifelong scars. One task of the adolescent is learning to cope with these physical and psychological growing pains, and with the sexual and social pressures that accompany them.

Motor Abilities

Growing up is in many ways a fight against gravity. Within a year the baby who could not even lift his head is sitting up, crawling around, and beginning to walk with a little help. And as soon as he can walk, he tries to jump and climb (first stairs, then trees and jungle gyms). At each stage his view of the world changes markedly. At 7 months the infant is curious about everything he sees; at 10 months he can put his curiosity into action, crawling through open doors and pushing ashtrays off the coffee table. Along the way, the infant works out a number of techniques he will abandon at later stages—like crawling.

In describing the infant's acquisition of motor abilities, psychologists focus on walking and grasping. Both appear as reflexes in the newborn baby, although neither is of much use to him at that point. Held up, with his body dangling, the infant pumps his legs up and down like a runner. This reflex seems to disappear after 7 to 8 weeks. When he begins practice-walking again at 10 or 11 months, his picture is quite different, for he is able to hold himself up (see Figure 3-6). Gradually his attempts become more deliberate, and with only a little support he begins to walk forward. He soon learns heel-to-toe coordination, and after practice (and quite a few falls) straightens up and walks.

Figure 3-6
The normal sequence of motor development. The newborn is capable only of simple reflexes. At about 1 month he begins to lift his shoulders, then starts to crawl at about 4 to 6 months. By 9 months the child can sit up alone. He can support himself in a standing position at about 10 months, and around 13 months begins to walk alone.
(*Suzanne Szasz*)

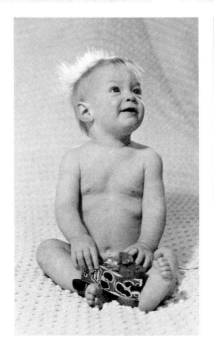

Figure 3-7

The stages of prehensile development. As his ability to control his fingers and thumbs increases, the child progresses from random reaching to grasping things with his fingers and thumb.
(Suzanne Szasz)

How effective is early encouragement or training in helping a child to walk sooner? A recent experiment indicated that early encouragement has results. A group of 1-week-old babies were trained in their own homes by their mothers in walking and foot-placing exercises each day for a 7-week period, while a second group of babies were not. The babies who had been helped through the motions of walking were significantly more active in step responses and, later, walked sooner than the others. Thus, this first 8-week period of life, before the newborn's walking reflex disappears, seems to be critical in promoting walking ability (Zelazo, Zelazo, & Kolb, 1972).

Mature grasping takes much longer to develop. The newborn infant has a surprisingly firm grip. From birth to 24 weeks many babies can hang by their hands like monkeys, and most can support 90 percent of their weight. Like newborn walking, this appears to be a reflex action. At about 6 months this primitive grasping disappears, but by this time the infant is reaching for things on his own. At first he can only close his hand around an object, but as his arm and hand muscles develop, he learns to hold things fairly securely in his palm. At about 9 months he is using his fingers to hold things, but not until the age of 12 months does the infant gain control of his thumb (see Figure 3-7).*

*This last step is particularly important. The fact that a human being's thumb is independent of his other fingers enables him to handle tools—to push a plow, swing a hammer, or control a pen.

At about 2 years, the infant begins to show a preference for one hand or the other. A few years ago, "handedness" was a controversial subject, with some researchers attributing stuttering and reading problems to parents' efforts to change a left-handed child into a right-handed one. Like many theories, the idea that left- or right-handedness is significant in the child's development has passed. Most infants will use both hands at first, gradually drifting into handedness as their skills increase.

When a person reaches the age of 3 or 4, we begin to speak of him as a child, not a baby. The 4-year-old child is ready to learn how to pitch a baseball, handle a paintbrush, write his name. During the next 8 or 9 years his speed and strength will increase, as will his ability to handle small objects like balls and tools. By the time he starts to grow rapidly again during adolescence, his motor abilities will be equal to those of an adult.

Perceptual Development

What does the world look like to an infant? The infant, as we have seen, cannot *tell* the researcher anything, but his body does send signals. When he is afraid, his heart beats faster, just like an adult's. Eye movements can be observed directly. Finally, the infant can be taught to perform some action that lets the researcher know when the baby has seen the stimulus. These methods have enabled psychologists to investigate the question of whether infants see only a meaningless swirl of images or whether they are born knowing, in some primitive way, the concepts of distance, depth, and so on.

Visual Discrimination

As a first step toward answering this question, researchers had to determine whether very young infants make any distinction at all between one thing and another. Perhaps their world is all "blooming, buzzing confusion," in William James's words.

(Rohn Engh, Photo Researchers)

To test this, psychologist Robert L. Fantz invented a number of "visual discrimination" experiments. His method was simple: he showed infants a variety of pictures and patterned cards to see if they preferred some to others. Preference was measured by the length of time the infant looked at a card. In one experiment he showed 1- to 15-week-old babies one card with a black and white pattern and one plain gray card. All the infants spent more time looking at the patterned card (Fantz, 1961). A recent study has shown that, as infants get older, they prefer increasingly complex patterns. Greenberg and O'Donnell (1972) showed patterns at three different levels of complexity to 6-week-old and 11-week-old infants. The 11-week-olds consistently spent more time looking at the complex patterns than the 6-week-olds did.

In a second experiment Fantz showed the babies three cards, one at a time (see Figure 3-8). The first was a simple drawing of a human

Figure 3-8

Fantz's experiment on pattern perception. Infants were shown the three shapes at the side of the graph. At almost every age the babies spent more time looking at the face and less time looking at the plain oval. (From "The Origin of Form Perception" by Robert L. Fantz. Copyright © 1961 by Scientific American, Inc. All rights reserved.)

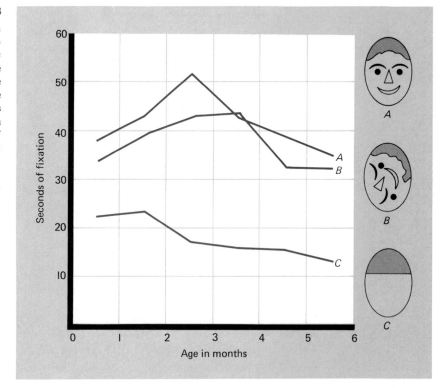

face; the second, the same shape but with the features scrambled; the third, an oval with a gray patch, but no features. Infants 4 days to 6 months old preferred the real and scrambled faces to the plain oval (Fantz, 1963).

What do these experiments tell us? First, that infants do see patterns and enjoy looking at them; second, that they seem to prefer patterns to plain shapes; and third, that they begin to recognize the human face at an early age. But what about dimensions? Before a baby begins to crawl and learns from experience that it takes effort to go from his crib to the door, does he realize that the door is far away? Before he has dropped his rattle from his crib a hundred times, does he perceive depth?

Depth Perception

Psychologists use a rather ingenious device—the visual cliff—for experiments on depth perception (see Figure 3-9). The basic apparatus is a table divided into three parts. The center is a solid board covered with a checkerboard pattern. On one side of this, the table surface is dropped an inch or so; on the other side (the visual cliff), the drop is about 40 inches. This side is covered with glass at the level of the

Figure 3-9
The visual cliff. The child pats the glass on the deep side, but is reluctant to crawl across it to his mother.
(William Vandivert)

centerboard so that if the infant should cross over, he will not fall. An infant is placed on the centerboard and his mother stands on one side or the other, encouraging him to crawl toward her.

All of the 6- to 14-month-old infants tested by Walk and Gibson (1961) refused to crawl over the deep side to their mothers. Some peered down over the cliff; others cried; still others patted the glass with their hands. When their mothers stood on the shallow side, the same babies crawled to them. Obviously, then, 6-month-olds perceive depth. What about younger babies? Because infants less than 6 months cannot crawl, researchers placed them on one side or the other and measured their pulse rates to see if they were reacting (Campos, Langer, & Krowitz, 1970). When they were placed on the deep side of the cliff, the infants' hearts slowed down, a reaction typical of infants and adults who stop to orient themselves in new situations. Thus small babies seemed to know that something was different, but not how to react.

Object Perception

All adults take for granted the fact that people and objects are solid and permanent. We know that if we put a box in the closet and lock the door, it will still be there when we come back. But does an infant?

T. G. R. Bower explored this question with infants who had been taught to turn their heads when they saw a familiar object.

To see whether infants know objects are solid, Bower devised a method for projecting an optical illusion of a hanging ball. His plan was first to give infants a real ball, one they could reach out and touch, and then to show them the illusion. If they reached out for the illusion and found empty air, undoubtedly they would show surprise and frustration in their faces and movements. If they did not expect the ball to be solid, they would not react. All the 16- to 24-week-old infants he tested were surprised when they reached for the illusion (Bower, 1971).

But do infants realize that things are permanent—that a ball that rolls under a chair does not disappear into never-never land? Apparently they do. When infants watch a toy train disappear behind the left side of a screen, they look to the right, expecting it to reappear. If the experimenter stops the train behind the screen, takes it off the table, and lifts the screen, the babies seem surprised that it is no longer there. If, when the train rolls behind the screen, the researcher substitutes a ball, 22-week-old babies seem puzzled; they look back to the left side for the original object. But 16-week-old infants do not seem to notice the switch.

Perceptual Set and Whole-Part Perception

Experiments with perceptual set and whole-part perception generally involve older children, for they rely on the child's being able to report what he sees. Studies in this area are thus particularly interesting with regard to the development and refinement of perceptual abilities. The focus in the two studies we will discuss here is on what the child sees when he looks at something that can be seen in different ways.

H. W. Reese (1963) was interested in how suggestions influence perception. He created a number of ambiguous drawings, such as the one shown in Figure 3-10. Depending on how you look at it, the figure could be a man's face or a rat. Reese paired the ambiguous drawings with sets of nonambiguous drawings that suggested one way of looking at them (the rat-man, for example, was paired with pictures that clearly showed human faces). First he showed the children the nonambiguous drawings; then he asked them to sort the ambiguous figures into piles of human, animal, and inanimate figures. Pre-school children were not influenced by the nonambiguous pictures. Older children almost always followed the suggestions, putting the rat-man in the human pile if they had seen nonambiguous human drawings first. This suggests that, given an idea, older children limit their perception along those lines: they accept a **perceptual set.** Younger children do not.

To test **whole-part perception,** Elkind, Koegler, and Go (1964) invented a set of pictures within pictures (see Figure 3-11). The first

Figure 3-10
One of the ambiguous drawings used by Reese to test perceptual set in children. The figure can be seen as either a rat or a man's face. (From Hayne W. Reese, "'Perceptual Set' in Young Children." *Child Development*, 1963, 34, 151–159.)

drawing, for example, can be seen as a heart (whole perception) or as two giraffes (part perception); the second as a plane or as a potato, two carrots, and some leaves. They found that young children tend to see wholes, while older children tend to name parts. Elkind and his colleagues suggest two reasons for this perceptual difference. First, young children cannot take in as much detail as older children, possibly because they have less facility with names. Second, young children need more cues. If they had seen the potato-airplane on a plate with a knife and fork, they probably would have realized the plane was made of vegetables. Seeing it out of a food context, they did not.

What can we conclude from these experiments? Does perception develop naturally, as the child gets older, as these studies suggest? Many psychologists think not.

The Role of Experience

All the babies in the experiments cited here were raised in normal homes, with mothers and fathers to play with them from the day they were born. What about babies raised without the learning experiences parents and siblings provide?

Putting this question to the test, White and Held (1966) studied two groups of institutional infants. The babies in one group were handled in the usual institutional way: they were washed, dressed, and fed—nothing more. The infants in the second group were handled an extra 20 minutes each day. The nurses talked to them, smiled at them, and so on. This special treatment was continued for a month. White and Held found that up to the age of 5 months, the handled babies showed much more interest in their environment than the others. In a second experiment, the handled babies were also given lively surroundings: pictures on the wall, colored and patterned sheets, mobiles over their cribs. The pads that protect institution babies from collisions with the sides of their cribs were removed for part of each day so that they could look

Figure 3-11

Some of the drawings used to test whole-part perception in children. (From David Elkind, Ronald R. Koegler, and Elsie Go, "Studies in Perceptual Development: II. Part-Whole Perception." *Child Development,* 1964, *35,* 81–90.)

around more. At the age of 3 months these babies were reaching out for things—2 months earlier than the other infants. Apparently, stimulation accelerated perceptual growth in these babies.

Other experiments have shown that perception improves with age. Shown rods of equal length at various distances, adults realized they were the same length far more often than 7- to 9-year-old boys (Zeigler & Leibowitz, 1957). Thus there is good evidence that stimulation, experience, and learning contribute to perceptual development. Depth and object perception may be inborn, but without experience they will not mature.

Language Development

Of all the changes a child goes through, none is more dramatic than the acquisition of language. Like motor abilities and perception, language depends on physical maturation (control of the mouth and tongue). But it also depends on experience.

A Brief Chronology

At about 2 months the infant begins cooing (a rather nondescript word for rather nondescript sounds). These early vocalizations are distinguished from the gurgling of the newborn baby by the fact that the infant moves his mouth and tongue to produce different sounds. In another month or two he enters the "babbling" stage—he starts to repeat sounds. Gradually his babbling begins to resemble the cadences of adult speech. Between 8 and 10 months he seems to take special pleasure in "talking" to himself as he works at grabbing hold of things and crawling. Vocalization at this age is primarily nonsocial. Soon, however, he begins to imitate sounds and to use his voice to get attention. By 10 or 11 months he shows signs of understanding things said to him.

At about 12 months the infant utters his first word, usually "Mama," "Dada," or "Papa." During the next 6 to 8 months the child builds a vocabulary of one-word sentences: (Pick me) "Up!"; (I want to go) "Out!"; (Tickle me) "Again!" This list of imperatives or commands is fairly typical—probably, some psychologists point out, because so many commands are given to the child. He may also use a number of compound words, such as "Awgone" (all gone). To these the child adds greetings, "Bye-bye" being a favorite, and a few exclamations such as "Ouch!" Most small children are also interested in possessives: (The shoes are) "Daddy's." But perhaps the overwhelming passion of 2-year-olds is naming. At play the child will say the word "block" or something like it over and over, looking at his mother for approval each time. Interestingly, children do not seem to be in any great rush to learn words associated with their needs: for these they rely on concrete action—crying and fussing.

Soon the child begins to formulate two- and three-word sentences of nouns and attributes. Typical beginner's sentences are "Baby crying," "My ball," "Dog barking." A number of psychologists have recorded mother-child dialogues at this age, to see just what the child picks up and what he omits. Most noticeably, children at this age omit auxiliary verbs—(Can) "I have that?" "I (am) eating it"—and prepositions—"It (is) time (for) Sarah (to) take (a) nap." Apparently children grab hold of the most important words, probably the words their mother stresses.

During the next few months the child begins to fill in his sentences. "Billy school" becomes "Billy goes to school." He starts to locate things in time, employing the past tense as well as the present; he asks more questions and learns to use "Why?" effectively (and sometimes monotonously). By age 5 or 6, he probably has a vocabulary of over 2,500 words and is making sentences of six or eight words.

Theories of Language Development

What prompts the child to learn to talk? Most psychologists feel the baby is born with a biological capacity for language that is stimulated into growth by the environment, by the talk he hears around him from the day he is born. This is not to say that the child learns by imitation alone. Rather, it seems that at the same time as the child learns words, he learns rules for putting them together in meaningful ways.

Cooing and babbling are spontaneous. Institutionalized children, who cannot expect the rewards of an adult's smile for their efforts, and deaf children, who do not have the self-satisfaction of hearing themselves make noises, babble like other children. However, the institutionalized child takes much longer to begin talking than the child who is raised in a family, and the deaf child requires special training. Clearly, "feedback," in the form of listening to oneself and others, influences language development.

When the child first uses actual words, he is very concrete: he identifies words with situations and functions. Stone and Church (1968) describe a child who called all red cars "engines" (for fire engines) long before he used the word "red" or had grasped the more abstract concept of colors. On word-association tests, where the subject is asked to listen to a word and say the first word that comes into his mind, adults associate the cue word "table" with "chair," "man" with "woman." Given the same cues, children associate "table" with "eat," "man" with "work." At this stage, then, the child is more aware of functions than of similarities (Brown & Berko, 1960).

Some researchers feel that by the time a child starts making two- and three-word sentences, he has developed simple rules for word order apparently by parroting adult sentences in telegraph form. Although he leaves a number of words out, he nearly always gets the main words in the right order. This is particularly remarkable because most parents do not seem to pay as much attention to word order as they do to content when they correct their children's speech (Brown, 1973).

At age $2\frac{1}{2}$ or 3 children commonly make certain mistakes that indicate they are beginning to learn more sophisticated grammatical rules. Often the child will proudly announce, "I saw some sheeps" or "I digged a hole." Obviously he did not learn the words "sheeps" and "digged" by imitating adults. Rather, he applied the rules for making nouns plural and verbs past tense in a logical way, not knowing yet that some words are irregular. Additional evidence that children learn grammatical rules at an early age comes from their understanding of how to use the words "I" and "you." When the child listens to his mother, she always uses the word "I" for herself, "you" for him. Somehow the child learns to reverse this. The child's apparent ability to learn such rules is surprising when we consider how long it takes him to learn other rules, such as telling time and counting, which have to be explained over and over. Psychologists differ in their explanations of this phenomenon.

Some feel the child is born with an innate sense of grammar—that he is preprogrammed to put words together in a correct and meaningful way (Chomsky, 1965). Obviously no 3-year-old child could understand the differences between verbs and nouns, nouns and adjectives if they were explained to him. Still, even the beginning talker makes sentences of his own.

Other researchers feel the child must learn each grammatical rule through observation and practice. Still others take a middle road. All children seem to enjoy making sounds and words, and all seem to pick up the rules for putting them together quite easily. This sensitivity to language seems to be inborn, but without a social environment—people to talk with—the child is slow to pick up the words and rules that enable him to communicate and learn.

Cognitive Development

The process of acquiring, storing, retrieving, and revising knowledge is called **cognition.** In this section we look at cognitive development, beginning with the theories of Jean Piaget.

Piaget's Approach

Jean Piaget entered the field of cognitive development through a back door: he was trained as a zoologist, and this perspective shows in his work. Piaget sees all behavior in terms of the individual's adaptation to his environment. Unlike animals, people have few reflexes and must figure out ways of dealing with their environment.

Piaget first became interested in human adaptations when he watched his own children playing. Observing them with the trained eye of a scientist, he began to see their games as confrontations with their surroundings. In other words, they were learning to adapt.

As Piaget's children grew, he noticed that the way they approached environmental problems at different ages changed dramatically. Was it simply that their coordination improved, or do older children think differently than their younger brothers and sisters? Piaget became an avid child-watcher: he played with them, asked questions about their activities, and devised games that would show how they were thinking.*
Gradually he discerned a pattern, a series of stages through which all children pass.

(Fritz Henle, Photo Researchers)

Sensory-motor stage (birth–2 years). As Piaget sees it, the baby's first step is applying the skills he has at birth (sucking and grasping) to a broad range of activities. Small babies delight in putting things into their mouths: their own hands, their mother's pearls, their toys. Gradually they divide the world into what they can suck and what they cannot. Similarly, a young baby will grasp a rattle instinctively. Then at some point he realizes that the noise he has been hearing comes from the rattle. He begins to shake everything he gets hold of, trying to

---

*Piaget's approach is unusual. In developing theories, most researchers test as many children as they can to arrive at solid generalizations. Piaget chose instead to study a small number of children intensively as they went about their daily lives. This is a form of naturalistic observation, which is discussed in Chapter 1.

reproduce the sound. He begins to distinguish between things that make noise and things that do not. In this way the infant begins to organize his experiences, fitting them into categories. *Schemata,* as Piaget calls these simple frameworks, are the first step toward intentional behavior and adaptive problem solving.

By the end of this stage, the child has developed a sense of object permanence (which we discussed in the section on perception). When a baby begins to look for a ball that has rolled under a chair, we know he realizes that the ball still exists. This awareness is crucial to cognitive development, for it enables the child to begin to see some regularity in the way things happen.

Preoperational thought (2–7 years). Entering the preoperational stage, the child is action-oriented. His understanding and thought processes are based on physical and perceptual experiences. But as his ability to remember and anticipate grows, he begins to form a consistent image of the world. Systematic methods for representing the external world internally are the major achievement of the preoperational stage. The most obvious example of *representation,* the use of symbols, is language, and it is in this stage that the child begins to use words to stand for objects.

(Suzanne Szasz, Photo Researchers)

Piaget notes a number of ways in which preoperational thinking differs from the thinking of older children and adults. Small children are extremely egocentric; they cannot distinguish between themselves and the outside world. They assume that objects have feelings, just as they do (animism); they consider their own psychological processes—for example, dreams—to be real, concrete events (realism).

Preoperational children cannot put themselves in someone else's place. Piaget demonstrated this quite simply. He set up three "mountains" on a table surrounded by four chairs. He then asked the child to sit down and gave him some drawing materials. Next he placed a doll in one of the other chairs and asked the child to pretend he was sitting in the doll's place and draw the mountains. None of the children realized that the display would look different from the other side (Piaget & Inhelder, 1956).

Piaget also found that children in this stage tend to focus on the one aspect of a display or event that attracts their attention, ignoring all others. In a now-famous experiment, Piaget asked children to fill two identical containers with beads (Figure 3-12). When they had finished, he poured the beads from one container into a tall thin glass and asked them if one had more beads. Invariably the children said yes, even though they realized he had not added or taken away any beads. One reason for this illogical response is that children can only think about one dimension at a time, height or width. Piaget calls this single-mindedness *centering.*

Another reason is that children's thinking is rigid and *irreversible.* An older child might reverse Piaget's steps to reach a conclusion. "If

Figure 3-12

In this experiment, Piaget pours the beads from one of the short wide beakers into the tall thin one. Children in the preoperational stage will usually say that the taller beaker contains more beads.

Figure 3-12

In this experiment, Piaget pours the beads from one of the short wide beakers into the tall thin one. Children in the preoperational stage will usually say that the taller beaker contains more beads.

we poured the beads back into the original container, it would look the same as before. The number of beads must be the same." The preoperational child is not able to retrace his steps. Phillips (1969) asked a 4-year-old boy if he had a brother; the child replied, "Yes." He then asked the brother's name; "Jim." "Does Jim have a brother?" The child responded with a definite "No." (This anecdote illustrates both irreversibility and egocentrism: the child could not think of himself as somebody else's brother.)

Concrete operations (7–11 years). During this stage the child acquires the flexibility preoperational children lack. He learns to retrace his thoughts, correct himself, and start over if necessary; to consider more than one dimension at a time; to look at a single object or problem in different ways. Three logical operations characterize thinking in this stage: combining, reversing, and forming associations.

Another bead game illustrates all these operations and shows how children between the ages of 7 and 11 have grown intellectually. Piaget gave children of different ages a box of 20 wooden beads: 2 were white, the rest brown. He then asked them whether the wooden beads or the brown beads would make the longest necklace. Children under 7 decided there were more brown beads, ignoring the fact that all the beads were wooden. Children 7 and older laughed at the question: they knew that *all* the beads were wooden (Piaget & Szeminska, 1952).

Although quite logical in their approach to problems, children in this stage can only think in terms of concrete things they can handle or imagine handling. In contrast, the adult is able to think in abstract terms, to formulate hypotheses and accept or reject them without testing them empirically. This ability develops in the next stage.

Formal operations (11–15 years). To demonstrate the development of abstract thinking, Piaget re-created a historical situation. He gave children an opportunity to discover for themselves Archimedes' law of floating bodies (Inhelder & Piaget, 1958).

Children in the concrete and formal operations stages were given a variety of objects and asked to separate them into two piles: things that would float and things that would not. The objects included cubes of different weights, matches, sheets of paper, a lid, pebbles, and so on. Piaget then let the children test their selections in a pail of water and asked them to explain why some things floated and others sank.

The younger children were not very good at classifying the objects, and when questioned gave *individual* reasons for each one. The nail sank because it was too heavy; the needle because it was made of iron; the lid floated because "it has edges."

ADOLESCENT THOUGHT

With the continued development of conceptual abilities, the adolescent's world begins to take on new dimensions. He begins to construct mental theories and systems. He is able to conceive of himself as a whole being, not just as a jumble of individual attributes. The world around him becomes an entire society rather than a collage of specific people, places, and activities. His morality is no longer limited to separate decisions on separate problems, but expands to encompass a complete ethical code. With this new cognitive ability often comes an idealistic sense of purpose and responsibility, a desire to construct a life style, to battle social and political injustices, to somehow make a mark on society.

In the beginning, however, the adolescent is not able to distinguish between his own thoughts and those of others, and he falls victim to a peculiar kind of egocentrism (Elkind, 1969). Because he is painfully preoccupied with himself, he believes that others are always thinking about him, too. He anticipates their negative reactions to his failures and positive reactions to his successes and continually plays to this "imaginary audience." At a football game a girl with a beautiful complexion and an attractive figure may be convinced that people are eyeing her instead of watching the game. A boy with an A in chemistry may believe that everyone around him is talking about his high grade.

Just as the adolescent fails to distinguish the real feelings of others, he tends to overvalue his own feelings, to believe that they are unique in content and intensity. This sense of uniqueness and self-importance constitutes what Elkind calls a "personal fable." No one else, the adolescent tells himself, can reach the same heights of ecstasy or depths of misery. His personal fable may lead him to indulge in lengthy soul-searching, to write anguished poetry or copious diaries for the enlightenment of posterity, or to engage in personal conversations with God.

It is not until the age of 15 or 16 that the egocentrism of early adolescence gives way to more mature thought. As the adolescent begins to distinguish the true thoughts of others, the real audience replaces the imaginary one. As he begins to reach out to others and to form more mature interpersonal relationships, he comes to realize that he is not so unique, and more realistic self-evaluation replaces his personal fable.

The older children seemed to know what would float. When asked to explain their choices, they began to make comparisons and cross-comparisons, gradually coming to the conclusion that neither weight nor size alone determined whether an object would float. Rather it was the relationship between these two dimensions. Thus they were able to approximate Archimedes' law (objects float if their density is less than that of water).

The fact that these children searched for a general rule is particularly significant. Younger children find reasons by testing their ideas in the real world; they are concrete and specific. Adolescents test their ideas internally with logic. This means that they are able to go beyond the here and now, to understand things in terms of cause and effect, to consider the *possibilities* as well as realities, and to develop concepts.*

Bruner's Approach

Psychologist Jerome Bruner, whom you will remember from the discussion of newborn babies, is also interested in concept attainment. Like Piaget, he studies children to see how thinking matures. His three developmental stages—enactive, iconic, and symbolic representation—are roughly equivalent to Piaget's preoperational, concrete operational, and formal operational stages. However, Bruner differs from Piaget in focusing on the representations a child uses rather than on the way he manipulates them.

Enactive representation. By this Bruner means the infant's representing objects and past events in terms of an appropriate motor response. He cites one of Piaget's case studies. A baby drops a rattle through the bars of his crib. He stops for a moment, brings his hand up to his face, and looks at his hand. Puzzled, he lets his arm fall and shakes it as if the rattle were still there; no sound. He investigates his hand again. Bruner suggests the infant is representing the rattle when he shakes his hand; that is, the rattle means shaking-your-hand-and-hearing-a-noise to him.

Iconic representation. In a few months the baby tries to look over the edge of his crib when the rattle drops and fusses if an adult takes it away. Bruner feels this sense of loss indicates the baby has an image of it in his mind, that he now distinguishes between shaking his hand and the rattle. Bruner calls picturing things to oneself iconic representation.

Symbolic representation. Symbols do not depend on images or appearances. The number 6 does not resemble the quantity six; the word "boy" neither looks nor sounds like a male child. Once removed from

*Concepts are discussed in detail in Chapter 6.

reality, symbols are infinitely more flexible than images. Consider a simple arithmetic problem: "A man has 4 apples; he buys 6 more. How many does he have?" The pre-schooler may solve the problem by drawing 4 circles and then 6 more circles on his paper and counting them up. The older child will write the numbers and add them up, without having to imagine the apples.

Bruner noticed that 7-year-olds talked to themselves as they worked on problems. He suggests that their success at problem solving resulted from their being able to come up with a verbal formula. But 4-year-olds can talk—why are they unable to construct such verbal formulas?

Integration and language development. The 4-year-old does have a vocabulary of symbols—both words and numbers—but he is still dominated by direct experiences. This can be demonstrated with the familiar game Twenty Questions. Children are allowed to ask 20 questions that can be answered yes or no to find out why a car went off the road and hit a tree. Six-year-olds approach this task with guesses: they propose complete solutions (Did a bee sting the man in the eye?), and if the answer is no, they go on to an entirely different solution. Eight-year-olds ask more general questions (Was something wrong with the man? Was it nighttime?).

Commenting on this, Bruner suggests that young children use words as "one-step substitutes" for concrete experience. The child who asked about the bee sting, for example, may have been remembering a television cartoon. The child who asked if something was wrong with the man has integrated a number of experiences into the concept "people who have something wrong with them." If the answer was no, he might ask if something was wrong with the car or the road. In each case he is using words to suggest classes of experiences or events; the answer will narrow the range of possibilities (Bruner, 1964).

Bruner's studies indicate that conceptual thinking and language develop together. The child begins to use words in an iconic way, to stand for specific experiences. Once he has a grasp of them and some practice in applying single words to a variety of experiences, he begins to use words in a symbolic way, to represent a large number of images. The words begin to assume a meaning of their own, independent of images. At this point he can begin to manipulate them without having to refer to experiences—to perform logical and abstract operations.*

Personality Development

The newborn baby is completely helpless, but he is also utterly self-ish. The only thing that matters to him is that his needs are satisfied. For years he cannot really distinguish between himself and his envi-

*We should emphasize the point that language use does not cause concept development. Deaf children, who use only limited sign language, are able to form concepts, although a bit more slowly than children who can hear (Furth, 1961).

THE GROWTH OF CONSCIENCE

Psychologists, like philosophers and theologians, have long been fascinated by the question of how children develop morality. How do they come to know right from wrong? In a word, how does a child develop a conscience?

Freud, as we have seen, equated conscience with the superego. As the child incorporated his parents' standards, Freud believed, the superego developed. Other psychologists have concentrated on the ways parents enforce discipline and how they affect the child's moral development. Some mothers use mostly physical punishment and others use mostly withdrawal of love to control their children. Sears, Maccoby, and Levin (1957) found that children are more likely to tell their mothers voluntarily when they do something wrong if the mothers have used withdrawal of love as the usual method of punishment. In fact, physical punishment was negatively related to the growth of conscience, as measured by the child's willingness to confess a wrongdoing.

Some of the most recent investigations indicate that children pass through several stages in the development of conscience. The stages seem to be fairly consistent from child to child. Piaget, for example, who thinks of conscience development largely as a cognitive process, has identified various stages in children's use of rules and in their awareness of rules. The stages correspond closely to Piaget's stages of cognitive development. At first children think of rules as specific examples; then, quite rigidly, as "sacred" dictates handed down by adults; and finally, in a more abstract way, as products of mutual consent.

Piaget felt that the younger children's "moral realism" stage (when they tend to regard parental rules as sacred taboos) could be inadvertently prolonged by parental behavior. Parents do punish children for breaking a dish, for example, even when it is accidental. But mature moral thinking does take motives into account. Parents can hasten this growth, said Piaget, if they stress cooperation and empathy with the feelings of others.

Kohlberg (1966) has extended Piaget's ideas to other, widely different cultures with different child-rearing practices. As children grow older, he finds, all go through the same three levels of moral development. The first is the *premoral* level, in which children tend to interpret good or bad behavior in the light of its physical consequences—either rewards or punishment. In the second, or *conventional,* level the child is concerned with maintaining a social order. The third, or *postconventional,* level is marked by an emphasis on the abstract moral principles themselves, quite apart from consideration of the power of those who enforce them or their effect on particular groups or societies.

ronment. He thinks he is the world; at the same time he realizes that he is powerless. This paradox of egocentricity and complete dependency is but the first in a series of conflicts the child must resolve. In doing so he establishes the feelings about the world and the image of himself that we call personality. Later, when he reaches adolescence, he will have to revise his self-image and integrate new feelings into his childhood personality.

Attachment

Nature supplies the infant with a mother who is able to care for him. **Attachment theory** suggests that the newborn's few activities—sucking, clinging, crying—serve to attach the baby to his mother, and the mother to her baby. The infant clings to his mother when she holds him; this triggers in her the desire to protect and provide for the child.

For a long time, child psychologists focused on feeding patterns. Feeding, they hypothesized, was the infant's first and most important experience of the world. His mother satisfies his need for food; he begins to view her in a positive way and thus forms the first social attachment of his life. Researchers no longer feel that oral gratification is so overwhelmingly important. The infant's parents also give him warmth and "contact comfort," and they talk to him and smile at him. Clearly all these are important to the child's development, but psychologists disagree as to which is most important.

We do know that institutionalized babies take longer than normal babies to learn how to walk and talk; that many more such babies are sickly and retarded. We also know that most infants raised in a family become very attached to their mothers; that they go through a period when they are terrified if she leaves the room; that attachment seems strongest between the ages of 6 months and a year, when most infants are very frightened of strangers.

Autonomy

But as soon as they are able to crawl, infants begin to leave their mothers—if only briefly. Exploration and separation are essential to the child's development. If he remained at his mother's side all the time, he would never learn to do things for himself; he would never develop a sense of **autonomy.**

However, the child's first efforts to be independent may not be entirely welcome to his mother. At about age 2, the infant begins to test his strength by refusing everything: "No, I won't take a bath." "I won't get dressed." "I won't go to sleep." At this point the child first encounters discipline. He must somehow learn to accept restraints without losing the feeling that his own desires are important.

Some psychologists—primarily psychoanalysts—feel that toilet training determines the child's feelings about authority, discipline, and self-control. Toilet training usually begins before the child can talk and understand reasons. It all probably seems very unnatural to him, but he knows it will please his parents. If he is pushed too fast, according to these psychologists, he begins to feel he is a weak and disappointing

(Thomas McAvoy, Time-Life Picture Agency, © Time Inc.)

IMPRINTING

In nature, young animals of many species follow their mothers around and stay close to them. Why? Because they have *imprinted* on their mothers. *Imprinting* is the process that takes place in the young animal whereby the first object that produces a social response (such as following) will be the object that calls forth that response later on.

From insects to mammals, many species show imprinting behavior. Species differ in their tendency to imprint, and even within one species, strains of strong imprinters and non-imprinters can be bred (Hess, 1959). A short "critical period," when imprinting is most likely, comes after the newborn is mobile and before he begins to fear strange objects. To imprint, the animal must be able to follow or at least walk toward the object. The time allowed for imprinting does not seem to matter, but Hess found that the distance ducklings had to cover to get to decoys did influence the strength of imprinting.

Imprinting differs from other learning in that the first object followed *always* elicits following, no matter how many other objects are introduced later. Moreover, punishment reduces most responses, but *increases* approach behavior in imprinting. Color, form, and sound will make a given model more or less likely to produce imprinting, but some animals have strange tastes. Lorenz was followed around by graylag geese, who treated him first as a mother, then as a potential mate. Hess discovered a breed of chickens that imprinted readily on a plain blue ball—and ignored a stuffed Leghorn rooster!

Human beings may not imprint in just this way, but at least one investigator thinks human babies may go through "critical periods" for social attachments. Stendler (1952) suggests that disruptions in nurturing relationships at age 8 to 9 months and age 2 to 3 years may cause overdependency in children and profoundly affect later personality.

"Oh, go away!"

(Reproduced by permission of Gahan Wilson)

(*Van Bucher, Photo Researchers*)

person. In later childhood he may react to authority and demands with "anxious conformity," trying desperately to please, or with "negativism," rejecting all demands so as to avoid failure. However, if his parents encourage and praise him, he will develop more positive feelings about himself.

Whether or not toilet training establishes behavior patterns is debatable. The child at this stage faces a number of constraints—eating at a particular time, learning that he may be able to get away with hitting his brother in the stomach but not with stepping on his head, that he can play with his father's pencils but not his coin collection, and so on. In working out each conflict between his desires and parental rules, the child establishes feelings about himself and the world.

During adolescence the drive for independence and autonomy becomes stronger. As Coleman (1974) points out, this is a necessary part of growing up in our society, where people are often geographically or socially separated from their parents and must be able to solve their own problems. Most adolescents do desire the external symbols of independence—a job, personal money management, a car, freedom to date—and most parents today seem fairly willing to respond to these wishes.

Even so, the transition to emotional independence and self-direction is far from easy. Our society has been criticized for expecting independence and yet encouraging dependency. For example, compulsory schooling and the value placed on higher education keep today's adolescents in school—and thus financially and emotionally dependent—for a long period of time. Depending on which state they live in, adolescents may drive, drink, and marry at quite diverse ages. For example, in New York, an adolescent can drink once he reaches 18, while in Missouri he must wait until he is 21. But a boy in New York cannot get his driver's license until he is 18, while his friend from Missouri got his at 16.

Not all theorists condemn our society's prolonged adolescence, however. Some consider it a "psychological moratorium," a period in which the young person is relatively free from responsibility and can experiment with various alternatives. However, it is doubtful that prolonged adolescence actually constitutes a psychological moratorium. The increasing pressures for economic independence, academic achievement, and social success make it difficult for the adolescent to "play the field" psychologically and philosophically for very long (Muuss, 1968).

Imitation and Identification

One of the ways a child solves conflicts is by imitating and identifying with the adults in his life. Parents, other adults, older siblings—and TV—provide him with **models** of acceptable behavior. For example,

ARE FIRSTBORNS BETTER?

Freud, Kant, Beethoven, Dante, Einstein, and Julius Caesar—what do they have in common? Of course, all were eminent. But they were also all firstborn children (Harris, 1964). Although many later-born children also become famous and accomplished, many studies hint that a firstborn child is more likely to excel.

More firstborns become National Merit Scholars, earn doctors' degrees, and rate mention in *Who's Who.* Twenty of the 36 United States presidents were firstborn sons. Even astronauts are likely to be first or only children.

Researchers suggest several explanations for the higher achievement of firstborns. Some believe that the reason is simply that firstborns are more likely than other children to go to college. They argue that economic factors alone could account for this educational difference. But studies show that firstborns consistently earn higher grades than their classmates do, *before* college. The higher marks may suggest a higher need to achieve—a fact that would help to explain why firstborns accomplish more in life.

Some research supports the existence of such a need, though not conclusively (Rosen, 1964). The need to achieve may be an outcome of the special relationship between firstborn children and their parents. Firstborns have their parents' exclusive attention; they receive more care and more protection than do later-born children and seem to interact more with parents (Gewirtz & Gewirtz, 1965). Parents of firstborns also seem to expect more of them (Hilton, 1967).

As a result, firstborns may come to depend more on others, particularly older persons, for affection and approval. The firstborn would thus seek approval by conforming to adult standards, including standards of achievement. The firstborn would be more likely than the later-born to look to adults for guidance; he would spend less time with peers, but would seek their approval more.

Whatever the reasons, firstborn children do tend to be more serious, more conforming, shyer, more anxious than their siblings—and more likely to outdo them.

he wants to strike out when he is frustrated or hurt, but frequently his mother inhibits his natural reactions. How does he learn to express these feelings? In large part, through **imitation,** the conscious copying of other people's behavior.

Stepping into the debate over whether violence on TV encourages aggression in children, Bandura, Ross, and Ross (1963) set up this famous experiment: four groups of children were taken to a room one at a time and asked to perform a simple task. The first group was allowed to work in peace; the other groups were exposed to different forms of aggression while they worked. While the second group of children worked, an adult came into the room and began beating up

(Vivienne, Photo Researchers)

(Wayne Miller, Magnum Photos)

(Katrina Thomas, Photo Researchers)

a large doll—yelling at it, throwing it in the air, sitting on its head. The third group of children were shown a film of this on TV. The fourth group saw a similar film, but the characters were costumed like cartoon characters. The children were then taken to a waiting room and told they could play with the toys there. But as soon as they had started to play, the experimenter said, "No, those are my favorite toys. I'm saving them for other children. You go into the other room." The other room contained the doll the adult had abused in the first part of the experiment. All the children in the second, third, and fourth groups took out their frustration on the doll, more or less imitating the adult's behavior. The children who had seen the realistic film—not those who had observed a live adult's tantrums—were the most aggressive.

Several later studies have confirmed that observing violence has an adverse effect on children (Liebert & Baron, 1972; Stein & Friedrich, 1972). In addition, a preference for violent TV programs in childhood was found to be significantly related to aggressive and antisocial behavior in adolescence (Lefkowitz et al., 1972). For most children, exposure to violent behavior comes mainly through television. At first glance, you may not think that's so bad. After all, there is a lot of violence in the world. Isn't it better that children learn about it safely, by watching it on TV, than by actually being exposed to it? But remember what Bandura and his co-workers found: the children who had seen the realistic *film* behaved more aggressively than the children who had seen a live adult's temper tantrum. The violence shown on TV is not threatening. It is oversimplified and, most important, it does not have the emotional trauma involved in real-life bloodshed. Children who watch it in their homes feel safe and relaxed. All these factors may contribute to reducing a child's inhibitions about displaying aggressive behavior that he has learned from watching TV. Thus, the problem with TV violence may not be due to its quantity but to its unrealistic presentation.

Identification may take a number of forms. The child may adopt his parents' characteristics because this may bring him love. Or he may fear rejection and punishment if he does not follow their model. Identification may also help the child overcome fear and frustration. If he identifies with his parents' commands, the commands begin to seem less formidable.

The child also looks to adults—especially his parents—for clues as to what he can reasonably expect from life. Children are constantly being told that there are some things adults may do that children may not do, and this is frustrating. The child works around these prohibitions in play and fantasy, by unconsciously **identifying** with "big people" and living through them. In this way he can take on some of adults' apparent omnipotence.

This is particularly important in the learning of sex roles. In the beginning, both boys and girls identify most with their mothers. But while the girl may go on modeling herself after her mother, at some point the boy is expected to switch over to his father. Sometimes this transition is successful—the boy who sees his father as nurturing may be more willing to "give up" his mother. Other times—for example, when the father is the parent who administers discipline and punishment—the child identifies with his father in a defensive way and will cling to his mother longer than is considered appropriate. At a later stage the girl begins to look to her father for confirmation of her feminine role.

(Robert E. Knopes, Nancy Palmer Photo Agency)

Peer Groups

In our society, children generally have few meaningful social relationships outside their family for their first 4 or 5 years. They may play with other children, but usually their mother is close at hand. School changes all this. The child's world is suddenly filled with "significant others"—his peers and teachers. The number of models for him to imitate and identify with increases. He finds he has lost some of the attention and freedom he had at home; he has to cope with other children's desires and aggression.

Gradually he transfers some of the feelings of attachment he worked out at home to the teachers and peer group. He begins to look to them as well as to his parents for approval. He asks his teacher to help him reach a goal; later he asks his friends. He begins to join groups. By adolescence the peer group has assumed primary importance. It seems that the adolescent compensates for his increasing independence from his parents by clinging to his friends until he feels more confident about being on his own. Unfortunately, however, his peers do not always give him the support he needs. Coleman (1974) aptly calls the high school "a cruel jungle of dating and rating" (p. 51), a place where only the fittest survive socially. Those who don't measure up find themselves left out, and pressure to be "in" and fear of being "out" can cause far greater emotional strain than the academic pressure parents typically worry about.

Even the socially successful adolescent may not be completely comfortable with his peers. Adolescents have their own subculture, with its own set of values, and these values are often very different from those of the family. Attitudes toward sex, drugs, alcohol, and grades are among the many possible sources of conflict. The adolescent must reconcile the two worlds of family and peers. He must sort out the numerous and often conflicting expectations of others and decide which values are really his own.

Development of Identity

A child has many fragmented "selves"—son, brother, friend, "Fatso," piano player, and so forth. As an adolescent, that same individual becomes capable of integrating these many roles into a single, unified

identity. To form a coherent self-concept, he must evaluate and choose from the vast number of beliefs, values, and roles available in modern society. This self-concept must have continuity with the past and future—with what he already knows about himself and what he can reasonably expect to become.

In simpler times, career, life style, and personal philosophies were largely determined by family background. There were clearly defined standards for sex roles and morality. In short, the adolescent had relatively few life choices to make. But our society has become increasingly complex and mobile and now offers a bewildering number of occupations, life styles, ideologies, and sex-role models. Today's adolescent can be nearly anything he wants to be, but choosing from so many alternatives can be extremely difficult. He must experiment with numerous roles and behaviors and must test himself in as many situations as possible. But eventually he must choose and integrate his choices into a whole, healthy personality. He must figure out who he is and how he fits in with or up against the world around him.

According to Erik Erikson (1968), this "quest for the identity" is the principal task of adolescence. If the individual fails to achieve identity, he will become the victim of **role confusion.** He will try to be all things to all men and will never really be himself. But to the extent that he succeeds in achieving identity, he creates a new sense of continuity that encompasses both the individual and his adult environment and that provides stability and confidence.

The Transition to Adulthood

As we have seen, the phenomena that introduce adolescence are biological and thus universal. But the phenomena that mark the end of adolescence and the beginning of adulthood are psychosocial and are thus determined by the individual and his culture. Adult status is not bestowed by an act of nature, it must be *earned.* In our culture it is not even very clear how or when it can be earned; there is no clear-cut border to cross. We have no formal rites of passage, and the indicators we do have—legal ages for drinking, driving, working, marrying, voting, and so forth—are inconsistent at best. Furthermore, just because an individual reaches the legal age doesn't mean that he will necessarily assume the responsibility of being an adult. For these reasons, there is a sort of no-man's land—termed "late adolescence" by some and "young adulthood" by others—in which the individual stabilizes his sense of identity and begins reaching out to others and to society, and the transition to adulthood gradually takes place.

The average American 20-year-old has almost three-fourths of his life left to live; yet the majority of psychological, social, and physiological studies have neglected development during the adult years. Although recently there seems to be an increased interest in adult development, there is at present little solid information on the subject.

Figure 3-13
According to Erikson, the primary task of young adulthood is to establish intimate relationships with other individuals. If a young adult fails to accomplish this, the result will be isolation.
(Left: Ken Regan/Camera 5; right: Van Bucher, courtesy Wagner College Department of Psychology)

(Photo Researchers)

Young Adulthood

Many an individual in his early twenties has been shocked to realize that he is approaching the quarter-century mark and still doesn't feel "grown up." But eventually most people reach a point when they feel relatively at home with themselves and with certain others in their society. This development is the core of young adulthood, though different psychologists describe it in somewhat different ways.

Erikson: Intimacy versus isolation. Erik Erikson (1968) views young adulthood as a crucial turning point toward *intimacy* on one hand or *isolation* on the other. He believes that the principal task of this stage is to form true interpersonal relationships—that is, to recognize others as unique human beings and to appreciate them for themselves, rather than to use them to define one's own identity. But before an individual can experience this sort of intimacy, he must first know who *he* is; he must accept himself before he can accept others. If he fails to establish intimacy, "he may settle for highly stereotyped interpersonal relationships and come to retain a deep sense of isolation" (p. 136).

White: Growth trends. Robert White (1966) identifies five interrelating "growth trends" that seem to him to typify young adulthood. *Stabilization of ego identity* involves bringing one's sense of self into focus and eliminating inconsistencies. White believes that this more mature identity is achieved, at least in part, by adopting stable social roles that are then reinforced by related social interaction. The next trend, *freeing of personal relationships,* is roughly equivalent to Erikson's concept of establishing intimacy. It involves stabilizing one's own identity and both narrowing the range and deepening the quality of interper-

(Miriam Reinhart, Photo Researchers)

(Josiah C. Hornblower, Photo Researchers)

sonal relationships. *Deepening of interests* involves increasing selectivity and deeper involvement with work and hobbies, rather than with other people. This growth is characterized by increasing skill and appreciation of the activity for its own sake. The fourth growth trend, *humanizing of values*, requires relating abstract moral philosophies to human life and thus establishing a highly personal system of values. The fifth and final trend is *expansion of caring*, which is a way of applying one's value system to create true empathy with others and a real concern for their feelings.

Keniston: Individuation versus alienation. Erikson's intimacy stage and White's five growth trends center around a movement toward deeper and more meaningful ties with society, by which they mean conventional society. They imply that if the individual establishes a firm sense of identity, he will automatically adopt mature and conventional social roles. Kenneth Keniston (1968), on the other hand, feels that it is entirely possible for a young adult to have a highly developed sense of identity and yet be unable to link this identity with adult roles and responsibilities. Keniston views young adulthood in terms of *individuation*— "the ability to acknowledge both self and society, personality and social process, without denying the claims of either." Individuation is contrasted with *alienation*—"a denial of the reality and importance of the self, or a repudiation of the existence and importance of social reality" (p. 270). To establish a personal link with his various social roles, a young adult must simultaneously examine himself and his society, but the keyword here is *balance*: if he leans too far inward, toward himself, he will become alienated from the world around him; if he leans too far outward, toward external roles, he will lose sight of himself. Kimmel (1974) suggests that with the increasing number of social norms comes greater freedom in selecting ways to create a "fit."

Adulthood

Arrival at adult status is by no means the end of human development. Rather, it is the beginning of a broader, more subtle form of personal, social, and intellectual maturation, characterized by simultaneous continuity and change.

Personality Development

According to Erikson (1968), *generativity* is the principal task of this period, which extends from young adulthood to old age. The individual must create something meaningful and permanent to perpetuate himself, and for this reason children and work become major concerns for most adults. With productivity comes a sense of fulfillment; without it, there is a sense of *stagnation*—of boredom, of missing out on something—and often an exaggerated preoccupation with aging.

As we have seen, the principal tasks of young adulthood center around establishing not only a self but a *social* self. Personality in the middle years is characterized by the establishment of a balance between the internal self and social roles. The adult develops a sense not only of who he is but also of how he relates to his society. As the person gets older, there is generally a tendency to turn inward as social roles and interactions become less and less important (Neugarten, 1968*b*).

Other psychological changes in the middle years include a decrease in psychic energy or self-assertiveness (Rosen & Neugarten, 1964) and a shift from activity to passivity (Gutmann, 1964). One study also uncovered a change in attitudes toward sex roles in adulthood: older women were more willing to acknowledge their aggressive tendencies, men to accept their submissive or nurturing feelings (Neugarten & Gutmann, 1958). Thus, older people do not seem to care so much about what society expects of them. It is interesting to speculate about whether today's young adults, who have greater freedom in choosing their sex roles, will show similar changes in their attitudes when they reach late adulthood.

Milestones of Adult Development

A recluse who spends his entire life alone in the same house in the same community, without working, marrying, traveling, or meeting new people, is unlikely to change very much in adulthood. But most individuals in our society continue to pass developmental milestones. These can be seen as crises, but they can also be developmental opportunities.

Most of us tend to think of development in terms of age norms. That is, we have general expectations for and attitudes about people simply because of their particular ages.

Such age norms have a powerful constraining influence on individuals. One study has shown that middle-class, middle-aged adults have strikingly similar ideas about the "proper" ages at which people should do things in life. There was general agreement that men should marry between 20 and 25 and women between 19 and 24, that most men should be settled in a career between 24 and 26 and should reach their vocational peak between 45 and 50, that a woman has the greatest number of responsibilities between 25 and 40 and accomplishes the most between 30 and 45, and that a woman is good-looking between 20 and 35 (Neugarten, Moore, & Lowe, 1965).

But despite this "social clock" (Neugarten, 1968*a*), chronological age is often a poor index of adult development. A 30-year-old may act like an 18-year-old in social settings; another individual who has unusually heavy responsibilities may seem middle-aged in his late twenties. Moreover, it is often more important to determine how an individual handles these developmental milestones, than to measure whether he "got there in time." Perhaps the two most significant sources of tasks that must be faced in adulthood are the family and work. Because of their nearly universal significance, we will examine these developmental tasks in some detail.

The family. If there is any real indicator of the boundary between adolescence and young adulthood, it is leaving the family to set out in the world. Whether the flight from the "nest" leads to a job, college, marriage, or a period of social and sexual experimentation, it involves a number of new experiences and a period of intense socialization.

The next developmental milestone is usually marriage. At this point, a couple begins the "establishment phase" of their own family cycle (Kimmel, 1974). This requires the adoption of new roles as well as the readjustment of old ones. Even couples who have lived together before marriage often find that the act of "making it legal" somehow changes the situation by adding a new sense of permanence and responsibility and, often, by creating a new social environment in the form of a new apartment, new friends, and a new "respectability." In most cases, the final task of the establishment period is the preparation for parenthood.

The birth of the first child is a crucial milestone. It requires numerous major adjustments as "husband" and "wife" become "father" and "mother" and "couple" becomes "family." For the woman, especially, parenthood can constitute a real crisis. If she has been involved in a career, her values may suddenly conflict—she may feel frustrated if she abandons her career and anxious or guilty if she continues to work.

Parenthood also involves many life-style adjustments. It often means increasing expenses by almost one-third while reducing income by roughly one-half, limiting mobility and freedom, giving up leisure time, and losing sleep. Inexperienced parents may be terrified by the responsibility, plagued by feelings of inadequacy, and stricken by guilt over mixed emotions about the baby. Even the most stable marriage is likely to suffer. The husband may feel "left out"; the wife may resent her husband's freedom and lack of responsibility. It should come as no surprise that in one study, 83 percent of the parents—and virtually all the working mothers—reported a severe crisis accompanying the birth of the first child. Even though the majority of the births had been planned and most of the marriages were considered stable, the results seem to indicate a lack of serious preparation for the new roles (LeMasters, 1957).

As the children grow up, new developmental tasks arise. Adolescent children particularly tend to precipitate family crises. Coming to grips with such issues as dating, sex, alcohol, drugs, and independence can be as challenging for parents as it is for adolescents.

Yet another family milestone is reached when the children leave home (Kimmel, 1974). We have already seen what this means for the children, but it is also a crucial turning point for the parents, especially for the mother if she has devoted the majority of her time to her home and family. Both parents must learn to let go, but the woman particu-

(Ken Regan/Camera 5)

(Leonard Lessin, Photo Researchers)

(Paul Fenton, Nancy Palmer Photo Agency)

(Rollie McKenna, Photo
Researchers)

(Al Satterwhite/Camera 5)

larly must undergo a major role change and adapt to the "empty nest." If this "launching period" occurs as the woman is going through menopause, it may constitute an acute crisis for her. To make things worse, her husband may be reaching the peak of his career at about this time, and he may be more concerned with his work than her problems.

If a couple weathers the launching phase, they must go through yet another series of changes in order to adapt to the post-parental years. Various studies have indicated that people express greater marital satisfaction after their children have become independent, although this may be because the more dissatisfied couples have already gotten divorces! Post-parental life may be further complicated by caring for, or mourning the death of, one's parents and by adjusting to becoming grandparents, with its implications of old age (Kimmel, 1974).

The final phase of the family cycle is old age. In these last years together a couple must often adjust to retirement, reduced finances and social status, and failing health. Eventually one member of the couple must face the death of the other.

The work cycle. An individual's career is directly or indirectly responsible for much of the quality and character of his life. For those who do not marry or have children, work is the primary creative outlet. For those who do, the work cycle parallels and interacts with the family cycle. For example, a job can be used to compensate for—or can greatly suffer from—an unhappy family situation. On the other hand, if the job is unsatisfying or unpleasant, it can cause a shift in emphasis to the family, sometimes enriching the home life, but sometimes creating additional pressures and frustrations within the family.

Beginning a career is an important milestone; it symbolizes adulthood and independence. When a young adult embarks on a career, he must often reconcile the realities of the job with his idealistic expectations. He must also take on various new roles and evaluate them in terms of his own expectations and the demands of others. To the extent that the individual's occupational success is the key to his sense of identity, any dissatisfaction he feels with himself or perceives on the part of others at work may constitute a severe crisis (Kimmel, 1974).

Another typical crisis occurs around the midpoint of the career cycle, when the individual realizes that he has only a certain number of years left until retirement. At this time he may have to readjust his goals and aspirations to coincide with the realistic possibilities.

At any point in his career, even if the individual is "doing well," he may suddenly realize that he is not doing what he *wants* to do, that his chosen career is not providing him with a sense of fulfillment. Thus, a successful lawyer may find that his creative aspirations are frustrated; a housewife who is well on her way to achieving her ideal of married life may discover that she is bored and resentful. These crises are typically characterized by the sense of stagnation described by Erikson and may be accompanied by severe emotional problems. Individuals

(Michael C. Hayman, Photo
Researchers)

(Joel Gordon)

may strike out in a new direction; the lawyer may take off for Hollywood to write film scripts, and the housewife may go back to school for her doctorate. They may find absorbing hobbies—the lawyer may practice astrology; the housewife may learn judo. Or they may stay on the job and in the home and resort to such escapes as alcohol or pills. The picture is not always so bleak, however. Neugarten (1967) has found that the middle years are often characterized by a sense of satisfaction and pride in accomplishments.

Every promotion or job change is a kind of milestone, and each new situation entails numerous adjustments, whether or not these constitute a real crisis. Being promoted can bring new responsibilities and tasks the individual may not feel able to cope with. After having been a competent salesman, feeling like an incompetent sales manager can be a shock. On the other hand, being fired, demoted, or passed over for promotion can completely undermine feelings of self-confidence and bring about a severe crisis. The individual must adjust to loss of economic status or future opportunity, and he must also reevaluate his self-concept and his aspirations. Anger, bitterness, resentment, and humiliation are only a few of the emotions he must deal with.

Retirement is a particularly significant milestone, since in our culture it typically marks the beginning of old age and thus brings with it a new awareness of one's mortality. For this reason the end of a career means far more to most individuals than a gold watch or increased amounts of free time. However, like many American rites of passage, retirement is somewhat ambiguous. In some industries, such as police work, an employee may retire after 20 or 30 years of service and thus may be in his forties or fifties when he leaves the job. In such a case retirement may mark the beginning of a new career or a period of great confusion. Other professionals may continue to work until death, and some notable individuals may still be active in their nineties.

The retired person must cope with a variety of psychological, social,

Figure 3-14

Being middle-aged doesn't necessarily mean being "over the hill." For example, George Blanda of the Oakland Raiders after 25 consecutive years in pro football, still holds the record for most career points scored. And Dame Margot Fonteyn, *prima ballerina*, still dances like a young woman of 25, though she is over 50.

(Left: Ken Regan/Camera 5; right: Wide World Photos)

and financial changes. For some, being retired may be a long-awaited opportunity to do all the things they never had the chance to do before; for others it may be a slow, lingering death. However, as Kimmel (1974) points out, since there is an ever-increasing number of retired people in our society, the pressure of sheer numbers may encourage society to take advantage of retired people's abilities, instead of simply relegating them to the "back burner."

Old Age

Aging of course begins when the infant draws his first breath, and it is a fact of life from that moment on. But it is less obvious that aging is also the major cause of death. If a cure for all forms of cancer were found, the average life span would increase by only $1\frac{1}{2}$ years. If all heart and kidney diseases were conquered, the average life span would only increase 7 years (Dublin, Lotka, & Spiegelman, 1949; Kohn, 1963; Myers & Pitts, 1972).

Physical Changes

(Steve Eagle, Nancy Palmer Photo Agency)

Despite this fact, it is not really known how we age. The most obvious theory is that our bodies simply wear out or run down. But aging is probably not simply a matter of bodily wear and tear, since stress can usually be counteracted by rest and a lower metabolism rate. Another theory attributes the process to increasing breakdowns of the body's self-regulating mechanisms, such as those controlling body temperature, hormone secretions, blood-sugar level, and kidney function. This gradual failure of physiological efficiency certainly provides one important key to the physical, social, and psychological changes involved in the aging process (Kimmel, 1974).

Sometimes, conditions traditionally attributed to the aging process may actually be the result of disease and attending social and psychological factors. Since disease prevails among the aged, it is often very difficult to distinguish its effects from those of aging per se. Recent studies have shown with striking consistency that the effects of aging are relatively insignificant if an individual is not suffering from disease (Kimmel, 1974). Unfortunately, few older people are perfectly healthy. Most are afflicted by some form of chronic illness, commonly arthritis, rheumatism, heart disease, or hypertension. Such chronic impairments as blindness, deafness, and disabilities due to injury also affect many old people. In fact, nearly two-thirds of the population over 75 years of age suffer from at least one chronic illness or impairment.

(Richard B. Klein, Nancy Palmer Photo Agency)

Whatever the reasons for aging, there are certain observable physiological changes that characterize the process. A slight decrease in stature, loss of teeth, wrinkles, "liver spots," baldness, gray hair, voice change, a decline in sensory abilities, and a slowing down of the central nervous system are sure signs of old age. All these physiological

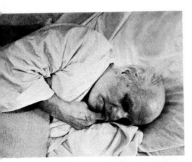

(Stanton, Magnum Photos)

(Lisl, Photo Researchers)

changes can have a drastic effect on self-image. Our society is largely youth- and beauty-oriented, and the idealized norms provided by the mass media can make even young, attractive individuals feel insecure. The denture adhesives and cleansers, cosmetics, wrinkle creams, scalp treatments, and hair dyes one sees advertised on TV help to cover up the outward signs of aging without doing much, if anything, to help resolve underlying problems.

Cognitive Changes

In many societies age is equated with wisdom. In our society, however, it is generally believed that to be old is to be "feeble-minded." Until quite recently it was an accepted fact that intelligence declines, beginning around age 30 and continuing to do so thereafter. But some longitudinal studies of people up to the age of 50 suggest that intelligence reaches a plateau between the ages of 25 and 30, but that it continues to grow, in ever-smaller amounts, during early adulthood. After that, people of above-average intelligence maintain or improve their abilities until the age of 50, while people of average intelligence decline somewhat (Botwinick, 1967). Still other studies suggest that intellectual growth can continue past the age of 70 (Baltes & Schaie, 1974).

These findings suggest that extraneous factors may cause older people to perform poorly on IQ tests. For example, such tests may seem more relevant to younger people, and this motivation might well explain their superior scores. It is also possible that higher education promotes more competent test performance, and many older people did not have the opportunity for advanced study. Also, a young adult might score better than a middle-aged or old person simply because he has attended school more recently (Kimmel, 1974).

What about memory? According to Botwinick (1967), memory does not necessarily decrease as you get older. However, there does seem to be an age-related decline in short-term memory. Conflicting studies make it difficult to tell whether the problem lies in absorbing new material or in retaining and recalling it. Probably all these processes are affected somewhat by aging.

A significant memory loss or decline in learning ability would contribute to a decline in creativity and other intellectual abilities. Most people have developed ways of compensating for slight impairment of these functions so that their daily performance is relatively unaltered, but they do tend to show a decline in concept attainment and in problem solving (Kimmel, 1974). Creativity also appears to decline. For example, one study indicates that in most fields the majority of high-quality output takes place in the thirties and declines thereafter; by the age of 50, subjects had made 80 percent of their superior contributions. However, in fields such as philosophy that build on accumulated knowledge, the creative peak comes between the ages of 60

Figure 3-15
Some people get better with age. Actress Marlene Dietrich, now in her 70s, could be considered ageless. And Sir Francis Chichester was nearly 70 when he sailed around the world alone in his boat, *Gipsy Moth IV*.
(Left: Springer/Bettmann Archive; right: Terence Spencer, Time Magazine, © Time Inc.)

(Al Satterwhite/Camera 5)

(Ann Zane Shanks, Photo Researchers)

and 64 (Lehman, 1953). These data point out that an apparent decline in ability (in this case, creativity) may be due as much to the nature of the tasks as to changes in individuals due to aging.

"Successful" Aging

There is some disagreement among psychologists as to what constitutes a successful adjustment to old age. The **disengagement theory** (Cumming & Henry, 1961) states that old age is characterized by a decline in involvement with society. In other words, elderly people have spent a long time fulfilling their social obligations and, as a reward, they are allowed by society to withdraw, to rest and relax, to be free. When disengagement by the society and the individual coincide, all is well. However, when one disengages before the other is ready, the individual's problems of adjustment will be greater.

Other psychologists disagree with this theory. For example, Maddox (1963, 1966, 1970) proposes an **activity theory** that takes the common sense position that the more active and productive a person is, the more satisfied he will be at any stage of life. According to this theory, old people want to be active and productive, but disengage simply because society provides no outlet for their energies. Because these theories are so contradictory, they have stimulated a good deal of research.

For example, Havighurst, Neugarten, and Tobin (1973) found that disengagement does consistently occur. But this may simply measure a fact of life, and, as we noted, some psychologists question whether the disengagement is really voluntary. Rather, they suggest, it may be imposed on the individual since society turns its back on older people and does not provide them with any way to continue being productive.

Neugarten, Havighurst, and Tobin (1965) found that personality characteristics had much to do with how well people adjusted to old age, whether they were disengaged or active. People with well-integrated personalities tended to adjust well to old age, while people who were not quite as satisfied with their lives tended to have more difficulty adjusting. In these latter cases, however, level of activity did appear crucial to satisfaction—those who were doing more were happier.

Death and Dying

Preparation for Dying

Erikson (1968) suggests that, at some point toward the end of life, there is a final developmental crisis: *integrity* versus *despair*. Death itself is seldom a central issue in the final years—it may be a more consuming consideration in the middle years, when the first awareness of mortality coincides with greater interest in living (Kimmel, 1974). According to Simone de Beauvoir (1972), for example, death may not be a horrifying prospect for the aged, who have often lost interest in life and have nothing to lose by dying. Instead, the elderly person, aware of the imminence of death, takes stock of his life, looking to the past in order to affirm the meaningfulness of his accomplishments. If he has been successful in the principal tasks of past life stages, he will be able to arrive at a sense of integrity. If he cannot accept his life as he has lived it, he will be submerged in despair, for it is too late for him to change.

Robert Butler (1963) asserts that the life review is a universal process among people nearing death. Ideally, such reminiscence leads to wisdom and peace; but it might also lead to depression, guilt, or obsession with the past. However, this does not mean that old people are preoccupied with the past. For example, Paul Cameron (1972) found that the past seems to be the least common orientation for all ages; most people, the elderly included, concentrate on the present.

Recent research indicates that nearness to death (apart from age or illness) may itself cause a number of psychological changes. Lieberman (1965) tells of a nurse who could predict the death of nursing home residents because they "just seemed to act differently." After giving old people psychological tests on several different occasions, Lieberman noticed a definite pattern of decline in those people who died quite soon after being tested. Similarly, a number of researchers have been startled to find a curiously accurate predictor of impending death called the "terminal drop." The terminal drop is a noticeable decline in assertiveness, cognitive organization, and IQ as measured by psychological tests. Researchers have found that the nearer a person is to death, the greater the decline in these functions (Jarvik & Falek, 1963; Kleemeier, 1961, 1962; Lieberman & Coplan, 1969; Riegel & Meyer, 1967).

Dying

Psychiatrist Elisabeth Kübler-Ross (1969) personally interviewed more than 200 dying people in an attempt to understand the process of dying. From these interviews she isolated five sequential psychological stages through which people pass as they react to their own impending death. The first stage is one of *denial*. The patient refuses to accept the prognosis, typically believing that it is a mistake, and consults other doctors or even faith healers. This denial is almost invariably replaced by "partial acceptance." In the second stage, the patient recognizes the verdict and feels intense *anger* and resentment. These emotions are directed at nurses, doctors, family—anyone the dying person comes into contact with. The patience and understanding of others is particularly important at this time. The third stage is characterized by *bargaining*— with the doctor, with the illness, or with God—in a desperate attempt to buy time. This brief stage is not obvious in all patients, but where it exists, it seems to be a healthy attempt at coping with the awareness of death. In the fourth stage, the patient has fully accepted the fact that he is going to die, and the result is *depression*. At least some depression appears to be necessary if the patient is to find acceptance and peace before death. Finally, the dying person arrives at full *acceptance*. This stage is characterized by "quiet expectation." The patient is typically tired, weak, and unemotional.

According to Kübler-Ross, our central problem in coping with death is that we fear and deny it. Because we do not believe we can possibly die of natural causes, we associate death with "a bad act, a frightening happening, something that in itself calls for retribution and punishment" (p. 2). She believes that we have depersonalized the dying person who so badly needs comfort and compassion, and that our institutions must rehumanize the process. In medical schools in recent years there has been a growing emphasis on helping dying people and their families accept death as a natural occurrence, not as a doctor's "mistake" to be put in a corner and forgotten. Increasingly there is a cry for a dignified death, for a peaceful and untroubled transition to whatever comes after.

Summary

1. *Developmental psychology* is the study of the stages of life from birth through childhood, adolescence, adulthood, aging, and death.
2. The newborn baby's body structures are all present and many are fully functioning at birth. The newborn is completely helpless when lying down, but when picked up, he immediately begins grasping quite hard, searching for a nipple—a reflex known as *rooting behavior*. Another important reflex is *sucking*, which appears shortly after birth.

3. Newborn infants show *individual differences* in both physical and emotional behavior.

4. *Maturation,* the process by which the body fulfills its genetic potential, involves both growth and changes in the physical character of the body that make new behavior possible. The timetable for these changes is preprogrammed, but in some cases—walking, for example—early exercise and training can result in earlier development.

5. Physical growth in adolescence is just as marked as it is in early childhood. While the rate of growth varies considerably from individual to individual, the sequence is fairly universal. The tremendous physical changes that occur are more stressful for the adolescent than for the child, because the adolescent is more concerned with how people perceive him and because the changes bring with them new challenges and responsibilities.

6. Some maturational changes occur spontaneously, such as walking and sexual development; others depend on learning, such as talking; still others require previous development, such as running.

7. Psychologists have established *developmental norms,* which show approximately when certain behaviors should appear. The norms may be useful for indicating either retarded or advanced development.

8. *Motor abilities,* like walking and grasping, develop according to a sequence. Walking progresses from lifting the head, sitting up, crawling around, and walking with help, to walking unsupported. Mature grasping takes longer to develop and proceeds according to the refined use of fingers, thumb, and fingertips toward holding and manipulating objects.

9. *Perceptual development* refers to how the baby sees the world and how his view changes. Depth perception, object perception, and visual discrimination appear to be inborn, but experience and physical maturation are necessary for them to develop and mature.

10. *Language development* depends on physical maturation and proceeds from a newborn's gurgling through an infant's cooing to formulation of concrete words and, finally, complete sentences. Most psychologists agree that a baby is born with a biological capacity for language that is stimulated to grow by the talk he hears around him.

11. Gaining the ability to acquire, store, retrieve, and revise knowledge is known as *cognitive development.* Jean Piaget's theory of cognitive development describes a series of stages through which all children must pass.

12. Piaget's series begins with the *sensory-motor stage,* from birth to age 2, during which the child responds with the reflexes of sucking and grasping, gradually acquires motor intelligence, and begins to explore and experiment, recognizing that his actions will affect things outside him.

13. During the *preoperational stage,* from 2 to 7 years, the child acquires systematic methods for representing the external world internally. During this stage the child is egocentric, and he centers on only one aspect of an event. He is unable to reverse a situation.

14. During the *concrete operations stage,* from 7 to 11 years, the child learns to retrace his thoughts, to consider more than one dimension at a time, and to look at a single object or problem in several different ways. He learns the operations of combining, reversing, and forming associations.

15. The *formal operations stage,* from 11 to 15 years, marks the development of abstract thinking and the ability to formulate concepts.

16. Jerome Bruner outlines three developmental stages in concept attainment: *enactive representation*—representing objects and events in terms of motor responses; *iconic representation*—the ability to picture things to oneself; *symbolic representation*—the ability to solve problems without having concrete objects present. Bruner states that conceptual thinking and language develop together.

17. As a child begins to establish his own feelings about himself and the world, he develops a *personality*. This personality will be further integrated during adolescence.

18. The *attachment* between a mother and an infant is the beginning of the child's social development. The mother satisfies the need for food and gives warmth, contact, and auditory and visual stimulation.

19. As soon as most babies can crawl, they begin to explore and to separate themselves from their mothers. They begin to develop a sense of *autonomy*. During adolescence, the drive for independence and autonomy becomes even stronger. The child's quest for autonomy may be limited by his mother's unwillingness to let him go, but the adolescent must overcome obstacles erected by society.

20. As the child becomes more autonomous, he is also subjected to greater discipline and thus faces many more conflicts. As he attempts to resolve these conflicts between his desires and parental rules, he begins to establish feelings about himself and the world around him, particularly other people.

21. One of the ways children solve conflicts is by *imitating* and *identifying* with parents, other adults, older brothers and sisters, and TV—all of which provide *models* for behavior. Later they begin to transfer some of their attachments to teachers and peer groups. By adolescence, the peer group has assumed primary importance.

22. An adolescent is intellectually capable of integrating the many roles he has into a unified *identity*. If the individual fails in this attempt, he will fall victim to *role confusion*. To the extent that he succeeds in achieving identity, he will have a sense of continuity that provides a feeling of stability and confidence.

23. The events that introduce adolescence are biological and universal. But the end of adolescence is generally determined by the particular culture and, moreover, must be earned. The ability to be economically independent is generally accepted as proof that the individual deserves adult status.

24. There are developmental norms for adulthood as there are for childhood. Although these are useful for indicating general trends, psychologists urge individuals not to take them too seriously. The real measure of adult development is the way in which the individual handles the various milestones, not in getting there "on time."

25. Principal milestones of adulthood include: leaving the family home, marriage, birth of the first child, coping with adolescent children, the children's leaving home, menopause, and post-parenthood and old age, including death of one's parents or spouse. The ups and downs of the work cycle, ending with retirement, parallel and interact with the family cycle. Retirement inevitably marks the beginning of old age.

26. Although there is disagreement about why we age, there are recognizable physical changes that mark old age—decrease in stature, loss of teeth, wrinkles, baldness, gray hair, voice change, decline in sensory acuity, and

a slowing down of the central nervous system. Because nearly two-thirds of the people who are over 75 suffer from one or more chronic diseases, it is difficult to isolate the effects of aging per se.

27. Contrary to popular belief, intelligence does not necessarily decline with age. People with above-average intelligence maintain or increase their IQs until age 50. Some psychologists have suggested that our current IQ tests are too youth-oriented to accurately measure the intelligence of an older person. Old people do show a decline in concept attainment, problem solving, and creativity.

28. Various theories have been advanced to describe successful adjustment to old age. The *disengagement theory* states that the elderly person voluntarily seeks to withdraw from society after a lifetime of fulfilling social obligations. The *activity theory*, on the other hand, proposes that old people want to continue to be active and productive, and that they disengage simply because society provides no outlet for their energies. Although disengagement is a consistent pattern, activity does seem to have a positive effect on old people's level of satisfaction. In general, however, personality characteristics seem to be the most crucial factors.

29. According to Kübler-Ross, there are five stages of dying: *denial, anger, bargaining, depression,* and *acceptance.* Not all people go through all the stages in this order, some may skip a stage, and some never achieve acceptance. People who are dying need dignity and emotional support, which are not always available.

Suggested Readings

Bee, H., *Social Issues in Developmental Psychology* (New York: Harper & Row, 1974). A collection of articles dealing with problems people face when they become parents, including sex differences, working mothers, and the role of fathers.

Bettelheim, B., *The Children of the Dream* (New York: Macmillan, 1969). After a 7-week stay on a kibbutz, the author describes this unique system of child rearing—how it differs from our own system and how it affects personality development.

Botwinick, J., *Aging and Behavior* (New York: Springer, 1973). A good overview of the characteristics and problems of old age.

Bruner, J. S., et al., *Studies in Cognitive Growth* (New York: Wiley, 1966). A collection of articles on how people gain and use knowledge, dealing especially with the questions of how man uses his past to plan his future, how the immediate culture shapes an individual's growth, and how man's growth is related to his evolutionary history.

Erikson, E. H., *Identity, Youth and Crisis* (New York: Norton, 1968). A challenging and provocative presentation of the theory that the identity crisis is a normal stage in the development of the individual.

Fraiberg, S., *The Magic Years* (New York: Scribner's, 1959). An absorbing and entertaining book about the child's first 5 years.

Kimmel, D. C., *Adulthood and Aging* (New York: Wiley, 1974). A very useful overview of development in adulthood and old age.

Kübler-Ross, E., *Questions and Answers about Death and Dying* (New York: Collier, 1974). A presentation of current knowledge about death and dying by an expert in the field in a question-and-answer format.

Maier, M. W., *Three Theories of Child Development*, rev. ed. (New York: Harper & Row, 1969). A stimulating and informative comparison of Erikson's psychosocial emphasis, Piaget's theory of cognitive development, and Sears's experimental approach to child development.

Newman, B. M., and Newman, P. R., *Development through Life: A Psychosocial Approach* (Homewood, Ill.: Dorsey Press, 1975). An excellent, readable text that summarizes developmental tasks, reviews selected research documents relevant to each age, and examines controversial social issues in the light of what is known about human development.

Papalia, D. E., and Olds, S. W., *A Child's World* (New York: McGraw-Hill, 1975). Illustrates development from conception to adolescence by following a little girl as she grows up.

Piaget, J., and Inhelder, B., *The Psychology of the Child* (New York: Basic Books, 1969). A concise summary of Piaget's theory of child development.

TWO

Psychology and Cognitive Processes

outline

CLASSICAL CONDITIONING 124

Pavlov's Conditioning Experiments
Classical Conditioning in Human Beings
Necessary Factors in Classical Conditioning
Extinction and Spontaneous Recovery
Generalization
Discrimination
Higher-Order Conditioning

OPERANT CONDITIONING 134

Acquisition of the Response
Reinforcement
Generalization
Discrimination
Extinction and Spontaneous Recovery
Shaping
Behavior Chains
Learning to Learn

NEW VIEWPOINTS ON LEARNING 150

The Cognitive Revolution
Social Learning Theory
Biological Factors in Learning

APPLICATIONS OF LEARNING PRINCIPLES 156

Autonomic Conditioning and Biofeedback
Behavior Modification in Education
Self-modification of Behavior

SUMMARY 166

SUGGESTED READINGS 170

Learning

There are many things that we recognize as learning tasks—learning to speak a foreign language, playing the piano, or cramming for an exam. But almost all activities that we do without even thinking consciously about them—talking, reading, sidestepping a puddle, driving a car—are also learned. Likes and dislikes, good and bad habits, superstitions and prejudices, far from being accidents, are learned. Some learning—such as "Don't touch a hot stove"—is very simple, and both people and animals can acquire the appropriate response very easily. Other learning—for example, why e equals mc^2—is exceedingly difficult, and very few people are able to grasp it. This is all *learning:* the process by which experience or practice results in a relatively permanent change in behavior. But learning is such a pervasive and continual process that we can easily overlook how much learning we actually do every day.

When we begin to talk of learning under the more controlled circumstances of the laboratory, the word *conditioning* often appears. Psychologists often use the word "conditioning" as a synonym for learning, in animals as well as human beings. Conditioning is a general term that refers to acquiring a pattern of behavior. But it is usually

(Van Bucher, Photo Researchers)

(Walter Chandoha)

used as part of an expression that describes a specific process of learning, like the two main types of learning we will discuss in this chapter—**classical conditioning** and **operant conditioning.**

Our discussion begins with the first of these processes—classical conditioning. This simple kind of learning, which takes place in many animals, including human beings, provides a convenient starting point for examining the learning process in general—what it is and how we can observe it.

Classical Conditioning

Classical conditioning was discovered almost by accident by Ivan Pavlov (1848–1936), a Russian physiologist who was studying the digestive processes. Since animals salivate when food is placed in their

Figure 4-1
Ivan Pavlov with his laboratory staff and canine subject.
(*The Bettmann Archive*)

mouths, Pavlov inserted tubes into the salivary glands of dogs so he could measure how much saliva they produced when given food. In the midst of this simple measuring experiment, Pavlov noticed that the dogs salivated before the food was in their mouths. The mere sight of food made their mouths water. In fact, so did the sound of the experimenter's footsteps. This aroused Pavlov's curiosity—what was making the dogs salivate before they had food in their mouths?

Pavlov's Conditioning Experiments

Pavlov's dogs always salivated when food was placed in their mouths. They did not have to learn to do this—their mouths watered naturally.

Pavlov was interested in discovering how to teach the dogs to salivate when food was not present. He devised an experiment in which he sounded a bell just before food was brought into the room. A ringing bell does not naturally make a dog's mouth water. But after repeatedly hearing the bell before getting food, Pavlov's dogs began to salivate as soon as the bell rang. They had learned that the bell signaled the appearance of food, and their mouths watered on cue, even if no food followed. The dogs had been conditioned to respond to a new stimulus, the bell, which would not normally have caused salivation (Pavlov, 1927).

Pavlov's experiment can be broken down into four separate elements that are always present in classical conditioning. The first element is an **unconditioned stimulus (US),** like food, which invariably causes the animal to react in a certain way—to salivate, in this case. That reaction is the second factor—the **unconditioned response (UR),** which takes place whenever the unconditioned stimulus is presented. Whenever the dog is given food (US), its mouth waters (UR).

Figure 4-2
Pavlov's apparatus for classical conditioning of a dog's salivation. The experimenter sits behind a two-way mirror and controls the presentation of the conditioned stimulus (bell) and the unconditioned stimulus (food). A tube runs from the dog's salivary gland to a vial, where the drops of saliva are collected as a way of measuring the strength of the dog's response.

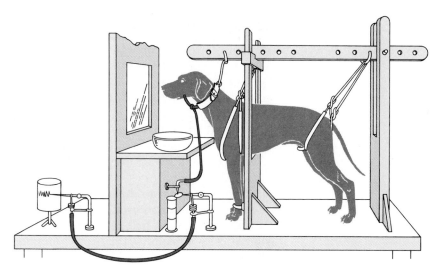

Figure 4-3
A paradigm of the classical
conditioning process.

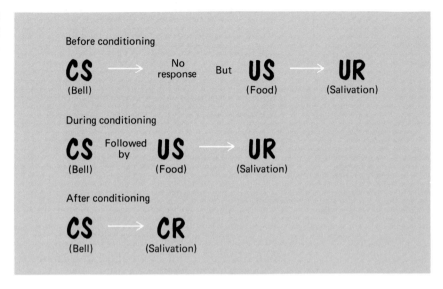

Before conditioning

CS $\longrightarrow$ No response   But   **US** $\longrightarrow$ **UR**
(Bell)   (Food)   (Salivation)

During conditioning

CS Followed by **US** $\longrightarrow$ **UR**
(Bell)   (Food)   (Salivation)

After conditioning

CS $\longrightarrow$ **CR**
(Bell)   (Salivation)

The dog has to learn to respond by salivating when it hears a bell ringing. This artificial stimulus is the third element—the **conditioned stimulus (CS).** A conditioned stimulus is an event—like a sound, a pressure, or an electric shock—that does not initially bring about the desired response. The sound of a bell ringing may cause a dog to perk up its ears, but it will not make the dog's mouth water—unless the animal has been conditioned to react in this way. Such a reaction is the fourth element—the **conditioned response (CR),** the particular bit of behavior that the dog has learned to produce to the conditioned stimulus. Although the response has changed names, it is still basically the same—the dog salivates.

Classical Conditioning in Human Beings

We begin to learn from the time we are born. Babies who are only 5 to 10 days old can learn to blink their eyes when they hear a tone (Lipsitt, 1971). Babies naturally blink when a puff of air is blown in their eyes. The puff of air is an unconditioned stimulus; blinking, the babies' natural reaction, is an unconditioned response. If a tone—a conditioned stimulus—is sounded immediately before the puff of air, the babies soon begin to blink their eyes whenever they hear the tone. By blinking as soon as they hear the tone, the babies are producing a conditioned response.

Adults can also learn by classical conditioning. One group of experimenters conditioned a group of asthma sufferers to react to substances that had previously had no effect on them. First they exposed the asthmatics to something they were allergic to, like dust or pollen (an unconditioned stimulus). Of course, the dust or pollen caused an attack of asthma (an unconditioned response). Then the experimenters presented a neutral substance (a conditioned stimulus). Initially, there was no reaction. But when the neutral substance was repeatedly followed by dust or pollen, the asthma sufferers began to wheeze and sniffle as soon as the neutral substance was presented. These attacks were conditioned responses—the people had learned to react in this way. In some cases, even a picture of the conditioned stimulus would trigger an attack of asthma (Dekker, Pelzer, & Groen, 1957). This study and others like it help to explain why asthma attacks are sometimes brought on by such seemingly unrelated events as hearing the national anthem, seeing a waterfall, or listening to a political speech.

Necessary Factors in Classical Conditioning

Conditioning is not automatic. Learning will not occur unless certain requirements are met. The most critical factors in classical conditioning are the strength and distinctiveness of the conditioned stimulus. If learning is to be effective, the conditioned stimulus must be strong enough for the learner to perceive it easily and distinct enough so he can pick it out from other things that may be going on at the same time. Pavlov's dogs obviously could not have been conditioned to respond to a bell they could not hear or one that they could not distinguish from other noises in the laboratory.

Another factor that can significantly affect the success of the learning process is the order in which the conditioned stimulus and the unconditioned stimulus are presented. The most effective method is the one used in all of the experiments we have described—presenting the conditioned stimulus before the unconditioned stimulus. Remember that Pavlov rang his bell before he gave the dogs their food. Presenting the conditioned stimulus and the unconditioned stimulus simultaneously is generally less effective. If the bell had rung at the same time the dogs got their food, they probably would not have salivated when the bell was later presented alone. Backward conditioning—presenting the unconditioned stimulus before the conditioned stimulus—very seldom results in effective learning. It would have been very difficult for Pavlov's dogs to learn to salivate when they heard a bell if they had already received their food before the bell rang.

The amount of time between the conditioned stimulus and the unconditioned stimulus is also critical to the success of learning. If this time lapse—called the **interstimulus interval**—is either too short or too long, learning will be impaired. The interstimulus interval that is most effective is usually somewhere between a fraction of a second and 2 seconds, depending on the animal that is being conditioned and the behavior it is supposed to learn. Pavlov found that if he waited too long after sounding the bell before he gave the dogs their food, the dogs would not learn.

BRAVE NEW WORLD

In Aldous Huxley's *Brave New World*, where Science rules and Man is its servant, where babies are bred in test tubes and "parent" is a dirty word, we find a fictional account of the use of classical conditioning to prepare children for their future roles as workers. Early in the book, the Director of Hatcheries and Conditioning gives his students a demonstration of how 8-month-old infants are conditioned to fear flowers and books:

> Infant Nurseries. Neo-Pavlovian Conditioning Rooms, announced the notice board. . . . Between the rose bowls the books were duly set out—a row of nursery quartos opened invitingly each at some gaily coloured image of beast or fish or bird. . . . The babies . . . began to crawl towards those clusters of sleek colours, those shapes so gay and brilliant on the white pages. . . . Small hands reached out uncertainly, touched, grasped, unpetalling the transfigured roses, crumpling the illuminated pages of the books. The Director waited until all were happily busy. Then, "Watch carefully," he said. And, lifting his hand, he gave the signal.
>
> The Head Nurse, who was standing by a switchboard at the other end of the room, pressed down a little lever.
>
> There was a violent explosion. Shriller and ever shriller, a siren shrieked. Alarm bells maddeningly sounded.
>
> The children started, screamed; their faces were distorted with terror.
>
> He waved his hand again, and the Head Nurse pressed a second lever. The screaming of the babies suddenly changed its tone. There was something desperate, almost insane, about the sharp spasmodic yelps to which they now gave utterance. Their little bodies twitched and stiffened; their limbs moved jerkily as if to the tug of unseen wires.
>
> "We can electrify that whole strip of floor," bawled the Director in explanation. "But that's enough," he signalled to the nurse.
>
> The explosions ceased, the bells stopped ringing, the shriek of the siren died down from tone to tone into silence. The stiffly twitching bodies relaxed, and what had become the sob and yelp of infant maniacs broadened out once more into a normal howl of ordinary terror.
>
> "Offer them the flowers and the books again."
>
> The nurses obeyed; but at the approach of the roses, at the mere sight of those gaily-coloured images of pussy and cock-a-doodle-do and baa-baa black sheep, the infants shrank away in horror; the volume of their howling suddenly increased.
>
> "Observe," said the Director triumphantly, "observe."
>
> Books and loud noises, flowers and electric shocks—already in the infant mind these couples were uncompromisingly linked; and after two hundred repetitions of the same or a similar lesson would be wedded indissolubly (Huxley, 1939).

In classical conditioning, as we have seen, learning a conditioned response involves building up an association between a conditioned stimulus, like Pavlov's bell, and an unconditioned stimulus, like food. It is not surprising, then, that one trial—one pairing of the bell and the food—is seldom enough for learning to take place. Pavlov had to pair the bell with the food several times before the bell alone would cause a dog's mouth to water. Conditioning is cumulative and each trial builds on the learner's previous experience. But this does not mean that learning will continue to increase indefinitely or that it will increase by an equal amount on each successive trial. At first, the strength of the conditioned response (one way of measuring the effectiveness of classical conditioning) increases a great deal each time the conditioned stimulus and the unconditioned stimulus are paired. Learning eventually reaches a point of diminishing returns—the amount of each increase gradually becomes smaller and smaller. Finally the learning levels off and continues at the same strength.

The spacing of learning trials over time is just as important as the number of trials conducted. Learning is more effective if the pairing of the conditioned stimulus and unconditioned stimulus is experienced at evenly spaced intervals, neither too far apart nor too close together. If trials follow each other very quickly, more trials are needed before learning can occur.

The more carefully these factors are controlled, the greater the likelihood that learning will occur. But this does not necessarily mean that the learned response will continue indefinitely.

Extinction and Spontaneous Recovery

Going back to Pavlov's dogs, what happens when the dog has learned to salivate upon hearing a bell, but repeatedly fails to get food? The dog's response to the bell—the amount of salivation—will gradually decrease until eventually the dog will no longer salivate when it hears the bell. This process is known as **extinction.** If the conditioned stimulus appears alone so often that the learner no longer associates it with the unconditioned stimulus and stops making the conditioned response, extinction has taken place.

Once a response has been extinguished, is the learning gone forever? Pavlov trained his dogs to salivate when they heard a bell, then caused the learning to extinguish. A few days later, the same dogs were again taken to the laboratory. As soon as they heard the bell, their mouths began to water—the response that had been learned and then extinguished reappeared on its own, with no retraining. This phenomenon is known as **spontaneous recovery.** The response was only about half as strong as it had been before extinction, but spontaneous recovery does indicate that learning is not permanently lost.

To understand why spontaneous recovery occurs, we have to take

LEARNING CURVES

Learning can be measured in many different ways. Usually we look for either an increase in the number of correct responses or a decrease in the number of errors when we want to know how much learning has taken place or how fast it has occurred. When we plot these measures on a graph, we have a *learning curve*.

The shape of the learning curve will vary, depending on what we are measuring. If we are counting the number of correct responses, the curve will be low on the left and move upward to the right. If we are measuring the number of errors, the curve will descend toward the right.

In most cases, whether we are drawing a graph of errors or of correct responses, the steepest part of the curve will be at the left. This is because the greatest amount of improvement comes early in the learning process. Then, as the increases in learning on each trial become smaller and smaller, the curve will gradually level off.

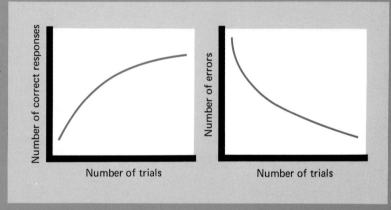

A typical learning curve based on number of correct responses (*left*). A typical learning curve based on number of errors (*right*).

a closer look at what happens during extinction. Let us begin with a dog that has learned a particular response, like salivating when it hears a bell. If the bell is rung over and over again, but is not followed by food, the conditioned response is extinguished—the animal's mouth no longer waters when it hears the bell. What happens is that the animal has gained an **inhibition,** which then suppresses the response that has been learned. Thus we are not simply adding learning and then taking it away again; we are adding learning—a pull in one direction—and then adding an inhibition—a pull in the opposite direction. As long as the learning pulls harder than the inhibition, the response will continue to be made. When the strength of the inhibition becomes equal to that of the learning, the animal will no longer produce the conditioned response, and we say that extinction has occurred.

Figure 4-4

From point A to point B the conditioned stimulus and the unconditioned stimulus were paired and learning continued to increase. From point B to point C, however, the conditioned stimulus was presented alone. By point C the response had been extinguished.

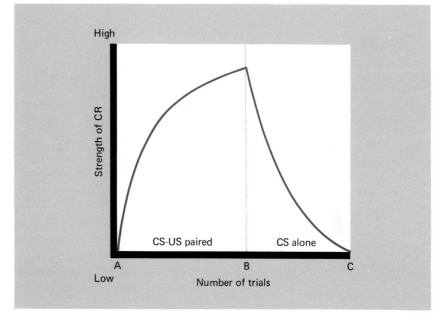

Figure 4-5

Up to point C this learning curve is the same as the one in Figure 4-4. Learning increases from point A to point B and is extinguished from point B to point C. But after a rest period (point C to point D), spontaneous recovery occurs—the learned response reappears at about half the strength it had at point B. If the conditioned stimulus is again presented alone, the response will extinguish rapidly (point E).

We have been talking about inhibition as something that temporarily blocks a response that has been learned. A sudden change in a learner's surroundings or routine can also block a conditioned response. When Pavlov's assistants would ask him to come and look over their projects to see how well the dogs were doing, the animals occasionally failed

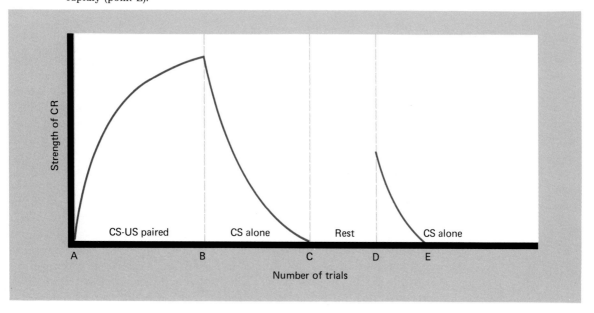

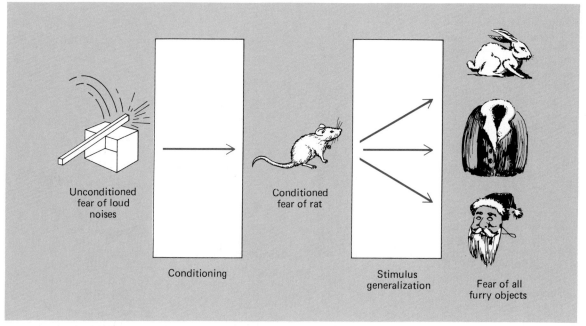

Unconditioned
fear of loud
noises

Conditioning

Conditioned
fear of rat

Stimulus
generalization

Fear of all
furry objects

Figure 4-6
Diagram of Little Albert's
laboratory experience.
He started with an
unconditioned fear of loud
noises, then learned to fear
a white rat. Finally his
fear generalized to all
furry objects.

to perform. Instead of blaming his students for a poor job, Pavlov realized that his presence had disrupted the dogs' usual routine and interfered with their performance. He called this effect an **external inhibition**—something in the dogs' surroundings (the presence of a strange person in the room) made it appear that extinction had occurred.

Generalization

Certain situations or objects may resemble each other enough so that the learner will react to one as he has learned to react to another. Pavlov noticed that after his dogs had been conditioned to salivate when they heard a bell, their mouths would often water when they heard a buzzer or the ticking of a metronome. Their conditioned response had been generalized to other sounds that were similar to the bell. Reacting to a stimulus that is similar to the one you have learned to react to is called **stimulus generalization.**

The well-known case of Little Albert provides a clear example of stimulus generalization (Watson & Rayner, 1920). The experimenters started by showing a white rat to Albert, an 11-month-old boy. At first the child demonstrated no fear—he crawled toward the rat and wanted to play with it. But every time he approached the rat, the experimenters made a loud noise by striking a steel bar. Since nearly all children are afraid of loud noises, Albert's natural reaction was to cry. After just a few times, he began to cry and crawl away whenever he saw the

(Ken Heyman)

rat. So far we have a simple case of classical conditioning—an unconditioned stimulus, the loud noise, caused the unconditioned response of fear; Albert learned to associate the loud noise with the rat; then the rat (conditioned stimulus) caused him to be afraid (conditioned response). Then the experimenters showed Albert a white rabbit. He cried and tried to crawl away—he had generalized from the white rat to the white rabbit, a similar stimulus. In fact, his fear generalized to a number of furry objects—a fur coat, for example, and even a Santa Claus mask.

Often a particular situation may lead to behavior that is similar to, but not exactly the same as, the originally learned behavior. Giving a different response to the same stimulus is known as **response generalization.** A dog in the laboratory is taught to raise its right front leg when given food. Then this leg is paralyzed so the dog is unable to move it. The dog will usually raise its left front leg or its right rear leg instead. In much the same way, people often begin eating candy when they are trying to stop smoking cigarettes.

Discrimination

It is also possible to train animals and people not to generalize, but to react only to a single, specific object or event. This process is called **discrimination.** The subject learns to distinguish among many stimuli and to respond to only one.

Pavlov's method for training an animal to discriminate was to present two similar sounds, but to follow only one of them with an unconditioned stimulus. He would first train a dog to salivate when it heard a tone. Then he sounded both a low-pitched tone and a high-pitched tone. When the dog salivated only when it heard the low-pitched tone and not when it heard the high-pitched tone, it had learned to discriminate.

Learning to discriminate is very important in everyday life. As we noted earlier, most children fear all loud noises. However, since thunder cannot harm a child, it would be helpful if he learned not to be afraid every time he heard it. Not all mushrooms are good to eat, not all strangers are unfriendly, and not all that glitters is gold. So, obviously, discrimination is one of the most important parts of learning.

Higher-Order Conditioning

After Pavlov's dogs had learned to salivate when they heard a bell, he decided to teach them to salivate when they saw a black square. But this time instead of showing them the square and following it with food, he showed them the square and followed it with the bell. The dogs eventually learned to salivate when they saw the square. The bell was used as an unconditioned stimulus and the black square was used as a conditioned stimulus. This procedure is known as **higher-order**

EXPERIMENTAL NEUROSIS

When an animal is taught to discriminate between two similar stimuli—two sounds or two shapes projected on a screen—it learns to respond to one but not to the other. In one experiment a dog learned to salivate when it saw a circle, but not when it saw an ellipse. Gradually the shape of the ellipse was changed, making it more and more circular. When the distinctions between the circle and the ellipse were too fine for the dog to detect them, discrimination broke down. The animal was unable to discriminate between the two shapes that were very similar and also lost the ability to discriminate between the original circle and ellipse.

At this point an interesting side effect began to appear. The dog became agitated and upset—it began to bark, tried to attack the conditioning apparatus, and acted fearful. Drawing an analogy to human neurotic behavior, we say that the dog was suffering from *experimental neurosis*. The prolonged stress of being unable to decide which shape to respond to had caused a breakdown and led to the animal's abnormal behavior. *Experimental neuroses* can persist for relatively long periods of time. In some cases, symptoms have lasted as long as 13 years (Liddell, 1956).

conditioning, not because it is more complex or because it involves any new principles, but simply because it is learning based on previous learning.

Higher-order conditioning is difficult because it is running a race against the extinction process. The dogs that are learning to respond to a square are no longer getting any food. Without the food, the dogs will soon stop salivating when they hear the bell. If this happens, they cannot learn to salivate when they see the square. To avoid this problem, food should be given to the dogs once in a while so their mouths will continue to water when they hear the bell.

Psychologists are still divided on the importance of classical conditioning in complex human learning. Could the conditioned response be the fundamental unit in all changes in behavior? Or, as many researchers believe, is classical conditioning too simple a process to have much bearing on the more complex types of learning that we humans are able to do? Regardless of the outcome of this debate, the fact remains that we are exposed to simple classical conditioning every day in education, advertising, and political socialization. And, because it is simple, classical conditioning is an important laboratory tool in the effort to isolate the factors involved in learning in general (Peterson, 1975).

Operant Conditioning

Classical conditioning is concerned with behavior that invariably follows a particular event—the salivation that automatically occurs when food is placed in the mouth, the eyeblink that always results when

(Courtesy of Ringling Brothers and Barnum and Bailey, Inc.)

a puff of air strikes the eye. It involves learning to respond to something that does not initially cause such a response—salivating to the sound of a bell, blinking to a tone. Classical conditioning is passive—something happens to us and we inevitably react in a certain way. The behavior is *elicited*—a specific, identifiable event causes it to occur. We learn to transfer this inevitable reaction to something that would not ordinarily produce it.

Clearly, all behavior is not inevitably elicited by external occurrences; everything we do is not so simple as salivating or blinking our eyes. In fact, most behavior seems to be *emitted* rather than elicited, voluntary rather than inevitably triggered by outside events. You wave your hand in class to get your teacher's attention; a dog begs at the dinner table to get a tidbit from its owner's plate; a child goes to bed at night without fussing, so his mother will not become angry and spank him. Actions like these are sometimes called **operant behavior**—they are designed to operate in some way on the surroundings or the course of events, to gain something that is desired or avoid something that is unpleasant.

To explain how operant behavior is learned, we turn to a second major kind of learning—**operant conditioning.** We must look at how this kind of learning occurs, in animals and in people.

Although they probably do not think of their work in these terms, animal trainers have been using operant conditioning for hundreds of years. If you send your dog to an obedience school, it will come back with a repertoire of new tricks—sitting up, "speaking," fetching, rolling over, playing dead. If you were to watch the trainer working with your dog, you would notice that whenever the animal does what it is supposed to do—when it produces the desired response—the trainer rewards the dog with food or a treat—he *reinforces* the behavior. If the dog failed to perform, the trainer might ignore the incorrect behavior or he might swat the animal with a rolled-up newspaper. This procedure illustrates the essence of operant conditioning: correct responses are reinforced; incorrect responses are either ignored or punished.

In the laboratory, psychologists use many different kinds of equipment in operant conditioning experiments. One apparatus that is employed frequently is the Skinner box. These boxes are named after B. F. Skinner, the American psychologist who invented them and developed many of the techniques of operant conditioning. They come in different sizes and styles for different animals. For rats, a typical box is small and bare except for a bar with a cup underneath it. The rat must learn to press the bar, which releases food pellets into the cup.

In Skinner's original conditioning experiment (1932), the rat was first allowed to get accustomed to the box so it would not be frightened. Then Skinner did not feed the rat for 24 hours and put the hungry animal into the box. The animal began to explore—sniffing about, standing on its hind legs—until it finally hit the bar and a food pellet dropped into the cup. The rat took the food and ate it, then continued

Figure 4-7
This laboratory rat has found the bar in his Skinner box.
(Will Rapport, courtesy of B. F. Skinner)

"Boy, do we have this guy conditioned. Every time I press the bar down, he drops a pellet in."

its exploration. After hitting the bar two or three times and seeing food appear, the animal learned that it could get food by pressing the bar. The food reinforced the bar-pressing response, and the rat pressed the bar again and again.

Acquisition of the Response

We have said that classical conditioning deals with behavior that is elicited. One implication of this fact is that it is relatively easy to produce the desired responses—all Pavlov had to do when he wanted his dogs to salivate was to put food in their mouths. But operant behavior cannot be inevitably elicited. Pressing a bar is not something that a hungry rat will do naturally, but until it presses the bar, it will receive no food and no learning will take place. Thus, the first thing we have to consider in operant conditioning is how to make the desired response occur so it can then be reinforced and learned. Many different methods are used by teachers in the classroom, scientists in the laboratory, parents with children, and all of us in everyday life. Many of the means of evoking responses are a matter of common sense, and we use them without even thinking about them.

Trial and error. One of the most common ways of getting the desired behavior is simply to wait for the subject to hit upon the correct response. The first time a baby says "mama," it is an accident. But if his mother smiles and hugs him, he will learn to repeat the sound. The trial-and-error method cannot be used if the experimenter is in a hurry, however, for it can take a long time for a subject to accidentally discover the correct response.

Increasing motivation. One way to speed up the process and maximize the likelihood that the correct response will be discovered is to increase motivation. A rat that is extremely hungry will move around more than one that has just been fed. This increased activity will make the rat more likely to discover the bar and press it, which will then release the food pellet. Motivation cannot always be used to produce a response. Some activities, like learning a series of nonsense syllables, are intrinsically hard to motivate. Under these circumstances, some of the following methods may be more effective.

Decreasing restraints. The fewer restrictions placed on a learner's movements or actions, the freer he is to respond. Decreasing restraints removes these restrictions and makes it much easier for the desired response to occur. Kenneth Koch teaches poetry-writing to young children in this way. He relieves them of the necessity of spelling correctly and of using traditional rhyme and rhythms. Because they are free to concentrate on the essence of the poem, even children who previously could not write poetry have produced good poems (Koch, 1970). But the method of decreasing restraints is not always appropriate. Student nurses learning how to give injections can hardly be freed from the necessity of sterilizing the needle.

Increasing restraints. Another method of simplifying the learning process is to prevent incorrect responses by restricting the environment. The fewer things to distract the learner, the more he can concentrate on what he is to learn. If the space in which an animal is placed is large and complex, he will spend more time exploring and take longer to discover the desired response. By making the space small and simple, the number of distracting elements is cut down. That is why one kind of Skinner box is almost bare except for the prominent bar that the animals must press for food.

Forcing behavior. Outside the laboratory it is rarely possible to arrange the environment so conveniently. In such situations, more direct action may be required to evoke the desired behavior. The experimenter or teacher can actively participate in the learning process by actually guiding the learner through the correct movements. If you want a child to learn to write his name, one way of teaching him is to guide his hand through the motions so that he will know how to do it in the future.

Verbal instruction. Explaining what is to be done is an important way of helping a person produce the desired response. Instructions can range from the "Say please" parents use with a small child to the college teacher's complicated description of what he expects on a term paper. Care must be taken to keep the instructions clear and appropriate.

(Erika Stone, Photo Researchers)

Modeling. Showing someone how to do something by demonstrating it can also be very effective. When the FCC banned cigarette ads from television, they showed their belief that modeling a response—lighting up a cigarette—would encourage other people to imitate it. They removed the model, so as not to encourage the habit. Adults often use the modeling method in teaching a child how to tie a shoe. Verbal instruction might not be enough, but if he sees how to do it, he can copy it.

Reinforcement

Once the desired response has been produced, how do we ensure that it will be repeated? We do just what the animal trainer does—we reward the correct response. Psychologists call this reward a **reinforcement,** since it strengthens the desired response and increases the likelihood that it will be repeated.

(Will Rapport, courtesy of B. F. Skinner)

Whenever something we do is followed closely in time by a reinforcement, we will tend to repeat the action—even if the reinforcement is not directly produced by what we have done. In one of Skinner's experiments, a pigeon was placed in a Skinner box that contained only a food hopper. There was nothing the bird could do to get food—no disk to peck or bar to press—but at random intervals Skinner dropped a few grains of food into the hopper. He found that the pigeon began to repeat whatever it had been doing just before it was given food—standing on one foot, hopping around, strutting about with its neck stretched out. None of these actions had had anything to do with getting food; it was pure coincidence that the food appeared when the bird was standing on one foot, for example. But that action would usually be repeated. Skinner said that the bird's behavior was "superstitious," because of its similarity to the way people sometimes learn to be afraid of black cats or the number 13 (Skinner, 1948).

Operant conditioning can be effective even when a person does not recognize a causal relationship between something he is doing and a reinforcement he receives. In one experiment, students were asked to name certain words. When they named plural nouns, the experimenter reinforced them by saying "hm-mmm." Without realizing it, the students began to name more and more plural nouns. They had learned that plural nouns would be reinforced (Greenspoon, 1955).

Reinforcement, then, strengthens the behavior that occurred just before it was given, even if that behavior was in no way the cause of the reinforcement. An action that is reinforced will tend to be repeated, even if the learner does not know he is learning.

(Walter Chandoha)

Following an action or response with something pleasant is called **positive reinforcement.** Most of the examples we have used so far have involved positive reinforcement—giving a dog a treat when it performs a trick, giving a rat food when it presses a bar, indicating vocal agreement with a subject who names plural nouns.

Following a response by removing something unpleasant is called **negative reinforcement.** In the laboratory, a rat can learn to press a bar to turn off an electric shock (negative reinforcement), and it can learn to press a bar to get food (positive reinforcement).*

Both positive and negative reinforcement result in learning. A child might learn to play the piano so that he will receive praise (positive reinforcement) or so that he will avoid the scolding he gets if he does not practice (negative reinforcement). A dog who learns to open the back door with its paws may be doing so either for the positive reinforcement of getting outside to play or for the negative reinforcement of avoiding a bath.

*Negative reinforcement should not be confused with punishment, which will be discussed later in this section. Punishment involves causing an unpleasant condition in an attempt to *eliminate* an undesirable behavior. In negative reinforcement the termination or easing of an unpleasant situation is used to *strengthen* a desired response.

(Wide World Photos)

In **escape training,** a person learns how to end an unpleasant condition—to take aspirin for a headache, for example. An end to the headache, or even a lessening of the pain, is a negative reinforcement. Nothing can be done to prevent the unpleasant event from starting. Only after it starts can anything be done to stop it. Escape learning is not simply a matter of getting away from a situation; it entails learning what to do in order to escape, like the rat that learns to press a bar to turn off an electric shock.

Avoidance training also uses negative reinforcement to promote learning. Unlike escape training, in avoidance training the unpleasant condition can be prevented from ever occurring. Avoidance training with animals usually includes some sort of warning device, like a light or a buzzer. An animal is placed in the box. First the experimenter sounds a buzzer; a few seconds later he turns on the shock. After the first few times, the animal will discover that the buzzer warns him of the shock to come. If the rat presses a bar after hearing the buzzer, no shock will be administered. Pressing the bar after the shock has already started will have no effect. In avoidance training, the animal must learn to press the lever after hearing the buzzer but before the shock starts in order to prevent it from occurring. This usually happens accidentally at first; but once the rat has learned that pressing the lever prevents the shock, it will run to the lever whenever it hears the buzzer and will avoid the shock altogether. Avoidance responses can be helpful, as when we learn to carry an umbrella when the weather forecast says it is going to rain or not to drink from bottles labeled "Poison." Sometimes avoidance learning persists even when it is no longer effective; a child who learns not to go into deep water may build up a fear that remains even after the child has learned to swim.

Punishment. From the time we are very young, we learn to expect punishment, either physical or verbal, from parents, teachers, peer groups, or society at large if we violate certain codes of behavior. Reinforcement will cause a response to become stronger. Will punishment cause a response to disappear?

Obviously punishment does not always work. Children often continue to misbehave after they have been punished repeatedly; many criminals come out of prison only to return to their previous way of life. The effectiveness of punishment depends entirely on how and when it is used. Punishment should follow as soon as possible after the undesirable behavior. A child who touches a valuable vase should be punished right away so he knows what he has done wrong. If punishment comes too late, the child may not know why he is being punished. It is also important to avoid inadequate punishment. If the mother merely tells the child not to touch the vase again, she may not accomplish as much as if she slaps his hand. The harder she slaps him, the quicker he will learn not to touch. She also should try to apply punishment consistently—to slap him each time he goes for the forbidden object. If the child is punished each time he touches the vase, he will learn much more quickly not to do it. If punishment is not applied consistently the behavior may reappear. If the child is not slapped every time he touches the vase, but is sometimes allowed to do it without being punished, he will probably continue to touch the vase. Rewards following punishment, such as hugging a child after spanking him, must be avoided. This can confuse him because he is being punished and rewarded at the same time.

One of the problems with using punishment is that it can often disrupt the learning process. When a child is learning to read and the teacher scolds him every time he mispronounces a word, she may only frighten him. As he becomes more frightened and confused, he mispronounces more words and receives more scolding. Eventually he may become so scared that he will not want to go to school any more.

By itself, punishment simply serves to inhibit responses. Ideally, punishment should be paired with reinforcement of the desired behavior to ensure the learning of a new and incompatible response. This is a more productive approach, since it teaches an alternative way of behaving to replace the old response that is being punished. The child who mispronounced words while reading might learn faster if the teacher, in addition to scolding him, also praised him for pronouncing other words correctly. The praise acts as a positive reinforcement for learning to pronounce words correctly and also makes the child less fearful about learning in general.

(Yerkes Regional Primate Research Center, Emory University, Atlanta, Georgia)

Primary and secondary reinforcers. A **primary reinforcer** is one that is rewarding in itself, without any association with other reinforcers. Food, water, sex, and the termination of pain are primary reinforcers. A **secondary reinforcer** is one whose value has to be learned through association with other reinforcers. It is referred to as secondary, not because it is less important, but because it is learned. A rat learns to obtain food by pressing a bar. Then a buzzer is sounded every time the rat presses the bar and gets food. Even if the rat stops getting food, it will continue to press the bar simply to hear the buzzer. The buzzer has no intrinsic value to the rat, but it has become a *secondary reinforcer.*

Money is a secondary reinforcer. In itself, money is just paper or metal. But through its association with food, clothing, and other primary reinforcers it becomes a powerful reward. Children come to value money only after they learn that it will buy candy (primary reinforcer); then the money becomes a secondary reinforcer. Chimpanzees have learned to work for poker chips, which they can insert into a vending machine to get the primary reinforcer, raisins. The poker chips have come to be secondary reinforcers for the chimps.

Figure 4-8
The typical pattern of responses on a fixed-interval schedule of reinforcement. As the time for reinforcement approaches, the number of responses increases and the slope becomes steeper. The rate of responding is low immediately after reinforcement, so the curve is nearly flat at that point.

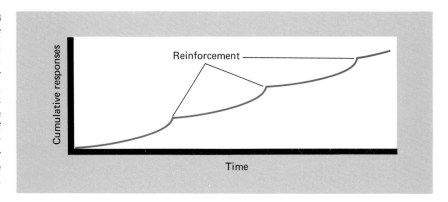

Schedules of reinforcement. Seldom in life or in the laboratory is someone rewarded every time he does something. And this is just as well, for *partial reinforcement,* where rewards are given for some correct responses but not for every one, is more effective than *continuous reinforcement.* The program for choosing which responses to reinforce is called the **schedule of reinforcement.** Schedules can be either fixed or varied and can be based on either the number of responses or elapsed time between responses. The most common reinforcement schedules are the *fixed interval* and the *variable interval,* which are based on time, and the *fixed ratio* and the *variable ratio,* which are based on the number of correct responses.

On a **fixed-interval schedule** the subject is reinforced for the first correct response after the passage of a certain amount of time. He learns to wait for a set amount of time before responding. On a fixed-interval schedule you may begin making responses shortly before the set amount of time has gone by, in anticipation of the reinforcement that is to come. A cake recipe may say, "Bake for 45 minutes," but you will probably start checking to see if the cake is done shortly before the time is up. Performance also tends to fall off immediately after the reinforcement and to pick up again as the time for the next reinforcement draws near. A rat learns to press a bar to get food, but it gets food only for the first response in any 5-minute period. The rat will stop pressing the bar right after it gets its food, but will begin pressing it more frequently as the time for getting the food begins to approach.

A **variable-interval schedule** reinforces correct responses after varying lengths of time. One reinforcement might be given after 6 minutes, the next after 4 minutes, the next after 5 minutes, then 3 minutes. The subject learns to give a slow, steady pattern of responses, being careful not to be so slow as to miss all the rewards. If he is too slow and fails to respond at the appointed time for reinforcement, he

Figure 4-9
On a variable-interval schedule of reinforcement, the rate of responding is relatively constant.

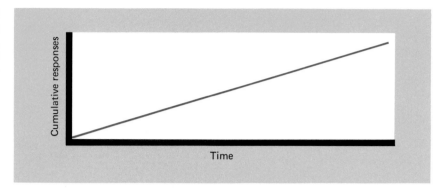

Figure 4-10
A high rate of responding and a moderate pause after each reinforcement are characteristic of the fixed-ratio schedule of reinforcement.

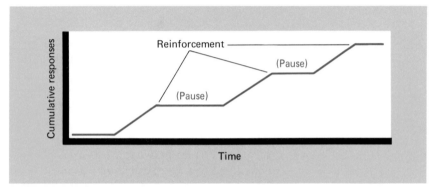

will not get his reward. When exams are given at fixed intervals, like midterms and finals, students will tend to increase their studying immediately before an exam and then decrease it sharply right after the exam until shortly before the next one. If, on the other hand, several exams are given during the course of a semester at unpredictable intervals, students have to keep studying at a steady rate all the time, because on any given day there might be an exam.

On a **fixed-ratio schedule** a certain number of responses must occur before reinforcement is presented. This results in a high response rate, because it is advantageous to make many responses in a short period of time in order to get more rewards. Being paid on a piecework basis is an example of a fixed-ratio schedule. A migrant worker might get $1.50 for every ten baskets of cherries he picks. The more he picks, the more money he makes. A fixed-ratio schedule results in a pause after reinforcement is received, then a rapid and steady response rate until the next reinforcement.

On a **variable-ratio schedule** the number of responses necessary to gain reinforcement is not constant. The slot machine is a good example of the variable-ratio schedule; it may pay off, but you have no idea when that reinforcement will come. However, there is always a chance of hitting a jackpot, so the temptation to keep playing is great. A person

Figure 4-11
The variable-ratio schedule of reinforcement leads to an extremely high rate of responding, with a slight pause after each reinforcement. Sometimes an animal will even forgo eating the food it has earned, preferring to get on with the business of earning the next reinforcement.

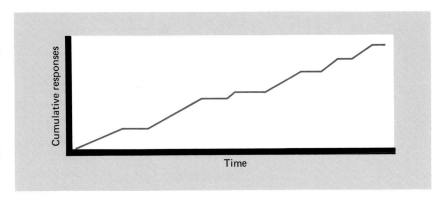

Figure 4-11
The variable-ratio schedule of reinforcement leads to an extremely high rate of responding, with a slight pause after each reinforcement. Sometimes an animal will even forgo eating the food it has earned, preferring to get on with the business of earning the next reinforcement.

on a variable-ratio schedule shows less of a tendency to pause after reinforcement and will exhibit a high rate of response over a long period of time. Since he never knows when reinforcement may come, he keeps on trying.

Generalization

As we saw in the discussion of classical conditioning, a response can generalize from one stimulus to another similar one and, conversely, the same stimulus will sometimes bring about different, but similar, responses. Both *stimulus generalization* and *response generalization* occur in operant conditioning too.

Stimulus generalization in operant conditioning is shown by the baby who is hugged and kissed for saying "mama" when he sees his mother and then begins to call everyone he sees "mama," including the mailman. The person he sees—the stimulus—changes, but he responds with the same word. In the same way, the skills you learn when playing tennis may be generalized to badminton; but they are not so likely to occur when you play football, because the stimuli are not similar enough.

Response generalization occurs when the same stimulus leads to different, but similar, responses. The baby who calls everyone "mama" may also call his mother "dada" or "gaga"—other sounds he has learned—until he learns that only "mama" applies to this particular woman. In response generalization, the response changes, but the stimulus remains constant.

(*Inge Morath, Magnum Photos*)

Discrimination

The ability to tell the difference, or **discriminate,** between similar stimuli (or even to determine whether or not the right stimulus is present) is essential in operant conditioning. Knowing what to do has little value if the learner does not know when to do it.

Figure 4-12
The rat has learned to discriminate between doors with vertical stripes and doors with horizontal stripes. If the rat jumps through the correct door, it will find food on the other side.
(Frank Lotz Miller, Black Star)

Discrimination is taught by rewarding one response and not rewarding others. In this way, pigeons have been trained to peck at a red disk, but not at a green one. First the pigeon is taught to peck at a disk. Then it is presented with two disks, one red and one green. The bird gets food when it pecks at the red one, but not when it pecks at the green one. Eventually the pigeon learns to discriminate between the two and will only peck at the red disk. The baby who called everyone "mama" eventually learns to discriminate between his mother and other people and to use "mama" only for his mother. This could, of course, be done by punishing the child when he calls other people "mama," but more commonly we teach a child to discriminate simply by reinforcing him only when he calls his mother "mama" and not reinforcing him when he uses this term for other people.

Extinction and Spontaneous Recovery

Extinction was discussed earlier in connection with classical conditioning. In operant conditioning, extinction is accomplished by withholding reinforcement. Withholding reinforcement does not usually produce an immediate decrease in the frequency of the response. When reinforcement is first discontinued, there is often a brief increase in responding before its decline. The behavior itself also changes at the start of extinction; it becomes more variable and often more forceful. If, for instance, you try to open a door by turning the knob and pushing, but find that it will not open, you may continue to try. You may turn the knob more violently and you may even kick or pound on the door. But if the door still will not budge, your attempts will decrease and finally you will stop trying to get the door open altogether.

QUALITY CONTROL THROUGH OPERANT CONDITIONING

The scene is a drug factory. A conveyor belt carries the tiny gelatin capsules that will soon be filled with one of our modern-day wonder drugs. A quality-control inspector stands by the moving belt and scrutinizes each capsule as it passes by. If a capsule is bumpy or dented, if its color is not quite right, the inspector pushes a button and the defective capsule is removed from the belt. There is nothing unusual about this situation—except that the quality-control inspector is a pigeon.

So far, no human quality-control inspector need worry about being replaced by a bird. But psychopharmacologist Thom Verhave has successfully conditioned pigeons to perform exactly the discrimination task outlined above—to look at drug capsules as they move by on a belt and signal by pecking at a disk whenever an imperfect capsule appears (Verhave, 1966). Verhave's conditioning procedure was very simple—he placed the bird in a cage that contained a small window, a lighted disk, and an automatic food hopper. When the bird correctly identified a defective capsule by pecking twice on the disk, it was rewarded with food. Eventually the bird learned to perform the whole inspection process—it would peck at the disk once to turn on a light behind the window so it could see the capsule. If the capsule was acceptable, the pigeon then pecked one more time at the disk, which turned off the light and moved the next capsule up. One out of every ten capsules was misshapen or off-color, and when the bird saw one of these, it pecked twice at the disk and was rewarded with food. Within a week, Verhave's pigeons were signaling defective capsules with 99 percent accuracy, no small achievement for any inspector—human or pigeon.

Several factors affect how easy or how difficult it is for learned actions to be extinguished. The stronger the original learning, the harder it is to stop it from being performed. The greater the variety of situations experienced during learning, the harder it will be to extinguish. Rats trained to run in a single straight alley for food will stop running significantly sooner than rats trained in several different alleys that vary in width, brightness, floor texture, and other features.

Complex behavior is also much more difficult to extinguish than simple behavior. Since complex behavior consists of many actions, each individual action that makes up the total behavior must be extinguished. Driving a car is a much harder behavior to extinguish than the behavior of simply pushing a button. Each action—locating the right key, putting the key in the ignition, and so on—must be extinguished.

The schedule of reinforcement used during conditioning has a major effect on the extinction process. Partial reinforcement creates stronger learning than continuous reinforcement. This is because the subject has not come to expect a reward for every response and has learned to continue responding in anticipation of eventual reinforcement. During extinction it will take him longer to learn that no reinforcement will be presented and to stop responding.

Avoidance training is especially difficult to extinguish, because it is based on fear of an unpleasant or painful situation. But what if the unpleasant situation no longer exists? In that case, continued response to the warning is pointless and may even be detrimental. The usual method of extinction—withholding reinforcement—will not work. Responding to the warning is reinforced because the unpleasant event *does not* happen. This reinforcement can obviously not be withheld by the event's ceasing to exist, because the subject has no way of ever finding that out as long as he continues to respond to the warning. For this reason, standard conditioning procedures are generally ineffective and special means must be used to extinguish avoidance responses.

Extinction will be easier if the nonreinforced experiences occur in rapid succession. This is just the opposite of learning, which occurs more rapidly if the experiences are distributed over time. Extinction can also be speeded up if the learner is put in a situation that is different from the one in which he learned. The response is weaker in a new situation, and it will disappear much more rapidly.

Taking away the reinforcement will eventually cause a response to be extinguished, but if you want to eliminate the response even faster, you can use punishment. Punishing a response adds an additional deterrent, and if the punishment is used correctly and consistently, the response will quickly be eliminated.

Spontaneous recovery, the reappearance of the original learning after it has been extinguished, occurs in operant conditioning too. Rats that have their bar-pressing behavior extinguished will sometimes spontaneously start pressing the bar when they are placed in the Skinner box again after a period of time.

(Ann Meuer, Photo Researchers)

Shaping

Operant conditioning is not limited to simple activities. It can be used to teach some very complex behavior patterns, but each part of the sequence has to be learned separately. In most instances, the learner will not produce all of a complex pattern immediately. Writing your name, for example, involves learning how to hold a pencil, how to form each letter, what letters make up your name and in what order, and so on. The procedure in teaching a complex behavior is to start by reinforcing partial responses—the smaller bits of behavior that make up the whole. Little by little, the complete response is **shaped.** The **method of successive approximation** is used to shape behavior. This means rewarding each bit of behavior that leads to the performance of the whole. It can also mean rewarding close hits, a method often used with children, as in teaching them to use a fork. A parent might praise a child just for picking up the fork instead of using his fingers, even if he does not hold the fork correctly. To teach a pigeon to walk in a figure-8, Skinner watched the bird's activity and gave it food when it moved in the proper direction. At first this meant that the pigeon got food for simply turning his head in the right direction, then for taking a step in the right direction, then for making the correct turn, and so on, until it had learned to do a complete figure-8.

Shaping was used successfully to get a boy who suffered from cataracts on his eyes to wear glasses. Without the special glasses, doctors predicted the boy would go blind. But he refused to wear the glasses and threw terrible temper tantrums at the mere mention of them. The glasses were left in his room and the child was given candy if he touched them in any way. Soon he began to carry them around, and eventually he started to wear them. He was rewarded each step of the way, until he learned to wear the glasses (Wolf, Mees, & Risley, 1964).

Behavior Chains

Operant behavior is usually not a matter of isolated actions. Rather, most operant behavior is a **chain,** or series of events. One event acts as a cue for the next event, which in turn stimulates the next part of the chain. Most behavior occurs in sequence, strung together by continuous response, stimulus, response, and so on, with reinforcement at the end of the chain.

The case of Barnabus, a laboratory rat at Columbia University, illustrates this point (see Figure 4-13). Barnabus has been trained to perform a complex chain of activities. At the signal of a flashing light, he dashes up a circular path to a landing. Here he crosses a moat and climbs a ladder to a second landing, where he hauls in a chain attached to a little red wagon. He gets into the wagon and pedals to the bottom of a stairway, which he climbs to a third platform. There he squeezes through a tube and enters an elevator. As the elevator descends, he pulls a chain, which raises the university flag. When he finally reaches the floor of his cage, Barnabus presses a bar and is rewarded with food (Pierrel & Sherman, 1963).

Every step of this complicated behavior chain was taught by shaping. Each action was rewarded, and each reward served to trigger the next activity in the chain.

Behavior chains are learned most readily if they are taught backward, if the last part of the chain is presented first. The best way to teach someone to hit a baseball is to tie the ball to a string that is suspended from a tree so that he can first learn to hit the ball when it is not moving. After this has been learned, he can then go backward in the chain and learn how to hit a ball thrown by a pitcher—how to judge its speed and direction, when to swing, and when not to.

Learning to Learn

The discussions of conditioning in this chapter give us some idea of how learning takes place. Everything we learn contributes to our lives in one way or another. The more we learn, the more we are capable

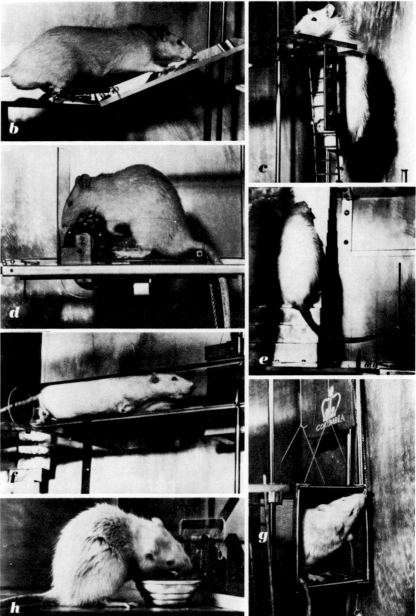

Figure 4-13
Barnabus runs through the behavior chain he has learned. He runs up a spiral ramp (*a*), crosses a moat (*b*), climbs a ladder (*c*), hauls in a little red wagon and pedals it to a stairway (*d*), climbs the stairs (*e*), squeezes through a glass tube (*f*), and rides down in an elevator while pulling a chain that raises the university flag (*g*). At the end of the chain, Barnabus presses a bar and is rewarded with food (*h*).
(*All photos from Wide World Photos*)

of building on previous learning to master more complex ways of behaving; we are in fact *learning to learn*.

When the learning of one task affects the ability to learn another, **transfer of learning** is taking place. The transfer may be either positive or negative; it may aid in learning another task or it may hinder learning another task.

Figure 4-14
One of Harlow's
experiments on learning set.
This monkey has learned to
choose the one object out of
three that is different from
the other two. When the
next set of three objects is
put in front of the monkey,
it will discover the right
solution much more quickly.
(*Both photos courtesy of Harry
Harlow*)

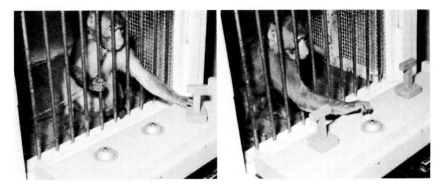

Figure 4-14
One of Harlow's
experiments on learning set.
This monkey has learned to
choose the one object out of
three that is different from
the other two. When the
next set of three objects is
put in front of the monkey,
it will discover the right
solution much more quickly.
(*Both photos courtesy of Harry
Harlow*)

When the skills that have been learned in one task make another task easier to learn, **positive transfer** is taking place. Positive transfer is often very important in formal education. When a child learns how to read *Mother Goose,* he is not expected to stop there, but to go on to read more complicated material. This task will be made easier because of the skills he has acquired in learning to read *Mother Goose.*

Sometimes learning one task makes another task harder to learn. This is called **negative transfer.** If you learned Spanish in high school and are now studying French, you probably find that Spanish words keep coming to mind when you are trying to learn French vocabulary. Motorists accustomed to driving on the right side of the road know how difficult it is to overcome this habit in a country that requires them to drive on the left side. The previous association between stimulus and response—a road and driving on the right—will interfere with learning the new response—driving on the left.

Learning to learn can also be demonstrated by the solving of discrimination problems. In one experiment, a monkey was shown two different objects, such as a red square and a green triangle. If the monkey lifted the red square, it found a raisin underneath. Lifting the green triangle produced no reward. The position of the two objects was randomly alternated; sometimes the red square was on the right, sometimes on the left. This forced the monkey to choose on the basis of the objects themselves rather than according to an irrelevant feature such as position. After the monkey had learned to select the red square consistently, he was presented with a new discrimination problem involving a different pair of objects, such as a large and a small wood block. The monkey solved the second problem much faster than the first, because it had learned how to learn (Harlow, 1949). Another way of explaining the monkey's improvement is to say that it had formed a **learning set.** The monkey had learned to solve one discrimination problem and was "set" to use the new skills in solving other discrimination problems. With each new problem, the monkey learned faster and took fewer trials to select the correct object.

This experiment demonstrates the fact that learning certain skills helps us when we have to work out similar problems. Even though the situation itself was changed, the basic task remained the same. The monkey still had to choose between two objects. What the monkey had learned was a technique for solving one particular type of problem, which could then be used on later, similar tasks.

New Viewpoints on Learning

The Cognitive Revolution

The theories of learning we have been discussing provide only "objective" definitions of the learning process and have little use for "inner causes" such as individual cognition. "If you can't measure it, forget it," as the behaviorists say. But some psychologists are no longer content with traditional objective descriptions of what goes on in learning. They feel that rigorous stimulus-response formulas leave many questions about human learning ambiguous or unanswered. Why does a particular change in behavior become "relatively permanent"? Granted that learning seems to have happened, how exactly did it come about? Isn't there more involved than the simple development of an association between an external stimulus and a visible response? Shouldn't we make a distinction between learning (what goes on inside the individual) and performance (what the individual does that tells you learning has taken place)?

In recent decades, psychological interest has begun to turn away from classical and operant conditioning and toward examination of **cognitive** or internal factors in learning. Cognitive psychologists distinguish between two kinds of learning: learning for retention, in which a person is *informed* of the correct response and is expected to be able to perform it at some later time; and problem solving, in which the person must *discover* the correct response for himself. The first can be explained by operant conditioning principles alone. But the second often appears to require something more than a stimulus-response description.

Cognitive theories have by no means done away with the classic notions of stimulus and response. But they have suggested that the two can be reversible, as when two words become associated and either can suggest the other. Another point these theories make is that any stimulus or response can become distinguishable through attention and practice without consistent associations with any other stimulus or response. For example, if you read a word you don't know in one sentence, you are able to recognize it again in other different sentences. It is not necessary for you to read the sentence where you first saw the word over and over again in order to learn to recognize the word.

However, when a stimulus *is* consistently associated with a response, a conceptual unit can develop, whereby the stimulus and the response become bonded to each other. One important feature of this attachment between a stimulus and a response is "boundary strength," which, like differentiation of individual stimuli and responses, can be increased by attention and practice (Saltz, 1971). The more boundary strength a particular stimulus-response unit has, the more resistant it is to interference from other learning.

These processes—differentiation and the formation of bonded conceptual units—are not isolated; they are integrated. They don't happen sometimes, but all the time, and in every learning situation. Thus, to cognitive theorists, learning involves much more than the performance of a certain behavior. Learning is the development of a bonded conceptual unit that can be distinguished from every other conceptual unit (Saltz, 1971). In this way, cognitive psychologists attempt to explain what they observe in terms of mechanisms that cannot be observed or measured—what actually goes on inside us when we learn.

Social Learning Theory

Despite the great influence that operant conditioning principles have had on the study of learning processes, some psychologists believe that cognition—our inner understanding—has a significant role in determining how we learn and why we do or do not learn. One such psychologist, Albert Bandura, has proposed what he calls **social learning theory** to explain how we learn in everyday life, outside the laboratory (Bandura, 1962). His theory brings together behaviorist and cognitive principles by focusing on human learning as a continuous interaction between the individual and the particular social environment in which he lives.

Although social learning theory does not investigate or explain the internal processes involved in learning in the detail that cognitive theory does, it does admit they are there. Thus, for social learning theorists, when we learn, we do much more than merely respond automatically and blindly to whatever the environment is doing. Humans have not only sight but also insight, foresight, and hindsight, and we use all three in interpreting our experiences. This is not always recognized by operant conditioning theorists, who apply the laws of learning equally to all living creatures, whether human, chimp, rat, or pigeon.

According to social learning theory, on the other hand, we can learn, not only through our own direct experiences with repetition and reward, but also by watching what happens to other people and by just being told about something. For example, imagine that you are going on a camping trip to Yellowstone Park. You remember a story your friend told you about the time he woke up in the middle of the night

(*Walter Chandoha*)

Such advice, combined with traditional discrimination training and reinforcement, can indeed provide a practical way to help people change their behavior into more constructive channels. Because social learning theory takes the best from operant conditioning and combines it with the "human element" ignored by traditional learning theories, it represents an important trend in learning research.

Biological Factors in Learning

Traditional learning theories have tried to establish general rules of learning that fit all learning, all situations, and all animals, including humans. As we have seen, psychologists are now breaking down these global theories and developing more specific theories to account for more limited situations. **Comparative psychologists** have been particularly discontented with the general theories. Their special interest is animal behavior. Having observed many different species of animals in the lab and in nature, they know that all species do not have the same general responses and abilities. As man is a species too, this perspective has bearing on human as well as animal learning.

One aspect of general learning theory that comparative psychologists disagree with strongly is the notion of **equipotentiality.** This is the idea that any response the animal can perform (such as a rat's pressing a bar) can be arbitrarily linked to any and all stimuli and reinforcements. Animals, however, do not behave quite so predictably. For example, it is not easy to get rats to press a bar to avoid a shock, though they learn to press a bar for food very readily.

Figure 4-16

A model like this was used by Tinbergen (1948) to study prepared fear responses in certain birds. When the model moved to the left (looking like a goose), the birds ignored it. When it moved to the right (looking like a hawk), the birds would give warning cries and would try to escape, even when they had never seen the model before.

What may account for these differences is the concept of biological **preparedness.** Comparative psychologists believe that a particular animal may be naturally more prepared by its biology and evolution to make some responses, while it may be unprepared or even contraprepared to make others. Thus, it is easier to condition a rat to jump to avoid a shock than it is to teach it to press a bar to avoid the shock. The rat is biologically prepared to jump when frightened—it would jump to avoid pain if it were in natural surroundings—and it must learn to control the impulse to jump before it can learn the response of bar-pressing. It *can* learn the response of bar-pressing to avoid shock, if that is what the experiment requires, but it takes many more trials than teaching the rat to bar-press for food.

Biologically prepared responses are also much harder to extinguish than artificial responses contrived by the psychologist. For example, pigeons learn very readily to peck at a key to get food. But unlike rats' bar-pressing, pecking is a natural response for the pigeon—it gets its food in nature this way. So, in extinction situations, while the rat will eventually stop pressing the bar if it receives no food for its efforts, pigeons will keep on pecking even when reinforcement stops. Williams and Williams (1972) arranged a situation where the pigeon's peckings

WHO'S AFRAID OF THE BIG BAD WOLF?

One interesting aspect of human learning is the formation of *phobias*. Phobias are irrational fears of things like high places, cats, spiders, snakes, and the dark. One of Sigmund Freud's most famous cases involved Little Hans, a 5-year-old boy with a horse phobia (Freud, 1909). Freud believed that Little Hans had an Oedipus complex: Hans saw his father as a rival for his mother's love, and he became afraid that his father would find out about this and destroy him. According to Freud, Hans found this conflict so upsetting that he denied his fear of his father and became afraid of horses instead. A different explanation has been suggested by Wolpe and Rachman (1960), who see Hans's phobia simply as a case of classical conditioning. Hans was a very sensitive, compassionate boy, and one day he had seen a horse that had been badly hurt. However, although phobias can be classically conditioned in this way, they do not behave according to most rules of classical conditioning.

In the first place, phobias are not affected by standard extinction procedures. For example, a woman has developed a fear of dogs because of one frightening experience in the past. According to traditional learning theory, each time she sees a dog and nothing frightening happens, her fear of dogs should decrease. But this does not happen. Her fear may become stronger each time she sees a dog or even thinks about a dog.

In the second place, phobias can be learned in one trial, which is not the case with typical laboratory fear conditioning. Also, phobias are irrational—simply telling the woman that dogs won't hurt her, or even showing her a dog and letting her see that nothing happens, does not usually work. With animals who have been conditioned to fear, often showing them once that they won't be hurt extinguishes their fear.

Another interesting aspect of phobias that does not conform to the laboratory model of learning is the limited range of stimulus objects that result in phobic fear. Classical conditioning theory would lead us to expect that any object could become a source of a phobia if it were paired with a trauma. But this is not the case with most phobias. "Only rarely, if ever, do we have pajama phobias, grass phobias, electric-outlet phobias, hammer phobias, even though these things are likely to be associated with trauma in our world" (Seligman, 1972, p. 455).

Seligman suggests that all these nonconformities can be explained by the concept of *preparedness*. Thus, all the common objects of phobia—heights, snakes, cats, the dark, and so on—represent "events related to the survival of the human species through the long course of evolution" (p. 455). Thus, humans are prepared to develop phobias about these things, just as a pigeon is prepared to develop a pecking response. And, as we have seen, a pigeon's pecking is also an easy response to elicit and a hard one to extinguish. Seligman suggests that creating true phobias in animals—for example, by exposing a rat to the sound of a snake's hissing instead of to the usual tone or light that signals a shock—and then studying new ways of extinguishing those phobias in animals might help pscyhologists to develop new therapeutic programs for phobic people.

(*Karl H. Maslowski, Photo Researchers*)

actually prevented food from being delivered. Even under these conditions where the response was counterproductive for the bird, it kept on pecking.

Some of the most compelling evidence for response differences in animal species has come from the experiences of Keller and Marian Breland. The Brelands, in addition to being psychologists, made a career out of training different species of animals to perform in shows. Their experiences provide delightful examples of how hard it is to ignore an animal's prepared responses (Breland & Breland, 1972).

For example, a bantam chicken that they tried to condition to stand on a platform for 12 to 15 seconds scratched so much that the Brelands had to bill it as a "dancing chicken." A raccoon, which had been trained to insert a coin into a container for food, unexpectedly became a miser. It reverted to its natural "washing" response, rubbing the coins together and refusing to drop them in the slot. A pig conditioned to deposit wooden coins in a "piggy bank" became increasingly disposed to dropping, nosing, and tossing the coin around, mindless of its loss of reward. These experiences refute basic assumptions of operant conditioning: the unimportance of species differences, the equipotentiality of responses, and the idea that any organism is, as it were, putty in the hands of the experimenter.

This is not to say that operant learning theory is invalid. But it does suggest that nature cannot be banished from the behaviorist's laboratory. Psychology can only profit from giving more attention to possible biological effects on behavior. As cognitive theorists have argued, S-R learning theory has been its own worst enemy by placing a "premium on the investigation of unnatural contingencies" (Seligman, 1972, p. 463). Comparative psychologists have been reporting differences among species for more than 40 years. General learning theorists are at last beginning to listen.

Applications of Learning Principles

Autonomic Conditioning and Biofeedback

The findings of comparative psychologists have not been the only things to cast a shadow on the long-held assumptions of general learning theory. The basic distinction of the two-factor theory of learning is that learning involves either *involuntary responses* (classical conditioning) or *voluntary responses* (operant conditioning). Skinner and others have made a clear distinction between involuntary behavior—classically elicited and controlled by the autonomic nervous system—and operant or voluntary behavior—controlled by the central nervous system and emitted by the organism of its own free will. There has been an assumption, based on this division, that operant learning is categorically superior to classical conditioning. All these ideas have fallen into question by recent work on *autonomic conditioning* and *biofeedback.*

Autonomic conditioning is the process by which voluntary control can be exercised over such physiological functions as blood pressure and heart rate, which were formerly thought of as involuntary processes. Numerous experiments in the past decade indicate that such autonomic behavior can indeed be *operantly* controlled, that both animals and human beings can—when given rewards and performance feedback—learn to control internal processes in the body.

One of the first successful experiments involved conditioning rats to change the rate of their heartbeat, the reward being electrical stimulation of a pleasure center in the rat's brain (Miller & DiCara, 1967). To make sure that skeletal muscles played no part in the changes, Miller and DiCara gave the rats curare, which made them unable to move. Some rats were rewarded for increasing their heart rate, others for decreasing it, and in both cases there was success. Six years later, baboons were conditioned to develop considerable and long-lasting changes in blood pressure to avoid electrical shock (Harris et al., 1973). Other autonomic responses that have been operantly conditioned include salivation, constriction of blood vessels, urine formation, and galvanic skin response.

The implications of autonomic conditioning are unquestionably exciting, particularly for our own species. But psychologists are not jumping to any hasty conclusions. One of the knottiest problems in all these revolutionary experiments is making certain that other mechanisms are not at work, that it is not some other physical system that is really responsible for the measured physiological changes. Monitoring several physiological systems in an experimental situation helps to eliminate such variables, as does using curare and having some subjects increase performance and others decrease it. For example, Miller and DiCara had amazing success in 1968 when they trained some rats to whiten the skin of the right ear only and other rats to whiten the left ear only!

Most of the research on autonomic conditioning has used some sort of *feedback,* such as bells, lights, or visual images on a screen, to let the subject know how he is doing. Because the bells, lights, and so on, are connected to the particular biological system being studied, this type of feedback is called **biofeedback.** Thus, when a person is learning to slow his heart rate, when the heart does slow down, the light goes on, and the person knows he is doing something right. In one study, the more feedback subjects were given, the better they controlled their heart rates (Brener, Kleinman, & Goesling, 1969). There has been a particular interest recently in using biofeedback to train humans to produce alpha brain waves, those waves associated with relaxed states of contemplation, yoga, and Zen meditation. But recent evidence shows

Figure 4-17
A man learning to control his autonomic responses through biofeedback. By watching the dials on the electronic equipment, which measures his autonomic activity, he can tell whether he is successful in controlling his physiological processes.
(Owen Franken/Stock, Boston)

that people are most alpha-productive when they just sit with their eyes closed in a dark room, and it is possible that alpha consciousness states may involve little more than forms of eye control (Hilgard & Bower, 1975).

Despite all the publicity and the fact that the research is already radically changing the old notions about self-control, biofeedback training is far from being universally successful, particularly in regard to lasting autonomic control. Even successful research is disputed. Have the effects of other body systems really been eliminated? What about the role of cognition in autonomic conditioning? How important is biofeedback to successful conditioning, and if it is important, how can patients learn to condition themselves without biofeedback outside the laboratory or hospital environment? And what about motivation in autonomic conditioning—is praise from the therapist enough of a reinforcement? These basic questions still need to be answered. For example, responses to questionnaires sent out after one experiment showed that subjects had had no idea that they had been controlling their own blood pressure nor even in what direction they had changed it (Schwartz, 1973).

But a door has been opened to a previously unknown world. It is possible that autonomic conditioning may help us to rediscover what one psychologist has called "the lost thread between mind and body" (Brown, 1974, p. 51).

Behavior Modification in Education

Classroom behavior. Most of us have observed at one time or another that the classroom is not the same as real life. Increasingly, the classroom is becoming more like a psychology laboratory as learning principles discovered in the lab are introduced into teachers' training pro-

TRUTH IS SKIN-DEEP: THE LIE DETECTOR

Our skin, superficial covering that it is, is also a giveaway of what is going on inside us. While monitoring heart rate tells us about the heart and measuring stomach contractions tells us about the stomach, monitoring the skin not only tells us about the skin, but also about our thoughts and emotions, including guilt and innocence.

The reason for this is that the skin undergoes changes in resistance to electrical current due to changes in blood vessels and sweat glands. These telltale changes, along with heart rate and breathing, are registered by the polygraph machine, commonly called a lie detector. Despite individual differences in skin electrical conductance, all skin "talks," as psychologist Barbara Brown puts it. "The skin will tell you when there is emotion, how strong the emotion is, and even just when you are lying" (Brown, 1974, p. 52).

Although polygraphs are used in business as well as by the police, it is their use as a police tool that most of us are familiar with. But are they being used as well as they could be? No, according to David Lykken (1975). During a polygraph examination, the suspect will of course be asked, "Did you kill Joe Blow?" Anyone, guilty or innocent, would respond strongly to such a question. But examiners neglect, Lykken says, to grill the suspect on details of the crime, facts that only the true criminal could know.

If a list of names of banks is read off, for example, a guilty suspect will react strongly to the name of the bank he actually robbed. According to Lykken, if a suspect shows such "guilty knowledge" on 6 of 10 such crime-detail items, the chances that he is innocent will be "only one in 1,000." Another virtue of this multiple-choice approach is that it avoids broad incriminating questions that can make an innocent person respond emotionally, causing him to "fail" the test. Since the multiple-choice approach requires knowledge of many details, there is less chance that an amoral psychopath could "beat" the lie detector.

Use of polygraph tests outside of police work has raised objections on moral and constitutional grounds, and both Brown and Lykken feel that such tests are less accurate outside police-lab conditions. In business, lie-detector tests are typically used to check the honesty of job applicants and employees suspected of pilfering. Lykken has two primary objections to this practice. First, the tests are not usually given and scored by psychologists. Second, in the police station, the lie-detector test is only one of many pieces of evidence that make up the police's case against a suspect. In business, on the other hand, the lie-detector test is often the only evidence against someone, and, on the strength of this alone, an employee may be fired and his future career put in jeopardy.

A better use of the polygraph may be as a psychotherapeutic tool. New research indicates that listening to "skin talk" can tell a therapist when the patient is emotionally disturbed during their therapy session. Watching his own skin responses during therapy may make a person more aware of his problems. Thus skin biofeedback may be useful for relieving guilt as well as for assigning it.

grams. In short, education is one fundamental form of **behavior modification.***

Teachers, as behavior modifiers, must determine which behaviors are to be encouraged and which discouraged. They must cope with the problems of scheduling reinforcement, choosing the most effective type of reward or punishment, knowing when a form of punishment has become counterproductive, and deciding when to intervene. Before beginning any program of behavior modification, the teacher must specify the behavior to be changed, what it should be changed into, how often the undesirable behavior typically occurs, and whether any event consistently precedes or follows the undesirable behavior. In analyzing behavior, the teacher should not simply note that Johnny is "immature" or "hyperactive." Precise descriptions of behavior, such as "He talks out of turn, particularly after recess," are much more useful than mere labels in behavior modification.

If there is a single key to behavior modification, it is probably judiciously applied reinforcement. For example, a 3-year-old nursery school child continually crawled or crouched on the floor with her face hidden. Rather than punishing her, teachers made a point of paying attention to her only when she behaved normally and ignoring her the moment she resorted to this behavior. Within a week she was walking in a normal manner (Harris, Wolf, & Baer, 1964). Shaping, or step-by-step conditioning, is also a major tool in behavior modification in schools, especially with so-called problem children. Shy children, for example, can be taught to be more active socially by giving them coins, first for any sound they make, then only for uttering syllables, and ultimately only for "mixing" and communicating (Hingten & Trost, 1966).

Punishments such as loud reprimands can frighten a child and make the school a place to be feared instead of a place to learn. But some children actually treat punishments as rewards, particularly if they get very little attention when they are not misbehaving. Research indicates that "don'ts" work best when backed up by "do's." One study with five

(Fritz Henle, Photo Researchers)

kindergarten children showed that cooperation increased when praise was given. When the praise was stopped, cooperation decreased. When praise was added again, cooperation increased sharply (Schutte & Hopkins, 1970). Activities can be used as reinforcers, for example, by rewarding children with a 15-minute play period after they have successfully finished their math lesson. One of the virtues of this is that, like a teacher's attention, activity reinforcers are already present in the school environment and often don't cost anything.

One specific form of behavior modification is the **token economy,** which is used in hospitals and businesses as well as in schools. In a

---

*Therapeutic applications of behavior modification principles are discussed in Chapter 15.

"HOW TO WIN FRIENDS AND INFLUENCE TEACHERS"
Believe it or not, behavior modification has undergone the ultimate reversal—students have successfully modified the behavior of their teachers! In a school in Visalia, California, eighth-graders learned to be behavior engineers (Gray, Graubard, & Rosenberg, 1974). They rewarded their teachers by smiling, sitting up attentively, and making eye contact whenever the teacher spoke nicely to them. They would directly try to train their teachers to be pleasant by commenting on how they liked to work when the teacher was nice. In one somewhat sneaky but effective technique, a student would pretend not to understand something the teacher was explaining. In the middle of the teacher's second try, the student would excitedly shout, "Aha!" and thank the teacher profusely for helping him understand something he had never been able to understand before. This had a very positive effect on the teacher's attitude toward that student. Apparently teachers need reinforcement as much as anybody else does.

The reason for this odd project? The students were all members of a special class for students with severe behavioral problems. Most had been labeled as incorrigible, and their past relations with their teachers had been exceedingly unpleasant. However, after a period of being reinforced by their students, the teachers began to treat them much more positively. Both teachers and students found school more rewarding. In addition, learning that they could control the way others behave gave the students a sense of self-confidence they had never had before. Similar conditioning techniques have been found to work effectively with parents and friends as well as with teachers.

token economy in a school, a child can be given play money or plastic chips as rewards for good behavior or scholastic achievement. These tokens can be exchanged for primary reinforcers, such as candy or an activity ticket. One benefit of such a system is that it enables teachers to provide different incentives for different individuals. Often students come to value the tokens more because they are earned than because they can be exchanged for something else. But, ideally, tokens are eventually replaced by more symbolic forms of reinforcement.

Token economies have been criticized by some psychologists as being undesirable last resorts because they have not been shown to produce real behavioral changes in the long run. These psychologists feel that once the tokens stop, the behavior does too. But tokens do give students immediate feedback, and token economies have been very successful in stimulating short-term changes in behavior (Macmillan, 1973).

Programmed instruction. Programmed instruction was invented by S. L. Pressey in 1926 and was later refined and developed by B. F. Skinner in the 1950s. In programmed instruction the material to be

CRITIQUE OF BEHAVIOR MODIFICATION

Most psychologists agree that behavior modification works well over the short term, but many are skeptical about the long-term effectiveness of behavior modification techniques.

One criticism has been that rewards are often misused and overused, and that this can have an adverse effect on the behavior you are trying to develop. For example, children may find certain tasks *intrinsically* interesting and will do them without being rewarded. But once rewards have been given for doing those tasks, the children come to expect them and, without the rewards, may no longer have much interest in performing something they once enjoyed doing. Thus, when an activity is an end in itself, "rewarding to death" can turn it into a means to an end, making joyless work out of play. In one experiment, some children were simply asked to draw and were told they would be rewarded. Although all the children had expressed equal interest in drawing before the experiment, the rewarded children later spent only half as much time drawing as the unrewarded children (Greene & Lepper, 1974). While more evidence is needed on the value of *unexpected* rewards, there is no question that indiscriminate use of token economies can result in token learning, or even in just learning how to earn tokens. Removal of tokens— which is the same thing as not giving a rat a food pellet for bar-pressing— often readily undoes success. "In a typical operant laboratory experiment, rats stop pressing the lever in a Skinner box when the food pellets stop coming. Why? The rats have learned how to earn pellets. They have not learned to value pressing the lever" (Levine & Fasnacht, 1974, p. 819). For just this reason, critics of behavior modification urge their colleagues to analyze the situation first. There may be reinforcers inherent in the situation or some intrinsic reward already present that could be used instead of contrived external rewards like tokens.

Levine and Fasnacht (1974) suggest that behavior modification may be most effective in dealing with inappropriate behavior that is inadvertently being reinforced. For example, a child who has temper tantrums may be completely ignored when he behaves well. By ignoring him when he's good and paying attention when he's bad, the child's mother is reinforcing his bad behavior without realizing that that is what she is doing. When parents or teachers unwittingly encourage undesirable responses by responding inconsistently or emotionally, short-term retraining is probably all that is needed to get things on the right track again. In such cases, behavior modification may actually be the most helpful way to effect behavior change.

learned is broken down into units or **frames,** which are organized so that the learner can go through the material step by step. Each frame is composed of a *statement* and a *question*. The question may be multiple-choice, fill-in-the-blank, true-or-false, and so on. The format of the question is not as important as its content. The question is not

Figure 4-18
Teaching machines. The machine on the left is similar to those developed by B. F. Skinner. The student reads the question in the left-hand opening and writes his answer in the opening on the right. If his answer is correct, he advances the machine to the next question by turning a knob on the left side of the machine. On the right is a photo of a computer being used as a teaching machine.

The student answers the computer's questions, which are visually displayed, by writing the answer on the typewriter. If he is correct, the computer automatically presents the next question. (*Left: courtesy B. F. Skinner; right: Hella Hammid, Rapho/Photo Researchers*)

about the statement; it is an *extension* of it. Here is a sample frame from a program designed to teach high school physics:

> *The important parts of a flashlight are the battery and the bulb. When we "turn on" a flashlight, we close a switch which connects the battery with the* _____. (*Skinner, 1968, p. 45.*)

The answer, of course, is "bulb." From this example you can see how the question builds on material given in the statement. In the same way, each frame in the program builds on information given in the frame just before it.

The other important characteristic of programmed learning is that the student gets immediate feedback. The answers to the questions are supplied by the programmer (usually in a second column beside the questions). They are to be covered with a strip of paper while the student is thinking. Once he has given his answer, he can lift the strip up and find out immediately whether he is right or wrong.

There are two main ways to organize a learning program. A **linear program** is arranged so that the learner acquires knowledge by going through the program in sequential order, frame by frame. A **branching program** allows more flexibility. Each question directs the student to a different frame later in the program. If he answers the question correctly, he can take one of several paths. After an incorrect answer on one of the branches, the student is referred back to the original question to make another choice. Each student can thus proceed at his own pace and in the direction that suits him best.

The essential thing to understand about learning programs is that they are *not* quizzes. Quizzes test you on knowledge you are supposed to have already acquired by studying. The questions in a learning program are designed to teach, not to test.

An example of personalized programmed learning is the Keller method of teaching, which is used at the college level in such diverse places as the United States, Canada, Mexico, Brazil, New Zealand, and Samoa (Ryan, 1974). In this method, performance standards are highly specific, testing is frequent and geared to individual progress, and lectures are given in a classroom atmosphere that encourages student participation. The course material is broken down into small units, and when the student feels he is ready, he asks to be tested on that unit. If he passes, he goes on to the next unit. If he fails, he may take the test again, without penalty, after a period of study and review. Thus each student is responsible for his own timetable and studies independently without teacher-imposed deadlines. Although the Keller system has the virtue of allowing each student to progress at his own rate, the giving and grading of tests at frequent and irregular intervals can be quite a burden on teachers.

Computer-assisted instruction. B. F. Skinner also designed teaching machines as tools for programmed instruction. Today, computers can be used to teach. When the student punches the correct response into the computer, it automatically reinforces him by presenting the next problem. The program is a carefully graded series of stimulus (question)–response (answer) frames. The advantages are clear: the learner must be active; feedback is immediate; the individual proceeds at his own pace and can learn without supervision. Teaching machines are used by very young schoolchildren (backed up by other reinforcers including candy and praise). They are also used throughout the school years and college and have become quite sophisticated. Movies have even been used, for example, to teach student technicians how to operate a new piece of equipment (Hilgard & Bower, 1975).

Self-modification of Behavior

Can an individual modify his own behavior? Indeed, yes. A remarkable instance of this is the case of a psychologist left confined to a wheelchair by an automobile accident in 1970 (Goldiamond, 1973). While he was still in the hospital, he undertook a behavioral analysis of his daily life and the new *contingencies* (possibilities for reinforcement or nonreinforcement) that he faced. To keep busy, he kept careful logs of his exercises, muscle movements, medication, and emotional states. These logs proved to be extremely valuable. For example, when he suddenly developed insomnia, his nurse blamed it on worry and anxiety. But Goldiamond carefully checked his day-to-day records and discovered that he was having trouble sleeping simply because he had recently stopped taking Valium, a mild tranquilizer. Without his daily logs, he

THE METHOD, BEHAVIORISTICALLY, IS NOT MADNESS

Stimuli, responses, and reinforcers are the stock and trade not only of learning theorists but of actors as well. At least of so-called Method actors at the famed Actors Studio in New York, whose graduates include Marlon Brando, Jane Fonda, Dustin Hoffman, Sidney Poitier, and Al Pacino. Here, taught by Lee Strasberg and his staff, pupils learn how to produce in themselves the feelings that make performances believable and compelling. It may be no coincidence that Stanislavski, the Russian who first worked out the principles of responsive or Method acting, knew Ivan Pavlov, the man who experimented with the dogs.

Stanislavski's two basic ideas were that acting is not simply imitation and that inspiration can be controlled through both internal and external stimuli. The internal stimuli can be imagined from memory, in which case the actor attempts to recapture relevant emotions by remembering moments in his own personal background.

To play a bereaved widow, for example, an actress may call up memories of the death of her own father. To effectively play Lady Macbeth's "Out, damned spot!" scene, she might imagine that she had a large spider on each hand. To communicate insanity, Strasberg told one performer trying to portray Salome to imagine that John the Baptist's head was "the cutest puppy you have ever seen."

Such "internal work" causes actual physiological changes, and it has been experimentally shown that Method actors have better GSR (galvanic skin response) control than other actors (Stern & Lewis, 1968). Method actors also learn and practice self-observation to be able to bring their real-life responses to the stage, and their teachers shape and reward them to increase this realism, gradually increasing the price of praise.

The actor also uses the external environment, particularly when he utilizes stage props to improvise or when he "relates" to what a fellow actor is doing. These help to eliminate stage fright, as does internal work and training in muscle relaxation. Strasberg not only shapes his students' behavior to be more spontaneous but he invites the actor's comments with questions such as "What did you work for?"

Method actors learn that our personal ways of expressing emotion are often complex and surprising. Fear responses, for example, can vary from smiling to blushing to rage. By making himself a behavioristic instrument and respondent, the Method actor creates an exciting environment for himself and, in the process, for his audience (Schulman, 1973).

might have stayed up all night worrying about why he couldn't sleep. Goldiamond found his system so effective that he began to apply it to other people who came to him for help in developing control over some aspect of their lives.

As in any program designed to change behavior, the first thing to do is to decide what behavior you want to acquire. Goldiamond particularly emphasizes a positive approach—which he calls "ignoring the deficit." He finds that much better results are achieved when the emphasis is on the behavior to be acquired rather than on the behavior to be eliminated. The next step is to analyze your environment, because changing the environment is almost always necessary if you are going to change behavior. The best way to pinpoint what needs changing in your environment is to keep a daily log, as Goldiamond did.

For example, say you are worried about gaining weight. You decide that you need to lose 10 pounds before summer comes. Picturing your slender new self—instead of telling yourself how fat you are and how badly you need help—is what Goldiamond means when he says "ignore the deficit." In your daily log, every time you eat something, you should write down what you ate, where you were when you ate it, what you were doing at the time, who was with you, and so on. After a couple of weeks you should begin to see a pattern. Suppose that you typically study in your room and that most of your overeating is composed of snacks that you nibble on while studying. Changing your environment by studying at a friend's house or at the library would be a good first step toward changing your eating behavior. Keeping the daily log going until you have achieved your goal will help you discover other ways to change your environment, which in turn will help you change yourself.

Summary

1. Learning is the process by which changes in behavior are brought about through experience or practice. The simplest kinds of learning are usually called *conditioning*—a general word referring to the acquisition of a particular response.
2. *Classical conditioning* involves learning to respond to some stimulus that would not invariably produce such a response. Ivan Pavlov first demonstrated this process when he conditioned a dog to salivate when it heard a bell.
3. In classical conditioning, the stimulus that invariably causes the desired response is called the *unconditioned stimulus* (US). The reaction to the unconditioned stimulus is called the *unconditioned response* (UR). The neutral stimulus that the subject learns to respond to is known as the *conditioned stimulus* (CS), and the response to the conditioned stimulus is called the *conditioned response* (CR).
4. A learned response will generally stop occurring if the conditioned stimulus continually fails to be followed by the unconditioned stimulus. This process is known as *extinction*. Extinction occurs because the learner has gained an *inhibition* that blocks the conditioned response. After a period of time, the inhibition weakens and the response may suddenly reappear on its own; this is known as *spontaneous recovery*.
5. Once a response has been conditioned to a particular stimulus, it can also be elicited by other similar stimuli. This phenomenon is known as *stimulus generalization*. In the same way, a particular stimulus may also elicit

similar but different responses without further learning—a phenomenon known as *response generalization*.

6. The opposite of generalization is *discrimination*. This is a process by which a subject can learn to respond to one specific stimulus and not to other similar stimuli.

7. After a response to a conditioned stimulus has been learned, the conditioned stimulus itself can be used as the unconditioned stimulus in further training—a procedure known as *higher-order conditioning*.

8. In *operant conditioning* the subject learns to operate on his surroundings in some way that will get him something he wants or allow him to avoid something he does not want. B. F. Skinner developed many techniques of operant conditioning and invented the laboratory apparatus—the Skinner box—most often used in this type of training.

9. Before operant conditioning can begin, the desired response must be made. There are several ways to get the correct response to occur. The most common method is *trial and error*—the subject tries various things until he discovers the correct action.

10. Other methods can be used when we want to speed up the process. By *increasing motivation* we can make sure that the subject will discover the required response more quickly. By *decreasing restraints*, we free the learner from rules or controls that might prevent him from finding the correct response. By *increasing restraints*, we eliminate distractions that might lead to incorrect responses.

11. The direct intervention of the experimenter or teacher can also help the learner acquire the desired response. In *forcing*, the subject is guided in making the response. In *verbal instruction*, he is told what to do. And in *modeling*, he is shown what to do so he can imitate the action.

12. Once the desired response has been made, *reinforcement* is used to ensure that it will be repeated and learned. Reinforcement can be either positive or negative. *Positive reinforcement* is something pleasant given to the learner after making the correct response. *Negative reinforcement* after a correct response is the easing or termination of a painful or unpleasant situation.

13. *Escape training* and *avoidance training* both use negative reinforcement. In escape training the subject learns how to terminate or escape from an unpleasant situation. In avoidance training the subject learns to do something that will prevent the unpleasant situation from occurring altogether.

14. *Punishment* is used to inhibit incorrect responses. Punishment should be applied soon after the undesirable behavior and should be applied consistently. Punishment is most effective when paired with reinforcement to teach an alternative response that is incompatible with the undesirable response.

15. A *primary reinforcer* is one that is rewarding by itself, without any association with other reinforcers, such as food or water. A *secondary reinforcer* is one whose value has to be learned through association with other reinforcers. Money is a good example of a secondary reinforcer.

16. Reinforcing every correct response is less effective than some type of *partial reinforcement*. *Schedules of reinforcement* can be based either on the number of responses (ratio) or the time elapsed between responses (interval). On a *fixed-interval schedule*, reinforcement is given for the first

correct response after a specific amount of time has passed. The amount of time always stays the same. On a *variable-interval schedule* the amount of time between reinforcements changes. On a *fixed-ratio schedule*, reinforcement is given after a certain number of responses. The number of responses always stays the same. On a *variable-ratio schedule*, the number of responses between reinforcements changes.

17. *Stimulus generalization, response generalization,* and *discrimination* occur in operant conditioning, just as in classical conditioning. Operant responses are extinguished by withholding reinforcement, but they may spontaneously recover.

18. Complex as well as simple tasks can be learned by operant conditioning. A procedure known as *shaping* is used for teaching complicated patterns of behavior. Each simple part of the total is built up step by step until the final behavior has been learned. Another name for shaping is the *method of successive approximation.*

19. Most behavior consists not of isolated actions, but of chains of events—one response becomes the stimulus for the next response, and so on. *Behavior chains* are most easily learned if they are taught bit by bit in backward order.

20. When the learning of one task affects the ability to learn another, *transfer of learning* is taking place. When what is learned in one task makes it easier to learn another task, *positive transfer* is happening. Positive transfer often involves what some psychologists call *learning set*—the learning of a specific approach that can be applied in solving similar kinds of problems.

21. In recent years, several new viewpoints on learning theory have been proposed. Most arose because psychologists felt traditional learning theory was unable to answer some of their questions about human learning. For example, *cognitive theories of learning* distinguish between simple learning for retention and problem solving. They also distinguish between learning (what goes on inside the individual) and performance (what the individual does that shows that learning has taken place). The cognitive theories focus particularly on the internal processes that go on during learning. They define learning itself as the formation of a conceptual unit with sufficient boundary strength to resist interference from other conceptual units. This conceptual unit is formed when a stimulus is consistently associated with a response.

22. A second new view is *social learning theory,* proposed by Albert Bandura, which combines elements of traditional operant conditioning and cognitive theory. One of Bandura's main departures from traditional learning theory is his emphasis on our ability to learn by watching other people's behavior. This is called *observational learning.* Research has shown that we learn many different types of behavior—from simple skills to complex behavior, values, and attitudes—by observing models. Social learning theorists also have a different view of reinforcement than traditional learning theorists have. In addition to primary and secondary reinforcers, social learning theorists also recognize *symbolic reinforcers* (such as attention and approval), *vicarious reinforcers* (whereby other people's being rewarded or punished encourages us to change our behavior), and *self-reinforcers* (such as pride or guilt).

23. A third new approach to learning theory is that of the *comparative psychologists*. Traditional learning theorists believe in the *equipotentiality* of responses—that any response an animal is capable of performing can be arbitrarily paired with any stimulus with no effect on learning and extinction. But comparative psychologists, who study the behavior of many animal species, have concluded that the unique biology and evolution of a species do influence learning. Comparative psychologists suggest that an animal may be more *prepared*—by its biology and evolution—to perform some responses and may be unprepared (and even contra-prepared) to perform others. The responses an animal is prepared to make are learned much more quickly and are much more resistant to extinction than are unprepared responses. As man is a species too, the work of comparative psychologists can do much to widen our understanding of how biology and evolution influence our ability to learn.

24. One distinction that used to be made between classical conditioning and operant conditioning has recently become somewhat blurred. It had been thought that classical conditioning only worked with involuntary responses such as salivation and heart rate, which are controlled by the autonomic nervous system, and that operant conditioning only worked with voluntary responses (which are controlled by the central nervous system). Recent research on *autonomic conditioning*—learning to voluntarily control involuntary responses—has suggested that this division is apparently overstated. People have been taught to lower their heart rate, change the constriction of their blood vessels, and change their brain waves, among other things. One of the problems in drawing conclusions from this research is the difficulty of making sure that some other physical system is not really causing these changes. Autonomic conditioning does have therapeutic potential for relieving such conditions as hypertension and high blood pressure.

25. Most of the research on autonomic conditioning uses some sort of feedback such as bells, lights, and visual images to let the subject know how he is doing. Because the bells and lights are connected to the particular biological system being studied, this type of feedback is called *biofeedback*. When a person successfully slows down his heart rate, for example, a light goes on. Although it appears that the more feedback people get, the better they learn, biofeedback training is far from being universally successful.

26. *Behavior modification* is one way learning principles are applied in the real world. One of its most important nontherapeutic uses is in education. Teachers are trained in behavior modification principles in an attempt to learn how to change their students' undesirable behavior effectively. In addition to scheduling reinforcement and punishment, teachers must know when to intervene and when to change their method.

27. One specific form of behavior modification that is used in hospitals and in businesses as well as in schools is the *token economy*. In a token economy in a school, a student is given tokens as a reward for good behavior or scholastic achievement. The tokens may be exchanged for primary reinforcers like candy or permission to use the gym during recess. Such a system gives the student immediate feedback and provides different incentives for different individuals. Token economies have been very

successful in achieving short-term changes in behavior, but their long-term effectiveness is still being evaluated. Some psychologists are very critical of them because they feel that the individual is really learning how to earn tokens rather than learning a new behavior, and that when the tokens stop, the learning may stop too.

28. Another way in which learning theory has been applied in education is *programmed instruction*. In this system, the student actually teaches himself by going through the learning program, which is composed of *frames*. He receives feedback by finding out immediately whether his answer is right or wrong and can proceed through the program at his own pace. There are two main types of learning programs: *linear programs*, in which the material to be learned is organized sequentially and the student must go through the frames in order; and *branching programs* in which the student is free to follow any of several paths as long as he continues to answer correctly.

29. *Computer-assisted instruction* is a more modern version of the teaching machine. Both are used as tools to program instruction. When the student answers correctly, the machine presents the next frame in the program. Teaching machines and computer-assisted instruction are currently being used by students of all ages, from nursery school through college.

30. You can learn to control your own behavior through behavior modification, just as teachers learn to control the behavior of their students. First, you decide on the behavior you want to acquire. Next, you analyze your environment to determine if anything in the environment either reinforces behavior you would like to eliminate or stands in the way of your acquiring the new behavior. The most effective way to do this is to keep a daily log. Then, you are in a position to change your environment so that it will provide the rewards and incentives you need to learn the new behavior.

Suggested Readings

Burgess, A., *A Clockwork Orange* (New York: Norton, 1963). A novel based on the attempt to apply classical conditioning in the rehabilitation of violent criminals. Stanley Kubrick's film version of the book appeared in 1972.

Hilgard, E. R., and Bower, T. H., *Theories of Learning*, 4th ed. (Englewood Cliffs, N.J.: Prentice-Hall, 1975). A comprehensive look at various theories that have been proposed to explain how learning takes place.

Hulse, S. H., Deese, J., and Egeth, H., *The Psychology of Learning*, 4th ed. (New York: McGraw-Hill, 1975). A detailed but clear treatment of the learning process and its elements.

Jonas, G., *Visceral Learning: Toward a Science of Self-Control* (New York: Viking, 1973). A well-written account of research on autonomic conditioning that focuses on the life and work of Neal Miller.

Mednick, S. A., Pollio, H. R., and Loftus, E. R., *Learning*, 2nd ed. (Englewood Cliffs, N.J.: Prentice-Hall, 1973). A concise introduction to the learning process.

Mikulas, W. L., *Concepts in Learning* (Philadelphia: Saunders, 1974). Emphasizes human learning and its applications and includes an excellent review of research on behavior modification.

Peterson, L. R., *Learning* (Glenview, Ill.: Scott, Foresman, 1975). A brief survey of classical and contemporary learning theory and research that contains examples of the application of learning principles to other areas in psychology such as motivation and emotion, social psychology, and abnormal behavior.

Skinner, B. F., "Teaching Science in High School—What Is Wrong?" *Science*, 1968, *157*, 704–710. In this relatively short paper, Skinner proposes the use of operant conditioning techniques—positive and negative reinforcement, shaping, and so on—to improve methods of teaching science.

outline

MEASURING RETENTION 174

Recall
Recognition
Savings

THE THREE LEVELS OF MEMORY 178

The Sensory Store
Short-Term Memory
Long-Term Memory

BIOLOGICAL BASES OF MEMORY 189

The Location of Memory
The Unit of Storage

FORGETTING 192

Decay of the Memory Trace
Interference
Motivated Forgetting
Organic Amnesia

SUMMARY 201

SUGGESTED READINGS 203

Memory

You are studying French vocabulary words. "Je t'aime" means "I love you." Close your eyes and say it again to yourself. You have learned the French sentence in one trial. Yet, if you want to use that sentence tonight, you'll have to practice it during the day. Why? You've already learned it, haven't you? Well, not exactly. From one point of view, learning is thought of as acquiring a response. So from that point of view, you have indeed learned something. But learning can also be considered as "keeping forgetting away." According to this point of view, if you cannot remember, you have not learned. Thus, learning and memory are intertwined.

All of us take for granted many aspects of human life. We only notice our breathing process when we have a cold or are "out of breath." Similarly, we don't think about digestion unless we have indigestion. Our tendency is to accept the physical workings of our bodies as casually as we browse through the morning newspaper. We pay attention only when things go wrong.

The same is true of memory. We accept as natural our ability to remember things. We dredge up the most amazing trivia from years past without feeling that we have done anything remarkable. But forget something, and what do we feel? Anger, frustration, powerlessness, and a fear that old age is sneaking up on us. This attitude toward memory is based on the assumption that memory is a simple, normal process that anyone (except perhaps the very young or the very old) should be able to do all the time.

In this chapter, we challenge this assumption. Memory is not a simple process. And, considering the amount of drill it takes for us to remember certain types of things, perhaps memory should not even be thought of as normal. It may be that forgetting is normal. In this chapter we talk about the different degrees and kinds of memory, the various ways we have of measuring retention, and the different levels of the memory process. From there, we move on to the physiological mechanics of memory, the biological "where" and "how" of storing and retrieving information. Finally, we talk about the occasions when memory fails to work—what we mean when we say that we have forgotten something, and what is involved in that forgetting.

Measuring Retention

The function of memory is **retention,** "holding on to" events and information from the past. But how do we know whether some experience or other has been retained? We can measure retention only through performance, and this performance can be affected by many things that have nothing to do with memory itself. If you are worried about giving

HIGH SCHOOL MEMORIES

Bahrick, Bahrick, and Wittlinger (1974) studied people's ability to remember high school classmates. The researchers tested 392 people who had graduated from 5 months to 48 years before the survey. Six tests were given, including tests for recall and recognition of classmates' names and photographs.

The results suggested that adults have a remarkable ability to recognize (though not recall) high school classmates. Recent graduates, as well as those who had graduated 35 years earlier, correctly identified nine out of ten of their classmates' pictures. And even elderly adults, who had graduated more than 40 years before, recognized three-quarters of their classmates. Size of the class made no difference in recognition rates. People from large classes performed just as well on these tests as people from small classes. Sex, however, did make a difference. The women consistently scored higher than the men on all tests except long-term retention (40 years or more).

DAX

VOH

PEL

QUS

BAF

FIC

GYT

TEM

WYB

REL

KUJ

JOD

Figure 5-1
Nonsense syllables like these are often used in studies of memory, both serial recall and relearning.

Figure 5-2
In studies of paired-associate learning, pairs of nonsense syllables are shown. Then a single nonsense syllable is presented alone, and the person's ability to recall the second member of the pair is measured.

PEL

PEL—QUS

FIC

FIC—TEM

REL

REL—KUJ

JOD

JOD—WYB

a speech, your anxiety may cause parts of it to become inaccessible at the critical moment, even though you may remember them after you have left the stage. Or motivation may influence performance. If you are training your dog to sit up, he may not seem to remember the trick if you are offering him a banana as a reward, yet he may perform the trick immediately if you offer him a dog biscuit.

What kinds of performance show retention? If someone asks you to recite a poem you once learned, you may be able to do it word for word without help—you have perfect **recall** of the poem. But suppose you get stuck halfway through and cannot remember some line or phrase. When someone tells you what it is, you **recognize** it as soon as you hear it. Or you may not think you remember the poem at all and you sit down to memorize it again. You may find that relearning the poem is easier than it was to learn it the first time. The **savings** in time and effort suggest some form of retention.

Recall, recognition, and savings are not three separate kinds of memory. They are three different ways of measuring retention. They differ in sensitivity to stored experience. In most cases, recognition is more sensitive than recall because recognition often provides evidence of retention when recall produces a blank. However, in certain testing situations, subjects have recalled items that they could not recognize (Hulse, Deese, & Egeth, 1975). Savings is the most sensitive of all. Often with material that we think we have forgotten entirely, or perhaps do not even remember having learned in the first place, savings will show that we have retained something.

Recall

Recall involves the reproduction or repetition of learned material. In its most obvious form, it is *verbatim* (word for word) recitation of learned material. But recall can also result from **reconstruction.** If you are writing an essay examination on World War II, and you recall that the United States entered the war in 1941 after the attack on Pearl Harbor, and that the atomic bomb was dropped on Hiroshima in 1945, you may be able to reconstruct the events that took place between these two times.

A distinction should be made between free recall and serial recall. In **serial recall,** you recall material in a very specific order, most often the order in which it was learned. Young children can sometimes remember lengthy songs when the verses follow each other in a recognizable sequence. **Free recall,** on the other hand, allows you to summon up pieces of information out of order. You may listen to a lecture and afterward remember a few important quotes, without recalling the order in which they were presented.

Figure 5-3
The memory drum is a device often used in laboratory experiments on memory. As the drum turns, one frame at a time, the woman sees a series of nonsense syllables or pairs of syllables through a small slot in the front of the machine.
(Van Bucher, Photo Researchers; courtesy Wagner College Department of Psychology)

Recognition

Recognition often demonstrates retention when recall draws a blank. Multiple-choice tests measure recognition. If you are asked to recall where the Arno River is, you may be unable to answer the question. But if you are given choices—Germany, Italy, or France—you may then recognize that Italy is correct. Once the remembered event or word is in front of you, you know that you have stored it away before. Sometimes, of course, recognition can be inaccurate, like thinking a stranger you pass on the street is your cousin George.

Savings

Even if you are unable to recall or recognize something you learned once, you may have a much easier time when you try to learn it again than you had the first time around. In one experiment, Burtt (1941)

TRADITIONAL STUDIES OF MEMORY

Among the classic studies of memory are the experiments on *serial learning* conducted by the German psychologist Herman Ebbinghaus in the late nineteenth century (Ebbinghaus, 1885). Like many of the psychologists of his day, Ebbinghaus used himself as his only subject. Therefore, he had to devise tasks that he could repeat over and over again, without being unduly influenced by prior learning. To eliminate the effects of meaningfulness, he composed a list of 2,300 nonsense syllables—like "zeb," "lef," and "dak." He then set about learning lists of nonsense syllables and measuring his own retention.

He would place a list of a dozen nonsense syllables in front of himself and read each word in order to the beat of a metronome—one syllable every two-fifths of a second. He continued to do this until he could repeat the entire list correctly from memory. He carefully noted how many trials it took before he could recall the list, then went on to another set of syllables. After a certain amount of time had passed, perhaps a day, Ebbinghaus counted how many of the nonsense syllables on the first list he could still recall. Then he proceeded to relearn the list and counted how many trials it took the second time. He called the difference between the number of trials required to learn the list the first time and the number required to learn it the second time the *savings*.

Ebbinghaus also experimented on the effects of overlearning his nonsense syllables. He would take two lists—List A and List B—of equal length. He would read through List A just until he could repeat it once correctly. Then he would practice with List B up to the same point, but did not stop there. After he was able to recall all the syllables on List B, he would continue to read through the list a few more times to overlearn the material. A day later he would test himself on both lists and measure the savings when he relearned the two lists. It took fewer trials to relearn the list that had been overlearned.

Ebbinghaus estimated the memory span to be 7 items, since that was the number of nonsense syllables he could recall correctly after reading through the list just once. To learn 12 items, he usually had to go through the list 15 times; to learn a list of 30 syllables, he had to go through it 50 times. He found that he added about one new syllable to the list of syllables he could recall for every two times he read through the list.

Another traditional approach to the study of memory is called the method of *paired associates*, developed by G. E. Müller, a follower of Ebbinghaus. In paired-associate learning, the subject is shown pairs of unrelated items, like nonsense syllables, in a series. He forms a connection between the items. To test retention, the experimenter then shows the subject the first word in a pair and asks him to respond with the correct mate. Paired-associate learning is what we do when we learn foreign vocabulary words—the English word "pencil" is associated with the German word *Bleistift*, for example, even though the two words are totally unrelated to begin with.

Sir Frederic Bartlett pioneered an alternate branch of memory research emphasizing *semantic memory*, the recall of meaning. While Ebbinghaus and Müller concentrated their studies on verbatim recall, Bartlett explored how a person remembers meaning and how that meaning is transformed during the process of recollection. For example, Bartlett (1932) had Cambridge undergraduates read a story about American Indians who went on a canoe trip to go seal hunting. When the students were asked to retell the story later, the canoes became boats and the seal hunt became a fishing expedition. Bartlett suggested that these changes occurred because canoes and seal hunts were not familiar things to the students. They substituted more familiar things like boats and fishing to fill in the blanks in the story caused by their inability to remember the exact words.

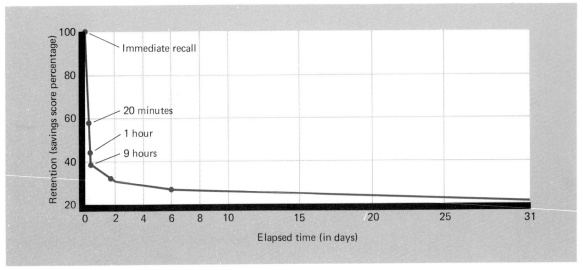

Figure 5-4

One of Ebbinghaus's retention curves. Retention decreases rapidly at first; yet even a month after learning, some evidence of retention remains. (Adapted from H. Ebbinghaus, *Memory: A Contribution to Experimental Psychology.* Leipzig: Altenberg, 1885.)

began teaching Greek to a 15-month-old infant. Burtt read 20 lines of Greek poetry to him, over and over, at various intervals until he was 3 years old. At that point the poetry readings were discontinued, and for the next 5 years the child had no contact whatever with Greek. Then, at the age of 8, he was given Greek poetry to learn—some of it lines he had heard as an infant, some of it new material. He had apparently forgotten his experience with Greek as a baby—he could not recall or recognize any of the lines. But the specific passages that had been read to him during his infancy were much easier for him to learn than those that were completely new. We call this difference between the difficulty of relearning once-known but "forgotten" material and the difficulty of learning something new the savings. Effort, as well as time, can be saved in the process of relearning.

The Three Levels of Memory

We have been discussing ways of determining what is in the enormous bank of stored experience called memory. But how does this bank come to exist in the first place? What does it consist of? And what are the processes, the techniques, by which stored information actually comes back to us? If we accept the analogy of memory as a vast information-processing system, like a giant computer, we can ask these questions in other terms: How do we feed information into the system? What happens to it then? How do we get the information back again?

Since the nineteenth century, people have been aware that there are several kinds of memory. William James distinguished between primary memory, which existed in the present and contained ideas that were current or momentary, and secondary memory, which could store past information. A contemporary of James noted that the primary memory-image is a brief impression, something we are aware of without paying attention to it. It does not have the permanence of secondary memory.

In recent years, especially as electronic computers have come into more general use, the idea of multiple memories has been expanded. Some theorists separate memory into three distinct levels—the **sensory store, short-term memory,** and **long-term memory.** They regard the levels as stages in a kind of refinery through which raw material passes. Each level is considered to be distinguishable from the others. At each level, the material receives certain kinds of processing, which eventually lead to its being either discarded or stored.

Recently, a number of theorists have questioned this view of memory as a series of distinct stages (Cermak, 1972; Melton, 1963; Postman, 1975). They suggest that the various kinds of memory are not easily distinguishable from each other. Rather, as information is processed in various ways, it takes on the characteristics of the sensory store, short-term memory, and, eventually, long-term memory. If future research establishes the validity of this viewpoint, the widely held definitions of the three stages of memory will need modification. For our purposes, however, we will describe the predominant view of memory in which

Figure 5-5
A diagram of the three levels of memory.

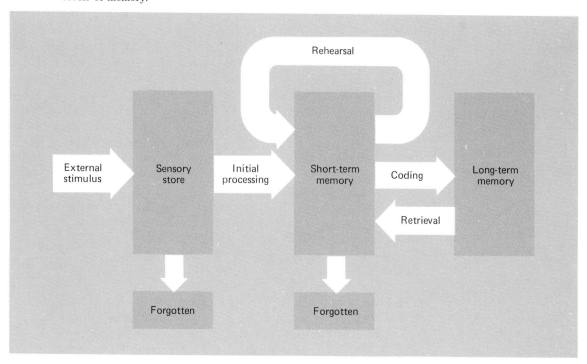

there are three relatively discrete levels. At the same time, we will temper our discussion in view of some of these more recent ideas.

The Sensory Store

We might be tempted to think of the sensory store as not being memory at all. It consists of the impressions that stimuli from the external world make on our senses, especially on the visual sense. The sensory store may be imagined as the "reception room" of the memory system, receiving almost everything that hits our senses. Some of these sensory impressions are admitted into a farther room, but most of them go away immediately, never to be heard from again.

The sensory store has a huge capacity for information, but its retention time is extremely brief. All the sounds, sights, and tactile impressions we receive decay rapidly, to be replaced by new ones. Only a tiny part of what enters the sensory store is processed from raw sensory data and passes into the next level.

Short-Term Memory

Short-term memory is temporary, active, and conscious. In everyday terms, it is our attention span. Short-term memory is more selective, and slightly more permanent, than the sensory store, but much less material can be held at this level. Keele (1973) states that material in short-term memory will disappear in 10 to 20 seconds, if it is not practiced.

A generally accepted theory (Miller, 1956) maintains that short-term memory can hold on to only seven items, plus or minus two items, at a time. It may seem to us that we are holding more items than that—when we are watching a circus or skimming a book, for example—but Miller's theory answers this by comparing short-term memory to a purse. The purse will hold seven coins—but it does not matter whether the coins are pennies or silver dollars. It could not hold 700 pennies, but if each 100 pennies is grouped into one coin, that coin counts as a single item and the purse can hold that. This way of grouping information is called **chunking.**

Processing a chunked item is more difficult than processing a single-unit item, because the chunk contains more information. But it can be done. Suppose you were asked to memorize 15 letters. This would be more than you could hold in short-term memory at once. But if you chunk together the first three letters, which are "S," "B," and "U"—that is, if you remember "SBU" as a single item rather than as three separate items—it will be possible to remember the five chunked items. Research by Murdock (1961) on chunking demonstrates that the critical variable for recall is the number of meaningful units, not the number of letters. In more simple terms, it is as difficult to recall three unrelated letters as it is to recall three unrelated words.

THE ZEIGARNIK EFFECT

Psychologist Kurt Lewin and some of his students noticed one evening that the waiter serving them in a Berlin beer garden could remember all the details of their orders—until the bill was paid. Once the transaction was completed, he could recall almost nothing. Bluma Zeigarnik, one of Lewin's students, investigated this phenomenon, which has become known as the *Zeigarnik effect.*

To determine why we are more likely to remember uncompleted tasks, she selected 32 subjects and gave each of them a series of simple tasks to perform, such as solving a riddle or doing mental arithmetic. They were allowed to complete half of the tasks, but were interrupted in the middle of the others. When they were questioned several hours later, the people all remembered the interrupted tasks better than the completed ones (Zeigarnik, 1927). The Zeigarnik effect seems to wear off in 24 hours, and it appears to work best under nonstressful conditions.

Lewin attributes the better recall of unfinished tasks to the tension that develops when one still needs to complete an action. This tension seems to depend on one's attitude: a person who is engrossed in the task or wants to do it well is more apt to recall it than a person who simply does not care if it is done or not.

A. J. Marrow (1938) was able to *reverse* the Zeigarnik effect by an ingenious use of instructions. People were told that they would be interrupted and allowed to go on to the next task if the examiner saw they were performing well. The instructions thus implied that being allowed to complete a task indicated poor performance and would lead to a lower total score. In this situation, where interruption was equated with accomplishment and completion meant failure, completed tasks were recalled more frequently than interrupted ones.

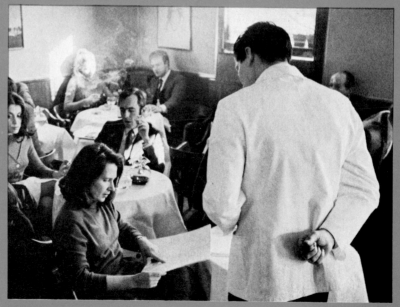

(Bruno Barbey, Magnum Photos)

(Margot Granitsas, Photo
Researchers)

Retention in short-term memory. Material that is repeated—either silently or out loud—can be retained for a while in short-term memory. The most obvious use of repetition is to hold on to information that you need only momentarily. You repeat a telephone number after you have looked it up. Then when you have dialed, you can forget it. If you get a busy signal, you may have to go back to the telephone directory before you dial again. Or you walk across the kitchen, from the recipe book to the flour canister, muttering "two-thirds of a cup" as you go. Psychologists have found some evidence to indicate that you can retain things you hear longer than things you see (Keele, 1973). That is why saying "two-thirds of a cup" out loud is more effective than trying to retain a visual image of the words on the page in the cookbook.

There are many factors that can interfere with the ability to retain information in short-term memory. One is the introduction of new material between the time you took in the information and the time it is to be recalled. It can be another event that takes your attention away. The importance of this event or new information has a direct effect on how likely you are to forget the old information. If a friend comes to the door unexpectedly while you are on your way to the flour canister, there is a good chance that you will forget the amount of flour you need for the recipe.

We have been discussing short-term memory in cases where it is the terminal point, so to speak, of information—things we need to know for a few moments and then can forget about. But suppose the telephone number you looked up belongs to someone you become friends with, or the recipe was so good that you make it often. In these cases, the material is likely to be transferred to long-term memory.

If material is to be stored in long-term memory, it must be repeated many times. This process is known as **rehearsal.** If information is rehearsed often enough and in constructive ways, it will be transferred from short-term memory to long-term, relatively permanent memory. But if rehearsal is interrupted, the material may be lost. Once information is discarded at the short-term memory level, it cannot be recalled.

A study by Cohen (1974a) pinpoints the effect of interruption of rehearsal on dream recall. One group of college students was instructed to call the weather report on the telephone immediately after they woke up and to write down the day's expected temperature. Then they were to write down anything they could remember about their dreams. A control group of students was instructed to lie still for 90 seconds upon waking (the approximate time the experimental group took to call the weather report), and then to write down their dreams. Only 33 percent of the experimental group could recall their dreams, while 63 percent of the control group remembered theirs. This finding supports the idea that if you are distracted or interrupted when the material is still at the short-term memory level, you are less likely to transfer it to more permanent memory and are therefore less likely to remember it.

(Wayne Miller, Magnum Photos)

Frequently, a person who has suffered a concussion is unable to recall the events that directly preceded the injury, even though he can remember things that happened some time before the injury. This condition is known as **retrograde amnesia.** The events right before the accident were at the short-term memory level and had not been rehearsed enough to be transferred to the long-term level. Thus, they were completely forgotten.

It is usually more difficult to retain information you have learned quickly than it is if you have some leisure to learn it. This may be a function of being able, if you have enough time, to rehearse gradually or cumulatively. If you are memorizing the names of American presidents, it is easier if you repeat the first three, then add the next name and repeat those four, and work slowly until you know the whole list.

Coding. Rehearsal is necessary if information is to be transferred to long-term memory, but there is another job that must also be performed. This is called coding. Coding is a way of processing information by compressing it into abbreviated form. If what you are coding is a word, it may be put into such physical categories as its length, the number of syllables it has, its sound, or its first letter. Or it may be coded according to its meaning and associations. Recent evidence, for example, suggests that short-term retention of words often involves coding based on their sound, while coding based on the meaning of words appears to be necessary for long-term retention (Hulse, Deese, & Egeth, 1975).

Most coding goes on continually without our being aware of it. Through this process, we fit new information into the organized material we already have in long-term memory.

Long-Term Memory

Like the sensory store, **long-term memory** has a vast capacity for information. But, as opposed to the sensory store, the information in long-term memory is highly organized and relatively permanent. It has been sifted, rehearsed, and coded and is now ready to find its place within a permanent body of remembered experience, which is constantly being revised and reorganized as new material flows into it. Instead of thinking of long-term memory as a set of pigeonholes, passive and finite, awaiting the arrival of new information, we should see it as a dynamic, interdependent, continually shifting network with a huge storage capacity.

What goes into long-term memory? Information from all the senses can be stored. What seems to be most important about what is stored in long-term memory is how it can be organized. This is why familiar information is more readily processed than unfamiliar information—it is easier to find a category to put it into.

SERIAL REPRODUCTION

Material in long-term memory has been broken down so it can be coded and stored. To recall it, we have to reconstruct the original material from all its parts. The nature of memory as a reconstructive process is demonstrated clearly by Frederic Bartlett's experiments on serial reproduction (Bartlett, 1932). Bartlett first showed a picture to one person, who was asked to study it and redraw it from memory. The redrawing was then given to a second person, who also redrew from memory what he had seen. A third person got this sketch, and so on. The drawings above show the results of one of Bartlett's experiments—in only ten steps, the owl was gradually transformed into a pussycat.

The same was true of verbal material. Bartlett would tell a story to one person and ask him to pass it on to someone else—like the children's game of "telephone," in which each participant hears a word or a sentence and passes it on to the next in line. Bartlett's subjects tended to change the stories to fit their own experiences and temperament. They omitted details, added morals, changed names, sometimes even altered the stories' endings. Yet they were unaware that they were inventing. This suggests that they remembered just what they wanted to remember and reformulated the information to fit into the framework of their own attitudes and experiences.

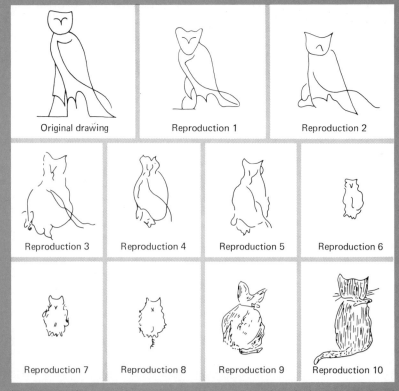

Original drawing

Reproduction 1

Reproduction 2

Reproduction 3

Reproduction 4

Reproduction 5

Reproduction 6

Reproduction 7

Reproduction 8

Reproduction 9

Reproduction 10

(From F. C. Bartlett, Remembering, 1932. Used by permission of Cambridge University Press.)

The same memory can be stored in many forms or categories, so that we can "call up" a single memory in various ways, depending on what sort of clues we have to it—you may get to "Iowa" through an association with corn, or hearing "Cedar Rapids" mentioned, or reading the word "Ionic" and recognizing the similarity of the initial sounds.

We have spoken mainly of how words are remembered. A recent article by Johnson-Laird (1974) poses the question of how we remember sentences: word by word, or as a whole unit, or by remembering the meaning of the sentence? Studies indicate that sentences with clear, logical meanings, such as "The doctor cured the patient," are easier to recall than less common sentences, such as "The doctor shook the author" (Rosenberg & Jarvella, 1970). These studies suggest that the memory of sentences is determined in part by their meaning. Even when the exact words cannot be recalled, the meaning of the sentence may still be retained.

But understanding how something is filed and stored in the bank of long-term memory only brings us to our next question. How do we get this material out again? How do we **retrieve** information?

The retrieval process. Can everything that is stored in memory be drawn up again when we need it? Most likely, no. Our capacity for retrieval appears to be smaller than our capacity for storage. Certainly, some retrieval is not immediate, as you know if you have ever searched your memory for an answer to a question and have come up with that answer a moment too late. If a piece of information does not seem to be retrievable, does that mean that it has gone away? Experiments suggest not.

During the course of brain operations performed on epileptics, it has been found that patients are often able to recall past experiences with amazing clarity when the brain is stimulated electronically (Penfield, 1959). In the strongest such reactions, it is as if the past and present were taking place at the same time. One woman heard an orchestra playing a popular song every time a certain part of her cortex was stimulated. Her retrieval of the song was so clear that she was convinced a phonograph in the operating room was being turned on and off. Under ordinary circumstances, the song would seem to have been "lost forever" in the woman's mind, but apparently this was not the case. It seems, instead, that long-term memory is more or less permanent, and when we talk about loss of long-term memory, we are really talking about the difficulty of retrieval.

But it is easy to overemphasize the problems of retrieving information. For the most part, we are pretty effective at retrieval (Norman, 1969). We often locate a word or name so quickly that we barely realize anything has happened. When confronted with the unfamiliar—a person we have never met before, a word whose form and meaning are new—we can usually determine rather quickly that we "don't know" the person or the word. And generally our instantaneous "hunch" is correct. This means that somehow, without being aware of it, we rapidly sort through parts of our long-term memory bank to see if a certain name or face or word is "in there" or not. Such capacity is remarkable and should not be taken lightly.

We should distinguish between memory that is *available* and memory that is *accessible* (Mandler, 1967). A memory may be available—it is there if we know how to get to it—but inaccessible if we have not found a process or route that will lead us to it. Not all the information in long-term memory is accessible at any given time, though apparently it is always available.

Cueing. We carry on the search for missing information by means of **cues.** As previously noted, a single item in memory may be grouped or organized under several different categories. Cueing may be seen as a way of checking each of a number of categories in turn, to see if one of them contains the information we are looking for. The better the information is organized, and the more categories it is filed under, the more likely it is that our search will lead to retrieval.

Suppose that long after you have read this paragraph, finished the chapter, and put away the book, you need some information about the search process in memory. You remember vaguely that such a process exists, but you don't remember what it is called. If you look at the book's index, you might find what you want under "retrieval" or under "memory." But if it had only been indexed under "cue," the term you cannot think of, you would not have been able to find it, unless your eye happened to fall on the word "cue" in the index and you recognized it as the term you were looking for.

By analogy, if you are trying to remember something and find that you cannot, you will increase your chances of eventually coming up with the memory by trying different approaches and different cues. If the information is indexed in several different ways, you will be more likely to retrieve it. When you cannot come up with something when it is needed, as during an exam, it may well be because none of the cues you tried were the right ones. But when the answer comes to you that night, it is usually because the search process has been continuing without your being aware of it, and eventually you have hit on the right cue to lead you to the memory.

An example of highly personal and arbitrary cueing is the **mnemonic device,** whereby we remember a fact by associating it with something else. If all other historical dates become inaccessible to us, that of Columbus's voyage sticks in our mind because somebody made up the mnemonic jingle "In fourteen hundred ninety-two, Columbus sailed the ocean blue." "Two" and "blue" have no logical connection with each other, but the cue of this rhyme assures us that it could not have been "ninety-three" or "ninety-four."

THE "TIP-OF-THE-TONGUE" PHENOMENON

"It's on the tip of my tongue, but I can't quite remember. . ." The frustration of almost, but not quite, being able to recall someone's name or a familiar word is something we have all experienced. Now this problem has received an official scientific name: the "tip-of-the-tongue" phenomenon (TOT).

In this state, people are likely to recall words that resemble the word they are searching for. Brown and McNeill (1966) gave some college students the definitions of words that are not in everyone's vocabulary: "sampan," for example. The words the students came up with when trying to recall the right word sometimes resembled the word in meaning (junk, houseboat), but most often in sound (Siam, sarong).

To put it more scientifically, in the TOT state we have some information about the word we want—even, sometimes, the number of syllables or its first letter. The closer we are to remembering it, the more accurate is our information. Thus, recall may occur a little at a time.

Brown and McNeill concluded that both *phonetic* (the sound of the word) and *semantic* (the meaning of the word) features are needed for word retrieval. Through remembering such features, an individual can eventually recall a word that is on "the tip of his tongue." Later research by Yarmey (1973) substantiates Brown and McNeill's findings, but also indicates that associations between words and events can help in the search for the correct word or name. For example, in identifying a well-known person from a photograph, a subject may realize: "I saw her on the morning news program last week. That's right; it's Barbara Walters." Such situational cues may assist the process of retrieval.

(Picture Collection, New York Public Library)

We have been talking about retrieval and cueing mostly in terms of conscious search for a piece of information. But, as with the woman undergoing brain surgery, it can be a less voluntary process. One cue can trigger different memories. If you are listening to a lecture on European history and the professor mentions Napoleon, you may remember some facts about the Battle of Waterloo. But "Napoleon" may also conjure up a kind of French pastry, a trip you once made to Naples, or a man you know who is shorter than you are. The opposite, too, can be the case: a variety of different cues can lead to the same memory. The smell of an apple pie in the oven, the taste of apple pie, or the words "apple pie" printed in a book can all lead you to remember a general or particular experience of apple pie.

Material stored in the memory is organized into **categories,** like the card index of a library. Memories are organized patterns, not just random facts. It has been shown that the recall of information is much better if it is stored in an organized fashion than if it is presented randomly. Categories are important for storing information in long-term memory, but they are even more important for retrieving stored information. The more categories you are able to store something under,

MNEMONIC DEVICES

Mnemonic devices are methods of organizing material that help us to remember it quickly and easily. When a person uses a mnemonic device, he consciously imposes some sort of systematic order on the material he wants to learn. He may use rhythm, meanings, or groupings as a means of organizing separate items.

Some of the simplest mnemonic devices are the rhymes and jingles we often use to remember dates and other facts. "Thirty days hath September, April, June, and November" helps us recall how many days there are in a month. "I before E except after C, or when sounded like A, as in neighbor and weigh" gives us a clue as to how to spell certain words. Other simple mnemonic devices involve making words or sentences out of the material to be recalled. The colors of the visible spectrum—red, orange, yellow, green, blue, indigo, violet—can be remembered by using their first letters to form the name ROY G. BIV. In remembering musical notes, the spaces in the treble clef form the word FACE, while the lines in the clef may be remembered by "Every Good Boy Does Fine."

Greek and Roman orators used a *topical system* of mnemonics to memorize long speeches so they could deliver them without the aid of written notes. They would visit a large house or temple and walk through the rooms in a definite order, noting where specific objects were placed within each room. When the plan of the building and its contents were memorized, the orator would go through the rooms in his mind, placing images of material to be remembered at different places in the rooms. To retrieve the material during the speech, he would imagine himself going through the building and, by association, would recall each point of his speech as he came to each object and each room.

Another kind of mnemonic system that helps in serial recall is the number-peg technique. Each number is visualized as a picture resembling the shape of the number: 1 is a candle, 2 is a swan, 3 a pitchfork, 4 a pennant, 5 a hand, 6 a snake, 7 a semaphore, 8 an hourglass, 9 a mailbox, and 10 a spoon and dish. The items to be remembered are linked, in order, to the pictures. The first item in a list might be visualized holding a candle, the second feeding swans, the third using a pitchfork, and so on. Then the items are recalled in order by re-evoking the mental images (Young & Gibson, 1962).

To investigate the effects of using a mnemonic system on the ability to remember, Smith and Noble (1965) divided their subjects into two groups. The first group was given a 1-hour lecture on a mnemonic system that involved linking items to visual images. Then they practiced the method for 4 days on their own. The second group received no training and were told not to use any particular system in learning. Both groups were then asked to learn a list of ten words. The words varied in meaningfulness. The people who had received instruction in mnemonics were able to recall the relatively meaningless words much better than the untrained group, and required less time to relearn them. On the more meaningful items, however, the mnemonic system did not appear to have any effect.

A later study by Bower (1973) demonstrates the greater effectiveness of mnemonic techniques as compared with rote learning. College students were asked to study five successive "shopping lists" of 20 unrelated words. They were given 5 seconds to study each word, as well as time to study each list as a whole. At the end of the session, they were asked to recall all 100 items. Subjects using mnemonic devices remembered an average of 72 items, but the control group (who generally relied on simple rote learning) remembered only 28. The subjects trained in mnemonic techniques were also much more successful at recalling the position of each item and the list on which it appeared.

the better. If two people are thinking about someone they knew in high school and cannot remember her name, one may be searching through the categories "red face," "curly hair," and "algebra class," while the other may be cueing in to "antique cars" and "tennis team." Pooling your categories will give you a much better chance of finally remembering the woman's name.

To say that the organization and number of categories available to the retrieval process facilitates that retrieval may seem like a mouthful, but it can also be said in very everyday terms. The more we know about something, and the more *ways* we know about it, the easier it is to remember it.

Biological Bases of Memory

Unfortunately, everyday terms cannot take us the whole way. Up to this point, we have been describing memory and the processes of memory metaphorically, likening them to computers and library card files. But we do not really carry computers inside our skulls. What, then, are the physiological processes that take place when we are remembering something? What is actually going on inside the brain? Where and how is memory stored and retrieved?

The Location of Memory

One of the most important things psychologists have been trying to find out for the last 100 years is whether memory is localized in a certain part of the brain. In Chapter 2 we learned that some functions, such as vision and speech, are localized in this way. Early in the nineteenth century, it was believed that this was the case with memory too. *Phrenology*—which held that specific mental operations took place in specific areas of the brain and could be determined by "reading" the shape of the skull—was fashionable then. Phrenologists believed that the "memory center" was located behind the eyes. A person with bulging eyes, they reasoned, would have a large memory center and thus a great capacity for remembering things.

This theory of memory is no longer current. By the 1920s it seemed apparent that no particular part of the brain was solely responsible for memory. In a pivotal experiment (Lashley, 1950), parts of rats' cerebrums were removed. Their memories were found to be weakened by having one or another part of the brain taken out, but the memories were still present. The degree or amount of recall, therefore, seemed to depend on the mass of the brain, regardless of what specific part was missing. A single memory, it was surmised, can be stored in numerous parts of the brain, so that removal of a part can diminish, but not erase, the memory. More recent experiments have supported this theory, although with some qualifications. In experiments with monkeys who had been trained to perform a certain task (Harlow, 1959), it was found that the removal of part of the brain affected some monkeys' competency at that task, while other monkeys were entirely unaffected. This suggests that a given memory may lodge in one of many

(Culver Pictures)

areas of the brain, but in no specific one. Further experiments have indicated that memory can, so to speak, be moved around—if one portion of the brain is removed, some other part of the brain may take up the job of remembering.

One possible explanation for the widespread storage of memories draws on the fact that a number of different senses seem to be involved in any one memory. A single experience might be stored in the brain's visual areas, its auditory areas, and its areas for smell and touch—all at the same time. Evidence to support this notion comes from studies in which one area of an animal's brain is damaged and then retrieval cues are limited to the particular sensory modality controlled by that area—perhaps the visual area is removed and the retrieval cues are limited to only black-and-white visual images, with no color, sounds, or smells to accompany them. In situations like this, retrieval does seem to be seriously impaired. Even without brain damage, limiting the retrieval cues to only one sense can reduce remembering. If you were to see a black-and-white silhouette of someone you know, you might well have more difficulty recognizing her than if you simultaneously saw her profile and the color of her hair, heard her voice, and smelled the brand of perfume she often wears.

The "holographic" theory of memory claims that memory failure does not occur because of destruction of the storage mechanism itself. Instead, it is caused by damage to the processing centers that act to *retrieve* the stored material. If there is localization, it is not localization of the stored memory itself, but rather of the processing centers that make the material available.

Where are these processing centers? The cerebral cortex seems to receive information from the separate senses. One section, near the back of the frontal lobe, takes this sensory information and organizes it. At the base of the cortex is another section called the limbic system. It appears that the hippocampus, one part of the limbic system, is instrumental in transferring verbal information from short-term to long-term memory. People damaged in this area can remember events that have just occurred, but often have to write everything down to remember it any longer, because the brain's ability to record this information is limited to the short-term span. Thus, much of the evidence about the input and retrieval function seems to point to the cerebral cortex.

The Unit of Storage

The second major question when we talk about the biological mechanisms of memory has to do with just what the individual unit of memory is. There is general agreement that memory involves a permanent alteration in the structure of the brain (Doty, 1974). Yet researchers disagree as to the nature of these changes.

(Richard B. Klein, Nancy Palmer Photo Agency)

One theory is that sensory experience produces a fragile, highly perishable neural response. This response is called a **memory trace** and is probably electrical in nature. It is as fleeting as a tiny shock we get from a doorknob if we have just walked across a thick carpet. But if this initial memory trace is strengthened in some way, as by repetition, it becomes something else. Instead of being simply a momentary response, it becomes an actual *change* in the nervous system. It is by now chemical or structural, not electrical, in nature. This more or less permanent structural change is called an **engram.** The development of the engram might be compared to a walk through the forest. If you take a given route once, you are unlikely to leave much trace of having been there. But if you take the same route again and again, a path is gradually worn down and the forest is changed.

Proponents of this theory think of the memory trace and the engram as active processes, not as tangible entities. They are dynamic and cannot be pinned down to any specific location. This is why we emphasize that engrams are changes.

Another theory has been touched upon earlier, in Chapter 2. If memory can be seen in terms of neural processes, then the sensory information coming into the brain would stimulate one neuron, which in turn would stimulate another, which in turn would stimulate another, until this stimulation came full circle and became a "reverberating circuit," which would permanently record the new information (Hebb, 1949). Upon repetition of this circuit, the memory would become more and more firmly entrenched, until it became a "cell assembly." Any part of this permanent assembly, when stimulated, would set off the entire circuit. If we received only a partial stimulus after that, the whole mechanism would go to work without individual bits of memory having to be triggered one by one. Hebb's theory, then, would account for the "associative" powers of memory. If several different units of information have been programmed into the same circuit, the stimulation of one would bring forth all the others.

Cermak (1972) notes that Hebb's theory has been frequently attacked because of physiological evidence that conflicts with the model. Cermak points out that "reverberation of single neurons actually lasts only a few seconds, not minutes" (p. 172). This means that neural reverberation cannot in itself be responsible for the circuit's continuing to reverberate. There must be some other internal or external mechanism to ensure that the process does not stop. Hebb has modified this (and other) aspects of his theory in the light of neurological findings. Yet Cermak argues that most evidence contradicts the theory of specific circuitry in learning and memory.

In addition, McGaugh (1974) has questioned all of the prominent theories concerning the neural bases of memory. He claims that, despite considerable speculation, there is no clear empirical evidence to support these theories.

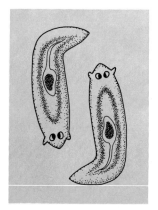

Planaria.

Other researchers have proposed a different view—that memory is carried by ribonucleic acid (RNA). As we saw in Chapter 2, RNA plays a vital role in protein production in the body's cells. Since RNA is capable of "remembering" the DNA's instructions for making proteins, it is a likely candidate for storing other kinds of memory.

Tests concerning the relevance of RNA to memory have been conducted with planaria (flatworms). If planaria are cut in half, the tail part grows a new head, and the head part grows a new tail. In these experiments (McConnell, Jacobson, & Kimble, 1959), planaria were conditioned to curl up in response to light. They were then cut in half. Some were left to regenerate in untreated water, and the others were put into water containing an enzyme that destroys RNA. When the two groups of planaria had grown their new heads and tails, they were tested to see whether they had retained their former learning. The regenerated planaria whose RNA had not been tampered with showed an ability to relearn quickly—both heads and tails remembered their previous conditioning. With the worms whose regeneration had taken place in treated water, it was a different story. Only the head ends that had grown new tails retained any of their previous conditioning. The tail ends that had grown new heads were "naïve" and showed no sign that they had ever been conditioned.

This seems to mean that the RNA in the tails of the plain-water planaria made it possible for the memory of the conditioning to be passed on to the new heads. But the planaria deprived of RNA did not have such a faculty—the head part retained the memory anyway, as might be expected, but the tail part was unable to grow a head that could profit from the tail's memory. In one study, planaria that had been conditioned were ground up and fed to other planaria (McConnell, 1962). Along with absorbing the first group, the cannibal planaria seemed to absorb what the first group had learned. The cannibals performed significantly better on the learning task than planaria that had been fed untrained worms.

Some doubt has been cast on these studies because other researchers have not been able to repeat them and consistently obtain the same results. Also, some psychologists object because the learning involved—response to light—is a natural response of the animal. These researchers want to see transfer of discrimination training before they will support McConnell's work (Deutsch, 1973).

Forgetting

You leave for a weekend visit, suitcase in hand, but you are troubled by the vague feeling that you have forgotten something—and more often than not, you have. You panic at a final examination, groping for the name of the Secretary of Agriculture, but it eludes you. Your old great-aunt inquires after the health of your grandfather, who died

"I'm getting close to the answer but can't for the life of me remember what the problem was."
(Copyright © 1969. Reprinted by permission of Saturday Review and Roland Michaud.)

5 years ago. You had something else on your mind when you put down your sunglasses, and now you cannot find them. You have not used a lawn mower in 2 years, and you have no idea how to start it. A friend coldly informs you that you had said you would meet him yesterday at four. A year ago you lost an important tennis match to your arch-rival, but now you have forgotten the anger you felt then, and you are the best of friends.

All of these are instances of the same phenomenon. Or are they? In all the examples above, something once learned or experienced has "slipped the mind." But are all the causes the same? What happens when we forget something? Has it gone away forever, or is there something standing in the way of remembering?

The commonest kind of forgetting is forgetting of an isolated fact, something that has nothing to do with anything else. If information is stored with a context of associations—filed in as many categories as possible, as we said earlier—it will be easier to remember, because there will be several alternate paths by which it can be recalled. Thus, if the name of the Secretary of Agriculture were the same as the grocer down the street, you probably would not have forgotten it, even under stress. Repetition, as we have also seen, makes it less likely that something will be forgotten—once you relearn how to start the lawn mower, it will be easier the next time you do it. Things can be forgotten, too, because we do not want to remember them, as with the tennis game. Or because we want to remember so badly that we search along the same memory route again and again—in which case the material will probably come to us later, when the need to remember is not so urgent and a new path to the forgotten information is found.

Psychologists have various theories of why we forget. Some of these are applicable to all kinds of forgetting, and some only to more special instances. Of course, theories of memory and theories of forgetting are really two sides of the same coin. Much information about forgetting has already been covered, by implication, in the material on memory we have already presented. But let us examine a few specific theories and questions.

Decay of the Memory Trace

We have already discussed the concept of the memory trace, and the transformation of that trace into a more or less permanent engram. The **trace-decay theory** of forgetting states that if the pathway is not used, the memory will fade and eventually disappear. It should be emphasized that the theory of trace decay is applicable only to short-term memory, where a very limited number of items are held for a very limited span of time. When memory traces decay here, the loss is permanent—the memory can never be retrieved. This sort of forgetting is usually just as well. If every passing detail of our lives went into

(*Picture Collection, New York Public Library*)

long-term memory, it would be a jumble of irrelevant, trivial, unrelated data, like a library so full of books that they could never be catalogued or arranged in order. In this sense, short-term forgetting is not a "problem" and has not received the attention that long-term forgetting has received.

But long-term forgetting can lead to serious problems. To do many jobs, for example, we must remember various facts, concepts, theories, names, addresses, and dates. Forgetting can impair performance on the job. In addition, our friends can become upset when we forget a birthday, or take them to a restaurant that they hate, or smoke in their presence when this always causes them to have coughing fits. Long-term forgetting can come from several causes: other things on one's mind, the passage of time without a task's having been repeated, senility, "absent-mindedness," or anxiety under stress. Several theories of the mechanics of long-term forgetting have been advanced, and we will discuss the major ones.

Interference

According to the **interference theory,** we forget things because other things get in the way. Interference may come from information we acquired before the item we are trying to remember or from new information we have acquired since. These two different types of interference are called proactive and retroactive inhibition (Cermak, 1972).

Proactive inhibition, according to this theory, is the major cause of forgetting information from long-term memory. Previous information or experience interferes with retrieval of something you have learned more recently. The more similarity there is between the old and the new learning, the more interference there will be. If you are trying to learn Italian and you have studied French for years, you may find yourself thinking of French words when you try to remember the Italian

Figure 5-6

A diagram of the experimental procedure used to measure proactive inhibition. The experimental group suffers the effects of proactive inhibition from List A and, when asked to recall List B, does not perform as well as the control group.

	Step 1	Step 2	Step 3
Experimental group	Learn List A	Learn List B	Recall List B
Control group	Rest or engage in unrelated activity	Learn List B	Recall List B

HOW TO IMPROVE RETENTION

Psychologists have isolated several factors that generally aid in learning effectively and improving retention.

Distribution of practice. For most kinds of material, spaced learning is more efficient than massed learning. Ebbinghaus (1885) found that four 15-minute practice periods, spaced a day apart, were more efficient than 1 solid hour of practice in learning nonsense syllables. However, the optimal distribution of practice and rest periods varies with the task.

Intervening activities. What we do during the time between learning and recall is a factor in retention. We are most apt to retain material if we go to sleep immediately after learning it, because there are no intervening activities to interfere with retention. Jenkins and Dallenbach (1924) found that six out of ten learned nonsense syllables could be recalled by people who had gone to sleep after learning them; people who had stayed awake could recall only one.

Knowledge of results. If we are informed of our progress, either by being told how well or poorly we are doing or by seeing the results directly, we can correct our errors. This is the principle behind programmed instruction—the learner receives immediate feedback, telling him how well he is doing. Feedback seems also to provide reinforcement. A delay in feedback does not in itself appear to influence retention, but it does allow intervening activities to interfere.

Whole vs. part learning. Whole learning is usually more efficient than learning by parts and then trying to put them all together, but much depends on the way the material is organized. Consider the following lists of words:

1. North, Man, Red, Spring, Woman, East, Autumn, Yellow, Summer, Boy, Blue, West, Winter, Girl, Green, South.
2. North, East, South, West, Spring, Summer, Autumn, Winter, Red, Yellow, Green, Blue, Man, Woman, Boy, Girl.

The second list is easier to learn because of the way it is organized (Deese & Hulse, 1967). Material can be efficiently learned by parts, however, if the parts are logical sub-units of the whole.

Meaning. It is easier to learn and remember something if you understand its overall meaning and can relate it to material you already know. The organization of learned material is crucial to both storage and retrieval.

Motivation. Continuous routine repetition will be less effective than fewer repetitions accompanied by an intent to learn. We are more receptive to learning if we know that the material will be useful to us later, though we may only remember it for a short time—long enough to take a test, for example.

word for "water." If you had chosen to study Russian, however, the amount of proactive inhibition would be less because Russian is not as similar to French.

In one experiment, two groups of subjects were tested for their

(Mimi Forsyth, Monkmeyer
Press Photo Service)

retention of a list of words they had been given to remember (Underwood, 1957). One group had previously learned several other lists, and the other had not. There was a great discrepancy between the ability of the two groups to recall the new list of words—the people who had had no other learning task to perform first retained 65 percent more than the others.

Retroactive inhibition, on the other hand, is caused by items that have been learned *after* what you are trying to remember. Experiments have indicated that the best time for learning something that you want to remember later is just before going to sleep. Sleeping is about the most inactive thing you can do, and the amount of retroactive inhibition would then be at its minimum. As an example, just before you go to sleep tonight, try concentrating on something—say, an errand you must

Figure 5-7
A diagram of the experimental procedure used to measure retroactive inhibition. The experimental group usually does not perform as well on tests of recall as the control group, which does not suffer from retroactive inhibition from the second list of words or syllables.

	Step 1	Step 2	Step 3
Experimental group	Learn List A	Learn List B	Recall List A
Control group	Learn List A	Rest or engage in unrelated activity	Recall List A

do tomorrow. You may not remember it the minute your eyes open tomorrow morning, but you should have recalled it by the time you leave the house.

When you are trying to learn new material, the rehearsal necessary to transfer the information to long-term memory can easily be disrupted. As with proactive inhibition, the more similar the interposed material is to what you are trying to remember, the more the new material is likely to interfere. If you go for a walk after studying ten pages of American history, the new material (buying a newspaper, seeing a Baltimore oriole) is dissimilar enough from American history that you will probably still be able to recall who was vice-president under Woodrow Wilson. But if you go from your American history book straight into a heated discussion of baseball statistics, which would also involve remembering names and dates, the name of the vice-president is much less likely to stay with you.

If there is a long list of material to be learned, we can see both sorts of interference at work at the same time. Their interaction produces what are called **primacy** and **recency effects.** If you are given a long list of nonsense syllables to learn, you will probably be able to remember more of the syllables at the beginning of the list (the primacy effect) and at the end of the list (the recency effect) than in the middle. The ones that come first are subject only to retroactive inhibition from the syllables that come later in the list; the ones at the end are subject only

Figure 5-8

Primacy and recency effects in learning a list of nonsense syllables. Fewer errors occur in remembering the items at the beginning and end of the list than in remembering those in the middle. (Adapted from J. W. McCary, Jr., et al., "Serial Position Curves in Verbal Learning." *Science*, February 6, 1953, pp. 131–134.)

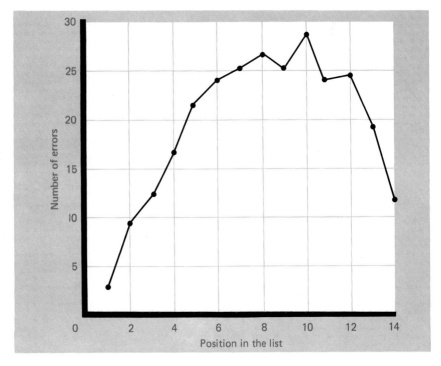

to proactive inhibition from the syllables that precede them. But the nonsense syllables in the middle of the list get hit from both sides— proactive inhibition from the syllables that precede them and retro-active inhibition from the ones that follow them. Thus they are much less likely to be retained. As you can see from this example, the inter-relationship of proactive and retroactive inhibition, and their effects on memory of learned material, can be fairly complicated.

Is there any way to overcome the forgetting that results from these kinds of interference? There may be. Tulving and Psotka (1971) tested the effects of retrieval cues on retroactive inhibition. Subjects were asked to learn lists of words that were grouped in specific categories, such as types of buildings and military ranks. They were given a variety of tests, including **cued-recall** tests (in which the names of the categories were provided as cues in order to spur memory). Results indicated that, in general, learning the subsequent lists did interfere with recall of previous lists. This is simply retroactive inhibition. However, when cued recall was used, memory for the early lists became nearly as good as it was immediately after the lists were originally learned. This suggests that, under certain conditions, some forgetting (in this case, due to interference) can be overcome through the use of appropriate retrieval cues.

Motivated Forgetting

So far, as we have talked about forgetting long-term memories, our discussion has had one assumption underlying it: that we *want* to remember things accurately. But go back again to the beginning of this section, and look at the situations we cited as examples. Does the assumption that we want to remember apply to all of them? The date with your friend might have been forgotten because you had something unpleasant to tell him, or to pay him back for keeping you waiting three-quarters of an hour last week. Your great-aunt might have been so grieved by your grandfather's death that she does not want to remember it. What you vaguely felt you had not put in your suitcase could have been the algebra notes that were going to spoil your week-end. And forgetting how furious you were when you lost the tennis match helped perpetuate your friendship.

Without realizing it, you may blank out memories that are unpleasant or that conflict with your own idea of the person you want to be or the world you want to live in. **Repression** defends you from remem-bering things that are so painful that you would rather not think about them. What if the name of the Secretary of Agriculture was the same as, not the friendly grocer on the corner, but the bully at a summer camp who pushed you into the water before you had learned to swim? Repression could well be a factor in your forgetting his name. There is a general, and probably praiseworthy, desire on the part of human

Figure 5-9
The nonsense syllables and words used by Glucksberg and King in their experiment on repression. In the first stage of the experiment, subjects learned the syllable-word pairs in columns A and B. In the second stage, they learned the words in column D, some of which were accompanied by mild electric shocks. The words in column C served as implicit links to the words in column B. The syllable-word pairs that were associated with shock became much harder to recall than the pairs that were not associated with shock. (From S. Glucksberg and J. L. King, "Motivated Forgetting Mediated by Implicit Verbal Chaining." *Science*, October 27, 1967, p. 518.)

| List 1 | | Inferred Chained Word | List 2 |
A	B	C	D
CEF	stem	flower	smell[*]
DAX	memory	mind	brain[*]
YOV	soldier	army	navy
VUX	trouble	bad	good[*]
WUB	wish	want	need
GEX	justice	peace	war[*]
JID	thief	steal	take[*]
ZIL	ocean	water	drink
LAJ	command	order	disorder
MYV	fruit	apple	tree[*]

[*] These words were paired with shock during the second stage of the experiment.

beings to see themselves, and to some extent, the world around them, as friendly, civilized, and reasonable. The memories that are in harmony with this view are acceptable to us, but those that are in conflict with it are often blotted out.

At its most extreme, repression can bring about **hysterical amnesia.** Screenwriters have gotten a lot of footage over the years with amnesia victims, and we are all familiar with some form of the story: a man wakes up in a strange city, unable to remember his name or where he came from or how he got there, but perfectly capable of reciting the alphabet or frying an egg. The memory of any personal information is gone. It makes a good melodramatic story—and it does happen. In hysterical amnesia, there is no apparent organic reason for the failure of memory, but usually something in the person's life has been so frightening or so unacceptable that he has totally repressed all personal memories rather than remember that one incident.

The conditions of hysterical amnesia have been approximated experimentally. In one study, college students were taught a list of word pairs. After learning the list of pairs, they were read a second list of words, some of which were consistently accompanied by a mild but unpleasant electric shock. This second list was composed of words that appeared to be related to the word pairs in the first list. If the students

(Esther Bubley, Time-Life Picture Agency)

had learned the pair "thief" and "steal," for example, the corresponding word on the second list was "take." When they were tested for their retention of the first list, the apparent association of the "shocked" word with the word pair led to a significant drop in their ability to remember the original pair, even though the paired words had had no shock directly attached to them (Glucksberg & King, 1967).

Organic Amnesia

Organic amnesia is memory loss caused by physiological factors: injury, disease, alcoholism, nutritional deficiencies, or brain damage. This sort of amnesia may be permanent or temporary, depending on the nature and extent of the damage. We do not know exactly why memory fails under these conditions, except that some vital processing center in the brain has failed to function and made retrieval impossible—just as the loss of your right index finger would hamper your ability to write.

Older people are sometimes absent-minded about the present. For instance, a student ran into Albert Einstein one day on the Princeton University campus. They chatted for a while, and then the student asked Dr. Einstein to join him for lunch. "Which way was I walking when you stopped me?" Einstein asked. "That way," pointed the student. "Oh," said Einstein, "then I've already eaten, thank you very much." This is an example of simple absent-mindedness. But older people sometimes experience **global demential amnesia.** In such cases, they are consistently absent-minded about the present, but have strong memories about things of personal importance in the past.

Amnesia can also occur as a brief, isolated episode, caused by severe temperature change, low blood sugar (hypoglycemia), epilepsy, insufficient flow of blood to the brain, or certain drugs. When this happens, it can be entirely without warning. The victim will be unaware that anything is wrong until the episode is over.

At the beginning of this section on forgetting, we asked whether an experience or a piece of information goes away forever when we forget it. In forgetting of material that has entered long-term memory, the answer seems to be that it does not. Rather, our paths to it are lost, sometimes temporarily, sometimes irretrievably. The stored item itself is still present. But for some reason—emotional or psychological, subjective or objective, external or internal—we have no means to get at it. Our discussion of forgetting, then, emphasizes a major point that we have tried to make throughout this chapter on memory. Memory, as it functions—or as it does not—is best seen in terms of processes. We said earlier that it was not to be thought of as a storage chest that things were randomly put into. Perhaps a better metaphor would be that memory is the key to that chest, or the act of opening it, to store or retrieve information. It is the *how* that is important—the order in which we have put the things away, and the ways we have of getting them out again.

REPRESSION

Freud often attributed the forgetting of names and places to repression. One of his patients, whom he called Mr. Y, fell in love with a woman who did not reciprocate his feelings. She married another man, Mr. X. Although Mr. Y was well acquainted with Mr. X before the marriage and had business dealings with him, he found himself unable to remember Mr. X's name and had to ask people what it was every time he had to write to him about a business matter. Since Mr. X was his rival and had married the woman he loved, Mr. Y, Freud believed, subconsciously did not want to know anything about him (Freud, 1938).

In another case reported by Freud, a student was questioned about the teachings of Epicurus on a philosophy examination. When asked to name a latter-day follower of Epicurus, the student recalled overhearing someone in a cafe mention the name Pierre Gassendi; he answered with that name. The professor was surprised and asked him how he knew this. Embarrassed to tell the truth, the student replied that he had been interested in Gassendi for a long time. This so impressed the examiner that he passed the student with high honors. Afterward, the student could never remember the name Pierre Gassendi because of his guilty conscience about the test episode.

In recent years, Freud's theory of repression as a cause of forgetting has come under attack. For example, Freud suggested that the forgetting of many dreams is due to repression. Cohen (1974b) has experimented with recall and non-recall of dream material, as explained earlier in this chapter. He has found that inability to recall dreams is not caused by repression. Instead, he points to two other factors that can limit dream recall—*interference* (when events after waking draw attention away from dream material), and *salience* (the impact of the dream on the dreamer; its intensity, pace, and emotional force).

Holmes (1974) argues more generally that, despite many research efforts, there has been no consistent evidence developed to support Freud's theory of repression. He agrees that we do recall selectively, but suggests that selective recall results more from selective attention, both during the experience and during later attempts at recall. For example, after watching two friends argue, you will not recall the same things that a trained therapist would recall. But you could not be charged with *repressing* information that you never truly focused on.

Summary

1. Memory is an active process that sifts, sorts, and reorganizes information and makes it available to us for use at a later time.
2. The function of memory is to retain or hold on to events and information from the past. Recall, recognition, and savings are three ways of measuring *retention*.
3. *Recall*, usually the least sensitive measure of retention, involves the reproduction of learned material either verbatim or through reconstruction.

In *serial recall* the material is remembered in a specific order; in *free recall* it may be remembered in any order.

4. *Recognition* is generally a more sensitive measure of retention than recall. Upon seeing or hearing the information, a person may remember having learned it, even though he could not recall it.

5. Even if recall and recognition fail, relearning may still be easier than the initial learning. The *savings* in time and effort to learn something a second time demonstrates retention.

6. Memory can be thought of as an information-processing system with three levels—the sensory store, short-term memory, and long-term memory. At each level, information receives certain kinds of processing and is either discarded or stored.

7. The *sensory store* receives sensory impressions from the external world. It has a huge capacity, but its retention time is extremely brief and only a portion of what enters it passes to the next level.

8. *Short-term memory* is more selective and slightly more permanent than the sensory store, but it has a much smaller capacity for material. It is possible to hold more information in short-term memory by *chunking* material together so that several bits of information form a single item. *Repetition* is used to retain items temporarily for immediate use. The interposition of new material can easily interfere with short-term memory. In order for material to be transferred to long-term memory, repeated *rehearsal* is necessary, as is *coding*—abbreviating and integrating new information into the material already in long-term memory.

9. *Long-term memory* has a vast capacity for information. It is highly organized and relatively permanent, and it assimilates new items by relating them to the categories it already contains. Whether something enters long-term memory depends mostly on how it can be organized; familiar information is assimilated more readily than unfamiliar information.

10. The *retrieval process* is the means by which a person draws upon the information in long-term memory. A memory is *available* at all times, but may not be *accessible* if no process or route leads to it.

11. Material stored in memory is organized into *categories*. The retrieval process depends on *cues*, which lead to the correct category. The *mnemonic device* is an example of a highly personal and arbitrary set of cues. A piece of information may be stored under more than one category; the more categories something is stored under, the easier it is to retrieve. Some material in long-term memory is organized by meaning (*semantic memory*) rather than by sound.

12. Experiments have found that memory is not located in one particular portion of the brain, but that a single memory can be stored in numerous parts. Some theories of memory claim that memory failure occurs because of damage to the processing centers that retrieve the stored material. The input and retrieval function seems to be located in the cerebral cortex.

13. There are several theories about physical changes in the brain when a memory is stored. One theory suggests that sensory experience produces a highly perishable neural response, probably electrical in nature, called a *memory trace*. If it is strengthened in some way, it produces a more or less permanent change, either chemical or structural, known as an *engram*.

14. Another theory sees memory in terms of neural processes—sensory information stimulates one neuron, which in turn stimulates another, until the

stimulation comes full circle and forms a *reverberating circuit.* With repetition, the circuit becomes a *cell assembly.* Stimulating any part of the assembly can set off the entire circuit, without individual bits of memory having to be triggered one by one.

15. A third theory holds that memory is carried by *ribonucleic acid* (*RNA*). Experimenters have found measurable changes in RNA molecules after learning has taken place. Experiments with planaria also point to RNA as the agent of memory transfer.

16. There are also several theories to explain why we "forget" items that have been stored. The *trace-decay theory* of forgetting helps to explain loss of information from short-term memory. This theory is based on the belief that if a memory trace is not developed, it will never form the more permanent engram and thus will be lost forever.

17. Other theories of forgetting apply to long-term memory. The *interference theory* says we forget things because other things we learn get in the way. *Proactive inhibition* occurs when previous information or experience interferes with retrieval of something we have learned more recently. *Retroactive inhibition* is caused by items that have been learned after what we are trying to remember. In both cases, the more similar the information, the greater the interference. Both types of interference can be at work at the same time, and their interaction produces what are called *primacy* and *recency effects.* We are apt to remember more items at the beginning of a list (the primacy effect) and at the end of a list (the recency effect) than in the middle.

18. *Motivated forgetting* refers to the inability to remember things that we do not want to remember. *Repression* is one method of defending ourselves from remembering things that are painful. Repression at its extreme can result in *hysterical amnesia. Organic amnesia,* on the other hand, is memory loss caused by physiological factors, such as injury or disease.

Suggested Readings

Cermak, L. S., *Human Memory: Research and Theory* (New York: Ronald Press, 1972). A good general text on memory that stresses, in particular, the view of memory as a continuum rather than as separate levels.

Keele, S. W., *Attention and Human Performance* (Pacific Palisades, Calif.: Goodyear, 1973). An experimentally oriented text with good discussions of levels of memory, coding, and retrieval.

McGaugh, J. L., "Facilitation of Memory Storage Processes." In F. Leukel (Ed.), *Issues in Physiological Psychology* (St. Louis: Mosby, 1974). An interesting article touching on a number of current concerns in the area of memory from a physiological point of view.

Norman, D. A., *Memory and Attention: An Introduction to Human Information Processing* (New York: Wiley, 1969). An analysis of memory in terms of the information-processing approach, stressing the levels of memory and the mental operations involved.

Underwood, B. J., "Are We Overloading Memory?" In A. W. Melton and E. Martin (Eds.), *Coding Processes in Human Memory* (Washington, D.C.: Winston, 1972). A good treatment of coding and recall vs. recognition phenomena by one of the significant researchers in the field of memory.

outline

THE UNITS OF THOUGHT 206

Images
Concepts
Language
Language Learning in Chimpanzees

DIRECTED THINKING 219

Logic and Reasoning
Steps in Problem Solving
Factors Affecting Problem Solving
Insight and Creative Problem Solving

ASSOCIATIVE THINKING 225

Daydreaming
Dreams
Creativity

SUMMARY 231

SUGGESTED READINGS 232

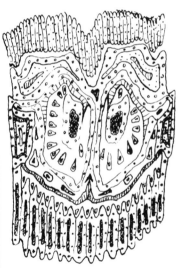

EIDETIC IMAGE

An eidetic image i...
of something that l...
imagery is sometin...
a person to describ...
even reading from...
imagery is much r...
possess the capab...

In a recent stu...
elementary school...
child was directed...
see all its various...
was told to look at...
needed at least 3 t...
when the picture v...
faded away. Image...
children could eras...

The quality of ei...
girl in Haber's stud...
recall them several...
images of three-dim...
eidetic image of one...
picture. Interesting...
formed no better th...

to a certain song. It...
elderly woman may...
her first big party, bu...

It is difficult to stu...
on people's reports o...
of course, are highly...
about imagery in thir...
think more in images...
physical scientists are...
while social scientists...
are present in most th...
it is possible to think...

Early in the twentie...
the image unnecessar...
of *imageless thought* ...
images, which we disc...
memory does not dep...
without them. They co...
people could solve simp...
they would name a g...
person being tested to...

Figure 6-1

An artist's drawings of two of his images after taking LSD. (From Mardi Horowitz, *Image Formation and Cognition*, p. 256. New York: Appleton-Century-Crofts, 1970. Used by permission of Prentice-Hall, Inc., Englewood Cliffs, N.J.)

Thinking

Thinking is one of our most frequent and least understood activities. We all do it and may even be somewhat proud of it. The English language is filled with clichés that only obscure the real nature of thought. You casually tell a friend, "Think for yourself!" as if somehow it were possible for a person *not* to think for himself. When someone disagrees or disappoints you, your anger may lead to the accusation, "You're just not thinking!"—meaning, of course, that he is not thinking in the precise way that *you* think. In fact, one of the reasons that psychologists are so interested in thinking is that it is such an individual process.

Thinking is also an incredibly complex process. Most of the time, we don't make a formal decision to think about something; we don't *think about thinking*. We just do it. It may only be when we look at the clock again and realize that half an hour has passed that it hits us—the last half-hour was spent *thinking*.

When psychologists study thinking, they ask two basic questions: What is it made up of? And, what does it do? In this chapter, we will talk first about what goes into thought and then go on to discuss how we use various kinds of thinking.

The Units of Thought

Images, concepts,
blocks of thought.
what does that th
him—probably hi
whistling. Second,
think about your b
are able to link hi
brothers or geome
about him. Finally
more," "egotist," "
him in your thinki

Images

We most often thi
can also employ ta
use more than one
forming visual im
Moreover, some pe
When thinking of t
it blinks its eyes; a
legs. A rarer form
identify one sense i
is light green" or "

Metaphor, like s
imagery (Pollio, 19
mon—in the Engli
examples as the *lo*
even a *hairy* eyeba
familiar idea in a c
in a familiar or ordi
images that are us
sensory understand

An image is our re
It need not mirror a
your image of a wall
lying on the sand, b
In addition, images
objects or sensation
ceptual distortions l
we can still have in

An image may be
or as dim as a kines

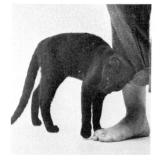

(Walter Chandoha)

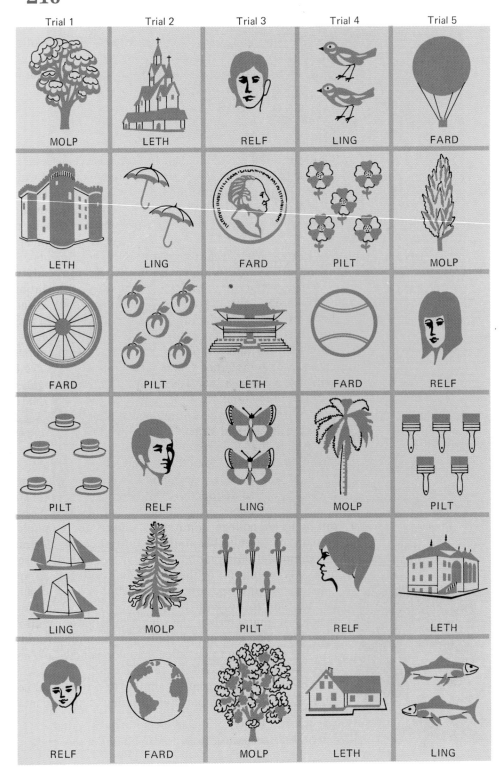

tive categories (for example, tall or short), we can see the relevant physical property (height) as being a continuum. Thus, people can be tiny, short, average, tall, gigantic, or anything in between. **Explanatory concepts** help us to understand and predict events and behavior by pointing out relationships between concepts. One example is the notion that jewelry is often expensive because the materials used to make it are rare. **Singular concepts** involve our understanding of a single object or event, such as the planet Mars, the Empire State Building, or the Emancipation Proclamation. Each person has particular associations with these terms. We may remember that the Empire State Building used to be the tallest building in the world, or that it was the location for dramatic scenes in the movie *King Kong*. Such memories are held together by their relationship to the singular concept "Empire State Building."

We have been talking about how concepts help us to think. But just as not all thinking is accurate or rational, not all concepts are either. Some are generally accepted as being correct until something comes along to modify them, as Columbus's voyage caused the earth to be moved from the concept "flat disk" to the concept "globe." Other concepts are held because of superstition or distorted perception. A gambler may base his bets on an elaborate system of concepts about which numbers and combinations are "lucky."

Certain concepts can lead to internal conflict. Saltz and Wickey (1965) presented persons who held liberal political beliefs with a person who apparently was both a liberal and an assassin. Many of the liberal subjects could not accept the fact that two such opposing concepts could coexist in the same person. The subjects' inability to resolve these contradictory concepts led to a kind of internal conflict known as "cognitive dissonance."* In an effort to resolve the conflict, some subjects claimed that the person was not really a liberal, but was actually working for the reactionary forces. Others denied that the person was really an assassin and insisted that he was being "framed."

◀ **Figure 6-2**
To find out how concepts are formed, Heidbreder showed these pictures to people one at a time, working down from the top of each column. The person being tested was asked to predict which of the nonsense words would be paired with each picture he saw. Since none of the pictures are the same, he had to learn to respond to the concepts of face, building, tree, and so forth. (Adapted from E. Heidbreder, "The Attainment of Concepts: III. The Problem." *Journal of Psychology,* 1947, 24, 93–138.)

Language

Our ability to think is strongly bound to language, the most sophisticated and intricate set of signs we have for things. Before we examine the function of language in thinking, we should know something about signs in general.

Signs are representations of what exists in the world of objects and situations. They *stand for* something or for the fact that such and such is the case. One kind of sign is language, but there are nonlinguistic signs as well. If someone shakes his head, you know he is responding negatively. If you see a man with a white cane, you know that he is blind. Mathematical symbols can represent distance, speed, and time—

*Cognitive dissonance will be discussed more fully in Chapter 16.

(Alex Webb, Magnum Photos)

all within the confines of a sheet of paper. Language is another system of signs, a set of arbitrary letters and sounds that, variously combined, represent the world around us and all of our experiences.

When something is actually present, of course, you can point to it, and this is the way we learn many words in the first place—the word "cat" would make no sense to a baby the first time he heard it, unless the cat were there to point to. But language can be used to represent things that are not actually present. After a while, the baby can talk *about* the cat without the cat's being in the room. Having a name for something, then, makes it easier to think about that thing.

The language we use for things can also influence the *way* we think about them. Compare the reactions that the following statements produce:

Finest quality filet mignon.	First-class piece of dead cow.
French armies in rapid retreat!	The retirement of the French forces to previously prepared positions in the rear was accomplished briskly and efficiently.
The governor appeared to be gravely concerned and said that a statement would be issued in a few days after careful examination of the facts.	The governor was on the spot.

These examples (Hayakawa, 1949, p. 85) illustrate how we can use "loaded" words—or intentionally obscure and "neutral" words—to color facts and stimulate certain desired responses from readers. The old baseball saying "I calls 'em as I sees 'em" might very well be reversed—sometimes we see things according to what we call them.

There are also psychologists who believe that the particular language we speak is crucial in structuring our perception and thought. For example, "machismo" in Spanish refers to a way of thinking about virility that no single word in English can express, and to call a girl a "poule" in French is much more insulting than to call her a "chick" in English, even though both words stem from "chicken." But Benjamin Whorf (1956) goes much further with this idea that people with different linguistic backgrounds think differently. His **linguistic relativity hypothesis** claims that thinking is patterned by language, and that the language one speaks determines one's view of the world. If a language lacks a particular expression, according to Whorf, the thought that the expression corresponds to will probably not occur to the people speaking that language. Whorf notes that the Hopi Indians of the Southwest United States have only two nouns for everything that flies.

Figure 6-3
Different languages have different words for colors. English divides the visible spectrum into seven segments, while Shona speakers use only three terms, and Bassa speakers use only two. The difference in the verbal labels, however, does not mean that a person who speaks Bassa or Shona is unable to distinguish between what we call "purple" and "blue." (From H. A. Gleason, Jr., *An Introduction to Descriptive Linguistics*, rev. ed. © 1955, 1961 by Holt, Rinehart & Winston, Inc. Reprinted by permission of Holt, Rinehart & Winston, Inc.)

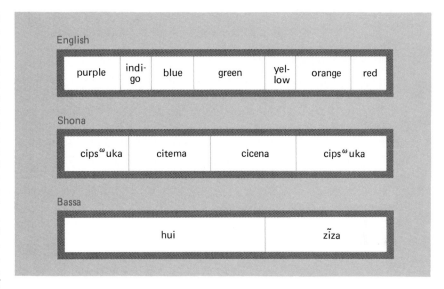

One noun refers to birds; the other is used for anything else—airplanes, kites, or dragonflies. Thus, according to Whorf's theory, the Hopi would interpret all flying things in terms of either of these two nouns—something in the air would be either a bird or a non-bird.

One interesting experiment that supports Whorf's view involved Japanese women who had married American servicemen (Farb, 1974). When talking to other people, especially to their families and neighbors, the women spoke English. However, when they talked together, the women spoke Japanese. Each woman was interviewed twice by a bilingual Japanese interviewer—the first interview was in Japanese, the second in English. The results showed that the women's responses to the same questions varied depending on which language they were speaking. One woman completed the following sentences in these two ways (Farb, 1974, p. 184):

"When my wishes conflict with my family's . . .
. . . it is a time of great unhappiness." (Japanese)
. . . I do what I want." (English)

"Real friends should . . .
. . . help each other." (Japanese)
. . . be very frank." (English)

The drastic changes in the women's responses could be accounted for by the shift in language. The study thus appears to support the theory that people think differently within different language worlds.

Nevertheless, serious objections have been raised to Whorf's hypothesis. Some critics insist that a need to think about things differently may bring about a change in language, and not vice versa. For example, if the Hopi Indians had ever been subjected to air raids, it is probable that they would have evolved a word to differentiate a butterfly from a bomber.

Another criticism of the linguistic relativity hypothesis asserts that while different languages encode experiences differently, any thought can be expressed in any language. In this view, words may affect interpretation, but not perception. A person living in the city may *call* all types of snow "snow," but he is capable of *perceiving* the difference between icy snow, slush, wet snow, and corn snow. It is not that language structures different views of reality, these critics say, but that certain languages, because of cultural differences that are already present, make one type of knowledge more readily available than another.

The problems we have been discussing have had to do with the interconnections between language and thought. **Psycholinguistics,** a relatively new field in its own right, came into being because psychologists and linguists wanted to understand these interconnections better. Psycholinguistics analyzes language in terms of its most basic components. We may take language for granted as we are using it, but it is actually a remarkable system of communication, and its basic components can be used to build fantastically complex structures.

The simplest unit of language is the **phoneme,** or basic speech sound. **Phonetics,** the study of phonemes, analyzes these sounds. In the English language, there are 46 phonemes, or possible sounds. If you are wondering how there can be 20 more phonemes than there are letters of the alphabet, ask yourself how many ways you can pronounce the vowel "e." Similarly, the phoneme for "ng" would be different from the phonemes for either "n" or "g"; it is more than just a combination of these two sounds.

Phonemes, in combination, make up **morphemes.** A morpheme is the smallest meaningful unit of speech. All words are morphemes, but not all morphemes are words. Consider the word "breadwinners," which contains four morphemes: the noun "bread," the verb "win," the suffix "er," and the plural "s." "Bread" and "win" are both *free* morphemes, words in themselves. "Er" and "s" are called *bound* morphemes; they can only appear connected to other morphemes. Thus, free morphemes can combine with other free morphemes or with bound ones to make new words.

Syntax is the study of grammar, the rules that govern how words are built into phrases and sentences. These rules of arrangement give order to a language and allow for the formation of relations between sentences, words, and phrases.

How do we learn this elaborate code of syntax, the sounds of phonemes, and the placement of morphemes that play such an important part in communication in any language—and in thought, which might

BLACK ENGLISH

In recent years, psycholinguists have realized that many ghetto blacks speak a particular dialect of English that they have named "Black English." Black English uses many sounds that are different from standard English. The consonant sound "th" is often pronounced as a "d" or a "t": thus, "they" is pronounced *dey*; "think" sounds like *tink*. An "r" sound between vowels is often dropped; the words "Paris" and "pass" sound almost alike in Black English. In addition, the "l" sound often is not used; word pairs such as *help–hep* and *toll–toe* cannot be distinguished.

Black English also has a distinctive grammar system. The verb form "is" is discarded in favor of the verb *be*. Thus, a Black English speaker will say *He be workin'* (meaning that he has been working for some time) or *He workin'* (meaning the subject is working at this very moment). These forms are not randomly interchanged, any more than verb tenses are in standard English.

As Farb points out:

> *Black English is neither a mispronunciation of standard English nor an accumulation of random errors made in the grammar of standard [English]. Utterances in Black English are grammatically consistent and they are generated by rules in the same way that utterances in standard English are generated by rules. Miss Fidditch may not regard utterances in Black English as "good English"—but that is beside the point, because Black English is using a different set of rules than those of standard English* (Farb, 1974, p. 160).

The white teacher is generally unaware of these properties of Black English and instead sees black children's use of their normal dialect as mistakes. Even black teachers may lose patience with their students' persistent use of Black English. Unfortunately, Black English-speaking children have problems not only in oral communication but also in learning to read, because books are written in standard English. This obviously makes it more difficult for them to succeed in school.

But the same teachers who take a dim view of Black English are likely to be patient with children of foreign-born parents. These children may have just as much trouble learning standard English as ghetto children do because, just like ghetto children, all they hear at home is their native dialect. Yet, because Polish, Chinese, and Yiddish, for example, are "real" languages—they have their own dictionaries and literature—teachers will go out of their way to help these students overcome their difficulties. Most important, teachers will not characterize *these* children as lazy, stupid, or unteachable.

This situation has led some linguists to propose teaching ghetto children the rules of English as if it were a foreign language, while others have insisted that such children should be trained in their native dialect, Black English, before they are taught standard English. Systematic study is required to determine which approach is better.

be called communication with oneself? Noam Chomsky (1965) believes that human beings possess an *innate grammar* that operates from the time of birth and gives the child the methods of organizing sensation into language. It is innate grammar, according to Chomsky, that makes it possible to learn foreign languages, because all languages share certain organizing principles, and these organizing principles are already, so to speak, built into us. Chomsky's theory has important implications for understanding the way we think, because it indicates that all people share ways of thinking; in this sense, it goes directly counter to Whorf's linguistic relativity hypothesis. Chomsky and his associates are now trying to discover exactly what these organizing principles are, and how we come to have them in the first place. Recently, the question of common organizing principles has gone even beyond the human level—in sending communications to outer space, scientists have wondered what "language" might be understood by beings in other worlds than our own.

Semantics is the study of the meaning of a language, the formal structure as well as the emotion and inflection employed in its use. For example, the sentence "How are you?" can be the merest formality at the beginning of a telephone conversation. Or, addressed to someone who is just getting over the flu, it can be a real request for information.

Because concepts are subjective, semantic misunderstandings can result. A word may not mean the same thing to other people as it does to you. For example, you and your friend have a loud, somewhat tense argument. You ask him why he's so angry. He insists he's not angry. You say, "Yes, you are," and there you go again. This is a classic case of semantic misunderstanding—to you, your friend is angry, but he says he is only annoyed or irritated. Because language is used to communicate ideas, as well as to think, it is important to minimize semantic misunderstandings, either by adapting yourself to your audience, or by defining your words carefully.

Language Learning in Chimpanzees

Language has long been regarded as one of man's unique capabilities, one of the powers that sets him apart from all other animals. But recent experiments with chimpanzees are raising questions about whether man is indeed the only species capable of using language.

Robert Gardner and Beatrice Gardner (1969) taught Washoe, a young chimpanzee, to communicate in American Sign Language (Ameslan), the system of gestures and hand movements used by many deaf people. From the time Washoe was a year old, all the humans she encountered used sign language among themselves and with her. By the time she was 4 years old, she knew more than 80 signs and could generalize some of them. The sign for "open," for example, was first learned with one particular door, but Washoe soon began to use it when referring

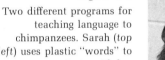

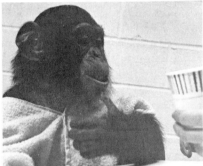

Figure 6-4

Two different programs for teaching language to chimpanzees. Sarah (*top left*) uses plastic "words" to communicate with her trainers. She must use words in the correct order to get a reward. Here she has "written," "Sarah give apple Amy." Nim is being taught to communicate in Ameslan. During the day, he goes to school and, at night, lives with a family. We first see Nim at about 6 months old, playing with one of his "siblings" (*top right*). He is now about 19 months old and is rapidly developing his signing vocabulary: when shown a cup, he makes the sign for "drink" (*bottom left*). In the last photo, we see him outdoors with one of his trainers. His trainer is eating a peach, but apparently Nim would rather play than watch her eat, because he is making the sign for "tickle."

(*Photo of Sarah by Ellen Arntz, courtesy David Premack; photos of Nim courtesy Herbert S. Terrace.*)

to all closed doors, briefcases, cupboards, boxes, and even faucets. She learned the sign for "dog" from pictures in a book, but extended this sign to refer to other pictures of dogs, to real dogs, and even to a dog she heard barking but could not see. Washoe learned to combine words in simple sentences to communicate her needs—"gimme drink" or "hurry open." Before she was 7, her vocabulary had increased to 175 words. She constructs six-word sentences, notes things that interest her, makes requests ("gimme sweet eat please"), and has even tried to communicate through sign language to other chimpanzees.

Nevertheless, psycholinguists have been skeptical of Washoe's achievements (Baur, 1975). A number of critics, including Eric Lenneberg, Ursula Bellugi-Klima, and Roger Brown, have stated that the multi-*sign* combinations formed by Washoe are not equivalent to the multi-*word* formulations of a child. For them, the way in which words are ordered is crucial in determining linguistic sophistication. Human children learn quickly that "Come Daddy home" is not proper word order. Because the Gardners never recorded data on word order during their years of work with Washoe, some psycholinguists are still unconvinced about whether Washoe is using sophisticated language.

A different approach to teaching language to a chimpanzee was devised by David Premack (1970), who chose to make his language written rather than gestured. The basic unit of the language is a "word" made of plastic backed with metal, which will adhere to a magnetic slate. Language training began with a feeding transaction. At first the experimenter simply looked on while Sarah, the chimpanzee, ate a piece of fruit placed on the table between them. After the feeding routine had been well established, a plastic "word" was placed next to the fruit, and the food was moved out of reach. Sarah quickly learned to place the "word" on the magnetic slate to get the fruit. Then she learned to associate different "words" with different fruits. Sentences were formed (in vertical order on the slate, because Sarah seemed to prefer it this way) by requiring Sarah to write the name of the person giving her the food. If the experimenter was Randy, Sarah would have to put "Randy apple" on the slate before she would get a bit of apple to eat. She would have to use correct word order—sentences like "apple Randy" were not acceptable. Sarah learned to form simple and compound sentences; to label things "same" or "different"; to answer questions; and to classify things by color, shape, size, and object class. She also learned some of the more abstract uses of language—how to employ the preposition "on," how to use plurals, when to use qualifiers (like "all," "none," "one," or "several"), and how to construct sentences that involve conditional relationships ("If Sarah take apple, then Mary give Sarah chocolate. If Sarah take banana, then Mary no give Sarah chocolate").

A more recent experiment suggests that baby chimpanzees who are raised almost from birth in the homes of deaf people can learn sign language at the same pace as human infants in deaf homes. Gardner and Gardner, whose original study of Washoe revolutionized the field, are supervising two baby chimps named Majo and Pili. After 6 months of training, one chimp has learned 13 words, and the other 15. They began making recognizable signs at the age of 3 months. The Gardners expect Majo and Pili to far surpass Washoe's linguistic achievements because they are starting training at a much earlier age and because their teachers can use Ameslan more fluently now than they could when they taught Washoe (Gardner & Gardner, 1975).

Perhaps the most significant of many current experiments with chimpanzees involves Herbert Terrace and a young chimp named Nim (Baur, 1975). Nim has been living with a New York City family virtually since birth. A staff of volunteer teachers works with Nim continually, helping him to learn an extensive variety of signs. In addition, Terrace insists on treating Nim just like a human child in all ways, including disciplining him when necessary. In this way, Terrace hopes to extend the time he and Nim can work together. (The Gardners had to stop living with Washoe when she was 6, because she had become somewhat spoiled and unmanageable.)

Terrace hopes to use Nim as the first part of an extensive program aimed at training and observing chimpanzees' language skills. When Nim has learned 30 signs, Terrace intends to test the relationship between his linguistic and mental development. Terrace also envisions a variety of future experiments, including communication between two Ameslan-equipped chimps; having a chimp who knows sign language teach another chimp how to use signs; and breeding two signing chimps to see if they will teach their baby the language of signing.

Directed Thinking

Directed thinking is aimed at solving a particular problem or reaching a certain goal. How do you get from Chicago to Des Moines? If you know the infinitive of a German verb, how do you make the second-person plural indicative? What is the best way to treat a sprained ankle? All these are problems that have defined limits. All can be approached by directed thinking, the application of past experience, available information, and learned methods to reach a solution. Thinking can be more directed or less, and, as we shall see, the distinctions between directed thinking and "freer" forms of thought are not absolutely rigid, and the two can often work in conjunction. Still, certain forms of thinking are more directed than others, and we will examine the more obviously directed ones first, and move from there to the less directed ones.

Logic and Reasoning

(Martha Swope)

"But that's just not logical!" When we make this exclamation, usually in a howl of exasperation, we mean that something does not seem to make sense. When we expect a thing to be logical, we are expecting it to follow certain rules, like the law of gravity or a code of accepted behavior. Logical thinking is thinking that adheres to rules of reasoning. At their most formal, these rules can be highly rigid and complex, and logicians have distinguished literally hundreds of different kinds of logical thought. But whether we have had formal training in logic or not, we apply it every day. You do not have to think, "If a and b, then c" to be using logic. If you say to someone, "Look at the sky—it's going to rain soon," and she nods, you are applying a shorthand form of logic. You do not have to go through all the steps of saying "If you look at the sky, you will see a buildup of dark gray clouds. Whenever dark gray clouds build up, there will soon be rain. Therefore, it is going to rain soon." But these are actually the logical steps between the two ideas "Look at the sky" and "It's going to rain soon." Without both of you going through these steps in your minds, and implicitly agreeing that the steps *are* logical, the two ideas would have no connection with each other.

In thinking like this, we use logic every day, almost without knowing it. But if you had gone through the whole process of spelling out the logical steps leading to your prediction of rain, you would have created a **syllogism,** which is the basis of formal logic. In the simplest form of syllogism, two sentences—called the *major premise* and the *minor premise*—are put together in such a way that a third statement follows from them. For example, if we say:

1. All eels slither. (major premise)
2. This is an eel. (minor premise)

we can conclude:

3. This eel slithers.

This is a correct syllogism, but a syllogism can sometimes be faulty. For one thing, the two premises must be *factually* correct for the conclusion to be accurate. If you start with:

1. All eels sing "O Sole Mio."
2. This is an eel.

you are forced to the logical, but factually wrong, conclusion:

3. This eel sings "O Sole Mio."

A second way a syllogism can be faulty is that, even though its premises are factually correct, they can be put together wrongly. They are *logically* incorrect. In the syllogism:

1. Dogs scratch when they have fleas.
2. I scratch my head when I think.
3. Therefore, thinking causes fleas.

the premises are both correct, but we have ignored the logical possibility that scratching can be caused by more than one thing.

Steps in Problem Solving

We have defined directed thinking as being aimed at the solution to a specific problem, and logical thinking as one method of getting to such a solution. But in concrete terms, what are the actual steps we go through when we have a complex problem to solve?

It is first necessary to *identify* the problem—to know that it exists and then to pinpoint and delineate it in order to see how you will direct your thinking to solve it. You first become aware of a problem as an obstacle or frustration—not always an unpleasant one, certainly, or sports and puzzles would not exist. Say you have just made a date to play tennis. After hanging up the phone, you realize that you have a dental appointment for exactly the same time. The problem is now identified—you are committed to being at two different places at 1:30 tomorrow afternoon.

After this, you begin to *search* for possible solutions. With some problems this search can be as simple as random trial and error, like fitting one key after another into a lock until you find the one that works. If you stumble upon the right solution by the trial-and-error method, of course, you need go no further. But many problems do not yield to such a mechanical solution, and trying every possible alternative is not a very economical approach. Still, to some extent trial and error probably does enter into your search for a solution. First you start restricting your alternatives. Can you simply not turn up at the dentist's? No. Not show up at the tennis court? Not a good idea either. Perhaps you had better call your friend back. Next, you *analyze* the situation: if you explain to your friend what the difficulty is, maybe you can work out another time for the tennis game.

You then move to the *attack* itself. You telephone your friend, and you agree to meet on the courts at 4:00 instead of 1:30. You no longer have to be in two places at once, and your problem is solved.

Sometimes, of course, the interval between the appearance of a problem and its solution is short enough that you think of it as all having happened in a single step. What has really happened is that these four steps have occurred so rapidly that the solution seemed to come instantaneously. Other times—if the problem is a very complicated one, such as finding a cure for cancer—the single problem must be broken down into many parts, and the steps must be gone through, over and over, by many people.

Factors Affecting Problem Solving

Directed thinking toward the solution of a problem is susceptible to many influences outside the limits of the problem itself. These include anxiety, anger, and frustration, whether from the problem-solving process itself or from other things that are in your life at that time. If these emotions are present to any noticeable extent, they may interfere with your finding a smooth solution to a problem. Severe anxiety may well impair your problem-solving ability on an exam, and frustration at not being able to work a crossword puzzle may interfere with the right word coming into your head. Occasionally these factors can help you arrive at the solution to a problem. If you are a very competitive person, the anxiety to succeed might actually increase your efficiency in solving a problem. Apart from these emotional factors, two other things may affect your ability to solve a problem. These are **set** and **functional fixedness.**

You usually approach a problem with some sort of direction or expectation that is the result of experience. This is a **set**—a kind of habit, the way you are used to perceiving certain situations. The value of previous experience in problem solving is that you have learned certain methods or ways of perception in the past, and you can apply them to the present situation. In the example of the conflicting ap-

CAN MACHINES THINK?

Hal, the emotional computer that ran amok in the movie *2001*, was clearly the star of the show. Ever since the invention of machines that can calculate faster than man can, many people have feared that these machines will one day outthink us and take over. Though no Hal yet exists, scientists do know that computers can think in surprisingly human ways.

One of the most sophisticated examples of machine thinking is the General Problem Solver, or GPS, a computer program developed by Newell, Shaw, and Simon (1960). The GPS and a human subject are given the task of proving a mathematical theorem. Both receive a set of axioms for developing their proofs. The human thinks aloud, giving the experimenter a record of the order in which he tries the rules and his reasons for accepting or rejecting his results. Both computer and human try and reject the rules in the same order. The one difference seems to be that the human can correct his mistakes by changing a previous decision, whereas the computer cannot.

This method of comparing computer behavior and human behavior in performing a task can also be used to test theories about human thinking. If the computer and the person solve the problem similarly, scientists assume that the computer program resembles actual human thought processes.

Computers have also been programmed to play chess and checkers the way people do. Like people, computers use heuristics—rules of thumb that enable them to limit the search for solutions by ignoring blind alleys. They select several possible moves, look ahead a certain number of moves, evaluate the board positions that would result from each possible move, and rule out some of the possibilities. Neither computer nor human considers all the results of every possible move. A computer could be programmed to do this, but such a program would take too much time, making a real game impossible. And heuristics produce good, though not perfect, results.

Hal, however, was a threat, not because his program was efficient, but because he had emotions—unsuspected impulses that upset the program and defied human control. No such impulses have been found in our computers, but we can give them instructions to interrupt a task under certain conditions: for example, when there is nothing left to try, or the computer finds a solution that meets certain minimum specifications. Computers can also be programmed to pursue a goal that will accomplish several objectives at once, like many human goals. However, neither computers nor people are very good at pursuing two incompatible goals (such as finishing an examination and writing a poem) at the same time.

pointments, one set you might have is that it is not polite to break appointments. Without that set, your solution might have been just to go off to the tennis court and forget the dentist entirely.

A set can function as a "hint" toward the solution to a problem. Maier (1930) conducted an experiment in which he asked his subjects to

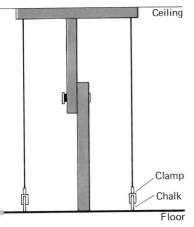

Figure 6-5

Maier gave his subjects two pieces of chalk, two kinds of clamps, some wire, and three lengths of wood and told them to construct pendulums that would swing across certain marks on the floor. Those who were given a head start—a set—found this correct solution more easily.

Figure 6-6

Here is an example of how our culture influences functional fixedness. To us, lightbulbs are simply lightbulbs, but to this girl from another culture they are jewelry.
(*Courtesy of the American Museum of Natural History*)

construct pendulums out of various materials. To one group he gave a set, a "head start"—not the solution to the problem, but a suggestion as to how it might best be approached. This group had significantly more success than the others in constructing the pendulum.

But to the extent that set is habit, it is not always an aid to problem solving. If a problem requires you to make new applications of your previous experience, too strong a set could blind you to all the possible solutions. If a man is an engineer, and has a very powerful set toward engineering as being a way to success, he may feel strongly that his son should be an engineer too. When the son receives his grades, the father is angry because he has only gotten a C in math. The A in music is ignored. In this case, the father's positive set toward engineering would not make it possible to perceive that another way to the ultimate goal—his son's success in life—might be to give the son a piano and encourage his desire to be a composer.

This is why many psychologists hold a negative view of set. They believe that set hampers creativity and makes it harder to see new methods and possibilities. Yet much of our education consists in the learning of sets, ways to solve problems, even though it may seem that we are learning only specific information. We are taught to integrate new information into forms we already have at our disposal, or to use methods that have proved effective in the past. In fact, the steps we use in problem solving are themselves a set—we have learned that approaching a problem in a certain logical sequence is the most successful way to reach a solution. The person who is most successful in solving problems is one who has a great number and variety of sets at his disposal and can judge when to change sets or when to break the set entirely. The great ideas and inventions come out of such a balance. Copernicus was familiar with the sets of his time, but he had the flexibility to see that they might not all be relevant. Only by putting aside these sets could he arrive at the discovery that the earth revolved around the sun. The important thing seems to be to use a set when it is appropriate, but not to let the set use *you*—not to be so controlled by learned ways of approaching the problem that you are closed to new methods of solving it.

One set that can affect problem solving is **functional fixedness.** The more you use an object, the harder it is to see novel uses for it. When you get accustomed to seeing something one way and one way only, you have assigned it a fixed function. Sometimes putting the object away for a while and coming back to it later will make you see it in a new light. But it is particularly hard to use an object in a new way if you have spent a lifetime using it in the accustomed way. You have a carful of groceries on a snowy day, and the driveway is not plowed. You will probably make four trips carrying grocery bags into the house, two at a time, each time passing a sled that would have carried them all at once, without stopping to think of the sled as anything but a child's toy.

To some extent, of course, part of the learning process is assigning correct functions to objects. We teach a child that the "right" function of a spoon is stirring, not pounding. Much of our formation of concepts is involved with learning the "right" functions of objects. But it is important to remain open enough to see that a coin can be used as an emergency screwdriver, or a book as a prop for a wobbly table leg.

We have been talking about the fixed function of objects, but the idea can also be applied to problems involving humans. The problem of the elderly has been given much attention recently. Putting older people into institutional homes can cause them to feel useless and to become depressed. At the same time, unwanted children live in institutional environments that cannot always give them the individual time and care that they need. Instead of seeing the elderly as people to be looked after, someone had the clever idea that they might serve as "foster grandparents" to the institutionalized children. This was a case of suspending the fixed function of both groups. The "grandparents" served to give the children love and attention, and the children provided the older people with the feeling of usefulness they lacked in conventional institutional life.

Insight and Creative Problem Solving

Not all forms of problem solving take place by means of thought that is as directed as the kinds we have been discussing. Especially in the fields of invention and science, a kind of thinking is often necessary that gets at the solution to a problem by a path that is different from the "steps" of purely directed thinking. This sort of thinking, called "creative," is to some extent still directed thinking (unlike "pure" creativity, which we shall discuss later). What is different about this kind of problem solving is **insight,** a seemingly arbitrary flash that presents, "out of the blue," a solution to the problem.

Figure 6-7
If you ever visit the University of Virginia at Charlottesville, you will see many examples of Thomas Jefferson's ingenuity. Here is one of them. The problem was how to construct a gate that would close automatically. Jefferson's solution was a novel combination of a metal ball, a chain, and a wooden post.
(Yvonne Freund)

Figure 6-8
To test the effects of functional fixedness, psychologists might give people the items shown on the table at the left. They are asked to mount the candles on the wall. When the tacks are presented in the box, people tend to think of the box only as a container and are less likely to see that it can be used as a candleholder.

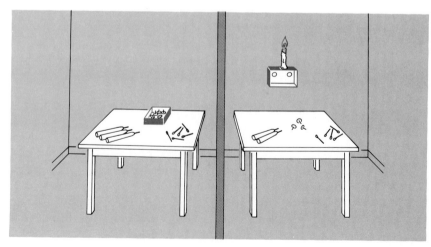

"Well, finally!"
(*Drawing by Robert Day;*
© *1972 The New Yorker*
Magazine, Inc.)

Most of us explain creative thinking in terms of inspiration. When we have an original idea and somebody says, "But how did you arrive at that?" we think back and realize that we did not arrive step by step. We answer something like, "The idea just came to me while I was walking home." But, psychologists ask, where did the idea come *from*? What is the process that enables certain people at certain times to find solutions that have not occurred to other people? Henri Poincaré, the French mathematician, has described his own creative process at work:

> *One evening, contrary to my custom, I drank black coffee and could not sleep. Ideas rose in crowds; I felt them collide until pairs interlocked, so to speak, making a stable combination. By the next morning I had established the existence of a class of Fuchsian functions, . . . I had only to write out the results, which took but a few hours* (Poincaré, 1924).

Many people have provided strikingly similar accounts of their own processes of creative thinking. One way of looking at these accounts is to identify the various stages of the creative experience (Wallas, 1926). The first is *preparation.* In this stage, we often try to use the steps outlined earlier, but they fail to lead us to a solution. Next comes a period of *incubation,* during which the individual is not actively or consciously thinking about the problem. The third stage is *illumination,* the seemingly spontaneous appearance of the creative insight or solution. In the fourth stage, *verification,* the solution is tested against the criteria of the problem.

In this process, unlike strictly directed problem solving, the solution does not, in any direct way, follow logically from the preparation. Poincaré's thinking was directed, in that he knew what the problem was and he had familiarized himself with the facts of the problem. In his hours at his work table, he may have tried to solve the problem by purely directed thinking. But such a solution did not come, and the way in which the thinking at the work table "led to" the sudden flash of insight that presented the solution is much less direct than the step-by-step method of problem solving. Note that Poincaré says not that he brought the ideas together, but that he "felt them collide." Something other than logic was involved, and that something is what we call "inspiration" or "insight."

Associative Thinking

We have seen that directed thinking is generally aimed at solving a particular problem of limited dimensions, and that creative problem solving, although some parts of it are directed, relies on an added factor, inspiration or insight, which goes beyond purely directed thinking. There are other forms of thinking that are even less directed—daydreaming, dreaming, and pure creativity. These forms of thought are called **associative thinking.**

Figure 6-9
Animals, too, solve problems through insight. The chimpanzee tries to reach the bananas by stretching, jumping, standing on one of the boxes, but nothing works. Then he realizes that he can pile one box on top of another and reach the bananas easily. (*Wide World Photos*)

Daydreaming

You are sitting in a classroom on a warm spring day, listening to a history lecture. But the windows are open, and outdoors the birds are singing and the trees are budding. The urge to gaze out the window is irresistible, and you think about what it would be like to be out there,

(*Inge Morath, Magnum Photos*)

sitting on the grass, relaxing, chatting with a friend in the sunlight. . . . Then the professor interrupts her discussion of the Holy Roman Empire to say, "Mr. Smith, just what is so interesting out the window?" Suddenly you are startled back to reality. Only what is it, exactly, that you have come back *from*?

It was not exactly that there was a specific thing out the window that interested you. Rather, the mood of the spring day set you off into daydreaming. Daydreaming and fantasizing are not quite the same. Fantasy is more self-directed (the "If I were . . ." or "If I could . . ." kind of thinking). In a daydream, however, your thoughts wander unconsciously in unexpected directions (Giambra, 1974).

The conditions under which such thoughts occur are usually situations in which you would rather be somewhere else, or doing something else—escaping from the demands of the real world for the moment. Sometimes you replay a scene from the past in your daydream, or you project into the future. Daydreams provide the opportunity to act, direct, stage-manage, and write the scenario for a private drama of which you are the only audience. For this reason, daydreams are known as **autistic thinking.**

Some psychologists believe that daydreams are a kind of wishful thinking that occurs when inner needs cannot be expressed in actual behavior. We daydream, they claim, when the world outside does not meet our needs, or when we are motivated to do something but cannot realize our goal. Freudian theorists have traditionally held that daydreams reflect repressed desires, generally about sex or hostility, that make us feel guilty (Giambra, 1974).

By contrast, other psychologists have stressed the positive value of daydreaming and fantasy. Pulaski (1974) suggests that daydreaming can build cognitive and creative skills and can help people get through difficult situations. She notes that daydreaming helped prisoners of war to survive torture and deprivation. Her view suggests that daydreaming and fantasy can be a constructive relief from everyday (and often unpleasant) reality, as well as a means of reducing internal tension and external aggression.

While autistic thinking can be a great source of creative ideas, in extreme cases autism can cut a person off from reality entirely, to the point where his whole life is his reveries, and he takes no notice of the world around him. But within normal bounds, daydreaming and fantasy can offer a relief from everyday reality and are often a source of ideas that logical thinking could not produce.

Dreams

The dreams we have at night are in many ways like the fantasies we have while we are awake. They may or may not be triggered by something in everyday waking life, but they reshape and re-create that

CAST OF DREAM

THE MONSTER . . . . . . YOUR FATHER
KIND WOMAN . . . . . . YOUR MOTHER
POLICEMAN . . . . YOUR ANALYST
FIRST STRANGER. . . . YOUR BROTHER
SECOND STRANGER . . YOUR SISTER
LITTLE BOY . . . . . YOU

Dana Fradon

*(Drawing by Dana Fradon;
© 1973 The New Yorker
Magazine, Inc.)*

material into new and "illogical" forms. A little boy who wishes his baby sister were out of the way knows it is unacceptable to have fantasies of killing her, much less to perform the act; but when he dreams that she is dead, the dream is "not his fault," because he had no say in whether or not to have it. A dream may reflect the unconscious wishes, needs, and conflicts of the individual. It may draw on any part of his history, from earliest childhood to the events of the previous day.

Dreams, like fantasies, can be a rich source of creative ideas. Franz Kafka got most of the material for his short stories from his dreams, and René Descartes "dreamed up" the axioms of analytic geometry while sleeping one night. The high regard in which dreams have been held throughout history can be seen in such biblical stories as the pharaoh's dreams of "fat and lean cattle," which the prophet Joseph interpreted as omens of 7 years of feast and 7 years of famine.

Creativity

We started this chapter by discussing the units of thought, the tools without which we are unable to think at all. Next, we discussed different kinds of thinking, moving from the most obviously directed kinds of thought to the "freer" kinds. You may have noticed the change of approach as you read on. We were able to give a strict definition to logical thinking and to define its limits. But as the kinds of thinking we were talking about moved more into the associative realm, definitions became less clear-cut, and distinctions between the various categories became less and less rigid. It may not be possible, for example, to say exactly where creative problem solving ends and daydreaming begins, just as between sleep and waking there is a state (called "hypnagogic") that is part dream and part daydream or fantasy. As you have read along, questions like "Just what is it that makes creative problem solving possible?" or "Where does the flash of intuition or the play of imagination come from?" may have occurred to you. This brings us to the question of creativity—what we might call "pure" creativity, as opposed to the creative problem solving we covered earlier.

It would probably be wrong to say that creativity is another *category* of thinking, as logic and daydreaming are. Perhaps we might call it a *character* of thought, or, looking at it another way, a *product* of thought or a *way* of using thought. We never really described the mechanics of, for example, Poincaré's insight into the nature of Fuchsian functions, because there is a sense in which creativity remains a mysterious quality that is present to a greater or lesser degree in our thought, and present in some people's thought more than in others' Perhaps it is best described as a capacity to *discover*.

We do know certain things about creativity, from experimentation and from the reports of people who are considered creative. There seem

WHAT'S IN A DREAM?

According to Freud, all dreams reveal hidden—and forbidden—desires. Aristotle believed they arose from the psychic activity of the sleeper. From ancient Egyptians to your Uncle Ben, most people have felt that the content of their dreams was significant—even if they did not know what they meant.

Today, investigators of dreams rely on what dreamers remember about their dreams just after waking. Such dream recall shows that individual differences and daytime experiences help to form the content of dreams, along with things that happen during sleep itself.

When your body is closest to waking, dreams are likely to be about recent happenings. In the middle of the night, when body temperature is lowest, more dreams incorporate childhood or long-ago events. The last dream before waking is the one most likely to be remembered.

Dreams vary according to age and sex. Children usually dream about their waking life, and 61 percent dream about scary animals. Very few adults (7 percent) dream about animals—except in primitive cultures. Men dream more about men than about women; women dream equally about both. Men's dreams are more adventurous and aggressive than women's and less emotional. Both sexes dream equally about being pursued or victimized. Before menstruation, women often dream about waiting. Before childbirth, they are more likely to dream about babies or their mothers than about their husbands.

Events near bedtime also affect a given night's dreams. We have all had dreams about snow when we were cold or deserts when we were hot. Eating salty food before bedtime made Freud dream of cold water—and thirsty people who dream about drinking water drink less upon waking up than do people who have not dreamed about drinking. Even films shown just before bed can influence dreams, especially their emotional tone.

to be different ways of being creative. The poet Stephen Spender distinguishes between "divers" and "diggers." Mozart, who had an instinctive flair for music, "dove" into it. Beethoven, on the other hand, struggled during the entire process of composition—he had to "dig" for the music, note by note.

There are not only different ways of being creative, there are different components of creativity (Johnson, 1972). Among these are sensitivity to problems (both in problem finding and problem solving), originality (the ability to develop a new solution), and ingenuity (the discovery of a solution in an unusually clever way).

Creativity itself is not simply stimulus-bound—it does not follow directly from external events. But the creative work is usually triggered by stimuli from the outside world. *War and Peace* would not have been written without Napoleon's invasion of Russia; the *Mona Lisa* is a painting of a woman who actually existed; Shakespeare did not create the plot of *Hamlet*, but based his play on an earlier story.

Figure 6-10

The musical scores of Mozart and Beethoven illustrate graphically the difference between the two composers' creative processes. Mozart's score (*top*) is clean and orderly, while Beethoven's (*bottom*) shows the signs of his struggle for each note.

(Photos from Mary Flagler Cary Music Collection, The Pierpont Morgan Library. Reproduced by permission of The Pierpont Morgan Library.)

Imagination, dreams, fantasies all have obvious connections to creativity. We may ask whether "pure" creativity has any relation to problem solving at all. Many artists have said that there was no "problem" presented to them at the beginning—that the work was somehow already *there* before it was begun. Thus, if any problem solving were involved, it would be in the *realization* of the work—putting the notes of the symphony down on paper, sculpting the form out of the marble.

Even logic can be present in the creative process. A novelist can realize that one of her scenes does not follow from the one before it, a passage in a concerto may or may not make sense in the context of the passages that precede it or follow it. This logic may be an aesthetic logic, but it is logic nevertheless. Thus creativity encompasses all of the processes we have discussed—imagination, problem solving, dreams, fantasies, even logic—and uses them to bring forth something that has never existed before.

Summary

1. The three major components of thought are images, concepts, and language.
2. *Images* are recollections or reconstructions of sensory experience and may employ sight, taste, touch, smell, and sound. They may be incomplete or even inaccurate, concrete or abstract, dim or vivid.
3. The theory of *imageless thought* held that thought did not depend on images and that it could occur without them. Later research showed that sensory images can exist below the threshold of conscious awareness, and therefore people might use images, yet not be aware that they are present.
4. *Concepts* allow us to classify specific people, things, or events on the basis of common elements. We form new concepts and revise and expand our existing network of concepts on the basis of new experiences. Concepts function to generalize, differentiate, or abstract in thinking. A *conjunctive concept* classifies all objects that have one or more features in common. A *disjunctive concept* classifies objects on an either/or basis. A *relational concept* classifies things on the basis of how specific attributes are related to other things. A *dimensional concept* lets us see a specific attribute as a continuum. *Explanatory concepts* point out relationships between concepts. A *singular concept* involves our understanding of a single object or event.
5. *Signs* are representations of what exists in the world of objects and situations and can be either linguistic or nonlinguistic. *Language* is the most sophisticated and intricate set of signs. Language is used to represent things whether they are present or not and to classify experience and objects. Language enables us to give names to things, which in turn makes it easier for us to think about them.
6. The *linguistic relativity hypothesis* maintains that thinking is patterned by language and that the language one speaks determines one's view of the world. According to this hypothesis, if a language lacks a particular expression, the thought corresponding to that expression will probably not occur to the people who speak that language. Others argue that language does not affect perception, but that any thought can be expressed in any language.
7. The interconnections between language and thought are the subject of a relatively new field of study called *psycholinguistics*, which analyzes

language in terms of its most basic components. The *phoneme*, or basic speech sound, is the simplest unit of language. When combined, phonemes make up *morphemes*. *Syntax* is the study of grammar, which gives order to a language and allows for the formation of relations between words, sentences, and phrases. *Semantics* is the study of the meaning of a language.

8. *Directed thinking* is aimed at solving a particular problem or reaching a certain goal. *Logical thinking*—thinking that adheres to rules of reasoning—is one method of accomplishing this. Logical thinking often takes the form of a *syllogism*—a series of statements, which, if accurate and combined correctly, lead to a logical conclusion.

9. If a problem is too complex for simple logic, we tend to use certain steps to arrive at a solution. First we *identify* the problem, then we *search* for possible solutions, *analyze* the situation, and finally *attack* the problem and arrive at a solution.

10. Various factors can affect problem solving. Anxiety, anger, and frustration may make a problem more difficult to solve, or they may increase efficiency in working out a solution to a problem. The way you are used to perceiving certain situations as the result of experience—your *set*—can also affect the way you approach problem solving. One type of set that can often hinder problem solving is known as *fixed function*—seeing something in only one way, which makes it harder to see new uses for it.

11. If the steps of problem solving do not lead to a solution, we sometimes see creative problem solving, which is characterized by insight. Creative problem solving can be described in terms of four stages—*preparation, incubation, illumination,* and *verification*.

12. *Associative thinking* is even less directed than creative problem solving. Daydreams, dreams, and pure creativity are not attempts to find specific solutions to specific problems.

13. *Daydreaming* is a kind of thinking that involves only your personal associations and allows you to create your own fantasies. Daydreams and fantasy are known as *autistic thinking*. They allow you to escape from the demands of the real world and be somewhere else in your mind. Daydreams and fantasies can be a source of creative ideas.

14. *Dreams* are even less directed and less bound by external events than daydreams or fantasies. Dreams reshape and re-create material into new and often illogical forms and can be a rich source of creative ideas.

15. It is difficult to classify *pure creativity* as just another kind of thinking. It is probably more correct to view it as a *character* of thought, a *product* of thought, or a *way* of using thought. Imagination, dreams, fantasies, and even problem solving and logic can be involved in pure creativity.

Suggested Readings

Beradt, C., *The Third Reich of Dreams,* trans. A. Gottwald (New York: Quadrangle, 1968). An analysis of the dreams of over 300 Germans during Hitler's rule in Germany, illustrating the impact of waking life on dream content.

Davis, G. A., *Psychology of Problem Solving* (New York: Basic Books, 1973). A good review of laboratory research as well as industrial and educational applications of problem solving, creativity, and brainstorming.

Deese, J., *Psycholinguistics* (Boston: Allyn & Bacon, 1970). A short, readable introduction to the science of psycholinguistics, including the fundamentals of generative grammar, the development of language in children, and the biological and social contexts of language.

Harman, G., *On Noam Chomsky* (Garden City, N.Y.: Anchor Books, 1974). A set of essays that explore the implications of Chomsky's thinking.

Mandler, J. M., and Mandler, G. (Eds.), *Thinking: From Association to Gestalt* (New York: Wiley, 1964). A look at the historical development of the psychology of thinking.

Manis, M., *Cognitive Processes* (Belmont, Calif.: Brooks/Cole, 1968). A concise examination of research on cognitive processes, including learning, memory, generalization, concept formation, language, thinking, and creativity.

Pollio, H. R., *The Psychology of Symbolic Activity* (Reading, Mass.: Addison-Wesley, 1974). A well-written book that covers a wide range of topics and includes reviews of experimental literature on signs, symbols, and concepts.

Postman, N., Weingarten, C., and Moran, T. P., *Language in America* (New York: Pegasus, 1970). A thought-provoking argument that the language of politics and advertising may be hurting our chance for survival by drawing us away from the reality the words stand for.

Ray, W. S., *The Experimental Psychology of Original Thinking* (New York: Macmillan, 1967). A collection of articles that provides a good sample of both research and theory on originality.

Rosner, S., and Apt, L. E. (Eds.), *The Creative Experience* (New York: Grossman, 1970). In interviews with 23 creative people in a wide variety of fields, the authors attempt to discover how these individuals experience their own creative processes.

Vinacke, W. E., *Psychology of Thinking*, 2nd ed. (New York: McGraw-Hill, 1974). A comprehensive examination of language, creativity, concept formation, and problem solving.

7

outline

THE NATURE OF INTELLIGENCE 236

Spearman's *g* Factor
Thurstone's Primary Mental Abilities
Guilford's Structure of the Intellect

THE NATURE OF CREATIVITY 239

The Creative Process
Intelligence and Creativity

MEASURING INTELLIGENCE AND CREATIVITY 242

Aptitude and Achievement Tests

WHAT MAKES A GOOD TEST? 245

Reliability
Validity
Standardization

INTELLIGENCE TESTS 247

The Stanford-Binet Scales
Performance Tests
The Wechsler Adult Intelligence Scale
Culture-Fair Intelligence Tests
Group Tests

TYPES OF CREATIVITY TESTS 259

DETERMINANTS OF INTELLIGENCE 260

Heredity
Environment
Race Differences: Jensen and His Critics
Sex Differences

SUMMARY 271

SUGGESTED READINGS 272

Intelligence and Creativity

When we say that someone is intelligent, we can mean a great many things. The person may be able, brilliant, clever, deep, expert, gifted, intellectual, knowing, nimble, quick-witted, smart, talented, or wise. We may use the term "intelligent" to describe a famous lawyer, an experienced football quarterback, a precocious 7-year-old girl, or the creator of an elaborate hoax. Many people consider television talk show host Dick Cavett to be "witty"; does that mean that he is intelligent? Conservative columnist William F. Buckley, Jr., has a marvelous command of the English language. Does this quality define intelligence?

There are no simple answers to such questions. Intelligence can mean knowing how to pack a canoe so it won't tip over, or it can mean knowing how to develop a cure for cancer. It can mean understanding the underlying symbolism of a movie or successfully balancing a checkbook. In other words, while we can recognize intelligence in ourselves and others, we are not really sure what it is or where it comes

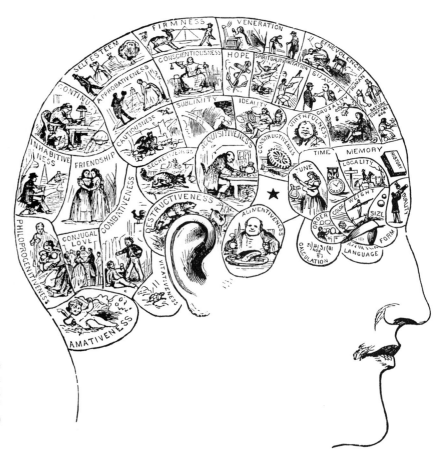

Figure 7-1
A phrenologist's map of the head, showing the location of various "mental functions."
(*The Bettmann Archive*)

from. In this chapter we look at what psychologists think intelligence is, how intelligence is influenced by heredity and environment, whether intelligence and creativity are related, and how both are measured.

The Nature of Intelligence

Modern studies of intelligence began, as we might expect, with the brain. In the early nineteenth century a number of scientists thought that differences in intelligence and ability could be explained in terms of physical attributes. Quite logically, they began measuring people's heads, searching for the bumps that made one man a great writer, another a mediocre general. *Phrenology,* as this "science" was called, enjoyed quite a vogue.

We mention it here for two reasons. First, phrenology did focus attention on the brain. For centuries people had thought of the mind in vague, abstract terms. Great ideas were attributed to divine inspiration; success in society or on the battlefield was considered the result of good breeding. Second, we have not quite gotten over the idea that intelligence is a thing you have inside you, something you possess more or less of—like a larger or smaller bump on the head.

When psychologists speak of intelligence, they are talking about a kind of behavior. Obviously, we cannot see the complex mental processes that are involved in intelligence. We have to approach the subject more indirectly—by watching what people (and animals) do in situations that require the use of intelligence. The subject of this chapter, then, really is intelligent behavior. We begin with theories on the nature of intelligence, touching on creativity. Next we consider the tests on which many of these theories are based. In the final sections we discuss the sources or determinants of intelligence and explanations of individual and group differences.

Spearman's *g* Factor

The concept of general intelligence, the notion that solving problems and reading novels have something in common, is largely based on the theories of Charles Spearman, a British psychologist. Spearman began working on a theory of intelligence around the turn of the century. The fact that people who are bright in one area are generally bright in other areas, Spearman argued, suggests that intelligence is more than an accumulation of specific skills.

In 1904 Spearman published his theory of general intelligence. He described general intelligence, which he called **g**, as a kind of well or spring of mental energy that flows into everything the individual does. The person who is "well endowed" is able to understand things quickly, make good decisions, carry on interesting conversations, and so on—he behaves intelligently in a variety of situations.

Once Spearman had established this foundation, he turned to the question of special abilities. Clearly, all of us are quicker in some areas than in others; we may find math easy, but spend hours puzzling over a modern poem. To account for these differences, Spearman hypothesized that g branches out into various activities in different degrees. The different manifestations of general intelligence in specific activities he called **s** factors. To return to the image of a well or spring, general intelligence is the fountain, from which specific abilities flow like streams of water into different thought processes.

Thurstone's Primary Mental Abilities

L. L. Thurstone, an American psychologist, more or less agreed with Spearman, but thought the concept of general intelligence required elaboration. After studying data obtained from various intelligence tests, Thurstone came up with a list of seven **primary mental abilities** (Thurstone, 1938).

Figure 7-2

Guilford's three-dimensional model of the structure of the intellect. The model is made up of 120 small cubes, or factors. Each factor can be classified according to operation, product, and content. (From J. P. Guilford, "Factorial Angles to Psychology," *Psychological Review,* 1961, *68,* 1–20.)

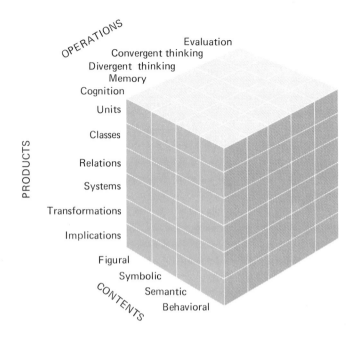

These different abilities, he thought, lay somewhere between what Spearman called general intelligence and specific abilities. They are

- S—Spatial ability*
- P—Perceptual speed
- N—Numerical ability
- V—Verbal meaning
- M—Memory
- W—Word fluency
- R—Reasoning

These abilities are relatively independent of one another. A person with high spatial ability might be low on word fluency, for example. But taken together, Thurstone felt, these primary mental abilities are what we mean when we speak of general intelligence. According to Thurstone, one or more of these abilities can be found in any intellectual activity. To read a book, you need verbal meaning, word fluency, and reasoning. To study that same book in preparation for an exam, you also need memory. Thurstone thus presented a somewhat more complex model of intelligence.

Guilford's Structure of the Intellect

J. P. Guilford found both Spearman's and Thurstone's models of intelligence incomplete. Guilford began by distinguishing between three basic kinds of mental ability: **operations,** the act of thinking; **contents,** the terms in which we think (such as words or symbols); and **products,** the ideas we come up with (Guilford, 1961). Within each category he

---

*The ability to perceive distance, recognize shapes, and so on.

identified a number of factors. The result is the three-dimensional model shown in Figure 7-2. At least one factor from each category, Guilford claimed, is present in all intellectual activities.

Say, for example, you read a newspaper column on the candidates in a mayoral election. Reading involves three operations: *cognition, memory* (you recall the candidates' speeches and ads), and *evaluation* (does the columnist make sense? do the candidates?). In carrying out these operations you employ two kinds of contents: *semantic* (the words) and *behavioral* (the activities or behavior described). The products of your reading are *inferences* (this person will make a good mayor, that person will not) and *classes* (two candidates are liberal, the third is conservative). You may also discover some *relationships:* perhaps the candidate born in the central city understands its problems better than the two who were raised in the suburbs.

The history of theories of intelligence is thus one of increasing complexity. Many current researchers are unhappy with definitions of intelligence that focus entirely on problem solving. They see the need to understand more fully the processes of cognition and thought. For example, Bouchard (1968) describes intelligence as a dynamic information-processing system. If this viewpoint becomes more widely accepted, we may come to view intelligence, not as a list of abilities or factors, but rather as a *system* for ordering and dissecting life's experiences and messages.

The Nature of Creativity

In ancient Greece, the mathematician Archimedes was asked by the king whether his crown was made of pure gold or whether it was alloyed with silver, a less expensive metal even then. Archimedes tackled the problem, but traditional geometry got him nowhere. Then one day he noticed that the water overflowed when he got into his bath. He suddenly realized that if he placed the crown into a basin full of water, he could measure how much water ran out. Since he knew that gold and silver have different densities, the amount of water that overflowed would tell him whether or not the crown was pure gold. Archimedes was so excited about his creative solution that he forgot his clothes and ran home shouting, "Eureka!" ("I have found it!"). Centuries later, the early impressionist painters noticed that as the sun moves across the sky, the light on a haystack changes. They realized that they could paint this light just as easily as they could paint the haystack. It had never occurred to their elders that light itself could be the subject of a painting. Creativity is not, of course, limited to inventors and artists. In everyday life, the housewife who scans the newspaper ads every morning and shops at the stores offering the best bargains is acting intelligently—she examines the available information and makes rational decisions. But the housewife who first thought of organizing a neighborhood co-op, with one family going to the whole-sale market every week to buy food for the group, came up with a creative solution.

The Creative Process

There have been numerous attempts to explain the creative process. One approach emphasizes the way people form associations between pieces of information (Mednick, 1962). The creative person, in this view, is the one who links things that would not normally be linked, who forms novel associations between highly unlikely elements. The un-creative person, on the other hand, tends to rely on associations he has encountered in the past.

Guilford (1959) speaks of creativity as a form of intelligence. He has isolated a number of special abilities that are related to the creative process. Most of these abilities—flexibility, originality, and fluency with words, associations, and ideas—are associated with **divergent thinking,** one of the five operations in his model of the intellect (see Figure 7-2). **Convergent thinkers** will examine the facts, decide which are relevant, and look for a single logical solution. **Divergent thinkers,** however, will look at the facts and expand on them, imagining where each piece of evidence will lead and producing a number of different solutions. For example, three people are lost in the woods. One of them argues that the only thing to do is to turn around and look for their trail. Another says that he knows the lake is to the west, so the only sensible thing is to follow the sun. The third camper looks off into the distance. He realizes that the lake is too far away, considers the possibility of going to the nearest stream and camping for the night, wonders if the ranger patrols the park, and thinks about ways of signaling. He quite suddenly looks at a tree and sees that he can climb it and find out where he is. This camper is engaging in divergent thinking. Instead of trying to find the one right solution, he "lets his mind go," expands the possi-bilities, and quite possibly finds a way out of the woods.

However, Guilford stops short of equating creativity with divergent thinking. Flexibility, originality, and fluency are associated with diver-gent thinking, but some of the other abilities that are related to the creative process lie outside that particular operation. For example, sensitivity to problems—the ability to see that a goal has not been achieved—falls into the operation called evaluative abilities. Redefini-tion—the ability to set aside our old ideas about familiar objects and use the objects in new ways—is, strangely enough, associated with convergent thinking. Thus Guilford's explanation of creativity, like his explanation of intelligence as a whole, draws together several distinct and interdependent abilities.

Subsequent writers have raised questions about the association between creativity and divergent thinking. For example, Brody (1972) argues that convergent thinking may actually be *more* essential for the

(*Inge Morath, Magnum Photos*)

creative person than divergent thinking. The primary aim of the scientist is not to generate a wide variety of theories, but to perfect one single theory that will adequately explain a large amount of data. Similarly, the artist's creativity is not a randomly "free" process; he must work within the specific limitations and constraints of his particular medium. Convergent thinking can be most useful in assisting the scientist or artist in narrowing his creative vision in a reasonable and productive way.

Intelligence and Creativity

Intrigued with these descriptions of the creative process, psychologists have begun to wonder if creativity is a special ability, distinct from general intelligence.

One interesting study was conducted in a private school in Chicago (Getzels & Jackson, 1962). At the beginning of their experiment the authors gave creativity and intelligence tests to a group of fifth- through twelfth-graders. Next they selected two groups, one from those who had scored high on creativity tests, another from those with high IQ scores. The two groups were equal in academic achievement. Getzels and Jackson found distinct personality differences between the two groups. The high-IQ children were conscientious, careful, and self-controlled. Their personal and career goals seemed to match those of their teachers. The creative children were playful, expressive, and independent. Although they often worked harder than the children with high IQs, doing more than was expected of them, they did not get along well with their teachers.

A few years later another team of psychologists conducted a similar investigation of the relationship between intelligence and creativity (Wallach & Kogan, 1965). The students in this study were fifth-graders in a middle-class suburban public school system. Believing that the creative person is penalized in a traditional test situation, Wallach and Kogan devised a series of gamelike activities to evaluate creativity, with no time limits imposed. These games included:

- *Instances*—a test in which the subject is required to list as many things as he can which are instances of something—for example, name all the round things you can.
- *Alternate uses*—for example, list all the uses of a knife.
- *Similarities*—a test requiring an individual to list all the ways two things are similar.
- *Pattern meanings*—a test in which the subject is required to list all the different things which various abstract images could represent.
- *Line meanings*—a test in which one is asked to name all the things which various line patterns make you think of (Brody, 1972, p. 131).

Students were divided into four groups: those who scored high in both creativity and intelligence, those with high creativity but low intelligence, those with low creativity but high intelligence, and those who were low in both creativity and intelligence. The students who were high on both dimensions were able to perform well in both free and controlled situations and with both childlike and adultlike behavior. The high-creative, low-intelligence children were most frustrated in the school environment, but were able to perform well in a freer context. The third group, those with low creativity but high intelligence, placed high value on achievement in school and worked hard to excel at their studies. The students who scored low in both creativity and intelligence tended to avoid their schoolwork and either concentrated on social activities or displayed regression or psychosomatic symptoms.* Like the earlier study by Getzels and Jackson, Wallach and Kogan's investigation suggested the existence of two somewhat different modes of thinking—creativity and general intelligence. The two modes appear to be distinct, yet both can generalize to many diverse activities.

A further study by Wallach and Wing (1969) supported the results of the earlier Wallach and Kogan research. Wallach and Wing studied the divergent thinking ability of a sample of college freshmen by using the students' scores on Scholastic Aptitude Tests as measures of intelligence. Again, there seemed to be little direct relation between intelligence and divergent thinking ability.

All of these studies rely quite heavily on ways of testing intelligence and creativity. Indeed, creativity studies are probably the direct result of widespread use of intelligence, aptitude, and achievement tests, which many people feel discriminate against originality. We now turn to this rather controversial subject—testing.

Measuring Intelligence and Creativity

No student can escape intelligence tests. They are inflicted on us in a variety of forms from the time we enter school until we graduate, and even then we may find a personnel office presenting us with a whole new set.

The tests themselves often seem to have little to do with what we regard as intelligence. What does putting puzzles together or answering multiple-choice questions about a paragraph on bees have to do with understanding the causes of the Civil War or designing a lab experiment or even with playing chess? Indeed, the whole business of having our intellects translated into numbers seems inhuman.

But whatever we think of them, it is hard to ignore tests once the scores are in. A C-student who does well on an aptitude test suddenly

---

*Regression—returning to behavior patterns characteristic of an earlier stage of development—and psychosomatic illnesses—physical disorders that have psychological origins—are discussed in more detail in Chapters 13 and 14, respectively.

INTELLIGENCE TESTS SHOULD HELP, NOT HINDER

Intelligence tests have generally been designed to predict students' performance in school and work situations. W. K. Estes challenges this prevailing approach. He laments that IQ tests have rarely been used to help us better understand how we process information and how we learn. Traditional IQ tests measure performance, and although performance does help us to predict later achievement, measuring it tells us nothing about the learning process itself, which Estes sees as the true measure of intelligence.

In a recent article (1974), Estes analyzed several important subtests used to determine IQ, including the Digit Span Test, the Digit Symbol Test, vocabulary tests, and word-naming tests. He pinpointed the operations involved in each of these tests and suggested reasons why students might encounter difficulty with each of them. For example, a student who is not skillful in grouping letters and numbers will be at a disadvantage on the Digit Span Test. More generally, some students think more slowly than others, and other students' frames of reference may be quite different from that of the test designer.

Estes argues that testing should be designed and used to locate the problem areas of students, rather than simply to predict their future attainments. He suggests that investigating why students fail to do well on these tests would be more fruitful for understanding intelligence than simply computing correlations between IQ and later success. In this sense, educational testing could assist social scientists in developing a better understanding of the way that humans learn (and fail to learn). This in turn could lead to programs that would maximize every student's potential.

Estes is not the only psychologist who feels that intelligence and aptitude tests are being badly used at present. David McClelland (1973) points out that, while amount of education is indeed a predictor of later success, achievement per se is not. Thus, simply finishing college appears to give a C student the same chance for success that an A student has. "The only difference I noted was that those with better grades got into better law or medical schools, but even with this supposed advantage they did not have noticeably more successful careers as compared with the poorer students . . ." (p. 2). Like Estes, McClelland feels that intelligence tests should be used to find out why a student has difficulty learning, instead of being used to cut his career short by telling school personnel that this student is not a "best bet" for further educational effort. On the contrary, this is the student who could benefit the most from continued education. Therefore, McClelland urges that tests be designed that will emphasize the individual's educational progress and that scores be used to help him improve in areas where he is weak. Test scores should not be a stigma. Rather, they should help a school to help all its students.

finds his teachers expecting more of him, his parents being disappointed with his merely passing grades. High school juniors anxiously wait for college board scores that may "make or break" their college careers.

"Sorry, your aptitude tests indicate you'd be too intelligent to stay with us long."

(Copyright © 1969. Reprinted by permission of Saturday Review and Roland Michaud.)

Many of our objections to tests are valid, but others are based on misconceptions. First, a score on an intelligence test is not an absolute measure. Many of us mistakenly assume that an IQ represents some absolute *quantity* of intelligence. This is wrong. A person's IQ is a comparison of his performance on a test to the performance of others his age. It can, and in most cases does, change over the years. Second, a score on an intelligence test should not be used by itself to forecast a person's chances for success.

Aptitude and Achievement Tests

Tests of general intelligence, which will be treated more fully later in this chapter, are designed to measure a person's scholastic aptitude. But not all of the tests given in schools and personnel offices are intelligence tests. We often want to determine where a person's specific strengths and weaknesses lie, both in **aptitude**—ability to learn—and in **achievement**—what has already been learned.

Aptitude tests are based on the multiple-factor theory of Thurstone and others, who, as we saw at the beginning of the chapter, defined intelligence as a combination of different abilities. Aptitude tests measure ability, and they are designed to identify specific strengths in different areas. Intelligence tests, for example, measure scholastic or intellectual aptitude.

Several kinds of aptitude tests are in use today. Some, called **multiple aptitude batteries,** test a number of abilities and give a profile of the individual. The SAT (Scholastic Aptitude Test) is an example of this kind of test. Others, called **special aptitude tests,** measure ability in one area only—music, art, mechanics, or even clerical skills. These are most often used for vocational guidance.

Achievement tests were pioneered in the 1920s. As the public school system grew, educators became increasingly dissatisfied with traditional ways of evaluating students—that is, the individual teacher's opinion. School administrators wanted a more general measure so that they could compare classes, programs, schools, and so on. The first in a long line of standardized achievement tests, and one still in use today, appeared in 1923: the Stanford Achievement Test.

Achievement tests, as the name implies, measure what a student *has* learned, not what he is capable of learning. A third-grade teacher decides to abandon traditional teaching methods and to let her students decide what they want to do and work at their own rate. An achievement test at the end of the year will tell her how the free-school method compares to traditional techniques. A school board ordered to integrate its schools through busing may use achievement tests to convince reluctant parents that the new system has not hurt their children's education.

Most often test scores are used to *predict* how an individual will perform in school or on a job. The Scholastic Aptitude Test, for example, tells an admissions board whether a student is likely to succeed in college-level work. A particular college may have found that students who score below a certain level have a difficult time with their program and decide on a cutoff point. Before hiring a Job Corps trainee, an auto plant may want to find out whether he has the coordination and ability to put things together that make a good mechanic. They might use a special aptitude test to measure mechanical ability.

Tests are also used for *diagnosis,* to identify individual strengths and weaknesses. If a teacher finds that a student has exceptional mathematical ability, he might decide on advanced placement. Tests can also identify problems, such as slow reading ability.

Finally, tests are used for *research.* Achievement tests can show school administrators how their program compares to others across the nation. In addition, achievement tests often furnish the standards on which aptitude tests are based.

How does a school principal or personnel director decide which test to use in a particular situation? How does he interpret scores once the test has been given? Over the years psychologists, in cooperation with testing services, have developed a number of sophisticated techniques for assessing the reliability and validity of tests and for evaluating scores.

What Makes a Good Test?

Reliability

How do we know if a test is reliable? That is, how can we tell if an individual's score is dependable and consistent?

If your alarm clock sounds off at 8:15 every morning, it is reliable. But if it rings at 8:00 one morning and 8:40 the next, you cannot depend on it. It is not reliable.

Similarly, if you take the same test twice and get the same score each time, the test can be said to be reliable; the results are consistent. If, however, you score 90 on a verbal aptitude test one week and 60 on the same or an equivalent test a week or two later, something is wrong.

Before any test is released, its reliability is measured by at least one of several techniques. The easiest method of determining reliability or consistency is to give the same test to the same subject twice, with a short interval in between. **Test-retest reliability** is of limited use, however, for most people will improve with practice. For this reason test-makers often compose **alternate forms,** two tests designed to measure the same ability or subject area. If an individual gets the same score on both forms, the test is reliable.

Not totally satisfied with this procedure—there is always a chance one form is easier than the other—testers also check reliability by splitting a single test in half, usually by odd- and even-numbered items, thus obtaining two scores from one test. If the two scores for an individual are the same, the test is said to have **split-half reliability.**

Psychologists express degrees of reliability in terms of **correlation coefficients,** which are nothing more than a way of expressing a comparison between two sets of scores. For example, the test-makers would compare the scores of a group of people on one form of a test with their scores on another form of the same test. If high scores on one version of the test were related to high scores on the other version, the correlation coefficient would be high, perhaps .90; if there were no relationship between the two sets of test scores, it would be zero.*

Psychologists are also concerned with inconsistencies that have nothing to do with the test itself: whether the person who reads the instructions enunciates clearly, what kind of mood you are in when you take the test, and so on. These chance factors can and do affect scores. Many testing services therefore provide the people who will administer and score a test with a range of scores that allows for variation due to chance factors. This might, for example, tell the person evaluating the test that all students who scored between 78 and 85 have the same aptitude for music.

Validity

A valid test is one that actually measures what it sets out to measure. This question is more complex than it seems, and researchers distinguish between several kinds of validity, some or all of which might be necessary for a given test.

For a test to have **content validity,** it must contain an adequate sample of the skills or knowledge it is supposed to measure. Consider, for example, an achievement test in American history. It is not enough that all items on the test have something to do with the main topic, they must cover all aspects of the field in the correct proportions. It should not overemphasize economics or the Colonial period or include too many questions that can be answered too easily. Careful preparation and review prevent this kind of error. A testing service might spend several months studying programs at representative schools and outlining the subject areas and approaches that must be covered in the test.

Face validity is the appearance of validity to the people taking the test. An intelligence test originally constructed for children might be an equally accurate measure of adult intelligence. But if adults find the test childish and silly, they will lose interest, and the test will not be a valid measure of their intelligence. In some cases face validity is not desirable. A clinical psychologist who wants to ensure valid

---

*For more information on correlation coefficients, consult the appendix on measurement and statistical methods at the end of this book.

results may not want his patient to realize what he is being tested on.

Construct validity refers to the ideas on which the test is based. If a school system wants to use a particular test to identify musically gifted children, they will first compare the test scores of children who have excelled in their music program with the scores of children who did poorly in music classes. If the scores of the musical children are consistently higher, as would be predicted from the teachers' *construct* of musical talent, the test is valid. If there is no difference between the groups, they may have to reconsider their notions about musical abilities.

The validity of a test is thus judged in terms of how well it measures up to certain criteria. Often the criteria are quite specific. An expanding business wants to hire high school graduates who will do well in clerical positions. They look for a test that has identified successful clerks in the past—a test that has **predictive validity.** A college admissions board finds that some students who score high on its advanced placement test for French do well in the subject, but others have trouble after the first semester. The French department then looks for a test that has long-range predictive validity.

Standardization

By itself, a score is just a number. We obviously would not compare a basketball player who scored 6 points a game to a hockey player who made the same score. It would make just as little sense to assume that a score of 65 on one test means the same thing as a score of 65 on an entirely different test.

If scores on an intelligence test are to be useful, the test must first be **standardized.** That is, it must be administered to a group of people who are representative of the people for whom the test is designed. A test of reading ability among third-graders, for example, would be given to a *standardization group* of students in a number of third-grade classes. The scores of these students provide a set of *norms,* or standards. We could then compare any student's score on the reading test with the norms, and we could say that one reader is average, another is exceptional, a third is in the lower 10 percent, and yet another is below average.

Intelligence Tests

The Stanford-Binet Scales

In the late nineteenth century the French public school system was struggling with the realization that some children who did badly in school just *couldn't* learn. With the school system growing, they needed some way to identify these retarded children so that they could be sent

Alfred Binet
(*Culver Pictures*)

to special institutions. The director of the first psychological laboratory at the Sorbonne, Alfred Binet, had long been interested in questions of intellectual development, so he and his colleague Theodore Simon were asked to design a test. Practical men, they decided to invent a large number of questions and try them out on Paris schoolchildren. Presumably, the retarded children would not be able to solve problems a normal child of the same age found easy.

The results of their preliminary tests were somewhat surprising: Binet and Simon found a much wider range of scores than they had anticipated. At this point they realized that the test might be used to measure normal children as well as to identify those who were retarded.

The first *Binet-Simon Scale* was issued in 1905. It consisted of a series of 30 tests arranged in order of increasing difficulty. With each child the examiner started at the top of the list and worked down until the child could no longer answer questions.* As the results came in, Binet and Simon began to see a pattern: for each age group a large number of children were able to reach a certain level, while a smaller number stopped answering questions before that point and some went beyond.

By 1908, they had tested enough children to predict what the normal or average child could do at each age level. Using these average scores, Binet developed the concept of *mental age*. If a child scores as well as an average 4-year-old, his mental age is 4; if he scores as well as an average 12-year-old, his mental age is 12.

In the next 10 years a number of Binet adaptations were issued, the best known of which was prepared at Stanford University by L. M. Terman and issued in 1916. Although Terman's plan was simply to Americanize the Binet Scale, he ended by substantially rewriting it. He replaced or revised nearly half of the Binet items and moved others from one age level to another.

In addition to revising the contents of the Binet Scale, Terman introduced the now-famous term **IQ** (intelligence quotient). Binet's mental age tells us something about a person's abilities, and perhaps where to put him in school, but it does not tell us how bright he is. An 8-year-old with a mental age of 12 probably has more potential than a 14-year-old with the same mental age. The IQ shows us how a person's mental age compares to his actual or chronological age. To compute an IQ we simply divide mental age by chronological age and multiply by 100.† The formula looks like this:

$$\frac{\text{mental age}}{\text{chronological age}} \times 100 = \text{IQ}$$

*In modern terminology, the level at which a person is able to answer all questions is called his *basal age*. The level at which he is no longer able to answer any questions is called his *ceiling age*.

†The only reason for multiplying by 100 is to avoid fractions.

For example, if a child's mental age is 9 and his chronological age is 8, his IQ is 112:

$$9/8 \times 100 = 112$$

A child of 8 whose mental age is 8 is average in intelligence:

$$8/8 \times 100 = 100$$

Thus someone of average intelligence will have an IQ of 100.

The Stanford-Binet Scale has been revised twice since 1916, for two reasons. First, any test must be updated as word meanings and styles (the test materials include a number of pictures) change. Second, after a test has been given to thousands of people, the authors can check their questions against the results. Terman and his colleagues found, for example, that some questions were easier for people from one part of the country than for people from other areas; that some were easier for boys than for girls (and vice versa). Still other questions failed to discriminate between age levels, since nearly everyone tested could answer them. Such questions were replaced.

By 1960, when the second revision was issued, IQ was much better understood than when Terman invented the term. Studies had shown that a person's IQ changes over the years, and that mental age seems to stop increasing sometime between the ages of 16 and 18. Adult scores were in fact somewhat embarrassing—for the adults as well as for the test-writers. Judging by his IQ, the average 25-year-old (whose mental age stopped increasing at 18) is "borderline mentally retarded" ($18/25 \times 100 = 72$). To correct this absurdity, the test instruction booklet suggests we use a chronological age of 18 for anyone 18 or over. Thus a 40-year-old whose mental age was 22 is given credit for better than average development: $22/18 \times 100 = 122$, a "superior" IQ.

The original Binet Scale and Stanford revisions are based on the idea that the ability to solve problems and to think in abstract terms constitutes intelligence. Do such tests actually measure intelligence? Are they valid measures?

Most psychologists and educators look for predictive validity: do children with high IQ scores do well in school? In general they do. The correlation between Stanford-Binet scores and predominantly verbal school subjects, such as English or History, is highest.* Thus, intelligence tests are useful as a predictive tool, but they are not perfect.

The appropriateness of intelligence tests seems to lie in the way they are used. If we consider an IQ an absolute measure of lifelong mental

*Correlation, as you will recall, is a comparison of two sets of scores. In figuring the correlation of an intelligence test to school achievement, we compare IQ scores with achievement test scores.

ability, we are making a serious mistake. Data collected over 60 years of testing show that a person's IQ scores change over the years. In fact, IQ scores can change quite dramatically from one day to the next. If we expect IQ alone to predict school achievement accurately in all instances, we may well be disappointed. Teachers must also consider that Susan's parents do not think it is feminine for girls to be smart or that Paul's older brother is at the top of his class and Paul would rather excel in sports than compete with him. But if we take the IQ for what it is—a person's ability to solve abstract, largely verbal problems (at a particular time) as compared with the ability of other people his age—it is a useful tool.

By this point you will have begun to wonder why we are talking almost exclusively about the correlation between IQs and school performance. One reason is that schools have used the Stanford-Binet Scales more than anyone else. We have very little conclusive data on the relationship of IQ to job performance and the skills of daily life, but everything we do know indicates that the correlation is very low.

Few psychologists are surprised by this low correlation. They argue that the Stanford-Binet measures not general intelligence but scholastic ability, especially verbal skills. At the lower levels, for example, the examiner asks the child to *name* objects or to *say* what is wrong with a picture. And there is even more emphasis on verbal skills in the upper levels.

Defenders of intelligence tests must concede that the Stanford-Binet *is* largely a measure of academic skill. But they point out that in our society these are the skills a child needs to go through school and prepare himself for a career, the skills an adult needs to evaluate a political candidate or an advertisement, to file taxes, to read a newspaper or enjoy a novel.

In recent years psychologists have become more and more dissatisfied with this argument. Researchers ask, do intelligence tests discriminate against people who do not speak English? against adults whose careers do not require verbal skills? against children who have attended poor schools? against creative children? Many argue that because these tests were written by well-educated, middle-class, white Americans they are suitable for use only with that group. Some in the anti-IQ camp have devised alternate tests to be used in special situations.

Performance Tests

A deaf child takes longer to learn words than a child who can hear; it is unfair to compare him with normal children his age. A recent immigrant, who may have been a lawyer or teacher in his own country, needs time to learn English. How can we test these people? We must use problems that do not involve words—**performance tests** that substitute visual puzzles for words.

THE MEANING OF AN IQ SCORE

An IQ score, like a score on a midterm or a final examination, must be interpreted if it is to be meaningful. What can we expect of a person if we find that his IQ is 75? How much can we raise our hopes if his IQ is 125?

Based on observations of many people who have taken the Stanford-Binet Intelligence Test, the following set of classifications has been suggested for various IQ ranges:

IQ	Description
Above 140	Genius
120—140	Very superior
110—120	Superior
90—110	Average, normal
80—90	Dull
70—80	Borderline mentally retarded
Below 60	Feeble-minded

Terman's classifications give us a general idea of what an IQ means, but it is possible to be even more precise. One way is to look at the expected school achievement of people with various levels of IQ. People with IQs below 50 are usually unable to do first-grade work—to learn elementary reading and arithmetic. Those with IQs in the 50s may reach the second-grade level. A person whose IQ is in the 60s can be expected to achieve a third-grade level by age 16, but someone with an IQ in the 70s will rarely complete work beyond the fourth- or fifth-grade level. Individuals with IQs between 80 and 89, if given special attention, may finish the seventh or eighth grade. People with IQs between 90 and 99 can complete eighth-grade work; those with IQs between 100 and 109 can finish high school. Someone with an IQ between 110 and 114 might have some difficulty in college, but a person whose IQ is above 115 should be able to finish college. Of course we must bear in mind that these are rough generalizations based on average achievements of large groups of people. They do not rule out the possibility that some people, if they are highly motivated or receive extra help, may exceed these expectations. Nor do they mean that a person will always do this well—someone with an IQ over 115 may never want to go to college or may fail because of social or emotional difficulties.

One of the earliest, the *Seguin Form Board,* was devised in 1866 as a test for the mentally retarded. The form board is essentially a puzzle. The examiner removes the cutouts, stacks them in a predetermined order, and indicates that he wants the subject to replace them as quickly as he can. Another performance test, the *Porteus Maze,* consists of a series of increasingly difficult printed mazes. The examiner asks the subject to trace his way through the maze without lifting his pencil.

Figure 7-3

This woman is taking one kind of form board test, a performance test to measure intelligence.

(Van Bucher, Photo Researchers; courtesy University of Florida Department of Clinical Psychology.)

Figure 7-4

In this test, intelligence is indicated by how fast a person can trace the maze while watching it in a mirror.

(Van Bucher, Photo Researchers; courtesy University of Florida Department of Clinical Psychology.)

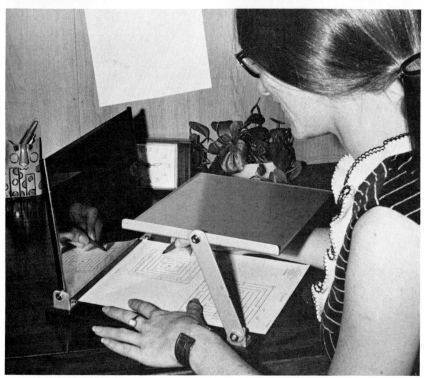

This test provides the examiner with something like a mental age based on the most difficult maze a subject negotiates.

Like the Stanford-Binet, performance tests assume that intelligence can be measured by observing a person's ability to solve problems, but unlike the standard intelligence test they have little obvious relation to the problems a child will encounter in school, or an adult will find

Figure 7-5
Equipment used to
administer the Gesell
Developmental Schedules,
an intelligence test for
infants.
(*From the Psychological
Corporation*)

in his career. However, performance tests can alert the examiner to possible problems, such as brain damage.

Performance tests are also used to evaluate infants and pre-school children who have only begun to understand and use words. An infant can neither understand directions nor answer questions. To test his intelligence (if we can use that word), an examiner has to observe what he does. Gesell, of the Yale Clinic of Child Development, worked out a detailed scale for assessing infant behavior and development. Using many of Gesell's measures, as well as questions from the lower levels of standard intelligence tests, Cattell devised an age scale. His *Infant Intelligence Scale* is basically a downward extension of the Stanford-Binet.

The results of infant tests are difficult to evaluate. For one thing, the infant does not realize he is being tested and is not motivated to do his best, as an older child would be. For another, we have no way of comparing these tests with other measures. The correlation between scores on infant tests and the Stanford-Binet given some years later is relatively low. In many cases, we can learn more about an infant's scholastic potential by looking at his parents' IQs and levels of education than we can by looking at his test scores. However, like other performance tests, infant tests are useful in diagnosing both physiological and psychological problems.

IQ AND OCCUPATION

Are lawyers more intelligent than dishwashers? Do you have to have a high IQ to be a dentist? Is there, in fact, any relationship at all between IQ scores and occupations?

One team of psychologists compared the IQ scores of a large group of Air Force enlisted men with their civilian occupations (Harrell & Harrell, 1945). They did indeed find a correlation between IQ and level of occupation, but the relationship was far from simple.

The table below gives the average IQ scores in each of the occupational levels; but it should not be interpreted as meaning that all professional workers had IQs of 120 or that all farmers had IQs of 94. Within each occupational level there was a range of IQs. For example, the highest IQ among public relations executives was 149 and the lowest IQ was 100. Among truck drivers the highest IQ was also 149, but the lowest truck driver scored an almost unbelievable 16. To perform well in an occupational level, a person had to have at least a certain minimum IQ, but there was no upper limit for any of the occupational levels. Nothing prevented the truck driver with an IQ of 149 from driving a truck, but the one with an IQ of 16 could hardly have succeeded in public relations.

Mean IQ	Occupation
120	Professional
113	Semiprofessional and managerial
108	Clerical, skilled, and retail
104	Semiskilled and minor clerical and business
96	Slightly skilled
95	Farm and nonfarm laborers
94	Farmers

Testing pre-school children is somewhat easier and more reliable. After the age of 2, the correlation with later IQ scores increases sharply. Children 3 to 5 years old understand instructions and are capable of working puzzles, copying block designs, naming objects, and so on. Many of the problems from the lower levels of the Stanford-Binet and other performance scales can be used with this age group. In most pre-school tests, puzzle and block problems are combined with tests for coordination and maturity. In general, then, pre-school intelligence tests measure "school-readiness."

The Wechsler Adult Intelligence Scale

The first intelligence test designed specifically for adults was published in 1939 by David Wechsler, a psychologist at New York's Bellevue Hospital. Most of Wechsler's patients were adults and many were

Figure 7-6
This woman is taking the
Wechsler Adult Intelligence
Scale (WAIS). She has been
given a set of picture cards
and must arrange them in
order so they tell a story.
*(Van Bucher, Photo Researchers;
courtesy University of Florida
Department of Clinical
Psychology.)*

undereducated and from the working class, that is, from the group many
feel the Stanford-Binet discriminates against.

Wechsler objected to using the Stanford-Binet for adults on a number
of grounds. First, the problems had been designed for children and
seemed juvenile to the housewife, the construction worker, the stock
market analyst—they lacked face validity. Second, the mental age
norms of the Stanford-Binet did not apply to adults (the method for
adjusting adult IQs was not devised until 1960). Finally, the emphasis
on verbal skills is inappropriate for adults. Teachers, lawyers, clergymen, doctors, and salesmen rely on words all their lives, but mechanics,
gardeners, factory workers, and cooks do not. Wechsler hypothesized
that adult intelligence consists more of the ability to handle the environment than of skill in solving verbal and abstract problems.

The Wechsler Adult Intelligence Scale (WAIS) is divided into two
parts, one emphasizing verbal skills, the other performance skills. The
verbal scale combines the usual problems—a vocabulary test, simple
arithmetic problems to be solved without pencil and paper, and a
memory test—with tests of information and judgment ("What would
you do if you saw smoke and fire in a crowded theater?").*

The *performance scale* is also composed of fairly routine tasks: block
designs, incomplete pictures, puzzles, picture cards to be arranged so
they tell a story.

Thus, although the questions and instructions might be more sophisticated on the WAIS than on the Stanford-Binet, the problems are

---

*You may have noticed that the verbal scale includes number problems. By "verbal,"
Wechsler simply meant tasks that required written or oral responses.

not especially adult. Wechsler's chief innovation was in scoring. First, the subject is given verbal and performance scores, as well as an overall IQ. In most cases, scores on the two scales are similar, but high performance and low verbal scores might indicate that a person had little education. Second, scores can be compared with an adult average, thus eliminating the impression of mental deterioration after the age of 18. The adult of average intelligence is given an overall IQ of 100. (The term "IQ" lingers on even where the mental age/chronological age ratio has been discarded.) Finally, on some items the subject can earn 1 or 2 points, depending on the complexity of his answer—thus giving credit for the reflective qualities we expect in adults.

The WAIS is often used in connection with placement in a job or training program. Here the separate scores for verbal and performance scales are particularly useful. Studies have shown a high correlation between occupation and WAIS subtests—professionals and white-collar workers generally score higher on the verbal than on the performance scale, and vice versa for blue-collar workers. A person with a high performance score might succeed as an auto mechanic, a TV cameraman, or an air traffic controller. Someone with an equal overall IQ but a higher verbal score might prefer managing a car repair shop, writing TV scripts, or holding an executive position with an airline.

The WAIS is also used in mental hospitals and clinics, in combination with other psychological tests. A person who has trouble with the block designs may be suffering from some kind of brain damage; someone who gives unusual answers to the judgment questions may have social or psychological problems.

Culture-Fair Intelligence Tests

As we saw in the preceding section, Wechsler defined intelligence as the ability to understand and deal with the environment, and designed a test specifically for the mature American. But, as we all know, America is a melting pot. Many U.S. citizens were born and raised elsewhere: to them the environment is bewildering.

(Constantine Manos, Magnum Photos)

Imagine that you were born in a small village in Greece. Most of your neighbors are farmers—and most are your cousins. The shop-keeper down the road remembers the day you were born; the school-teacher, who has taught all your brothers and sisters, keeps reminding you of your good family name. For as long as you can remember, you have tried to be like your father and looked forward to the day you would leave school and join him in the vineyards. But one day he calls you inside for a serious talk. He tells you you are going to live with your uncle in America, where you can get a good job and maybe one day have a store of your own. Quite suddenly you find yourself in a strange land where you do not understand the language or the customs.

After a few months, you learn enough English to get around, and you decide to apply for a job-training program.

The first day is a disaster—an insult. The woman who interviews you can see that you are nearly a man, but what does she do? She takes you to a small room and gives you some American children's toys (a performance test). But you want to do the right thing, so you start putting pieces together—and then, before you have even had time to think, she tells you to stop because the time is up. She writes down some numbers and asks you to come back tomorrow.

This young Greek, who was considered exceptionally promising in his village, had learned English, but not American ways. He expected the woman interviewing him to ask about his character, his family. In Greece no one would have asked him to play with toys, and he had always had time to talk, to understand why someone had asked him to do something, to think about how his father would have done it.

This is the situation of many immigrants who learn the language of their new country, but not its values and customs. This is also the situation of people who grow up within the borders of a country, but learn a very different culture—the children of immigrants who created an Italian or Chinese village in the heart of New York; poor children who grow up in the back country of Mississippi or Appalachia or on the streets of Harlem.

Culture-fair tests attempt to measure the intelligence of people who are outside the culture in which the test was devised. Like performance tests, they are language-free. (Even if a person becomes fluent in English as a second language, he may find idioms, nuances, and slang confusing.) In addition, they attempt to eliminate skills and feelings—such as the need for speed—that vary from one culture to another.

A classic example of this is the *Goodenough Draw-a-Person Test,* which requires only knowledge of the human body. The subject is asked to draw the best picture of a person he can. His drawing is scored for proportions, correct and complete representation of the parts of the body, detail in clothing, and so on—not artistic talent.*

Cattell's *Culture-Fair Intelligence Test* is based on a distinction between two different kinds of general intelligence. According to Cattell, **crystallized general ability** is what we use when we are required to apply prior knowledge to new information, as in taking an achievement test in history or geography. **Fluid general ability,** on the other hand, comes into play when we have to adapt to new situations, where crystallized abilities are not very helpful. Crystallized ability, Cattell felt, is what is measured by standard intelligence tests. But since it depends on skills and habits that have already been learned, it is strongly influenced by cultural experiences. A test that is truly culture-fair, according to Cattell, has to measure fluid general ability, which he believes is largely innate. The Culture-Fair Intelligence Test

---

*The Draw-a-Person test is often used as a supplement to the Stanford-Binet and as a personality test—a child's drawing may reveal more about his feelings than anything he will tell an adult.

thus contains materials that will be unfamiliar to all subjects, regardless of cultural background. It includes performance problems (such as identifying the item that does not belong in a series or completing a pattern), as well as questions that require verbal skills and cultural knowledge. Like the WAIS, this scale provides both verbal and performance scores, as well as an overall IQ.

To date, attempts to construct a test that is totally free of cultural bias have not been altogether successful. For one thing, we cannot assume that just because a test does not use words, it is culture-fair. Hopi Indian children, for example, score several points higher than white children on Goodenough's Draw-a-Person Test (Dennis, 1942). Second, characteristics of the test situation itself may bias the results. Even Cattell's Culture-Fair Test, despite its isolation of fluid and crystallized abilities, may be easier for those cultural groups whose members are accustomed to working with pencils and paper or who are motivated to do well when taking a test. Until these problems are solved, we must be very careful about making direct comparisons of intelligence test scores in different cultural groups.

Group Tests

The Stanford-Binet, the WAIS, and most of the performance tests discussed so far are individual tests. The examiner takes the subject to an isolated room, spreads the materials on a table, and spends anywhere from 30 to 90 minutes giving the test. He may then spend another hour or so scoring the test according to detailed instructions in the manual. Obviously this is a time-consuming, costly operation. And there is always a chance that the examiner's feeling will influence the score.

(Van Bucher, Photo Researchers)

For these reasons, test-makers have devised written intelligence tests that can be given to large groups by a single examiner. Instead of a person sitting across the table asking you to name an object, the test booklet gives you a choice of four words; instead of building a design with blocks, you choose one of four shapes that will complete a design.

Schools are among the biggest consumers of group tests. From fourth grade through high school the *School and College Ability Tests* (SCAT) are used to measure students' specific abilities. The *Scholastic Aptitude Tests* (SAT) are designed to measure a student's ability to perform college-level work. The *Graduate Record Examination* (GRE) plays the same role in graduate admissions.

Group tests have some distinct advantages. Bias in the examiner is eliminated. A computer or a clerk who never saw the subject can score marks on an answer sheet quickly and objectively. More people can be tested in this way and better norms established. At the same time, there is less chance that an examiner will notice if a student is tired or ill or if he has not understood the directions. Group tests are used widely in industry, civil service, and the military, as well as in schools.

Types of Creativity Tests

To many people, the idea of testing creativity will seem utterly ridiculous. How can we squeeze imagination into a question that can be answered *true* or *false, a* or *b*?

The answer is that we do not. Creativity tests are usually open-ended; instead of asking for the correct solution to a problem, the examiner asks how many solutions the subject can see. Scores are based on the number and originality of his answers.

For example, in the *Torrance Test of Creative Thinking* the examiner shows the subject a picture and asks him what questions he would ask to find out what is happening, to explain how the scene came about, and to speculate on its consequences. The *Christensen-Guilford Test* asks him to list as many words with a given letter as he can; to name things belonging to a class (such as liquids that will burn); to write four-word sentences beginning with the letters *R, D, L, S* (Rainy days look sad, Red dogs like soup, Renaissance dramas lack symmetry, and so on); to name unusual ways of using an everyday object, such as a newspaper (starting fires, stuffing packing boxes, training puppies, and so on); and to imagine what would happen if some bizarre situation came about (if people stopped wanting and needing sleep, for example). The second half of this test requires drawing: the subject is asked to make the most interesting picture he can from a given geometric shape or a few printed lines.

(Fritz Henle, Photo Researchers)

The most widely used creativity test, Mednick's (1962) *Remote Associates Test* (RAT), asks the subject to produce a single verbal response that relates to a set of three apparently unrelated words. For example, the three stimulus words may be "poke," "go," and "molasses." The subject must answer with a single "creative" response which can be linked to all three of these words. In the example given, the desirable response (though not necessarily the only answer) is "slow" (*slow*-poke, go *slow, slow* as molasses). Arriving at such responses is no easy process, especially since the stimulus words have no apparent connection to each other.

The correlation between scores on these tests and the products we associate with creativity—paintings, poems, operas, inventions, cures for cancer—is low. Many psychologists explain these disappointing results by pointing to the fact that creativity appears to be dependent on more than just certain kinds of intellectual abilities. For example, Tryk (1968) sees *motivation* as a critical factor in creative output. The great artist, scientist, or writer has more than simple "talent" or "genius"; he has intense dedication, ambition, and perseverance.

Of course, there are many other problems associated with creativity tests. We lack a generally accepted definition of creativity, and thus many tests that we lump together as "creativity tests" are, in fact, measuring a wide variety of skills and qualities. In addition, the scoring of creativity tests is often complicated by the absence of a single, correct answer. An intelligence test may have easily determined "right" answers, but a creativity test rarely does (Tryk, 1968). Because of this, scoring—and, hence, definition—cannot be precise.

Determinants of Intelligence

In 1969 psychologist Arthur Jensen wrote a critique of compensatory education programs like Head Start. Such programs, he felt, were failing. Jensen went on to argue that heredity accounted for a significant proportion of the 15-point difference between the average IQ scores of blacks and whites. Within days Jensen made headlines in the South. Lawyers fighting school integration in Virginia used the article as proof of black inferiority. Many social scientists felt that Jensen's conclusions were at the very least premature.

Thus began a new round in the debate between *nativists,* who believe that heredity determines intelligence, and *environmentalists,* who argue that heredity is only part of the story. We will return to the question of race differences at the end of this section. First let us look at the evidence on each side of the heredity/environment controversy.

Heredity

In Chapter 2 we noted that inherited characteristics are carried by genes; that an individual gets half his genes from each parent; that the genes of two parents can combine in different ways, producing variety in their offspring; that some genes are dominant, others recessive; and so on. But until recently scientists knew little about how genes affect abilities and about which genes are important in determining intelligence.

In a few cases specific traits have been attributed to single genes. For example, the disease phenylketonuria (PKU) has been linked to a recessive gene that controls an enzyme. If both of a child's parents have this gene and pass it on to their child, his body will be unable to break down a substance that then accumulates in his blood and brain, causing severe retardation. If diagnosed early enough, this situation can be corrected through diet. But PKU is an exception in this way. Even simple traits, as we saw in Chapter 2, depend on several genes **(polygenic inheritance);** the number involved in intelligence is potentially enormous.

But we are jumping ahead here. How do we know that intelligence has anything at all to do with heredity?

Some 30 years ago R. C. Tryon began wondering if the ability to run mazes could be bred into rats. Horse breeders and cattle farmers have long known that selective breeding—for example, crossing a fast horse with a strong one—can change the physical characteristics of animals.

INTELLIGENCE, FAMILY SIZE, AND BIRTH ORDER

A recent article by Zajonc (1975) presents some striking findings about the relationship between intelligence, family size, and birth order. After reviewing research conducted by Belmont and Marolla (1973), who collected intelligence and birth-order statistics on 386,114 young men in the Netherlands, Zajonc concluded that:

> *Intelligence declines with family size; the fewer children in your family, the smarter you are likely to be. Intelligence also declines with birth order; the fewer older brothers or sisters you have, the brighter you are likely to be* (p. 37).

Zajonc and Markus (1975) have constructed a model of the intellectual environment of a family in order to account for these findings. Their model suggests that when a newborn baby enters a family, the average intelligence of the family is lowered. Previously, each parent had arbitrarily been scored at a level of 100. But the zero score assigned to the newborn baby lowers the average intelligence in the family to a level of 67. If a second child is born 1 year later, the family's score will drop to 50. One simple way to explain this is to imagine the intelligence of the parents being spread around among a number of young children. The more children there are, the more the parents' intelligence will be passed to each in small doses. Also, as younger children are born, there is less and less to go around.

To maximize the intellectual environment of your children, Zajonc suggests that you have no more than two children and that you have them at least 3 years apart. One of the benefits firstborn children have is the opportunity to teach things to their younger siblings. Contrary to popular belief, Zajonc has found that only children are not better off intellectually, probably because, although they have their parents' undivided attention, they do not have this teaching opportunity.

Chance (1975) makes an interesting connection between Belmont and Marolla's data and the debate over racial differences in IQ. He hypothesizes that, if those data are reliable, then blacks may score lower on IQ tests than whites merely because of their larger family sizes. The 1973 census shows an average family size of 2.52 children for blacks and 2.13 for whites, which doesn't seem like a big difference. But blacks are three times as likely as whites to have six or more children in a family. Chance suggests that this may explain the differential between whites and blacks on IQ tests and thus may put quite a different perspective on the debate about race and IQ.

Could the same technique be used to alter mental abilities? Tryon isolated eligible pairs of "maze-bright" rats in one pen and "maze-dull" rats in another. The animals were left free to breed. Within a few generations the difference between the two groups was astounding: the maze-dull rats made many more mistakes learning a maze than their bright counterparts (Tryon, 1940; see Figure 7-7).

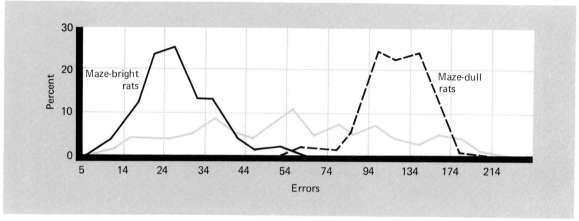

Figure 7-7

Errors made in learning a maze by the rats Tryon bred to be maze-bright and maze-dull. The color line shows what percentage of the parent group made each number of errors. The black lines show the results of the eighth generation of rats. Notice that almost all of the maze-dull rats made more errors than the maze-bright rats. (After R. C. Tryon, "Genetic Differences in Maze-Learning Abilities in Rats." In *39th Yearbook, Part I, National Society for the Study of Education.* Chicago: University of Chicago Press, 1940, 111–119.)

It is difficult to say exactly how maze ability had been transmitted. Perhaps the brighter rats inherited better eyesight, larger brains, quicker reflexes, a greater desire to succeed, or a combination of these and other subtler abilities. Still, Tryon did show that a specific ability can be passed down from one generation to another.

For obvious reasons laboratory experiments in selective breeding of humans are impractical. Fortunately, nature provides us with the perfect experimental subjects for measuring heredity in man: identical twins. Unlike siblings and fraternal twins, whose genes come from the same parents, but have combined differently, identical twins have exactly the same genetic inheritance. If, as Tryon's experiment suggests, intelligence is inherited, they will have identical IQs. Any difference between them can be attributed to environment.

Studies of twins begin with a comparison of the IQs of identical twins who have been raised together. The correlation, shown in Figure 7-8, is very high. But these twins grew up in the same environment: they shared parents, home, schoolteachers, vacations, and probably friends and clothes as well. Maybe these common experiences explain their similarity. To check this possibility, researchers look for identical twins who were separated early in life (generally before they are 6 months old) and raised in different families. The correlation between IQs of separated twins is nearly as high as that between twins raised together, but there is some evidence of environmental influence.

Heredity clearly has a significant effect on intelligence. But what about fraternal twins, brothers and sisters, parents and their new child? The correlation between their IQs is not nearly as high as that for identical twins. As final proof, researchers compare the IQs of unrelated children raised in the same home and of adopted children and their foster parents: the correlations here are very low.

At this point the case for heredity seems to be won: identical twins think alike, even when they have not lived together. Twin studies,

Figure 7-8
Correlations of IQ scores
and familial relationships
(Adapted from L.
Erlenmeyer-Kimling and
L. F. Jarvik, "Genetics and
Intelligence: A Review,"
Science, 1963, 142,
1477–1479.)

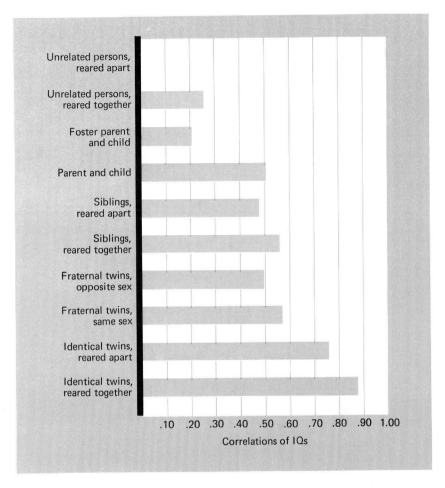

however, are not "final proof," for several reasons. First, it is difficult to find identical twins who were separated at birth. The largest study to date was based on only 53 pairs (Burt, 1966). Few scientists would consider the data from so limited a sample conclusive. Second, adoption agencies tend to match natural and foster parents. If the twins were born to middle-class, educated parents, it is highly likely that the adopted twin was placed with middle-class, educated foster parents. Finally, even if the twins grew up in radically different environments, for 9 months they lived in the same mother: their prenatal experiences were identical. It is at this point that the environmental case begins.

Environment

Environmentalists do not deny that some part of intelligence is inherited, but they feel this is only the start. Each person inherits a certain body build from his parents, but his actual weight depends on what he eats and how much he exercises. Similarly, environmentalists argue, people inherit certain mental capacities, but how their intellectual abilities develop depends on what they see around them as infants, how their parents respond to their first attempts to talk, the schools they attend, the books they read, the TV they watch—and even what they eat.

The environmental case begins with the fetus. A number of studies show that prenatal nutrition affects intelligence. One group of psychologists, for example, studied a group of pregnant women who were poor and therefore rarely got "three square meals a day." Half the women were given a dietary supplement, and half were given placebos (to guard against the possibility that merely taking pills would make women feel better and that this, not nutrition, would affect their babies). When given intelligence tests between the ages of 3 and 4, the children of the mothers who had taken the supplement scored significantly higher than the other children (Harrell, Woodyard, & Gates, 1955).

Extreme malnutrition during infancy can lower intelligence and may lead to retardation that cannot be cured by improved diet in later years. Severely undernourished children in South Africa, for example, averaged 20 points lower in IQ than similar children who had had adequate diets (Stock & Smythe, 1963). If a child does not get an adequate diet in the early stages of development, his mental as well as his physiological growth will be stunted.

None of this is surprising: common sense tells us that a person needs food to grow. But is that all he needs? Apparently not. Many psychologists think that surroundings are as important to mental development as diet. The first hint of this came from studies of the effect of light deprivation on sight. Chimpanzees, kittens, rabbits, and other animals raised in total darkness for 16 to 18 months and then moved to a normal environment were never able to see as well as animals exposed to daylight from birth. There was nothing wrong with these animals' eyes at birth; it seems the cells and nerves we use to see do not develop without stimulation (Wiesel & Hubel, 1963).

Even more revealing was a study of Tryon's maze-bright and maze-dull rats conducted in the 1950s. Psychologists raised one group of mixed bright and dull rats in absolutely plain surroundings, another group in an exceptionally stimulating environment that contained toys, an activity wheel, and a ladder. When the rats were grown, they were tested on the mazes. There was *no* difference between the formerly bright and dull rats who had been raised in a restricted environment (indicating that the inherited abilities of the bright rats had failed to develop) and little difference between the rats raised in a stimulating environment. The researchers performed autopsies on both groups and found that the rats brought up in a stimulating environment had heavier brains than the others, whether or not they had inherited maze-brightness (Cooper & Zubek, 1958).

Figure 7-9

This cage, with all its opportunities for activity, represents an enriched environment for animals such as rats, mice, and gerbils (shown here). When raised in such an environment, maze-dull rats can learn to perform in mazes as well as rats that were selectively bred for maze-brightness.

(Courtesy M. R. Rosenzweig and E. L. Bennett; reprinted by permission of John Wiley & Sons, Inc.)

Quite by accident, one researcher found evidence that intelligence, like sight and maze-brightness, depends on stimulation. In the 1930s, psychologist H. M. Skeels was investigating orphanages for the state of Iowa. Then as now the wards were terribly overcrowded: often three or four attendants were responsible for washing, dressing, feeding, and cleaning up after as many as 35 children. There was rarely time to play with the children, to talk to them, or to read them stories. Many of the children were classified as subnormal; it was fairly common for the state to transfer them to institutions for the mentally retarded when the orphanages ran out of space. Skeels became interested in two such children who, after a year and a half in an orphanage, were sent to a ward for adult women whose mental ages ranged from 4 to 9. When Skeels first tested these girls they did indeed seem retarded, but after a year on the adult ward their IQs were normal (Skeels, 1938). This was quite remarkable: after all, the women they had lived with were themselves severely retarded. Skeels decided to repeat the experiment and placed 13 slow children as house guests in adult wards (Skeels, 1942). Within 18 months the mean IQ of these children had risen from 64.3 to 92 (within the normal range), all because they had had someone to play with them, to read to them, to cheer when they took their first steps, to encourage them to talk. During the same period the mean IQ of a group of children who had been left in orphanages dropped from 86 to 61. Such dramatic changes could not occur if intelligence were stable and hereditary. Thirty years later Skeels found that all 13 of the children raised on adult wards were self-supporting, their occupations ranging from waitress to real estate salesman. Half of the contrasting group were unemployed, four were still in institutions, and all those who had jobs were dishwashers (Skeels, 1966).

Figure 7-10

Changes in IQ of the institutionalized children studied by Skeels. (Adapted from H. M. Skeels, "The Study of the Effects of Differential Stimulation on Mentally Retarded Children: A Follow-up Report," *American Journal of Mental Deficiencies*, 1942, 46, 340–350.)

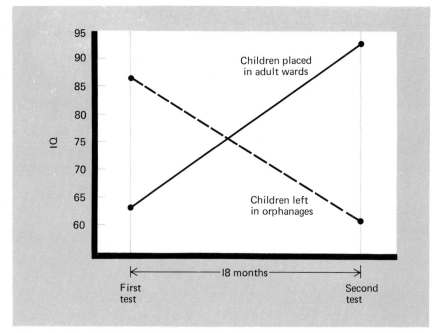

Taking their cue from Skeels, some researchers suggest that child-rearing patterns explain class differences in IQ. Lower-class mothers, especially mothers with large families, they point out, often do not play with their children as much as middle-class mothers do. Nor do they reward them consistently for development (such as learning to crawl or to tell time). Middle-class parents encourage their children to talk. They ask them to describe what they are building with blocks, to identify shapes, colors, and sizes. Those who accept the idea that intelligence depends on stimulation explain the lower IQs of poor children in terms of thwarted curiosity, underdeveloped attention span, and a general mistrust of adults.

This is the essence of the environmentalist argument. True, some general capabilities are inherited, but without stimulation a child's intelligence, like the eyes of animals raised in darkness, will not develop. The effects of early deprivation—whether the extreme loneliness of the institutionalized child or the relative isolation of the lower-class child—may not be reversible in later life.

Race Differences: Jensen and His Critics

Operation Head Start was conceived as a kind of foster middle-class environment for disadvantaged children. The idea was not only to teach basic concepts (color, size, shape), but also to encourage children to put their perceptions and wondering into words; to teach them to trust adults, to feel comfortable in a schoolroom, to exercise their curiosity—to make them ready for school. The apparent failure of this program was the occasion for the article by Jensen that we mentioned at the beginning of this discussion.

The IQs of the first graduates of Head Start had not gone up as anticipated; their scores on achievement tests after a year or two in school were no higher than those of similar but untutored children.

In the first part of his article Jensen examines the evidence that intelligence is inherited (studies of twins and maze-bright rats) and concludes that heredity accounts for at least 80 percent of the variation in IQ. He then turns to the question of race differences: black Americans average 15 points lower than whites on IQ tests. Noting the extreme reluctance of social scientists to consider the possibility of "innate racial differences," Jensen argues that such taboos are scientifically irresponsible. He goes on to say that socioeconomic class does not explain race differences: blacks in the upper and middle classes, as well as those in the lower class, average lower than their white counterparts; American Indians, who are worse off in every way, score higher than blacks. Nor do discrimination and prejudice explain the gap: the fact that blacks are isolated in our society suggests that their gene pool differs from that of the general population. Jensen concludes that heredity is strongly implicated, but cautions against drawing any conclusions about individuals on the basis of group generalizations.*

Critics feel that Jensen's argument is logical, but totally unrealistic. Any comparison of blacks and whites in America must take discrimination into account—on several levels.

First, for generations blacks have been told that they belong to an inferior race. The lower-class white who came to America as a young boy and went right to work as a laborer had no reason to feel that he could not have been a doctor or lawyer if he had been able to go to school. He probably expects his children to do better in life than he has. For blacks it is the opposite: the argument goes, "Everyone says blacks are inferior, so they must be inferior. Well, they were slaves, weren't they?" The effects of such discrimination have been documented in comparisons of blacks living in the South with those in the North: Northern blacks score significantly higher on IQ tests than Southern blacks, suggesting that a higher level of discrimination in the South depresses intelligence (Vernon, 1969).

Second, teachers tend to expect less from black students and will communicate this, however subtly. The effects of low expectations and

---

*Although most of the controversy over Jensen's article centers on the question of race and intelligence, it should be pointed out that this issue occupied only about 10 pages out of 123 in his article.

low self-esteem accumulate over the years. One psychologist tested 1,800 Southern black students between the ages of 5 and 13. The average IQ of 5-year-olds was 86; the average IQ of 13-year-olds was 65 (Kennedy & Lindner, 1963).

Jensen assumes that if the blacks and whites we test are in the same socioeconomic class, their environments are equal. Few researchers would agree with him on this. Take housing: the average white construction worker owns his own home, with a little help from the bank. A black man with the same income and references has a much harder time finding a home and getting a mortgage. His living conditions are likely to be quite different from those of his white co-worker.

But let us set aside differences in physical environment. We still must be certain that the testing situation was the same for the two groups we are comparing. Many psychologists feel black children are frightened of tests and of examiners, who are usually white. One researcher found that when black adolescents thought they were being tested for coordination they did better than when they knew the problems were part of an intelligence test. The idea of taking an intelligence test from a white examiner affected their performance (Katz, 1964).

Jensen's work has led to a raging controversy among educators and social scientists over the validity of IQ testing, the heritability of intelligence, and the relationship between race and intelligence. Between 1969 and 1973, as Jensen (1974) notes, 117 articles have been published in response to his original piece (1969) in the *Harvard Educational Review*. In addition, the Jensen controversy has led to protests, sit-ins, and even disruption of speaking engagements on many campuses.

Jensen (1974) has defended his controversial speculations on the grounds that conservatism in generating hypotheses "has not made for progress as often as a more adventurous approach" (p. 921). On the other hand, Dworkin (1974), in a criticism of Jensen, notes that the risks of these adventures will not be experienced by the scientist. "Jensen faces only the risk of being wrong in his speculations; others face the risk of increased political, economic, and educational oppression" (p. 921). Essentially, Dworkin argues that continued propagation of Jensen's theories will only contribute to prejudice and discrimination against black Americans.

It is difficult to sort out the conflicting data and claims involved in the argument over Jensen's work. This is especially true since most of the participants, including Jensen and many of his critics, agree that both hereditary and environmental factors do have *some* impact on intelligence. Dobzhansky (1973a) insists that we simply don't have conclusive evidence to prove that there is, or is not, a genetic component to racial differences in intelligence. In addition, as Jensen himself points out, we should remember that comparisons of *average* scores of any group tell us very little about what we can expect of the *individual* member of any group.

IQ AND TEACHER EXPECTATIONS

Many psychologists and educators feel that the dismal school records of deprived children are the result of a self-fulfilling prophecy—the children realize that their teachers expect them to fail, so they do.

One team of psychologists (Rosenthal & Jacobson, 1968) decided to test this hypothesis in a public elementary school in San Francisco. Most of the students in the school came from lower-class homes; 17 percent were of Mexican descent. In the spring of 1964 Rosenthal and Jacobson tested all the children in the school. They explained to the teachers that the test scores would reveal "late bloomers," children who would very soon begin to make startling academic progress. Before the next semester began, each teacher received the names of several children in her class and was told they could be expected to make an unusual intellectual gain. What the teachers did not know was that the names given to the teachers had simply been chosen at random. The only difference between these children and the others was in the minds of the teachers.

Rosenthal and Jacobson went back to the school in January and again in May of 1965 and retested the children. The children who had been described to their teachers as "late bloomers" had indeed made striking intellectual gains, especially in the first and second grades. Teachers were asked to rate their students on academic performance and classroom behavior. Not surprisingly, they gave more favorable ratings to the children they had expected to do well. But even more revealing were their ratings of the other children. Children who had gained in IQ but had not been expected to do so were rated unfavorably. The more they had gained, the lower their teachers rated them.

The teachers had not spent more time with the children who had been designated "late bloomers," but their attitude had obviously had an effect on them. Perhaps the teachers' expectations were communicated by their tone of voice, expression, touch, or posture, all of which could conceivably change a child's self-image or motivation.

In a followup study, Rosenthal (1973) found that 242 studies have been conducted to test the validity of this self-fulfilling prophecy, which has been called "the Pygmalion effect." One study found that swimming instructors in a summer camp made better swimmers out of a supposedly "high potential" group than out of a control group. The Pygmalion effect was also noticeable in studies involving institutionalized adolescent girls, United States Air Force Preparatory School airmen, and supervisors of disadvantaged workers in electronics plants.

Although many questions are still unanswered, these experiments show that IQ gains can take place in a school without special educational enrichment programs. Thus, some of the deficiencies that have been attributed to the deprived background of the disadvantaged child can perhaps be blamed on the attitudes and expectations of his teachers. Perhaps if each teacher gave each schoolchild, not just the "good" ones, warmth, positive feedback, and attention, the school performance of disadvantaged children might show real improvement without contrived and expensive programs.

Sex Differences

In the past few years women in America have begun to see themselves as an oppressed minority. They argue that the idea that men are more capable, more aggressive—in a word, smarter—is a myth. But have generations of domesticity left women, like the maze-dull rats, intellectually underdeveloped? IQ tests show that this is not the case: in overall intelligence the sexes are equal.

However, there are differences in particular abilities. Young girls are more verbal than boys: they talk earlier, do better in English, and outperform boys on verbal intelligence scales and on verbal achievement tests. A higher proportion of boys than girls have reading problems. One researcher suggests this is because boys think school is feminine and "sissyish" (Kagan, 1966). On the other hand, boys have more skill with spatial, mechanical, and mathematical problems. These differences continue through grade school, with boys excelling in history, geography, and math, and girls excelling in English and languages. Interestingly, at the primary school level, boys and girls show equal aptitude for science; in grade school, girls move ahead somewhat; but by high school, girls are falling behind. In fact, this pattern seems to characterize female intellectual development in general: girls do well in grade school and high school, then seem to level off and sometimes retrogress.

Many researchers account for differences in school performance by pointing out that girls mature earlier than boys. They reach puberty about two years before boys do, and even in earlier years girls are taller, heavier, and have more mature interests than boys. According to this argument, girls thus have a slight head start when they begin school. This might explain girls' superiority in school achievement, but why does their advantage taper off? Why are there so few eminent women scientists? So few successful businesswomen? So few great female artists? For an explanation of women's lack of achievement after the school years, most psychologists look to cultural and social influences. Women have seldom enjoyed an equal opportunity to excel in intellectual achievements. The personality traits that have generally been approved in women, including submissiveness and docility, might well lead to higher evaluations by teachers, but are unlikely to result in intellectual achievements. Boys, on the other hand, are expected to be more aggressive and competitive, traits that would aid them in achieving excellence in many fields. As our culture changes toward sexual equality, we expect these differences between men and women's achievement to decrease. But, although the situation has changed for the better, it will be many years before women will be equipped to accomplish as much as men have in the past.

Thus with sex differences, as with racial and cultural differences, achievement depends on more than equality of general intelligence.

Summary

1. Since intelligence cannot be seen directly, psychologists are concerned with intelligent behavior. Intelligence is usually considered to be the ability to perform well in a variety of situations.

2. Spearman presented a theory of general intelligence, which he called g. He explained differences in specific abilities by introducing s factors, into which g branches out unequally. Thurstone compiled a list of seven *primary mental abilities*, which he felt together constituted general intelligence. Guilford devised a three-dimensional *model of the intellect* to show the interactions of three classes of mental ability.

3. Creativity involves the ability to go beyond the conventional and find original solutions to problems. One way of explaining creativity emphasizes the formation of unlikely associations. Guilford's approach draws on a number of the operations in his model of the intellect, but is centered around *divergent thinking*—an approach that leads to several different solutions instead of focusing on one right answer. Recent studies suggest that convergent thinking may also be important for creativity.

4. Investigations of schoolchildren indicate that creativity and intelligence are two distinct abilities, and that being high in one does not necessarily mean that a person will be high in the other.

5. *Aptitude tests* are used to measure ability to learn and to identify specific strengths. *Multiple aptitude batteries* yield an overall profile of a person's abilities; *special aptitude tests* concentrate on ability in a particular area; *intelligence tests* measure intellectual aptitude. *Achievement tests*, on the other hand, are used to measure what has already been learned.

6. Tests can be used for several purposes: to *predict* how an individual will do in certain situations; to *diagnose* problems; or as part of a *research* program to design curriculum materials or other tests.

7. A test must meet certain criteria if it is to be useful. It must be *reliable*—the results must be consistent and dependable. It must be *valid*—it must really measure what it is supposed to measure. It must be *standardized*—there must be norms to use in interpreting an individual's score.

8. The first test of intelligence was the *Binet-Simon Scale*, prepared in France in 1905. A child's score on this test was called his *mental age* and was based on a comparison of his answers with the average performance of children of various ages.

9. The *Stanford-Binet Scale*, prepared by L. M. Terman, is an American adaptation of the Binet-Simon Scale. Terman also introduced the term *IQ* (intelligence quotient) as a means of comparing a person's mental age with his chronological age. The formula for computing IQ is:

$$\frac{MA}{CA} \times 100 = IQ$$

The most recent revision of the Stanford-Binet Scale uses a mental age of 18 for anyone 18 or over.

10. In general, children who score high on the Stanford-Binet Scale do well in school. The correlation with job performance is much lower, since the test measures scholastic ability and places heavy emphasis on verbal skills.

11. *Performance tests* have been developed for testing people who are unable to take standard intelligence tests. These tests, which are used to test the handicapped, people who speak a foreign language, and children who have not yet learned how to talk, generally substitute puzzles or mazes for word questions.

12. The *Wechsler Adult Intelligence Scale* (WAIS) was designed especially for adults. It includes a verbal scale and a performance scale; it yields separate scores on the two scales, as well as an overall IQ.

13. *Culture-fair intelligence tests* are designed to measure the intelligence of people who are not part of the test-maker's own culture—immigrants or members of subcultures. They attempt to include only materials that will be equally familiar to all cultural groups and to eliminate skills that depend on cultural training, but have not yet been very successful.

14. *Group tests,* like the *Scholastic Aptitude Tests* or the *Graduate Record Examination,* are designed to be administered to many people at one time. Two advantages of group tests are efficiency in testing and the elimination of bias on the part of the examiner. One disadvantage is that of keeping the examiner from discovering specific problems the subject might have at the time of the test.

15. *Tests of creativity* usually ask for a number of solutions to a problem, rather than one right answer. A person's score depends on the number of solutions and their originality. Correlations between tests of creativity and creative production are low; many psychologists feel the tests do not measure the personality characteristics that are important in determining creativity, for example, motivation.

16. Psychologists have long debated the question of whether intelligence is primarily inherited or developed by environmental influences. Selective breeding experiments with rats and comparative studies of identical twins suggest that intelligence can indeed be passed on from one generation to the next. However, further studies have shown that without the proper environmental stimulation, inherited capacities will not develop to the fullest extent.

17. In 1969 Arthur Jensen proposed that the 15-point difference between the IQs of black and white Americans could be attributed primarily to inheritance. Jensen's critics, however, have argued that the effects of racial discrimination must be taken into account, no matter how similar black and white environments appeared to be.

18. Intelligence tests show that the overall intelligence of males and females is equal, but that boys and girls usually do have different abilities in specific areas. To explain sex differences in intellectual achievement, most psychologists emphasize social and cultural influences.

Suggested Readings

Black, H., *They Shall Not Pass* (New York: Morrow, 1963). A skeptical but balanced evaluation of the uses of intelligence tests in the schools.

Butcher, H. J., *Human Intelligence: Its Nature and Assessment* (London: Metheun, 1968). A good overall treatment of intelligence—what it is, what affects it, and how it is measured.

Ehrman, L., Omenn, G. S., and Caspari, E. (Eds.), *Genetics, Environment, and Behavior: Implications for Educational Policy* (New York: Academic Press, 1972). An extremely good collection of papers on the effects of social and educational policy on intelligence and on the relationship between genetics and environment.

Herrnstein, R. J., *IQ in the Meritocracy* (Boston: Atlantic–Little, Brown, 1973). A controversial book that supports the heritability of IQ and foresees a society organized around intelligence as the primary determinant of status.

Jensen, A. R., *Educability and Group Differences* (New York: Harper & Row, 1973). In addition to summarizing the recent evidence for the heritability of intelligence, Jensen suggests that "educability"—the ability to learn in a conventional classroom setting—may also be inherited. Educators have traditionally assumed that ability to learn is environmentally influenced. Jensen proposes changes in the educational system that would reflect his point of view.

Kamin, L. J., *The Science and Politics of IQ* (New York: Halsted, 1974). A presentation of the argument against the heritability of intelligence and a discussion of the implications of an uncritical acceptance of heritability.

Taylor, C. W. (Ed.), *Creativity: Progress and Potential* (New York: McGraw-Hill, 1964). A stimulating set of essays on such topics as the characteristics of the creative person, creativity in the schools, and ways of increasing creativity.

Tuddenham, R. D., "The Nature and Measurement of Intelligence," in L. Postman (Ed.), *Psychology in the Making* (New York: Knopf, 1962). An interesting account of the development of intelligence tests and the theories behind them.

Tyler, L. E., *Tests and Measurements*, 2nd ed. (Englewood Cliffs, N.J.: Prentice-Hall, 1970). A concise, readable introduction to psychological testing and the statistics involved in interpreting test scores.

Tyler, L. E. (Ed.), *Intelligence: Some Recurring Issues* (New York: Van Nostrand Reinhold, 1969). A collection of articles that deal with controversial topics in the study of intelligence and testing.

Wolfle, D. (Ed.), *The Discovery of Talent* (Cambridge, Mass.: Harvard University Press, 1969). A series of lectures on intelligence and talent by well-known psychologists, including Guilford, Terman, and Vernon.

outline

THE NATURE OF SENSATION   278

General Characteristics of Sensation
Measurement of Sensation
Sensory Adaptation

VISION   281

The Eye
Rods and Cones
Neural Connections
Adaptation
Color Vision

HEARING   290

Sound
The Ear
Neural Connections
Theories of Hearing

THE CHEMICAL SENSES   295

Smell
Taste

THE BODY SENSES   299

Kinesthesis
The Vestibular Sense

THE SKIN SENSES   302

Receptors and Neural Connections
Pressure
Temperature
Pain

SUMMARY   306

SUGGESTED READINGS   309

Sensation

Sensation has many facets. It includes the sight of a rainbow, the feel of oozing mush of a mud puddle, the icy chill of a hard rainstorm, the smell of the ocean, the sting of the salt water in your eyes, the throbbing pain of a toothache, the dizziness that comes after a ride on a roller coaster, the sweet taste of ice cream, and the splitting headache that you get if you eat cold ice cream too quickly.

All of us use our senses continually, but usually we are unaware of most of our sensations. Moreover, we do not usually question how various sensory experiences are caused; how it is, for example, that a rose causes such a delicate and delightful smell. But the psychologist does more than merely accept these reactions. He tries to determine how various forms of energy affect the receptor cells within the sense organs and how the receptor cells translate that energy into messages to the central nervous system. The psychologist studying sensation wants to learn how information from the outside world gets through to us—how we see and hear the things around us, how we taste and smell the foods we eat, how we know when we are moving or when we have lost our balance, and, literally, how we keep in touch with our external environment.

The Nature of Sensation

Our senses do not all work the same way—the way we smell is very different from the way we see; the way we hear is quite unlike the way we taste. But before we turn to the specific characteristics of each of the sensory processes, let us look at the general characteristics common to all sensations.

General Characteristics of Sensation

Described in general terms, the sequence of events that produces a sensation seems quite simple. First, some form of energy, either from an external source or from within the body, stimulates a receptor cell in one of the sense organs—such as the eye or the ear. A receptor cell is specialized to respond to one certain form of energy—light waves of certain lengths, air pressure, the energy from chemical activity, thermal energy, or mechanical pressure. There are several different kinds of receptor cells. Some—like the receptors in the eye and nose—are specialized neurons; others—like those in the ear and the tongue—only activate neurons that are adjacent to them or enclosed within them. What all receptors have in common is the ability to change the energy they receive into the only form of energy the nervous system can understand—an electrochemical neural impulse. This process of translating energy from one form—for example, sound waves—to another—an electrochemical neural impulse—is known as **transduction.**

During the process of transduction, the neural impulse is also **coded** in some way. During its transmission to the central nervous system, the neural impulse is coded further, so that by the time it gets to the brain, the message is quite precise and detailed. Without this coding process, all the receptors would be able to say to the brain is, "Hey, you! Pay attention!" The coding lets the brain know what exactly to pay attention to. Some codes may be temporal—how fast or how slow the neural impulses are—while in other codes the important factor may be magnitude—how weak or how strong the neural impulses are (Uttal, 1973).

In any case, after it has been coded, the neural impulse travels along the sensory nerves to the central nervous system—the brain and the spinal cord—ultimately headed for the appropriate sensory projection area of the cerebral cortex (see Chapter 2).

Not just any energy will trigger this sequence. Each receptor cell responds to energy that falls within a certain range. Energy that falls outside that range will not be sensed. Even when the energy falls within the right range, it must be of a certain intensity or the receptor cell will simply ignore it. A whisper on the other side of the room will cause sound waves, but they will probably not be strong enough for your ear to pick up what is being said.

(Jean Renoux)

Measurement of Sensation

Since the various kinds of sensation are so common and so widespread, measuring sensation would seem to be a very simple task. But in fact the very universality of the sensory processes makes the measurement of sensations quite complicated. For one thing, people do not usually use only one sense at a time. They get information from several senses simultaneously. When you bite into an apple, you see its color and size and shape; you feel its hardness and weight; you hear the crunch; you taste it, smell it, and feel your jaws chewing. It thus becomes extremely difficult to isolate just what kind of energy each separate set of sense receptors is responding to. Another factor that complicates the measurement of sensation is that people do not all have the same experiences when they bite into the same kind of apple. Even the same person does not experience the same sensations from one day to the next.

THE DOCTRINE OF SPECIFIC NERVE ENERGIES

The modern study of sensation started in 1838, when Johannes Müller formulated his doctrine of specific nerve energies. Müller said that we are not aware at all of sensory stimuli as such. What we are aware of is the state in our nerves that the sensory stimuli cause. Moreover, he stated, when a given nerve is stimulated, the sensation that results is determined by the nature of the nerve, not by what stimulated it. Thus, pressing on the eye or looking at a colorful scene can both result in seeing something; listening to a symphony or trickling water into the ear can both result in hearing something.

Müller was not sure whether the differences between the various senses are determined in the sense organs themselves or in the brain or spinal cord. He was certain, however, that there are specific "nerve energies"—each responsible for a different kind of sensation.

The influence of Müller's doctrine was enormous. Scientists began searching for the specific parts of the brain where the specific nerve energies might be found or for the specific sense receptors that might be the source of the differences between kinds of sensations. Müller's notion of specific energies of nerves was extended to the nerves of each sense organ. Specific nerve fibers were assigned as the mediators of the specific qualities within each sensory system—some proposed a pitch perceiver within the sense of hearing, for example; others credited specific nerve endings with the sensations of heat, cold, pressure, and pain. Still others began mapping the tongue in search of the separate receptors for various tastes.

Not everybody, of course, accepted Müller's doctrine, and not everyone does today. Some of the research it prompted has been successful in locating specific receptors for different sensations; other studies have turned up distinctly contradictory evidence. But the question is still compelling enough to sustain the search and the controversy today.

Figure 8-1
Determining a sensory threshold. The dotted line represents an ideal case—at all intensities below the threshold the subject reports no sensation or no change in intensity; at all intensities above the threshold he does report a sensation or a change in intensity. More often, the results resemble the solid line. The point where the subject reports a sensation or a change in intensity 50 percent of the time is the threshold.

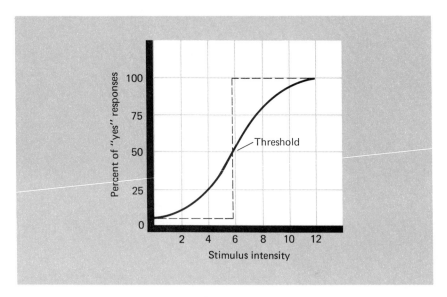

Efforts to isolate sensory experiences from one another and to measure the effects of different kinds and intensities of stimulation have led to the development of the science of **psychophysics.** When the psychologist is using psychophysical methods, he controls the kind and intensity of stimulation and measures that intensity against the way his subjects react or against the sensory experiences they report.

The first question the psychologist usually asks when he is studying sensation is how much stimulation it takes to trigger a sensory process in the first place. How loud does a sound have to be in order for a person to hear it? How bright does the "blip" on a radar screen have to be in order for the operator to detect it? The minimum intensity of physical energy required before a person will report any sensation at all is called the **absolute threshold.** Because people do not all respond the same way to the same degree of loudness, softness, and so forth, the absolute threshold will vary from person to person and from time to time for the same person. To find the absolute threshold, a psychologist conducts several tests, using varying intensities of stimulation. The level of intensity at which a person reports noticing the stimulus 50 percent of the time is his absolute threshold (see Figure 8-1).

Then the psychologist can proceed to measure the **difference threshold**—the smallest change in stimulation that a person can detect, called the **just noticeable difference,** or **j.n.d.** Like the absolute threshold, the difference threshold will vary from person to person and from time to time. To find the difference threshold, the psychologist will again conduct several tests and then determine what amount of difference is required for the person to report a change in 50 percent of the trials. The absolute threshold is thus a measure of the "yes or no" of sensation; the difference threshold is a measure of "more or less."

(*Wide World Photos*)

Some psychologists feel that such thresholds do not accurately measure the limits of sensation. Because you are asking people to tell you whether or not they have sensed anything, they say, you get subjective, not scientifically valid results. Thus, rather than measuring sensitivity, thresholds only measure the willingness of the subject to tell you what he senses (Uttal, 1973).

Sensory Adaptation

With each of our senses, what we notice most often is change—the change from no stimulation to stimulation, the change from less stimulation to more, and vice versa. But when the intensity of stimulation remains constant for a period of time, we get used to the constant level of stimulation. If you walk into a darkened movie theater, you probably will not be able to see much of anything—until your eyes have become accustomed to the dark. This phenomenon is known as **adaptation.** When the receptor cells become adapted to a constant level of stimulation, they become less sensitive. Then, when the level of stimulation is reduced, the receptor cells become more sensitive again. Sensory adaptation may complicate the task of the psychologist who is trying to measure sensations, but it is actually one of the body's most important mechanisms for adjusting to the external environment. The miner who works underground does not lose his way in the dark; the people who live in a town whose main industry is a pulp mill usually do not even notice the putrid smell that repels a visitor.

All sensations, then, occur as a result of the same sequence of events. Yet each of the body's sensory systems is unique—the receptor cells are different and respond to different kinds of stimulation, the way they transduce energy into neural impulses varies, the pathways to the brain are more direct or less so, and, most obviously, the sensations we experience are quite different.

Vision

Animals vary in their relative dependence on the different senses. Dogs rely heavily on the sense of smell, bats on hearing, some fish on taste. But for humans, the ability to see is probably the most important sense. And, of all the senses, vision has been most thoroughly studied by psychologists and physiologists.

The physical stimulus for the sense of vision is light—a small part of the spectrum of electromagnetic energy. The total spectrum extends from the range of energy used in radio communication at one end all the way down to minute cosmic rays at the other (see Figure 8-2). The receptors in the eye are sensitive to only one small segment of this spectrum—known as **visible light.**

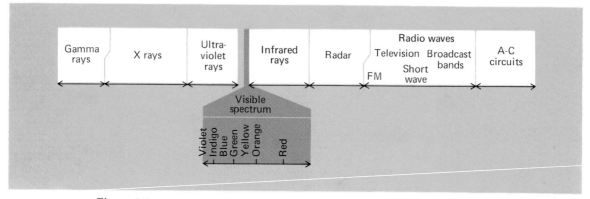

Figure 8-2

The electromagnetic spectrum. The eye is sensitive to only a very small segment of the spectrum, known as visible light.

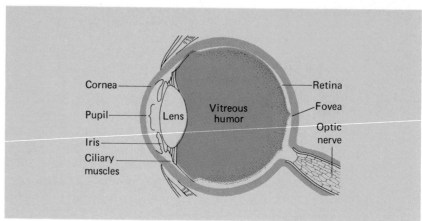

Figure 8-3

A cross section of the human eye.

The Eye

The structure of the human eye is shown in Figure 8-3. Light enters the eye through the **cornea,** the transparent protective coating over the front part of the eye. Then it passes through the **pupil,** the opening in the center of the **iris,** the colored part of the eye. In very bright light, the muscles in the iris contract to make the pupil smaller and protect the eye from damage. In dim light they extend to open the pupil wide and let in as much light as possible.

Inside the pupil, the light passes through the **lens,** which focuses it onto the **retina,** the inner lining of the back of the eyeball. The lens changes shape to focus on objects that are closer or farther away. Ordinarily, it is adjusted to focus on fairly distant objects. To focus on an object that is very close to the eyes, tiny muscles around the lens contract and make the lens rounder. The retina contains the receptor cells that respond to light. But before the light can reach the receptor cells, it must pass through a layer of nerve cells and blood vessels and a layer of neurons that make the connections between the receptor cells and the nerve pathways to the brain (see Figure 8-4).

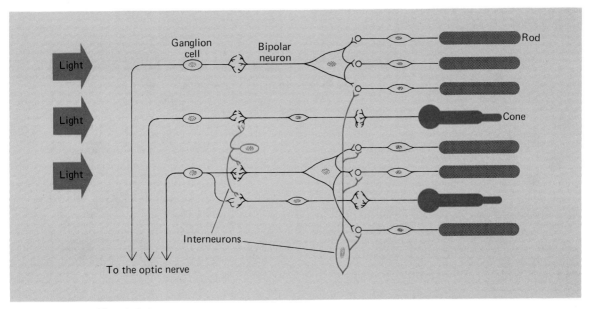

Light

Light

Light

Ganglion
cell

Bipolar
neuron

Rod

Cone

Interneurons

To the optic nerve

Figure 8-4
The layers of the retina.
Light must pass through the
ganglion cells and the
bipolar neurons to reach the
rods and cones. The sensory
messages then travel back
out again from the receptor
cells, through the bipolar
neurons, to the ganglion
cells, the axons of which
gather together to form the
optic nerve.

Rods and Cones

There are two kinds of receptor cells in the retina—**rods** and **cones**—named for their characteristic shapes. Cones are less sensitive to light than rods are. Cones operate mainly in daylight and respond to colors. The better the lighting, the more cones will be stimulated. When more cones are stimulated, **visual acuity**—the ability to distinguish fine details and small spatial separations—is increased. Rods are mainly responsible for night vision, when there is not enough light to stimulate the cones. Rods respond only to varying degrees of light and dark, not to colors. Each eye contains about 130 million rods and cones.

The depressed spot on the retina, directly behind the lens, is called the **fovea.** The fovea is packed with millions of cones, but contains no rods. Daytime vision is most acute when light is focused directly on the fovea. One reason for this is the high density of cones in the fovea. Another is that, in this one spot on the retina, light reaches the receptor cells directly. Around the edge of the fovea is an area where rods predominate. As we move outward from the fovea, toward the edges of the retina, both rods and cones get sparser. At the extreme edges there are no cones at all, only rods. The edges of the retina are most sensitive at night, after the eye has adjusted to seeing in the dark. This is why we can often see things better at night if we look a little to one side so the light is focused on the rods in the periphery.

The rods and cones differ from one another in more than just shape. For one thing, they contain different chemical pigments. The pigment found in rods is called *rhodopsin.* When light strikes a rod, rhodopsin

Figure 8-5
To locate the blind spot, hold the book about a foot away from your eyes. Close your right eye, stare at the X, and slowly move the book toward you and away from you until the black line appears to be solid. Light from the break in the line is then projected directly onto the blind spot.

breaks down into *retinene* and a number of other chemical substances. The chemical activity is thought to stimulate the bipolar neurons* connected to the rods, thus starting the sensory message on its way to the brain. Then the chemicals get back together again—the retinene recombines with the other substances to form rhodopsin. Vitamin A is essential to this recombination, which is why a deficiency in vitamin A often causes "night blindness." The chemical activity of the cones appears to be more complex, in part because the cones have a more difficult job to do in sending messages about colors to the brain. The pigment found in the cones is *iodopsin*. Light striking the cones causes a similar chemical breakdown, but the recombination occurs much faster in the cones than in the rods.

Neural Connections

Another difference between rods and cones is in the way they connect to the nerve fibers that carry their messages to the brain. Some bipolar neurons connect to both rods and cones. In the fovea, however, cones generally connect with only one bipolar neuron, a sort of "private line" arrangement. Rods are usually on a "party line"—several rods share a single bipolar neuron. This helps to explain why the rods operate better than the cones in dim light. Each rod may receive only a small amount of light, but the combined effect of all the rods may be enough to cause the bipolar neuron to fire off a message.

Things are starting to get a bit complex now, as rods and cones combine with bipolar neurons in different numbers and in different combinations. The subject becomes even more confusing when we add the two layers of cells that form horizontal connections—one between different receptor cells and one between bipolar neurons and other bipolar neurons. The maze of connections is fantastically intricate, but of course the neural impulses do somehow find their way out of the eye. The bipolar neurons connect to the ganglion cells, whose axons make up the **optic nerve** and carry the neural messages to the brain. The place on the retina where the axons of all the ganglion cells come together to leave the eye is called the **blind spot**—it contains no receptor

---

*A bipolar neuron is one that has only two fibers extending out of the cell body—one axon and one dendrite.

Figure 8-6
The neural pathways of the
visual system. Messages
from the left visual field of
each eye travel to the right
occipital lobe; those from
the right visual field of each
eye go to the left occipital
lobe. The crossover point is
the optic chiasma.

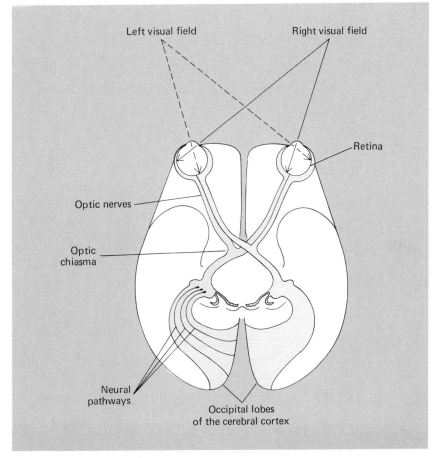

cells. Ordinarily, we are not aware of the blind spot, but when light
is focused directly on it, the object the light is coming from will not
be seen (see Figure 8-5).

After they leave the eyes, the fibers that make up each optic nerve
separate and some of them cross over to the other side. The nerve fibers
from the right side of each eye travel to the right hemisphere of the
brain; the fibers from the left half of each eye travel to the left hemisphere. The place where the fibers cross over is called the **optic chiasma**
(see Figure 8-6).

Having crossed over, the fibers of the optic nerves carry their messages to several different parts of the brain. Some of the messages reach
the area of the brain that controls the reflex movements to adjust the
size of the pupil. Others reach the area that directs the eye muscles
to change the shape of the lens. But the main destinations for the
messages from the retina are the visual projection areas of the cerebral
cortex, where the pattern of stimulated and unstimulated receptor cells
is registered, integrated, and interpreted.

Adaptation

Luckily for our safety, as well as our pleasure, adaptation is rarely total in the receptors of the eye. This is true, not because the receptors in the eye are less subject to adaptation than the receptors for the other senses, but because light is rarely focused on the same rods and cones for a long enough time for them to become wholly insensitive. In normal vision, the eyes are in constant motion. Small, involuntary eye movements keep the image on the retina drifting slowly away from the fovea, then bring it back again with a tiny flick. And, at the same time, the eyes continually show a slight, extremely rapid tremor. It is virtually impossible to stop these eye movements without damaging the eye. The combined effect of these involuntary eye movements is to keep the image moving across the retina, from one group of receptors to another and back again, allowing all of the receptors some time to rest and restore their chemical balance between active periods.

Also happily for our safety and pleasure, the receptors of the eye do adapt partially to light and dark. Adaptation to dark after daylight takes place in two stages, the first about 5 minutes long, the second taking up to a half-hour. When you first go from bright light into the dark, you frequently cannot see a thing. There is not enough light to stimulate the cones of the eyes, and the rods are not sensitive at all. After having been exposed to very bright light, all the pigment in the rods has been bleached. If you stay in the dark for a time, however, the cones and rods have an opportunity to become dark-adapted—to build up their pigments again.

(Hiroji Kubota, Magnum Photos)

The cones recover first; after about 5 minutes they will become as sensitive as they are going to be at detecting objects in the dark. The rods catch up more slowly (remember that we said earlier that the recombination of rhodopsin in the rods occurs more slowly than the recombination of iodopsin in the cones). After the first 5 minutes, the rods are able to begin functioning, but they do not reach their maximum sensitivity until 20 to 30 minutes after encountering the dark. There is not enough energy in the dim light to stimulate the cones to respond to colors, so you see a black and white world of different brightnesses.

When you go out into bright light again, your eyes will be very sensitive, perhaps even painfully so. In the dark, the light-absorbing pigments in both cones and rods have had a chance to build up a good supply, and the light affects them immediately. All the neurons fire at once, and you are overwhelmed by light. You squint and shield your eyes, the muscles of the eye squeeze the pupil smaller, and, as some of the iodopsin that was stored up in the cones while you were in the darkness is used up, your eyes become less sensitive. Pretty soon the sunny day seems only ordinarily bright. By this time, the eye's receptors are light-adapted—their sensitivity has decreased.

Color Vision

The ability to see colors depends on the eye's capacity for sending different messages to the brain in response to different wavelengths of the visible spectrum (see Color Plate 1). The fact that the visible spectrum is arbitrarily divided into seven colors does not mean that the eye is sensitive to only seven wavelengths. Within the range of wavelengths that we call blue, for example, we can detect many differences among stimuli, though we don't have labels for all of them. The question of how we see colors is dominated by two main theories—the **trichromatic theory** and the **opponent-process theory.** Each theory explains part of the way we see colors, but neither is able to fully account for all we know about colors and the way we experience them.

At the beginning of the nineteenth century, Thomas Young, an English physicist, conducted an impressive experiment. He mixed three lights that lay far apart from one another in the spectrum—red, green, and blue—and found that practically any hue we can detect could be produced by adjusting the relative intensities of the three lights. He surmised that this is precisely what the eye must do when we see colors—mix three basic colors to arrive at all the different colors in the spectrum.

Young's explanation impressed German physiologist Hermann von Helmholtz, who in turn elaborated on the theory. Helmholtz proposed that we see colors because the eye contains three different kinds of color receptors—cells that respond to red, cells that respond to green, and cells that respond to blue or violet. All the rest of the colors we see, he believed, are a result of mixing by the three receptor systems. The Young-Helmholtz trichromatic theory of color vision remains one of the major explanations of color vision.

Somewhat later, in 1878, Ewald Hering proposed that color vision did not depend on the mixture of three basic colors, but rather that we see colors by means of three *opponent processes*. Hering accepted the notion that there are three separate kinds of color receptors, but he differed from Young and Helmholtz in his description of how they operate. Each set of receptors, he believed, is capable of responding to either member of three basic color pairs. The receptors in one set can deliver one kind of message for red, another kind of message for green. The second set sends one kind of message for yellow, another for blue. The receptors in the third set respond to different intensities of light, sending messages about brightness. But the colors in each pair oppose each other, he felt—a yellow-blue receptor cannot send messages about both yellow and blue at the same time, nor can a red-green receptor send both red and green messages at the same time. This, Hering maintained, explains the fact that we never see a reddish green or a bluish yellow.

COLOR PROPERTIES AND COLOR MIXING

The physicist can describe colors quite precisely in terms of wavelengths and amplitude. But most of us, when we describe what colors we see, use terms that are much less exact. When we talk about colors, we generally refer to three basic dimensions, which are represented spatially on the color solid shown in Color Plate 3.

The first thing that usually comes to mind is *hue*—the particular name of the color, like green or blue. This is what the physicist is talking about when he refers to different wavelengths. Then we might mention the *saturation* of the color—how pure it is. A yellowish green is less saturated than a pure green; a grayish blue is less saturated than a pure blue. Light waves that are made up of many different elements result in colors that are low in saturation. The third dimension of a color is its *brightness*—how dark or light it is. Forest green is brighter than avocado, navy blue is darker than sky blue. The brightness of a color depends mainly on the strength of the energy source—the more light an object reflects, the brighter it will be.

When an artist mixes colors, he usually starts with red, yellow, and blue pigments and combines them to create all the colors he needs. The psychologist also starts with three colors, but he uses lights instead of pigments. Any three colors that are widely separated on the spectrum can be combined to produce all the other colors. The psychologist usually starts with red, green, and blue.

The reason for the difference is that the artist's color mixing is a *subtractive process*—each of the pigments he uses absorbs a different part of the spectrum, thus subtracting from the total range of wavelengths reflected to the eye. Mixing red and green pigments, for example, results in a mixture that absorbs both the green and the red wavelengths and reflects only gray. Mixing lights, on the other hand, is an *additive process*—the wavelengths of one color are added to the wavelengths of another to produce yet a third. Projecting red and green lights together onto a white surface, for example, will result not in gray, but in yellow (see Color Plate 4).

Among the phenomena of color vision that Hering felt were not adequately explained by Young and Helmholtz's trichromatic theory were **afterimages.** If you look at Color Plate 5 for about 30 seconds and then look at a sheet of white paper, you will experience an afterimage. Hering's explanation is that the receptors in the red-green set have reversed themselves—that when you were looking at the figure, they were sending "green" messages, but when the stimulation was withdrawn, they began to readjust and, in the process, sent "red" messages. The reason for this appears to be that the opponent-process system is designed to reestablish equilibrium when the balance of neural activity has been disturbed. This is why the strength of the afterimage increases the longer you look at Color Plate 5.

The opponent-process theory is also somewhat more successful in explaining **color blindness.** A person with normal vision is a **trichro-**

mat—given three hues, his visual system can reproduce all the colors of the spectrum. At the other extreme is the **monochromat**—the rare person who sees no color at all and responds only to black and white or brightness. Much more common than the monochromat is the **dichromat,** the person who responds to only two hues and can see only the colors that can be produced by mixing those two. Red-green color blindness, which we described in Chapter 2 as a sex-linked inherited characteristic, is the most common form of dichromatism. People with this form of color blindness may see red and green as a kind of yellowish gray, or they may just confuse red and green a bit because they do not see them very vividly (see Color Plate 6). The difficulty with the Young-Helmholtz theory of color vision is that it maintains that yellow is produced by the combined activity of the red and green receptors, yet the person who can see neither red nor green is still able to see yellow. The opponent-process theory, on the other hand, explains red-green color blindness by saying that the set of receptors that respond to either red or green simply do not function in the retina of the red-green dichromat.

The two theories have existed side by side for over 50 years, with no resolution in sight. But modern investigations have produced evidence that both theories may, in fact, be true, but at two different stages in the visual process. Measurement of the responses of individual receptor cells has revealed cells with distinctly different responses to wavelengths in the blue, green, and red-yellow areas of the spectrum (Brown & Wald, 1964; Marks, Dobelle, & MacNichol, 1964). Young and Helmholtz, it seems, were not altogether wrong after all.

Other studies, however, recording the electrical activities of the bipolar neurons and the ganglion cells in the retina, indicate that colors are coded neurally in an opponent-process way. The first indication that the ganglion cells play a very active role in coding visual messages came when it was discovered that they show some level of electrical activity at all times. They do not, that is, just sit there and wait for a message to come along from the bipolar neurons. Rather, since they are conducting nerve impulses all the time, they can respond in two opposite directions—they can turn "on" by increasing their rate of firing or turn "off" by decreasing it. Some cells have been found, for example, that turn "on" to yellow or green, but turn "off" to blue. These cells are paired with others that respond in the opposite way—"on" to blue, "off" to yellow or green (Hurvich & Jameson, 1974). So, Hering was not all wrong either.

It seems plausible now that there are, as Young and Helmholtz believed, three kinds of receptor cells for color. The messages they transmit, however, seem to be translated by the bipolar neurons or by the ganglion cells into opponent-process form. These patterns of "on" and "off" firing of certain groups of neurons then carry the messages to the brain, and we see the colors of all the separate areas in our field of vision.

Incidentally, the opponent-process concept may be relevant not only to visual activity. As we stated earlier, opponent processes restore equilibrium by providing a push when there has been a pull. Two psychologists who have been studying emotions have used opponent processes to describe emotional phenomena (Solomon & Corbit, 1973). They suggest that fear and joy, for example, may work in somewhat the same way that red and green color perception does. Thus, joy could be described as the afterimage of fear, as red is the afterimage of green.

Hearing

There's an ancient question that asks, "If a tree falls in the woods, and there is no one there, is there a sound?" What do you think? A psychologist would say "Yes, but there is no noise."

Sound

The physical stimuli for the sense of hearing are **sound waves**—the changes in pressure caused when molecules of air or fluid collide with one another, transmitting energy at every bump, then move apart again.

The simplest sound wave—what we hear as a pure tone—can be pictured as a sine wave (see Figure 8-7). The tuning fork vibrates, causing successive compression and expansion of the molecules of air. The **frequency** of the waves is measured in cycles per second, expressed in a unit called Hertz (Hz). Frequency primarily determines the **pitch** of the sound—how high or low it is. The human ear responds to frequencies from about 20 Hz to 20,000 Hz. A bass viol, as a reference point, can reach down to about 50 Hz. A piano can reach as high as 5,000 Hz. The height of the wave represents its **amplitude,** which, together with pitch, determines the **loudness** of a sound. Loudness is measured in **decibels** (see Figure 8-8).

Figure 8-7
The tuning fork, as it vibrates, alternately compresses and expands the molecules of air, creating a sound wave.

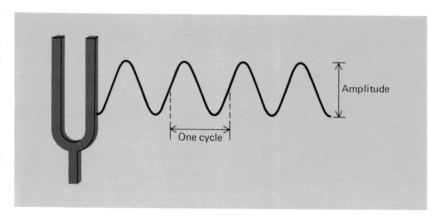

Plate 1
Sunlight contains the wavelengths for all the colors we can see. When it is passed through a prism, the wavelengths are bent at different angles and the light is separated into a color spectrum. *(Fritz Goro, Life Magazine, © Time Inc.)*

Plate 2
A natural spectrum, a rainbow, occurs when sunlight is deflected by the atmosphere. *(Fritz Henle, Photo Researchers)*

Plate 3
The color solid. The dimension of hue is represented around the circumference. Saturation ranges along the radius from the inside to the outside of the solid. Brightness varies along the vertical axis. *(Photos courtesy of Inmont Corporation)*

Plate 4
Mixing light waves is an additive process. When red and green are combined, the resulting hue is yellow. When all three basic colors are mixed, we see white. *(Fritz Goro, Life Magazine, © Time Inc.)*

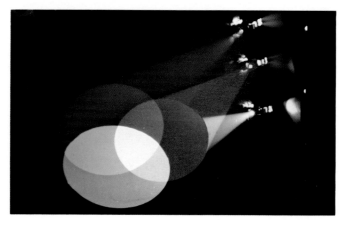

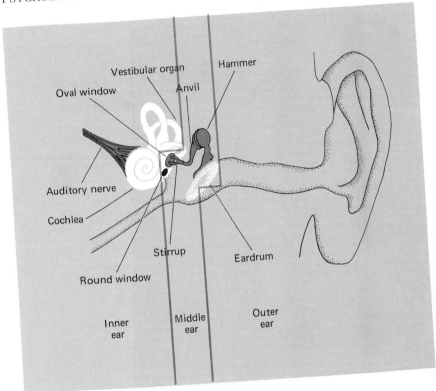

Figure 8-9
...of the
... ear.

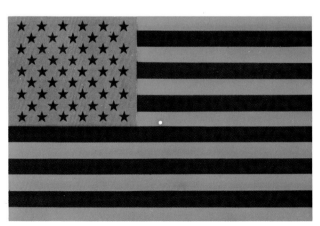

Plate 5
Stare at the white
spot in the center of this
flag for about 30 seconds.
Then look at a blank piece
of white paper to see an
afterimage.

is attached to another membrane—the **oval window.** Just below the oval window is another membrane, called the **round window,** which equalizes the pressure in the inner ear when the stirrup hits against the oval window.

The air pressure waves are magnified during their trip through the middle ear, so when the oval window starts to vibrate at the touch of the stirrup, the effect in the inner ear is powerful. There, the vibrations are transmitted to the fluid inside a snail-shaped structure called the **cochlea.** The cochlea is divided lengthwise by the **basilar membrane,** which is narrowest near the oval and round windows and gets gradually wider as it coils inward toward its other end. When the fluids in the cochlea begin to move, the basilar membrane is pushed up and down, bringing the vibrations further into the inner ear.

Lying on top of the basilar membrane, and moving with it, is the **organ of Corti** (see Figure 8-10), and it is here that the messages from sound waves finally reach the receptor cells for the sense of hearing. The receptors—millions of tiny hair cells—are pushed and pulled by the vibrations of the fluid inside the cochlea. The hair cells ca... their adjacent bipolar neurons to fire, sending out through the aud... nerve a coded message about the particular pattern of vibration... sound has created.

Plate 6
The Dvorine Pseudo-
Isochromatic Plates are
used to detect color blindness.
People who are color
blind cannot see the figure
inside the circle. To show
what this means in
everyday life, we have
printed this picture of a
butterfly as someone with
red-green color blindness
would see it. *(Color-blind
test reproduced by
permission of the
Scientific Publishing Co.,
Baltimore, Maryland;
photo by Karl Maslowski,
Photo Researchers)*

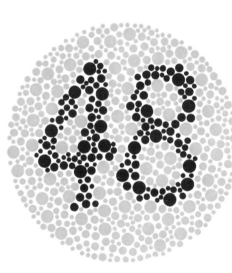

Figure 8-8
A decibel scale for several
common sounds. Prolonged
exposure to sounds above
85 decibels can cause
permanent damage to the
ears. As a further point of
reference, one Rolling
Stones concert was
measured at 136 decibels.

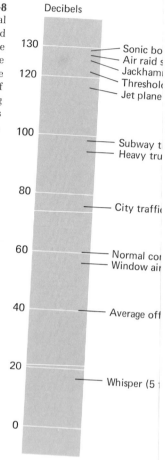

Decibels

130 — Sonic bo
— Air raid s
— Jackhamı
120 — Threshol
— Jet plane

100 — Subway t
— Heavy tru

80 — City traffi

60 — Normal co
— Window ai

40 — Average off

20 — Whisper (5

0

The sounds we hear, how
fundamental tones also car
panying sound waves that
frequency. A violin string,
whole. It also vibrates in h
same time. Each set of vib
pattern of overtones determ

The Ear

The process of hearing begir
eardrum (see Figure 8-9) and
eardrum causes three tiny bo
the **anvil,** and the **stirrup**—to
vibrations to the inner ear.

Figur
The structure (
huma

Figure 8-10
If the cochlea were uncoiled
and stretched out, it would
look something like this.
The basilar membrane gets
gradually narrower as it
stretches out from the oval
window.

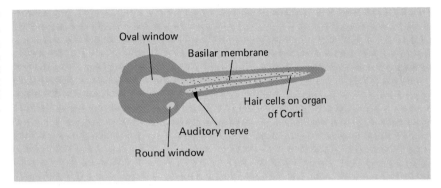

Neural Connections

The sense of hearing is truly bilateral—each ear sends messages to both cerebral hemispheres. The switching station where the nerve fibers from the ears cross over is in the medulla, part of the hindbrain. From the medulla, other nerve fibers carry the messages from the ear to the higher parts of the brain. Some messages go to the brain centers that coordinate the movements of the eyes, head, and ears. Others travel through the reticular activating system, which probably tacks on a few special "wake up" or "ho-hum" postscripts to the sound messages. The primary destinations, of course, are the auditory projection areas in the temporal lobes of the two cerebral hemispheres.

Along the way, the auditory messages pass through at least four levels of neurons, a much less direct route than we saw in the visual system. At each stage, the coding of auditory information becomes more precise. Each nerve cell in the auditory system responds to a certain range of frequencies. Some of the higher cells in the auditory system fire only in response to certain combinations of attributes—to a sound of a certain frequency *and* a particular intensity *and* a particular duration, for example. At each step up, the range becomes narrower, and only the most exact information is allowed to pass.

Theories of Hearing

So far we have said nothing about exactly how the many different sound wave patterns that reach our ears are coded into neural messages—how the tiny organ of Corti can tell the brain how loud a sound is or what pitch it has. The millions of tiny hair cells send messages about almost infinite variations in the pitch, loudness, and timbre of sounds, as well as their location and duration. The loudness of a sound seems to depend on how many neurons are activated—the more neurons firing, the louder the sound seems to be. The same principle applies to all the senses—the intensity of the sensation depends primarily on the number of nerve impulses sent to the brain.

The coding of messages about pitch, however, is not so simple a matter. Theories of pitch discrimination tend to fall into two major types—**place theories** and **frequency theories.**

Place theories. Helmholtz, the physiologist who helped develop the trichromatic theory of color vision, was also interested in how the ear sends messages about pitch. He thought of the basilar membrane as having fibers arranged rather like the strings on a harp—those at the narrow end, near the oval window, would resonate for high tones, and those at the wider end would resonate for low tones. The nerve fibers, Helmholtz thought, carried to the brain an exact copy of the pattern of firing, and the brain determined pitch by noting the *place* on the basilar membrane where the messages originated.

Helmholtz did not know, however, that the cochlea is filled with fluid and that it is impossible for nerve fibers to resonate. A more recent form of the place theory, Georg von Békésy's **traveling wave theory** (1957), holds that the sound wave, as it travels through the cochlear fluid, causes the different places on the basilar membrane to move in direct proportion to the pitch of the sound wave. Von Békésy cut holes in the cochleae of guinea pigs and watched, under a microscope, to see where and how much the membranes moved in response to sounds of different pitches. He saw that only the narrow end moved when the sounds were high. For sounds in the middle range, the movements occurred farther toward the wide end. Low sounds set the basilar membrane into motion along its entire length, with the maximum amount of movement at the wide end. Thus, he demonstrated clearly that different pitches are registered by maximum vibrations at different places on the basilar membrane.

Frequency theories. The second type of theory of pitch discrimination holds that the *frequency* of vibrations of the basilar membrane is translated into an equivalent *frequency* of nerve impulses—each time a hair cell is pushed or pulled, its neuron fires off a message to the brain. The problem with the frequency theory is that neurons simply cannot fire as rapidly as the frequency of the highest-pitched sounds we can hear.

To overcome this difficulty, frequency theorists have developed a **volley principle**—the nerve cells, they maintain, fire in sequence, not individually. For example, one neuron fires, then a second one, then a third. By then, the first neuron has had time to recover and it fires again. Thus pitch is registered, according to this theory, not by the frequency of firing of a single neuron, but by the volleys of impulses coming in sequence from the group of nerve cells.

Neither theory alone fully explains pitch discrimination, so some combination of place theory and frequency theory is needed. The volley principle, for example, works quite well to explain the ear's responses to frequencies up to about 4,000 Hz. Above that, however, the place theory provides a better explanation of what is happening.

The Chemical Senses

Smell and taste are called the chemical senses because both are activated by chemical substances. Less is known about the chemical senses than about vision or hearing, largely because the nature of the chemical stimuli makes it difficult to experiment with smell and taste.

Smell

The receptors for the sense of smell are located high in each nasal cavity, in a patch of tissue called the **olfactory epithelium** (see Figure 8-11). The olfactory epithelium is only about half the size of a postage stamp, but it is densely packed with millions of receptor cells. Airborne molecules, carried into the nasal cavities as we breathe, activate the receptors in the epithelium, which are specialized neurons. The axons of the receptors carry the messages, without synapse, directly to the olfactory bulbs in the brain. These fibers do not seem to pass through the thalamus, as other sense fibers do, so the sense of smell's route to the cerebral cortex is the most direct.

Unlike the optic and auditory nerves, the fibers from the nose travel only to the olfactory bulb on the same side, without crossing over. The olfactory bulbs can communicate "across the hall" to each other and

Figure 8-11
The location of the olfactory epithelium.

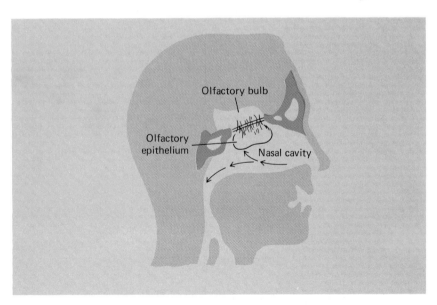

Figure 8-12
Since dogs have a much more sensitive sense of smell than humans, they are often used for searching or tracking. This dog has just found a mail package containing marijuana. (*Wide World Photos*)

"upstairs" to the olfactory projection areas in the cerebral cortex. The connections from the olfactory bulb to the cerebral cortex are extremely intricate: for every thousand nerve fibers that enter the olfactory bulb, only one fiber leaves the bulb headed for the cortex.

We know very little about what kinds of molecules carry what kinds of odors. One of the problems psychologists studying smell have is that there are no commonly accepted names for odors as there are for colors. This makes odors difficult to describe and makes it hard to evaluate what people say they smell. Several classifications of odors have been proposed, but none has been totally successful.

Since odors are difficult to classify, it is hard to develop a theory of how our sense of smell really works. Not knowing how odors are physically and chemically similar makes our understanding of how the receptor cells in the nose translate chemical stimulation into nerve impulses equally sketchy. Some believe that there is a chemical reaction between the odorous molecules and the receptor cell. Others propose that transduction occurs as a result of infrared rays being absorbed by the receptor cells. Still others point to ultraviolet rays or to the vibrations of molecules. What actually happens is still to be discovered.

The sense of smell is subject to rather rapid adaptation. We get accustomed to smells fairly quickly, especially very strong smells. The rate of adaptation appears to be different for different odors. Women's senses of smell are generally more acute than men's. Researchers have also found that sensitivity to odor decreases with age and will change in women depending on their menstrual cycle (Engen, 1973).

The sense of smell is rather a luxury for people. Although we use our sense of smell to tell whether food has spoiled, unlike animals we do not depend on smell to find food, to tell a friend from an enemy, or to determine when the females of our species are receptive to sexual advances. In some fish, for example, the whole cortex is devoted to registering messages about smells; in the dog, the olfactory cortex, as a proportion of the whole cortex, is more than seven times as large as it is in humans. This may be why—compared with vision and hearing—little research has been done on smell. In humans, the sense of smell seems to be most important when it is used in conjunction with the other chemical sense—taste.

Taste

The receptor cells for the sense of taste lie inside the **taste buds,** most of which are found on the tip, sides, and back of the tongue. The taste buds normally die and are replaced approximately every 7 days. An adult has about 10,000 taste buds. Children have more taste buds than adults, and the number decreases with age. It may well be that older people who lose interest in food do so simply because they cannot taste it as well.

THE STEREOCHEMICAL THEORY OF ODOR

One of the most promising explanations of the sense of smell is the stereochemical theory of odor proposed by John E. Amoore and his colleagues (1964). According to these researchers, the molecules of each primary smell category have a distinctive shape, size, or electrical charge. Each fits into a corresponding "hole" in the olfactory epithelium. Chemicals that smell alike, they propose, have the same shape and will fit into the same type of socket much as a key fits into a lock. Amoore and his colleagues have identified five primary odor qualities and their shapes—camphoraceous, a spherical shape that fits into a bowl-like hole; musky, a larger disk shape; floral, a disk with a tail, somewhat like a kite; ethereal, a rod shape fitting into an elongated trough; and minty, a wedge shape. The other two basic odors seem to depend on their electrical charge rather than their molecular shape. Pungent substances are positively charged; putrid ones are negatively charged. Complex odors—such as lemon or cedar or garlic—result from molecules that can fit into more than one receptacle depending on how they lie.

The theory does not attempt to tell us how fitting a molecule into a particular receptor cell triggers a nerve impulse. Nor does it explain why some people are able to smell one substance from a primary odor group but not another—one kind of musk, for example, but not another. It may be that there are many more than seven primary odors and that a complete understanding of the sense of smell will have to wait until all the different molecular shapes are identified.

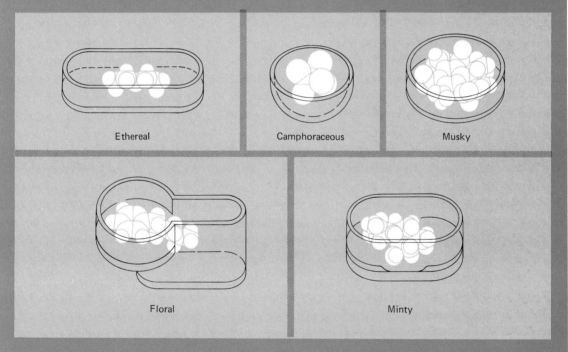

Ethereal   Camphoraceous   Musky

Floral   Minty

(Courtesy of J. E. Amoore, "Current Status of the Steric Theory of Odor," *Annals of the New York Academy of Science*, 1964, 116, 457–476.)

Each taste bud contains a cluster of taste receptors—hair cells (see Figure 8-13). Each taste cell thrusts a single hair into the crevice between the *papillae* of the tongue—the small bumps you can see in the

Figure 8-13
A diagram of a single taste bud.

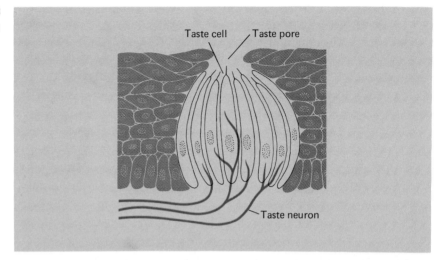

Figure 8-14
A schematic map of the tongue, showing the locations most sensitive to the four basic taste qualities.

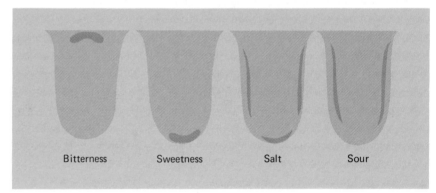

mirror. The chemical substances in the foods we eat are dissolved in saliva and carried down into these crevices, where they come into contact with the hairs of the taste receptors. The chemical interaction between these substances and the taste cells depolarizes adjacent neurons and causes them to fire, sending a nerve impulse to the brain. Several nerve fibers enter each taste bud; one nerve fiber may send branches to several different taste buds. The same nerves that carry messages about taste also conduct information about chewing, swallowing, and the temperatures and textures the tongue can feel.

It was established very early in the course of experiments on the sense of taste that we experience only four primary taste qualities—sweet, sour, salty, and bitter. All other tastes result from combinations of these four qualities. The tip of the tongue is most sensitive to sugar, the back is most sensitive to bitterness, and the sides are most sensitive to sourness. The tip and the sides of the tongue are most sensitive to salt (see Figure 8-14).

The next step was to try to isolate four kinds of taste receptors that correspond to these four basic taste qualities. These efforts have been largely unsuccessful. It seems that taste is coded by the overall pattern of firing in a number of fibers, not by the activation of a single fiber for each single taste quality. One possible explanation is that further processing occurs at higher levels in the sensory system for taste, but exactly where or how is not yet known.

The sense of taste adapts very quickly, and in very complicated patterns. Adaptation to one kind of salt, for example, does not lower the thresholds for other salts; but adaptation to one kind of acid usually does affect our sensitivity to other acids. Cross-adaptation in the sense of taste will probably not be fully understood until more is known about the activities of the taste cells and how their messages are coded and interpreted by the nervous system.

The Body Senses

The body senses—**kinesthesis** and the **vestibular sense**—help us maintain our balance as we stand or walk. They tell us how to reach for things accurately and how to manipulate them. They help us adjust when something we lift turns out to be heavy and to compensate when we stumble or when someone bumps into us.

Kinesthesis

Close your eyes and extend your arm. How do you know where your hand is when you can't see it? You know through your *kinesthetic sense*. The sense of kinesthesis is ordinarily taken for granted, but kinesthetic receptors are scattered throughout the muscles and joints of the whole body. The receptors in the muscles and tendons provide information about whether a muscle is stretched out or contracted. Receptors in the joints respond to different angles of position, thus telling us about position and movements of body parts. Nerve fibers from the kinesthetic receptors join together with the nerve fibers from the skin just before they enter the spinal cord, and all the messages from one part of the body travel together to the cortex.

The Vestibular Sense

In birds and fish, the vestibular sense is extremely important to orientation—they rely on it to tell them which way is up and in what direction they are headed when they cannot see well. In higher vertebrates, and in man, the vestibular system provides information about body position and movement, but seems not to be essential for survival. People who have had one or even both vestibular organs removed seem to function normally, as long as they have visual and kinesthetic cues to rely on.

Figure 8-15
The vestibular organ.

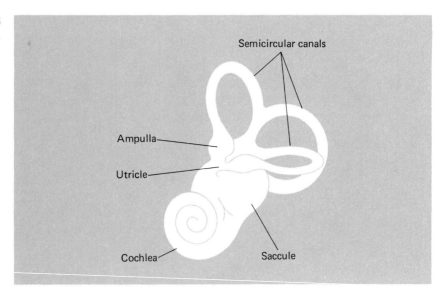

Figure 8-16
An amazing example of a well-developed vestibular sense—Phillippe Petit, walking on the high wire strung between the two towers of the World Trade Center in New York City. (*Sygma*)

(Courtesy of NASA)

EFFECTS OF WEIGHTLESSNESS

When gravity is absent, the vestibular organ cannot function. The visual and kinesthetic senses must be used to determine position and movement of the body. As space flight has developed, scientists have been able to determine the effects of weightlessness on living organisms. The astronauts on the U.S. Apollo 14 mission lost weight and showed marked circulatory deterioration, but recovered a few days after returning to earth. The astronauts who took part in the Apollo 15 flight in 1971 learned to adapt to lunar gravity. By the second day, walking was easier and their heart and metabolic rates had returned to normal. However, they took longer to readapt to earth's gravity than previous crews. Many astronauts describe a "full feeling," which wears off in a few days and may account for weight loss.

In 1971 scientists from twenty countries attended a symposium in Armenia to exchange their knowledge about the biological effects of extended space flight on man (Kopanev, 1972). Some astronauts were reported to have experienced no reactions to weightlessness, or ones that lasted only a few seconds. Others experienced illusions, accompanied by feelings of anxious joy and ease. Still others experienced extended spatial illusions, such as a feeling of flying upside down. Fine muscle coordination was often affected, especially in the hands and fingers, making writing difficult. It was harder to perform motions while floating than while strapped in a fixed position. Many experienced a lack of appetite and mild nausea that did not impede their functioning. The body, it appears, seems to realize that it no longer needs the kinds of bones and muscles required to cope with earth's gravity. So calcium is withdrawn from the bones, the muscles atrophy, and dehydration sets in. At present, the consensus is that man *can* gradually adapt to the adverse effects of weightlessness. The greatest problems seem to be in readapting to the earth's gravity. After returning from 18 days aloft, for example, one Russian cosmonaut found his whole body so heavy that it was difficult to rise from an armchair. It took him 10 days to return to normal.

The receptors for the vestibular sense, the sense of equilibrium, lie in the inner ear. There are two subsystems for this sense, both of which are contained in the **vestibular organ** (see Figure 8-15). The first subsystem includes the three **semicircular canals** and the **ampulla.** The canals are arranged at right angles to one another in three different planes and all are filled with fluid, which shifts when the head is moved in any direction. The movement of the fluid in the semicircular canals stimulates the receptors in the ampulla—tiny hairlike projections that are pushed and pulled by the moving fluids. The hair cells stimulate the nerve cells around them to fire, sending messages about the speed and direction of bodily rotation.

The second subsystem includes the two **vestibular sacs** that lie just below the ampulla—the **utricle** and the **saccule.** Both sacs are filled with a jellylike fluid. Inside this fluid are tiny crystals, called **otoliths,** which brush against the hairs of the receptor cells when the head is inclined toward the front or back or toward one side or the other. The hair cells, stimulated by the otoliths, cause the nerve cells at their base to fire, sending messages about the position of the head with respect to gravity—how far from the vertical it is and in which direction.

The nerve fibers from both of these subsystems hitch a ride to the brain on the auditory nerve. Once they get there, they seem to go their own ways, and their ultimate destinations are not fully understood. Some messages from the vestibular system go to the cerebellum, which controls many of the reflexes involved in coordinated movement. Others go to the areas of the brain that control eye movements. Still others go to the areas that send messages to the internal body organs, and some go to the cerebral cortex for analysis and response.

The Skin Senses

What we ordinarily think of as touch is actually made up of several different sensations—**pressure, warmth, cold,** and **pain.** All other sensations result from some combination of these four elements. Usually messages from all these senses are combined, but it is possible to separate them and to map the different areas of the skin that respond most strongly to each. Some areas of the skin are extremely sensitive to pressure, others to warmth or cold or extreme heat. Generally, the most numerous are the spots that respond to pain, then the spots that record pressure, and finally the spots that are sensitive to cold and warmth. Each of these touch spots is surrounded by areas that are much less sensitive to tactile stimulation.

Some parts of the body are more sensitive than others to all of these sensations. The hands and feet, for example, and the face (especially the lips and tongue) are much more sensitive than the back, the upper arms, or the calves of the legs. The most sensitive areas are represented in the cerebral cortex by many more fiber endings, and they also seem to contain a higher concentration of receptor cells.

Receptors and Neural Connections

Many different kinds of receptors have been located in the skin. At one point, physiologists quite confidently pointed to one receptor or another as the specific receptor for each of the four skin sensations. However, studies have been unsuccessful in revealing a consistent set of relationships between the various types of receptors and the separate sensations. What was once thought to be clearly understood now appears not to be so clear a picture at all.

The receptors in the skin fall into three general categories (see Figure 8-17). The first, **free nerve endings,** are found just below the surface

Figure 8-17
The three types of sensory
receptors in the skin.

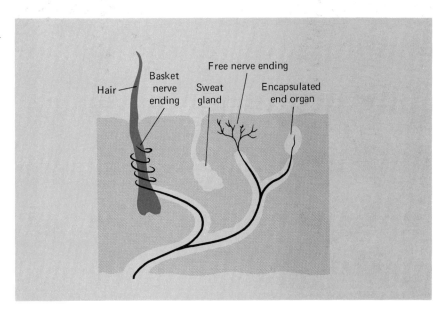

of the skin, where they branch out and intertwine to provide pretty much complete coverage of the whole skin area. Free nerve endings are traditionally thought to be involved in the sensation of pain, but they probably also play a role in sensations of warmth and cold, and may even participate in sending messages about pressure.

A second type of receptor is the **basket nerve ending**—a nerve fiber that wraps around the base of a hair. Basket nerve endings are widely distributed over all the areas of the body that are covered with hair— about 90 percent of the body's surface. They respond to touch or light pressure—when the hair they entwine is moved, they fire off a message about the intensity and direction of the touch. But, lest we jump to the conclusion that the basket nerve endings are the primary source of touch sensations, we should also recall that some of the most sensitive areas of the body—such as the lips and the fingertips—have no hair at all, and thus no basket nerve endings.

The third general glass of receptors in the skin are called **encapsulated end organs.** Many different versions have been located and named, and they show immense variations in size and structure. But they all share one common feature—a nerve fiber ends inside some sort of capsule or shell. Most kinds of encapsulated end organs are found quite near the surface of the skin. They usually appear to be responsive to sensations of pressure, but some are also sensitive to temperature.

The nerve fibers from all of these different receptors travel to the brain through the spinal cord. At various points along the way, some bundles of nerve fibers cross over. By the time they reach the top of the spinal cord and enter the brain, all have crossed. All the messages from the left side of the body reach the projection areas in the right cerebral hemisphere; all the messages from the right side of the body go to the left hemisphere.

Pressure

To map the areas of the skin that respond to pressure, psychologists touch the skin with stiff hairs or tiny hammers. Most humans are aware of very slight pressures, especially on the lips, tongue, and fingertips. Like the other senses, the sense of touch shows rapid adaptation. Adaptation to a weight applied to the skin, for example, occurs quite rapidly if the area it covers is large. The heavier the object, the longer adaptation takes, but even quite heavy weights are eventually not felt at all.

Temperature

The temperature sense appears to depend on at least two different kinds of receptors. One spot on the skin may be sensitive only to objects that are at least 1 or 2 degrees Centigrade warmer than body temperature; another area will respond only to objects that are 1 or 2 degrees Centigrade colder than the body. When one set of receptors sends in messages, the brain reads them as "warm." When the other set sends messages, the brain reads "cold." But if both sets are activated at the same time, the brain reads their combined pattern of firing as "hot."

(Phyllis McCutcheon, Photo Researchers)

Thus, in certain situations, you may think you are touching something hot when you really are touching something warm and something cool at the same time. This phenomenon is known as **paradoxical heat.**

It is easier to study cold receptors than warm receptors because cold receptors are easier to find. These receptors are always firing at about 5 to 15 impulses per second. This rate increases to over 100 impulses per second when there is a sudden temperature change. However, there is still doubt about whether the degree of coldness is coded by the number of impulses arriving at the brain (intensity) or by the speed of the receptor's firing or both (Hahn, 1974).

Pain

Pain is quite different from all the other senses. For one thing, it seems to be much more subject to individual interpretation. To one person a wound or injury might be a sensation so overwhelming that it literally blocks out all other sensations. But another person, or even the same person at a different time, might hardly notice the pain at all.

Until recently, psychologists believed that the primary pain receptors were the networks of free nerve endings that overlap and penetrate many layers of skin. According to this theory, a painful stimulus activates several networks at once and sends a number of messages to the

ACUPUNCTURE—SHUTTING THE GATE ON PAIN
Acupuncture, as most of us know, is an analgesic (or pain-killing) technique in which special needles are inserted at specific sites in the body. These needles may be rotated rapidly or used to conduct mild electric currents. Even though the needles are inserted in areas distant from the area of pain, the technique has been shown to be effective in pain relief. In one documented thyroid operation, analgesia was induced by inserting one needle into each forearm of the patient. In another case, four needles were inserted into the patient's external ears during an operation to remove his stomach (Dimond, 1971). Unlike patients who are anesthetized during surgery, these patients are conscious and alert throughout their operations. Postsurgical pain seems to be decreased, as the pain-relieving effects last for several hours after the needles have been removed. There is also some evidence that healing after surgery is accelerated. According to Chinese tradition, acupuncture brings the *yin* (spirits) and the *yang* (blood) forces back into harmony. But why does it work?

While the specificity theory of pain cannot explain the success of acupuncture, Melzack and Wall's gate-control theory (1965) recognizes that there are neurological pathways between distant sites of the body, and that there are trigger areas from which pain can be referred. Thus, people may experience pain in the shoulder when they have a heart attack. Needle stimulation of these trigger sites results in what Melzack (1973*b*) calls "hyperstimulation analgesia." "The stimulation of particular nerves or tissues by needles could bring about an increased input to the central biasing mechanism [located in the brainstem], which would close the gates to inputs from selected body areas [including areas involved in surgery]" (Melzack, 1973*b*, p. 189). Once the gate has closed, no further pain messages will be received by the brain. If the gate-control theory is valid, it means that pain can be controlled by stimulating, rather than disrupting, the normal activities of the body.

brain simultaneously. Moreover, pain receptors were considered to be immune to adaptation, which was fortunate, since they play such an important role in protecting us from bodily harm.

Yet recently, some psychologists have suggested that there are no specific pain receptors at all. Pain results, they argue, from excessive stimulation of any of the sense receptors. This recent view explicitly challenges the **specificity theory** of pain. That theory holds that an injury to the arm, for example, will affect specific pain receptors in the arm, which relay signals directly to the brain (Melzack, 1973*b*). Under the specificity theory, the individual is expected to feel pain precisely at the point of the injury.

An alternate model, known as the **gate-control theory,** has been proposed by Ronald Melzack and Patrick Wall (1965; Melzack, 1973*b*). They hypothesize that our pain-signaling system contains a gatelike mechanism that, depending on the level of activity of sensory fibers, may be open, partially open, or closed. If the "gate" is closed, the signals that normally transmit pain messages from injured tissues will not reach the brain, and thus the sensation of pain will not result.

Melzack and Wall believe that large fibers exist in the sensory nerves that can "close the gate" when stimulated. In addition, certain areas of the brainstem can send out signals to fibers connected to the spinal cord, which can effectively block pain. Thus, the gate-control theory offers the hope that methods can be developed to diminish pain through manual or electronic stimulation of these large fibers. Research in such pain-reducing techniques has been under way throughout the last decade.

The gate-control theory also explains how pain messages can be modified considerably on their trip to the brain. Messages from the other senses can inhibit or enhance the nerve impulses from the pain receptors. Interference in the higher brain centers can also reduce, or even block out, sensations of pain. For example, people who have been hypnotized and told that they will experience no pain do not feel pain (Hilgard, 1969). The same principles may be important in the dramatic success of acupuncture in China.

But pain sensations are one thing and the agony of being in pain is quite another. The first is purely a physical process, more or less the same for everybody. The second depends largely on each person's evaluation of and reaction to the painful situation. This suggests that more areas of the cerebral cortex are involved in the suffering of pain than merely the sensory areas, and that pain is a complex sensation, both in its physiology and in the way that it is experienced.

Summary

1. The study of sensation is the study of how the body's various receptor cells translate physical energy into neural messages, how those messages reach the central nervous system, and the experiences that result.
2. In all the sensory processes, some form of energy stimulates a receptor cell in one of the sense organs. The receptor cell then changes the energy it receives into an electrochemical neural impulse, a process known as *transduction*. The neural impulse then travels through the sensory nerves to the central nervous system. During the process of transduction and transmission, the neural impulse is also *coded,* so that by the time it gets to the brain, it is quite precise.
3. *Psychophysical* methods are used to measure sensation. One measure is the *absolute threshold*—the minimum intensity of physical energy at which a person reports noticing a sensation 50 percent of the time. Another is the *difference threshold*—the smallest change in stimulation that a person can detect, called the *just noticeable difference* (j.n.d.), 50 percent of the time. Some psychologists have questioned the validity of thresholds as

measures of sensation. They suggest that thresholds really measure only the subject's willingness to report what he senses.

4. When the intensity of stimulation remains constant for a period of time, we get used to the constant level of stimulation and the receptor cells become less sensitive. This phenomenon is known as *adaptation*.

5. The physical stimulus for the sense of vision is light. The amount of light entering the eye is controlled by the *pupil*, which expands or contracts to allow more or less light to pass through. Inside the pupil, the light passes through the *lens*, which focuses it onto the *retina*.

6. There are two kinds of receptor cells in the retina—*rods* and *cones*. Cones operate mainly in daylight and respond to colors. Rods are primarily responsible for night vision when there is not enough light to stimulate the cones. The *fovea*—the depressed spot on the retina directly behind the lens—contains millions of cones, but no rods. Moving outward from the fovea, both rods and cones get sparser. At the extreme periphery there are only rods.

7. Rods and cones differ in shape, chemical pigments, and neural connections. The pigment in rods is *rhodopsin*, that in cones is *iodopsin*. Both break down into retinene and other chemical substances when struck by light, then recombine. The chemical activity is thought to stimulate the *bipolar neurons*, which connect to the *ganglion cells*, whose axons make up the *optic nerve*. After they leave the eye, the fibers that make up the two optic nerves separate and cross at the *optic chiasma*. The nerve fibers from the right side of each eye travel to the right hemisphere of the brain, and vice versa.

8. Adaptation is rarely total in the receptors of the eye. Light is almost never focused on the same rods and cones for very long, because the eyes are constantly moving. But the receptors of the eye do adapt partially to light and dark. The cones adapt to dark after about 5 minutes, the rods in about 20 to 30 minutes.

9. Color vision is dominated by two main theories. According to the *trichromatic theory*, the eye contains three different kinds of color receptors that respond to red, green, and blue light. By mixing these three basic colors, the eye can detect any color in the spectrum. The *opponent-process theory* accepts the notion of three separate kinds of receptors, but holds that each responds to either member of three basic color pairs—red and green, yellow and blue, and black and white (dark and light). Recent studies indicate that both theories may be correct at different stages of the visual process.

10. The physical stimuli for the sense of *hearing* are *sound waves*. The *frequency* of the waves determines the *pitch* of a sound; their *amplitude* determines *loudness;* and their *overtones* determine *timbre*. Sound waves cause the *eardrum* to vibrate, which sets in motion the *hammer, anvil,* and *stirrup*. The stirrup strikes the *oval window*, which transfers the vibrations to the *cochlea*. The *basilar membrane* then moves up and down, and the receptor cells in the *organ of Corti* cause their adjacent bipolar neurons to fire. The nerve fibers from the ears cross in the medulla. The auditory messages pass through at least four levels of neurons on their way to the brain, each of which codes the information more precisely.

11. The loudness of a sound depends on how many neurons are activated. There are two major types of theories of pitch discrimination. *Place theory*

states that sound waves, depending on their pitch, cause different places on the basilar membrane to move. *Frequency theory* says that pitch is determined by the frequency of firing of nerve cells. Neither theory alone explains pitch discrimination fully.

12. *Smell* and *taste* are termed *chemical senses* because they are activated by chemical substances. Millions of receptor cells for the sense of smell are located in the *olfactory epithelium,* high in the nasal cavity. Airborne molecules activate these specialized neurons, which then carry the messages directly to the brain without crossing over.

13. The receptor cells for the sense of taste lie in the *taste buds* on the tongue. Each taste bud contains a cluster of taste receptors—hair cells—which cause their adjacent neurons to fire when activated by the chemical substances in food. We experience only four primary taste qualities—sweet, sour, salty, and bitter—and these combine to form all other tastes. Taste seems to be coded by the overall pattern of firing in a number of fibers, not by the activation of a single fiber for each single taste quality.

14. The *body senses* include *kinesthesis* and the *vestibular sense.* Kinesthesis tells us what position one part of the body is in in relation to the other parts; its receptors are scattered throughout the muscles and joints of the whole body. The vestibular sense tells us what position we are in with respect to gravity. The receptors for this sense are located in the vestibular organ in the inner ear.

15. The sense of touch is made up of several different sensations—*pressure, warmth, cold,* and *pain.* Some parts of the body—such as the hands, the feet, and the face—are more sensitive to all these sensations than other parts—such as the back, the upper arms, and the calves.

16. The receptors in the skin fall into three general categories. *Free nerve endings* are found just below the surface of the skin and are traditionally thought to be involved in the sensation of pain, but may also play a role in sensations of warmth and cold, and perhaps even pressure. The *basket nerve ending* wraps around the base of a hair and responds to touch or light pressure. In *encapsulated end organs* a nerve fiber ends inside some sort of capsule or shell. Most are found quite close to the surface of the skin and appear to respond to sensations of pressure, but some are also involved in sensations of temperature. The nerve fibers from all these different receptors travel to the brain through the spinal cord, crossing over at various points so that messages from the left side of the body reach the right cerebral hemisphere, and vice versa.

17. The sense of *temperature* depends on two different kinds of receptors—one set for warmth and one set for cold. If both sets are activated at the same time, the brain reads their combined pattern of firing as hot.

18. *Pain* is more subject to individual interpretation than the other senses. Until recently, psychologists thought that the primary pain receptors were the networks of free nerve endings. But recently, some psychologists have suggested that there are no specific pain receptors, and that pain results from excessive stimulation of any of the sense receptors. According to the *gate-control* theory of pain, our pain-signaling mechanism contains a gatelike mechanism that, depending on the sensory fibers' level of activity, may be open, partially open, or closed. If the gate is closed, no pain message will get through to the brain and there will be no sensation of pain.

Suggested Readings

Geldard, F. A., *The Human Senses,* 2nd ed. (New York: Wiley, 1972). A comprehensive account of the sensory processes in man.

Gregory, R. L., *Eye and Brain: The Psychology of Seeing* (New York: McGraw-Hill, 1966). A clear and sophisticated discussion of the visual sense.

Melzack, R., *The Puzzle of Pain* (New York: Basic Books, 1973). A readable book that describes the various theories of pain, including the author's own gate-control theory, and discusses psychological and physiological aspects of various pain phenomena.

Mueller, C. G., *Sensory Psychology* (Englewood Cliffs, N.J.: Prentice-Hall, 1965). A thorough introduction to the basic facts and theories of sensory psychology.

Mueller, C. G., and Mae, R., *Light and Vision* (New York: Time, Inc., 1966). An interesting and well-illustrated account of the nature of light and the visual process.

Scharf, B., et al., *Experimental Sensory Psychology* (Glenview, Ill.: Scott, Foresman, 1975). A collection of advanced papers on each of the five sensory systems, all written by experts in the area.

Stevens, S. S., and Warshofsky, F., *Sound and Hearing* (New York: Time, Inc., 1965). A basic description of the nature of sound and the sense of hearing.

Wilentz, J. S., *The Senses of Man* (New York: Crowell, 1968). An entertaining account of sensory phenomena, including discussions of drug effects and extrasensory perception.

outline

ATTENTION 312

The Focus of Attention
Marginal Attention
Selective Attention
The Information-Processing Model of Perception

ORGANIZATION OF PERCEPTION 317

PERCEPTION OF DISTANCE AND DEPTH 322

Monocular Cues
Binocular Cues

PERCEPTION OF MOVEMENT 327

PERCEPTUAL CONSTANCY 329

FACTORS AFFECTING PERCEPTION 335

Motivation
Expectations
Personality and Perception
Cultural Differences

ALTERED STATES OF CONSCIOUSNESS 338

Sensory Deprivation
Sleeping and Dreaming
Hypnosis and Meditation
Drug-Induced Experiences

SUMMARY 350

SUGGESTED READINGS 353

9

Perception

Every second our sense organs are bombarded by millions of pieces of information from the outside world. Light waves trigger chemical reactions in the retina, sound waves set the eardrums vibrating; heat and pressure are registered by innumerable receptors in the skin. We need this critical information to decide when to take shelter, when to eat (and what to eat), and when to perform a host of other functions. But these sensations usually arrive at the brain simultaneously, competing with one another for a place in the spotlight of attention. The brain must take this information and identify it, analyze it, classify it, and interpret it before a response can be made. The eye records a pattern of light and dark, but it does not "see" a tree. The eardrum vibrates in a particular fashion upon the arrival of a given set of sound waves, but it does not "hear" a baby's cry or a Bach fugue. These tasks belong to the brain, and all the processes involved in creating meaningful patterns out of a jumble of sensory impressions fall under the general category of **perception.**

Most of the discussion in this chapter is based on the assumption that the perceiver is in a normal state of consciousness—alert, awake,

311

and generally drug-free, except for mild, common drugs such as caffeine, nicotine, and the chemicals found in most American food. Nobody, however, is in a normal state of consciousness all the time; our state of consciousness is altered, for example, when we go to sleep. Nevertheless, we continue to perceive. Therefore, in this chapter, after our study of perception in the normal state of consciousness, we examine the altered states of consciousness—sensory deprivation, sleeping, dreaming, hypnosis, meditation, and drug-induced experiences.

Attention

Perception requires attention. So, the first step in the perceptual process is to narrow the field, to select certain messages from the constant jumble of sensory information, to decide which set of messages to pay attention to at any given moment.

The Focus of Attention

Focusing attention involves selecting one object or event from all the many things going on around us. The focus of attention can and does shift very easily and rapidly. It moves around like a television camera, centering first on one event or object, then on another. Generally, the focus of attention is attracted to objects or events that possess unusual characteristics or that provide strong stimulation to the sense organs. This has been called "involuntary attention" (Kahneman, 1973). In general, we tend to give only casual notice to anything relatively commonplace and uninteresting—until it moves or changes in some way. A parked car rarely draws our attention unless it is an unusual model or color, but a car careening down the street will immediately attract our attention.

(Myron Wood, Photo Researchers)

In addition, just as we give attention to something, we can also give attention to nothing. For example, when it suddenly becomes quiet after a period of noise, the sense receptors don't simply shut down—they send a "nothing is happening" message to the brain. Such a message can be quite arousing—we have all probably been in positions where we were made uncomfortable by an extended period of silence. In these cases, we are actually paying more attention to nothing than to the somethings also present in the situation.

The focus of attention is also affected by certain characteristics of the individual—his interests, his motivation, his past experiences. If you are preoccupied with some personal problem, you might read a page of a book without perceiving a single word. If you have just finished a big meal, the smell of pizza from a stand around the corner might not affect you as strongly as it would someone who had skipped lunch.

Another type of focused attention is related to effort connected with goals. This "voluntary attention" (Kahneman, 1973) differs from involuntary attention in that it is determined by deliberate choice rather than by physiological arousal such as that caused by novelty or change in the environment. For example, if you want to learn, you will deliberately pay more attention to your professors than you might otherwise. In this sense, the more meaningful the stimulus is in terms of your goals, the more likely you will be to give attention to it.

Marginal Attention

Even when a person's attention is focused on something, he is usually aware of other things in his environment. Occasionally, he may be attending so intently to a project he is working on or be so absorbed in a novel or a movie that he seems almost oblivious to anything and everything else that may be happening. But even though his attention is taken, he is still receiving sensory messages and registering a great deal of information about his surroundings. He is probably aware of where he is, for example—whether he is in a library, a cave in the mountains, or the corner bar. He senses the presence of other people around him, the sounds and temperature of the room, and so on. Occasionally messages such as these may come to occupy the focus of your attention, if only for a moment. If you are with friends at a restaurant that provides piano music to entertain the customers, your attention may be focused on your conversation with your friends or on the taste of the food you are eating. But you might recognize a snatch of melody now and then, and you might even pick up bits and pieces of the conversations at other tables, especially if your name is mentioned. Thus we still sense events and objects even when our attention is focused elsewhere. We are sensing them at a low level of awareness, but we are not perceiving them.

Selective Attention

As we saw in Chapter 2, the primary function of the reticular activating system in the brain is to filter incoming messages and to alert the higher brain centers when important messages are received. The filtering process that goes on in the reticular activating system is known as **sensory gating**—input from one set of sense organs is allowed to pass, while other information is temporarily held back. In addition, the reticular activating system seems to provide some sort of feedback to the sense receptors. It appears to tell them not to send in any conflicting messages (at least for the moment)—to hold all calls until the brain can get around to handling them. Which information passes through the sensory gates determines where our attention will be directed.

The brain, it seems, is able to attend to only one set of messages at a time, to tune in on only one channel at any particular moment. Hernandez-Péon and his associates (1956), interested in finding out what happens in the brain when more than one set of sense organs is stimulated at the same time, implanted electrodes in the auditory nerve of a cat. They sounded a click at regular intervals and measured the electrical activity of the cat's auditory nerve. Each time the click was sounded, the activity of the nerve increased, producing the sharp spike in the recording shown in Figure 9-1. Then they placed some mice in front of the cat. As they had expected, the mice immediately attracted the cat's attention. The visual messages must have been judged more interesting or more important than the auditory ones, for as long as

Figure 9-1

When a click is sounded, the electrical activity in the cat's auditory nerve increases markedly, producing a sharp peak on the recording. But when the cat is presented with a jar of mice, the same click causes a much weaker response. (After R. Hernandez-Péon, H. Scherrer, and N. Jouvet, "Modification of Electric Activity in the Cochlear Nucleus during 'Attention' in Unanesthetized Cats." *Science*, 1956, *123*, 331–332.)

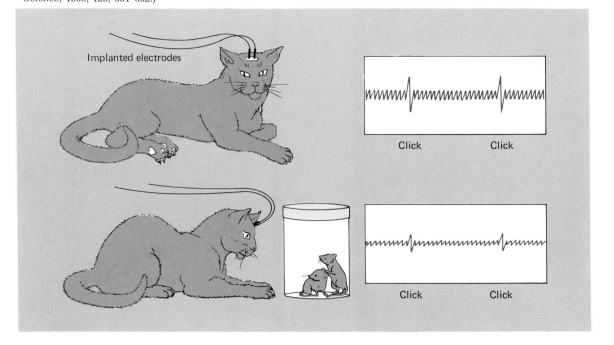

Implanted electrodes

Click   Click

Click   Click

the mice were present, the sound of the click caused a much smaller increase in the electrical activity of the auditory nerve. It was almost as if the cat's ears had been turned off. And, to some extent, they probably had been—the reticular activating system, by opening the gates to the visual messages and by inhibiting the sensitivity of the auditory system, seemed to have tuned out the ears to focus the cat's attention on the mice. In humans, as in cats, vision is the dominant sense. If we are simultaneously exposed to a sight and a sound, in general the visual stimulus will be given more attention (Colavita, 1971).

In such situations, two distinct sensory systems are in competition for our attention. What happens when competing information is simultaneously presented to the *same* sensory system? To study this question, Stroop (1935) set up a very ingenious experiment. One group of people were shown drawings of rectangles of various colors and were asked simply to tell the experimenter what color each of the rectangles was. A second group of people were assigned the same task, but were shown words printed in various colors instead of rectangles. As an added complication, the words were color words that were different from the colored ink the words were printed in. For example, the word "red" was printed in green ink. As you might expect, the response rates of the second group were significantly slower than those of the first group. It is generally agreed that the reason for this is that it takes time to sort out the two conflicting responses caused by such a double stimulus.

Psychologists have found similar effects for the perception of simultaneous aural stimuli. To study this, people are given earphones and a different message is presented to each ear; this is called **dichotic listening.** In one study, Anne Treisman (1964) asked people to repeat the passage they heard in one ear and ignore a passage simultaneously presented to the other. As you might expect, Treisman found that this task was easy as long as there was a lot of difference between the two passages. If, however, the two messages were in the same language or were spoken by the same speaker, the task was much more difficult. When the dichotic messages were in different languages, the results were particularly interesting. Listeners who knew both languages found it much more difficult to ignore the unattended message than listeners who knew only one. Thus, the ability to selectively attend depends on the similarity of the information. In Treisman's study, for example, either similarities in the physical properties of the messages (speakers) or similarities in the level of meaningfulness (language), or both, make the task difficult.

The Information-Processing Model of Perception

Computers were originally valued for their ability to simulate human thought processes at a superhuman rate. But computer research has also generated a tremendous amount of exciting and potentially fruitful work on human perception. The major computer model currently in use is **information processing** (Haber & Hershenson, 1973; Vinacke, 1974). Using computer terminology, information processing describes behavior in terms of "input" and "output" variables and attempts to trace the connecting processes that are brought to bear on information from the time it enters the system to the time it leaves. Although we will look at information processing here solely in terms of the light it sheds on perception, the model has been applied to a broad range of human activity.

The information-processing approach to perception rests on four major assumptions (Haber & Hershenson, 1973):

1. Perception is the result of processing over a period of time, and is not an immediate result of exposure to the stimulus.
2. Researchers can design experiments that will demonstrate the change (or lack of change) in the stimulus information at each point in the processing sequence.
3. At each point in the processing sequence, the amount of information that can be contained or processed in a certain time period is limited.
4. These limitations usually result in selectivity; when the information presented exceeds capacity, some of it will not be processed as thoroughly, and some will be shut out entirely.

As we discussed in Chapter 5, we can handle an excessive amount of information if, instead of treating each item separately, we combine them into larger units, or *chunks*. In information-processing terms, chunking is called **recoding** (Vinacke, 1974). The chunks or codes, are stored for short- or long-term use in formulating responses according to established *programs,* or rule systems.

Haber and Hershenson (1973) have developed an information-processing model of visual perception that draws on the three levels of memory we discussed in Chapter 5. The first stage is called **brief visual storage.** Information from light waves striking the retina is represented internally. Because the eye is in constant involuntary motion, the perceiver has at most one-quarter of a second in which to process the information for brief visual storage (as well as for further use). Next, a visual image is constructed; this is "conscious awareness of the experience of perceiving." The second step, which may occur after construction of the visual image or simultaneously with it, is **short-term memory.** This involves encoding the visual information into concepts or words. Then, some, but not all, of the contents of short-term memory are sent to **long-term memory.** Some information in long-term memory is called into use daily, and some is simply stored there for years on end. Finally, a response is formulated by the **output process.** If a spoken response is called for, the motor program of the speech apparatus will be drawn upon; if a written response is required, a different program will organize the response.

Figure 9-2
An information-processing model of visual perception. Feedback from both long- and short-term memory is needed to analyze, classify, and identify the visual image before the response program is activated and the response itself, or "output," is performed. (From R. N. Haber and M. Hershenson, *The Psychology of Visual Perception*. New York: Holt, Rinehart & Winston, 1973, Fig. 7.1 © 1973 Holt, Rinehart & Winston. Reprinted by permission.)

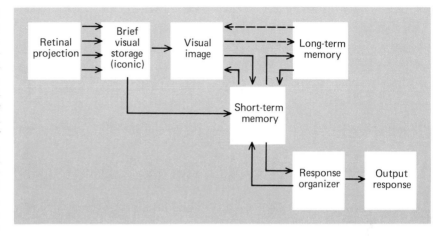

Information can sometimes flow in both directions, as illustrated by the arrows in Figure 9-2. For example, look at the relationship between the visual image and short-term memory. One can generate the other; the name in short-term memory can stimulate reproduction of the visual image even when it is absent, and we can give a name to the image, even if we learned the name after seeing the image.

Organization of Perception

In Chapter 1 we noted that the Gestalt psychologists were particularly interested in studying perception to determine how sensory impressions are organized. They believed that the whole, or "gestalt," was more than the sum of its parts—that a perception was more than simply the sum of a number of sensory impressions. They found that individuals tend to follow certain basic principles in organizing the sensations they receive from their surroundings.

According to the Gestaltists, these organizational principles serve to arrange the elements of a figure in ways that minimize uncertainty and that maximize **redundancy.** The more redundant a figure is—that is, the more the information in it is repeated—the less ambiguity it has and the more predictable it is. The Gestaltists feel that making simplicity out of complexity is a natural human process that is carried out without our being conscious of it. (Note that this is analogous to recoding in information-processing terminology.) Haber and Hershenson (1973) report that, when shown a figure that could be seen in both simple and complex ways, people were more apt to report seeing the simple version. This can be helpful, because it allows us to make rapid responses to what we perceive and to accommodate much more information than would otherwise be possible. But, as we shall see, we can also be fooled and may misinterpret what we perceive.

Probably the most fundamental principle in the organization of sen-

Figure 9-3
These two spirals show how we can be fooled if we do not think about what we perceive. These spirals look alike, but they are not. The one on the left is formed of a single continuous line, but the one on the right is actually composed of two lines. If you don't believe us, take a pencil and trace both spirals for yourself. (From B. Julesz, "Experiments in the Visual Perception of Texture." Copyright © 1975 by Scientific American, Inc. All rights reserved.)

sations is the distinction between a **figure** and the **ground** it appears against. A figure is often distinguished from the ground by its shape or its color, or because it seems closer while the ground seems farther away. A colorfully upholstered chair will stand out as a figure against the ground of darker furniture in a room. A marble statue will be perceived as a figure against the ground of a red brick wall.

Figure 9-4
Figure and ground are clearly distinguished at the top and bottom of this woodcut by M. C. Escher, but in the middle, they alternate. (*Haags Gemeentemuseum, The Hague*)

Figure 9-5
In another Escher woodcut,
reversible figure and ground
cause us to see first devils,
then angels in each of
the rings.
(*Escher Foundation*)

Figure 9-5
In another Escher woodcut,
reversible figure and ground
cause us to see first devils,
then angels in each of
the rings.
(*Escher Foundation*)

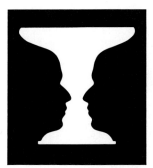

Figure 9-6
Reversible figure-ground
drawing. This figure can be
perceived either as a white
vase against a black ground
or as two black faces
against a white ground.

Sometimes the contrast between figure and ground does not give us enough cues to determine which is figure and which is ground. In those instances, we have a **reversible figure,** like the ones shown in Figures 9-4, 9-5, and 9-6. At one moment we see white figures against a black ground, at the next, black figures against a white ground.

The figure-ground relationship extends to senses other than vision. It helps to distinguish the sound of a solo instrument, like a violin or piano, against the ground of a symphony orchestra, for example. Similarly, the raised dots in a Braille reader are felt as figures against the ground of the surface of the page.

When we receive sensations that do not form a finished figure, our inclination is to overlook the incompleteness and perceive the figure as a finished unit. **Closure,** then, refers to this tendency to fill in the gaps. If we see only partial outlines, as in Figure 9-7, for example, we tend to fill in the missing lines and perceive the objects as wholes. The same thing happens with aural sensations. Someone listening to a conversation over a very bad telephone connection may hear only bits and pieces of what the other person is saying, but he will fill in the gaps and perceive these sounds as whole words and sentences.

Figure 9-7
We tend to perceive all these figures as "closed" objects, not as separate lines.

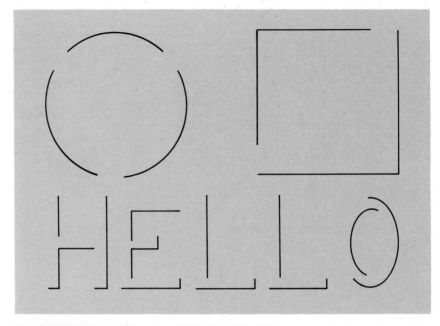

Figure 9-8
Most people perceive a continuous wavy line, not the two separate lines shown at the right.

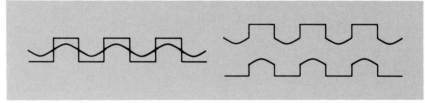

Figure 9-9
By moving your eyes along the curved lines, the principle of continuity will make it difficult for you to find the hidden letters and number in this figure. You should be able to find the letters A, I, L, V, Y, and the number 4.

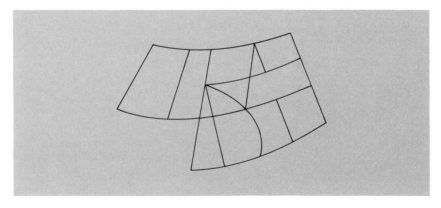

Items that continue a pattern or direction tend to be grouped together with the preceding items that set the pattern. In Figure 9-8, we tend to perceive a wavy line crossing three square humps, even though the figure could justifiably be described as two separate lines. The principle of **continuity** can sometimes lead to inaccurate perceptions. Try to find the hidden letters and numbers in Figure 9-9. In order to

Figure 9-10
Figures that are in close proximity to one another tend to be perceived as patterns.

Figure 9-11
Similarity of shape or color can lead to the perception of patterns in these figures.

Figure 9-12
This portrait was "drawn" by a computer. Can you tell who it is? Try holding the page farther away or unfocusing your eyes, and you will see how the principles of proximity and similarity will help you to recognize this familiar face.
(*Courtesy of Bell Telephone Laboratories*)

perceive the hidden letters and numbers you must break continuity or you will be drawn off the track.

When objects are close to each other, the tendency is to perceive them together rather than separately. Figure 9-10 illustrates the grouping of visual sensations. The principle of **proximity** also applies to aural sensations. "Did he tell you what the night rate is?" means something quite different from "Did he tell you what the nitrate is?" Both sentences contain the same sounds, but the way the speaker groups the sounds—where he pauses—will usually determine how the sounds are perceived.

Similarity can also cause elements that are similar to each other to be grouped together. Items that have the same color, the same shape, or the same size tend to be perceived as parts of the same pattern, as in Figure 9-11.

The principle of **common fate** describes the tendency to group together several items that are moving in the same direction. The planes in a precision flying team, for example, tend to be perceived as a whole unit, distinct from the clouds or trees behind them.

So far, in our study of perception, we have looked at the phenomenon of attention and how an individual comes to focus on a certain few of the many sensory messages the sense organs are constantly transmitting. Then we have described ways in which an individual processes information and imposes a basic structure on the meaning-less jumble of sensations. The question we turn to now is how we form simple judgments about objects—how we determine how far away they are, how large they are, whether they are fixed or moving, whether they remain stable over time.

Perception of Distance and Depth

A person is constantly faced with situations in which he has to judge the distance between himself and other objects. When he walks through a classroom, his perception of distance helps him avoid bumping into desks or tripping over a wastebasket. If he reaches out to pick up a pencil, he automatically judges how far to extend his arm. We also constantly judge the depth of objects—how much total space they occupy. In doing so, we seem to ask ourselves (often without being aware of the question) "How big is this object? How thick or thin is it?"

Many of the same cues are used to determine how far away objects are and how large they are. Some of these cues depend on visual messages that one eye can transmit; they are called **monocular cues.** Others—**binocular cues**—depend on the interaction of both eyes.

Monocular Cues

Having two eyes enables a person to make more accurate judgments about distance and depth, particularly when he is dealing with objects

Figure 9-13
Because the king of clubs has been superimposed on the blank card, we perceive it as being closer. When the cards are spaced out. however, we can see that the cards have been notched to create an illusion, and that the king of spades is actually the closest card.

(Burk Uzzle, Magnum Photos)

that are relatively close, but the monocular cues to distance and depth often enable him to successfully judge distance and depth by using only one eye.

Superposition, when one object first partially blocks a second object, is an important distance cue. The first object is perceived as being closer, the second as more distant (see Figure 9-13).

As all students of art know, there are several ways **perspective** can help in the estimation of distance and depth. Two parallel lines that extend into the distance seem to come together at some point on the horizon. This cue to distance and depth is known as *linear perspective*. In *aerial perspective*, objects that are far away have a hazy appearance and a somewhat blurred outline. On a clear day, mountains often appear to be much closer than they do on a hazy day when their outlines become blurred. The *elevation* of an object is another perspective cue to depth. An object that is on a higher horizontal plane seems to be farther away than an object on a lower plane (see Figure 9-14).

Still another helpful monocular cue to distance and depth is **texture gradient.** An object that is quite close often appears to have a rough or detailed texture. As distance increases, the texture becomes finer until finally the original texture cannot be distinguished clearly, if at all. A person standing on a pebbly beach, for example, will be able to distinguish the gray stones and gravel beside his feet. As he looks off down the beach, however, the stones will seem to become smaller and finer until eventually he will be unable to identify individual stones.

Figure 9-14
Because of its higher elevation, we tend to perceive the tree on the right as being farther away.

Shadowing can provide another important cue to distance and to the depth and solidity of an object. Ordinarily, shadows appear on the parts of objects that are farther away. The shadowing on the outer edges of a spherical object, like a ball or globe, for example, gives it a three-dimensional quality. Without this shadowing, the object might be perceived as a flat disk. The shadow an object casts behind itself can also provide a cue to its depth. And the presence of shadows either before or behind objects can help to indicate how far away they are.

Figure 9-15
Shadowing as a cue to depth makes the hieroglyphics on the left seem to be etched into the surface, while those on the right seem to protrude. Actually, you have been fooled again. Both pictures are the same—the one on the right has simply been turned upside down.
(*The Bettmann Archive*)

Figure 9-16
Several different distance
and depth cues are at work
in this picture—linear
perspective, aerial
perspective, elevation,
shadowing, and texture
gradient.
(*Arthur Tress, Photo
Researchers*)

People traveling on trains or buses often notice that the trees or telephone poles that are close to the road or the railroad tracks seem to flash past the windows very rapidly, while buildings and other objects that are farther away seem to move fairly slowly. You can observe the same effect if you stand still and move your head from side to side. The objects close to you are perceived as moving very quickly; those that are farther away seem to move much more slowly. These differences in the speeds of **movement** of images across the retina as you move provide an important cue to distance and depth.

In the process known as **accommodation,** the lens of the eye changes its curvature to focus different objects on the retina. If the object is close, the lens is made rounder; if the object is farther away, the lens is flattened. Kinesthetic sensations from the muscles that cause these changes provide another cue to how near or far away an object is.

Binocular Cues

All the cues discussed so far depend on the action of only one eye. Many animals such as horses, deer, and fish, although they have two eyes, are dependent entirely on monocular cues. Because their eyes are

EXTRASENSORY PERCEPTION

Extrasensory perception, or ESP, has been defined as "a response to an unknown event not presented to any known sense" (McConnell, 1969). It covers a wide variety of phenomena, including *clairvoyance*, seeing an unknown object or event; *telepathy*, knowing someone else's thoughts or feelings; and *precognition*, foreknowledge of future events.

Modern experiments on ESP often use a deck of 25 cards, each containing five symbols. To test clairvoyance, the target cards are arranged randomly. The order is unknown to both the subject and the experimenter. The subject is asked to "call" the cards in order. If the number of correct guesses, called "hits," is consistently greater than would be expected by chance, ESP is presumed to be operating. To test for telepathy, the sender concentrates on a symbol and the subject writes down what he "receives." In testing for precognition, the subject calls out the order of cards in advance, then the experimenter selects cards at random, using a computer or a pair of dice, and checks to see if the subject called them in correct order.

Physical factors, such as electromagnetic radiation and distances of space and time, appear to have no effect on ESP. But physiological factors that decrease body functions, such as depressants or lack of oxygen, tend to lower ESP scores. Stimulants cause greater variations, but do not seem to raise the level of ESP. Psychological factors seem to have the most effect. Subjects who are eager, spontaneous, well adjusted, and who have a positive attitude toward ESP have higher ESP scores than withdrawn, hostile, neurotic subjects with negative attitudes. A close congenial relationship between agent and perceiver seems essential for telepathy to work. ESP ability may be constant or intermittent and varies widely with the individual.

C. E. M. Hansel, a severe critic of ESP experiments, has expressed the doubts most psychologists have about the whole subject of ESP. The experiments, he feels, are poorly designed—there were not enough safeguards against dishonesty. The reports of results often are inadequate. Many psychologists feel that ESP researchers select data to support their own beliefs and slight the evidence to the contrary. Hansel is also dismayed by the inability of researchers to use their findings to predict how subjects would perform on future tests. Another of his objections is that results often are not confirmed by conducting follow-up experiments, either with the same team or with different subjects. Yet, despite all these objections, Hansel does admit that "subjects when trying to guess card symbols have obtained scores that cannot be attributed to chance" (Hansel, 1966). Still, most psychologists are not convinced, and more and better experiments are needed before the scientific validity of ESP will be generally accepted.

set on the sides of their heads, the two visual fields do not overlap. But humans, apes, and many predatory animals (such as lions, tigers, and wolves) have a unique physical advantage over these animals. Because both eyes are set in the front of the head, the visual fields do overlap. This **stereoscopic vision** obtained from the coalescence of the two retinal images makes the perception of depth and distance more accurate.

Because our eyes are set approximately $2\frac{1}{2}$ inches apart, each one has a slightly different view of things. The difference between the two images the eyes receive is known as **retinal disparity.** The left eye receives more information about the left side of an object, the right eye more about the right side. You can easily prove to yourself that each of your eyes receives a different image. Close one eye and line up a finger with some vertical line, like the edge of a door. Then open that eye and close the other one. Your finger will appear to have moved a considerable distance. However, when you look at the finger with both eyes, the two different images coalesce into one.

Another binocular cue to distance comes from the muscles that control the **convergence** of the eyes. When we look at objects that are fairly close to us, our eyes tend to converge—to turn slightly inward toward each other. The kinesthetic sensations from the muscles that control this movement of the eyes provide an additional cue to distance. If the object if very close, like the end of the nose, the eyes are unable to converge and two separate images are perceived. And if the object is more than 60 or 70 feet away, the sight lines of the eyes are more or less parallel and convergence does not occur.

Up to this point we have considered only stationary objects—how we locate them in space and how we perceive their depth. Now let us examine how we perceive motion.

Perception of Movement

The perception of movement is a complicated process, involving both the visual messages from the eye as an image moves across the retina and the kinesthetic messages from the muscles around the eye as they shift the eye to follow a moving object. At times, too, our perceptual processes play tricks on us and we think we perceive movement when the objects we are looking at are actually not moving at all. In our discussion of movement, therefore, we must distinguish between real movement and illusory movement.

Real movement means the physical displacement of an object from one position to another. The perception or real movement depends only in part on the movement of images across the retina of the eye. If a person stands still and moves his head to look around him, the images of all the objects in the room will pass across his retina. Yet he will probably perceive all these objects as stationary. Even if he holds his head still and moves only his eyes, the images continue to pass across the retina. But the messages from the eye muscles seem to counteract the messages from the retina, and the objects in the room are perceived as motionless.

Therefore, the perception of real movement seems to be determined less by images moving across the retina than by changes in the position of objects in relation to a background that is perceived as stationary. When we perceive a car moving along a street, for example, we see the street, the buildings, and the sidewalk as a stationary background and the car as a moving object. Quite remarkably, the brain is able to distinguish between these retinal images of an object moving against an immobile background and all the other moving images on the retina.

It is possible, under certain conditions, to see movement in objects that actually are standing still. One form of **illusory movement** is the *autokinetic illusion*—the apparent motion created by a single stationary

Figure 9-17
How can we perceive
movement in a stationary
object like this painting
(*Current* by Bridget Riley,
1964)? One theory is that the
perceived movement is due
to the constant involuntary
motion of the eye.

(*Collection, The Museum of
Modern Art, New York; Philip
C. Johnson Fund*)

object. If a person stands in a room that is absolutely dark except for
one tiny spot of light and stares at the light for a few seconds, he will
begin to see the light drift. In the darkened room, his eyes have no
visible framework; there are no cues to indicate that the light is actually
stationary. The slight movements of the eye muscles, which go on
unnoticed all the time, make the light appear to move.

Another form of illusory movement is *stroboscopic motion*—the
apparent motion created by a rapid series of images of stationary
objects. A motion picture, for example, is not actually in motion at all.
The film consists of a series of still pictures, showing persons or objects in slightly different positions. When the separate images are projected in sequence onto the screen, the persons or objects seem to be
moving because of the rapid change from one still picture to the next.

Stroboscopic motion is also responsible for a perceptual illusion
known as the *phi phenomenon*. When a light is flashed on at a certain
point in a darkened room, then flashed off, and a second light is flashed
on a split second later at a point a short distance away, most people

will perceive a single spot of light moving from one point to another. Of course, the distance between the two points, the intensity of the two lights, and the time interval between them must be carefully controlled if the illusion is to be achieved. The same perceptual process causes us to see motion in neon signs or theater marquees where words appear to move from right to left as different combinations of stationary lights are flashed on and off.

Perceptual Constancy

(Wide World Photos)

Perceptual constancy refers to the tendency to perceive objects as relatively stable and unchanging, despite changing sensory images. Without this ability, the world would be completely confusing. Every time a person moved, he would perceive the size, shape, and color of objects differently. In perceptual constancy, what we have learned from our past experiences with certain people and objects seems to compensate for the changing sensory images, allowing us to perceive things accurately under changing conditions.

Our perceptual experience of an object usually stays constant, even though the information to our sense organs may vary greatly. To quote Gertrude Stein, "a rose is a rose is a rose" whether it is seen in clear sunlight or by moonlight. This is called **object constancy.**

Essentially, once a person has formed a stable perception of an object, he is able to recognize it from almost any position, at almost any distance, under almost any illumination. As a sightseeing boat circles the Statue of Liberty, for example, a series of changing images are projected onto the retina of a passenger at the rail. Yet he does not perceive a number of different statues. From all angles, he perceives the same Statue of Liberty. The sensory images change, but the object is perceived as constant.

Objects tend to be perceived in their true size, regardless of the size of the retinal image they cast. As Figure 9-18 illustrates, the farther away an object is from the lens of the eye, the smaller the retinal image it casts. For example, a 6-foot man standing 20 feet away casts a retinal image that is only one-half the size of the retinal image he casts at 10 feet. Yet he is not perceived as having shrunk to 3 feet tall. **Size con-**

Figure 9-18
The relationship between distance and the size of the retinal image. Object A and Object B are the same size, but A, being much closer to the eye, casts a much larger image on the retina.

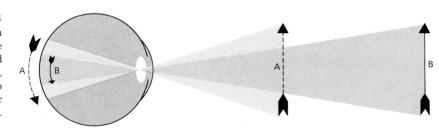

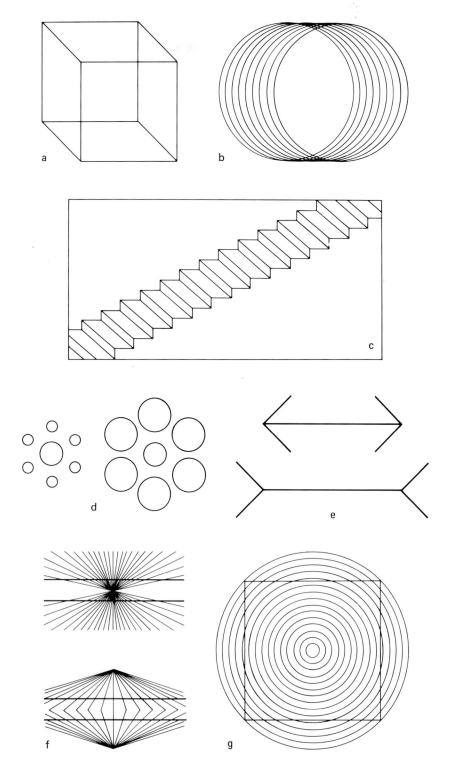

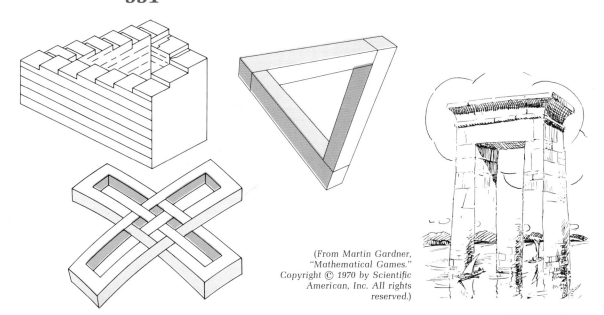

(From Martin Gardner,
"Mathematical Games."
Copyright © 1970 by Scientific
American, Inc. All rights
reserved.)

PERCEPTUAL HYPOTHESES

Is the cube facing to the left or to the right (Figure *a*)? Which way through the coils—left or right (Figure *b*)? Do you see a flight of stairs or an overhanging cornice (Figure *c*)? The answer in all cases, of course, is "both." Our perceptions keep changing—first we see the figures one way, then we see them the other way. Reversible figures like these illustrate quite clearly that perception is not just a simple replication of visual stimuli. As we look at each of these figures, we are actively searching for the best way to interpret them. According to R. L. Gregory (1966), a perception is, in effect, a *hypothesis* that is suggested by the sensory information. But a reversible figure can be explained by either of two different hypotheses. Since the figures do not provide any clues to tell us which hypothesis is correct, we keep shifting from one to the other.

This view of perceptions as hypotheses also gives us a way of describing visual illusions. Which of the center circles in Figure *d* is larger? Which of the two lines in Figure *e* is longer? In Figure *f*, are the horizontal lines straight? Does the square that is superimposed on the concentric circles in Figure *g* have straight sides or are they bowed inward? In all of these figures we tend to be misled in our perceptions. We choose a perceptual hypothesis that is wrong, so we do not perceive the figures accurately. Exactly why visual illusions occur is not very clearly understood and no single explanation has been widely accepted. Some (like Figure *d*) seem to depend on the size of an object in relation to the surrounding objects. Others (like Figure *e*) might arise from interpreting the angles at the ends of the lines as perspective cues, which causes the brain to compensate for the nonexistent distance and perceive the top line as shorter. What does seem clear, however, is that the source of the illusions must be sought in the brain, not in the eye—the error lies in the way the visual sensations are interpreted and perceptual hypotheses formed.

Some of the most perplexing visual illusions are the drawings known as "impossible figures," four of which are shown on this page. In these drawings, each individual part is acceptable and seems to be a perfectly normal representation of a three-dimensional object. But, as we follow along the surface lines we must continually form new perceptual hypotheses to adapt to the ever-changing apparent distance of the object.

"Let's have another look at the blueprint."
(Reproduced by special permission of Playboy Magazine. Copyright © 1974 by Playboy.)

stancy depends partly on experience—information about the relative sizes of objects is stored in the memory—and partly on distance cues.

When there are no distance cues, size constancy has to rely solely on what we have learned from our previous experiences with an object. Naturally, more errors occur when no distance cues are present, but considerably fewer than one would expect in view of the radical changes in the size of the retinal image. We might guess a man's height to be 5'8" instead of 6'2", but hardly anyone would perceive him as being 3 or 4 feet tall, no matter how far away he was. We know from our experience with people that adults are seldom that short.

Familiar objects also tend to be seen as having a constant shape, even though the retinal images they cast change as they are viewed from different angles. A dinner plate is perceived as a circle, even when it is tilted and the retinal image is oval. The only time a rectangular door will project a rectangular image on the retina is when it is viewed directly from the front. From any other angle, it casts a trapezoidal image on the retina, but it is not perceived as having suddenly become a trapezoidal door. These are examples of **shape constancy.**

Brightness constancy is related to the light reflected by an object. Most objects are only visible because of the light they reflect. The

Figure 9-19

The Ames room, specially designed to test size constancy. Most people watch with disbelief as the man seems to grow taller as he crosses the room. But the room actually has a tilted floor, which makes our normal distance cues unreliable.

(William Vandivert; reprinted by permission from Scientific American.)

amount of light changes constantly, as night follows day, yet we tend to perceive objects at characteristic brightnesses that do not change. A sheet of white paper is perceived as white, whether it is viewed by candlelight or under a light bulb. A piece of coal is perceived as black, whether it is viewed in the darkness of a cellar or out in the noonday sun, even though coal in sunlight reflects more light than white paper in candlelight. The reason is that a white object—or a black or gray one—will reflect the same percentage of the light falling on it, no matter whether the light is from a candle, from a match, from a fluorescent lamp, or from the sun. What is important here is not the absolute amount of light that any particular object reflects, but the relative reflection in comparison to surrounding objects.

When comparisons with surrounding objects are not possible, brightness constancy often fails. If a spotlight is directed at a black

(*Herman Eisenbeiss, Photo Researchers*)

THE MOON ILLUSION

The moon appears larger when it first rises than when it is high in the sky. Yet, photographs show us that its size does not actually change. Holding a pencil at arm's length and measuring the moon when it is in different positions in the sky will also reveal that its size does not change. The question of why the moon, the sun, and the constellations all appear larger near the horizon than when they are higher in the sky has been asked since antiquity. There are many theories but, as yet, no single definitive explanation of the moon illusion.

Kaufman and Rock (1962) favor the *apparent-distance theory*, based on the knowledge that an object appears smaller when it is farther away and seems to grow larger as it approaches us. To most people, the horizon seems farther away than the sky directly overhead. Thus, we perceive the horizon moon to be larger in order to compensate for its apparently greater distance from us. When the terrain is blocked out, the horizon moon does not appear larger than the zenith moon. According to Kaufman and Rock, the impression of distance is created by the terrain. Regardless of whether it is flat and barren or full of objects, it affects the moon's apparent size. This theory has recently been contested by Gilinsky (1971) who claims that the distance cues used are ambiguous. According to Gilinsky's *adaptation-level theory*, the perceived size of an object depends primarily on its perceived distance and the "angle of regard" (viewing angle). For all objects, we have a normal viewing distance and a normal viewing angle. When these aspects are changed, we perceive the object as larger or smaller than usual. For example, if you place your hand right in front of your eye, it seems enormous. We also have a "maximum perceived distance," which can range from 0.5 to 300 feet, depending on the individual and the situation. Our perception of a "normal" moon is that which is seen when the moon is at a 20-degree angle in the sky. At that point, the viewing distance is equal to the maximum perceived distance. The maximum perceived distance is longer at lower eye elevations and is shorter at higher eye elevations. Thus, according to Gilinsky, there are actually two moon illusions: the horizon moon, viewed at a low elevation, appears to be both larger and nearer than it actually is; and the zenith moon, viewed at a higher eye elevation, appears smaller and farther away.

disk and there are no shadows or other objects to compare it with, the disk will usually be perceived as white (Woodworth & Schlosberg, 1954). But if a piece of white paper is placed over one edge of the disk, the disk will be seen as black. Remove the paper, and it appears white again, although the observer now "knows" the disk is black.

The same principle holds true for colors, which are determined by the wavelengths of light that stimulate the eye. Under different kinds and intensities of illumination, the actual messages that reach the eye may be quite different from the way the color is ultimately perceived. Because of **color constancy,** we tend to perceive familiar objects as retaining their color, no matter what information reaches the eye. Someone who owns a red automobile, for example, perceives his car as red whether he sees it parked in an unshaded parking lot or under a shade tree, even though in shade the eye may actually receive information that more closely approximates "brown" or "black" than red.

Color constancy does not necessarily occur with unfamiliar objects, however, or when ordinary color cues are lacking. People who buy clothing in a store illuminated by fluorescent light often realize later that the color is quite different in daylight.

Factors Affecting Perception

Throughout this chapter we have emphasized that perception depends on more than just the messages sent to the brain by the various sense organs. Perceptual constancy, we noted, depends in large part on experience and learning. Several other factors can also affect perception, sometimes making our interpretations inaccurate, sometimes distilling perceptions still further by choosing the features of an object that are of greatest importance at the moment. **Selective perception,** as this process is called, depends largely on an individual's particular motivations and values, his expectations, his cognitive style, and the experiences he has had while growing up in a certain culture. Many psychologists have become critical of the Gestalt approach to perception because it does not deal adequately with these cognitive and motivational factors.

Motivation

A person's desires and needs may exert a strong influence on his perceptions. The individual who is in a state of need is more likely to perceive something that he thinks will satisfy that need.

Several interesting experiments have been conducted to determine the influence of hunger on perception. Sanford (1937) found that if persons were deprived of food for some time and then shown vague or ambiguous pictures, they were apt to perceive the pictures as related to food. Similarly, McClelland and Atkinson (1948) showed blurred pictures to people who had not eaten for varying numbers of hours. Some had eaten 1 hour previously; others had gone as long as 16 hours without food. Those who had not eaten for 16 hours perceived the blurred images as pictures of food much more frequently than the people who had eaten only a short time before.

Another experiment demonstrates how strongly perceptions can be affected by a person's values. Children of nursery school age were shown a poker chip. Each child was asked to compare the size of the chip to the size of a circle of light. The experimenter adjusted the size of the light until the child perceived the chip and the circle of light

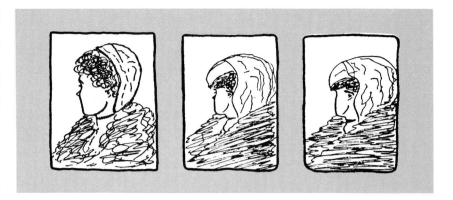

Figure 9-20

Look first at the drawing on the left and ask a friend to look at the one on the right. When you both look at the one in the middle, you will probably perceive it differently, because your expectations are different. (From R. W. Leeper, "A Study of a Neglected Portion of the Field of Learning." *Pedagogical Seminary and Journal of Genetic Psychology*, 1935, 46, 41–75. Courtesy of Journal Press.)

as being the same size. The children were then shown a machine with a crank. When a child turned the crank, he received a poker chip, which he could then exchange for candy. Thus the children were taught to value the poker chips more highly. After the children had been rewarded with the candy for cranking out the poker chips, they again were asked to compare the size of the chips to a circle of light. This time the chips appeared noticeably larger to the children (Lambert, Solomon, & Watson, 1949).

Expectations

Knowing in advance what we are supposed to perceive can influence our perception. Siipola (1935) demonstrated the effects of prior expectations in a study of individuals' responses to certain words. He told one group of people that they would be shown words related to animals. For a brief moment, he showed them combinations of letters that really did not spell anything—like "sael," "dack," or "wharl." Most of the group perceived the letters as the words "seal," "duck," and "whale." He then told a second group that he was going to show them words pertaining to boats and showed them the same letter combinations. This group, expecting to see nautical terms, perceived the same letter combinations as the words "sail," "deck," and "wharf."

Personality and Perception

As an individual matures, he develops a **cognitive style**—his own general method of dealing with the environment. Some psychologists distinguish between two general approaches people use in perceiving the environment (Witkin et al., 1962). The first is the "field-dependent" approach—the person perceives the environment as a whole and does not differentiate clearly the shape, color, size, or other qualities of the individual items around him. If a field-dependent person is asked to draw a human figure, he usually does not draw the figure so that it stands out clearly against the background. People who are "field independent," on the other hand, tend to perceive the elements of the environment as separate and distinct from each other and to draw each element as standing out from the background.

Another way of describing differences in cognitive styles is to distinguish between "levelers" and "sharpeners"—those who level out the distinctions between objects and those who magnify them. To investigate the differences between these two approaches, Klein (1951) showed individuals sets of squares of varying sizes and asked them to estimate the size of each of the squares. One group, the "levelers," failed to perceive any difference in the size of the squares. The "sharpeners," however, were aware of the differences in the size of the squares and changed their size estimates accordingly.

Cultural Differences

A person's cultural background can influence his perceptions. The language a person speaks, as we note in Chapter 6, can affect the way he perceives his surroundings and his experiences. Other cultural differences can influence the way a person uses perceptual cues.

In the Western world, for example, the square and the rectangle are the most commonly used shapes. Most buildings are constructed on rectangular lines; the round church or the round barn is the exception rather than the rule. Furniture is usually square or rectangular—rectangular beds, tables, desks, and bureaus to fit into rectangular rooms. Streets usually run at right angles to one another; the farmer plows his rectangular field in neat, straight furrows.

However, in other societies other shapes predominate. In the Zulu culture, for example, the circle is much more prevalent than the rectangle. The Zulu people live in windowless round huts with round doors, arranged in circles. They plow their ground in curved furrows that follow the contours of the land. Their language has no words for squares or rectangles. They are thus much less likely to use linear perspective cues accurately, if at all, to judge distance or depth.

(Hubertus Kanus, Rapho/Photo Researchers)

Other perceptual judgments depend on cues that may be more prevalent in one culture than another. The Mbuti pygmies of the Congo, for example, seldom leave the forest and rarely have an opportunity to look at objects that are more than a few feet away. On one occasion, Colin Turnbull (1961), an anthropologist, took a pygmy guide named Kenge on a trip out onto the plains. When Kenge looked across the plain and saw a herd of buffalo, he asked what kind of insects they were. He refused to believe that the tiny black spots he perceived were buffalo. As he and Turnbull drove toward the herd, Kenge believed the animals were growing larger because of some kind of sorcery. Because of his lack of experience in dealing with distant objects, he was unable to perceive the buffalo as having constant size. Kenge's eyes transmitted the same messages as the eyes of the people who had grown up in Western cultures, but the way he interpreted those messages—the way he *perceived* the situation—was radically different.

Altered States of Consciousness

At the beginning of this chapter, we stated that most discussions of perception assume a normal level of awareness and alertness. However, in the last 15 years, scientists and the general public have become increasingly interested in **altered states of consciousness (ASCs).** These states include sensory deprivation, sleeping and dreaming, hypnosis and meditation, and drug-induced experiences. They all affect perception, as well as a broad spectrum of other human functions from respiration to motor coordination to cognition and memory. Although most societies operate on the assumption that the majority of its citizens function in a "normal" state of consciousness, altered states seem to have an appeal for some people in all classes of all societies. For example, little children all over the world have been observed to play at making themselves dizzy by turning rapidly in circles and eventually falling down to watch the world spin. The means used to achieve ASCs may have varying degrees of social acceptability, but the interest itself is commonplace.

An ASC has been broadly defined as any mental state caused by physiological, psychological, or pharmacological intervention, which can be recognized either by the person himself or by an objective observer as a substantial deviation from the individual's behavior when he is in a normally alert, awake state of mind. According to Ludwig (1969), most ASCs demonstrate one or more of the following general characteristics: impaired cognitive functions and reality testing; distorted sense of time; loss of self-control; change in emotional displays; change of body image; perceptual distortions such as hallucinations and increased visual imagery; change in the significance given to experience; sense of having experienced something that cannot be verbalized or communicated; feelings of rebirth; and hypersuggestibility.

(Michael Gamer, Photo Researchers)

Ludwig (1969) also lists three general functions of ASCs that historically have been socially acceptable: healing; gaining new knowledge; and providing an outlet for a group's ritualized conflicts and goals. Weil (1972) adds a controversial fourth function: counteracting the negative and limiting effects of "straight," logical, uninsightful thinking. With this brief general introduction, we now turn to an examination of four major kinds of ASCs.

Sensory Deprivation

We have discussed in detail the processes utilized by the brain to cope with the quantities of sensory information it receives, but what happens when the number of stimuli are drastically and systematically reduced? Does the brain go into a resting state, thankful for the opportunity, or does it actually need stimulation to maintain all its functions?

These questions have been probed during the last two decades in a series of experiments that carefully limited sensory input by a variety of means. The primary study was done at McGill University in the late 1950s. Student volunteers who were paid $20 a day were put in special cubicles and were masked and bandaged, thus severely restricting their

Figure 9-21
A sensory deprivation chamber. The subject lies on a cot with cardboard cuffs over his hands and forearms and translucent goggles over his eyes. The only sound is the monotonous noise of the exhaust fan. A microphone allows experimenters to monitor his speech, and the wires attached to his head record his brain waves. (After W. Heron, "Cognitive and Physiological Effect of Perceptual Isolation." In P. Solomon et al. (Eds.), *Sensory Deprivation.* Cambridge, Mass.: Harvard University Press, 1961, p. 9, Figure 2-1.)

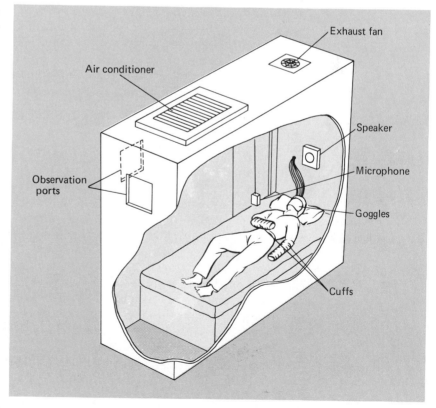

visual, auditory, and tactile stimulation. The subjects were released from the constraining devices for three meals a day and for trips to the toilet. The results were dramatic. The subjects were increasingly unable to do the tasks that they had set for themselves to while away the time (like reviewing their studies or thinking about a paper they had to write); they grew increasingly irritable and eventually began to hallucinate. When released from this sensory deprivation, they performed poorly on a number of tests, compared with a control group (Heron, 1957). From these results, researchers drew the broad conclusion that a monotonous environment is definitely harmful and that one of the general functions of sensory stimuli is to maintain a continual arousal condition in the brain.

Subsequent research (Suedfeld, 1975; Zubek, 1973) has modified these initial findings, particularly the data on hallucinations. While subjects in later experiments often reported *visual sensations* (like dots and geometric forms), real hallucinations involving meaningful objects and integrated narratives have not occurred with the frequency reported in the McGill study (Zubek, 1973). Zubek also found that while visual acuity and perception of brightness remained relatively unimpaired, color perception and reaction time were more vulnerable to the effects of sensory deprivation. However, some faculties, according to Zubek, are actually heightened by systematic deprivation. Auditory vigilance, tactile acuity, pain sensitivity, and taste sensations have all been improved in this kind of experiment. Furthermore, the negative effects of deprivation can sometimes be canceled out by counter-measures including drugs, prior experience in isolation, and pre-isolation training. In sum, sensory deprivation has both adverse and beneficial effects on perception, depending on the experimental model used, the length of deprivation, the subject's expectations, and other factors.

(George Butler, Rapho/Photo Researchers)

Sleeping and Dreaming

We spend about one-third of our lives in an ASC, namely, sleep. Throughout history, varying degrees of respect have been paid to sleep and its product, dreaming. Some societies believe great universal truths are revealed in dreams, while others view sleep as an essential, but basically nonproductive, kind of activity. Only recently have sleep researchers begun to analyze the fascinating complexity of the sleeping and dreaming processes, the functions that they serve, and the impact they have on human perceptual activity.

Scientists do not usually enter people's homes to study how they sleep. Instead, they find volunteers who are willing to spend some nights in a "sleep lab." With electrodes painlessly attached to his skull, the volunteer sleeps comfortably while his brain waves, eye movements, and other physiological data are monitored.

Using information gathered from these "sleep labs," researchers have

Figure 9-22
The brain wave patterns
typical of the five stages of
sleep. Because the brain
waves in REM sleep closely
resemble those of Stage
One—but the person in
REM is very deeply asleep,
hard to wake up, and
extremely relaxed—REM
sleep has been called
"paradoxical sleep." (From
Sleep by Gay Gaer Luce and
Julius Segal. Reprinted by
permission of Coward,
McCann & Geoghegan, Inc.
© 1966 by Gay Gaer Luce
and Julius Segal.)

identified several stages that everyone goes through while sleeping (Kleitman, 1963). "Going to sleep" means losing awareness and failing to respond to a stimulus that would produce a response in the waking state. Often, this involves a floating or falling sensation, followed by a quick jolt back to consciousness, especially if the sleeper is nervous. Once sleep has begun, the sleeper has entered *Stage One,* which is characterized by irregular and low-voltage brain waves, slower pulse rate, muscle relaxation, and side-to-side rolling movement of the eyes. This eye movement is the most reliable indication of the initial sleep process (Dement, 1974). Stage One only lasts a few minutes, and the sleeper is easily awakened at this point. If he is awakened, he may not realize he has been asleep. Stages Two and Three form a continuum of deeper and deeper sleep. In *Stage Two,* brain waves show bursts of activity called "spindles." In *Stage Three,* these disappear and brain waves become long and slow, about one per second. At this stage, it is hard to wake up the sleeper, and he is unresponsive to stimuli. Heart rate, blood pressure, and temperature continue to drop. *Stage Four* is **delta sleep,** the deepest stage, characterized by slow, even brain waves.

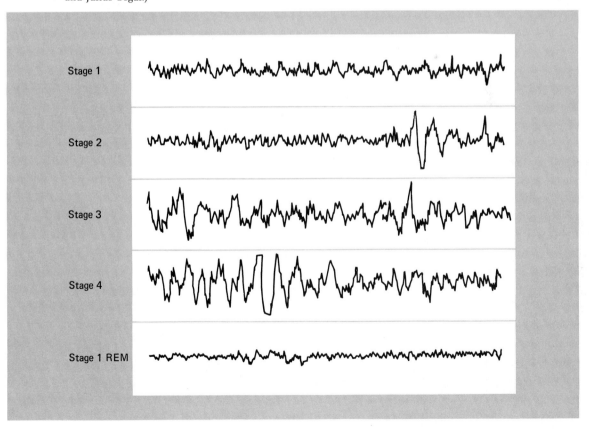

In young adults, delta sleep occurs in 15- or 20-minute segments (interspersed with lighter sleep) mostly during the first half of the night. Delta sleep lessens with age, but continues to be the first sleep to be made up after sleep has been lost.

Thirty or 40 minutes after going to sleep, the sleeper begins to ascend from Stage Four, a process that takes about 40 minutes. At the end of this time, the brain waves exhibit a saw-toothed quality, the eyes move rapidly, and the muscles are more relaxed than they have been at any previous point. This is called **REM** (rapid eye movement) **sleep,** as opposed to the other four, non-REM (**NREM**) stages. The first REM period lasts about 10 minutes and is followed by Stages Two, Three, and Four of NREM sleep. This cycle continues all night long, averaging 90 minutes, but the configuration shifts. At first, NREM Stages Three and Four dominate, but as time passes, the REM periods gradually become longer, up to 60 minutes, with NREM Stage Two the only interruption. Dreams occur in both NREM and REM stages, although they occur much less frequently in NREM sleep and are much less detailed, sequential, and vividly recalled than those reported during REM sleep (Dement, 1974).

Can we say that there appears to be a need for REM sleep? Apparently so. One theory is that the brain cannot stand long periods of relative inactivity, such as occur during NREM sleep, and that, if it were not for REM sleep, our brain's need for activity would cause us to wake up every 90 minutes. Then what happens when researchers systematically interfere with REM sleep? When people have been deprived of REM sleep and then allowed to sleep undisturbed, the amount of REM sleep nearly doubles—this phenomenon is called "REM rebound." During the period of REM-sleep deprivation, people generally become more anxious and irritable and have trouble concentrating. However, Dement notes that "a decade of research has failed to prove that substantial psychological ill effects result even from prolonged selective REM sleep deprivation" (1974, p. 91). Dement finds no evidence that REM-type dreams break through into other stages of sleep or into waking consciousness, except in the case of alcoholics suffering from acute withdrawal and *delirium tremens* (the DTs).

Most dreams last about as long as the events would in real life; they do not flash on your mental screen immediately before waking. Generally, they consist of a sequential story or series of stories. Stimuli, both external and internal, may modify an ongoing dream, but they do not initiate dreams. One interesting experiment used three different external stimuli on REM-sleeping subjects—a 5-second tone just below waking threshold, a flashing lamp, and a light spray of cold water. The water was incorporated in 42 percent of the dreams, the light into 23 percent, and the tone into 9 percent (Dement & Wolpert, 1958). Another experiment by Dement and Wolpert (1958) showed that when a tape recording of the subject's voice was played back to him during REM sleep, the principal actor in the dream became more active and self-assertive. Thus, while these external stimuli are perceived during REM sleep, their origin is often not perceived as being external. They are interpreted as being part of the dream.

Are the dreams in a single night interrelated? Unfortunately, experimenters run into a methodological problem when they try to explore this question, because each time the subject is awakened to be asked about his dream, the natural course of the dream is interrupted and usually lost forever. However, if one particular problem or event is weighing heavily on the dreamer's mind, it will often manifest itself in a variety of dreams throughout the night (Dement, 1974).

More than one desperate student has gone to sleep with a tape recorder conjugating foreign verbs in his ear, with the hope of somehow painlessly absorbing such boring material. Although such external stimuli are incorporated, the incorporation is unpredictable and incomplete. Similarly, attempts to influence dream content through pre-sleep suggestions have had mixed results. Success seems to turn on subtleties like the phrasing of the suggestion, the tone in which it is given, the relationship between the suggester and the subject, and the setting (Walker & Johnson, 1974). But, if these variables can be refined and controlled, the pre-sleep suggestion technique could have important ramifications for both sleep researchers and psychotherapists.

Hypnosis and Meditation

Hypnosis and meditation are two of the more controversial ASCs, and, indeed, psychologists cannot even agree on whether they are in fact ASCs or whether they are something else.

Hypnosis first came to general attention in mid-eighteenth-century Europe, when Anton Mesmer, a Viennese physician, fascinated continental audiences by putting patients into trances and curing a variety of ills. Although some scientists tried to study and apply Mesmer's techniques to a variety of medical problems, for years hypnosis remained largely a sideshow amusement. However, when Freud successfully used hypnosis to cure symptoms of hysteria, scientific interest in the subject revived in earnest.

In the trance state, people may appear to be blind, deaf, or immune to pain. They may be able to perform seemingly impossible feats. Told to relive their childhood, for example, persons under hypnosis can talk baby talk or recite forgotten childhood memories. When awakened, they may be unable to recall anything that happened during the sessions. The trance state thus seems unique and capable of giving extraordinary powers to ordinary people.

The dispute over the nature of hypnosis is confusing and unresolved,

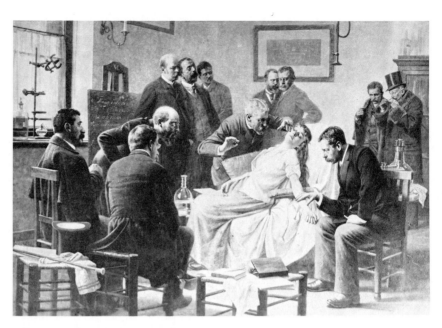

(The Bettmann Archive)

in part, because of two major research problems. First, unlike REM and NREM sleep, there is no physiological condition that can clearly be characterized as unique to a hypnotic state (Hilgard, 1974). In addition to raising the question of whether hypnosis is an ASC at all, it makes it difficult to know when the hypnotic trance state has occurred, and thus makes it difficult to study. Second, researchers must rely, at least in part, on the reports of people who have experienced hypnosis, and their subjective reactions can differ according to their hypnotists and the way in which they are asked about their experience (Dalal & Barber, 1970). Nevertheless, some objective measures of perception and performance under hypnosis have been devised. While this research has not resolved the theoretical debate over hypnosis, it has shown that, for whatever reason, some people's perceptions can be dramatically altered by systematic forms of suggestion.

Some people are more susceptible to hypnosis than others. One leading researcher (Hilgard, 1975) finds the best subjects to be those with vivid imaginations, often people who had imaginary childhood playmates or who used their imagination as an escape from unpleasant realities. Hilgard hypothesizes that an active imagination may enable the subject to so thoroughly create another world that objectively observable stimuli from the external environment are shut out.

Differences among people in hypnotic susceptibility were demonstrated in a recent experiment by Hilgard (1974). First, the subject in a waking state immersed his hand and forearm in ice cold water and rated the intensity of pain he felt. Next he received hypnotic suggestions

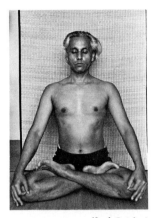

(Joel Gordon)

(René Burri, Magnum Photos)

that the hand and arm were insensitive. He then immersed them again and rated the pain a second time. Hilgard found that 67 percent of the "highly hypnotizable" subjects showed a 33 percent reduction in pain, while only 13 percent of the least hypnotizable subjects obtained such dramatic results.

Unlike hypnosis, **meditation** produces an identifiable cluster of physiological changes. A lower rate of metabolism is evidenced by reduced consumption of oxygen and elimination of carbon dioxide. Alpha and beta brain waves noticeably increase during meditation, and there is a decrease in blood lactate, a chemical that may be linked to stress. Wallace and Benson (1972) have reported a sharp rise in skin resistance and interpret this as a sign of increased ability to cope with or shut out stressful occurrences, but other research (Schwartz, 1974) does not support this finding.

There are many forms of meditation—Zen, Yoga, Sufi, Christian, and the currently popular transcendental meditation (TM)—and each focuses the meditator's attention in a slightly different way. Zen and yoga concentrate a great deal on respiration. The Sufi discipline, on the other hand, involves both frenzied dancing and another technique that is similar to the use of a mantra in TM (Schwartz, 1974). A *mantra* is an Indian sound specially picked for a student by his teacher. Concentrating on the mantra, according to proponents of TM, keeps all other images and problems at bay and allows the meditator to achieve progressively deeper relaxation (Deikman, 1973b; Schwartz, 1974).

Meditation quite often results in a sense of unity between the individual and his surroundings. The meditator may experience increased sensory awareness, euphoria, strong emotions, and a sense of timelessness and expanded awareness (Deikman, 1973b). Some studies have indicated that a high percentage of meditators abandon the use of drugs, and that the longer a person meditates, the more likely it is that he will completely abstain from drugs (Schwartz, 1974).

Drug-Induced Experiences

The use of drugs to alter consciousness for social, religious, medical, and personal reasons has a long history. Wine is mentioned often in the Old Testament, and marijuana first appeared in the herbal compendium of a Chinese emperor in 2737 B.C. Today, with widespread education about psychology and a great deal of interest in (and misinformation about) drugs, many people take drugs in a conscious effort to alter their cognitive and perceptual styles, to get away from "straight" modes of thinking (Weil, 1972). Some of these drugs have variable effects that may depend on **set** (the expectations that a person brings to the drug experience and his emotional state at the time) and **setting** (the physical, social, and emotional atmosphere in which the drug is taken). Other drugs affect everybody in rather similar ways.

(*Leonard Freed, Magnum Photos*)

(*Joel Gordon*)

Alcohol. Are you surprised that alcohol is in this section? In our society, we recognize many appropriate occasions for the use of alcohol: to celebrate important life events, to reduce tension, to break down social distance and promote group harmony (National Commission on Marihuana and Drug Abuse, 1973b). According to a government survey, 39 percent of American adults and 34 percent of American youth do not regard alcohol as a drug, and only 7 percent of the public see alcoholism as a serious social problem (compared to 53 percent who hold this attitude toward all other drugs). Yet alcoholism is the most serious drug problem in the United States today. Users of alcohol outnumber users of all other drugs, largely because alcohol is readily available, aggressively marketed, and highly "reinforcing"; that is, it tends to encourage repeated use and can result in both physical and psychological dependence. One out of every ten Americans uses it compulsively, and half of them are seriously dependent on it (NCMDA, 1973a). Furthermore, there are many signs of a sharp upsurge in alcoholism among adolescents.

Alcohol is a depressant and can result in a lessening of the person's normal inhibitions. Because people may feel freer to display certain behaviors when drinking, they may think that the drug is a stimulant. It's not, but the excitement of feeling "free" certainly can be. During the period of euphoria, the person's diminished self-control can result in social embarrassment, injury, or automobile accidents. Prolonged and excessive use of alcohol can result in damage to the brain, liver, and other internal organs and can change the general character and personality of the alcoholic.

Alcohol has mixed effects on visual perception. It heightens perception of dim lights, but it impairs perception of the differences between brighter lights, colors, and depth. The same is true of auditory perception. Some aspects of hearing, like perception of loudness, are not affected, while the ability to discriminate between different rhythms and pitches is impaired by a single dose of the drug. Smell and taste perception are uniformly diminished. Perception of time is also distorted; most people report that time seems to pass faster when they are "under the influence" (NCMDA, 1973b).

Marijuana. Although use of marijuana in the United States has risen markedly in the last 15 years, there is no indication of significant compulsive use (NCMDA, 1973a), and there is an impressive amount of research showing that moderate use produces no mental or physical deterioration (Grinspoon, 1969).

Marijuana is far less potent than the hallucinogens—LSD, peyote, mescaline, and psilocybin—and affects consciousness far less profoundly. A user who becomes "high" for the first time is likely to experience initial anxiety, which is usually followed by euphoria, a heightened sense of humor, a feeling of being bodiless, a rapid flow

(Geoffrey Gove, Rapho/Photo Researchers)

(Joel Gordon)

(Richard Klein, Nancy Palmer Photo Agency)

of ideas but confusion in relating them (due to impairment of short-term memory), heightened sensory sensitivity, visual imagery, and distortion of the sense of time. Synesthesia frequently occurs; stimuli normally perceived in one mode are transformed into another. A person may say he "sees" music or "feels" light. Cognitive tests administered to subjects after use of marijuana show mixed results; some functions are unaffected, some are mildly impaired, and others may be slightly heightened (Grinspoon, 1969).

Amphetamines and barbiturates. Amphetamines (or "uppers") produce feelings of optimism and boundless energy. They are thus a highly reinforcing kind of drug. However, compulsive use can eventually lead to psychosis.

Amphetamines have a stimulating effect, while barbiturates, or "downers," are depressants. Barbiturates are pharmacologically similar to alcohol and have the same potential for creating physical and psychological dependence (NCMDA, 1973a). They have the effect of relaxing all muscles (including the heart) and are therefore used to alleviate anxiety. An overdose can relax muscle function so completely that death results.

Both amphetamines and barbiturates affect perception, primarily the perception of time. In addition, people's self-perceptions can be affected—a user of amphetamines may rate his abilities higher than they really are. Both drugs also affect memory—barbiturates can cause amnesia, but they can also enhance long-term memory ("truth serums" are barbiturates) (NCMDA, 1973a). Amphetamines can make it hard to concentrate and thus disrupt both attention and perception.

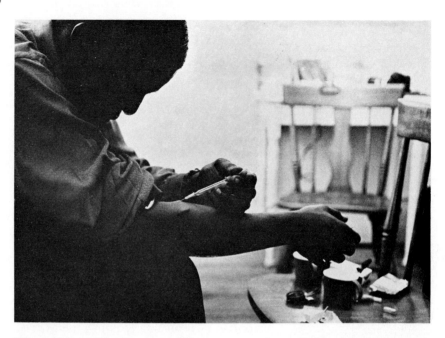

(Bob Combs, Rapho/Photo Researchers)

The opiates. The most well-known member of the opiate family is **heroin.** Heroin use has tremendous social implications because the people most likely to become addicted are young men in cities who are at the age when they might otherwise be seeking an economic and social niche in the larger society (NCDMA, 1973a). And because it is illegal and expensive, heroin, more than any other drug, generally results in undesirable changes in personality and life style, most noticeably criminal behavior. Most people who use heroin inject it intravenously, which leads relatively quickly to physical dependence and addiction. Overdoses can kill.

Heroin generally results in euphoria and relaxation. However, because of the rapid development of tolerance, the addict must take increasingly larger doses to achieve these euphoric effects; smaller doses simply avoid the pains of withdrawal. Because of the high cost, an addict must spend so much time and energy getting the drug that when he does get it, the primary feeling is generally relief, rather than euphoria. At this stage, it is no longer a means to alter consciousness; it is medicine, a pain-killer.

Cocaine. Cocaine is a stimulant and is the most reinforcing of all drugs. It has the greatest potential for psychological dependence. Because it appeals generally to the same personality type that is attracted to heroin, its use also has potentially negative social implications (NCMDA, 1973a). Cocaine's appeal is heightened because it is not physiologically addicting and because it has a mystique—it is the drug of the elite.

Cocaine's immediate effects are similar to those of the amphetamines: increased alertness, impulsivity, and suppression of hunger and fatigue. In addition, cocaine results in a heightened sensitivity to sensory experience—colors are brighter, music more beautiful, touch more exciting. A person's self-perception may also be altered—he may feel stronger and braver than usual. But, like the amphetamines, abuse of cocaine can result in psychosis, particularly paranoia.

Hallucinogens. The hallucinogens include LSD ("acid"), mescaline, peyote, psilocybin, and other drugs. These drugs have a rather low dependency rate (NCMDA, 1973a) and contrary to some popular thinking only rarely induce psychosis, particularly in people with no previous history of instability (Barron, Jarvik, & Bunnell, 1964). Their effects last considerably longer than those of most drugs—12 hours or longer is common. This length of time can cause unstable people to panic unless reassured and reminded that the effects are indeed temporary. Pahnke and Richards (1969) feel that the sense that the experience is only temporary is one of the important distinctions between the psychedelic experience and psychosis.

Even more than most drugs, the effect a hallucinogen will have is determined by the properties of the drug itself, the individual's set, and the setting in which the drug is taken. An additional problem in doing research on the effects of hallucinogens is that subjects under the influence of these drugs often find a researcher's questions hilarious or irrelevant and either refuse or are unable to give a response (NCMDA, 1973a).

Hallucinogens have profound effects on visual and auditory perception. At a minimal level, colors seem more vivid and surface details stand out more. With a higher dosage of the drug or greater individual sensitivity to it, the person may see kaleidoscopic patterns and images or fully integrated and often bizarre scenes (Barron, Jarvik, & Bunnell, 1964). Spatial distortion and changed body image also are common. Sometimes these visual effects are described as breathtakingly beautiful, but others may be extremely unpleasant and upsetting.

Auditory perception also undergoes a fascinating variety of alterations. Some people report hearing imaginary conversations, or fully orchestrated and original symphonies, or foreign languages previously unknown to them. Aural acuity may be increased, making the person keenly aware of low sounds like breathing, heartbeats, or the light rustle of leaves in the wind (Barron, Jarvik, & Bunnell, 1964).

Some students of hallucinogens view all the above as the shallower aspects of the drug experience, compared with the mystical and transcendental qualities that are often noted. For example, Pahnke and Richards (1969) say that the synesthetic experience of music as a series of visual images is insignificant compared with the consciousness attained when one goes *through* the pattern toward a mystical sense of harmony, unity, and serenity. Deikman (1973b) cites the LSD experience as another means of achieving "deautomatization," the abolition of the psychological structures that normally limit, select, and interpret sensory stimuli.

It should be noted in conclusion that scientists are still debating whether or not any or all of the hallucinogens have harmful physiological effects.

Summary

1. Messages from the sense organs arrive at the brain in a complicated order and usually from several senses at the same time. The process of making a meaningful pattern out of the jumbled sensory impressions is called *perception.*
2. The perceptual process begins with narrowing the field, selecting which messages will receive *attention* at any given moment.
3. When one object or event is selected from all the things going on around us, the attention is said to be *focused.* Usually objects or events that possess unusual characteristics or that provide strong stimulation to the sense organs attract our attention, but the focus of attention is also affected by our interests, motivation, and past experiences.
4. Even when attention is focused on something specific, a person is usually aware of other things going on around him. *Marginal attention* to events and objects outside the focus of attention is at a low level of awareness.
5. The reticular activating system in the brain acts as a filter for incoming messages and alerts the higher brain centers when important messages are received. This filtering process is known as *sensory gating.* Input from one set of sense organs is allowed to pass, while other information is temporarily held back. When competing stimuli are presented to the same sensory system, response time is significantly lengthened.
6. The *information-processing* model of perception is based on computer technology. According to this model sensory stimulation is "input," responses are "output," and what goes on in between is called "processing." During processing, sensory data are coded into *chunks* so they can be handled more easily by short-term memory.
7. Information from the sense organs is organized according to certain basic principles. *Figure-ground* refers to the distinction between a figure and the ground against which it appears. *Closure* refers to the tendency to fill in the gaps and perceive a figure as a finished unit. The principle of *continuity* applies to the tendency to group together items that follow a pattern or direction set by preceding items. The tendency to perceive objects that are close to each other as a group rather than separately is known as *proximity.* *Similarity* is the tendency to group together items that resemble each other. The principle of *common fate* describes the tendency to group together several objects that are moving in the same direction.
8. The eye records information in only two dimensions—height and width—but we can also perceive *distance* or *depth* through *monocular cues*—from one eye, or *binocular cues*—depending on the interaction of both eyes.

9. Monocular cues include *superposition, aerial* and *linear perspective, elevation, texture gradient, shadowing, movement of the observer,* and *accommodation.*

10. Binocular cues increase the accuracy of depth and distance perception. Two eyes provide a much wider visual area and also have a slightly different view of things. The difference between the images the two eyes receive is known as *retinal disparity.* Other binocular cues to distance include *stereoscopic vision* and *convergence.*

11. Perception of *movement* is a complicated process involving both the visual messages from the retina and the kinesthetic messages from the muscles around the eye as they shift to follow a moving object.

12. The perception of *real movement*—the actual displacement of an object from one position to another—seems to be determined principally by changes in the position of objects in relation to a background that is perceived as stationary.

13. *Illusory movement* involves the perception of motion, under certain conditions, in objects that are actually standing still. The *autokinetic illusion* refers to the apparent motion created by a single stationary object. *Stroboscopic motion* is the apparent motion created by a rapid series of images of stationary objects. Stroboscopic motion is also responsible for a perceptual illusion known as the *phi phenomenon.*

14. *Perceptual constancy* refers to the tendency to perceive objects as relatively stable and unchanging, despite changing sensory images. Past experience seems to compensate for the changing sensory images, leading to *object constancy, size constancy, shape constancy,* and *brightness* and *color constancy,* despite changing sensory information.

15. Several other factors can also affect perception. Perception is selective. How an object is interpreted and certain features selected depend on a person's *motivation, expectations, cognitive style,* and *cultural background.*

16. *Altered states of consciousness* include sensory deprivation, sleep, dreaming, hypnosis, meditation, and drug-induced experiences. Altered states in general are characterized by impaired thinking, particularly reality testing; distorted sense of time; loss of self-control; change in emotional behavior; change of body image; perceptual distortions; change in the significance attributed to experiences; sense of having experienced something that cannot be verbalized or communicated; feelings of rebirth; and hypersuggestibility. The desire to alter one's state of consciousness is nearly universal, but the means chosen are not always socially acceptable.

17. *Sensory deprivation* has been found to result in disruption of thought processes, irritability, and hallucinations. Recent research has indicated that hearing, touch, sensitivity to pain, and taste become more acute.

18. There are four stages of *sleep.* Stage One occurs only in the initial minutes of sleep and is a borderline between true sleep and waking. True sleep begins with Stage Two and Stage Three, which are characterized by a progressive slowing and lengthening of the brain waves and by decreases in heart rate, blood pressure, and body temperature. Stage Four, *delta sleep,* is the deepest stage. Delta sleep is especially critical for younger people, and the quantity of it per night decreases with age. As the person passes from Stage Two through Stage Four, he becomes increasingly unresponsive to the environment and it is harder to wake him up. After Stage Four, *REM*

(rapid eye movement) *sleep* begins. The other stages of sleep are referred to as *NREM* (non-rapid eye movement) *sleep*. After a period of REM sleep, the sleep cycle begins again with Stages Two, Three, and Four, with the REM periods getting longer throughout the night. NREM sleep seems mainly related to the restoration of physiological functions, while REM sleep appears to aid in the restoration of psychological functions.

19. *Dreams* can occur in both NREM and REM sleep, but are more frequent and detailed in REM sleep. Dreams generally last about as long as the events would in real life and usually consist of a sequential story or series of stories. People can perceive external stimuli while dreaming, but they are usually incorporated into the dream and not recognized as being external. Research on the effectiveness of pre-sleep suggestions has been inconclusive.

20. Psychologists disagree about whether the trance induced by *hypnosis* is a true altered state of consciousness. One reason for this is that there are no consistent physiological signs that accompany hypnosis. In any case, the trance state seems unique and capable of giving extraordinary powers to ordinary people. Hypnosis has been shown to affect people's perception of pain, visual clarity, depth, and time.

21. Unlike hypnosis, *meditation* entails an identifiable cluster of physiological changes: lower metabolism rate; increase in alpha and beta waves; and a decrease in blood chemicals associated with stress. The many different forms of meditation all involve rigidly focused attention. Zen and yoga focus the meditator's attention on breathing; transcendental meditation uses an Indian sound called a *mantra*. The goal of meditation is to achieve deep relaxation without drugs, which these disciplines feel is an essential prerequisite to transcendental experience.

22. The use of *drugs* to alter consciousness has a long history. The effect any drug has on consciousness depends on *set* (the person's state of mind at the time he takes the drug) and *setting* (the physical, social, and emotional atmosphere in which the drug is taken).

23. The most commonly used drug is *alcohol*. Alcohol is a depressant and can result in a lessening of the person's normal inhibitions, which has a temporary stimulating effect. Prolonged use results in extensive damage to the brain and the liver, and changes the personality. Alcohol impairs perception of brightness, color, depth, smell, taste, and time.

24. *Marijuana,* if used moderately, does not appear to cause mental and physical deterioration or result in compulsive use. Its effects on perception are much less striking than those caused by the hallucinogens, but are similar in kind, if not degree. These are: euphoria, heightened sense of humor, a feeling of bodilessness, rapid flow of ideas, impairment of short-term memory, heightened sensory sensitivity, visual imagery, distortion of sense of time, and synesthesia. Some cognitive processes are impaired; others are enhanced.

25. *Amphetamines* produce feelings of optimism and boundless energy. Amphetamine use can become compulsive and may eventually lead to psychosis. *Barbiturates* are depressants and have the same potential for creating physical and psychological dependence that alcohol does. Both drugs affect the perception of time, self-perception, and memory.

26. *Heroin* use results in physical and psychological dependence. Its users

become tolerant of the drug and need ever-larger doses. Heroin's effects are pleasant: euphoria and extreme relaxation. But because the addict develops tolerance, he needs larger and larger doses to achieve these effects. Getting the drug becomes a necessity simply for relief from pain.

27. *Cocaine* is a stimulant and has the greatest potential for psychological dependence of all drugs. It is not physiologically addictive. Its effects are similar to those of the amphetamines: increased alertness, impulsivity, and suppression of hunger and fatigue. Cocaine also results in heightened sensory awareness and changes in self-perception. As with the amphetamines, use of cocaine can result in psychosis.

28. The *hallucinogens* include LSD, mescaline, peyote, and psilocybin. They do not result in physiological dependence and do not generally cause psychological breakdowns in stable people. Unstable people, however, can be severely upset by the great changes caused by these drugs unless they are reminded that the effects are only temporary. The influence of set and setting are more important with the hallucinogens than with other, less volatile drugs. Hallucinogens have profound effects on visual and auditory perceptions: colors are brighter, spatial distortions and changes in body image are also common, and aural acuity is increased. But the most striking effects of these drugs are mystical and transcendental.

Suggested Readings

Bartley, S. H., *Principles of Perception,* 2nd ed. (New York: Harper & Row, 1969). A complete analysis of human perception, covering all the senses.

Dement, W. C., *Some Must Watch while Some Must Sleep* (San Francisco: Freeman, 1974). A concise, well-written summary of sleep research and sleep disorders by a pioneer in the field.

Gibson, J. J., *The Senses Considered as Perceptual Systems* (Boston: Houghton Mifflin, 1966). A new approach that separates perception from the sensory processes.

Gombrich, E. H., *Art and Illusion: A Study in the Psychology of Pictorial Representation* (New York: Pantheon, 1960). An art historian examines the relations between the artist, his subject, his painting, and the viewer.

Gregory, R. L., *The Intelligent Eye* (New York: McGraw-Hill, 1970). An entertaining and well-illustrated analysis of the effects of learning on visual perception, especially perceptual illusions.

Kaufman, L., *Sight and Mind: An Introduction to Visual Perception* (New York: Oxford University Press, 1974). A comprehensive, up-to-date text that discusses visual perception at a more advanced level.

Moray, N. *Listening and Attention* (Baltimore: Penguin, 1969). A concise but thorough account of attention, including selective attention.

Ornstein, R. E., *The Psychology of Consciousness* (San Francisco: Freeman, 1972). A lucid, brief overview of human consciousness that gives attention to expanded consciousness and altered states.

Weintraub, D., and Walker, E. L., *Perception* (Belmont, Calif.: Brooks/Cole, 1966). A brief overview of the phenomena of visual perception.

FOUR

Psychology of Motivation and Emotion

outline

PHYSIOLOGICAL MOTIVES 359

Hunger
Thirst
Sleep and Dreaming
Pain
Sex
The Maternal Drive

STIMULUS MOTIVES 367

Activity
Exploration and Curiosity
Manipulation
Contact

LEARNED MOTIVES 372

Fear
Aggression
Social Motives
Consistency

UNCONSCIOUS MOTIVES 381

A HIERARCHY OF MOTIVES 382

SUMMARY 384

SUGGESTED READINGS 387

10

Motivation

To watch motivation manipulated at a very sophisticated level, we might turn to a detective story. All we know at the beginning is that an act has been committed: after eating dinner with her family, sweet little old Miss Jones collapsed and died of strychnine poisoning. "Now, why would anyone do a thing like that?" everybody asks. The police are asking the same question, in different terms: "Who had a *motive* for doing Miss Jones in?" In a really good murder mystery, the answer is, "Practically everybody."

The younger sister (now 75 years old) still bristles when she thinks of the tragic day 50 years ago when Miss Jones stole her sweetheart. The next-door neighbor, a frequent dinner guest, has been heard to say that if Miss Jones's poodle tramples his peonies one more time, he'll . . . . The nephew, a major heir, is deeply in debt. The parlormaid has a Guilty Secret that Miss Jones knew. All four people were in the house on the night that Miss Jones was poisoned. And all four had easy access to strychnine, which was used to kill rats in Miss Jones's basement.

These are the first things that come to mind when we think of motivation in a murder mystery. But look at some of the ordinary things

357

Figure 10-1
The stages of motivation.
First a stimulus (a bodily
need, a cue in the
environment) triggers a
motive. The motive leads to
behavior. When the
behavior results in goal
attainment, the organism
achieves a state of rest, or
freedom from tension, until
the next stimulus.

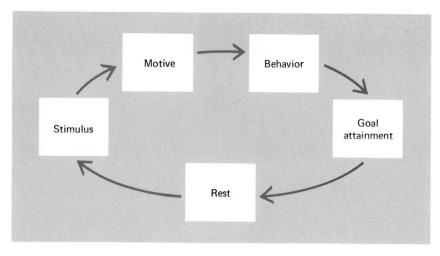

that are happening in the same story. Motivated by hunger, the family gets together for meals. The next-door neighbor is lonely and visits because he wants company. The parlormaid's Guilty Secret involves her sex drive. The poodle's presence in the peonies may spring from the physiological need to eliminate wastes or from sheer curiosity. When Miss Jones dies, the tragedy draws the family together; their need for affiliation makes them seek each other out. Yet, quickly, they become fearful; the drive for self-preservation makes each wonder if the other is actually the murderer. In all these less spectacular forms of behavior, motivation is also present. In this chapter we discuss all these motives, from the most basic to the most complex.

Why do certain motives lead to certain acts? The network of motives that governs our behavior is not a simple one. A motive may be as basic as hunger or as complex as the set of factors that leads to the choice of one career over another. Motives may be internally or externally triggered. One motive may reinforce another, or be in conflict with it. Motivated by the same thing—ambition, say—one person may go to law school and another might apprentice himself to the local crime ring. On the other hand, the same behavior may spring from different motives—you may buy liver because you like it, because it is cheap, or because your body "knows" that you need iron.

We might best think of motivation as a series of stages that we are continually going through. Each series begins with a *stimulus* (perhaps a bodily need or a cue in the environment). The stimulus triggers a *motive*—a sort of arousal to action of one kind or another. The motive, in turn, activates *behavior*. When this behavior leads to *goal attainment,* the motive is satisfied and the chain of motivation is complete. It should be noted, however, that this process takes place whether we are aware of it or not. We do not have to know we are feeling hungry to go to the refrigerator, or be conscious of a need for achievement to study for an exam.

Physiological Motives

For sheer survival, the body must have a certain amount of food, water, and sleep. Other basic physiological motives include the need to maintain proper body temperature, to eliminate wastes, and to avoid pain. We call these physiological motives **primary drives.** A primary drive is unlearned and common to every animal, including man. It expresses the need to sustain life. A certain physiological state—brought on by lack of food or sleep, cold, the presence of pain—activates these primary drives. How we behave once they have been triggered may be simply a reflex, like shivering when we are cold, or it may be the result of learning. A baby does not have to be taught to be hungry or sleepy, but he can learn to eat certain foods and to sleep at certain times. All such behavior is aimed at reducing the state of arousal, but the patterns of that behavior may vary according to learning and experience.

(Culver Pictures)

Hunger

When you are hungry, you eat. If you cannot do so, your need for food will increase the longer you are deprived of it. You may skip lunch if you are busy with something else, but it is likely that by dinnertime no concern will seem as overriding as getting something into your stomach. When we talk of a need for food, we do not mean feeling hungry. The obvious signs of **hunger**—a growling stomach or hunger pangs—may make you remember you forgot lunch, but they are not the same as the need for food. For example, if the body is deprived of food, it continually needs food, but the hunger pangs that we feel are only intermittent.

Physiological mechanisms of hunger. Laboratory experiments demonstrate that the hunger drive is set in motion by a chemical imbalance in the blood. A simple sugar called *glucose,* which forms the basis of carbohydrates, can be stored in the liver only in small quantities and for a short time. When the amount of glucose in the blood (the blood-sugar level) falls below a certain point, an area in the hypothalamus is activated, signaling you to eat and replenish your glucose supply. After eating, when the blood-sugar level has risen, the hypothalamus seems to turn off the hunger drive. When the blood of an animal that has eaten is transferred to an animal that has been deprived of food, the animal will refuse to eat, even though it still needs food (Davis, Gallagher, & Ladove, 1967). Similarly, when a hungry human is injected with glucagon, a hormone that raises the blood-sugar level, he ceases to eat, even though he still needs food (Schulman et al., 1957).

This hunger mechanism regulates our day-to-day intake of food. But there appears also to be a second hunger regulator, one that operates on a long-term basis to regulate the body's weight. With the exception of humans and some of the animals we have domesticated, very few

Figure 10-2
A very fat rat, weighing five times its normal weight. This rat's obesity is the result of damage to the part of its hypothalamus called the ventromedial nucleus.
(Courtesy Neal E. Miller)

animals ever become grossly overweight. The body seems to have a way of monitoring its own fat stores and regulating the intake of food to provide just enough energy to maintain normal activities without storing up excessive fat deposits (Kennedy, 1953).

The primary parts of the brain that monitor the level of blood sugar and the amount of body fat are located in two areas of the hypothalamus—the *lateral hypothalamus* and the *ventromedial nucleus*. These two areas seem to balance each other and to work together to control the intake of food. Experiments with animals suggest that the lateral hypothalamus sends out "eat" messages, and the ventromedial nucleus counteracts or inhibits those messages. For example, if the lateral hypothalamus is stimulated electrically, a satiated animal may continue to eat and gain weight. If that area is damaged or removed, however, the animal may stop eating or reduce its intake of food to maintain a lower body weight. On the other hand, when the ventromedial nucleus is electrically stimulated, the animal may stop eating. And, if that area is damaged or removed, the animal may overeat and gain weight. The gains or losses in weight seem to be due to changes in metabolism as well as to increased eating. However, they do not continue indefinitely. After a few weeks, the animal's weight will level off and be maintained at a new level. It is as though the regulating mechanisms had been turned up or down like a thermostat. Interestingly, if the animal is already obese before the ventromedial nucleus is damaged, it may not overeat or gain weight (Hoebel & Teitelbaum, 1962).

Recent research has indicated that the hypothalamus is probably not the only area that controls food intake (Balagura, 1973). Although the roles of other brain structures involved—such as the limbic system and the temporal lobe—have not been precisely defined, it is now clear that all the questions about hunger cannot be answered by studying only the hypothalamus.

Specific hungers. If you have ever let yourself get so hungry that you begin to feel faint, you have probably grabbed at a chocolate bar. You may not "know" that sweets are the fastest way to raise your blood-sugar level—or even that you have a blood-sugar level that needs raising—but, in fact, candy is one of the most efficient foods for restoring glucose to your blood as quickly as possible. Similarly, cattle and deer will travel long distances to find salt licks. **Specific hungers** like these seem to indicate that, to some extent, the body itself knows what foods it needs to maintain itself. In one study (Davis, 1939), infants were given free choice from among nutritional foods. By and large, they selected their diet as if they had studied the seven basic food groups at school. They may not have "balanced" every meal, but over the long run they ate the combination of foods that their bodies needed. In another experiment (Richter, Holt, & Barelare, 1938), rats fed a diet deficient in vitamin B were given a choice of bottles, one of which was

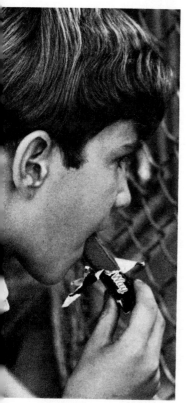

(Bob S. Smith, Rapho/Photo Researchers)

a very strong vitamin B solution. They showed an unerring preference for this bottle.

To some extent, then, the survival and evolution of each species must be dependent on the selection of the right foods, and there seems to be some way every individual of that species "knows" what those foods are. But it would not be a good idea to get overconfident of this theory and conclude that your body needs a hot fudge sundae every afternoon. The "sweet tooth" seems more likely to be a learned preference, not a physiological drive. Culture can also influence the way in which specific hungers are satisfied. For example, Americans love milk, but the Chinese have a great aversion to it (Balagura, 1973). Pregnant women's cravings may or may not be for their, or their babies', good. And the desire to eat things that are specifically harmful to the organism has caused much concern in urban areas especially, as more and more babies have been found to have lead poisoning from eating paint that was peeling off the walls.

Learning and hunger. The hunger drive and the need for food are, as we have said, unlearned. But they can be modified by learning. If you are used to eating three meals a day at more or less regular intervals, your body will accommodate itself to this pattern and develop a rhythm of expectation. Say your usual dinner time is six o'clock, but you have to catch a train then. You will have to choose between eating at 5:00, when you have no real desire for food yet, or waiting till you reach your destination at 7:30, by which time you will be ravenous. Nor is hunger solely dependent on physiological need. In some cases, external cues can trigger the hunger drive. One explanation of why people become overweight suggests that the fat person is more easily aroused by the sight or smell of food than the person whose weight is normal (Schachter, Goldman, & Gordon, 1968).

To a large extent, what we choose to eat is governed by learning and habit—a cola drink may provide the sweetness of orange juice and the stimulation of coffee, but it is unlikely that you would have it with bacon and eggs for breakfast. Emotional factors can also affect hunger—you may sit down to the table starving, but have an argument that "turns off" your desire to eat. Social factors can make a meal a ceremony, and elaborate rituals have grown up around offering and accepting food. But all these kinds of behavior are responses to a need we are born with and to a basic drive to satisfy that need.

Thirst

The physiology of **thirst** is very similar to that of hunger. When you are hungry, your stomach growls. Similarly, when you are thirsty, your mouth is dry and your throat is scratchy. However, as we have seen with hunger, the thirst drive goes much deeper than that. It is controlled by delicate biochemical balances within the body, and has been linked to the level of salt (sodium chloride) in the bloodstream. Salt causes water to leave the body's cells, and a high level of salt in the blood would therefore cause the cells to become dehydrated. When the level of sodium chloride in the blood reaches a certain point, indicating that the tissues need more water, a *thirst center* in the hypothalamus is stimulated, thus activating the thirst drive. After a drink has been found, the chemical balance returns to normal, and a *thirst satiety center,* also in the hypothalamus, is activated.

Scientists have recently discovered that, as with hunger, there seems to be a second thirst regulator. Although this mechanism is not yet fully understood, a reduction of the amount of fluid *outside* the body's cells

(*Margot Granitsas, Photo Researchers*)

THE FAT OF THE LAND

There are two fundamental theories as to why people become fat. One view, proposed by Stanley Schachter and his colleagues (1971*a*, 1971*b*), stresses the importance of food as a powerful stimulus affecting obesity. In Schachter's opinion, fat people are particularly sensitive to environmental food cues, perhaps because their hypothalamus is not working properly. An alternate explanation, offered by Donald Thomas and Jean Mayer (1973), presents obesity as an internally controlled, physiological phenomenon. Thomas and Mayer see the obese person as being unable to rely on normal internal signals of hunger and satiety.

Schachter's theory is supported by a number of important studies. In one such effort, subjects were given either a vanilla milkshake or a milkshake that had quinine in it. Obese subjects drank more of the vanilla milkshakes than did normal-weight subjects, but they drank less than normal subjects when the milkshakes were filled with quinine. This supported Schachter's view that obese people are more sensitive to external stimuli (such as the taste of food). In another study, subjects were offered almonds in bags. Some of the almonds had shells, while others did not. Normal subjects ate nuts more or less equally from both batches. But while 19 of the 20 obese subjects ate almonds without shells, only 1 ate the almonds that had shells. This suggests that obese people do not like to work very hard for food and will only eat when food is easily available.

Thomas and Mayer feel that Schachter has isolated an important characteristic, not a cause, of obesity. They see surplus energy—mainly due to inactivity—as an important cause of weight problems. One of their studies found that overweight girls ate several hundred calories *less* per day than girls of normal weight. The cause of their obesity seemed to be a lack of exercise; the overweight girls engaged in only one-third as much physical activity as the normal-weight girls. Thomas and Mayer (1973) feel that opportunities to be inactive are built into our automobile- and convenience-oriented culture. Their advice? "Walk, don't ride. Take the stairs, not the elevator" (p. 79).

appears to be involved. When the level of extracellular fluid drops, less blood flows to the kidneys. These react by emitting a substance—probably a protein called *renin*—which in turn releases another chemical, *angiotensin*, into the bloodstream. The bloodstream carries angiotensin to certain areas of the brain, which then activate the thirst drive (Epstein, Fitzsimmons, & Simons, 1969). The control mechanisms for this second system also seem to be located in the hypothalamus. To some extent, the two thirst controls are independent—one can be damaged without affecting the other. But gross interference with the hypothalamus will inactivate both mechanisms. Under normal conditions, the two regulators appear to interact and to augment one another.

Learned, individual, and cultural factors can also affect how we respond to the thirst drive. Some people avoid coffee, having been brought up to believe that stimulants are harmful; for others, a cup of coffee symbolizes a welcome 10 minutes' break from work. As flipping through magazine advertisements indicates, our self-image is linked to what we choose to drink—one beer may appeal to a "man's man," another to someone who wants to "stay on the light side." In many cases, these preferences involve other, more subtle, motives, which we shall touch upon later.

Sleep and Dreaming

People have often lamented what a waste it is that we spend a third of our lives asleep. Think what we must be missing! What we are actually missing by being able to sleep is the following: visual, auditory, and tactile sensory disorders; vivid hallucinations; inability to concentrate; withdrawal; disorientation of self, time, and place; lapses of attention; increased heart rate and stress hormones in the blood; and the onset of psychosis. This alarming list, of course, refers to extreme instances—people who have stayed up, on a bet or for a television marathon, for upwards of 200 hours. But if you have ever been up all night, you may fall asleep in class the next day and be slower in taking notes or answering questions on an exam. In short, the human body needs **sleep** to function, just as it needs food and water.

The **need to dream** appears to be as basic as the need to sleep. People dream about 2 hours a night on the average, whether or not these dreams are remembered. In one experiment people were consistently awakened for five consecutive nights just as the periods of REM (dreaming) sleep began (Dement, 1965). They became anxious and irritable, were hungry, and had difficulty concentrating. Some began to experience hallucinations. Prolonged deprivation from dreaming will make people dream as soon as they shut their eyes. There seems to be a strong need to compensate for dreaming time that has been lost (Dement, 1960). Many people who take drugs or alcohol, or who lose dreaming time because of illness or worry, say that when these inhibit-

BIOLOGICAL CLOCKS

What does the birth rate have to do with crime? Not much—except that both are linked to inner body cycles that scientists are just beginning to understand.

One such cycle we all share is the 24-hour circadian cycle of body activity (from the Latin *circa dies*, "about a day"). The cycle seems to be inherited and to relate to hormones, body chemistry, and DNA-dependent RNA synthesis. At the high point of the cycle, functions like white cell formation, pulse, and the production of glycogen and other substances are greatest. People feel best at this high point, sometime during the day. For human beings, the low point comes at night, during sleep. Scientists have found that post-surgical deaths and ability to withstand stress and illness are lowest at the low point of the cycle and that many more babies are born in the wee hours than at midday.

If our personal daily rhythm is upset, we may feel tired and irritable or even become ill. Pilots, stewardesses, and frequent international travelers know that crossing time zones can cause physical problems, but people can adapt to these disruptions up to a point. (The night watchman, for example, can get used to sleeping during the day.)

Scientists are sure that other cycles also affect our behavior, though they have not yet fully identified and classified all of them. The menstrual cycle, clearly, can affect mood, but there may be "mood cycles" of varying lengths in all people. Depression or elation, accident proneness, and efficiency have all been shown to vary cyclically.

Even old wives' tales about the moon's influence may turn out to have some foundation. The full moon may not cause lunacy, but it does seem to be associated with destructive behavior, even crime. Moon phase has also been related to conception and rainfall. More cycles, and more human behavior that depends on these "biological clocks," are sure to be discovered.

ing factors are removed they compensate by dreaming more intensely, often having nightmares.*

Pain

Hunger, thirst, and sleepiness are drives that cause a person to seek food, drink, or sleep. **Pain,** on the other hand, leads not to seeking but to escape or avoidance. Escape from or avoidance of pain are as necessary to survival as are eating, drinking, and sleeping. When we feel pain, we know we are in some sort of danger and we seek to escape from it. If you have a headache and your throat and legs are sore, you may be coming down with the flu. Therefore you take measures (going to bed, taking aspirin, calling the doctor) to fight the illness.

*Sleeping and dreaming are discussed in greater detail in Chapter 9.

(*Walter Chandoha*)

To what extent are the experience of pain, and the behaviors of escaping or avoiding pain, learned? Some experiments by Melzack and Scott (1957) provide partial answers. One set of puppies was brought up under normal circumstances; a second set grew up in isolated cages that made the usual sensory stimuli, experience, and learning—especially the normal bumps and scrapes from puppy play—impossible. Upon maturity, both groups were exposed to pain—shock, a match held under the nose, being pricked with a needle. The dogs that had been raised normally showed awareness of pain—yelping, wincing—and took measures to avoid its source. The isolated group, on the other hand, did not seem to know how to avoid the pain and in many cases did not even seem to experience it. When a needle was jabbed into the leg of one of these dogs, a localized twitch was the only sign of pain.

In humans, also, responses to pain are conditioned by learning and experience. Some people are more sensitive to pain than others, as dentists surely know. And responses to pain can be culturally conditioned as well. The physiological process of childbirth is presumably the same everywhere, but in some societies a pregnant woman will work until the last minute, have her baby without apparent discomfort, and return to work immediately afterward.

Sex

Sexual motivation is many things, in humans especially, but first and foremost it is a physiological drive, just as hunger, thirst, and pain are. But while those three drives are vital for the survival of the individual, the sex drive is important for the survival of the species.

In animals, hormones (principally *testosterone* for males and *estrogen* for females) are undeniably essential to the sex drive. Both hormones are present in both the male and the female, but in greatly differing quantities. In most animals, the female is receptive to sex only during certain times—when she is *in heat* or, in more technical language, during the **estrus cycle.** At this time, her ovaries are secreting a greater quantity of estrogen into her bloodstream, and she is receptive to the advances of the male. Only during the period of estrus can she become pregnant.

Human females differ in this respect from most other animals. A woman is receptive to sexual arousal during her whole hormonal cycle, not just when reproduction is possible. Hormones affect her fertility as they affect the fertility of lower animals, but the sex drive itself operates more or less independently of the physiological fertility cycle.

The pituitary gland in the brain controls the onset of puberty and the development of secondary sex characteristics. Sexual arousal and behavior, on the other hand, are controlled by the hypothalamus. The more highly evolved the animal, the more the cerebral cortex also plays a part in such arousal and behavior.

(*Magnum Photos*)

As the cerebral cortex becomes more and more involved, experience and learning become more and more instrumental in sexual arousal and behavior. This accounts not only for the fact that the human sex drive is noncyclical, but also for the fact that the stimuli that activate the sex drive are almost numberless—the phrase "soft lights and sweet music" immediately comes to mind. The stimulus need not be the sexual partner—it can be a visual, auditory, or tactile sensation, a picture, or a fantasy. Human sexual behavior is also affected by a wide range of variables—social experience, experience with the sexual act, poor nutrition, emotions (particularly one's feelings about the sex partner), and age.

The picture that emerges of sexual motivation, then, is one of decreasing involvement of purely physiological factors the higher one moves up the evolutionary scale. In humans, the role of hormones is at a minimum compared with the importance of learning and experience, both in the stimuli that elicit the drive and the behaviors that result.

The Maternal Drive

Maternal behavior is so complex that it is difficult to attribute it to a single "maternal drive." It would be hard to say, for example, whether the mother's impulse to nurse her child springs from a motive to nourish her child, directly from some hormone, or from a desire to relieve the discomfort of her full breasts. In all animals, including humans, hormones influence nursing, at least to the extent that the hormone *prolactin* stimulates the mammary glands to produce milk. And, if prolactin is injected into a nonpregnant female of the same species, it can bring about a variety of maternal behaviors. Yet prolactin alone cannot account entirely for maternal behavior, for when the mammary glands are removed from animals they still try to suckle their young.

(*Suzanne Szasz, Photo Researchers*)

It seems likely that much of the "maternal instinct" is not instinctive at all, but learned. In one experiment, a group of monkeys was raised in isolation, with no maternal attention (Harlow & Harlow, 1966). When these monkeys matured, many were unreceptive sexually. Many of those that did give birth seemed to have no maternal interest in their babies. Out of 20 such mothers, only 5 were on the borderline of adequate maternal care, and 3 of those 5 had had at least some contact with other monkeys while growing up. Seven others were indifferent to their young, and 8 actually brutalized them. Even when the babies actively sought their attention, the un-mothered mothers would have little or nothing to do with them.

In higher animals, then, maternal behavior, and apparently the maternal drive as well, seem to require learning and experience. Moreover, it seems probable that "mother love" reflects not a single drive but a complex set of motives and emotions—responsiveness, protectiveness, tactile contact—which come together to bring about a range of behavior that is as wide as the range of motives themselves.

Stimulus Motives

A second set of motives seems to be largely innate, but in all species these motives depend much more on external stimuli than on internal physiological states. Moreover, unlike the primary drives, their function extends beyond bare survival of the organism or species to a much less specific end—dealing with information about the environment in general. Motives such as *activity, curiosity, exploration, manipulation,* and *contact* are apparently innate. They push us to investigate, and often to alter, the environment. Most often, external stimuli—things in the world around us—set these motives in action, and we in turn respond with **stimulus-seeking behavior.** Our need for sensory stimulation has been demonstrated in laboratory studies of sensory deprivation (Bexton, Heron, & Scott, 1954). When subjects were prevented from receiving any external stimulation, their behavior became quite bizarre. For example, after being deprived of visual stimulation, the subjects began to have extraordinary hallucinations.*

Activity

If you get a flat tire late at night when you are driving through a small town whose sidewalks were rolled up hours ago, you go into the gas station and wait for the tire to be repaired. At first you are comfortable just sitting there, but then you get up and begin to wander around. You jangle your car keys or the coins in your pocket. You drum on a table top. You go over and read the fine print on the windshield-wiper ad. You pace about. Confined in a small space without much to do, you

---

*The effects of sensory deprivation are covered in more detail in Chapter 9.

IS WORK A STIMULUS MOTIVE?

A number of studies suggest that rats, pigeons, and children will sometimes perform work to gain rewards even when they can receive the same rewards without working (D'Amato, 1974).

> Rats will run down an alley tripping over hundreds of food pellets to obtain a single, identical pellet in the goal box [Stolz & Lott, 1964], . . . and pigeons will peck a key, even on intermittent schedules of reinforcement, to secure exactly the same food that is freely available in a nearby cup [Neuringer, 1969, 1970]. Given the option of receiving marbles merely by waiting an equivalent amount of time for their delivery, children tend to prefer to press a lever . . . to obtain the same marbles [Singh, 1970; Singh & Query, 1971] (p. 95).

Why would animals or humans work for food or other rewards when they can get the same payoff without working? Isn't there an inherent tendency to "freeload"?

Apparently, just the opposite is true; there seems to be an inherent need to work. The reason may lie in the importance of controlling the environment in order to survive. Such control is basic in all animal and human existence. The need to be in control seems to persist in animals and children even in situations where it is not immediately necessary. Thus, it may be that the work is the reinforcement, not the food. Another explanation suggested by D'Amato is that the individual's *perception* of a reward changes. "The very same wine often tastes better when drunk from a stem glass than from a paper cup" (p. 96). Thus, although they are physically the same, the free food and the worked-for food may be perceived as different.

exhibit all the signs of boredom. When the tire is changed and you are ready to drive off again, you are likely to do so with great relief, and probably 10 miles an hour faster than you should.

The need for **activity** is apparent in all animals, but scientists cannot determine whether it is a motive in itself or a combination of other motives. Most of the experiments that have been conducted to determine whether there is a separate "activity motive" have been done with rats. A rat put into a cage so small that it cannot move around will be more active than normal when it is released (Hill, 1956). But before we draw the conclusion that activity is an innate motive, we should consider other experiments. Food deprivation also increases activity—especially running activity (measured on the cylindrical "squirrel cage"). But restless activity (pawing, climbing, moving around aimlessly) increases less. Experiments with female rats (Wang, 1923) show that the sex drive also affects activity—peak activity and peak sexual receptivity coincide.

We do not quite know where this leaves us with human beings. Age, sex, health, genetic makeup, and temperament all seem to vary the need for activity—one person may be comfortable sitting in the same position for hours, while another may begin to fidget in 5 minutes, as any professor knows.

Exploration and Curiosity

Where does that road go? What is that dark little shop? How does a television set work? What is that piece of farm equipment for? Finding answers to these questions holds no obvious advantage to you. You do not expect the road to take you anywhere you particularly need to go, or the shop to contain anything you really need. You are not about to become a television repairman or help out in the hay harvest. You just want to *know*. **Exploration** and **curiosity** appear to be motives activated by the new and unknown and directed toward no more specific goal than "finding out." Exploration tends to be more spatial, and curiosity may be more intellectual, but the two motives are so similar that we consider them together.

An animal will learn a behavior not only to get food or drink but also to earn the privilege of being allowed to explore its environment. The family dog will run around a new house, sniffing and checking things out, before it will settle down to eat its dinner. Exploration and curiosity thrust us forward to get to know things. They drive us to find out about new stimuli and, once the old ones are familiar, they impel us to find new stimuli to explore. Placed in a maze that is painted black, a rat will explore it and learn its way around. The next time, given a choice between a black maze and a white one, it will choose the white (Dember, 1965). Apparently the unfamiliarity of the unknown maze has greater appeal—the rat seems to be curious to see what the new one is like. The parent of a bored 2-year-old on a rainy day can also tell you—if not too exhausted to speak—how important novelty is.

Similarly, animals seem to prefer complexity, presumably because more complex forms take longer to get to know and are therefore more

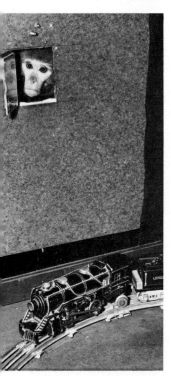

Figure 10-3
This monkey has learned to unlock a door simply in order to watch an electric train on the other side. (*Courtesy Wisconsin Primate Laboratory*)

Figure 10-4
On the first trial, a rat explores either black arm of the maze at random. On the second trial, however, given a choice between black and white arms, a rat will consistently choose the unfamiliar white arm. (After W. N. Dember, "The New Look in Motivation." *American Scientist*, 1965, *53*, 409–427.)

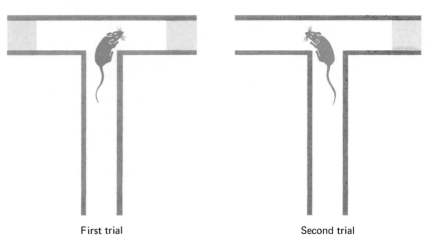

First trial

Second trial

interesting (Dember, Earl, & Paradise, 1957). We can "do more" with something complex than with something simple.

There are, of course, reservations. We have all been in situations where the unknown was distressing rather than stimulating, or when we shook our heads because something—an argument, a symphony, or a chess game—was getting too complicated for us. A child accustomed only to his parents may withdraw from a new face and scream with terror if that face has a beard. A very unusual dress style or a revolutionary piece of art or music may evoke rejection, scorn, even anger. But here learning enters the picture again. Acquaintance with the face, dress style, or symphony may reduce its novelty from an unacceptable to an interesting level. A child who at 2 years of age is only up to "Three Blind Mice" welcomes the complexity of a popular song at 12, and perhaps a Beethoven string quartet at 22. As we learn—and as we continually explore and familiarize ourselves with our environment—our threshold for the new and complex is raised and our exploration and curiosity become increasingly more ambitious.

Manipulation

Why do you suppose that museums have "Do Not Touch" signs all over the place? It's not because the curators are afraid some people might touch the exhibits. It's because they *know*—by hard experience—that touching is one of our more irresistible urges, and that we *all* might give in to it unless specifically asked not to. The desire to manipulate differs from curiosity and exploration in that it is directed toward a specific object that must be touched, handled, played with, and felt before we are satisfied. **Manipulation** differs from curiosity and exploration in another way, too—it is a motive that seems to be limited to primates, who have the physical structures of agile fingers and toes.

Figure 10-5
Although these locks do not open anything and lead to no tangible reward, the monkeys will work diligently to open them, providing evidence of the existence of a manipulation motive.
(Courtesy Harry Harlow)

The desire to manipulate seems to be related to two things—a need to know about something at a tactile level and sometimes a need to be soothed. The Greek "worry beads"—a set of beads on a short string that are moved back and forth in the course of conversation or thought—are examples of the second sort of manipulation. Under stress, people "fiddle"—with a cigarette, a paper napkin, a fountain pen. Children are always manipulating the objects of their environment. Eyeglasses, earrings, flowers, dogs' tails—everything must be touched, played with manually. The brighter the object, the more mixed its colors, the more irregular its shape, the more appealing it is as a potential object for manipulation. But monkeys too will take a puzzle apart for no apparent reason other than manipulation (Harlow, 1950).

Contact

People want to be in touch with other people. The need for **contact** is much broader and more universal than the need for manipulation. Furthermore, it is not limited to digital touching, but can involve the whole body. While manipulation is active, contact can also be passive.

In one of the most famous series of psychological experiments of all time (Harlow, 1958; Harlow & Zimmerman, 1959), baby monkeys were separated from their mothers at birth. In place of their real mothers, they were given two "surrogate mothers." Both were the same

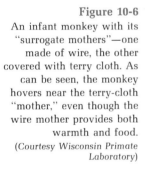

Figure 10-6
An infant monkey with its "surrogate mothers"—one made of wire, the other covered with terry cloth. As can be seen, the monkey hovers near the terry-cloth "mother," even though the wire mother provides both warmth and food.
(*Courtesy Wisconsin Primate Laboratory*)

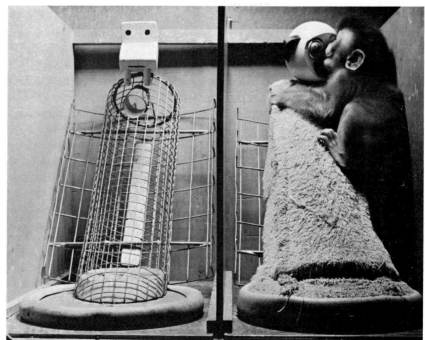

shape, but one was made of wire and offered no soft surfaces. The other was cuddly—over the wire structure there was a layer of foam rubber covered with terry cloth. A nursing bottle was put in the wire "mother," and both "mothers" were warmed by means of an electric light placed inside them. Thus the wire "mother" fulfilled two physiological drives for the infant monkeys: the need for food and the need for warmth. But it was to the terry-cloth "mother," which did not provide food, that the babies gravitated. When they were frightened, they would run to it, and they clung to it as they would to a real mother.

Since both mothers were warm, it seems that the need for affection, cuddling, and closeness goes deeper than a need for mere warmth.

Learned Motives

If all the motives that caused us to act were the ones we were born with, the police in our detective story would have a pretty slim list of clues to lead them to Miss Jones's murderer. But as we develop, our behavior comes to be governed by new motives. Although these new motives are learned, not innate, they exert just as much control over our behavior as physiological drives and stimulus motives do.

Fear

Fear is a complex motivation with a simple goal—to avoid or escape the source of the fear. If we were not afraid of certain things, we would probably not be around very long. We are brought up to be afraid of some things because they are dangerous. More often than not, we learn fear by association with pain. If a child has once been bitten by the big dog down the street, he learns to be afraid of it and he avoids it when he sees it approaching. He may also extend this particular fear to a fear of all dogs, or of all large or strange dogs. Thus, fear is important to us in dealing with the hazards in our environment.

How actually is fear learned? In one experiment (Miller, 1948), rats were taught to escape from a painful stimulus. They were put into a white compartment, and an electric shock was applied to the compartment's grid floor. Then they were allowed to escape to a black compartment, which was shock-free. When the rats were put back into another white compartment, also shock-free, they showed all the signs of fear, such as trembling and crouching. Although there was no actual pain the second time, the white compartment had become *associated* with pain, and therefore triggered fear in the rats. Fear can be attached to almost any stimulus. A bell ringing at the time of the shock would have made the rats afraid of bells too.

The fact that association plays a strong role in fear, and the fact that potential or even imagined harm can trigger it, set fear apart from simple pain avoidance. Once fear has been learned, it is very hard to unlearn, and it extends to things other than the feared object itself.

Figure 10-7
The apparatus used by Miller to condition fear in rats. An electric shock can be administered in the white compartment. The rats learn to escape the shock by rotating the wheel that opens a door into the adjoining black compartment. The rats also learn to fear the white compartment itself, even when no shock is given. (After N. E. Miller, "Studies of Fear as an Acquirable Drive. I." *Journal of Experimental Psychology,* 1948, *38,* 89–101.)

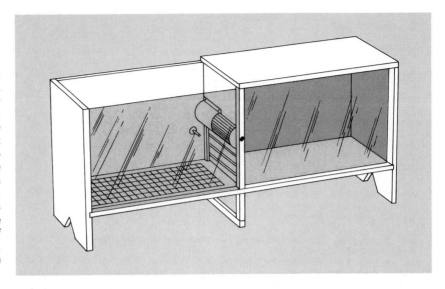

People are said to have "irrational" fears, but in many cases these fears were learned in particular, actually dangerous situations and then extended by association to other objects or situations where the element of real danger is minimal or nonexistent. A fear of heights, for example, may have been learned from one fall or a close escape from a fall. If you are afraid of the dark, you may have once awakened in an unfamiliar dark room and been unable to find your way around. As human beings are not simple, neither are the situations that trigger fear. But behavior in response to fear is simple—we try to get away from whatever it is that is causing our fear.

Aggression

If you have ever seen a toddler wham his baby sister on the head with a block, you might suppose that aggression is innate. Skimming the newspaper might give you the same impression. Some, but by no means all, psychologists go along with this view. According to those who do, like Freud and Lorenz, we are born with an **aggressive drive** and this innate motive expresses itself in destructiveness, war, and sadism.

As Lazarus (1974) points out, certain implications about human life follow from the conclusion that an aggressive drive is innate. An innate drive cannot be eliminated. Thus, it must be "sublimated" into socially acceptable and productive activities. According to Freud, civilization as we know it is actually an elaborate channeling device for our sexual and aggressive energies. Competitiveness in the work world or controlled and limited violence in a football game can be seen as ways of redirecting innate aggression into forms that are either useful and enjoyable or, at least, of limited harm.

The innate drive concept is unpopular among many psychologists because it poses a rather negative and deterministic view of human beings. We are pictured as inherently dangerous and destructive animals whose natural instincts must be controlled or else chaos will result. Humanistic psychologists such as Fromm and Maslow see people in a more positive light and emphasize the distinctly human, cooperative tendencies in our basic nature.

The innate drive theory can also be questioned scientifically. Lazarus (1974) points out that there is no substantial research to demonstrate that people have a built-in drive to attack or fight that cannot be controlled. Under the innate drive concept, aggression is constantly generating energy. If this energy is not released, the person will experience great tension and pain. Yet studies suggest that the release of aggression through behavior tends to increase, rather than decrease, the likelihood of future attack.

Another view of aggression suggests that aggression is not a motive at all, but simply a form of behavior. Aggression, according to this viewpoint, results from the nonfulfillment of other motives, which produces frustration. This frustration is then directed into aggressive behavior. According to this **frustration-aggression hypothesis,** when the stimuli associated with frustration are not present, aggressive behavior does not appear, so aggression cannot be considered a motive.

Many theorists and researchers have pointed out that laboratory studies do not support the idea that frustration inevitably leads to aggression. Bandura (1973) notes that frustration can lead to a wide variety of behaviors other than aggression. Among these are a search for help and support; achievement strivings; withdrawal and resignation; and escapism into drugs or alcohol. Bandura suggests that frustration will generate aggression in those people who have previously developed aggressive attitudes and actions as a means of coping with unpleasant situations.

In any case, aggressive *behavior* is in part learned. A child raised in a competitive climate is likely to learn to fight. The little boy who hits his little sister with a block was probably hit by someone else.

(Ian Cleghorn, Photo Researchers)

Aggressive behavior sometimes is learned because it is reinforced. In the animal kingdom, much aggressive behavior results from competition for limited resources such as food, territory, or sexual partners. Deprivation leads to competition, and the means of eliminating that competition is aggression. In addition, aggression can be learned through imitation. A child is punished for aggressive behavior, but, of course, this punishment is in itself a model of effective aggression. Children who are severely punished for aggressive behavior are found to act aggressively toward others, even toward dolls.

Social Motives

Another class of learned motives centers around our relationships with other people. Observing everyday behavior, we see that **social motives**

(Mary Rosenfeld, Nancy Palmer Photo Agency)

play a very great part in our lives and that social motives are numerous and complex. Our discussion will focus on two of the most important social motives.

Achievement. Climbing Mount Everest "because it is there," sending rockets into space, making the honors list, rising to the top of a giant corporation—these are actions whose underlying motives are probably mixed. Achievement can, of course, be sought because of other, quite different motives—curiosity, fear of failure, and so on. But in all the activities mentioned above, the desire to perform with excellence is certainly present. It is this interest in achievement for its own sake that

PRESIDENTS AND POWER

One important type of achievement motivation is the power motive. Generally, we think of achievement in terms of specific skills—the ability to compose a sonnet, throw a football, or solve a complex physics problem. Yet some people have a strong achievement striving that aims at gaining power over others.

Winter (1973) studied the power motives of 12 American Presidents, from Theodore Roosevelt through Richard Nixon. His technique was to score the concerns, aspirations, fears, and ideas for action of each President as revealed in his inaugural speech. The highest scorers in terms of power drives were Theodore Roosevelt, Franklin Roosevelt, Harry Truman, Woodrow Wilson, John Kennedy, and Lyndon Johnson. Except for Theodore Roosevelt, all were Democrats and all six men are known as action-oriented Presidents. All also scored high in need for achievement. By contrast, Republican Presidents (such as Taft, Hoover, and Eisenhower) are known more for restraint and tend to score much lower in power motivation and in need for achievement. Richard Nixon scored quite high in need for achievement but relatively low in power motivation. According to Winter, the effect of this is a tendency toward vacillation and hesitancy when faced with a power-oriented issue.

Winter makes a number of interesting correlations between the power motive and specific presidential policy decisions and actions:

> Those Presidents in power when the country entered wars tended to score high on power motive.
>
> Power scores of Presidents seem significantly related to the gain or loss of territory through wars, expansion, treaties, and independence struggles.
>
> Presidents with high power scores tend to have the highest turnover in Cabinet members during their administrations.

Winter does not suggest that we avoid electing Presidents with high power motives. Nor does Winter feel that Presidents high in power motives are always preferable, although Presidents who had high power motives are rated as more effective by historians. Rather, it is more a matter of electing the right person at the right time.

leads psychologists to suggest a separate achievement motive. **Need for achievement,** or *nAch* as it is abbreviated, varies widely from person to person. McClelland (1958) has developed techniques to measure *nAch* experimentally. For example, one picture in the Thematic Apperception Test (TAT, see Chapter 12) shows an adolescent boy sitting at a classroom desk. An open book lies on the desk, but the boy's gaze is directed outward toward the viewer. Subjects are asked to make up stories about this picture. One person responded:

> *The boy in the picture is trying to reconcile the philosophies of Descartes and Thomas Aquinas—and at his tender age of 18. He has read several books on philosophy and feels the weight of the world on his shoulders.*

Another response was in sharp contrast:

> *Ed is thinking of leaving home for a while in the hope that this might shock his parents into getting along.*

The first response comes from someone with a very high need for achievement, the second from someone whose need for achievement is very low.

From psychological tests and personal histories, psychologists have discovered some general traits of the high-*nAch* individual. Such a person functions best in competitive situations and is a fast learner. What drives him is not so much the desire for fame or fortune as the need to live up to a high self-imposed standard of performance. He is self-confident, takes on individual responsibility willingly, and is relatively resistant to outside social pressures. He is energetic and lets little get in the way of accomplishing his goals. But he is also likely to be tense and to suffer psychosomatic illness.

(Robert De Gast, Rapho/Photo Researchers)

Once we know that a person is high in need for achievement, the question remains: how did he get to be that way? Two major factors have been suggested (McClelland et al., 1953). First, a child must see his actions or efforts as leading to successful changes in the environment. Second, he must have the success of these actions reinforced by adult standards for excellence. A child who is exposed to such standards will soon learn how to differentiate between good and poor performance and will know that he will be praised for achievement or punished for lack of it. This may lead to a desire to do things well.

It is important to remember that our standards of achievement are often biased by our culture (Maehr, 1974). On many psychological tests, the lower-class black child shows a low achievement motivation. Yet the same black child may demonstrate an intense achievement drive on a basketball court. Similarly, disadvantaged children who exhibit language difficulties in school may be quite skillful in the use of familiar dialects within their own communities. Any serious study of the achievement needs of various Americans must avoid the dangers of *ethnocentrism*—the attitude that one's own culture is superior to all others. If white, middle-class standards are the only yardstick measuring achievement motivation, we can expect that white, middle-class children will consistently appear more achievement-oriented. Such studies will not help us to understand the ambitions and desires of many children who are not from the white middle class.

The motive to avoid success. Is there a motive to *avoid* success? Modern women who want challenging jobs are now freer to take them than ever before. However, many intelligent, skilled women fail to achieve according to their talents—especially some of those who most desire success. According to Matina Horner, women have a motive to avoid success. Where men develop the need to achieve, Horner says, women feel a "fear that success in competitive achievement situations will lead to negative consequences, such as unpopularity and loss of femininity" (Horner, 1969). This fear, however, goes hand in hand with a strong *desire* to achieve.

To tap feelings about success, Horner studied the responses of 90 female and 88 male undergraduates at the University of Michigan. The men were asked to finish a story that began: "After first-term finals, John finds himself at the top of his medical school class." The women got the same story, but with "Anne" substituted for "John."

Only about 10 percent of the men gave responses revealing doubt or fear about success. But the women (who had also scored much higher than the men on an independent measure of test anxiety) did reveal much fear in their stories. They worried about social rejection, picturing Anne as "acne-faced," lonely, dateless—even subject to physical attack after her victory! They also expressed doubts about her femininity: "Anne feels guilty. . . . She will finally have a nervous breakdown and quit medical school and marry a successful young doctor." A third group of women refused to admit that Anne could have succeeded. They misread the story, writing about Anne as a "nurse" or as second in score to a male student, and so on.

In another test, women performed better when asked to do some solitary tasks than when paired with men, against whom they had to compete. Working alone, they were free from anxiety that could interfere with performance.

Horner believes the source of this anxiety to be the way women are brought up in our society. Taught that her proper role is that of housewife and mother, the girl grows up hearing women who achieve outside the home called "sexless," "unfeminine," or "hard." It is not surprising that achievement—or the prospect of it—makes her feel guilty and anxious. Women would rather be liked than be successful. Unless these feelings can be resolved, Horner believes, women are unlikely to make full use of their opportunities.

Horner's work has received widespread publicity, but some of her methods and conclusions have recently been questioned. Tresemer (1974) stresses the small size of Horner's sample and various inconsist-

Figure 10-8

These women could serve as models for women who are worried about success. Margaret Mead, the well-known anthropologist, had to fight to be granted tenure because her male colleagues felt it would be inappropriate to have a female professor in their department. But times have changed. Mary Wells Lawrence runs her own advertising agency in a way that has earned her praise from her staff and her competitors, both male and female. And Billie Jean King, in addition to being one of the world's greatest tennis players, successfully fought to have women's tennis put on a par with men's tennis.

(Left: Sahm Doherty/Camera 5; center: courtesy of Wells, Rich, Greene, Inc.; right: Jill Krementz)

encies and problems in the coding of fear of success (FOS). He notes that there has been no satisfactory scoring manual devised to ensure uniform coding of sample stories.

Tresemer is also skeptical of Horner's connection between FOS imagery and nonachievement or failure in women's actual behavior. He claims that Horner's work has not established fear of success as a clear *motive* for lack of achievement in women. Tresemer poses alternate explanations for some of the same behavior that Horner sees in terms of FOS. For example, he believes that nonachievement imagery in women subjects may represent "fear of sex-role inappropriateness" rather than "fear of success."

Despite these difficulties, Tresemer acknowledges the pioneering importance of Horner's work. He and his colleagues at Harvard are currently developing a more effective scoring system and manual for FOS testing and are designing more ambiguous story lines such as "After much work, Joe (Judy) got what he (she) wanted." Their efforts should aid researchers in expanding on Horner's studies and clarifying the unresolved issues.

Affiliation. Sometimes you want to get away from it all—to spend an evening or a weekend alone, reading, thinking, or just being by yourself. But, generally, people have a **need for affiliation,** a need to be with other people. If a person is isolated from social contact for any considerable length of time, he will become anxious. Why is it that people seek each other out? How do groups come into being, and under what circumstances does a handful of isolated individuals become a group?

For one thing, the affiliation motive is aroused when people feel threatened. Esprit de corps—the feeling that you are part of a sympathetic group—is an important sentiment to encourage among troops

(*Wayne Miller, Magnum Photos*)

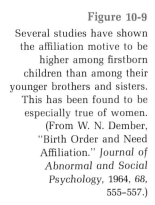

(*Burk Uzzle, Magnum Photos*)

going into a battle. Henry V's speech to his men before the battlements of Harfleur and a football coach's pre-game pep talk are both examples of an effort to make people feel they are working for a common cause or against a common enemy.

Often, affiliative behavior results from another motive entirely. For example, you may give a party to celebrate getting a promotion, or you may go around the office handing out cigars when your first child is born, because you want to be praised for your achievement.

It has also been suggested that fear and anxiety are closely linked to the affiliation motive. When rats, monkeys, or humans are placed in anxiety-producing situations, the presence of a member of the same species who is not anxious will reduce the fear of an anxious one. If you are sitting in a plane during a bumpy flight and are nervous, you may strike up a conversation with the unalarmed-looking person sitting next to you, because the erratic flight of the plane does not seem to be worrying him. In a study of female college students (Schachter, 1959), the subjects were divided into two groups: one high-anxiety, the other low-anxiety. The high-anxiety group was told the experiment they were participating in would involve their receiving a severe electric shock. The low-anxiety group was told the sensation of shock would be merely a tickle. Over two-thirds of the high-anxiety group, given the choice of waiting alone or with others, chose the latter. Out of the low-anxiety group, only one-third chose to wait among other people.

Figure 10-9
Several studies have shown the affiliation motive to be higher among firstborn children than among their younger brothers and sisters. This has been found to be especially true of women. (From W. N. Dember, "Birth Order and Need Affiliation." *Journal of Abnormal and Social Psychology*, 1964, 68, 555–557.)

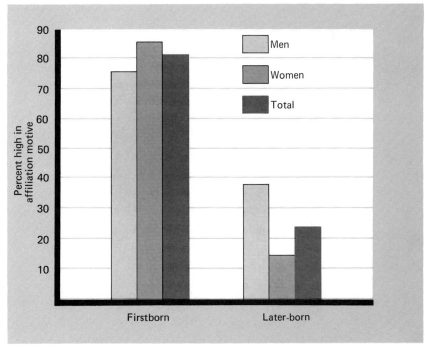

How does the motive for affiliation develop in people? It has been found (Sarnoff & Zimbardo, 1961) that firstborn or only children have stronger affiliation motives than those born later, perhaps because they were used to receiving more parental attention during the early years. Children who are brought up to be dependent, or raised with close family ties, show stronger affiliation motives than those coming from more loosely knit families that encouraged early independence. Many conclusions about the arousal of the affiliation motive are still tentative, but the evidence points to the fact that the desire to be with others goes back to the family, the first group we were ever in.

Consistency

"I was really shocked when she said that," you might remark of someone. "It just wasn't like her." You mean, of course, that it was not like what you know of her. People have a strong desire for things to be consistent. Any disparity produces a condition known as **cognitive dissonance.** Suppose you do not believe in astrology, but you let a friend chart your horoscope, and you find it amazingly accurate. You have several alternatives—you can dismiss the whole thing as a coincidence, you can decide your friend based the horoscope on things he found out about you behind your back, or you can switch over entirely and study astrology. In the first case, you have rejected the evidence entirely; in the second, you have brought in an "explanation" to reconcile the dissonance; in the third, you have changed your beliefs in the face of the evidence. Whatever you do, you have relieved the cognitive dissonance between the opinion you held and the contradictory new evidence; you have restored **consistency.**

The steps a person takes when faced with cognitive dissonance can depend on a number of factors. One of them is how strongly he holds his belief—what it "costs" him to give it up. If someone makes a good argument for cantaloupe being more nutritious than watermelon, the person might change his belief accordingly because it does not matter very much to him anyway. But if he is told that his much-admired older sister has been caught cheating on an exam, he may reject the information entirely rather than change the image he holds of her. Self-image, too, is relevant—people with low self-esteem will feel a stronger need to retain their own ideas intact, while more confident people are more tolerant when faced with conflicting situations.

In terms of the pattern of motivation we have been discussing, then, we might sum up the need for consistency in this way: faced with a fact or event that is not in accord with something we believe, we experience the tension of cognitive dissonance. The tension elicits a desire for consistency, a need to restore the balance between our beliefs and the new experience. This need for consistency, in turn, activates behavior. The behavior can take several tacks. We can reject or play

FUNCTIONAL AUTONOMY

Dog owners know that their pets will at times pick up something and shake it—just what they would do if they wanted to kill prey. But dogs do not shake things just when they are hungry. Anyway, how long has it been since Rover killed rabbits for food? People, too, may keep on doing things even when the original motives for doing them seem to have disappeared (for example, the miser who counts his money over and over, even though he knows how much is there).

R. S. Woodworth (1918a) was the first to suggest that some skills we learn can become motives of their own, no longer reflecting any basic motive. A person learns to play chess because he is curious, for instance, and the skills he develops become, in effect, drives that propel him to play chess again and again.

Gordon Allport (1937) described behavior with no apparent motive beyond itself as having *functional autonomy*. Such behavior, he said, may originally have been a response to a biological need or a secondary drive, like the need for approval, but it continues to take place even though the original motivation no longer exists. Moreover, it has no present motive beyond itself. (Thus, if the chess player plays to win money, his behavior cannot be called functionally autonomous.)

Critics say that terms like functional autonomy only describe behavior, but do not explain it. Others feel that different theories will work just as well to explain specific behavior. Meanwhile, the question of why a given person skydives, studies math, or tastes wine remains open.

down the dissonant fact, we can alter our beliefs, or we can bring in some new factor that reconciles the two. Whichever behavior we choose, the balance is restored and the tension is relieved.*

Unconscious Motives

A new brand of car is advertised, and a man decides he would like to own a BTX Super Panther II. Why? He may tell you that his old car was running down and this one looks "pretty good" to him. But there may be other reasons, of which he is unaware.

Theories of **unconscious motivation** vary. Freud's is probably the most extreme. According to his theory, every act—however trivial—derives from a host of unconscious motives. A Freudian might perceive the man's choice of a car as the desire to conquer a sexual object—a desire encouraged by advertisements touting it as "sleek," "purring," and "packed with power." Or Freudian theory might have cited aggression, the man's need to zoom down Main Street with as many horsepower as possible under his control.

*For a fuller discussion of cognitive dissonance, see Chapter 16.

(Stephen Frisch, Photo
Researchers)

But we do not need to interpret all acts in Freudian terms to realize that they can spring from motives we are not aware of. The man may be expressing a desire for social approval—"Be the first one on your block to own one!"—or a desire to reward himself for hard work. He could be trying to bolster a sagging self-image. He could be giving himself a present after the loss of a promotion or a girlfriend.

It should be emphasized that unconscious motives are not a particular *class* of motives, as physiological, learned, and stimulus motives are. Especially in the discussion of physiological drives, we pointed out that we do not have to be aware of hunger and thirst to act in such a way as to satisfy them. An unconscious motive is any motive that we are acting to satisfy without knowing quite why we are doing so.

A Hierarchy of Motives

You will have noticed that throughout this chapter we have been gradually working along lines leading us from very primitive motives, shared by all creatures, to motives that are more and more sophisticated, complicated, and human. Maslow (1954) has proposed that all motives can be arranged in such a hierarchy, from lower to higher. The lower motives are relatively simple, and they spring from bodily states that *must* be satisfied. As the motives become higher and higher, they spring from other things—the desire to live as comfortably as possible in our environment, to deal as well as we can with other human beings, and to present ourselves to others as well as we can. Maslow's hierarchy of motives is diagrammed in Figure 10-10.

According to Maslow's theory, higher motives will appear only to the degree that the more basic ones have been satisfied. This is true

Figure 10-10
Maslow's hierarchy of motives. The stages, from the bottom up, correspond to how crucial the motive is for survival and how early it appeared in both the evolution of the species and the development of the individual. The higher motives appear only to the extent that the ones below them have been satisfied.
(After A. H. Maslow, *Motivation and Personality*. New York: Harper & Row, 1954.)

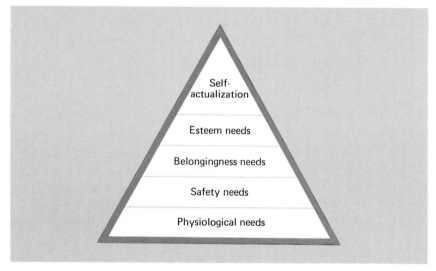

THE SELF-ACTUALIZING PERSON

Abraham Maslow, studying a number of famous people and a group of college students, compiled a list of 15 traits that he believed were characteristic of the self-actualizing person (Maslow, 1954).

1. *More efficient perception of reality.* The self-actualizing person judges persons and events realistically and is better able than others to accept uncertainty and ambiguity.
2. *Acceptance of self and others.* These people take others for what they are and are not guilty or defensive about themselves.
3. *Spontaneity.* This quality is shown more in thinking than in action. In fact, the self-actualizing person is frequently quite conventional in behavior.
4. *Problem centering.* Self-actualizing people are more concerned with problems than with themselves and are likely to have what they consider important goals.
5. *Detachment.* Self-actualizing people need privacy and do not mind being alone.
6. *Autonomy.* The self-actualizing person is able to be independent of culture and environment.
7. *Continued freshness of appreciation,* even of often-repeated experiences.
8. *Mystic experiences, or the oceanic feeling.* This feeling, which Maslow includes under the heading of "peak experiences," frequently involves wonder, awe, a feeling of oneness with the universe, and a loss of self.
9. *Gemeinschaftsgefühl, or social interest.* This is a feeling of unity with humanity in general.
10. *Interpersonal relations.* Deep, close relationships with a chosen few characterize the self-actualizing person.
11. *Democratic character structure.* These people are relatively indifferent to such matters as sex, birth, race, color, and religion in judging individuals.
12. *Discrimination between means and ends.* The self-actualizing person enjoys activities for their own sake, but also appreciates the difference between means and goals.
13. *Sense of humor.* The self-actualizer's sense of humor is philosophical rather than hostile.
14. *Creativeness.* The self-actualizer's creativity in any field consists mostly of the ability to generate new ideas.
15. *Resistance to enculturation.* The self-actualizing person is not rebellious, but is generally independent of any given culture.

Maslow does not maintain that these persons are perfect—disregard of others is one possible fault, for example. Moreover, having the characteristics on this list does not mean that you are self-actualized, only that self-actualization is important to you and that you are the type of person who tries to achieve it.

on an evolutionary scale, and also on an individual one. If you are starving, you will probably not care what people think of your table manners. If you are being approached by a speeding car, you will get out of the way fast and not worry about whether you look graceful.

Maslow believes that the most "evolved" motive in the hierarchy is **self-actualization.** This may be described as a desire to make the best one can out of oneself. It does not concern the respect of other human beings and their judgments of us, but rather what we ourselves want to be. People differ in how important self-actualization is in their behavior, but to some extent all of us are motivated to live according to what is necessary for our individual growth. The people who are the most self-actualizing, Maslow says, think of themselves as whole beings, not as parcels of hunger, fear, ambition, and dependency. We have all, at one time or another, had what Maslow calls *peak experiences*—moments when we felt a flash of joy or fulfillment at being at one with the world about us, but particularly with ourselves.

Summary

1. *Motivation* consists of a series of stages: first a *stimulus* triggers a *motive*, which in turn leads to *behavior*. If the behavior results in *goal attainment*, the motive is satisfied and the chain is complete.
2. *Physiological motives,* also called *primary drives,* are activated by certain physiological states, such as the need for food, water, and sleep.
3. The *hunger drive* is aroused when the body's need for food is registered in the brain. There appear to be two hunger regulators in the body. The first monitors the blood-sugar level. The second operates on a long-term basis to regulate the body's weight by monitoring fat stores. Two parts of the hypothalamus—the *lateral hypothalamus* and the *ventromedial nucleus*—balance each other and work together to control the intake of food. Other brain structures, such as the limbic system and the temporal lobe, also may be involved in this control. *Specific hungers* indicate that the body "knows" what foods it needs to maintain itself. The hunger drive and, often, the need for specific foods are unlearned, but how that drive is expressed in behavior is governed by learning, habit, and culture.
4. *Thirst,* like hunger, is controlled by delicate biochemical balances in the body, and has been linked to the level of salt (sodium chloride) in the bloodstream. When the level of salt in the blood reaches a certain point, a thirst center in the hypothalamus is stimulated, thus activating the thirst drive. A second thirst regulator seems to involve a reduction in the amount of fluid outside the body's cells. This appears to trigger the kidneys to release certain chemicals, which, when carried to the brain, activate the thirst drive. Learning also has a large influence on how we act to satisfy the thirst drive.
5. *Sleep* is also vitally important to survival, and the need to *dream* appears to be as basic as the need to sleep. Being deprived of either for long periods can result in disorientation, anxiety, poor concentration, and even hallucinations.

6. *Pain* acts as a warning signal that something is wrong with the body and motivates us to escape or avoid the danger. Responses to pain are conditioned by learning and experience. Other aversive drives include suffocation, fatigue, and elimination of body wastes.

7. *Sexual motivation* is a combination of many factors, but it is first and foremost a physiological drive. In lower animals, hormones are absolutely necessary to the sex drive, but as one moves up the evolutionary scale the role of purely physiological factors diminishes. The role of hormones in the human sex drive is minimal compared with the importance of learning and experience, with regard to both the stimuli that elicit the drive and the behaviors that result.

8. The complexity of maternal behavior makes it difficult to isolate a single *maternal drive.* Hormonal influence is present in all animals, including humans, in the form of *prolactin,* which stimulates the mammary glands to produce milk. But prolactin alone cannot account for the wide range of maternal behavior, and it seems more likely that much of it is learned.

9. A second set of motives that is largely innate depends much more on external stimuli than on internal physiological states. These *stimulus motives,* such as curiosity, activity, exploration, manipulation, and contact, push us to investigate, and often to alter, our environment.

10. External stimuli set stimulus motives into action. Experiments indicate that stimulus motives lead us to seek out sensory stimulation. In the face of *sensory deprivation,* we will sometimes create stimulation for ourselves in the form of hallucinations.

11. All animals apparently need *activity,* but scientists have not yet been able to determine whether activity is a motive in itself or whether it results from other drives.

12. The motives of *exploration* and *curiosity* appear to be activated by the new and unknown and to be directed toward finding out something. Unfamiliar and complex things seem to have greater appeal to animals than the familiar or simple, but sometimes the unknown can be distressing or even frightening. As we continually explore and familiarize ourselves with our environment, our threshold for the new and complex is raised and our exploration and curiosity become increasingly more ambitious.

13. *Manipulation* is directed toward a specific object that must be touched, handled, played with, and felt before we are satisfied. It appears to be limited to primates, who have fingers and toes. The desire to manipulate relates to a need to know something at a tactile level and sometimes to a need to be soothed.

14. The need for *contact* with others is much broader and more universal than the need for manipulation. It is not limited to touching, but can involve the whole body. It can be passive, whereas manipulation is active.

15. All motives are not inborn; many are learned as we develop. *Fear* is a motive that is often learned through association with pain.

16. Some psychologists hold that *aggression* is innate, while others suggest that aggression results when the nonfulfillment of other motives produces frustration, which is then directed into aggressive behavior. According to this *frustration-aggression hypothesis,* when the stimuli associated with frustration are absent, aggressive behavior does not appear. More recently, some psychologists have suggested that frustration does not necessarily

lead to aggression, but that aggression is a learned way of responding to unpleasant situations and is, therefore, neither innate nor inevitable. In any case, aggressive behavior is in part learned.

17. The desire to perform with excellence is present in many activities, but the interest in achievement for its own sake suggests a separate *achievement motive.* The need for achievement—*nAch*—varies from person to person. If a child sees his actions or efforts lead to successful changes in the environment and then has these actions reinforced by adult standards for excellence, he is more likely to develop a high need for achievement. At one time, most psychologists believed that women had a motive to *avoid* success. Recent research has called this into question. Some psychologists also question the tests used to measure *nAch* because they feel they are slanted in favor of the white middle class.

18. The *affiliation motive*—the desire to be with others—is usually aroused when people feel threatened. Fear and anxiety are closely linked to the affiliation motive. Development of the affiliation motive seems to begin in the family, the first group we are ever in.

19. The *motive for consistency* is elicited by the tension of *cognitive dissonance,* which occurs when we are faced with a fact or event that is not in accord with something we believe or expect. This need to restore the balance between our beliefs activates behavior—we can reject or play down the dissonant fact, alter our beliefs, or bring in some new explanation that reconciles the two. Any of these alternatives will restore the balance and relieve the tension.

20. Many things we do spring from motives we are not aware of—*unconscious motives.* Unconscious motives play an important part in Freud's theory of personality. Any motive that we are acting on without quite knowing why we are doing it constitutes an unconscious motive.

21. Abraham Maslow has postulated that all motives can be arranged in a *hierarchy,* from lower—relatively simple motives springing from bodily states that need to be satisfied—to higher—the desire to live comfortably, to deal easily with other people, and to present ourselves to others as well as we can. According to this theory, higher motives will appear only to the degree that the more basic ones have been satisfied. The most evolved motive in Maslow's hierarchy is *self-actualization*—the desire to make the best we can out of ourselves, not in respect to other human beings, but in respect to what we ourselves want to be.

Suggested Readings

Balagura, S., *Hunger: A Biopsychological Analysis* (New York: Basic Books, 1973). A readable, physiologically oriented overview of hunger.

Birch, D., and Veroff, J., *Motivation: A Study of Action* (Belmont, Calif.: Brooks/Cole, 1966). A concise and original approach to experiments on motivation.

Fowler, H., *Curiosity and Exploratory Behavior* (New York: Macmillan, 1965). An excellent introduction to the motives of curiosity and exploration.

Knutson, J. S., *Control of Aggression: Implications from Basic Research* (Chicago: Aldine, 1973). Deals with the physiology of aggression and the learning of aggressive behavior.

Lorenz, K., *On Aggression* (New York: Harcourt Brace Jovanovich, 1966). An interesting argument for the theory that humans have an innate drive to be aggressive.

McClelland, D. C., *The Achieving Society* (Princeton, N.J.: Van Nostrand Reinhold, 1961). A fascinating analysis of the economic effects on a society when many of its members have a high need for achievement.

Montagu, M. F. A. (Ed.), *Man and Aggression* (New York: Oxford University Press, 1968). A collection of reviews critical of Lorenz's hypothesis that human aggression is innate.

Murray, E. J., *Motivation and Emotion* (Englewood Cliffs, N.J.: Prentice-Hall, 1964). A clear, well-organized introduction to motivation and emotion.

Stacey, C. L., and DeMartino, M. F. (Eds.), *Understanding Human Motivation*, rev. ed. (Cleveland: Howard Allen, 1963). An engrossing collection of articles on motivation by several psychologists.

Winter, D. G., *The Power Motive* (New York: Free Press, 1973). A comprehensive study of the need for power, including an analysis of the fabulous lover, Don Juan, in terms of the power motive.

outline

THE NATURE OF EMOTION 390

The Physiology of Emotion
The Psychology of Emotion
Basic Emotional Experiences

THE FUNCTION OF EMOTION 407

Emotions and Attitudes
Emotions: Disruptive or Adaptive?
Emotions as Motives

THE COMMUNICATION OF EMOTION 410

Verbal Communication
Nonverbal Communication

SUMMARY 416

SUGGESTED READINGS 418

Emotion

Suppose a friend of yours has been away all weekend for a family reunion. When he gets back, you ask, "How was it?" "All right, I guess," he might answer. This rather neutral reply sums up a situation that probably evoked a broad range of emotions, strongly or dimly felt, pleasant or unpleasant, consistent or conflicting. He may have felt grief because his grandfather, who had always sat at the head of the table, died last year, and this was the first reunion that was held without him. His older brother, a doctor, was there, and his admiration for his success was tinged with envy, not to mention anxiety that if he did not do better in biology he might not get into medical school himself. He concealed his anger and embarrassment when his aunt addressed him by a childish pet name he hoped everybody had forgotten years ago. When the dinner-table conversation turned to state politics, he knew more about the party structure than anyone else and was elated at everybody's obvious respect for his opinions. He had a long talk with a cousin he had not seen for a while and was gratified to find that the two of them were on the same wavelength after so many years. He was angry that his grandmother could have forgotten he hated stewed rhubarb, but he felt such guilt for that anger that he ate the rhubarb and even asked for a second helping. He wanted to die when the family photograph album was brought out and everybody said how cute he looked in a diaper, but he smiled bravely and pretended to be amused. So many emotions were in play during this weekend. But what exactly is an emotion?

The Nature of Emotion

Love, hate, fear, joy, anger, worry—we can reel off the names of emotions easily enough. But what do the names really tell us? Where would poets get their subject matter if "love" were not burning and freezing, joy and agony, feeling 10 feet tall and groveling at the beloved's feet? And what do we mean by love, anyway, when we can say that we love a person, a novel, or lemon chiffon pie? If we are trying to define an emotion, or emotion itself, the words we use are as likely to trip us up as to enlighten us. For the moment, let us say that an **emotion** is a complex affective experience that involves diffuse physiological changes and can be expressed overtly in characteristic behavior patterns. To realize how complex, interconnected, subtle, and contradictory emotions can be, think of how you feel toward yourself. Not simple, is it?

Emotion is a difficult field for psychologists to study. The effects of emotion on behavior can be measured, but emotion itself is not easy to analyze objectively. In a recent summary of research in emotion, K. T. Strongman (1973) notes that human responses in the laboratory setting are obviously not the same responses you would get in "real life," and that many psychologists doubt that the results from animal studies can tell us much about human emotion.

In spite of these problems, psychologists have had some success in isolating and describing the physiological changes that occur during the experience of emotion. So let's start there as we attempt to define and describe what emotion is.

(*Joel Gordon*)

The Physiology of Emotion

The physiological changes that are associated with emotion are controlled by the endocrine glands and the autonomic nervous system. These two systems are responsible for the wide range of symptoms that accompany most emotional states—the faster heart rate, the enlarged pupils, the deeper or shallower breathing, the flushed face, the increased perspiration, the butterflies in the stomach, the gooseflesh sensation as the body's hairs literally stand on end.

For example, there is some evidence that the physiological patterns associated with fear are different from those associated with anger. In one experiment (Funkenstein et al., 1953), a group of college students was given a set of very difficult problems and told to solve

(Rita Freed, Nancy Palmer
Photo Agency)

them without using paper and pencil. They were then accused of stupidity when they were not able to complete the tasks. Three different kinds of reactions occurred. Some of the students showed fear and anxiety at not being able to solve the problems and at being scolded by the experimenters. Others expressed anger at the experimenters. A third group also expressed anger, but they turned it upon themselves—they blamed themselves for their failure. The cardiovascular pattern—heart and pulse rate, circulation of blood—of all three groups was then tested. The individuals who had expressed anger at the experimenters showed the physiological changes that would have occurred if they had received an injection of norepinephrine. Those who had become angry with themselves showed the pattern that would have accompanied an injection of epinephrine.* The students who had become anxious showed an exaggerated epinephrine pattern.

Some emotions are caused by a combination of physiological and environmental factors. Anxiety and depression are often a result of environmental stress, which causes certain chemical changes in the brain; these chemical changes, in turn, bring on the emotional disturbance. For example, Weiss and his colleagues (1974) were able to show that stressful conditions cause norepinephrine levels in the brain to go down, and that this lowered level of norepinephrine brings on immobility and depression. They also found that it was possible to control depression by giving test animals a drug called *pargyline*, which prevents the body from breaking down norepinephrine under stressful situations such as inescapable shock.

*Epinephrine and norepinephrine are hormones produced by the adrenal medulla; see Chapter 2.

The nervous system. When we watch a football player make a touchdown, or see a car wreck, or are embraced, what happens in the nervous system that results in our feeling elation, fear, or pleasure?

The external stimulus is registered by the reticular activating system, whose function is simply arousal. At this point, only the dimension of intensity is involved—it is immaterial to the reticular activating system whether you just cut your hand or got an A in chemistry. But as the message of arousal reaches the limbic system, the emotion is differentiated. The limbic system knows the difference between pleasure and pain and controls whether the stimulus is to be approached or avoided. The hypothalamus is particularly important here. Experiments have shown that damage to the hypothalamus can result in extreme placidity, even under conditions that would normally produce strong emotion; stimulation of the hypothalamus, on the other hand, can result in "sham" rage. With no external stimulus, a cat will react by hissing, spitting, and arching its back when the hypothalamus is stimulated (Wheatley, 1944). The hypothalamus is also involved in activating the endocrine system, and it is a pathway to and from the cerebral cortex.

An important experiment by Olds and Milner (1954) located points in the brain that register pleasure and pain. The researchers implanted electrodes in the hypothalamus of rats' brains and then placed the rats in Skinner boxes and allowed them to electrically stimulate themselves by pressing a lever. They found that the rats experienced intense pleasure; they would press the lever at rates up to several thousand times an hour. Further research (Olds, 1956) revealed that the intensity of the shock was more important than how often it occurred; the rats would press the bar far more eagerly for strong shocks, even if they occurred infrequently. Later experiments found nearby regions that produced pain. The rats would press the lever for hours to avoid the stimulus, finally developing ulcers if the experiment continued.

Further self-stimulation studies support the idea that the limbic system is at the physiological center of emotion. Delgado (1969) has been able to produce a variety of emotional reactions in humans by electrically stimulating various areas of the limbic system. He found that stimulating the posterior hypothalamus creates the most intense pleasure sensations; stimulating the septal region produces sexual sensations that can approach orgasmic intensity. Delgado maintains that far more of the human brain is geared to register pleasure than pain. He has determined that 60 percent of the human brain is neutral—that is, it registers neither pleasure nor pain; 35 percent registers rewarding and pleasurable sensations exclusively; and only 5 percent registers pain.

The exact connections between these physiological components are not yet known in detail. We know the functions of various areas of the brain and nervous system, and the circumstances that bring them

"THE PHYSIOLOGY OF VIOLENCE"

Until recently, psychologists have worked primarily with two theories of aggressive behavior. The first is based on heredity: Aggression is an innate drive and it is society's task to provide an acceptable outlet for it. The second involves learning: Experience and environment teach people to be aggressive, but society can control aggressive impulses through behavior modification techniques.

New research, however, has suggested that every human being, regardless of heredity or experience, has a built-in aggression system that can be activated by a number of external and internal stimuli. For example, electrical stimulation of the part of the human brain called the *amygdala* causes subjects to become hostile and aggressive (Charles Whitman, who killed 14 people and wounded 31 others during a shooting spree at the University of Texas, was discovered to have had a tumor near the amygdala).

Moyer (1973) has suggested that the sensitivity of these built-in aggressive systems varies from extremely insensitive to extremely sensitive, and that this variation in sensitivity determines how violently a person will react to aggression-provoking stimuli. If the system is totally insensitive, such as in mice castrated before puberty, no aggression will be shown. At the other extreme, the system may be extremely sensitive, as when the aggression cells are spontaneously "firing." People in this state are restless, feel hostile, and will act aggressively as soon as they are presented with an appropriate stimulus. However, most people have selective sensitivity, and their neural aggression cells can be activated only by a very limited range of stimuli. But, in spite of this selectivity, every individual's neural sensitivity fluctuates up and down between these extremes.

The sensitivity of the neural aggression system is controlled by four factors: heredity, other neural systems in the brain, blood chemistry, and learning. Experimenters have bred aggressive strains of rabbits, mice, and monkeys, and Moyer believes that humans also inherit aggressive tendencies. As for other neural systems, electrical stimulation of the reticular formation and lateral hypothalamus has intensified aggressive behavior in laboratory animals; stimulation of the brain's septal region inhibits hostility in some psychotic patients. Hormones are another physiological factor that can effect violent behavior. For example, premenstrual tension makes many women irritable and some violent, and testosterone levels in the blood determine a man's readiness to fight. Finally, learning and experience are such powerful controllers of aggression that they can nullify all the other factors; human beings can be taught to exhibit or inhibit their hostile impulses.

While behavior modification can control aggressive behavior, it does not shut off the neural bases of aggression. This would require surgery, altering the endocrine balance, or electrically stimulating those portions of the nervous system that inhibit aggression. So far, these techniques have not been widely applied because they are ethically questionable and offer great opportunities for abuse.

(The Bettmann Archive)

into play. Someday it may be possible to diagram them as we would a computer circuit, but that day has not yet come. There are several theories about how these physiological changes relate to the psychological experiences of emotion.

James-Lange theory. In the 1880s, William James announced the first formal theory of emotion, and almost simultaneously a Danish psychologist, Carl Lange, arrived at essentially the same conclusions. The James-Lange theory reversed what was previously believed about how emotions are aroused. Before, it had been thought that the sequence of arousal was *You see a bear, you feel afraid, you run.* According to the new theory, the order was changed to *You see a bear, you run, you feel afraid.* Emotion, according to James and Lange, springs out of physiological reactions. The perception of the stimulus (the bear) causes your body to undergo certain physiological changes. Then, and only then, do you feel the emotion (fear), which is caused, not by the direct perception of the bear, but by the physiological responses.

The James-Lange theory did not identify any special centers of the brain. A receptor is stimulated by an object and impulses are sent to the cortex, where the stimulus is perceived. Impulses are then relayed to the muscles, skin, and viscera, which undergo change accordingly. When these physiological changes are sent back to the cortex, the result is emotion. All this, of course, happens almost instantaneously and in a reflexive, automatic way. But if the bodily responses were bypassed, according to James and Lange, no emotion would be felt.

Cannon-Bard theory. In the 30 years after the James-Lange theory was formulated, additional knowledge was accumulated concerning the centers of emotion. In 1927 another psychologist, W. B. Cannon, was able to question the James-Lange theory in these terms: If the same visceral changes—increased heartbeat and sweating, for example—are experienced for emotions as different as fear, anger, and excitement, how can we account for the differences between these emotions? The implication of the James-Lange theory had been that different physiological cues produce different emotions. Not so, stated Cannon—the *same* physiological cues can result in different emotions. His experiments disclosed that if the viscera of a laboratory animal were separated from its central nervous system—that is, if the James-Lange "feedback" were cut off—the animal continued to display emotional behavior. Also, Cannon pointed out, the viscera are composed largely of smooth muscles. The changes these muscles undergo, as in the digestive process, are very slow—too slow to account for how quickly we feel emotion.

Later, reinforced by L. L. Bard's work on the thalamus, the Cannon-Bard theory was elaborated to propose that there are specific brain centers which are involved in the emotional processes. These are the thalamic-hypothalamic regions. According to this theory, emotions and bodily responses occur *simultaneously*, not one after another. After the stimulus is perceived, nerve impulses pass through the thalamus. There they split—some of the impulses go to the cortex, where the stimulus is perceived and the emotional response is experienced, and some go to the muscles and viscera, where the physiological reactions take place. Thus, *You see the bear, you run* and *are afraid*, with neither reaction preceding the other.

Schneirla (1959) suggests that the James-Lange and Cannon-Bard theories may both be right in certain circumstances. The James-Lange theory may be most useful for explaining emotion in young animals, including children. The Cannon-Bard theory, on the other hand, may explain later emotional development, when perception and motivation become more important factors in the experience of emotion.

Measurements of the physiological changes in emotion certainly have their "scientific" uses, as we all know from reading police stories in which the lie detector plays a star role. But the changes in your pulse rate, heartbeat, and blood pressure would probably not be much different if you suddenly met a bear than if you met your girl- or boyfriend after 6 months' separation—although the emotion you would feel would be different. Most of the physiological "signs" of emotion say only that emotion is there and how intense it is. They cannot tell us whether we are feeling rubbery knees from terror or joy.

The Psychology of Emotion

So far we have talked about the involuntary physiological changes that occur when we experience an emotion, and about some of the early formal theories that attempted to explain the sequence of arousal. But how do we acquire our emotions in the first place? Are we born with them, or do we learn our emotional responses by imitating others? What role does memory play? What is the connection between our thoughts and emotions, and what part does perception play?

(Bruce Buchenholz, Photo Researchers)

Emotional development. There is evidence that the more advanced an animal is on the evolutionary scale, the greater are the number and complexity of stimuli that will arouse its emotions, and the more important the role of learning is in arousing emotion. For example, with many animal species, certain emotional responses seem to be instinctive. In Chapter 4, we mentioned the goose/hawk shape that evokes signs of fear in birds. Still another experiment (Hebb, 1949) involved exposing chimpanzees to a clay model of a detached chimpanzee head. There was nothing in the chimpanzees' experience that would make such an object frightening, yet adult chimpanzees responded to the head with terror. What is most interesting is that infant chimpanzees showed no fear, and adolescent chimpanzees were much less frightened

LEARNING TO LOVE

Learning how to respond to emotional stimuli, and which stimuli to respond to, is nowhere more clear than in the case of love. All of us are brought up to believe that we should love our parents, and our choices of friends and mates are strongly influenced by what we have learned about emotional stimuli, particularly love.

Harlow and Harlow (1966) have identified five affectional systems in the social development of monkeys. In each system, the monkeys become attached to different members of their group and respond differently to them. Normal development of each system is vital to the next.

1. *Infant-mother affectional system.* Born with reflexes that help him feed and cling to the mother, the young monkey gradually shows more voluntary attachment to her and finally becomes able to explore the environment as long as his mother is near. Eventually he leaves her entirely, though some have noticed continuing mother-offspring ties in the wild (Van Lawick-Goodall, 1971).

2. *Peer affectional system.* The laboratory monkey raised without mothering is reluctant to play at first, but soon joins in. More serious is early separation from peers, which does permanent damage to social relationships. Normally, young monkeys start with eye contact and clinging and progress to real play, including immature sex play. Friendships formed at this stage may persist, even affecting later sexual choice. Laboratory play groups cohere, especially when strange youngsters appear (Harlow & Harlow, 1966).

3. *Heterosexual affectional system.* Lack of early peer group contact does serious harm to later sexual behavior. Sex behavior needs to be practiced, and monkeys raised in isolation rarely mate (Harlow, 1962). Monkeys raised alone, when paired, treat each other like brother and sister, but behave hostilely toward normal monkeys who try to mate with them.

4. *Maternal affectional system.* Normally, primates begin to nourish and protect their offspring immediately. Care is intense during the early months, gradually becoming mixed with punishment, which eventually drives the young to spend more time with peers. Females raised without mothering and away from peers, as we saw in Chapter 10, are often brutal or indifferent to their babies—though Harlow and Harlow (1966) were surprised to find that mothers are better with later offspring, having apparently learned from the first ones.

5. *Paternal affectional system.* Males, especially dominant males, may defend the young. Frequently, they tolerate behavior from the young that they would punish in an adult. Males in the wild have even been known to adopt infants or to attach themselves to adolescents that have separated from their mothers (Harlow & Harlow, 1966). Recently this situation was re-created in the laboratory (Mitchell, Redican, & Gomber, 1974). Male parental behavior was found to be different from female parental behavior in several significant ways. First, while the bond between mother and infant usually decreases as time goes by, that between father and infant increases. Second, when the baby is threatened, a mother will typically scoop it up and run away, while the father will move to attack the threat. Third, the fathers play with their infants more often and with more enthusiasm than mothers do. Even a male raised in isolation was able to successfully raise an infant. Being raised by a male rather than by a female does not seem to injure the infants' later social development in any way. It must be noted, however, that this paternal interest is displayed only toward motherless infants; when the mother is present, the adult male monkey's reaction is typically indifference or hostility.

than the adults. To what extent, then, can we say that the fear of such an object is "instinctive"? The chimpanzees' response was unlearned, yet they were not born with it, either. What the experiment does seem to indicate is that the capacity to respond emotionally to a given

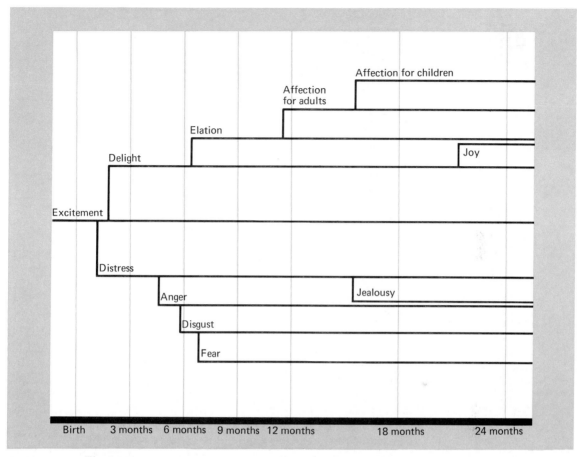

Figure 11-1

A diagram of the differentiation of emotions in infancy. (After K. M. B. Bridges, "Emotional Development in Early Infancy," *Child Development*, 1932, *3*, 324–334, 340.)

stimulus increases as we grow older, even when there is no specific experience we have had that teaches us to fear the object.

This growth of emotional "sophistication" can be seen not only along the evolutionary scale, but also within the human lifetime. A newborn baby's emotional range seems to include only one emotion—a state of generalized excitement. A baby will react with this diffuse excitement to a red rattle, a large dog, a loud noise, or his mother's breast. One study (Bridges, 1932) tried to make a "chronology" of emotional development. By observing many babies, Bridges found that all the basic human emotions appear at particular times in a definite pattern between birth and the age of 24 months. After the first generalized excitement, this pattern branches off in two ways: the emotions that develop around distress (unpleasantness, avoidance) and the emotions that develop around delight (pleasantness, approach). The child will show delight before he is 3 months old. (Actually, we can only *assume* that his gurgling, smiling, and cooing express delight, since he cannot tell us.) Between 3 and 6 months, anger, disgust, and fear will be dis-

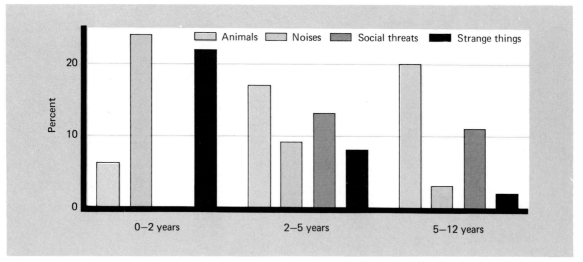

Figure 11-2
The situations that cause fear in children. Note the change in the kinds of stimuli that evoke fear as children grow older. (After A. T. Jersild, F. V. Markley, and C. L. Jersild, *Children's fears, dreams, pleasant and unpleasant memories. Child Development Monographs* 1933, No. 12.)

played. Elation and affection are shown between 6 and 12 months. At about 16 months the child will express jealousy.

As the range of emotions increases, the number of stimuli that trigger the emotions increases too. Much of this occurs simply because the child's capacity to assimilate experience increases—his world is getting larger every day. Which stimuli produce which emotions is also learned, either directly or by imitation. A child bitten by a snake will, of course, fear it in the future (direct experience). But a mother who screams when her 3-year-old presents her with a wriggling garter snake will probably also teach this response to the child (imitation).

Emotions toward something can also be triggered by stimulus generalization. Suppose you dislike a person named Eric. He may be a perfectly nice fellow, and nothing you have learned about him ought to make him distasteful to you. None of your friends sees anything wrong with him, so your response cannot be imitative, either. But Eric happens to look very much like the playground bully who always pushed you off the swings in kindergarten, and without knowing it you may be responding to your Eric as you did to the bully you were scared of 15 years ago. In a sense, of course, your dislike of Eric *is* learned—only you learned it, not from Eric himself, but from your association of him with someone else. You are generalizing your response (fear) from one stimulus (the bully in kindergarten) to another (Eric).

Aronfreed (1968) suggests that being able to internalize emotional stimuli may actually be the first step toward emotional self-control and thus represents an important milestone in a child's development. As Aronfreed describes the process, the child learns to associate his behavior with the way other people respond to it and how that makes him feel. The child internalizes this sequence and may begin to feel pleasure or fear when he only thinks of doing something that he has

(*Olive R. Pierce, Photo Researchers*)

learned will be either praised or punished. For example, a little boy wants to take a toy away from his sister but decides not to, because his fear of punishment outweighs the pleasure he might get from playing with the toy. Aronfreed notes that internalization is facilitated when the child has a close and rewarding attachment to an adult.

Another theory explains emotional development in terms of the balance between epinephrine and norepinephrine. Earlier we noted that a high level of norepinephrine is associated with anger that is outwardly directed and that a high level of epinephrine is associated with inner-directed anger (Funkenstein et al., 1953). In later research, Funkenstein and his colleagues (1957) noted that there seems to be an overabundance of norepinephrine in childhood. Usually this imbalance has been corrected by the time the person reaches adulthood. Funkenstein and his co-workers suggest that this gradually achieved balance could account for the development of emotional control. However, little research has been done in this area, and these ideas should be considered tentative.

Cognitive theory. As you will recall, the James-Lange theory of emotion held that you feel no emotion unless your body first undergoes certain physiological changes that are unique to the emotion you are experiencing. Seeing the bear is not what makes you afraid; you feel afraid because of your particular muscular and visceral reactions to seeing the bear. The Cannon-Bard theory, on the other hand, stated that the physiological responses are the same for every kind of emotion ranging from anger to delight, and that the stimulus is perceived and the emotion experienced in a certain part of the cerebral cortex in the same instant as, but completely independent of, the general physiological reactions occurring in the body.

Stanley Schachter (1970) has suggested a third description of emotional experience. He believes that our physiological arousal together with our perception and judgment of situations (cognition) jointly determine which emotions we feel. All our emotional states consist of a diffuse and general arousal of the nervous system. The situation we are in when we are aroused (the environment) gives us clues as to which particular name we should use for this general state of arousal. Thus, our cognitions tell us how to label our diffuse feelings in a way suitable to our current thoughts and ideas about our surroundings. On the other hand, although we have ideas about fear, sexuality, anger, and so on, we will not experience them as distinct emotions and call them such unless we are physiologically aroused to begin with.

Schachter and Singer (1962) performed an experiment to test the interaction of cognition and physiological arousal and to study how emotional states come to be labeled. The experimenters led a group of subjects to believe that they would be injected with a dose of "Suproxin" (a fictitious vitamin compound that was supposed to affect vision) and that they would be tested for its effects. They divided the subjects into two groups. They gave one group a placebo that had no physiological effect whatever. Then they gave the rest of the subjects injections of epinephrine, which produces general physiological arousal similar to emotional states. They divided these latter subjects into three subgroups. They accurately informed the first subgroup of epinephrine's effects; they told the second subgroup nothing; and they misinformed the third subgroup by telling them to expect side effects other than those epinephrine would produce. The placebo group was not told to expect any side effects.

The experimenters then exposed each subject separately to a stooge, supposedly another subject, who pretended to be either euphoric and friendly or angry and resentful. The experimenters observed the subjects through a two-way mirror in order to determine the extent to which they appeared to adopt the stooge's emotional state. Afterward, they gave the subjects a self-report questionnaire to find out how angry and irritated or happy and contented they felt.

Schachter and his co-workers discovered that those who were ignorant or misinformed about the effects of epinephrine-Suproxin were much more emotionally aroused—that is, more euphoric or angry—than those who knew what the drug would do and knew what to expect. These data support Schachter's idea that, if there is little physiological difference between emotional states, then our cognitions (perceptions and expectations) must tell us what emotion we are experiencing.

Schachter (1970) supported his theory by showing that people have to learn from others which emotions to experience when smoking marijuana. Marijuana is similar in a way to epinephrine, in that it produces vague, diffuse physiological arousal that first-time users find difficult to describe. The beginning smoker learns to label his physiological symptoms as "high"—that is, other people teach him to identify the physiological changes and to interpret them.

Stuart Valins (1966) performed an interesting experiment that shows the extent to which even minor cues control an individual's emotions. Valins showed a group of male subjects pictures of female nudes and arranged his equipment so that the subjects could hear their own heartbeats as each slide was shown. He deceived one group by substituting a recording that contained first increasing, then decreasing heart rates. He found that his deceived subjects found those nudes most attractive that had been accompanied by what they thought was their own increasing heart rate.

Magda Arnold (1960) also believes that cognitive processes control how we interpret our feelings and how we act on them. She emphasizes the function of appraisal: we first evaluate an incoming stimulus on the basis of whether it is "good," "bad," or "indifferent." If it is good we approach it, if bad we avoid it, if indifferent we ignore it. Our appraisal of any new stimulus is determined by our memories of past

Figure 11-3
A summary of the four
major theories of emotion.
According to the
James-Lange theory, the
body first responds
physiologically to a
stimulus, and then the
cerebral cortex determines
which emotion is being
experienced. In the Cannon-
Bard theory, impulses are
sent simultaneously to the
cerebral cortex and the
peripheral nervous system.
Thus the stimulus is
responded to and the
emotion is experienced at
the same time, but
independently. Stanley
Schachter proposes that the
cerebral cortex and the
peripheral nervous system
work jointly to determine
which emotions we feel.
Magda Arnold emphasizes
our appraisal of the
situation and thus feels that
the emotions we experience
and our physiological
responses are both
determined by the cerebral
cortex.

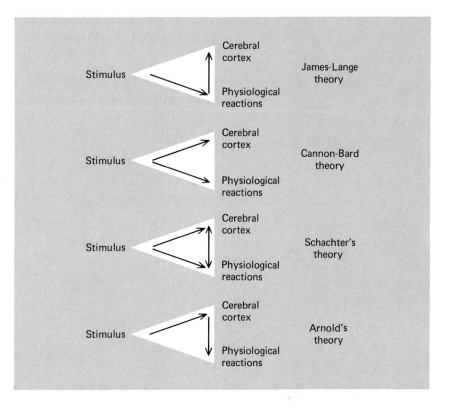

experiences and our simultaneous imagining of various ways of coping with the situation and whether it will be good or bad for us. These appraisals are thought to be almost instantaneous, and they precede any physiological responses, emotional feelings, or actions. For example, if you are picnicking in a field and see a bull is coming toward you, your appraisal of the situation will be based on memories of being told that bulls are dangerous, of crossing traffic intersections in front of fast-moving trucks, of seeing accident victims or wounded matadors, imagining what will happen if you stay where you are, and so on. You will then have a physiological response—you will feel afraid—and this will produce a direct action—you will get up and run for your life.

Richard Lazarus (1966, 1968; Lazarus, Averill, & Opton, 1970) carries Arnold's position a few steps further. He grants that cognitive appraisal governs our emotional responses but believes that each emotion requires a different kind of appraisal. He also breaks emotional responses down into separate components, unique to each particular emotion. These components include many different physiological changes and responses such as facial expressions and body postures that result from the urge to action. He also analyzes in detail the way our appraisals interact with the environment. Each of us is predisposed to look for and respond to certain stimuli, and these predispositions

(Jim Jowers, Nancy Palmer
Photo Agency)

Three basic "families" of emotion are present in that little scene. A is frustrated and angry. B is fearful and anxious. C is happy and experiencing a sense of release and joy.

Psychological studies have made still finer distinctions between emotions. One study (Plutchik, 1962) lists eight basic emotions: destruction, reproduction, incorporation, orientation, protection, deprivation, rejection, and exploration. Other studies have maintained that there are more, still others that there are fewer. It does not appear that any single scheme for classifying emotions is likely to be very successful in dealing with the complexity of our emotional experiences.

As an alternative, there are several *dimensions* of emotion, which may help us to make distinctions among them. We will treat three here: approach/avoidance, intensity, and pleasantness/unpleasantness.

Approach/avoidance. When you see someone you like coming down the street, you walk toward him. When a car in the opposite lane looks as if it is out of control, you do what you can to stay out of its path. When you see your dog making off with the steak that was on the kitchen counter, you run after him.

To some extent we can classify emotions in terms of whether they cause us to turn toward or away from the object that arouses them (Arnold, 1960). If we are using the idea of three basic emotions cited in the thunderstorm example, this is very clear. The person who loves storms goes to the window and wants to go out in the lightning and rain. The person who fears them would hide in a closet if he could and wants to avoid a confrontation with the lightning by turning off the electricity in the house. The person who is angry is frustrated because he cannot "get at" the storm itself, so he uses the television set as a substitute (he would probably like to kick it). In general, it can be said that the emotional "family" that includes such things as love, affection, and pleasure makes us want to approach something. The second broad category—the one that includes things like fear and anxiety—makes us want to *avoid* something. With anger, the third category, we are again moved to approach something, but in an aggressive or attacking way.

The Funkenstein experiment we described earlier noted some physiological differences between fear and anger. Another way they have been differentiated is by the response of *flight* or *fight*. Whether we move away from something because we fear it or move toward it because we are angry seems to depend on how we feel about the object and about ourselves in relation to it. If we feel we are helpless, that we have no hope of controlling the object or situation, we want to avoid it. If the appearance of an obstacle to our wishes makes us feel we want to pit ourselves against it, we move toward it so as to grapple with it. The same situation, of course, can evoke flight reactions in some people and fight reactions in others. Consider a burning apartment house. Some of the residents may feel helpless to stop the fire from spreading and will try to save themselves by running away. Others may feel so angry that they stay and fight. Fear and anger toward a specific object can be mixed in ourselves as well. A person who meets a mugger on a dark street may be undecided whether he should try to run or fight off the assault.

Intensity. Another dimension of emotion—a way of explaining how we can have such a wide range of emotional experience if there are so few basic kinds of emotion—is intensity. If you get to the post office one minute after closing time, your basic emotion could probably be categorized as anger. If you only wanted to buy some stamps, the anger will take the form of mild annoyance. But if you are mailing in your income tax form and it has to be postmarked by midnight that night, you will feel something stronger—rage or fury.

Some psychologists believe intensity to be the sole characteristic of emotion, that the level of arousal is the only thing that makes it possible to tell one emotion from another. This **activation theory** holds that all behavior lies along a continuum of activity, from the low level of sleep to high excitement, with all the stages in between. Duffy (1941) rejected emotion as a separate class of behavior. In her view, the only thing that distinguishes emotion from other forms of behavior is a much higher level of intensity. This idea was amplified by Lindsley (1951). A particular brainwave (EEG) pattern, he declared, appears in all emotional arousal. This he termed the "activation pattern." In 1970,

Figure 11-4
Plutchik's three-dimensional model of the emotions. Intensity is represented on the vertical dimension, ranging from maximum intensity at the top to a state of deep sleep at the bottom. The model tapers inward at the bottom to indicate that emotions are less distinguishable at low intensities. (From *The Emotions: Facts, Theories, and a New Model,* by Robert Plutchik. New York: Random House, 1962, p. 111.)

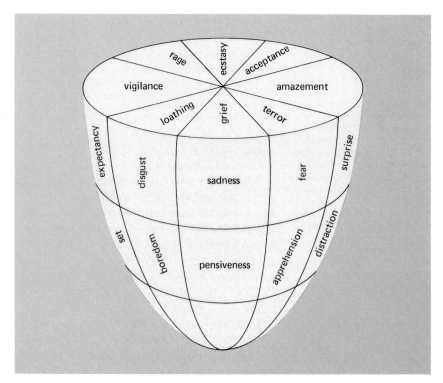

Lindsley revised his theory to include the influence of the reticular activating system, the thalamus, and the cerebral cortex on the processing of emotion.

Most psychologists, however, consider intensity to be only one aspect of emotion. We mentioned earlier that Plutchik proposes eight broad groups of emotion, which he believes are founded on basic human and animal instincts. Within these groups, he feels, it is intensity that distinguishes one emotion from another. Under "deprivation," for example, he lists, in descending order of intensity, grief, sorrow, sadness, dejection, gloominess, and pensiveness. Of all these emotions it could be said that we feel something lacking in our lives. But whether we feel deprived of a beloved person or money to buy a new car would determine the intensity of our emotion.

Pleasant/unpleasant. Photographs of the faces of patients undergoing electroshock therapy and of the faces of people at the height of physical ecstasy show such similar physical characteristics that it would be impossible to distinguish one from the other. It has also been suggested that Mona Lisa's smile might have been caused by a slight case of indigestion, not by contentment. This brings us to the most obvious dimension we use in classifying emotion: Is what we are feeling pleasant or unpleasant? Sometimes, of course, pleasant and unpleasant emotions can be intermingled, as in poets' descriptions of love, or when

you get a B minus on a paper when you had hoped for a B but feared it would be a C. But usually, when we say we have "mixed feelings" toward something, it is quite easy to separate those feelings and describe each of them as being pleasant or unpleasant.

The Function of Emotion

Imagine a world entirely without emotions. This book would be a little shorter to get through, yes—but what would it be like to move through a world of things you felt nothing about, like flipping through the pages of an unused coloring book? The nearest we might get to imagining such an environment might be thinking of sitting alone in a large white box, with no stimuli whatever. But even given such an environment, you would feel things—probably boredom in particular.

Anyway, emotion *does* exist, and this raises our final question. How does it function in our lives? What is it good, or bad, for?

Emotions and Attitudes

When we discussed the cognitive theory, we were talking about how cognition affected emotion. But that question can also be turned around. How does emotion affect the way we think? One interesting study by Rosenberg (1960) explored the relations between emotions and attitudes. Rosenberg took a group of people whose attitudes toward blacks' moving into their neighborhoods were very negative. Then he hypnotized the people and told them:

> *You will be very much in favor of Negroes moving into white neighborhoods. The mere idea of Negroes moving into white neighborhoods will give you a happy, exhilarated feeling* (Rosenberg, 1960).

After the subjects were brought out of the hypnotic trance, Rosenberg found significant changes in their values and in their beliefs about blacks. The same people who had previously reacted negatively to the suggestion of blacks' moving into white neighborhoods would now vigorously defend their new belief that blacks would *not*, after all, cause a lowering of property values. When confronted with their earlier beliefs, they indicated that they had simply been wrong. Rosenberg went on to demonstrate the same results with people's attitudes toward U.S. foreign aid—once again he found that changing people's feelings led to a change in their beliefs and attitudes. In both cases, after the posthypnotic suggestion was removed, the beliefs shifted back toward what they had been before the experiment.

Emotions: Disruptive or Adaptive?

Under what circumstances does emotion hinder what we do? Under what circumstances does it help? There seems to be no single, simple answer. It is largely a question of degree—both the strength of the emotion and the difficulty of the task. The *Yerkes-Dodson law* formulates it this way: The more complex the task at hand, the lower the level of emotion that can be tolerated without interfering with performance. You may feel very angry while boiling an egg and it may not make much difference, but the same degree of emotion may interfere with your ability to drive safely.

Some psychologists feel that a certain minimum level of emotional arousal is necessary for good performance. Thus, if you did not care at all about an exam you were taking, you would probably not do as well as you would if you were at least somewhat aroused. On the other hand, a high level of anxiety may affect your performance for the worse. On the most mechanical level, if your hands are trembling and your palms are sweaty, the normally automatic job of writing legibly will occupy the attention you could otherwise direct toward the questions to be answered. In one study (Sarason, 1961), children were asked, "Do you worry a lot when you are taking a test?" Sarason found that those who did—the high-anxiety children—did not perform well on conventional tests of mental ability, verbal learning, or creative reasoning.

We have all probably had the experience of being in a situation where we desperately wanted to think rationally but were unable to

SHOULD YOU HOLD IT IN OR LET IT OUT?

Some influential psychotherapists believe that a person who lets out his pent-up anger and aggressiveness will free himself of inhibitions, tensions, and muscular aches and pains and enjoy deeper, healthier relationships with others. According to this view, people who are afraid to express their hostilities directly should either fantasize situations where they physically attack the object of their anger or overtly express their anger by beating a pillow. This kind of therapy encourages people to "ventilate" their emotions spontaneously without guilt.

However, according to Leonard Berkowitz (1973), some behavior theorists have questioned the value of ventilation techniques in reducing internal aggression. They cite experimental evidence which shows that while people who are rewarded for acting out anger in therapy sessions do lose their inhibitions and have less anxiety, they also become more, not less, aggressive in the outside world. The acting out of emotions verbally or physically, therefore, may not purge people of their aggressiveness, but instead may reinforce it and ensure that people resort to it more often in the future. These psychologists recommend instead that a person resolve his anger by describing his feelings to the other person instead of attacking him verbally or physically.

because our emotions had disrupted our concentration. Sometimes the emotion is related to the task at hand—as when you are so eager to get a job that you put your foot in your mouth during the interview. Sometimes the emotion is entirely irrelevant to the task. "I can't sleep, I can't eat," says the popular song about someone who has just fallen in love—even less likely is it that he could do a decent job of changing a typewriter ribbon.

On the other hand, the proposal has been put forth that emotions can organize and direct behavior, just as motives can. Leeper (1948) gives the example of a family who heard that an arsonist was in the neighborhood. First the family perceived the situation as it related to them, finding that one of the rooms of their house was a firetrap. They learned about possible protective devices and had them installed. Their performance was focused because of their anxiety about fire.

Emotions as Motives

The example of the family threatened by the arsonist brings us to another way that emotion can function in our lives. It can motivate us—give us reasons for approaching or avoiding things. It is a truism in advertising that people can be made to buy a given product by manipulating one of two emotions—desire or fear. A car may be advertised as a sexual object, so that the emotion of desire is aroused. On the other hand, a mouthwash commercial may make us afraid that if we do not use that product, people will shrink from us on the street.

EMOTION: PRO AND CON

Psychologists generally agree that most of our behavior is irrational—that is, it is controlled by emotion. But Leeper (1948) points to a curious contradiction. Traditionally, psychologists (and most others in our society) have held the emotions in low repute. Popular psychology tells us to gain maturity by "controlling our emotions." In the laboratory, too, psychologists usually think of emotional responses as a disorganized—and disorganizing—aspect of behavior.

Why? One reason may be that in Western society, technology is king. Technology requires facts. Thus, intellectual skills are highly valued, and we look down upon those who seem to be swayed by their feelings. Behind this lies the Western philosophy of rationalism, which sees reason as the one thing that sets us apart from the animals. As a result, Western culture has often viewed emotions as nasty, frightening, and destructive.

Leeper, however, refuses to accept the notion that reactions like fear and anger are "disorganized." On the contrary, they seem to mobilize the person to act (though not necessarily the way the researcher wants him to!).

Our culture, too, shows some signs of changing its low opinion of feelings. "Jesus freaks" have resurrected the revival meeting, with all its fervent outbursts. Staid teachers, bankers, and businessmen undergo sensitivity training to get in touch with their own and others' feelings. Anti-intellectualism is sweeping the campus, as students practice Yoga instead of studying logic. Whether these are trends or fads is still not clear, but meanwhile psychologists (using rational methods) may be clearing emotion's bad name.

We approach or avoid something and respond to its pleasantness or unpleasantness according to the emotion we feel for it. If we think of emotion as what makes action—for or against, backward or forward—possible, we realize that a world without emotion would be almost entirely static. Dante ends his *Divine Comedy* on perhaps the most cosmic and universal application of emotion to motivation that there could be: he speaks of "the love that moves the sun and other stars." Our way of saying it would be, "Love makes the world go round." So do hate, fear, contentment, rage, anxiety, guilt, and joy.

The Communication of Emotion

Sometimes you are vaguely aware that a given person makes you feel ill at ease. When pressed to be more precise, you might say, "You never know what he is thinking." But you do not mean that you never know his opinion of the movie he saw last week or what he thought about the election. Probably it would be more accurate to say that you do not know what he is *feeling*. Almost all of us conceal our emotions to some extent, to protect our self-image or conform to social conventions. But usually there are some clues to help us determine another person's emotions.

Verbal Communication

It would be simplest, of course, if we could just ask someone what he is feeling. Sometimes we do, with more or less successful results. If your mother finishes drying the dishes and says acidly, "I hope you are enjoying your novel," her words are perfectly clear, but you know quite well that she is not saying what she really means. If she were to say, "I'm furious that you didn't offer to help," she would be giving you an accurate report of her emotions at that moment.

For various reasons, we may not be able or willing to report our emotions accurately. There are some situations in which people simply do not know what their emotions are. The parent of an abused and battered child may sincerely profess his affection for the child, yet his actions reflect an additional set of emotions, which are otherwise hidden, even from the parent himself. Sometimes, even when we are aware of our emotions, we diminish the degree of emotion we are feeling—as when we say we are "a little worried" about an upcoming exam, when actually we are terrified. Or we may deny the emotion entirely, especially if it is negative. This may be done out of politeness or out of self-protection, as when we claim to like someone either because we do not want to hurt him or because we feel we *should* like him.

Psychologists have traditionally considered verbal reports to be inadequate because people can use the same word in so many different ways. Joel Davitz (1969, 1970) investigated what exactly people refer to when they label their emotional states. He interviewed 1,200 people, asking them to remember times when they had experienced a certain emotion and to describe that experience. He then compiled a checklist of thousands of short statements, each one describing some aspect of a particular emotional state. For example, here is part of the composite definition of "happiness":

> *There is an inner warm glow, a radiant sensation; I feel like smiling; there is a sense of well being, a sense of harmony and peace within; I'm optimistic and cheerful; the world seems basically good and beautiful. . . . I think about beautiful things; I feel safe and secure. . . . My movements are graceful and easy; I feel especially well coordinated; there is a general release, a lessening of tension. . . .*
>
> *There is a sense of being more alive, I am excited in a calm way. . . . There is a particularly acute awareness of pleasurable things, their sounds, their colors, and textures. . . . Colors seem brighter, sounds clearer, movements more vivid.*
>
> *. . . I have a sense of sureness, I feel strong inside, taller, stronger, bigger; there is a sense of being important and worthwhile, a sense of more confidence in myself. . . . I feel clean, as if I look especially good; there is a sense of being more substantial, of existing, of being real (Davitz, 1970, pp. 254–255).*

Davitz discovered that there is widespread agreement about what emotional labels mean in terms of physical sensations, perceptions, relationships to others and oneself, actions, self-expression, and, finally, how long the experience lasts and how it changes while it is occurring. He then analyzed the results statistically and discovered a definite, logical order in all the verbal descriptions. Four dimensions consistently emerged in every emotional experience: *activation,* which includes impulses to act or not to act; *relatedness to the environment,* meaning whether one feels like moving toward, against, or away; *hedonic tone,* which reflects the degree of pleasure in terms of comfort, discomfort, or tension; and *competence,* the degree to which one feels adequate, inadequate, competent, incompetent, satisfied, or dissatisfied.

Nonverbal Communication

At a county fair, a political rally, or a football game, a pickpocket goes to work. Standing behind someone, he is preparing to relieve him of his wallet. Slowly the hand moves toward the back pocket, is almost touching the wallet, then—he pulls his hand back empty and moves casually away through the crowd, whistling unconcernedly. Why did he stop? What gave him a clue that the man was ready to catch him in the act? To any pickpocket skillful enough to stay out of jail, it could have been one of a number of signs. The hairs on the back of the intended victim's neck might have bristled slightly. There might have been a slight stiffening of the back, a twitch in a neck muscle, a subtle change in skin color, an outbreak of perspiration. The man might not yet have been aware that his pocket was being picked, but these physiological signals indicated an awareness that something was afoot.

As we noted earlier, these physiological changes are not normally under our control. They tend to function independently of our wanting them to, often, indeed, against our will. Actions speak louder than words, as the saying goes, and people are often more eloquent than they realize or intend. We transmit a great deal of information to others through our facial expressions, body postures, vocal intonations, and physical distance, and our bodies often send emotional messages that contradict our words.

Facial expressions are the most obvious emotional indicators. We can tell a lot about a person's emotional state by observing whether he is laughing, crying, smiling, or frowning. Many facial expressions are innate, not learned; children who are born deaf and blind use the same facial gestures to express the same emotions as normal children do. Charles Darwin observed that most animals share a common pattern of muscular facial movements—for example, dogs, tigers, and men all bare their teeth in rage. Some human facial expressions of emotion are universal; others are unique (Izard, 1971).

In his study of facial movements, Ray Birdwhistell (1952) has determined that the most expressive emotional signals are transmitted by

(Walter Chandoha)

the shape and disposition of the mouth, nose, and eyebrows. While most people can recognize widely differing emotions in facial expressions, they do tend to confuse some emotions with others, such as fear with surprise (Tomkins & McCarter, 1964). Thompson and Meltzer (1964) designed an experiment to see if certain emotions were easier to express facially than others. They found that most people have no trouble expressing love, fear, determination, and happiness, but suffering, disgust, and contempt are significantly more difficult to express—and to recognize. In another experiment with male and female subjects, Drag and Shaw (1967) found that women were better than men at recognizing happiness, fear, love, and anger in facial expressions.

Most people consider the eyes to be the most expressive part of the face. One of the surest indicators of someone's mental state is the size of the pupils; the pupils of your eyes enlarge involuntarily whenever you see something pleasant or attractive. This item of information has enabled TV advertisers to make more effective commercials by first showing trial commercials to selected viewers and noting what makes their pupils widen (Fast, 1970).

The rest of the body also sends significant messages, particularly through position and posture. This has been called *body language.* When we are relaxed, we tend to sprawl back in a chair; when tense, to sit more stiffly with our feet together. Slumping, crossing of the arms and legs, straightness of the back—all these supply clues to which emotion someone is feeling. Ray Birdwhistell (1952) has made the study of body language into a science called *kinesics.* He believes that every movement of the body has a meaning, that no movement is accidental, and that all of our significant gestures and movements are learned.

Birdwhistell has also studied the relationship between verbal and body languages. Every ethnic group has its own characteristic set of body motions; the differences between, say, French, German, and English body gestures are as great as those between their respective

NONVERBAL CUES AND YOUR ABILITY TO DETECT THEM

Beier (1974) studied nonverbal cues between 50 newlywed couples to determine the degree of harmony or conflict in each relationship. During videotaped interviews, he observed that contented harmonious couples showed their feelings of security and well-being by talking to each other more, looking into each other's eyes more often, sitting close together, and touching each other more than themselves. Couples who were having trouble getting along communicated their anxiety and insecurity by touching themselves more than each other, avoiding each other's eyes, and sitting with their arms and legs crossed.

In another study, Beier (1974) tested people's ability to project their emotions accurately. He had his subjects act out on videotape six emotions: anger, fear, seductiveness, indifference, happiness, and sadness. He found that most of his subjects could successfully portray at most two out of the six and that the rest of their portrayals did not reflect their intentions. One girl appeared angry no matter what emotion she tried to project; another invariably appeared seductive. This finding supported his belief that we often misinform others around us by our "discordant" behavior—that is, we may want to express one emotion, such as affection, but we actually communicate a contradictory one, such as dislike.

Just as people send out complex and contradictory emotional messages by nonverbal cues, so do they show considerable variety in their ability to read the messages. Rosenthal and his co-workers (1974) developed a test of sensitivity to nonverbal cues—the Profile of Nonverbal Sensitivity (PONS)—that assesses the ability to judge the meaning of vocal intonations and face and body movements.

The subjects watch a film that shows an actress or actor portraying various emotional states; sometimes the portrayal is accompanied by spoken phrases, but certain tones and rhythms that identify them as distinct words have been removed. The viewer that selects one of two possible interpretations of the scene.

The study revealed that women were consistently better than men in understanding nonverbal cues, although men in the "nurturant" professions—psychiatrists, psychologists, mental hospital aides, and teachers—along with artists, actors, and designers scored as highly as women. The authors offer some explanations for women's superior performance. One is that motherhood seems to demand an ability to interpret nonverbal behavior in very young children. Another explanation is that women are traditionally an oppressed group, and oppressed groups have always had to learn to be subtle and vigilant in order to survive. The study also showed that sensitivity to nonverbal cues increases with age, probably because the young have not had the necessary experience in judging vocal tones and observing body movements.

vocabularies. Birdwhistell noted this in old newsreels of Fiorello La-Guardia, New York City's famous mayor who was fluent in Italian, Yiddish, and English. Birdwhistell found that with the sound track off, he could identify which language LaGuardia was speaking by simply observing his accompanying hand gestures (Birdwhistell, 1974). On the other hand, many body gestures that accompany speech often contradict the verbal message. In a family, for example, one might notice first that the mother seems always to defer verbally to her husband and children by asking for and taking their advice; but a closer inspection reveals her to be the true leader as she crosses her legs first, and all the other family members unconsciously imitate her (Fast, 1970).

Another kind of body communication is *distance*. The normal distance between people definitely differs from culture to culture. Two Swedes standing around and talking would ordinarily stand much farther apart than two Arabs or Greeks. Within every culture, there seems to be a distance which is generally agreed to be appropriate for normal conversation. If someone is standing closer than usual to you, it may indicate aggressiveness or sexuality; if farther away than usual, withdrawal or repugnance.

Figure 11-6
An example of body language. Three members of this group are showing cohesiveness by the way they have copied each other's posture. The man on the right is partially mimicking his friends, but apparently prefers to be somewhat aloof.
(Jerry Dantzic)

CULTURAL PATTERNS OF EMOTIONAL EXPRESSION

When angry, some Americans speak loudly and wave their arms about. Others speak softly, and look around for the culturally prescribed big stick. Most of us are aware that different persons and groups in our culture have different ways of physically expressing their emotions. Physical expressions of emotions also vary among cultures.

The psychologist Otto Klineberg (1938) became interested in these cultural differences and devised a unique method to study them. His "novel" approach was to take several classic and modern Chinese works of fiction and examine how the emotions of the characters were represented in physical descriptions. He discovered both similarities to and differences from Western styles of expressing emotion.

Fear, for example, is described in similar fashion in Chinese and Western literature. Chinese examples include "Everyone trembled with a face the color of clay" and "Every one of his hairs stood on end, and the pimples came out on the skin all over his body."

Other emotions were manifested quite differently. "They stretched out their tongues" conveys surprise to the Chinese, not the insolence or teasing it suggests to us. Anger is shown in Chinese fiction by the eyes growing round and opening wide. Indeed, the Chinese assume that people can die of anger.

Fainting is as common in Chinese novels as in Western fiction, but the Chinese faint in anger. From the Chinese viewpoint, the delicate Victorian maidens who cultivated the fine art of fainting from fear would have been responding inappropriately.

Klineberg's study, with its innovative methodology, demonstrated the cultural variability of overt expressions of emotion. Similar gestures, body postures, or physical movements often convey drastically different emotional meanings in different cultures. We express our emotions in the style we have learned.

(Suzanne Szasz, Photo Researchers)

(Rene Burri, Magnum Photos)

Our explicit *acts* themselves, of course, also serve as nonverbal clues. A 2:00 A.M. telephone call indicates that the caller feels what he has to say is urgent. A slammed door tells us that the person who left the room is angry. If someone comes over for a visit and you ask him into the living room, you are probably not as much at ease with him as if you were to sit down together at the kitchen table. *Gestures*, like a slap on the back or an embrace, can indicate feelings. Whether a person shakes your hand briefly or for a long time, firmly or limply, can tell you something about what he feels toward you.

A word of caution is necessary here. Although overt behavior can be useful as a clue to emotion, it is not always infallible. The sound of laughing and crying are similar, for example, and we bare our teeth in smiles as well as snarls. Crying can "mean" sorrow, joy, anger, nostalgia, or that you have just been slicing an onion. Moreover, as with verbal reports, it is always possible that someone is putting out false clues. And we have all done something thoughtlessly—turned our backs, frowned because we were thinking about something else, laughed at the wrong time—that has given offense because these acts were taken to express an emotion that we were not, in fact, feeling at that time.

Summary

1. Emotions are complex affective experiences that involve diffuse physiological changes and can be expressed overtly in characteristic behavior patterns.

2. Emotion begins with the registration of an external stimulus in the reticular activating system, whose function is arousal. At this point only the dimension of intensity is involved, and the emotion is not differentiated until the message of arousal reaches the limbic system. The hypothalamus is extremely important in the differentiation process, in activating the endocrine system, and as a pathway to and from the cortex, which interprets the incoming messages and organizes them into systematic reactions. This is particularly important in the experience of pleasure and pain. The exact connection between these physiological components is not yet known in detail, but there are several theories about how these physiological changes relate to the psychological experiences of emotion.

3. According to the *James-Lange theory*, emotion is the result of visceral reactions. The perception of a stimulus causes the body to undergo certain physiological changes, and these changes are the cause of emotions.

4. The *Cannon-Bard theory*, unlike the James-Lange theory, holds that emotions and bodily responses occur simultaneously, not one after another. When a stimulus is perceived, nerve impulses pass through the thalamus, where they split, some going to the cortex (where the stimulus is perceived and the emotional response is experienced) and some to the muscles and viscera (where the physiological reactions take place).

5. The more advanced an animal is on the evolutionary scale, the greater the number and complexity of external stimuli that will arouse its emotions and the more important the role of learning in arousing emotion. Other evidence indicates that the capacity to respond emotionally to a given stimulus increases with age. As we become more sophisticated emotionally, both the range of our emotions and the number of stimuli that triggers them increase. Which stimuli produce which emotions is often learned, either through direct experience or by imitation.

6. The *cognitive theory* holds that emotion results from the interaction of cognitive and physiological processes. Most emotional states are quite diffuse, and many emotions are accompanied by essentially the same physiological reaction. According to the cognitive theorists, our interpretation is affected by events and people in the environment, by memories of past experiences, and by our predisposition to look for and respond to certain stimuli, and our culture.

7. Various attempts have been made to classify emotions, but no single scheme has yet been wholly successful in dealing with the richness and complexity of emotional experiences. There are, however, several *dimensions* of emotion that may help to make distinctions among them— approach/avoidance, intensity, and pleasantness/unpleasantness.

8. The *approach/avoidance* dimension differentiates emotions on the basis of whether we tend to move toward or away from the object that is causing the emotion. Such emotions as love, affection, and pleasure make us want to approach something, while emotions such as fear and anxiety make us want to avoid the object. Fear and anger have also been differentiated by the responses of *flight* or *fight*. Whether we want to move away from something we fear or move toward it because we are angry depends on how we feel about the situation and about ourselves in relationship to it.

9. Another way to differentiate emotions is by their *intensity*. The *activation theory* states that all behavior lies along a continuum of activity, from the low level of sleep to high excitement, and that the only way to distinguish

one emotion from another is by its intensity. Most psychologists, however, consider intensity to be only one aspect of emotion.

10. The most obvious dimension used in classifying emotion is whether what we are feeling is *pleasant* or *unpleasant*. We usually know whether we like or dislike what we are responding to. Even when we have mixed feelings about something, it is usually quite easy to separate them and describe each of them as being pleasant or unpleasant.

11. Emotions function in our lives in several ways. The way we feel about something affects our attitudes toward it. Experiments have shown that when emotions are changed, attitudes and beliefs may also change. Emotions can be either disruptive or adaptive. The *Yerkes-Dodson law* says that the more complex the task at hand, the lower the level of emotion that can be tolerated without interfering with performance. On the other hand, emotions can organize and direct behavior just as motives can. Emotions can provide strong motivations to approach or avoid things.

12. *Verbal reports* do not always give a complete picture of what a person is feeling, because people may be unable or unwilling to report their emotions accurately. Recent research into people's descriptions of various emotions has demonstrated, however, that there is wide general agreement among laymen about what our emotional labels mean.

13. *Nonverbal communication*—facial expressions, position, posture, distance between people, explicit acts, and gestures—can all be useful clues to emotion. In many cases, nonverbal communication can contradict a person's verbal message. Many facial expressions do not appear to be learned, and many are universal. Although each culture has its own distinct "vocabulary" of facial expressions and gestures, most people have only minor difficulty in recognizing many emotions when they are nonverbally displayed by people from other cultures.

Suggested Readings

Arnold, M. B., *Emotion and Personality,* 2 vols. (New York: Columbia University Press, 1960). A thorough discussion of contemporary views of emotion, with a detailed presentation of Arnold's theory that the emotion we feel depends largely on our cognitive appraisal of a situation.

Cofer, C. N., *Motivation and Emotion* (Glenview, Ill.: Scott, Foresman, 1972). A short overview of current issues in emotion.

Darwin, C., *The Expression of the Emotions in Man and Animals* (Chicago: University of Chicago Press, 1965). A reprint of Darwin's 1872 classic, with an introduction by Konrad Lorenz.

Davitz, J. R., *The Language of Emotion* (New York: Academic Press, 1969). A good discussion of labeling, language, and attribution in the learning and use of emotion.

London, H., and Nisbett, R. E., *Thought and Feeling: Cognitive Alteration of Feeling States* (Chicago: Aldine, 1974). A good summary of cognitive theory.

Plutchik, R., *The Emotions: Facts, Theories, and a New Model* (New York: Random House, 1962). An interesting presentation of the notion that there are eight basic emotions common to all animals, including humans.

Schachter, S., *Emotion, Obesity, and Crime* (New York: Academic Press, 1971). A stimulating account of the author's research in these three areas and his reasons for supporting the cognitive theory of emotion.

Selye, H., *The Stress of Life* (New York: McGraw-Hill, 1956). An excellent explanation of the role of the endocrine glands and the nervous system in adjusting to the constant changes people encounter.

FIVE

Psychology and the Individual

outline

CONSTITUTIONAL THEORY 424

PSYCHOANALYTIC THEORY 425

Sigmund Freud
Carl Jung
Alfred Adler
Karen Horney
Erich Fromm
Erik Erikson

SELF THEORY 438

Origin of Personality
Development of the Self

TRAIT THEORY 439

Development and Classification of Traits
Measurement of Traits
Alternate Views of Trait Theory

PERSONALITY ASSESSMENT 448

The Interview
Observation
Objective Tests
Measuring Values
Projective Tests

SUMMARY 458

SUGGESTED READINGS 462

Personality

Personality is one of those words that roll easily off our tongues. But try to define personality, and it seems like you have been asked to remove a piece of chewing gum from your mouth and divide it with a knife into 16 equal pieces. For our purposes here, we may say that personality consists of the characteristic behavior patterns, attitudes, motives, tendencies, outlooks, and emotional responses with which an individual reacts to others and to the environment. Personality is not just individuality; it is *consistency* of individuality. It is what accounts for our *usual* behavior. We might say that understanding another individual's personality is like an annual visit to some relatives: we don't know exactly what will occur during our visit, but we have a pretty good idea of what the atmosphere and possibilities will be.

But where does personality come from? Since the days of the ancient Greeks and Romans, philosophers and physicians have speculated about the causes of human behavior. But it was not until the late nineteenth century that scientists began to write down their clinical findings about personality and, on the basis of these observations, to formulate theories to explain the full range of a person's mental and emotional life. Personality theorists differ widely in their approach to problems of human behavior. Some emphasize the lasting influence of childhood experiences; others think that either heredity or the immediate environment is more important. Some theories were developed in therapy situations, from work with troubled people; others were formulated under the controlled conditions of the laboratory. In this chapter, we look briefly at some of the theories that have had the greatest impact on modern psychology.

Constitutional Theory

(© 1959 United Feature Syndicate, Inc.)

Probably the oldest theory of personality is one that suggests that there is a relationship between a person's body physique and his behavior. William Sheldon, an American psychologist who has studied the problem since 1924, has provided the most carefully researched and documented theory of personality based on body types.

Sheldon concluded that the human physique could be measured according to three basic dimensions: **endomorphy,** the size of the digestive organs; **mesomorphy,** the size of the skeleton and muscles; and **ectomorphy,** the area of the skin and nervous system. An extreme endomorph has a round, soft body with a large abdomen and relatively weak muscles and bone structure. An extreme mesomorph has a sturdy, upright body with strong bones and muscles. An extreme ectomorph is thin and fragile, with slender bones and poorly developed muscles. Most people have characteristics of all three types, though one of the three usually dominates.

Sheldon then devised a means of measuring temperament, or personality traits. He concluded that temperament could be rated according to three basic dimensions representing clusters of traits: **viscerotonia,** indicating general traits of sociability, relaxation, and love of food and physical comforts; **somatotonia,** characterized by aggressiveness, physical courage, love of adventure, and directness of manner; and **cerebrotonia,** indicating restraint, love of privacy, self-consciousness, and hypersensitivity. Sheldon observed that a person's somatotype compared very closely with his temperament. A chubby endomorph was apt to rate highest in characteristics of viscerotonia; those who rated high in somatotonia proved to be athletic mesomorphs; and the thin ectomorph was strongest in traits of cerebrotonia. It was Sheldon's belief that the psychological traits were in fact caused by the body types and that both traits and types were inborn and inherited.

The accuracy of Sheldon's findings has been questioned by other researchers. For example, Sheldon did not have a person's physique and temperament rated independently by two separate researchers. The same investigator measured both the body build and the personality traits of an individual and could conceivably have assumed that a fat person had a jolly temperament or might unconsciously have associated cerebrotonic traits with an obvious ectomorph.

Figure 12-1
Sheldon's three basic somatotypes. The person on the left ranks high in endomorphy, the person in the center is high in mesomorphy, and the person on the right is high in ectomorphy. (After W. H. Sheldon, *The Varieties of Temperament.* New York: Harper & Row, 1942.)

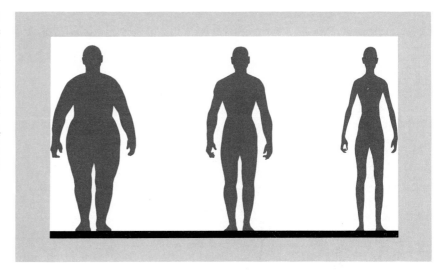

Sheldon's theory has also been criticized because it does not take into account a person's natural reaction to his own physique. An undersized ectomorph, for example, will not usually adopt the role of domineering bully because he does not have the muscles. Also, society has formed stereotypes of persons with particular physiques, and often people are influenced to act in a certain way because that particular behavior is expected of them. However, Sheldon's work does indicate that there is some relationship, whatever the cause, between body physique and personality.

Psychoanalytic Theory

Sigmund Freud

To this day, Sigmund Freud continues to be the best-known and most influential of the personality theorists, for he opened up a whole new route for the study of human behavior. Up to his time, psychology had centered its attention on consciousness. Freud, however, stressed the unconscious. While many of his views have been modified by later research and Freud himself revised and expanded his beliefs throughout his life, his ideas still form the basis of psychoanalysis and have influenced our language, literature, customs, and child-rearing practices.

Freud came upon the technique that inspired his theory in a rather indirect way. He received his medical degree from the University of Vienna and then studied in Paris with Jean Charcot, a French psychiatrist who was successfully using hypnosis to treat patients with hysteria. When Freud began his own practice as a specialist in nervous disorders, he was dissatisfied with the results of conventional methods of treatment. At the suggestion of a friend, Dr. Josef Breuer, he began

Figure 12-2
The structural relationships of the systems of the mind. The ego is situated partly in the unconscious, partly in the conscious, and receives knowledge of the external world through the senses. Thoughts repressed by the ego are driven down into the unconscious. The superego lies partly in the conscious and partly in the unconscious. The id has contact with the external world only through the ego; the open space at the bottom of the diagram indicates the limitlessness of the unconscious id. (Adapted from a diagram by S. Freud, *The Complete Introductory Lectures on Psychoanalysis.* Trans. and ed. by James Strachey. New York: Norton, 1966.)

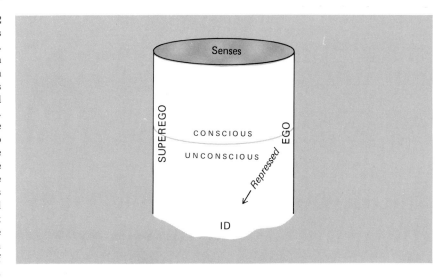

to use hypnosis to induce his patients to talk about their problems. Finding that he was unable to hypnotize all his patients, Freud encouraged them to talk directly about their difficulties, and from this he developed his psychoanalytic technique of "free association of ideas." He found that as patients mentioned their thoughts and described their dreams, they began to remember thoughts or events that they had forgotten or had repressed. Once these events were remembered, the patients could deal with them successfully. From his clinical work, then, Freud developed his theory to explain the structure of the personality.

The threefold structure of the mind. Freud believed that personality is composed of three interrelated parts: the id, the ego, and the superego. Unfortunately, through popular usage each of these terms has almost come to assume an identity of its own—somewhat as if id, ego, and superego were three little gremlins vying for control of the individual. But the three are actually parts of one integrated whole, and they interact so closely that few of their functions can be separated.

The **id** is the basic system of personality, the storehouse of energy from which the ego and superego develop. The id is completely unconscious and consists of all the basic drives or instincts an individual is born with. Since it is completely unconscious, the id can only be known indirectly, as it reveals itself in a person's dreams, actions, and behavior. Even the absent-minded mistakes we all make—the funny little errors known as "Freudian slips"—arise from the unconscious, and Freud considered them to have great significance in revealing the workings of the id.

Freud believed that the instinctual drives of the id—such as hunger, thirst, sex, and self-preservation—are the source of energy for personality. This energy is set in motion by a condition of deprivation, which results in discomfort or tension. The id has two means of relieving the discomfort. One is by reflex actions, such as coughing, which provide immediate relief for unpleasant sensations. Another is what Freud termed wish fulfillment or **primary process thinking:** the person can form a mental image of an object or situation that will relieve the uncomfortable feeling. Primary process thought is most clearly evident in dreams, but a person may also have a mental picture of a wish-fulfilling object or situation. On a hot, dusty day, for example, a very thirsty person may have a mental picture of himself lying under a shady tree, sipping a cool drink. However, although a mental image may give momentary relief, it cannot actually satisfy a need. Merely thinking about water does not reduce dehydration. Therefore, the id by itself is not very satisfactory in gratifying instincts. It must ultimately have contact with reality if it is to satisfactorily relieve its discomfort. The id's link to reality is the ego.

The **ego,** Freud thought, controls all thinking and reasoning activities. Through seeing, hearing, and touching, the ego takes in information about the external world. And the ego controls the ways of satisfying the id's drives in the external world. In seeking to rid itself of discomfort and to return to a comfortable state, the id acts according to the **pleasure principle.** The ego operates by the **reality principle**—that is, it acts to protect the person against dangers that might result from indiscriminate satisfaction of the cravings of the id. For example, a thirsty person who sees a bottle filled with liquid would be apt to pick up the bottle and drink the liquid. It does not occur to the id to see what is in the bottle first. The id only knows it is thirsty and wants a drink *now.* It is the ego that says, "Wait! That's poison! Let's go into

Figure 12-3
The pleasure principle expresses the basic tendency in human nature to avoid unpleasant experiences and seek only pleasant ones. The reality principle modifies the pleasure principle by using rational thought to find a safe means of satisfying the desire for pleasure.

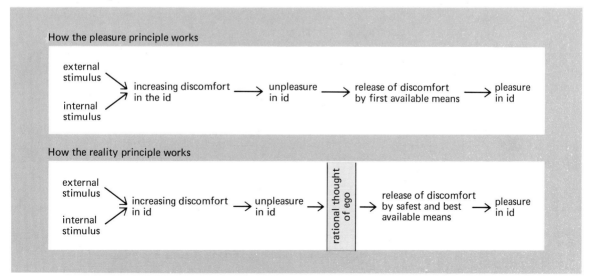

(*William Carter, Photo Researchers*)

the kitchen and get a drink of water instead." Thus, the ego tries by intelligent reasoning to delay appeasing a desire of the id until a means of successfully and safely satisfying that desire is at hand. Freud called this type of realistic thinking **secondary process thinking.**

The ego, then, has a directorial function in the personality. It derives its energy from the id and its task is to satisfy the desires of the id—but it must control the id and direct its energy into effective, realistic channels. Freud, who was very fond of analogies, compared the relationship of ego and id to that of a rider trying to guide a spirited horse. However, a personality consisting only of ego and id would be completely selfish—it would function effectively, but behave unsocially. Fully adult behavior is governed not just by reality but also by morality, that is, by the conscience or the moral standards that a person attains through interaction with his parents and with society. Freud referred to this moral guardian as the superego.

The **superego** is not present in a child at birth. A young child is amoral and reaches for anything that appears pleasurable. As the child matures, he assimilates, or adopts as his own, the judgments of his parents as to what constitutes "good" and "bad," and eventually the external restraint exercised over him by his parents is replaced by his own internal self-restraint. The superego, then, acting as conscience, takes over the task of observing and guiding the ego, just as the parents observed and guided the child.

According to Freud, in addition to its role as conscience, the superego has a second function—it compares the ego's actions to an "ego ideal" of perfection and then rewards the ego or punishes it. Unfortunately, the superego sometimes tends to be unduly harsh in its judgments. A person with a dominating superego may be so self-critical that he finds it almost impossible to do anything. He may like to paint, but knows that he can never equal a Rembrandt or a Michelangelo, and so he does not even try.

Ideally, the id, ego, and superego work in harmony, with the ego satisfying the demands of the id in a reasonable, moral manner approved by the superego. The person is free to love and to hate, and to express his emotions sensibly without guilt. When the id is dominant, the emotions are unbridled, the person is subject to violent fluctuations of mood, and he is apt to be a danger to himself and to society. When the superego dominates, behavior is checked too tightly and the person is unable to enjoy a normal life.

"All right, deep down it's a cry for psychiatric help—but at one level it's a stick-up."
(© *Punch, London*)

Occasionally, Freud felt, the ego may be threatened from within, either by excessive moral pressure from the superego or by impulses of the id that it fears it cannot control. Or it may be threatened by persons or events in the external world. To protect itself, then, the ego may resort to defense mechanisms, such as repression, projection, and regression. These and other defenses of the ego will be treated more fully in Chapter 13.

Dynamic forces. Freud maintained that the id's energy arises from unconscious forces, or instincts, which are the experience of inborn needs. He differentiated two classes of instincts: **life instincts** and **death instincts.** Little is known about the death instincts, which reveal themselves principally in self-destructive or suicidal tendencies when they are directed toward the self, or as aggression or war when they are directed toward other people. Under life instincts Freud included all those impulses involved in the survival of the individual and of the species—hunger, pain, sex, self-preservation—with particular emphasis on the sexual instincts. The energy generated by the sexual instincts he termed **libido.** However, Freud interpreted the sexual instincts in a broad sense, as including not only the actual genital sexual function, but also impulses arising from other areas sensitive to erotic stimulation, such as the mouth and lips, the anal region, and the genital area. And he considered the sexual instincts to be the most important drives for the development of personality, because they are subject to taboos and regulations in society.

We can distinguish four aspects of an instinct: its source, its aim, its object, and its intensity. Its source is the bodily need or excitation (experienced as tension); the aim is the satisfaction of the need (tension reduction); the object is the means of satisfying the need; and the intensity is the strength of the compulsion to satisfy the need. In the case of hunger, for example, the source of the instinct is the bodily need for food, which is experienced as tension. The aim is to reduce the tension, the object is usually food, and the intensity is the energy to be expended to obtain the food—a starving man will seek food much more eagerly than a person who ate a hearty meal just a few hours ago.

Although the source of the instinct, according to Freud, remains generally the same throughout a person's life, except for natural changes that occur as he matures, the aim, object, and intensity can change considerably. For example, a person may choose to substitute a different object to satisfy the need. The energy generated by the need is then displaced onto the new object. This **displacement** of energy is the principal cause of differences in human behavior. According to his own interests, tastes, attitudes, and talents, each individual chooses different objects on which to expend his energy. The only instincts that cannot be displaced or be deferred for very long are hunger and thirst. A special kind of displacement, which occurs when a person gives up one object for a higher cultural or social object, is known as **sublimation.** A person may choose, for example, not to marry and have a family, but to remain single and devote his energy to helping others. Very often, Freud believed, artistic accomplishments result when sexual drives are sublimated into acceptable social activities.

Freud theorized, then, that all energy originates in the urges of the id. Some energy passes into the ego, where it is used in transactions with the external world. The ego stores up the excess energy it receives

FREUD'S PSYCHOSEXUAL STAGES AND PERSONALITY DEVELOPMENT

According to Freud (1949), our personalities go through critical developmental stages during childhood. In each of these stages *libido* is localized in a different erogenous zone. No two people experience these psychosexual stages in quite the same way, but what happens during the infantile period—up to the age of 5 or 6—greatly influences later personality.

During the first of these periods, the *oral* period, sexual activity is centered around the mouth. This is where the baby has most contact with his environment. The id derives pleasure from biting, sucking, and spitting out. In later life, such actions may be reflected in aggression, acquisitiveness, and contempt, respectively. An adult's habit of chewing gum or smoking may be a carryover from his having been weaned too early as a child. A person who does not easily trust other people may have been fed less than he wished or was fed on an undependable schedule in infancy.

The second of the infantile stages is the *anal* stage, when the child finds pleasure in expelling or in retaining feces. In learning to control his bowels, the child has his first significant encounter with authority and social pressure. Freud suggests that if his parents are very strict about this, the child will learn to value holding back and may grow into a stingy, miserly adult. If his parents push him to control himself before he is really able to, the child may use expulsion to express hostility. This experience may result in the child's becoming cruel and bad-tempered as an adult.

During the *phallic* period (after the age of 3 or so), the child discovers his genitals and the pleasure of masturbation. (Despite the name, this stage applies to girls as well.) It is at this time that the child develops a marked attachment for the parent of the opposite sex and becomes jealous of the parent of the same sex. Freud called this the *Oedipus complex* (in the case of a boy) and the *Electra complex* (in the case of a girl). Oedipus, according to Greek mythology, killed his father and married his mother and thus is a model for boys, who, according to Freud, all sexually desire their mothers and would like to do away with their fathers because they stand in the way of their achieving this goal. Because, in our society, children can't kill their fathers and get away with it, the boy has no choice but to repress these unacceptable impulses. At the same time, he becomes afraid that his father knows what he is thinking and is going to punish him for it. This situation—where the boy is attracted to (but repelled by) his mother and afraid of (but violently jealous of) his father—is the crux of the Oedipus complex. The Electra complex follows more or less the same pattern. In either case, the child eventually resolves the conflict by identifying with the parent of the same sex. At this point, Freud believed that the *latency* period—when children avoid intimate contact with the opposite sex—begins.

At puberty, we enter the last stage, which Freud called the *genital* stage, and our sexual impulses reawaken. In lovemaking, the adolescent and adult are able to satisfy unfulfilled desires from infancy and childhood. But it is during the three infantile stages, Freud says, that the die of adult personality is cast (Hall & Lindzey, 1970).

from the id and uses it for its rational processes—thinking, remembering, choosing, and acting. Part of the id's energy is also channeled into the superego, which uses it to oppose the id's improper urges.*

Freud's beliefs were not completely accepted even by those who are considered members of the psychoanalytic school. Two early followers of Freud who later broke with him and formulated their own theories of personality are Carl Jung and Alfred Adler.

*Other aspects of Freud's theory of personality are discussed in Chapter 10 and the chapters that follow in this section.

Carl Jung
(*Culver Pictures*)

Carl Jung

Carl Jung became a close associate of Freud in 1909. However, he left Freud's circle in 1913 and established his own school of analytical psychology.

Jung's beliefs differed from Freud's in many ways. Jung contended that libido, or psychic energy, represents all the life forces, not just the sexual ones, and that it arises in the normal course of body metabolism just as physical energy does. Both Freud and Jung emphasized the role of the unconscious in determining human behavior, but where Freud saw the id as a "cauldron of seething excitations" requiring control by the ego, Jung saw the unconscious as the ego's source of strength and vitality.

Jung distinguished two levels of the unconscious: a personal unconscious and a collective unconscious. The **personal unconscious** contains our repressed thoughts, forgotten experiences, and undeveloped ideas. These ideas may rise again to consciousness if some incident or sensation triggers their recall.

The **collective unconscious,** which is perhaps Jung's most original concept, consists of the memories and behavior patterns inherited from past generations. Jung believed that just as the human body is the product of a million years of evolution, so over the centuries the human mind has developed "thought forms" or collective memories of experiences that have been common to people since prehistoric times. He called these thought forms **archetypes.** The archetypes are not in themselves mental images, but they give rise to certain typical mental images or mythical representations. Since all people have mothers, the archetype of "mother" is universally associated with the image of one's own mother, with Mother Earth, with a protective presence. The archetype of the hero figure who rallies his people can be equally represented in a primitive tribal chieftain, in a Joshua at the battle of Jericho, or in a John F. Kennedy, depending on the particular moment in history.

Figure 12-4
One of Jung's most important archetypes is the *mandala,* or magic circle, which represents the total unity of the self. The mandala takes various forms in different cultures and is represented here by the stained-glass "rose window" from the Gothic cathedral at Chartres, France.
(*Photo from Scala New York/Florence*)

In differentiating between people, Jung proposed that there are two general attitude-types of personalities—the **introverted** and the **extraverted.** The extraverted individual is concerned with the external world—he is a "joiner," interested in people and events. The introvert is more concerned with his private world, tends to be unsociable, and lacks confidence when dealing with people. Everyone, Jung felt, has characteristics of both attitude-types, but one is usually dominant in a personality, while the other is largely submerged in the unconscious.

Within these two general types, Jung further differentiated people as *rational* or *irrational*. The rational individual regulates his actions by the psychological functions of thinking or feeling. In making decisions, he may be guided principally by thought, or he may give more weight to emotional factors and value judgments. In contrast, the irrational person bases his decisions either on perception through the senses (*sensation*), or on perception through unconscious processes (*intuition*). Most individuals express all four psychological functions—thinking, feeling, sensing, and intuiting—to some degree. However, Jung felt that one or more of the four functions usually dominates at the expense of the others. Thus, a predominantly thinking type of person is rational and logical and bases his decisions on facts; the feeling person is sensitive to his surroundings, acts tactfully, and has a balanced sense of values; the sensing type relies primarily on surface perceptions, rarely employing imagination or deeper understanding; and the intuitive type sees beyond the obvious facts and predicts future possibilities.

In contrast to Freud's emphasis on the sexual instincts, Jung's analytical psychology stressed our rational and spiritual qualities. Where Freud considered development to be determined in childhood, Jung thought that we reach full psychic development only at middle age. Jung had a sense of historical continuity. He believed that the roots of the human personality extend back through our ancestral past, but he also contended that the individual human being moves constantly toward a goal of self-realization, toward the blending of all parts of the personality into one harmonious whole. Because Jung broke with Freud, whose theories have dominated the study of personality, and because of the symbolism and mysticism that characterizes his theory, Jung's ideas have been somewhat neglected by psychologists. Recently, perhaps because of increased popular interest in mysticism, Jung has been "rediscovered," and, of late, there is a renewed interest in his theory of personality.

Alfred Adler

Alfred Adler
(*The Granger Collection*)

Alfred Adler broke with Freud in 1911 and established his own school of individual psychology. Like Freud and Jung, he believed that our behavior is shaped by unconscious inborn forces, but for Adler these forces were social urges. He considered the individual to be essentially a social being, exposed to interpersonal relationships from the moment of birth and adjusting constantly throughout life to the society he lives in. Adler also stressed the role of consciousness in shaping personality and gave far more importance to the ego than Freud did. He believed that we are not at the mercy of instinctual urges, but that each individual is free to choose his own destiny, to create his own life plan, and to develop those traits, attitudes, and abilities that will help him achieve the goals he sets for himself. Thus the musician will organize his life to allow himself uninterrupted hours for daily practice; the gossip columnist will be gregarious.

Adler also believed that the driving force motivating the individual is a striving toward **superiority,** based in part on feelings of **inferiority.** Every infant is completely dependent on adults for food, shelter, and

NEUROSIS AS A LEARNED RESPONSE

Psychoanalysts and behavior theorists often seem worlds apart in their approach to personality. John Dollard and Neal Miller, however, have tried to bridge the gap by translating clinical concepts like conflict and repression into stimulus-response theory, which concerns itself with how we learn.

Like the psychoanalysts, Dollard and Miller are concerned with neurotic behavior and see the first few years of life as crucial (Dollard & Miller, 1950). They too feel such behavior has its roots in the infant's earliest experiences, especially feeding, toilet training, sex training, and control of aggression. They regard hunger, sex, elimination, and aggression as strong *primary drives* with which the infant is born. Parents often keep these drives from being satisfied, causing the child to feel anxious and guilty when these drives arise.

Dollard and Miller explain the way the infant's hunger drive, for example, can give rise to many adult reactions that seem to have nothing to do with food, by saying that when a baby feels hungry, he reacts in the most instinctive way—usually by crying. If crying does not get results, he will try something else. The response that brings the food is thus reinforced, and the infant also learns to associate satisfaction with, for example, his mother's presence, because she brings the food. Desire to be with others thus becomes a *secondary drive,* originally associated with food, but now having motivating force by itself.

If the baby is fed but has digestive upsets, he may learn to associate the presence of other people with pain and perhaps become reclusive or distrustful in later life. Failure to get food may result in fear of being alone (as the baby originally feared the pain of going hungry), or in a general passivity ("What's the use of crying if I'm not going to get fed anyway?").

But Dollard and Miller point out that being frustrated can have positive results, too. When none of our old responses is rewarded, we must come up with new ones. In this way, an association can be broken and a neurosis unlearned.

protection, and throughout his early development the child is constantly reminded of his inferior position as his parents, teachers, and other meaningful adults point out his faults and correct him. A physical defect, the presence of older brothers and sisters, or an unhappy home environment may intensify the child's inferiority reaction. To compensate for this "inferiority complex," Adler said, the child sets himself a goal, whose achievement will give him a sense of superiority or personal fulfillment or a feeling of power over others. The goal may be realistic, such as becoming a teacher, a scientist, or a bank president. Or it may be unrealistic, as when an individual with limited musical ability aspires to become a concert artist or someone with poor eyesight wishes to be an airline pilot. In some instances, the striving for power

Karen Horney
(*Association for the Advancement of Psychoanalysis of the Karen Horney Psychoanalytic Institute and Center*)

may be neurotic, as in the individual who uses illness as a means of dominating others. But once a goal is chosen, all the person's activities consciously and unconsciously are oriented toward achieving it. The striving toward the goal provides the momentum of his life.

Three of the more prominent neo-Freudians, or "new Freudians," who accepted many of Freud's principles but developed their own theories of the driving forces motivating human behavior, are Karen Horney, Erich Fromm, and Erik Erikson.

Karen Horney

Karen Horney, while acknowledging her great debt to Freud, disagreed strongly with some of his ideas, particularly his analysis of women and his emphasis on the sexual instincts. From her experience as a practicing psychoanalyst in both Germany and the United States, she concluded that environmental factors are the most important influence in shaping personality and that the most vital of these factors are the human relationships in which the child grows up.

Horney believed that overemphasizing the sexual drives gave a distorted picture of human relationships. Feelings and drives do indeed arise from sexual desires, she said, but they may also arise from non-sexual sources. A mother, for example, may have purely maternal and protective feelings of love for her child. For Horney, a stronger motivating force than sexual drives is *anxiety,* which represents the desire for safety. The feeling of anxiety originates in childhood, when the child is dependent on others for survival and unable to defend himself against critical adults and a generally hostile world. The child therefore builds up defensive attitudes, which enable him to obtain a certain amount of satisfaction but also keep him "safe." A child with domineering parents may adopt a submissive attitude that frustrates his own desires somewhat, but keeps his parents from becoming angry with him. He learns that if he is "good," his parents may reward him with a bicycle. He can feel safe as long as he does not disobey. Or a child who feels neglected may act aggressively to attract his parents' attention. Horney identified three general "neurotic trends," all of which are attempts to resolve emotional problems and to secure safety at the expense of personal independence: moving toward people (submission), moving against people (aggression), and moving away from people (detachment).

Freud had theorized that a woman's emotional life was governed by her childhood desire for a penis. But Horney declared that if women express any desire to be masculine, it is probably because they wish to enjoy the same privileges men have in society, such as independence and sexual freedom. She believed that feelings of weakness and dependence in women are encouraged by such notions as "woman's place is in the home."

Erich Fromm
(Jill Krementz)

Erik Erikson
(Jill Krementz)

Erich Fromm

Erich Fromm is a sociologist as well as a psychologist. Fromm believes that personality is determined largely by social needs. The theme underlying much of Fromm's writing concerns our *loneliness* in the universe. We occupy a unique and isolated place in the world of nature: we possess all the instinctual drives common to animals, yet we alone also possess reason, self-awareness, and imagination. As Fromm puts it, "The whole life of the individual is nothing but the process of giving birth to himself," that is, striving to realize his "humanness" (1955).

Fromm feels we share five specifically human needs:

1. *Relatedness*—the need to unite with other human beings, to feel part of a group. This need underlies all experiences that can be called love in its broadest sense.
2. *Transcendence*—the need to be a creative person in some way, whether by building a better mousetrap, by creating art or music, or by planting seeds to create new life.
3. *Rootedness*—the need for a home, for lasting ties, for security, which may be found in a family, a clan, a nation, a church.
4. *A sense of identity*—a sense of "I." An individual may achieve an individual sense of identity ("I am John Jones of Jonesville") or he may attain identity through conformity to a particular group ("I am an Elk") or through a specific occupation ("I am a fireman").
5. *A frame of reference*—a consistent way of viewing and understanding the world that gives order and purpose to one's actions. The frame of reference may be religion, or philosophy, or even an illusory concept such as being a member of a superior race, so long as it offers the individual stability.

Fromm believes that we can satisfy these human needs only by associating with other people in a society and that an individual's personality is determined by the structure of the particular society in which he lives. A person living in a dictatorship will be unlike a person living in a democracy. But, ideally, the individual should be able to relate to others in his society in a loving, brotherly way that permits him to retain his own integrity as a person.

Erik Erikson

Erik Erikson, who studied with Freud in Vienna, takes a more social view of personality development and places more emphasis on the workings of the ego than Freud did. While he agrees with Freud's theory of sexual development, he feels this is only part of the story. Equally important is the child's sense of trust—in himself and in others. Erikson points out that different societies value different characteristics. In some cultures mothers ridicule male children who cry; in others boys are

THE ALIENATED BUT "TOGETHER" PERSONALITY

The young adult who is going through the life stages that Erikson calls *identity versus role confusion* and *intimacy versus isolation* is particularly concerned with strength of identity. Erikson says that a sense of identity must be achieved before you can successfully establish interpersonal relationships at an intimate level. "True engagement with others is the result and the test of firm self-delineation" (Erikson, 1959, p. 95). However, Erikson and many other personality theorists implicitly assume that acceptance of conventional social roles is an essential step in achieving identity and thus intimacy as well.

How mature or intimate can a person be if he goes against the conventions of society?

In a recent study, Jacob Orlofsky, James Marcia, and Ira Lesser (1973) interviewed more than 50 college men in an attempt to determine what effect the way they had resolved their identity crises had had on their being able to sustain intimate relationships with others. After analyzing the interviews, Orlofsky and his associates assigned each man to one of the four identity categories developed by Marcia (1964) or into a new, fifth category that they had developed and wanted to investigate. Men in the first category, *identity achievement,* expressed strong vocational and philosophical commitments that affirmed the goals of established society. The commitments of men in the second category, *foreclosure,* on the other hand, were also conventional, but had been acquired secondhand from parents or other authority figures. Because such people had uncritically accepted the roles given them by others, they were not considered to have resolved the identity crisis described by Erikson. Men in the *moratorium* category were still in the midst of an identity crisis and had only a vague sense of commitment. Such men wanted to be free, but at the same time wanted guidance and help in making decisions. Those in the fourth state, *identity diffusion,* tended to be purposely uncommitted. Some preferred a "playboy" life style, which increased their chances of avoiding commitment, while others seemed to be just drifting and somewhat out of touch. Such people can be easily swayed from one goal to another and may or may not have gone through an identity crisis.

The new, fifth category to which the experimenters assigned some of the men was called *alienated achievement.* This category is very much an outgrowth of the disenchantment of the 1960s. Men in this category were vocationally uncommitted and were typically opposed to the "system." But, because they also had strong philosophical reasons for their cynicism, they were enthusiastic and involved, rather than depressed or aggressively rebellious.

How had all this affected the personal relationships of these men? Interestingly, the results of this study showed that alienated achievers scored highest in autonomy, had the least need for social approval, but were the least socially isolated of all the groups. Moreover, they had as high levels of intimacy and ego strength as those in the identity achievement category, who have traditionally been seen as the model for the healthy resolution of the identity crisis. The identity diffusion group scored lowest on intimacy. None of the people in that group had established an intimate relationship, and that group contained more socially isolated individuals than any other. Like the identity achievement group and some of the moratorium subjects, the alienated achievers had open and intimate relationships with women. But, while men in the identity achievement and moratorium groups tended to describe themselves in terms of their occupational goals and political beliefs, the alienated achievers emphasized the quality of their relationships with other people. "It is as if he chooses to forego the identity crisis in favor of the intimacy crisis, his stance toward the latter becoming the basis of his identity" (Orlofsky, Marcia, & Lesser, 1973, p. 217).

Is the alienated achiever a new phenomenon in our society, produced by the sociopolitical upheavals of the past two decades? These psychologists believe in the validity of their new category, although they admit that their sample was small. Their study at least suggests that one can stand off from established society, refuse to "play the game" of traditional middle-class values, and yet still have a relatively mature, integrated, person-oriented personality.

encouraged to express emotion. The important point is that the child should feel that his own needs and desires and the needs of his society are compatible. Only if the child feels competent and valuable, in his own and society's eyes, will he develop a sense of identity. This, in Erikson's view, is crucial.

In contrast to Freud's emphasis on the childhood years, Erikson feels that personality continues to develop *throughout* life. In explaining this view, he outlined "eight ages of man" and suggested that success in each stage depends on the individual's adjustments in the stages that came before (Erikson, 1963).*

1. *Trust versus mistrust.* In infancy the baby must acquire an "inner certainty" that his mother will care for him, that she loves him. He must also learn that he can rely on himself. These are the bases of social trust and identity.
2. *Autonomy versus shame and doubt.* During his first 3 years, when the child learns to walk and begins to talk, he is exploring his own powers. If his parents ridicule him—if they laugh when he falls down, taunt him for wetting his bed—he will lose the sense of being a competent, autonomous being.
3. *Initiative versus guilt.* Between the ages of 3 and 6 the child acquires motor skills, practices being an adult in play and fantasy, and develops a conscience. It is in this period that he learns to control *himself.* If his parents are overly restrictive, if they discourage his explorations, he loses the will to try. Failure in this stage is experienced not as the loss of parental love so much as the loss of self-esteem.
4. *Industry versus inferiority.* During the next 6 or 7 years the child learns the skills and values of his culture—in school, in the fields, or on a fishing boat. All children receive formal instruction in this stage; the need for self-discipline increases. If the child has learned to trust himself and his world in the earlier stages, he identifies himself with the goals of his society and finds great satisfaction in his accomplishments. If he has not, his feelings of inadequacy and mediocrity may be confirmed.
5. *Identity versus role confusion.* At puberty, childhood comes to an end; the responsibilities of adulthood seem close at hand. The adolescent begins to question the feelings and beliefs he has depended on through childhood; he compares his image of himself to the way others see him, his role at home to his role among peers. He must work out a sense of inner continuity, an identity.
6. *Intimacy versus isolation.* The trusting youth who has a firm sense of identity is able to risk himself in associations with others, to commit himself to relationships and affiliations, and to maintain those commitments. If he cannot, he experiences isolation.

*Erikson's stages of development are also discussed in Chapter 3.

7. *Generativity versus stagnation.* Adulthood is characterized by an expansion of interests and concerns. The individual is able to give himself over to guiding the next generation, directly and indirectly. He raises offspring and works to improve the world, to contribute to his society. If he is still struggling against mistrust, still unable to establish intimate relationships, he experiences stagnation.

8. *Integrity versus despair.* Only the person who has been able to trust, to adapt to "triumphs and disappointments," to contribute to his world, experiences what Erikson calls "ego integrity" in old age. Others fear death, having lost the chance for self-fulfillment.

Self Theory

The **self theory** of Carl Rogers is similar to the theories of Freud, Jung, and others of the psychoanalytic school in that it developed out of Rogers's work with troubled individuals.* Briefly stated, the basic idea is that the troubled individual knows more about himself and his problems than anyone else does and that he is thus the person best able to find ways of successfully resolving his problems. Rogers (1959) has carried the same idea over to his theory of personality.

Origin of Personality

According to Rogers, as infants we possess certain basic attributes. First, we create our own environment, in that our own experiences constitute our reality. Second, we have an inborn tendency to protect and maintain ourselves and to develop our capacities. This tendency involves not only the basic life processes such as eating and sleeping but all activities that lead to personal growth, reproduction, creativity, movement toward personal goals. This inborn tendency serves as the motivating power of the personality. Third, each of us exercises this inborn tendency within his own world of reality, and we form value judgments about our experiences. We value as good those experiences that satisfy our needs or help us grow; we react negatively toward those that hinder our growth or are unpleasant.

Carl Rogers
(Courtesy of Carl R. Rogers)

Rogers has explained these concepts by describing an infant who is picked up by a friendly adult he has never seen before. If the child is unaccustomed to strangers, he may perceive this experience as frightening, even though the adult means to be friendly. In the child's world of reality, the stranger is a threat to his safety and the child behaves accordingly, howling in fear. Eventually, the child will learn that smiling strangers can be very pleasant and he will revise his value judgment, but at that time his perception of the adult will have changed.

*For more details about Rogers's client-centered therapy, see Chapter 15.

An individual's behavior, then, reflects his reaction to reality as he perceives it at any particular moment. As a person's perception of reality changes, his behavior changes accordingly.

Development of the Self

As the infant matures, Rogers believes, he gradually acquires awareness of being and awareness of functioning. A portion of his private world then becomes differentiated to him as "me" and becomes his conscious **self.** Probably the infant's awareness of self begins with his feeling of having control over some part of his body or some part of his private world. At the same time, he forms value judgments and becomes aware of pleasurable and unpleasurable experiences.

However, the values the child develops are of two kinds—some values he has experienced directly and others he takes over from other people, but erroneously perceives as his own. When he takes over other people's values that are opposed to his own, he becomes disoriented. For example, a child likes to tear up the daily newspaper, particularly before his father and mother have read it. For him, this is a very pleasurable experience, which he values highly. But his father and mother indicate by words, gestures, and facial expressions that they do not approve of this behavior, and the child then begins to view himself and his behavior in the same way his parents do. In effect he says to himself, "When you tear up the newspaper, you are a bad boy," but at the same time he feels, "I like to tear up newspapers—it's fun." These conflicting emotions cause the child to lose touch with his own feelings and to become confused.

Under ideal conditions, this disorientation of the child's feelings need not occur. The parents could explain to the child that they respect his feelings but also have regard for their own, and that they cannot allow him free expression when his wants disregard the feelings of others. The child could then experience his own destructive feelings without guilt, but could also choose to please his parents by leaving the newspaper intact, rather than please himself by destroying it. Whichever course of action he chose, he would remain in touch with his feelings of satisfaction or of dissatisfaction. However, once the infant begins to adopt disorienting values, his concept of self becomes distorted and the pattern continues through adulthood. The individual's behavior is not regulated solely by his own perceptions and feelings, but also by the values taken over from others, and his personality becomes divided.

Trait Theory

If someone asked us to describe a certain person, we would probably identify certain behavior patterns or **traits.** Thus, to the question "What kind of person is John?" we would reply that he is moody or friendly,

THE MASKS WE WEAR

All the world's a stage,
And all the men and women merely players:
They have their exits and their entrances;
And one man in his time plays many parts.

Sociologists and social psychologists echo Shakespeare's words from *As You Like It* when they talk about the "roles" we play. Though we all play many roles, at the same time we are supposed to maintain one strong, central identity, or self. Without it, we may be called "alienated," "phony," or even "neurotic."

At least one psychologist, however, feels that it may be more natural to be—in effect—several selves at once. Kenneth Gergen (1971) and his colleagues have conducted a series of experiments that reveal how self-identity changes with circumstances and how people feel about these apparent inconsistencies in their personalities.

The basic technique Gergen and his colleagues used was to have people fill out a checklist designed to measure self-image, then to take part in an experiment that required them to rate themselves or describe themselves again. Afterward, each person was asked whether he had been completely honest in his self-evaluation. Though people did rate themselves differently in different situations, most were not aware of presenting a false self-image.

Not surprisingly, the desire to impress someone can change self-image. So can the presence of others. Gergen and Morse (1970) got male college students to apply for a desirable summer job. They asked the men to fill out a self-rating questionnaire, telling them that their answers would not affect their chances of employment. While they were doing this, another young man walked into the room and sat down. In some cases the newcomer was handsome and clean-cut, in others a slob—but the applicants assumed he was a rival for the job. The applicants who filled out their questionnaires with "Mr. Clean" in the room rated themselves significantly lower than did the others.

A setting can also influence the role we choose. Even the "life of the party" does not cavort at a funeral—and he probably *feels* like a different person, too. Likewise, Gergen and Taylor (1969) told some men to work with a partner on a problem. These men rated themselves highly on persistence and other work-related qualities, while men told to "get along with" their partners stressed social strengths in their self-ratings.

aggressive or reserved, energetic or lazy—whatever characteristic types of behavior he has exhibited to us.

The trait theorists believe that this simple, natural way of identifying a person by his traits is the best means of describing and evaluating an individual's personality. They maintain that a unique pattern of traits exists within each personality and that these traits play a dominant role in determining the person's behavior. They are more interested in a person's conscious motives than in his unconscious drives, and they are concerned principally with his contemporary behavior—how he acts "here and now." They also emphasize that no two individuals possess precisely the same traits to the same degree.

Traits are relatively permanent and relatively consistent general behavior patterns, which an individual exhibits in many situations and which reveal his adjustment to his environment. Traits are only "relatively permanent" because, even though an individual's personality has an underlying structure of stability and consistency, personality is constantly developing and changing as the individual matures. Traits are also only "relatively consistent" because contradictory traits, such as aggression and submission, often exist within the same person and are exhibited at different times. An army sergeant who is meek and mild toward majors or colonels, for example, may be aggressive and rude to a private. Under stress, a person may exhibit unusual traits—the typically calm, methodical person may become flustered when trying to catch a plane or a train. And traits are "general" because they are activated by many situations and can provoke a wide range of responses.

It is their quality of generality that distinguishes traits from habits and attitudes. A **habit** is a person's unvarying response to a particular situation. A lecturer, for example, may twirl a button on his jacket as he speaks, or a student may always pull a certain lock of his hair as he concentrates on his studies. An **attitude** expresses a favorable or unfavorable point of view toward something. For example, a person may have an unfavorable attitude toward smoking, or a favorable attitude toward pollution control of Lake Erie. But a trait indicates a person's response to many situations and covers a far wider area. A man has a kindly attitude toward his own dog or cat. But if he extends this feeling to all people and animals, then he exhibits the general trait of kindliness.

Gordon Allport
(UPI)

Traits cannot be observed directly—that is, we cannot see a trait such as sociability directly in a person in the same way that we can see that he has blue eyes and brown hair, wears button-down shirts, and so on. But we can *infer* the existence of the trait from the person's behavior over a period of time. When we observe that an individual chooses an occupation in which he has to deal with the public, that he goes out of his way to make friends, and that he organizes his leisure activities so that he is regularly in the company of other people, we may safely conclude that he possesses the trait of sociability.

Development and Classification of Traits

How do trait concepts fit into a theory of the development of the whole personality? According to Allport (1955, 1961), the normal person is born with three groups of dispositions: first, he has all the instinctive drives common to the human species; second, he has all the traits inherited from his family; and third, he is born with the capacity to learn and to develop a sense of self, a conscience, and a personal set of traits. The foundations of a child's character, says Allport, are established between the ages of 3 and 5 and are strongly influenced by early family relationships and the sense of security, or insecurity, he develops. But from his earliest days, the child is torn between two opposing needs: his need for love and security, which can only be obtained by affiliation with his family and with society; and his need to break away from the restrictions imposed by his family and society and be an individual. The struggle to reconcile his own wants with what best serves the common good continues throughout his life.

Traits are difficult to classify, first, because there are so many of them. Allport and Odbert (1936) compiled a list of 17,953 English words that could be used to indicate personal behavior traits. Second, because they are closely intermingled in every individual, we cannot easily pinpoint where one trait stops and another begins. And, third, no two people possess the same traits in exactly the same form. Nevertheless, some general trait categories have been established.

Common traits are those that everyone possesses to some degree. These are traits such as intelligence, gregariousness, introversion, submission, and all those related to social adjustment. **Individual traits** are specific to one person. Albert Einstein, for example, possessed unique traits that enabled him to develop the theory of relativity.

In the individual personality, Allport (1937) distinguished cardinal, central, and secondary traits. A **cardinal trait** is so strong that it colors all of a person's actions. Thus, "sadistic" implies a person as cruel as the Marquis de Sade, "quixotic" refers to an impractical idealist like Don Quixote, and a "narcissistic" individual loves himself excessively, like the legendary youth Narcissus. **Central traits** are those most typical of an individual. According to Allport, each of us usually has from five to ten central traits that distinguish us. **Secondary traits** are the less prominent ones that are not really typical of an individual and that he usually shows only under special circumstances, as in times of stress.

Dynamic traits impel the person to activity. The egotist, for example, enjoys bragging about his latest triumphs, and the hypochondriac will describe his ailments to anyone within earshot. **Stylistic traits** indicate a person's manner of behavior—whether he is polite, forceful, careless, skillful, irritable, and so on. Interestingly, what begins as a stylistic trait may also become dynamic. A naval officer's skill at seamanship and navigation, which is a stylistic trait, could also become dynamic if the officer is an avid amateur yachtsman in his spare time.

Measurement of Traits

(© 1959 by the United Feature Syndicate, Inc.)

The trait theorists have sought to develop a method of accurately measuring personality traits. If an individual's personality could be measured at a given moment, and then measured again at a later date, a comparison of the two sets of measurements would show what changes had taken place in the personality. And if accurate measurements of many personalities could be obtained, dependable laws on how the personality grows, changes, and operates could eventually be formulated. But how could the thousands of traits observable in the personality be reduced to a workable number so that reasonable measurements could be obtained? The trait theorists, particularly Raymond Cattell, have attempted to do this by the statistical method of factor analysis.

Cattell (1965) believes that there are a few basic traits, which he calls **source traits,** that serve as the essential structures of the personality, just as chemical elements form the basic structures of the physical world. These source traits are the underlying source of each individual's behavior. Cattell's method of discovering the source traits was to have a few hundred young men and women rated, by people who knew them well, on about 60 different trait elements. When the ratings were subjected to factor analysis, between 12 and 20 source traits were determined and tests were then devised to measure these traits. On the basis of this research, Cattell constructed several personality inventory scales. The most comprehensive is the Sixteen Personality Factor Questionnaire (16 PF), which yields scores on the 16 source traits Cattell identified.

Alternate Views of Trait Theory

There has been considerable controversy concerning trait theory in recent years. Is the average individual really a patchwork of internal traits? Or are these specific personality characteristics only descriptive conveniences for the psychologist? It is important to remember that traits can only be inferred; they are not definite and observable the way that a particular response in a laboratory is, and many psychologists question their validity for that reason. The dispute over the validity of traits has centered on whether consistencies in personality are due to the consistency of these internal factors we call traits, or whether consistencies in personality are due to consistencies in the external environment. In other words, does your personality come from "inside" you or "outside" you? For example, if you feel angry when your parents do not seem particularly grateful for a gift you have carefully chosen for them, is your anger due to some general "need for appreciation" trait that you possess, or does it arise because of the particular situation and circumstances of that day?

Many psychologists today feel that a trait theory of personality, if not actually wrong in focus, is at least too simple. The human being is more complex, they say. He cannot be categorized as an entity that is now, always was, and always will be a certain way because of stable personality traits. Don't we all act differently in different situations, around different people, at different times of our life? Another criticism

(© 1972, The New Yorker
Magazine, Inc.)

of trait theory is that it tends to suggest that a personality characteristic has existed all along even though it may not be reflected in overt behavior, that is, that one may be a "latent" homosexual or a "potential" criminal (Byrne, 1974, p. 310).

Situationism. One perspective on personality theory that has developed in opposition to trait theory is **situationism.** Situationists reject the notion that personality is stable and unchanging regardless of the person's environmental context. According to the situationists, it is the particular situation that determines behavior, not internal personality variables. Traits are considered to be "constructs," useful labels, but they are not considered to be real entities. One psychologist, George Kelly, had some strong feelings about our common tendency to confuse constructs with real, observable things:

> When I say that Professor Lindzey's left shoe is an "introvert," everyone looks at his shoe as if this were something his shoe was responsible for. Or if I say that Professor Cattell's head is "discursive," everyone looks at him as if the proposition had popped out of his head instead of mine. Don't look at his head! Don't look at that shoe! Look at me; I'm the one who is responsible for the statement. After you figure out what I mean you can look over there to see if you make any sense out of shoes and heads by construing them the way I do (Kelly, 1958, p. 40).

According to the situationists, individual behavior is not necessarily consistent, despite our temptations to accept it as such. You yourself, for example, may be buoyant and outspoken around certain friends but reserved and cautious around others. Even when others seem to us to act consistently, it may be because we encounter them only in certain, limited types of situations. Situationists also recognize that personality varies over the dimension of time. Thus, the fact that you may have been an outgoing child does not mean that you are an outgoing adult.

Small wonder, then, that we hesitate on a personality test when faced with a yes-or-no question such as "I'd rather go to a sporting event than to a concert." (What kind of sport? On what day of the week? With whom? What kind of concert?) The most insidious aspect of personality labeling, it has been pointed out, is that "the trait explanation makes it unnecessary to examine any aspect of our political or economic or interpersonal traditions to seek either the problem or the solution" (Byrne, 1974, p. 323).

An example of a situationist analysis of personality is the learning theory approach of B. F. Skinner and others. Trait theorists believe that "you do what you are." Skinner and other learning theorists, on the other hand, believe that just the opposite is the case, that "you are what you do." For behaviorists, only observable and measurable behavior is relevant in psychology. And in view of the fact that historically the field of personality has developed more from clinical and case-history study than from laboratory research, learning theorists hold that a more scientific approach to personality is needed. ". . . The early study of personality has distinguished itself from other branches of psychology by being more speculative and less subject to careful controls, that is, based more on intuition than experience" (Lundin, 1974, p. 2).

While learning theorists do not deny that there are biological determinants of behavior (such as the effects of being taller or shorter than other people, for example), they reject structural or body-type theories, such as Sheldon's, and the trait theories that describe us as being a collection of certain characteristics. Although behaviorists reject Freud's idea of a self divided into several parts, they share with Freudian personality theory an emphasis on *development*. Both Freud and Skinner would agree that what happens to a person in his early life greatly influences his later behavior. Learning theorists also agree that there are periods of life that are particularly critical to personality development, for example, the stage when attachments to other people are formed. Specifically, learning theory recognizes that behavior learned in infancy may be carried into adulthood, and that the effects of deprivation or punishment during our earliest years are stronger and more lasting.

For example, one behavioral response that we as well as animals make is escape. Removing heavy clothing when it is hot, putting our fingers in our ears when a train passes, squirming when we are uncomfortable—all these are attempts to escape unpleasant stimuli. But escape is not always that simple, and as we mature, we adopt subtle and

(Ken Regan/Camera 5)

sometimes habitual escape mechanisms. We may "arrange" our behavior in certain ways in order to avoid certain people or situations. Thus, a child who fears being questioned in school may learn to say, "I don't know," in many fearful situations. This response may generalize as the child grows up, thus resulting in a shy, evasive, and escape-oriented adult personality (Lundin, 1974).

On the other hand, learning theorists believe that data based on free association, dream content, or personal observation are scientifically unreliable and that the hypotheses of Freud (and his successors) are conjectural and unverifiable. But learning theorists face the same problem that all personality theorists face: the difficulty of gaining actual experimental data about human beings under controlled conditions. The problem is even greater when the psychologist wants to study human behavior over a long period of time.

Interactionism. So far, we have looked at two perspectives on personality—internal traits and the external, situationist orientation. A third point of view, interactionism, recognizes both traits and environmental factors and thus represents a synthesis of these two viewpoints.

Generally speaking, interactionism accounts for an individual's behavior by studying the influence of the *physical environment*—the objective, social world outside a person—and the *psychological environment*—the subjective or cognitive world of the individual, his perceptions of the physical world. While two different people may live in identical physical environments at identical times, the way they perceive the world around them will obviously be different, and, thus, their psychological environments will be different. This is particularly true if one person is, for example, 10 years old and the other is 40 years old.

The physical and psychological environments interact to create a "behavior space" (Jessor, 1958). According to this view, concepts such as traits, motivations, or needs must be related to the physical environment. In a recent comment on this idea, the prominent trait theorist Gordon Allport admitted that his earlier views on personality "seemed to neglect the variability induced by ecological, social, and situational factors" (Allport, 1966, p. 9).

An example of an interactionist theory is Walter Mischel's social behavior theory (1968, 1971). Mischel not only criticizes the methods used to classify people in terms of their traits, but also disputes the very existence of traits. According to Mischel, a personality will be consistent to the extent that the surrounding conditions and the individual's perception of those conditions remain constant. In fact, according to Mischel, the reason we are believed to have traits in the first place is probably due to the simple fact that the contexts of our day-to-day lives remain relatively unchanged most of the time. His theory is "social" in the sense that the way a person behaves in a given situation is very much determined and maintained by the responses of other

GENETIC FACTORS IN PERSONALITY

Both situationists and interactionists recognize the effects of external influences on personality, from parental behavior to physical settings to social and cultural forces. But what about constitutional and genetic influences? Does heredity have a hand in the formation of personality? Comparative studies of identical and fraternal twins suggest that genetic inheritance does influence personality.

A general conclusion from research on twins has been that those twins with identical genetic characteristics are behaviorally more alike than fraternal twins. Although some psychologists argue that this probably occurs because identical twins are treated more alike than fraternal twins, there is little direct evidence of this as yet. In fact, it is quite possible that some parents of identical twins go out of their way to encourage different environments for their children. After reviewing the recent research on twins, Brody (1972) concludes that "variations in the environment are of little or no significance as sources of individual differences in personality" (p. 176). Brody suggests that if environment does have any influence, it occurs while the child is still in the womb rather than after birth. For example, the twin who is heavier at birth is usually stronger and somewhat more independent in later life (Tienari, 1966). In addition, it has been shown that the twin who weighs less at birth tends to have lower verbal IQ and performance scores when tested between the ages of 8 and 10 (Willerman & Churchill, 1967).

At least one psychologist (Bell, 1968) has suggested that personality characteristics are not only inborn in children (whether because of genes, the prenatal environment, or the circumstances at birth), but that such characteristics can influence the parents' behavior toward the child. For example, some children may be born with a higher degree of assertiveness than other children. These highly assertive children will be more difficult for the parents to manage and thus the parents will be more likely to use physical punishment to control them. Thus, contrary to the traditional assumption that parents mold the child, Bell suggests that the child may mold the parents.

Similarly, a major long-term study of personality development by Alexander Thomas and his associates suggested that "temperamentally difficult" children tend to affect parental behavior in such a way that the personality development of these children is affected (Thomas, Chess, & Birch, 1970; Thomas et al., 1963). These difficult children were found to be relatively irritable, very upset by changes in the environment, and irregular in their sleeping and feeding habits. Thomas and his co-workers suggest that parents are likely to treat such children differently than their more pleasant-tempered brothers and sisters. For example, they describe a situation in which the difficult child's demands are first ignored because the parents are annoyed at the child's constant screaming, shrieking, and fussing. After a time, however, the parents become unable to go on ignoring the child, and at this point whatever attention they give him serves to reinforce those constitutional characteristics that made the child so unlikable in the first place. In addition, the child's extreme signals of distress and general crankiness and irritability may cause the parents to worry about their competency as parents, and they may react to the child with unconscious hostility.

Thus, Thomas and his colleagues take a more interactionist approach to personality than Bell does. They accept Bell's idea that the child's behavior influences the parents' behavior toward the child. But they go further and say that the parents' behavior toward the child can in turn modify the child's constitutional personality characteristics. Brody (1972) suggests that the interactionist model that takes genetic and constitutional factors into account is the most effective means we have of understanding how personality is acquired and developed.

people. For example, a man who has doubts about himself at work may exhibit a confident personality when he is around his parents.

Mischel's approach does not suggest that we are all pawns whose behavior is controlled entirely by this or that circumstance. Rather, Mischel stresses that each of us is adaptable to our environment, and that the range and manner of our adaptation is the core of our personality. What is important is to *relate* environmental changes to behavioral changes, instead of trying to establish general rules that will apply to all situations.

The personality theories we have discussed represent the efforts of various psychologists to explain in an orderly and coherent manner the characteristic behavior of persons. But interest in personality centers not only on how and why people behave as they do but also on how to evaluate and measure characteristic behavior patterns.

Personality Assessment

In our daily lives we are constantly assessing people's personalities informally. In any form of competition—sports, a chess game, business—our strategy depends on how we evaluate our opponent's ability and how accurately we can predict his behavior. Does he tend to "go to pieces" under stress? Is she steady and reliable in a crisis? In choosing a partner for marriage, for a business deal, even for a vacation trip, we try to find someone who is compatible with us.

Our own assessments of people are informal and subjective, based largely on our own experience or hearsay and apt to be strongly influenced by our own biases. But there are many occasions when an objective, unbiased, and accurate assessment of an individual's personality is very valuable and highly desirable. A reliable measure of personality is extremely helpful, for example, in a business firm's selection of employees. When choosing an employee for a sensitive post in a developing country, an employer should know if the person has the tact needed to deal with people raised in a different culture, the stability to live in a less developed area, and the ability to work without supervision. A school counselor who has an accurate assessment of a student's personality can more wisely advise the student in his choice between a large state university and a small college. A clinical psychologist can use personality assessments to help choose the best therapy for his patients.

However, there are special difficulties in measuring personality that are not encountered in measuring intelligence and academic ability (see Chapter 7). As we mentioned earlier in the chapter, an individual's personality reflects his *characteristic* behavior traits and the way he *consistently* reacts to his environment. In assessing personality, then, we are not interested in a person's *best* behavior. We want to find out what his *typical* behavior is—how he usually behaves in ordinary situations. All of us will occasionally alter our behavior patterns in times of illness, personal misfortune, or family troubles. Then, too, most of us want to appear at our best before others. A person who is being questioned about his personality may be reluctant to disclose information that will show him in an unfavorable light. Any measurement of personality, therefore, must take into account the possibility that the person being assessed may not be displaying his characteristic way of behaving.

Another difficulty lies in the subject matter of personality testing. To obtain an accurate picture of a person's personality, the psychologist often must ask questions about sensitive areas, such as the person's emotional adjustment to life, his relations with other people, his intimate family history, and his attitudes. The question of invasion of privacy arises: how far, in the interests of science, may a psychologist delve into the personal life of another individual? The privacy of the person being evaluated must be respected and protected.

In the intricate task of measuring personality, psychologists use four basic types of tools—the personal interview, direct observation of a person's behavior, objective tests, and projective tests. All these tools measure personality at one particular time. For this reason, they have limited value for helping psychologists study how a personality changes over time, how earlier experiences may have influenced the development of personality. To measure change in personality over time, psychologists often use *longitudinal studies* (see Chapter 1). Because such studies are costly and time-consuming, and because "the investigation may outlive the investigator" (Holzman, 1974, p. 247), very few have been done. Most of our knowledge about personality has come from the use of the tools and procedures we are about to discuss.

The Interview

Essentially, an **interview** is a conversation, during which an interviewer seeks to elicit information about another person and to evaluate him in general terms. Within the limited time of the interview, the interviewer has an opportunity to observe certain aspects of a person's behavior, such as his manner of speaking, his poise, his tendency to be outgoing or withdrawn, or his tenseness about certain topics. Ideally, the interviewer should try to direct the conversation over a wide range of subjects, encouraging the individual to talk about his personal experiences and to express his feelings and attitudes.

Interviews may be either structured or unstructured. In the **unstructured interview,** the interviewer is free to develop the conversation along the lines that seem most suitable to him. He is able to take advantage of openings provided by the person being interviewed to probe deeply in certain areas and to touch only lightly upon other topics. The flexibility of the unstructured interview is desirable in clinical situations or in vocational guidance sessions, for example, where the interviewer wishes to encourage the person to talk as freely as possible about his needs and desires.

In the **structured interview,** the interviewer follows a predetermined plan of questioning. He may use either a list of questions or a checklist of general topics as a guide. Usually the interviewer can use his own discretion to decide in what order the topics should be brought up. The structured interview has certain advantages. It ensures that essential topics will be covered and lessens the probability that an unskillful interviewer will ignore many important areas of inquiry. Also, it is easier to compare interviews when all interviewers have covered the same topics. The structured interview is used in employment situations, for instance, where the employer requires specific information about a prospective employee's schooling, work experience, special abilities, and reasons for leaving his former positions.

The success of the interview technique depends in large measure on the skill of the interviewer. He should establish a sympathetic relationship with the person being interviewed. He should be sensitive in reading the person's unconscious cues, such as the unexpected change in tone of voice, twisting of the fingers, clenching of the fists at mention of certain topics. Yet he must not become so emotionally involved in the interview that he injects his own personality into the conversation and influences the person's answers.

Observation

Another way to find out how a person usually behaves is to **observe** his actions in everyday situations over an extended period of time. Since most adolescents and adults are inclined to be self-conscious if they suspect they are being watched, observational techniques are most frequently and most successfully used with young children or with people who have difficulty in verbal communication. But observation can be used with some degree of success with people of almost any age and in a variety of settings—a company cafeteria, an assembly line, or wherever individuals work or play in a natural social setting.

Observation can be used to assess a person's general behavior, or it can be confined to special situations provoking a particular response, such as the way an individual acts under stress or within a group. The observer must make a sufficient number of observations to provide a good "average" of the person's behavior. The observer must also try to ensure that his presence is not altering the behavior he is observing. We all drive more carefully when we see a police car at a traffic intersection and work harder when the boss is watching.

The advantages of direct observation are that the observer sees the person's behavior at first hand and does not have to rely on the person's own description. And if several careful observers provide unbiased, factual accounts of a person's behavior over a period of time, the composite picture of that individual's personality can be quite accurate. The disadvantages are that an observer may misinterpret the real meaning of some act. For example, he may think a child is being hostile when the child is merely protecting himself against the taunts of the class bully. And observation must be selective. Only a relatively small number of people can be observed for a limited period of time.

Objective Tests

In an attempt to devise measuring instruments that do not depend on the skill of an interviewer or the interpretive abilities of an observer, psychologists have created **objective tests,** or personality inventories. These are generally paper-and-pencil tests that are administered and scored according to a standard procedure. Usually the tests are constructed so that the person merely chooses between a "yes" and "no" response or selects one answer among multiple choices. Since the administration and scoring procedures are standardized, the results of the tests are less likely to be influenced by the biases or prejudices of the persons administering them.

Personality tests came into general use during World War I, when a Personal Data Sheet developed by R. S. Woodworth (1918b) was used by the armed forces to screen out men who were emotionally unfit for military service. The data sheet consisted of a list of questions on topics ranging from an individual's general health to his attitude toward life and his social adjustment. The questions were simple and direct, such as:

1. Do you make friends easily?
2. Was your childhood happy?
3. Do people find fault with you much?
4. Do you suffer much from headaches or dizziness?

"No" to questions 1 and 2 and "Yes" to questions 3 and 4, for example, would be scored as unfavorable. It was found that neurotic individuals gave an average of 36 unfavorable answers to the 116 questions on the test, while normal men gave only 10 unfavorable responses.

The difficulty with such a direct questionnaire is, of course, that its effectiveness depends on the honesty and frankness with which it is answered. The "correct" answers can be faked. To overcome this shortcoming, efforts have been made to devise tests that include rating scales to show if a person is distorting his answers. One of the most widely used tests with built-in correction scales is the Minnesota Multiphasic Personality Inventory.

Minnesota Multiphasic Personality Inventory. The Minnesota Multiphasic Personality Inventory (MMPI), published in 1942 by Hathaway and McKinley, was developed originally to aid in the diagnosis of psychiatric disorders. The authors prepared a number of test items and presented these to patients in a mental hospital. The same items were also administered to a control group of 724 normal men and women who were visiting friends or relatives at the hospital. When the replies of both normal and abnormal groups were compared, only those items with clearly different replies were included in the final version of the test.

The final test consists of 550 items to which the person answers "true," "false," or "cannot say." Some typical items are "Once in a while

Figure 12-5
An MMPI profile. (From
S. R. Hathaway and J. C.
McKinley, *The Minnesota
Multiphasic Personality
Inventory.* Minneapolis:
University of Minnesota
Press, 1942. Reprinted by
permission. Copyright 1948
by the Psychological
Corporation, New York,
N.Y. All rights reserved.)

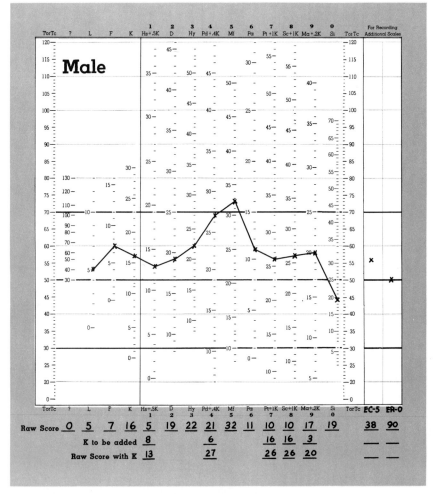

I put off until tomorrow what I ought to do today," "At times I feel
like swearing," "There are persons who are trying to steal my thoughts
and ideas." Some of the items repeat almost the same question in
different words—"I tire easily," "I feel weak all over much of the time."
This was done for ease of scoring and to check on the possibility of
faking and of inconsistency in answers. The test is scored according
to ten personality scales. The scale measuring hysteria, for example,
was constructed so that persons with this disorder scored much higher
on these items than normal individuals.

In addition, the MMPI has four scales that check on the validity of
the responses. The ?, or question, scale consists of the total number
of items the person put in the "cannot say" category. If the "cannot
say" responses are too numerous, the test is considered invalid. The
L, or lie, scale is scored on 15 items scattered throughout the test.
Sample items rated on this scale would be "I do not always tell the

truth" and "I gossip a little at times." Most people would admit that they do gossip occasionally and they do lie once in a while. If a person indicates that he does *not* do these things and marks an excessive number of the items this way, he is believed to be consciously or unconsciously distorting the truth to present himself in a more favorable light. The F, or validity, scale is rated on the items that were seldom marked "true" by the normal individuals in the control group, for example, "Everything tastes the same" and "My soul sometimes leaves my body." An unusually high score on this scale would indicate that a person had marked the test carelessly, was extremely confused, or was trying to "look bad." The K, or correction, score is based on items measuring the individual's attitude toward the test. It is related to both the lie and validity scales, but is more subtle. A high K score would indicate that a person had denied his personal inadequacies and tried to fake a good appearance. A low K score would indicate an extremely self-critical individual who exaggerated his weaknesses and was trying to look bad.

The results of the 14 scales are plotted on a profile sheet. Any score above 70 or below 30 is generally cause for consideration of some possible psychological difficulty. However, the scores must be evaluated very carefully, for a normal person may have a high score on certain scales. Only someone trained in the test scoring should attempt to interpret the results.

Measuring Values

A different approach to personality measurement is used in the measurement of values. One test of values—the Allport-Vernon-Lindzey Study of Values—is based on the premise that an individual's value standards are a key to his personality traits, for his values regulate his choice of behavior. As their value standards, the test authors selected the six classifications proposed by Eduard Spranger (1928):

- *theoretical*—emphasizing critical and intellectual interests
- *economic*—preferring the useful and practical
- *aesthetic*—valuing grace, form, and harmony
- *social*—essentially interested in helping others
- *political*—emphasizing power and influence
- *religious*—basically mystical, interested in universal truths

They then devised a test to measure an individual's strength in these six areas, by requiring him to choose between alternative values.

The first part of the test consists of a series of questions, each followed by two alternative answers. The person taking the test is to rate the answers according to the degree to which he favors one over the other. Each answer is related to one of the value scales. When all the test items have been scored on the value scales, the individual's

Figure 12-6

A hypothetical profile of a person's scores on the Allport-Vernon-Lindzey Study of Values. Based on these scores, a psychologist might advise this person to become a philosophy teacher instead of an engineer.

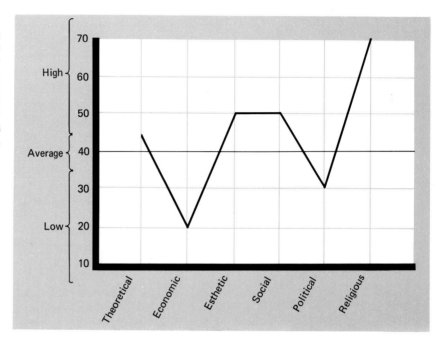

total preference for each of the six values can be plotted on a profile to show the relative importance of the values to him.

While some scoring norms are available, the Study of Values test is not so much intended to provide comparison scores as to reveal the areas in which an individual's values are strongest. It has proved particularly helpful, therefore, in student counseling and vocational guidance work. A student who scored high on the aesthetic scale and very low on the economic scale, for example, might have second thoughts about becoming a business administration major. The validity of the test has been demonstrated with different occupational groups. Theological students tend to score relatively high on the religious and social scales, and engineers tend to score higher on the theoretical and economic scales. The test has proved to be suitable primarily for college students and persons with fairly high educational backgrounds.

Essentially these objective tests of personality try to measure "how much" of various traits, attitudes, interests, and conflicts a person has. A different approach is used in projective tests, which attempt to assess the organization of the total personality.

Projective Tests

Most **projective tests** of personality consist of a simple unstructured task that can elicit an unlimited number of responses. The person may be shown some essentially meaningless material or a vague picture and be asked to tell what the material means to him. Or he may be given two or three significant words, such as "My brother is . . ." and be asked to complete the statement. He is given no clues as to the "best way" to interpret the material or finish the sentence. It is believed that in devising his own answers, he will "project" his personality onto the test materials.

Projective tests offer several advantages in testing personality. Since the tests are not rigidly structured and can be treated somewhat as a game or a puzzle, they can be administered in a relaxed atmosphere, without the tension and self-consciousness that sometimes accompany paper-and-pencil tests. Sometimes the actual purpose of the test can be hidden—the person may be told, for instance, that he is being measured on his powers of imagination—so that responses are less likely to be faked. The projective test is believed to be able to uncover unconscious thoughts and fantasies, such as latent sexual difficulties or family conflicts. However, the tests have the obvious disadvantage that the accuracy of the evaluation depends on the skill of the examiner.

Rorschach Test. The Rorschach Test is probably the best known of the projective personality tests. The test is named for the Swiss psychiatrist who in 1921 published the results of his research on the interpretation of inkblots as a key to personality. A great deal of work on the inkblot technique had been done by the time Rorschach began his clinical practice, but he was the first to use the technique to evaluate the individual personality as a whole. For 10 years he tested thousands of

Figure 12-7
Designs similar to this one are used in the Rorschach Test.

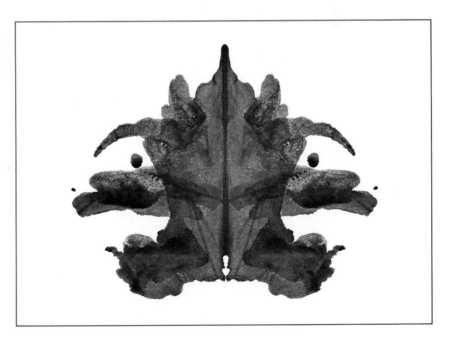

Figure 12-8
A clinical psychologist
administering the
Rorschach Test.
*(Van Bucher, Photo Researchers.
This photo has been slightly
retouched.)*

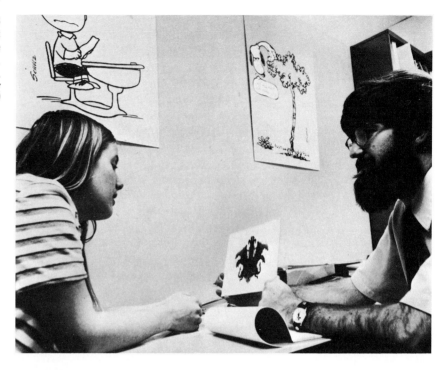

blots and finally chose ten that seemed to arouse the greatest emotional response in people.

Each inkblot design is printed on a separate card and has unique characteristics of form, color, shading, and white space. Five of the blots are black and gray; two contain red splotches; and three blots contain patches of several colors. The cards are presented to the person one at a time and in a specific order, and he is asked to tell what he sees in each blot. The test instructions are kept to a minimum so that the individual's responses will be completely his own. Although he is not specifically told that he may do so, he is permitted to turn the card and look at the blot from any angle and he may make as many interpretations of each blot as he wishes. After he has finished his interpretation of all the blots, the individual goes over the cards again with the examiner and identifies which part of each blot determined his response.

The responses to each blot are usually scored in five general categories:

1. *Location.* Did the response relate to the whole blot or to only a small part of it?
2. *Determinants.* What qualities of the blot determined the response—the shape, the color, the shading? Did the response indicate motion—a bird in flight, an animal running, two people dancing?
3. *Content.* Was the subject matter a human figure, an animal, an inanimate object, or a sexual symbol?

4. *Popularity-Originality.* Was the response a common one often cited by other persons taking the test? Or was it strikingly original?

5. *Form level.* How accurately was the concept seen—was it clear or an impressionistic blur? Was the concept elaborate or very simple?

The scoring also includes subscores within each of the categories, such as use of details, response to white space, color response, and so forth. The number of interpretations for each blot also counts in the scoring.

The Rorschach Test is believed to be useful in uncovering information about a person's general intellectual and emotional processes. Responses to the blots can indicate, for example, whether he is creative and original or whether he has a limited range of ideas. If he is creative, are his ideas linked to reality or are they bizarre? The consistent use of the entire blot in the interpretations is believed to indicate an ability to organize material well. Responses based on color, texture, and shading are usually linked to emotional control.

Thematic Apperception Test. Somewhat more demanding is the Thematic Apperception Test (TAT), developed at Harvard by H. A. Murray and his associates. The test consists of 20 cards containing pictures of one or more human figures in various poses. Some of the pictures suggest a basic story line, others give very few plot hints. As a person is shown the cards one by one, he is to make up a complete story for each picture, including the events leading up to the scene in that picture, what the characters are doing at the present moment, what their thoughts and feelings are, and what the outcome will be.

When shown a picture of a boy contemplating a violin lying on a table, two men in their forties told these stories:

Figure 12-9
A clinical psychologist administering the Thematic Apperception Test.
(*Van Bucher, Photo Researchers*)

*This is a child prodigy dreaming over his violin thinking more
of the music than anything else . . . of wonderment that so much
music can be in the instrument and in the fingers of his own
hand. I would say that possibly he is in reverie about what can
be or what he can do with his music in the times that lie ahead.
He is dreaming of concert halls, tours, and appreciations of
music . . . of the beauty he will be able to express and even now
can express with his own talents.*

*The story behind this is that this is a son of a very
well-known, a very good musician and the father has probably
died. The only thing the son has left is this violin which is
undoubtedly a very good one and to the son the violin is the
father and the son sits there daydreaming of the time that he
will understand the music and interpret it on the violin that his
father has played* (Henry, 1956).

For the first storyteller, the boy is the central figure, but the story action
moves outward into the exciting world of concert halls and tours. In
the second story, the central figure is the father, and the boy achieves
identity only through the father who is no longer present. The first
storyteller was an active business executive. The other had held the
same job for several years and was considered unpromotable.

Although various scoring systems have been devised for the TAT,
usually the examiner interprets the stories in the light of his personal
knowledge of the story, or with one of the minor characters. Then the
examiner must determine what the attitudes and feelings of the character reveal about the storyteller. The examiner also assesses each story
on its content, language, originality, organization, and consistency.
Certain themes, such as need for affection, repeated failure, or parental
domination, may recur in several of the plots.

Summary

1. *Personality* refers to the characteristic behavior patterns, emotions, motives, thoughts, and attitudes with which an individual consistently reacts
   to the environment.
2. Probably the oldest theory of personality is the *constitutional theory*,
   which suggests that there is a relationship between a person's body physique and behavior. William Sheldon devised three basic dimensions of
   a person's *somatotype: endomorphy, mesomorphy,* and *ectomorphy.* He
   then devised three basic dimensions of temperament: *viscerotonia, somatotonia,* and *cerebrotonia.* Sheldon found that somatotype ratings often were
   related to temperament ratings.
3. Sigmund Freud proposed the first major *psychoanalytic theory* of personality. He believed that personality is composed of three interrelated
   parts—the id, the ego, and the superego—which form an integrated whole.

4. The *id* is the storehouse of energy from which the ego and superego develop. The energy from the instinctual drives of the id is set in motion by a state of deprivation, which causes discomfort or tension. The id relieves this discomfort by reflex actions or by wish fulfillment, which Freud called *primary process thinking.* The id acts according to the *pleasure principle.* The *ego* operates on the *reality principle.* It controls all the thinking and reasoning activities and has a directorial function in the personality. The ego derives its energy from the id, but also controls the id and directs its energy into effective, realistic channels, a process known as *secondary process thinking.* The *superego,* the moral guardian of behavior, develops through learning from parents and society. It compares the ego's actions to an *ego ideal* and then rewards or punishes the ego.

5. The dynamic forces of this threefold structure arise from two classes of unconscious drives or instincts—*life instincts* and *death instincts.* Freud placed greatest emphasis on the *libido*—energy generated by the sexual instincts. Freud distinguished four aspects of an instinct—its source, its aim, its object, and its intensity. The last three account for differences in human behavior, because an individual may *displace* the energy onto new objects. *Sublimation* occurs when a person gives up one object for a higher cultural or social object.

6. Carl Jung, a close associate of Freud, stressed the rational and spiritual qualities of man. He contended that libido represents all the life forces, not just the sexual ones, and that it arises in the normal course of body metabolism just as physical energy does. Jung saw the unconscious as the ego's source of strength and vitality and divided it into two parts: the *personal unconscious* and the *collective unconscious.* Jung believed that the human mind contains thought forms called *archetypes,* made up of the collective memories of experiences common to man since prehistoric times. Jung proposed two general attitude-types of personalities—the *introverted* and the *extraverted.* He further differentiated people as *rational* or *irrational.*

7. Alfred Adler believed that man's unconscious inborn forces are social urges. Adler placed greater importance than Freud did on the ego in shaping personality, stating that man is not at the mercy of instinctual urges but that each individual is free to choose his own destiny and to develop whatever means necessary to achieve the goal he sets for himself. Adler believed that the driving force motivating the individual is a striving toward *superiority,* based in part on feelings of *inferiority.*

8. Karen Horney, one of the more prominent neo-Freudians, believed that environmental factors (especially the human relationships in which a child grows up) are the most important influence in shaping personality. She felt that *anxiety* is a stronger motivating force than sexual drives. She called a person's attempts to resolve emotional problems and to secure safety at the expense of personal independence *neurotic trends,* distinguishing three general types: moving toward people (submission), moving against people (aggression), and moving away from people (detachment). She took exception to Freud's theory that a woman's emotional life is governed by her desire for a penis and held instead that if women express any desire to be masculine, it is probably because they want the same privileges that men have in society.

9. Another prominent neo-Freudian, Erich Fromm, believes that personality is determined largely by social needs. According to Fromm, we occupy a unique and isolated place in the universe, possessing the instinctual drives common to animals and reason, self-awareness, and imagination. He proposes five specifically human needs—relatedness, transcendence, rootedness, a sense of identity, and a frame of reference—which can be satisfied only by associating with other people in a society.

10. Erik Erikson's view of personality is more social than Freud's and places more emphasis on the workings of the ego as it intercedes between the id and the real world. In contrast to Freud, Erikson feels that personality continues to develop throughout the life span. He describes eight stages of personality development, each of which involves the resolution of a crisis: *trust versus mistrust,* during which the infant acquires a sense of security; *autonomy versus shame and doubt,* during which the child begins to test his abilities; *initiative versus guilt,* during which the child develops a conscience and learns to control himself; *industry versus inferiority,* during which the child learns about and develops identification with the goals of his society; *identity versus role confusion,* during which the adolescent struggles to develop individual identity; *intimacy versus isolation,* during which the adolescent develops his ability to sustain commitment to other people; *generativity versus stagnation,* during which the adult gives himself to the next generation by raising children and/or trying to contribute something to the world; and *integrity versus despair,* during which the elderly person comes to terms with his life and to the idea of approaching death. The first term in these labels represents the result of successful resolution of that stage's crisis; the second term represents the result of an unsuccessful resolution. According to Erikson, a successful outcome at any stage depends on how successfully the crises that preceded it have been resolved.

11. The *self theory* of Carl Rogers asserts that every individual is the center of his own personal, private world of experience. This private world consists of both conscious and unconscious experiences; it can only be known by the individual whose world it is; an individual's experiences constitute his reality. According to Rogers, personality originates from certain attributes that all infants possess—we all create our own environment, in that our experiences constitute our reality; we have an inborn tendency to protect and maintain ourselves and to develop our capacities; and each of us exercises this inborn tendency within our own world of reality, where we form value judgments about our experiences. As the infant matures, a portion of his private world becomes differentiated to him as "me," and becomes his conscious self. He also becomes aware of pleasurable and unpleasurable experiences and forms two kinds of value judgments: values he has experienced directly and values he takes over from others, but erroneously perceives as his own.

12. *Trait theorists* maintain that a unique pattern of traits exists within each person and that these traits play a dominant role in the person's behavior. Trait theorists are primarily interested in conscious motives and in behavior here and now. They define traits as relatively permanent and relatively consistent general behavior patterns, which an individual exhibits in many situations and which reveal his adjustment to his environ-

ment. They hold that a person inherits the tendency to develop certain traits, but that he may also develop certain traits as a result of his environment or his personal experiences, or by integrating several specific habits with the same general significance.

13. Gordon Allport's theory of personality development is based on the interrelationship of traits and the uniqueness of the individual. From the start, the child is torn between two opposing needs: the need for security and the need to assert himself as an individual. The struggle to reconcile his own wants with what best serves the common good continues throughout his life.

14. Traits can be categorized as *common*—those that almost everyone possesses to some degree, or *individual*—those that are specific to one person. An individual person may show *cardinal traits*—those that are so strong that they are reflected in all of a person's actions; *central traits*—general traits most typical of an individual; and *secondary traits*—less prominent traits that an individual usually shows only under special circumstances. Traits can also be categorized as *dynamic*—those that impel a person to activity, or *stylistic*—those that indicate a person's manner of behavior.

15. There has been considerable controversy over the trait theory in recent years. The central dispute involves the question of whether behavior is consistent because traits are consistent or because environment is consistent. Psychologists who believe that the environment determines consistency are called *situationists*. Learning theorists are particularly committed to this view and are the most critical of trait theory. For learning theorists, understanding personality is a matter of determining the laws and conditions of how behavior is learned. Although they reject Freud's theory of the id, ego, and superego, they do agree with him that personality is developed over time and that learning at certain critical periods of childhood may be more resistant to extinction.

16. *Interactionism* represents a synthesis of trait theory and situationism. From this perspective, an individual's behavior is determined by the interaction of the *physical environment* and the *psychological environment* (the unique way in which the individual perceives the physical environment). Analysis of this interaction, with the added element of the reinforcement provided by the responses of other people in the environment, forms the basis of the *social behavior theory* of personality proposed by Mischel.

17. Psychologists use four basic tools to assess personality—personal interviews, direct observation of a person's behavior, objective tests, and projective tests.

18. During an *interview*, an interviewer seeks to elicit information about another person and to evaluate him in general terms by listening to what he says and observing his behavior. Interviews may be *unstructured*, in which the interviewer is free to develop the conversation along the lines that seem most suitable to him, or *structured*, in which the interviewer follows a predetermined plan of questioning. The success of an interview depends largely on the skill of the interviewer, who must establish a sympathetic relationship with the person being interviewed, but at the same time maintain a detached, objective viewpoint.

19. Another way to assess behavior is to observe a person's actions in everyday situations over an extended period of time. *Observation* can be used for

general behavior or confined to special situations. The observer must make a sufficient number of observations to provide a good average of a person's behavior, and he also must be careful to ensure that his presence does not alter the behavior he is observing and that he does not misinterpret the meaning of some act. The main advantage of direct observation is that the observer does not have to rely on the person's own description of his behavior.

20. *Objective tests* of personality are administered and scored according to a standardized procedure. One type of objective test is a direct questionnaire requiring yes-or-no responses or selection of one answer among multiple choices. The effectiveness of this type of test depends on the honesty with which it is answered. Other objective tests provide ways to determine if a person is distorting his answers. One of the most widely used is the *Minnesota Multiphasic Personality Inventory (MMPI)*.

21. The *Allport-Vernon-Lindzey Study of Values* takes a different approach to personality assessment, by concentrating on a person's values. It is based on the premise that an individual's value standards are a key to his personality traits, for his values regulate his choice of behavior.

22. *Projective tests* of personality consist of simple, unstructured tasks that can elicit an unlimited number of responses. It is believed that a person will project his personality onto the test material. Projective tests can be administered in a relaxed atmosphere, and the purpose of the test can be hidden to avoid faking. One major disadvantage is that they depend on the skill of the examiner for accuracy of evaluation and assessment of data. Two well-known projective tests are the *Rorschach Test*—consisting of ten inkblot designs, which subjects are asked to interpret—and the *Thematic Apperception Test*—consisting of 20 pictures, which subjects are asked to make up stories about.

Suggested Readings

Allport, G. W., *Letters from Jenny* (New York: Harcourt Brace Jovanovich, 1965). A gripping collection of letters, demonstrating the value of personal documents in understanding personality dynamics.

Allport, G. W., *Pattern and Growth in Personality* (New York: Holt, Rinehart & Winston, 1961). A presentation of Allport's view that personality is a complex and unique system that reflects the individual's pursuit of growth and fulfillment.

Brenner, C., *An Elementary Textbook of Psychoanalysis*, rev. ed. (Garden City, N.Y.: Anchor Books, 1974). A clearly written explanation of Freud's theoretical works.

Byrne, D., *Introduction to Personality: Research, Theory, and Applications*, 2nd ed. (Englewood Cliffs, N.J.: Prentice-Hall, 1974). A comprehensive introduction to personality that gives particular attention to the situational determinants of behavior.

Hall, C. S., and Lindzey, G., *Theories of Personality*, 2nd ed. (New York: Wiley, 1970). A thorough analysis of all the major theories of personality, from Freud to the present.

Hall, C. S., and Norgby, V. J., *A Primer of Jungian Psychology* (New York: New American Library, 1973). An introduction to Jung's theory of personality that explains Jung's ideas in a clear, readable way.

Janis, I. L., Mahl, G. F., Kagan, J., and Holt, R. R., *Personality: Dynamics, Development, and Assessment* (New York: Harcourt Brace Jovanovich, 1969). A comprehensive discussion of personality, how it develops, and how it is measured.

Mischel, W., *Introduction to Personality* (New York: Holt, Rinehart & Winston, 1971). A behaviorist-oriented overview of personality theory and research.

Ostrovsky, E., *Self-Discovery and Social Awareness* (New York: Wiley, 1974). A look at the basic ideas and concepts of personality through an analysis of real or fictionalized examples of people's actual behavior.

White, R. W., *Growth and Organization in Personality* (New York: Holt, Rinehart & Winston, 1972). A warm and readable introduction to the subject of human personality.

White, R. H., *Lives in Progress*, 2nd ed. (New York: Holt, Rinehart & Winston, 1966). An outstanding casebook, following the lives of several people through middle age and using their experiences to raise various theoretical issues.

outline

WHAT DO WE HAVE TO ADJUST TO? 466

Stress
Pressure
Anxiety
Frustration
Conflict

WAYS OF ADJUSTING 476

Direct Coping
Defensive Coping

THE WELL-ADJUSTED INDIVIDUAL 486

SUMMARY 487

SUGGESTED READINGS 489

Adjustment

In everyday usage, the word "adjustment" has come to stand for an ideal: the outgoing, well-rounded child or the happy and successful adult. In psychology, **adjustment,** like adaptation in biology, refers to an individual's relationship with his environment—the ways he attempts to achieve harmony between his own drives and desires and the demands or restraints of the environment. All animals and plants must adapt to their environment; if that environment changes, they too must change to survive. Similarly, the individual must adjust to his physical and social environment.

Even the best technology cannot prevent disasters—floods, droughts, epidemics, and man-made disasters like pollution and war. Accidents happen. People we love die. A change in government policy or a sudden shift on the stock market puts men thousands of miles away out of work and threatens the most carefully planned lives.

The life cycle presents additional problems. Every child finds he must obey his parents to win their approval, control his impulses if he is to get along with friends, delay more pleasant activities and go to school. The rules seem endless; often the child's needs and those of others conflict.

The child who had always depended on his parents must learn first to support himself, then perhaps to support a family. When his own children are grown, his life changes once again as he begins to face retirement and old age. Thus, natural disasters, accidents, social change and social demands, maturation—all require adjustment.

People adjust to their lives and problems in a variety of ways. The flood victim who has lost everything, for example, may call his insurance man, look for a second job, move to a mountaintop, or collapse entirely and find himself in a hospital. All of these reactions—including collapse—are adjustments.

We begin this chapter with a description of the kinds of problems people face. We then consider various direct and defensive ways of coping with these problems. In the final section we turn to the question of how psychologists determine whether someone is well adjusted.

What Do We Have to Adjust to?

Stress

When a person feels he is unable to cope with the demands of his environment, when he faces a situation that threatens to harm him physically or psychologically, he begins to feel tense and uncomfortable. He is experiencing **stress.** The term "stress" is used to describe the situations in which a person feels in conflict or threatened beyond his capacities, as well as his emotional and physiological reactions to such situations. Psychologists have found that coping with psychological stress places just as much of a burden on the body as coping with physiological stress.

Some things, of course, are inherently stressful—like wars and natural disasters. Here the danger is very real: people's lives are threatened and there is little or nothing they can do to save themselves. Some people fall apart in such situations; others regain their composure almost immediately; still others refuse to admit that they are threatened.

(Walter Chandoha)

Rescue workers invariably find families who have totally ignored hurricane or flood warnings.

But stress is not limited to life-and-death threats. The man who loses his job may feel just as threatened as the soldier caught behind enemy lines; the patient dying of cancer may experience less anxiety than the husband who suspects that his wife is having an affair. The degree of stress a person feels depends on how much danger he perceives, and this in turn depends on learning. The child who has been frightened by a large vicious dog has learned to be terrified every time he sees a dog; the child who sleeps with his beagle every night has not. The visitor who has just arrived in New York City may be delighted when he discovers Central Park and decides to take an evening walk. The New York resident knows the park is dangerous.

Figure 13-1

People adjust to natural disasters in many different ways. Here people are searching for victims in the ruins of a Florida trailer park destroyed by a tornado.
(*Wide World Photos*)

Stress also depends on the person's evaluation of his ability to cope with whatever is threatening him. A girl who is taking judo lessons feels relatively safe walking home alone at night. Because she feels she can cope with a physical assault, she does not feel tense or frightened. A student who knows he can study when he has to and has been successful in the past is calmer the night before an exam than one who failed two subjects the semester before.

Several studies of stress indicate that responsibility is also a determining factor. Porter and his colleagues (1958) provided the classic example in a series of experiments with "executive monkeys." Two rhesus monkeys with similar backgrounds were strapped into adjacent chairs. Both were given painful shocks every 20 seconds. One of the monkeys, the "executive," could delay the shocks to both himself and his partner by pressing a lever. The other monkey was also given a lever, but it did not work; there was nothing he could do to avoid pain. Within a short time, the executive monkey developed severe stomach ulcers; the strain of being responsible for his own comfort and that of his companion was too much for him. The non-executive monkey, who did not experience the same stress, did not develop ulcers.

In some of the experiments, the researchers varied the time monkeys spent strapped in the chairs and the length of the rest periods. After a number of trials, they began to notice that the level of stomach acid in the executive monkeys was highest during the rest periods. Apparently the anticipation of danger was more stressful for these animals than the experience itself (Brady et al., 1958).

However, a later study by Weiss (1971) reversed these findings. Weiss

Figure 13-2
The monkey on the left—the
"executive"—can push a
lever to prevent a shock
from being given to himself
and his comrade. He
developed an ulcer. The
monkey on the right, whose
lever had no effect, did not.
*(Medical Audio Visual
Department, Walter Reed Army
Institute of Research)*

(Wide World Photos)

found that those rats that were *deprived* of control were the most likely
to develop ulcers. His study raises questions about the methods used
by Porter and Brady and their colleagues. These researchers pre-tested
all their monkeys, and those monkeys that had the highest response
rates were assigned to the "executive" category (Lefcourt, 1973). These
monkeys may have been higher in anxiety than the other monkeys.
Thus, their getting ulcers under stress may have occurred despite
(rather than because of) the control that they had over the shocks.

On the other hand, when Seymour Epstein (1962) studied the effects
of anticipation of stress on a group of 28 parachutists, he found much
the same pattern as Porter and Brady did. Each man was asked to
describe his feelings the night before the jump, as he was boarding the
airplane, at the moment he was tapped on the shoulder (the signal that
his turn to jump had come), in free fall, when the chute opened, and
upon landing. Going through with the jump would enhance their
prestige among friends and thus their self-esteem, but even with the
best precautions a parachute jump is dangerous. All reported increasing
fear and desire to escape as the jump approached. However, once they
were in line and realized they could not turn back, they began to calm
down. By the time they reached the most dangerous part of the jump—
when they were in free fall and waiting for the chute to open—their
fears had subsided.

Similar findings on the effects of anticipation of stress were reported
by Nomikos and his colleagues (1965). Subjects were shown two versions of a movie about a woodworking shop and were told that they
would see three serious accidents during the movie. In the first version,
there were 20 to 30 seconds of film before each accident. In the second

MEASURING LIFE STRESS

Is it more difficult to survive the death of a spouse, or to experience simultaneously a serious illness and a marital reconciliation? Is the strain of being fired from a job harder to cope with than a series of minor stresses, such as arguments with family members, finding a new place to live, and problems with income taxes?

Normally, we would have no way of answering such questions; there has been no "magic formula" for measuring stress. But Holmes and Rahe (1967) have developed a Social Readjustment Rating Scale (SRRS) to do exactly this job. The SRRS is a questionnaire on which the person lists which of 43 possible change events he has experienced in recent months. Each experience has a rating for the number of "life change units" (LCUs) involved. For example, the most severe type of stress, death of a spouse, has an LCU rating of 100. Other LCU ratings are: divorce, 73; marital separation, 65; death of a close relative, 63; major injury or illness, 53; fired from job, 47; retirement, 45. Not all experiences rated by Holmes and Rahe are unpleasant. Christmas, for example, was given a 12 LCU rating, and the birth of a new baby was rated 39.

Based on these ratings, we can estimate the stress to which a person has been exposed over a particular period of time. A score of 0 to 150 is normal. A score of 150 to 199 indicates mild stress; 200 to 299 suggests a moderate life crisis; and a score of over 300 indicates a major life crisis. Thus, based on Holmes and Rahe's system, it should be easier to cope with the death of a spouse than with simultaneously being seriously ill and reconciling with one's spouse. The chance that an individual will be able to cope effectively decreases as the potential life crisis becomes more serious. While there is a 66 percent chance that you could effectively cope with mild stress, there is only a 20 percent chance that you could cope effectively with the combination of events that constitutes a major life crisis. Thus, SRRS scores may potentially have practical value in predicting periods of vulnerability in people's lives.

version, only a few seconds of anticipation were provided in the scenes involving the first two accidents. The researchers reported that periods of long anticipation, or *suspense,* led to greater stress, as measured by heart rate and sweat-gland activity. In addition, most of the stress reaction was found to occur during the moments of anticipation, rather than while the actual accidents themselves were on the screen.

One reason why psychologists are interested in stress is that, in general, people do not perform as well when they are upset as they do when they are feeling confident. Lazarus and Erickson (1952) demonstrated this with a group of students. All were given an intelligence test and told that their scores would indicate how well they would do in college. A few days later the students were called back. Some were told they had done very poorly and would be given another chance; others, that they had done well and the experimenters wanted to know

Figure 13-3
Chess champion Bobby Fischer. He decided when he was 6 years old that he would become champion of the world. He studied so hard that, as he admits, he could not be called a well-rounded, well-adjusted adult. To achieve his goal, he had to cope with strong internal pressures to be the best, as well as with the external pressure of competition. These apparently took their toll: after becoming champion, he apparently lost all interest in chess for over a year and in 1975 lost the title because of his refusal to defend it against the Russian challenger, Anatoly Karpov. Karpov became champion by default.
(*Harry Benson*)

if the tests were a true example of their ability. On the second test the students who felt threatened made many more mistakes than those who had been encouraged and praised. Clearly the students in the first group did not feel capable of dealing with the test; stress interfered with their normal performance level.

Pressure

Pressure is a form of stress in which the individual feels that he must live up to a particular standard of behavior or adapt to rapid change. Our *internal pressures* often are related to maintaining self-esteem. Because of our feelings about our own intelligence, attractiveness, popularity, or athletic or artistic skills, we may push ourselves to conform to an ever higher standard of excellence. Internal pressure can be constructive. It may lead, for example, to a serious effort to learn to play a musical instrument, which can ultimately bring us great pleasure. On the other hand, internal pressure can be destructive if our ideals are impossible to achieve. *External pressures* hit us from all sides. Among the most significant and consistent are the pressure to compete, the rapid rate of change of our society, and expectations held by family and close friends.

The pressure to compete affects all relationships in American life. Wherever we look, some group is proclaiming that "We're Number One," and others are trying to gain that status. We compete for grades, jobs, sexual and marital partners, popularity, and even for the status of being the "best dresser" in the crowd. We are taught to see failure in terms of shame and worthlessness; thus, the pressure to "win" can be intense.

Our society is also very complex and in a rapid state of change. For example, television was virtually nonexistent in the 1940s. But in the 1970s, nearly every family in the United States has a television set. Our patterns of family life are also changing rapidly, and our divorce rate is skyrocketing. But it is not change itself that is hard to adjust to. Detroit has prepared us to adjust to "new and improved" models of automobiles every year, and this philosophy has spread to most types of consumer goods. But living in the midst of constant and pervasive change is a very real pressure on an individual. The extremely rapid rate of change has led Alvin Toffler (1970) to coin the term "future shock" to describe the deep emotional trauma that results from living in the midst of a rapidly changing society.

In addition, we often face pressures from family and close friends. When people are emotionally involved in our lives, they are especially likely to place demands on us and to expect them to be met. In particular, being a marital partner and being a parent are among the most difficult and pressure-packed roles in our society. A husband or wife may expect the spouse to satisfy all unresolved psychological, social, and sexual needs. And children clearly need an enormous amount of

Figure 13-4
A diagram of frustration.
The person (represented by
a dot) is prevented by a
barrier (the vertical line)
from reaching a goal that
attracts him (+).

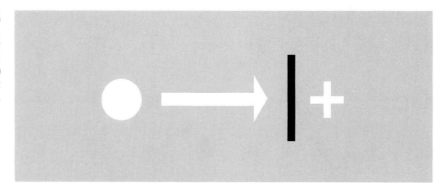

affection, time, understanding, and support from parents. These roles require us to constantly face demands from others that we may not always be able or willing to satisfy.

Anxiety

Anxiety is a particularly difficult and puzzling form of stress. In all the examples in the preceding section, the individuals knew *why* they were frightened and upset. The anxious person does not. He experiences all the symptoms of stress—butterflies in his stomach, shallow breathing, muscle tension, inability to think clearly, and so on—but he does not know why. He feels angry when his roommate says "good morning," guilty for not calling his parents even though he called last week, depressed in spite of the fact that he has saved enough money to go to Europe. In short, his feelings seem to contradict a rational analysis of his situation. Anxiety is thus very private and disturbing.

Many psychologists refer to psychoanalytic theory in explaining anxiety. According to this view, anxiety is a sign of internal, unconscious conflict. Some wish or desire that conflicts with the person's conscious values is struggling to the surface. For example, a girl is furious at her mother, but firmly believes it is wrong to feel angry toward one's parents. If her inhibitions are particularly strong, she may use all her energy to keep from realizing just how angry she is. But the emotion persists. She feels depressed and tired, blows up at her sister, goes on a shopping spree. Psychoanalytic psychologists argue that none of these displaced solutions will work effectively. Only by becoming aware of her real feelings will the girl be able to relieve her anxiety and make a more successful adjustment to her situation.

Frustration

Still another cause of stress is **frustration.** In frustration an individual is somehow prevented from reaching a goal—something or someone is standing in the way (see Figure 13-4). A 13-year-old girl may give up when she reads that Mick Jagger is happily married. A student who

Figure 13-5
An everyday example of frustration. The man is prevented from getting at his money by the locked bank door. The frustration is heightened by the fact that he just missed getting there in time. If the money was an important ingredient in his evening's activities, that could be a further source of frustration.
(Courtesy of the Bulova Watch Company and Steve Horn)

does poorly on his College Boards may not get into his father's alma mater. In each case, the person's goal is unattainable. He must either give up his goal or find some way to overcome the obstacles that are preventing him from reaching it.

The love-stricken 13-year-old will probably recover quickly. But what about the student? Most likely, his first reaction will be to get angry: angry at himself for not having studied more, angry at his father for pushing him to apply to the college he had attended, angry at the Admissions Board for not considering the fact that he had a bad cold the day of the exam. He may not be able to express his anger directly—society does not approve of sons punching their fathers. He may not even realize or admit how disappointed he is. In either case, the damage is done, and he must either change his goal and be satisfied with another school or find a new way to reach his goal.

Coleman and Hammen (1974) identify five basic sources of frustration. *Delays* are difficult for us to accept because our culture stresses the value of time. Also, because advertising makes consumer goods so attractive, we may become frustrated if something we would like to own is out of our immediate economic reach. *Lack of resources* is especially frustrating to low-income Americans who cannot afford new cars, color televisions, or vacations in Europe. *Losses,* such as the end of a cherished friendship or love affair, are frustrating because they often seem beyond our control and may reflect on our sense of worth and importance. *Failure* is a constant source of frustration in our competitive society. The most difficult aspect of failure to cope with is guilt. We feel we should have done something differently and thus feel responsible for our own and someone else's pain and disappointment. Finally, some people have a sense that life is *meaningless.* Finding a meaningful and fulfilling life style is often more difficult than we expected. This can be a source of frustration, particularly if we feel that society is to blame and that there is nothing we can do about it. This feeling of powerlessness can result in alienation, despair, and a feeling that nothing we do is really important.

Conflict

Of all life's troubles, **conflicts** are probably the most common. A student finds that both the required courses he wanted to take this year meet at 10 A.M. Monday, Wednesday, and Friday. In an election, one candidate's views reflect our own on foreign policy, but his opponent proposes domestic programs that we agree with. A child does not want to go to his aunt's for dinner, but does not want to listen to his mother's complaints if he stays home. A man hates living in New York City, but has to because of his work, which he enjoys very much.

Conflicts arise when a person faces two incompatible demands, opportunities, needs, or goals. There is no complete solution to conflicts: the individual must either give up one of his goals, modify one or both, delay one, or learn to live with the fact that neither is fully satisfied.

Writing in the 1930s, Kurt Lewin described conflict in terms of two opposite tendencies: *approach* and *avoidance*. When something attracts us, we want to approach it; when something frightens us, we try to avoid it. Lewin showed how different combinations of these tendencies produce three basic types of conflict (Lewin, 1935).

The first, diagrammed in Figure 13-6, he called **approach/approach conflict.** The individual (the circle) is simultaneously attracted (the arrows) to two desirable goals (the plus signs). For example, a recently married woman may want to pursue a career, but may also want to raise a family. A rational person, she considers the alternatives. She could accept a job now and delay having children, or she could have children now and look for work when the children start going to school. Alternatively, she could modify both goals by hiring a housekeeper and working part-time. Or she and her husband could share child-care duties. Here the solutions are numerous. This is not always the case. Suppose the same woman wanted to be a psychiatrist, a profession that

Figure 13-6
A diagram of approach/approach conflict. The person is attracted to two incompatible goals at the same time.

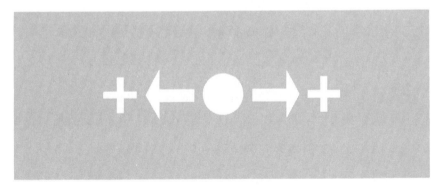

Figure 13-7
A diagram of
avoidance/avoidance
conflict. The person is
repelled by two fears or
threats at the same time.
His inclination is to try to
escape (the black arrow),
but often other factors
prevent him from escaping
the conflict.

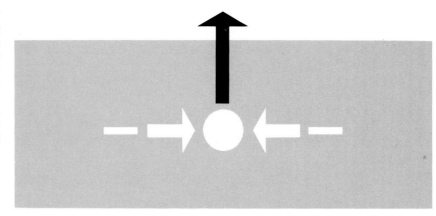

Figure 13-8
A diagram of
approach/avoidance conflict.
The person is both repelled
by and attracted to the
same goal.

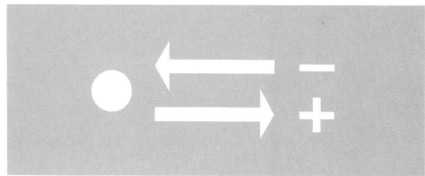

requires years of training. She might not be able to meet both this goal and that of motherhood.

The reverse of this dilemma is **avoidance/avoidance conflict,** when a person is faced with two undesirable or threatening possibilities (Figure 13-7). When faced with an avoidance/avoidance conflict, people will usually try to escape from the situation. If escape is impossible—if other factors are keeping them in the situation—they will cope with the situation in a number of ways, depending on the severity of the conflict. The student who must choose between studying something he finds terribly boring and flunking an exam will probably decide to study, at least for a while. (Otherwise he might have to repeat the course, an even more unpleasant alternative.) But the choice is not always easy. The Army pilot who knows he risks his life with each mission, but risks his buddies' lives (and his own self-esteem) if he stays behind, has a more difficult decision.

People caught in avoidance/avoidance conflicts often vacillate between one threat and the other, like the baseball player caught between first and second base. He starts to run, realizes he will be tagged, turns around only to realize he will be tagged on first if he returns. In no-exit situations like this, many people sit down and wait for the inevitable,

Figure 13-9
Both approach and
avoidance increase as the
distance to the goal
decreases. At the point
where the two lines cross,
the person in the conflict
will begin to waver, unless
he is forced to decide or the
situation changes.

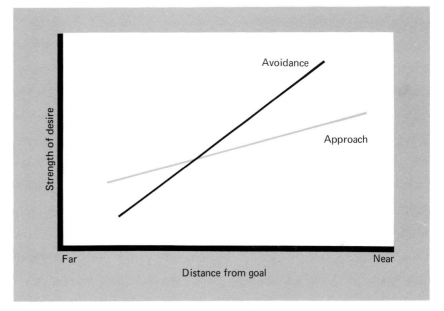

hoping that something will happen to resolve their conflict for them.

Approach/avoidance conflicts (Figure 13-8), in which an individual is both attracted and repelled by the same goal, are rarely so easily resolved. A football player recovering from an operation may want to return to his team, but knows he may limp for the rest of his life if he is injured again. A girl may know she will hurt a boy she really likes if she goes out with others, but realizes she will feel resentful toward him if she does not. A boy whose parents have taught him that sex is dirty and sinful may find himself attracted to and repelled by girls at the same time.

The desire to approach a desired goal grows stronger as the person gets nearer to it. But the desire to avoid the goal also grows stronger as he gets nearer. The avoidance tendency usually increases in strength faster than the approach tendency. Thus in an approach/avoidance conflict, the person will approach the goal until he reaches the point where the two gradients intersect. Afraid to go any closer, he will stop, fall back, approach again, continuing to vacillate until he is forced to make a decision or until the situation changes (see Figure 13-9).

Often approach/avoidance conflicts are mixed up together in complex patterns. A mother who adores classical music may dream that her son will be a great pianist. His father might be convinced that all musicians are homosexuals and push him to go out for sports and "be a man." If the child practices on the piano, he pleases his mother but infuriates his father; if he stays after school for football practice, his mother cries while his father beams. **Double approach/avoidance conflict,** as Lewin called this, is diagrammed in Figure 13-10.

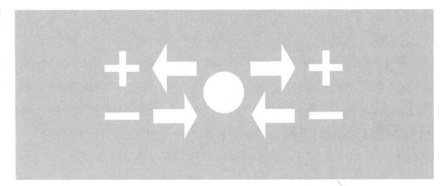

Ways of Adjusting

Psychologists distinguish between two general types of adjustment: **direct coping** and **defensive coping.** The first refers to any action a person takes to alter an uncomfortable situation. When his needs or desires are frustrated, he attempts to remove the obstacles between himself and his goal, or he gives up his goal. Similarly, when he is threatened, he tries to eliminate the source of fear—either by attacking it or by escaping.

Defensive coping refers to the different ways people convince themselves that they are not really threatened, that they did not really want something they could not get. A form of self-deception, defensive coping is characteristic of internal, often unconscious conflicts. The person feels unable to bring a problem to the surface and deal with it directly—it is too threatening. In self-defense, he avoids the conflict.

Direct Coping

A person who is threatened, frustrated, or in conflict has two basic choices for coping directly: he can either attempt to change the situation in which he finds himself, or he can try to change himself. Both approaches are forms of direct coping. For example, a college graduate is turned down for a job. He knows he is qualified for the work and thought the interviewer liked him. He calls someone he knows at the company and learns that one of the bosses refused to hire him because of his appearance. Long hair and jeans are the obstacles between him and his goal. He has several alternatives.

He might decide that he wants the job badly enough to compromise by cutting his hair and buying a suit. Reminding himself that the student volunteers for Eugene McCarthy in the late sixties went "Clean for Gene," he heads for the barber. Of course, he may decide that he would be uncomfortable in such a conservative atmosphere. In this case, he would probably decide to withdraw from the conflict and look for

(*Springer/Bettmann Film Archive*)

another job. But if both the job and the right to dress as he likes are important to him, he will probably choose a third route—he will attack the problem directly by calling the person who rejected him and arguing his case. He might begin by pointing out that the company cannot afford to discriminate against youth styles for long. He might even appeal to some outside agency if he feels he is being discriminated against. This kind of behavior is approved in our society. No one would blame the young man for arguing in his own behalf.

Aggression. Few would blame the young man in this example even if he got angry and yelled at the man who was standing in his way. But he will control his anger on the phone, walk out to his car, and kick one of the tires with all his might. Afterward, he will probably feel better. Why? As we noted in Chapter 10, some psychologists feel that man is innately aggressive, that it is part of his nature to want to defend himself and his territory, to destroy his enemies and demolish anything that stands in his way. But society says he cannot, so, frustrated, he kicks tires, honks and yells in traffic jams, cheers football teams, and far too often starts wars.

The theory that aggression is innate is debatable. Perhaps aggression is man's innate response to frustration, but social inhibitions usually prevent his acting on this impulse. Indirect expression of anger is more common than direct attack.

Whether physical or verbal, direct or indirect, the success of aggressive action depends on two conditions. First, the person must know who or what threatens him or stands in his way. This is not always possible. The man who gets an incorrect computerized bill every month may fold, spindle, and mutilate the bill, but with little effect. He will have difficulty finding out who is responsible for the mistake. Ghetto riots often provide examples of aggression with no clearly defined adversary. Rioters attack the symbols of oppression—policemen and stores—sometimes hurting members of their own community.

Second, aggression will be successful only when the person is at least equal to his enemy. People seldom attack (even verbally) when they know their adversary is in a position to reciprocate effectively. The student who argues vehemently with a graduate assistant over grades or an assignment would probably be more timid if he were taking a course with the head of the department. The housewife may yell at her grocer (she can always go to another store) but not at her landlord, who can hurt her by neglecting repairs. However, if the student has been elected to a committee on the curriculum and the housewife is a leader of a neighborhood action group, each will feel stronger.

Compromise. One of the most common ways of coping with a conflict or frustration directly is to compromise. The college graduate in our earlier example could work out a compromise with the man who disapproved of his appearance—"I'll wear a suit to work if you'll put up with my hair style." Each of them gives up a bit of his own goal to reach a satisfactory solution. Or, if the job is important enough to him, the student could compromise one of his goals by accommodating his dress and the length of his hair to the desires of his employer. If he decides instead that he would rather take a different job, he is compromising by selecting a new goal.

Withdrawal. In many situations it is more practical to withdraw from a conflict. The child whose parents argue about whether he should play piano or football might end up spending his afternoons in the woods with his dog. Often we equate withdrawal with "copping out," with refusing to face problems. But when a person realizes that his adversary is more powerful than he is, that there is no way he can change the situation or compromise his own goals, and that any form of aggression would be self-destructive, withdrawal is a positive and realistic adjustment.

Resignation or apathy is probably the rarest kind of direct coping. Most people keep trying to the end. However, in completely hopeless situations, such as submarine and mining disasters, few people panic (Mintz, 1951). Realizing that there is nothing they can do to save themselves, they give up. But is this direct coping? Yes. First, it relieves the symptoms of stress. The person who gives up stops trembling and struggling. He is in a better position to take advantage of an opportunity to escape if one comes along. Second, the person is aware that his situation is hopeless. If he denied that he was in any danger—both to himself and to those around him—psychologists would say that he was coping defensively.

Defensive Coping

Defensive coping is characteristic of ambiguous situations, when the individual cannot tell who or what is threatening him, and of internal conflicts that threaten the individual's sense of identity and self-esteem. A young girl wants to go camping with a group of high school classmates, but her parents refuse to let her go. She runs to her room in tears and slams the door. She knows that if she defies her parents and goes without their approval, she will feel guilty, but that if she does not go, she will disappoint her friends and hurt her own sense of independence. Still, part of her wants her parents to say no. Some of the girls who went the year before have been talking about couples going off alone to sleep, and she does not feel sure of herself sexually. She turns on the radio and tries to forget the whole thing.

Forgetting is one way that people cope with complex problems they feel unable to solve. By denying that a threat exists, blocking out painful memories, and repressing unacceptable impulses (like wanting to hit a child or sleep with a friend's husband), people protect their self-image and feelings of integrity. Some people are unable to face the fact that they are sometimes helpless and sometimes mean; giving up strong inhibitions requires major internal changes. Both situations are painful, so people try to avoid them.

Sometimes, of course, a problem cannot be ignored. In this situation people tend to distort their perception of things, translating the problem into a form they can handle. For example, a girl talks her boyfriend into taking LSD. It is a bad experience for both of them. Days later she insists that it was he who pushed her. She is not lying—she really believes that he did. Probably she feels guilty for insisting they take the drug, angry at him for not talking her out of it, disturbed by what she felt during their trip. To pull herself back together, she locates the responsibility outside herself. **Projection** (as this is called), like forgetting, is a form of defensive coping.

The self-deceptive element in such adjustments led Freud to the conclusion that they are entirely unconscious. Freud was particularly interested in distortions of memory and in irrational feelings and behavior, all of which he considered symptoms of the struggle against unconscious impulses. Suppose a man quite suddenly develops a chronic fear of falling. Perhaps as a child he had fantasies about pushing a younger brother out the window; perhaps he feels guilty about wanting to unseat his superior at work (who has an office with a window on the twentieth floor) and unconsciously wants to punish himself; perhaps he is afraid of "falling" in love. All these explanations are oversimplified. The point is that Freud believed our ways of defensive coping always spring from unconscious conflicts and that individuals have little or no control over them.

Not all psychologists agree with this interpretation. Often people realize that they are pushing something out of their memory or transferring emotions. (Everyone has had the experience of blowing up at one person when they knew they were really angry with someone else.) The transfer is conscious: if questioned, the person could explain his behavior quite lucidly. Despite this difference in approach, psychologists agree on the descriptions of certain basic types of defensive coping, called **defense mechanisms**—the ways people react to frustration and conflict by deceiving themselves about their real desires and goals in an effort to maintain their self-esteem and avoid anxiety.

Denial. One common defense mechanism is denial—refusing to acknowledge painful or threatening circumstances. Lazarus (1969) cites the example of a patient who was dying from severe burns. At first the woman was depressed and frightened, but after a few days her attitude began to change. She felt sure that she would soon be able to return home and care for her children, although all medical evidence was to the contrary. By denying the extent of her injuries, this woman was able to remain calm and cheerful. It is important to emphasize that the patient was not merely putting on an act for her relatives and friends—she *believed* she would recover. C. T. Wolff and his colleagues demonstrated the effectiveness of denial in a similar situation. Parents of children dying of leukemia were asked to participate in a study. By interviewing the parents, Wolff determined which of them were facing their children's condition and which were denying it. Physical examinations revealed that those who were denying the illness were not suffering the physiological symptoms of stress—such as excessive stomach acid and so on (Wolff et al., 1964).

Most psychologists would agree that in these situations denial is a positive solution. This is not always so. The student who uses denial to cover the fact that he spends most nights at the movies may well fail his exams. The heroin addict who insists that he is merely experimenting with drugs is similarly deluding himself.

Intellectualization. This defense mechanism is a subtle form of denial. A person realizes that he is threatened, but detaches himself from his problems by analyzing and intellectualizing them. Parents who sit down to discuss their child's difficulties in a new school and, hours later, find themselves in a sophisticated discussion of educational philosophy may be intellectualizing. They appear to be dealing with their problems, but may in fact have cut off their emotions.

Like denial, intellectualization can be a valuable defense. Doctors see pain and suffering every day of their lives. They must retain some degree of detachment if they are to be objective and clear-headed. Psychologist Bruno Bettelheim, once a prisoner in a Nazi concentration camp, reports feeling completely detached on the journey to prison. He simply did not feel that it was happening to him (Bettelheim, 1943).

Reaction formation. The term "reaction formation" refers to a behavioral form of denial: the person expresses emotions that are the opposite of what he or she really feels. The classic example of this defense is a line in *Hamlet,* "The lady doth protest too much, methinks." In this case, the Queen's exaggerated protestations of loyalty to her husband reveal the fact that she feels guilty about having betrayed him. Exaggeration is the clue. Examples of this behavior are common. The person who praises a rival extravagantly may be overreacting—covering up hostility about his opponent's success. Reaction formation may also be a way of convincing oneself that one's motives are pure. The mother who feels ambivalent about her role may devote all her time to her children in an attempt to prove to *herself* that she is a good mother.

Repression. Perhaps the most common mechanism for blocking out painful feelings and experiences is repression. Repression, as we saw in Chapter 5, is one form of forgetting. The most extreme form of this defense is amnesia—total inability to recall a part of the past. Soldiers

REACTION FORMATION: AN EXAMPLE
Jules Masserman, a psychologist who used cats as experimental subjects for research on alcoholism, once received the following letter from an ardent anti-vivisectionist. The woman's warmhearted interest in the welfare of cats appears to be a cover-up for her very bitter and hostile attitudes toward people:

I read . . . your work on alcoholism. . . . I am surprised that anyone who is as well educated as you must be to hold the position that you do would stoop to such a depth as to torture helpless little cats in the pursuit of a cure for alcoholics. . . . A drunkard does not want to be cured—a drunkard is just a weak-minded idiot who belongs in the gutter and should be left there. Instead of torturing helpless little cats why not torture the drunks or better still exert your would-be noble effort toward getting a bill passed to exterminate the drunks. They are not any good to anyone or themselves and are just a drain on the public, having to pull them off the street and jail them, then they have to be fed while there and it's against the law to feed them arsenic so there they are. . . . If people are such weaklings the world is better off without them. . . . My greatest wish is that you have brought home to you a torture that will be a thousandfold greater than what you have, and are doing to the little animals. . . . If you are an example of what a noted psychiatrist should be I'm glad I am just an ordinary human being without a letter after my name. I'd rather be just myself with a clear conscience, knowing I have not hurt any living creature, and can sleep without seeing frightened, terrified dying cats—because I know they must die after you finish with them. No punishment is too great for you and I hope I live to read about your mangled body and long suffering before you finally die . . . and I'll laugh long and loud (Masserman, 1946, p. 35).

who break down in the field often block out the experiences that led to their collapse (Grinker & Spiegel, 1945). But forgetting that you are supposed to appear at a job interview Thursday morning or forgetting the embarrassing things you said at a party the night before may also be instances of repression. Repression is never entirely successful; repressed drives cause anxiety and irrational behavior.

Many psychologists feel that repression is a signal that a person is struggling against impulses that his conscious values prevent him from expressing. A girl who has been taught that nice women do not experience sexual desires may flirt with a man and then act shocked when he becomes sexually aroused. She may not be conscious of the conflict between her values and her actions.

Displacement. The redirection of unrealizable drives into other areas, called displacement, is closely related to repression. With displacement, repressed feelings find a new, more acceptable outlet. The woman who

(Roir, Ben Roth Agency)

learns she cannot bear children and feels inadequate as a result might become extremely attached to a pet. Loving a dog may not be a totally satisfactory substitute, but it enables the woman to carry on.

Displacement is characteristic of situations in which a person is unable to defend himself directly. The man who must smile and agree with his boss all day to hold his job may come home and yell at his innocent children. Bettelheim cites an interesting example of this type of defensive coping in his study of former concentration camp prisoners. At one point during the war, English and American journalists began to report on the inhumane treatment of prisoners in Nazi Germany. Learning of this, camp guards punished the prisoners severely. In later years the former prisoners blamed the journalists rather than the guards for the bad treatment they received. Bettelheim suggests this is because the prisoners had been completely at the mercy of their captors. They blamed the journalists, who were "safer" targets (Bettelheim, 1960).

Sublimation. Freud believed that the redirection of sexual drives, or sublimation, is essential to personality development—and to civilization. At about age 7 the child begins to suppress his Oedipal feelings and learn the skills of his culture. Sexual curiosity becomes a desire for knowledge; unexpressed hostility toward the mother or father becomes the driving force behind a hammer or baseball bat; the need for approval leads to a talent for acting. Without these transformations, Freud argued, men would continue to live on a very primitive level and could never build societies.

According to psychoanalytic theory, then, sublimation is both necessary and desirable in some instances. The conflict between an individual's desires and society's demands is inevitable. Only when a person finds an acceptable way to express and release these drives can he find internal peace.

Projection. The displacement of one's own motives onto others is known as projection. The person attributes feelings he does not want to have to someone else, thus locating the source of conflict outside himself. A corporation executive who feels guilty about his own unscrupulous means of achieving power may project his own motives onto his business associates. He is simply a man doing his job, he may believe, but the people he works with are all two-faced connivers who cannot be trusted.

Dana Bramel (1962) demonstrated projection with an experiment in which male subjects were exposed to a homosexual threat. Each subject was given a partner, and both were connected to a machine they were told would measure sexual arousal while they looked at a series of pictures. Actually, the machine was a fake—the experimenter controlled the dial. Some of the subjects were led to believe they had

SUBLIMATION: A CASE HISTORY

In his very early years an infant was observed by a number of people to possess a considerable amount of aggressiveness and hostility. This was quite evident in his later ideas, his behavior, fantasies, and in repeated incidents with playmates. There were also several episodes of cruel and sadistic treatments of pets. His reading and hobbies confirmed these trends as well.

As he grew older, he became quite interested in hobbies, first in guns, and later in knives and sharp instruments. His hostility, sadistic trends, and his aggressive trends met with overwhelming parental and social disapproval and, almost inevitably, his own. By the time he had traversed the latent stage of development there appeared to be little outward trace of these drives left.

There was, however, some growing interest in the work of physicians in the field of medicine. In adult life this man eventually became a highly successful and respected surgeon. The repressed instinctual strivings had been successfully sublimated into surgical work of high caliber. The process of sublimation had not only been successful, but had also proved highly valuable from personal, cultural, and social standpoints (Laughlin, 1963, p. 98).

measurable homosexual tendencies; others were not. In interviews after the experiment, the subjects who had been threatened were more inclined to attribute homosexual feelings to their partners than were the control subjects. Bramel feels this was because they could not deny evidence about themselves from the machine. Trapped, they projected the unacceptable self-image onto their partners.

Identification. The reverse of projection is identification. Through projection, a person rids himself of undesirable feelings by attributing them to someone else. Through identification, he takes on the characteristics of someone else in order to share in that person's triumphs and avoid feelings of personal incompetence. The admired person's actions become a substitute for actions of his own. Identification is considered a form of defensive coping because it enables people to resolve conflicts vicariously. A woman who gives up career ambitions to raise children may share emotionally in her husband's professional life. When he is promoted, she may feel as if *she* had triumphed. The musician who still feels that his father wanted him to be a lawyer and who sometimes wishes he had become one may temporarily identify with Clarence Darrow as he reads his biography.

Identification is a very natural part of growing up. All children imitate adults in their play, often with disturbing accuracy. A game of cowboys and Indians, for example, allows children to practice the moral values they are learning. Sex roles are also developed in part

PROJECTION: A CASE HISTORY

A 36-year-old elementary schoolteacher was perhaps best known by her colleagues for her bitter condemnations of anyone in whom she observed signs of poor organization, lack of orderliness and meticulousness, or inability to cope with difficult situations. Becoming easily emotional or unnerved was an anathema to her.

It had been long and painfully obvious to her friends that she possessed herself the attributes so readily ascribed to others, and so much the cause for censure. Her appearance was unkempt; her desk was generally in disarray; and she readily "flew off the handle" when things did not go smoothly.

Her fellow teachers recognized implicitly that she was projecting her inadequacies and shortcomings to others. This endeavored to spare her the anxiety and intolerable burden of self-censure which otherwise would result were she to consciously recognize them in herself (Laughlin, 1970, p. 227).

through play. Girls may be punished more for fighting than boys. When play becomes too rough, a girl's tears may get more parental sympathy than a boy's.

But identification is more than imitation. The child *internalizes* values long before they have any direct meaning for him. A 6-year-old may not care about his mother's collection of china figurines, but he warns his friends to stay away from the shelf because he identifies with his mother and wants her approval. He feels it is wrong to play with them, even though he has no sense of their artistic or sentimental value. Identification is thus a primary source of moral values.

Freud felt that part of the reason children identify with their parents is self-defense. Freud believed that the child goes through a stage of considering the same-sex parent a rival. The child wants to do away with that parent and fears reprisal for his fantasies. Identification with that parent resolves the conflict and removes the fear. The Little League star who has absorbed his father's competitiveness feels confident of his father's approval. By identifying with his father, specifically with his father's fantasies about sports and his view of proper male behavior, the child also shares vicariously in his father's adulthood and power.

Identification is also prominent in adolescence. The 13- or 14-year-old is no longer satisfied with games and make-believe success. His goals are adult, but society says he is not yet ready to function as a full member. Both sex and full-time work are prohibited. Adolescents typically resolve the conflict between what they think they can do and what society and their parents allow by identifying with rock and movie stars, politicians, and other visible public figures.

Of course, identification goes both ways in the parent-child relationship. Even if parents do not have ambitions for their children, they may identify with their youth. A mother may enjoy her daughter's popularity or political activism; a father may share his son's bent for poetry, science, or motorcycles. Just as the adolescent gains a sense of autonomy by identifying with Mick Jagger, the adult regains his youth and hopes by identifying with his children. Identification is thus a way of coping with being too young or too old to do everything one wants.

It is also a way of coping with situations in which a person feels utterly helpless. Bettelheim describes how prisoners in concentration camps gradually came to identify with the Nazi guards. Unable to retaliate against their captors, prisoners turned on each other. Over the years they began to copy the speech and mannerisms of the guards, and sometimes even their values. Old prisoners put in charge of new internees were sometimes more vicious than their models.

Bettelheim explains this puzzling behavior in Freudian terms. The prisoners were completely dependent on the guards, who could treat them however they liked. The relationship between prisoner and guard was similar to that between son and father. Bettelheim suggests that the guards may have consciously made their wards feel like children. For example, prisoners had to ask permission to go to the bathroom. Sometimes that permission was denied, forcing on grown men the indignity of wetting their pants. Reduced to a childlike, helpless condition, prisoners reverted to a pattern developed in childhood—identification with the aggressor (Bettelheim, 1943, 1960). Like boys in conflict with a stern and cruel father, they grew to admire their enemy.

Regression. The prisoners were exhibiting symptoms of regression, the reversion to childlike, even infantile, behavior. No form of adult behavior would have worked for the prisoners: they could not argue with their oppressors or appeal to their humanity. Direct action was sure to make the situation worse. With all else failing, these victims found some relief in regressing to immature patterns. Why? Some psychologists feel it is because an adult cannot stand feeling helpless. Children, on the other hand, are made aware of their dependency every day. By regressing to childhood emotionally, these people made an intolerable situation more bearable.

But regression is not always the result of imposed dependency. The adult woman who cries when her arguments fail may expect those around her to react sympathetically, as her parents did when she was a child. The executive may use temper tantrums in the same way. In both examples the individual is drawing on experiences long past to solve current problems—in the hope that someone will respond and take care of him. Inappropriate as it may seem, such behavior often works—which brings up the final point in this section.

Is defensive coping a sign that a person is immature, unstable, on the edge of a breakdown? The answer is no. All people act childishly on some occasions, intellectualize on others. We could not get along from day to day if we allowed ourselves to fully realize the dangers of flying in an airplane or driving on a superhighway. Sublimation and identification, at least according to the psychoanalytic view, are essential to growing up. However, when any of these defenses *interfere* with a person's ability to function, when they create more problems than they solve, psychologists consider the defense a maladjustment. But what is successful adjustment?

The Well-Adjusted Individual

Psychologists differ in their ideas of what constitutes effective adjustment. Some base their evaluation on an individual's ability to live according to social norms. All people have hostile and selfish wishes; all people dream impossible dreams. Those who learn to control such impulses and to limit their goals to those society allows and provides for are well adjusted. The girl who grows up in a small town, attends her state university, teaches for a year or two, and then settles down to a peaceful family life is, according to this view, well adjusted. She is living by the values of her society.

Other psychologists disagree strongly with this "conformist" viewpoint. Barron (1963), for example, argues that "refusal to adjust . . . is very often the mark of a healthy character." Society is not always right. To accept its rules blindly (to say, for example, "My country, right or wrong") is to give in. Barron suggests that the well-adjusted person enjoys the difficulties and ambiguities of life—rather than avoiding them by conforming. He is able to accept challenges and to feel pain and confusion. Confident of his ability to deal with problems in a realistic and mature way, he is able to admit primitive or childish impulses into his consciousness. Temporary regression does not threaten him. Barron sees flexibility, spontaneity, and creativity as signs of healthy adjustment.

This view is based primarily on the psychoanalytic theory that overcontrol produces anxiety. Antisocial impulses do not disappear when a person pushes them out of his mind. The individual who lives by a strict code of values and works all his life to accommodate society's demands is very likely repressing his own needs. Unable to feel or express his emotions, he is tense, defensive, overly anxious to please—and probably uncomfortably neurotic. The man who really wanted to be a painter but yielded to pressure to go into business, marry, and raise a family—and at age 50 develops a heart condition—is an example.

But not all psychologists feel that the way a person copes with his life determines whether or not he will be happy and self-fulfilled. All that matters is that he learn how to get along. One woman finds happiness in marriage; another in working her way to the top of a corporation; still another in tending her garden in the evenings and on weekends. In this view, the absence of tension indicates healthy adjustment.

Not content with this negative definition, still others suggest the following pattern. The well-adjusted person has learned to balance conformity and nonconformity, self-control and spontaneity. He is able to let himself go, but also able to control himself in situations where acting on his impulses would be damaging. He is able to change when society demands it, but also to change society when this seems the better course. One explanation of this flexibility is that the person is realistic in his appraisal of the world around him *and* of his own needs and capabilities. He knows his strengths and admits his weaknesses. As a result, he has chosen a role in life that is in harmony with his inner self: he does not feel he must act against his values in order to be successful. This self-trust enables him to face conflicts and threats without excessive anxiety and, perhaps more important, to risk his feelings and self-esteem in intimate relationships.

Another means of evaluating adjustment is to use specific criteria, such as these (Coleman & Hammen, 1974).

1. *Does the person's behavior really meet the stress, or does it simply postpone resolving the problem?* Various forms of escapism—drugs, alcohol, and even endless fantasizing through books, movies, and television—may divert us from our pain. But they do not eliminate the causes of our difficulties. Thus, escapism can never be a truly effective adjustment to a stressful situation.
2. *Does the action satisfy the individual's own needs?* Often we act to eliminate external pressures in our lives without considering our own needs. A wife may abandon her career goals because of her husband's. In the short run, external pressure on her may be reduced, but she may experience frustration and disappointment for the rest of her life. A solution that creates such inner conflict is often not really an effective adjustment.
3. *Is the action in harmony with the individual's environment?* Some individuals satisfy their needs in a way that hurts other people. The young executive who uses people and manipulates co-workers may "get ahead" through such actions. But, even if he does succeed in becoming vice-president of his company, he may find himself without friends. He may become afraid that others will treat him as he treated them. Ultimately, this situation can become quite stressful and frustrating. An effective adjustment must take into consideration both individual needs and the well-being of others.

Summary

1. The way an individual attempts to adapt to his physical and social environment and to achieve harmony between his own desires and motives and the demands and constraints placed on him by his environment is called *adjustment*.
2. An individual who faces a situation in which he feels unable to cope often begins to feel tense and uncomfortable. *Stress* describes situations in which a person feels threatened, frustrated, or in conflict, and his reactions to

such situations. Stress is particularly important to psychologists because people do not perform as well when they are upset.

3. *Pressure* is a form of stress in which the individual feels he must live up to a particular standard of behavior or adapt to rapid change. Pressures can be *internal* or *external*. We may pressure ourselves to live up to some internal standard of excellence. External pressures include competition, change, and the expectations and demands of family and friends.

4. *Anxiety* is a form of stress in which the individual experiences all the symptoms of stress, but cannot identify what is frightening or upsetting him. Some psychologists explain anxiety in terms of psychoanalytic theory—as a sign of internal conflict between a person's conscious values and his unconscious desires.

5. In *frustration* the individual is somehow prevented from achieving his goal. He must either give up his goal, find some new way to achieve it, or adjust to living with his disappointment.

6. *Conflicts* are probably the most common problems to which people must adjust. Conflicts occur when an individual is faced with two incompatible demands, opportunities, needs, or goals.

7. One way of describing conflict is in terms of two opposite tendencies—*approach* and *avoidance*. Developed by Kurt Lewin, this theory says that we want to approach things that attract us and avoid things that frighten us. These contradictory feelings produce three basic types of conflict.

8. In an *approach/approach conflict*, the individual is attracted to two goals at the same time and must either make a choice between them or modify one or both of them in some way.

9. In an *avoidance/avoidance conflict*, the individual faces two undesirable or threatening, yet unavoidable, alternatives and must either choose the one that causes the least discomfort or, in certain extreme instances, sit the situation out and wait for the inevitable.

10. In an *approach/avoidance conflict*, the individual is both attracted to and repelled by the same goal.

11. There are two general types of adjustment—*direct coping* and *defensive coping*.

12. Direct coping refers to any action a person takes to alter an uncomfortable situation, either by trying to change the situation or by trying to change himself. *Aggression, compromise,* and *withdrawal* are all ways of coping directly.

13. Defensive coping is one way that people deal with complex situations that they feel unable to solve. They may deny that a threat exists, block out painful memories, or repress unacceptable impulses.

14. Defensive coping can take several forms, called *defense mechanisms*. In using defense mechanisms, people react to frustration or conflict with self-deception about their real desires and goals in order to maintain their self-esteem and avoid anxiety.

15. *Denial* is refusing to acknowledge that a painful or threatening situation exists. *Intellectualization* is a subtle form of denial by which a person detaches himself emotionally from his problems by analyzing them in purely rational terms. *Reaction formation*, a behavioral form of denial, is exhibited when a person expresses emotions that are the opposite of what he really feels.

16. *Repression,* or motivated forgetting, is probably the most common means of blocking out painful situations. *Displacement,* the redirection of unrealizable drives into other areas, is closely related to repression. *Sublimation* goes one step further—instead of simply forgetting, the person redirects his drives into acceptable forms of behavior that allow him to express and release these drives.

17. *Projection* involves the displacement of one's own motives onto others. The reverse is *identification*—assuming the characteristics of someone else in order to share that person's successes and avoid feelings of personal incompetence.

18. *Regression* refers to the reversion to childlike, even infantile, behavior when no form of adult behavior will work in a certain situation.

19. Some psychologists believe that healthy adjustment depends on an individual's ability to live according to social norms, to control his drives and limit his goals to those society allows. Others feel that a person is well adjusted when he is able to face the difficulties and ambiguities of life by demonstrating flexibility, spontaneity, and creativity. Some claim that the absence of tension indicates effective adjustment, while others suggest that the well-adjusted person is able to balance conformity and nonconformity, self-control and spontaneity.

Suggested Readings

Appley, M. H., and Trumbull, R. (Eds.), *Psychological Stress: Issues in Research* (New York: Appleton-Century-Crofts, 1967). A comprehensive collection of articles that explore many approaches to the study of stress.

Blatz, W. E., *Human Security: Some Reflections* (Toronto: University of Toronto Press, 1966). A unique theory of human development as a search for security and competence.

Coleman, J. C., and Hammen, C. L., *Contemporary Psychology and Effective Behavior* (Glenview, Ill.: Scott, Foresman, 1974). A well-written and positive overview of adjustment that emphasizes effective coping.

Frazer, M., *Children in Conflict* (Garden City, N.Y.: Doubleday, 1973). Deals with the ways in which children in Northern Ireland have learned to cope with the stress caused by the strife between the Catholics and the Protestants.

Goldstein, M. J., and Palmer, J. O., *The Experience of Anxiety: A Casebook,* 2nd ed. (New York: Oxford University Press, 1975). A set of cases that illustrate the ways in which people may fail to adjust effectively.

Lawson, R. (Ed.), *Frustration: The Development of a Scientific Concept* (New York: Macmillan, 1965). A collection of readings on the experimental approach to studying frustration.

Lazarus, R. S., *Patterns of Adjustment and Human Effectiveness* (New York: McGraw-Hill, 1969). An excellent, thorough description of the kinds of things we have to cope with and our ways of adjusting to them.

Toffler, A., *Future Shock* (New York: Random House, 1970). A fascinating analysis of the rapidly increasing demands for adjustment in a world of ever-accelerating social change.

outline

WHAT IS ABNORMAL? 491

Historical Views of Abnormal Behavior
Current Views of Abnormal Behavior

NEUROSES 497

Anxiety Neurosis
Phobias
Dissociative Neurosis
Conversion Reaction
Obsessive-Compulsive Neurosis
Neurotic Depression
Individual Differences and Neurotic Behavior

CHARACTER DISORDERS 506

Sexual Deviation
Alcoholism and Addiction
Sociopathic Behavior

PSYCHOSES 513

Affective Psychosis
Schizophrenia
Organic Psychosis
The Causes of Psychosis

SUMMARY 522

SUGGESTED READINGS 525

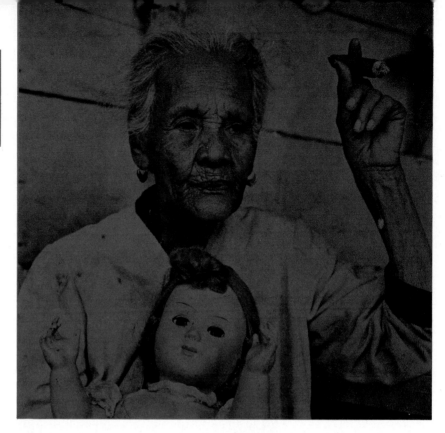

14

Normal and Abnormal Behavior

What Is Abnormal?

There is no clear dividing line between normal and abnormal behavior. Most of us consider people "disturbed" when they habitually act in a bizarre and irrational manner that we cannot understand—like the old woman who stands on the street corner arguing loudly with the air or the man who thinks he is Napoleon.

But psychologists point out that what is bizarre or abnormal for one person, under one set of circumstances, may be normal for another person in other circumstances. If a man takes off all his clothes and goes for a walk down the main street of his town, he will probably be arrested and held for a psychiatric examination. But if a hundred young people decide to swim nude at a public beach, the reaction will be quite different. They may be arrested or chased away, but few people will think they are "crazy."

491

Figure 14-1
Playing music is not in itself
considered abnormal
behavior. But what about
Nero's singing while Rome
burned?
(*The Bettmann Archive*)

What is generally considered normal behavior thus varies from time to time and place to place, and society sets the standards. But in a complex society such as ours, different cultures and different values exist side by side. This fact makes it difficult for a psychologist to derive a general definition of "normal," using social standards.

To some extent, psychologists turn to *intrapersonal standards* of normality—that is, they try to evaluate each person in terms of his own life. Consider the following examples:

A housewife is unable to keep up with her work because no matter how often she washes the dishes or cleans the bathrooms, she cannot get them clean enough. Her husband and children do not understand. Finally one morning she cannot get out of bed.

The adolescent son of a wealthy suburbanite has a substantial bank account of his own, yet one night he is arrested for trying to hold up a gas station. He insists that there is nothing wrong with his actions.

A quiet, well-behaved child quite unexpectedly covers the living room walls with fingerpaint. When questioned, he explains that "Johnny" did it. Within a few weeks, the child is spending all his time alone in his room talking with his imaginary friend.

Each of these individuals is acting in a dysfunctional, self-defeating manner. The housewife has set herself an impossible task. Her perception of the danger of germs is so exaggerated that she cannot possibly win the battle against them. The suburbanite's son is surprised at people's concern. "Why all the fuss?" he asks. "So I got caught." His complete failure to internalize certain basic social values is also considered a psychological problem. All children make free use of their imaginations—they invent people when they play and make excuses for unacceptable behavior. But the child in the example above is unable (or unwilling) to turn his imagination off. Perhaps Johnny protects him from punishment, loss of love, loneliness. Johnny does all the things he cannot.

Figure 14-2
Moondog, an eccentric
Manhattan poet who walks
the streets dressed as a
Viking.
(*Curt Kaufman, Photo
Researchers*)

The behavior of these people is considered abnormal because their perception of reality is distorted and their ability to cope appropriately is impaired. The housewife is struggling with an unseen—and invincible—foe. The adolescent can comprehend neither the effects of his action on the victim nor the basic immorality of his behavior. The child, on the other hand, perceives his own normal impulses as terribly wrong, but, since he is unable to control them, he invents a second self. The important point about abnormal behavior is that, in each case, the person's *interpretation of reality* makes adjustment impossible. Within that interpretation of reality, the person *is* trying to cope effectively. But each of these people is behaving in a way that creates more problems than it solves. Distorted perception, inappropriateness, and discomfort are three criteria for abnormal behavior.

Figure 14-3
Our word "lunacy" comes from the early belief that abnormal behavior was caused by the influence of the moon. Interestingly, some researchers in recent years have found that patients in mental hospitals often become quite restless and violent crimes sometimes increase on nights when the moon is full.
(*The Bettmann Archive*)

A fourth is danger—to oneself and to others. The person who is likely to attempt suicide or to harm a friend or stranger in a sudden outburst is a threat. So too, in a more general sense, is the person who behaves in an irrational way. We all depend on being able to predict how people will act. We expect drivers to stop for red lights, grocers to give us food in exchange for money, friends to understand our feelings and react sympathetically. When a person violates these written and unwritten rules, he creates problems for himself and for those around him. When violations are extreme, we consider such people in need of help. But this has not always been the case.

Historical Views of Abnormal Behavior

No one knows precisely what ancient man considered abnormal or how he explained unreasonable behavior to his children. However, we can hazard a general description based on studies of contemporary primitive tribes. In such cultures, nearly everything is attributed to supernatural powers. Madness is a sign that spirits have taken possession of a person. Sometimes the possessed person is seen as sacred and his visions are considered messages from the spirit world. Other times the tribal wisemen diagnose the presence of evil spirits. Presumably, this supernatural view of abnormal behavior dominated early man.

The ancient Greeks viewed unreasonable behavior quite differently. Madness, they felt, was a disease of the spirit. Like other illnesses, it could be cured with rest, proper diet and exercise, and a little magic.

Figure 14-4

The arrest of a woman
accused of witchcraft in
Salem, Massachusetts.
(*The Bettmann Archive*)

Not all Greeks, however, accepted this view. The most notable exception was Hippocrates (c. 450–c. 377 B.C.). Sickness, he argued, is a natural event arising from natural causes. So is madness. Epilepsy, he reasoned, is caused by the brain melting down into the body, resulting in fits and foaming at the mouth. Hysteria, he felt, was a woman's disease that occurs when the womb wanders from its natural place in the body in a frustrated search for sex and children; marriage is the obvious cure. Melancholia, an imbalance in the body fluids, can be cured with abstinence and quiet. Because of the influence of Hippocrates' ideas, the mentally disturbed were treated with quiet and kindness for centuries.

Then, in the Dark Ages, the primitive idea that abnormal behavior was the work of demons was revived and given a new respectability by the Church. The ravings of madmen, the curses of old women, the sudden impotence of soldiers, the melancholy of young girls—all were attributed to the Devil and his agents. Over the years, sincere and pious men developed a battery of cruel techniques for exorcising the Devil, the most common of which was burning at the stake.

However, the fifteenth and early sixteenth centuries saw a return, in some circles, to the humanistic ideals of Greek culture. One writer after another suggested that such practices were cruel and inhuman. Some argued that madness was an illness and should be treated as such. Gradually, major cities began to establish asylums, where the insane—as they were called—were confined instead of tortured. By the late 1700s, pressure for a reevaluation of attitudes was mounting.

Most contemporary views of abnormal behavior derive from this revolutionary period in the history of psychology and medicine. In 1793 Philippe Pinel unchained the patients in a mental hospital in Paris (only

Figure 14-5

Philippe Pinel demanding
the removal of chains from
the patients in the Bicêtre
Hospital in Paris.
(*The Bettmann Archive*)

Figure 14-6
Charcot demonstrating hypnotism to his students. Although Sigmund Freud is not in this picture (which hung in his study), he did study with Charcot, and much of his early work was based on the effects of hypnosis on his patients. (*Inge Morath, Magnum Photos*)

11 years after the last witch-burning in Switzerland). He argued that disturbed people should be given pleasant surroundings, enjoyable occupations, kind treatment, and a chance to discuss their problems. The "moral cure," as this was called, rested on the idea that abnormal behavior was the result of problems in living.

At about the same time, another Frenchman, Franz Anton Mesmer, was achieving considerable fame for his success in curing everything from melancholy to blindness through hypnosis. Mesmer himself was something of a showman, but a number of doctors took him seriously—among them Jean-Martin Charcot. A neurologist, Charcot sought connections between the workings of the brain and the miraculous effects of hypnosis. Sigmund Freud, who studied under Charcot, based much of his early psychoanalytic work on the effects of hypnosis on disturbed people.

Meanwhile, in America, Dorothea Dix had launched a crusade against the imprisonment and mistreatment of the insane in state institutions. It was largely through her efforts that people began to think of disturbed persons as "mentally ill." Gradually, this country's asylums were turned into hospitals, staffed by doctors, nurses, and attendants.

One of the earliest hints that abnormal behavior might have an organic or physiological basis came in 1875. In that year, Fournier published an explanation of *paresis*—an overall breakdown of mind and body common among nineteenth-century merchants and soldiers. Most of them, he found, had at some point contracted syphilis. Fournier determined that syphilis was indeed the cause of the massive mental deterioration that characterized paresis. Thus began the search for a medical cure for all forms of madness.

Current Views of Abnormal Behavior

By the 1920s, three explanations of abnormal behavior had acquired a substantial following—explanations that continue to influence psychological research and theory today. At one end is the **organic model:** abnormal behavior has a biochemical or physiological basis. In part, this view rests on the evidence that a tendency to schizophrenia can be inherited (see Chapter 2). Over the years a number of researchers have discovered chemical differences between normal and disturbed people. Some types of retardation have been traced to dietary deficiencies. The extensive use of drugs in mental institutions today also rests on the organic model of abnormal behavior.

At the opposite extreme is the **psychoanalytic model** developed by Freud and his followers. According to this model, behavior disorders are symbolic expressions of internal unconscious conflicts. To recover, the person must trace his problems to their origins in childhood and infancy.

The **medical model** of abnormal behavior has adherents in both the physiological and psychoanalytic camps. A perspective more than a theory, the medical model suggests that the person who behaves abnormally is sick. This approach has led to the classification of psychological symptoms and the naming of diseases—a procedure that enables doctors to compare cases and methods for treating them. It has also promoted the idea that disturbed people are not responsible for their behavior—that they are fundamentally different from normal people.

In recent years, several new viewpoints on behavior disorders have appeared. The medical model has been attacked by learning theorists, who argue that abnormal behavior, like all behavior, is the result of learning. By reversing this process, fear, anxiety, frigidity, hallucinations, and so on, can be *unlearned*—without the probing of the analyst (which can take years) or the use of drugs. By implication, the **learning theory model** suggests that the only thing that separates the normal from the "sick" is experience.

Thomas Szasz has also attacked the medical model. He says that the idea of mental illness is a myth equivalent to the demonic myth of the Middle Ages. Because most of us find it difficult to deal with people who are deviant when someone behaves in a way that disturbs our view of how things should be, society can simply dispose of him by labeling him sick and closing him off in an institution. Szasz (1974) particularly deplores the government's use of the medical model as an excuse to create laws that determine what is or is not mentally healthy behavior.

R. D. Laing takes an even more radical view. According to Laing, most of us refuse to admit our own craziness, preferring to live in an artificial world of logic, neat explanations, and happy endings. The so-called mentally ill, Laing says, have dared to step over the bound-

Thomas Szasz
(Photo by Gabor Szilasi)

R. D. Laing
(Jill Krementz)

aries of this world into their minds. Laing sees their journey into the unknown and chaotic parts of the self as an act of heroism.

Whether or not these new views of abnormal behavior will replace the traditional models remains to be seen. At present, most psychiatrists think partly in terms of the medical model, partly in terms of "problems in living." Many psychological disorders begin as social problems—loss of love or self-esteem, frustration, unresolved conflicts. But when a person copes with these problems in a way that makes him feel more nervous and unhappy, or escapes them by distorting reality and cutting himself off from other people entirely, a problem in living has become a psychological problem. Some disorders tend to relate more to one model than another. For example, the organic model seems to be most relevant to schizophrenia (Siegler & Osmond, 1974).

As you read the descriptions of the various disorders summarized in this chapter, you may occasionally feel an uncomfortable twinge of recognition. This is only natural. Much abnormal behavior is simply normal behavior that is greatly exaggerated or displayed in inappropriate situations. Moreover, the similarities between yourself and a person with psychological problems are likely to be as instructive as the differences.

Neuroses

The term **neurosis** derives from the now-discarded idea that anxiety, depression, and so on, are physiological disorders—specifically, a disease in the nervous system. Today psychologists consider neurotic behavior a symptom and expression of emotional problems.

Neurosis is characterized by inappropriate emotions and behavior. The neurotic person is not "crazy" in the way we ordinarily use the word. For the most part, he is able to get along from day to day and acts and thinks like everybody else. But at some point there is a collapse. He may be terrified of being in closed rooms; he may go off for several days and be unable to remember where he went or what he did; quite suddenly, he may be unable to move one of his hands.

What causes such behaviors? Psychoanalytic theorists feel they are reactions to internal threats. The person is fighting impulses that contradict his self-image and values. The man who cannot move his hand, for example, may have been punished severely for masturbating as a child. Now, after 7 years of marriage, his eye begins to wander. He is sure his wife suspects his fantasies and begins to feel as he did as a child when his father slapped his hand and said he was disgusting. The impulse to masturbate returns. In this instance, the paralysis is self-protective: it prevents the man from doing something that would make him feel guilty. According to the psychoanalytic view, then, neurotic behavior is a symbolic and indirect expression of unconscious conflict.

The Shriek by Edvard Munch: Collection, The Museum of Modern Art, New York; Mathew T. Mellon Fund.

Behavior theorists take a somewhat different perspective. According to them, a person who behaves neurotically has learned to associate fear and anxiety with an apparently innocuous situation or object. The man who fears closed rooms may have been punished as a child by being locked in a closet. Perhaps the experience was repeated: a principal asked him to wait in a small, windowless room while his parents were being told that he was a troublemaker; years later a doctor closed the door before telling him that he was very ill. These incidents reinforce the man's early experiences to the point where he is fearful and anxious in all closed places.

Whether they view neurotic behavior as an expression of internal conflict, as learned behavior, or as influenced by personality factors, most psychologists agree that the behavior itself becomes a trap. The person realizes that his fears and actions are unreasonable, but he finds it difficult or impossible to change. Tiredness, irritability, and high levels of tension are characteristic of neurosis, though not all tired or irritable people are neurotic. We turn now to a description of the most common neuroses.*

Anxiety Neurosis

Anxiety neurosis is a chronic state of apprehension. All people are afraid at times, but usually they know why. This knowledge enables them to attack or escape the source of fear. Of course, as we noted in Chapter 13, direct action is not always possible. A student who does not like to go home because he always fights with his parents, but does not want to spend Christmas alone, can neither attack nor escape comfortably. But at least he knows why he is tense. Anxiety, on the other hand, is apprehension without an identifiable source of danger. Like fear, it is a common experience—and for most people, a brief one. The student stops being anxious once he decides that he would rather go home than be alone. However, when anxiety persists, when a person is unable to sleep or relax for days at a time, or when anxiety attacks are so severe that he is virtually paralyzed, the condition may be described as anxiety neurosis.

Phobias

A **phobia** is an intense, paralyzing fear of something in the absence of any real danger—a fear of something most people find tolerable. Few of us like snakes, but this distaste does not interfere with our lives. But when a person is so afraid of snakes that he cannot go near a zoo, go camping with his family, or even look at pictures of snakes on

*The various therapies used to treat psychological problems are discussed in the next chapter.

ANXIETY NEUROSIS: A CASE HISTORY

Miss J. K., aged 24, while at her work, suddenly feels a pressure on her chest. She has to sit down, as she is seized with giddiness, is afraid of falling, and gasps for breath. She is possessed by an indescribable dread. This must be death—a pulmonary stroke. She begins to pant spasmodically. Her forehead is bathed in a cold sweat. After a few minutes the oppression gives way to a fit of weeping.

Ever since this attack she suffers from a chronic lack of breath. She is obliged to take deep breaths, gasping for air, often ten times consecutively until she can get the "right" breath. She grows thin. She cannot eat much because food "weighs" in her stomach. Her sleep, hitherto tranquil and deep, becomes restless. She goes to sleep with difficulty and is troubled with uneasy dreams. She sees corpses, is attacked by burglars, somebody thrusts a knife into her stomach, she is pursued by raging dogs, wild bulls, and neighing horses. She awakes with palpitations and covered with perspiration, out of these (typical) anxiety dreams. By day, also, she is tormented by groundless fears, palpitations, and giddiness. At times a fever seems to run through her veins.

The organs are perfectly sound. But her young employer, with whom she is secretly in love, married a few weeks ago. Her first attack took place a quarter of an hour later, within a neighbouring room, after she had surprised the young couple in a passionate embrace. On leaving the business there was a conspicuously rapid disappearance of all the symptoms described (Stekel, 1950, pp. 29–30).

(Tom McHugh, Photo Researchers; courtesy Steinhart Aquarium)

(Carl Frank, Photo Researchers)

television without trembling, he is phobic. The fear of heights, water, closed rooms, fire, and cats are all common phobias.

Psychoanalytic theorists see phobias as a kind of displacement. The phobic person is frightened by his own unconscious wishes. Unable to face his wishes or the fear of them, he transfers the fear to something outside himself. Displacement brings relief on two levels. First, he has an outlet for his emotions; he does not have to keep them bottled up. Second, it is possible (if difficult) to avoid heights, snakes, or closed rooms, but nearly impossible to escape one's own impulses.

Other psychologists believe that phobias are learned in a more direct way. For example, a child is savagely attacked by a large dog. Because of this traumatic event, he is now terribly afraid of all large dogs, even friendly, gentle ones. As we noted in Chapter 4, because phobias are usually learned after only one such experience and are extremely resistant to extinction, some learning theorists see them as *prepared responses*—responses built into us biologically over ages and ages of evolution. Seligman (1972) suggests that this is why there is such a relatively limited range of phobic objects. Common objects of phobias—such as darkness, snakes, large dogs—were once very real threats to our survival. But few people develop phobias about electric outlets, hammers, and knives, even though all of us have probably had unpleasant experiences with these objects. Two aspects of modern life that people do seem prepared to become phobic about are cars and airplanes.

One way that people deal with phobias is to force themselves to confront the situation that frightens them and conquer it. A man who fears heights climbs mountains on the weekend; a man who fears water goes sailing. Counterphobic behavior such as this may restore the person's self-esteem for a time, but it often leads to very real dangers. The mountain climber may push himself beyond his abilities in the desperate attempt to conquer his fear. More often, phobic people try to avoid the thing they fear, even though this may become impossible. A woman who is afraid of driving a car may find that she is beginning to get tense about walking on the sidewalk—someone else's car might go out of control. In a month or two she begins trembling every time she starts out her front door. Phobias tend to generalize in this way.

Dissociative Neurosis

Dissociative neurosis is perhaps the most puzzling form of neurosis—both to the observer and to the person experiencing it. Dissociation may take the form of a loss of memory, somnambulism (sleepwalking), a complete change in identity (usually temporary), or the presence of several distinct personalities in one person. In each case, a part of the individual's personality is separated from the rest and, for whatever reasons, he is unable to reassemble the pieces.

Amnesia, or loss of memory without an organic cause, may occur as a reaction to intolerable experiences. The person blocks out something he did or a period of his life. During World War II, a number of hospitalized soldiers were unable to recall the events leading up to their injury or collapse. But war and its horrors are not the only source of amnesia. The man who betrays a friend in order to complete a business deal and the housewife who calls an airline and reserves a single ticket for Tahiti may also forget what they have done. Near total amnesia—when a person forgets everything and wanders around not knowing who he is or where he is—is quite rare, despite its popularity in old movies.

Fugue states are also a popular subject for drama. The term literally means "flight" and describes an escape into a new, less confining, less responsible life, which the person had dreamed of but could not pursue without guilt. Temporary amnesia frees him to follow his impulses. Of course, in recent years a number of people have "taken off," abandoning their careers and sometimes their families to start a new life. But they are fully aware of the consequences of change. In contrast, most of

(The Bettmann Archive)

the people who experience fugue states are unable to make firm decisions and are just as unable to control their impulses.

The term **somnambulism** refers to anything a person does while asleep. Often a somnambulist's activities reflect emotions he cannot express during his waking hours. Walton (1961) tells of a young architectural assistant who began attacking his wife in his sleep. Awakened by her struggles, he remembered that he had been having a nightmare, but not what he had done. It seems the man associated his wife with his domineering mother, but was unable to stand up to either of them. Somnambulism is rare and is found most often in children and adolescents.

Multiple personality is even less frequent. It involves extreme forms of amnesia and a variation on the fugue state. The individual's personality is split into two or more distinct characters. Of course, all people play different roles. We behave one way at work, another way among friends, and still another way with our parents—but through it all we remember who we are. This is not the case with a person exhibiting multiple personality. In effect, he has within him several personalities, and he cannot remember what he did in one role when he is in another. Usually this neurosis is attributed to conflicting values and desires. A man who always supresses anger and frustration may periodically go "berserk," acting out the violent impulses he usually represses; a quiet, modest young woman may occasionally abandon her morals, change her posture and voice, and go to bars for the express purpose of picking up strange men. In each example the two personalities are incompatible, so each is acted out independently.

Conversion Reaction

Conversion reaction, or **hysteria,** was common among the Greeks and Romans and persisted through the Middle Ages and the Renaissance. In the 1880s and 1890s a few hypnotists achieved widespread fame for curing hysteria. Then, about 1900, Freud began to publish the results of his "talking cure." Today hysterical neurosis is comparatively rare.

Hysteria is paralysis, blindness, or deafness without biological basis. The person is healthy, his muscles and nerves intact. But he may be unable to move, to see, to talk, or to hear. Psychoanalysts see hysteria as a transplantation of emotional problems to the body. After treating a number of hysterical patients, Freud came to the conclusion that the physical symptom was always related to traumatic experiences buried in the person's past. The man who had been punished for masturbating loses the use of his hand; the woman who years before saw her mother being seduced by a traveling salesman loses her sight.

By unconsciously developing a handicap, the person punishes himself for forbidden desires or behavior, prevents himself from acting on these desires or repeating the behavior, and at the same time regresses to an earlier stage, when people took care of him. Although there is no real physical cause for the handicap, hysteria can result in physical damage. When muscles are not used for extended periods, as in hysterical paralysis, they can become weak and may ultimately atrophy.

Sometimes it is easy to determine that a handicap is hysterical rather than organic. Some hysterical disorders are anatomically impossible, as in "glove anesthesia," a lack of feeling in the hand from the wrist down. There is no way that damage to the nerves running into the hand could cause such a pattern of anesthesia. Another clue to hysteria is the fact that the person is unusually cheerful about his disability. Most people are quite upset when they find they cannot move or see. Characteristically, the hysteric is not; psychologists call this attitude *la belle indifférence*.

Today hypochondria and psychophysiological disorders are far more common than hysteria. **Hypochondria** refers to the continued belief that one is sick—in the absence of symptoms. **Psychophysiological** or **psychosomatic disorders** are very real biological problems that seem to result from prolonged anxiety and stress. Ulcers, migraine headaches, asthma, high blood pressure, and heart conditions can all result from psychological problems.

Obsessive-Compulsive Neurosis

The term **obsessive-compulsive neurosis** applies to a wide range of behavior. Obsessions are recurring thoughts and fantasies that are almost impossible to get rid of. Compulsions are strong, uncontrollable inpulses that go against a person's conscious intentions. A typical obsessive-compulsive neurotic is rigid, hyperactive, and meticulous. He likes everything to be in order, from his office to his social life. Threatened by change, he insists that things be done the way they always have been done. He is exceptionally good at details, but often loses sight of long-range goals. He is tortured by doubt and indecision, for he is more aware than other people of the vast possibilities for error.

All of us sometimes engage in similar behavior—we organize drawers, clean the living room twice when someone we want to impress is coming to dinner, insist on maintaining traditions that have outlived their significance. This kind of behavior becomes neurotic when it begins to dominate a person's life. The woman who checks her watch five or six times when she is waiting to pick up an old friend on the six o'clock train is excited; the woman who constantly checks all the clocks in her house and gets nervous and upset if one is slightly inaccurate is obsessed with time and compulsive about correcting clocks.

Psychoanalytic theorists explain obsessive-compulsive neurosis in terms of defenses. It begins when repression fails to work and the person must try to deal with an uncomfortable emotion or fantasy. For example, a young man who is about to finish his medical internship

Figure 14-7

Humphrey Bogart as Captain Queeg in *The Caine Mutiny*. Whenever he was anxious, Captain Queeg would compulsively rub two steel balls together. His obsessions about neatness and doing things by the book so angered the crew that they mutinied.
(*Penguin Photo*)

is tortured by the thought that he has made a mistake. He and his wife have struggled for years to put him through school, but he cannot help thinking about the life he might have led if he had not gone to medical school and married early. Fantasies about murdering his wife begin to interfere with his work—he cannot concentrate. Then one day he discovers that if he concentrates on a list of symptoms he memorized years ago, he can escape his worries about his life. This recitation of lists becomes more and more frequent. Later he realizes that his wife is hinting that she wants a baby. He becomes tense and disappears into the bathroom to wash his hands. This too may reduce his anxiety, and more and more often he responds with this behavior as a way of escape. Soon these trivial rituals—the reciting and washing—are holding his life together and, at the same time, taking up a disproportionate amount of his time. In other words, repeated thoughts and actions—obsessive-compulsive behavior—have helped control the impulses that are unacceptable and they have become problems in themselves.

Although the event that triggers obsessive-compulsive neurosis usually occurs in adulthood, Freud looked back to childhood events to find the source of the disorder. Freud (1924) claimed that the obsessive-compulsive behavior was the result of the individual's unpleasant experiences during toilet training. However, this has been tested, and so far no consistent relationship has been found between methods of toilet training and later obsessive-compulsive neurosis (Beloff, 1957; O'Connor & Franks, 1960; Sewell, Mussen, & Harris, 1955).

Learning theorists believe that this type of behavior is learned in response to trauma. The behavior may be learned by trial and error—as when the intern in our example discovered by accident that reciting lists reduced his anxiety—or it can be an exaggeration of some responses that had successfully reduced anxiety in the past (Dollard & Miller, 1950). This reduction of anxiety is reinforcing and encourages the obsessive-compulsive to repeat the behavior. Carr (1974) agrees with this theory in part, but finds it inadequate because it does not deal with the cognitive factors involved, does not explain the "ritualistic character" of the behavior, or how a single trauma can result in the common finding of more than one compulsive behavior in the same person.

Carr suggests instead that personality factors may be the critical element in the development of this disorder. He describes the obsessive-compulsive person as being abnormally cautious, very fearful of taking risks, and always sure that the worst will happen in every situation. These traits account for the individual's extreme anxiety and explain why, though excessive, the obsessive-compulsive's behavior is so real-world-oriented. According to Carr, the ritualistic behavior is simply an overdeveloped superstition, and just like any other superstition, it gives the individual a feeling that he is able to control events in some magical way. This can be compared to the avoidance training situation. As we saw in Chapter 4, avoidance training is very hard to extinguish because as long as the individual continues to respond, he has no way of ever finding out that the original threat no longer exists. When the expected catastrophe does not happen, the obsessive-compulsive feels he has been successful and so continues to behave in those ways that "worked." However, Carr himself recognizes that although there is little doubt that obsessive-compulsives have these abnormally high expectations of unpleasantness in all situations (Steiner, 1972), as yet there is no explanation for how these expectations arise.

Neurotic Depression

With phobias, dissociative neurosis, hysteria, and obsessive-compulsive rituals, people cast off internal problems—by projecting them onto objects, separating off a part of themselves that they dislike, translating their fears into physical symptoms, or blocking disturbing thoughts with rituals and mind-absorbing chores. In **neurotic depression,** this process is reversed: the person fully acknowledges—and exaggerates—his guilt and helplessness. Depression is characterized by sadness, feelings of worthlessness, and varying degrees of inactivity. The person feels that he has failed utterly. His ability to become involved with other people and in his work or studies declines. He may turn to friends for consolation, but he blames his troubles entirely on himself. He is tired and apathetic most of the time. Depression is a self-perpetuating state of mind: self-doubting, the depressed person feels unable to call a friend or start a new project—actions that might restore his self-confidence.

Exaggerated depression is often a reaction to a real loss or failure—the death of a loved one, losing a job, failing an exam, the sudden realization that one's children are leaving home. But this is not always the case. Some people get depressed when everything seems to be going well, and some people are depressed all the time.

(Joel Gordon)

Psychoanalysts offer the following explanation: as a child, the depressed person was never sure that he was loved and wanted. He felt angry about the lack of warmth in his family, but was afraid that if he expressed his hostility, he would only drive his parents further away. He grew up doubting that he was a lovable person and mistrusting the affection and confidence others offered him. In later life a sudden loss or a slow accumulation of disappointments tap this well of need and anger, and depression follows. According to this view, depression is an expression of ambivalence. The person wants love, but he never believes that anyone loves him and resents the people on whom he depends.

Psychoanalytic theorists emphasize the self-punishing side of depression and suggest a number of reasons why people want to do themselves harm. Sometimes self-punishment is payment for sinful fantasies and behavior. Other times people seem to feel that if they punish themselves, that if they are visibly miserable, no one else will hurt them. In this case, self-punishment is both a way of protecting oneself and an assertion of self-mastery and independence. As a child, the person knew that he would be punished for a particular action. If he sent himself to his room, without waiting for orders from his parents, he felt better, more adult. In effect, he was usurping his parents' role. Others feel that depression is displaced aggression. The person is furious at someone, but unable to express his anger. By turning his hostility against himself, he eliminates the possibility of retribution.

Behavior theorists agree that mistrust causes depression, but offer a somewhat different interpretation. Over the years, they say, the depressed person has learned that he is unable to keep friends, and that no matter how hard he tries, he fails with every project. Gradually he learns to expect loss and failure and begins to think of himself as a worthless, unlovable, incompetent person.

For example, Seligman (1973) notes that passivity is the most prominent symptom of depression. The depressed person is pessimistic about his ability to affect his environment in any positive way. He lacks aggressiveness and competitive drive. All of these symptoms resemble the behavior of dogs and rats in *learned helplessness* studies. In such a study, no matter what the animal does, it gets shocked. When the animal is later given electric shocks, it behaves passively and does not attempt to excape, even when it is given the chance.

Weiss, Glazer, and Pohorecky (1974) reviewed Seligman's experiments and came to a different conclusion. When dogs were tested 24 hours after the first inescapable shock, they did not try to escape. But when other dogs were tested for the first time 48 hours after the shock, they were able to escape. Weiss and his colleagues thus conclude that the dogs' behavior was not any form of permanent learned helplessness, but rather a symptom of a temporary neurochemical imbalance: a decrease in the amount of norepinephrine in the brain, which is a normal characteristic of reactions to stress. Schildkraut and Kety (1967) have related a chronic decrease in norepinephrine to depression in humans, and Weiss and his colleagues feel that their findings are further confirmation of this idea.

Other psychologists have suggested that there is a connection between depression and a particular personality type, called the *cyclothymic personality* (White & Watt, 1973). The cyclothymic person, in general, is energetic, affectionate, loyal, and outwardly confident. However, these people have one major flaw: they are extremely dependent on one "love-object" and cannot cope with frustration or disappointment connected with that love-object. The love-object is generally a person, but may be the individual's work, religion, or even some powerful symbol. Although they are otherwise well adjusted, their overdependence on one source of love and self-esteem makes them quite vulnerable.

None of the behavior we have described in this section is neurotic or abnormal in itself. All of us have periods of anxiety and depression; all of us are compulsive at times; and most of us are a little phobic about snakes, rats, roaches, and other relatively harmless creatures. Psychologists consider a person neurotic only when this kind of behavior dominates his life, increasing his problems, and when the person himself feels unhappy and ineffective much of the time.

Individual Differences and Neurotic Behavior

White and Watt (1973) pose an interesting question about the many different styles of neurotic behavior.

> Why does one person have plain anxiety attacks, another a circumscribed phobia, a third a crippling set of obsessions and compulsions, a fourth an amnesia for personal identity, while a fifth blossoms forth with an hysterical paralysis of the lower limbs? (p. 231)

Eysenck (1970) has made the most extensive studies of how personality may relate to neurosis. After much research, he concludes that whether a person is extraverted or introverted does relate significantly to his "choice" of neurosis. As Eysenck describes it, the extravert is sociable, changeable, and spontaneous. Such a person may develop hysteria and dissociated states under extreme conditions. By contrast, the introvert is quiet, introspective, and reserved. When stress occurs, he is apt to lapse into phobias and obsessive neuroses.

Korner (1971) has also related personality factors to the way individuals respond to stimulation, but he uses the terms "reflection" and "action" instead of introversion and extroversion. Thus, reflective people tend to mull things over, to dislike new or excessively strong stimulation, and to spend a good deal of time analyzing and sorting out their experiences. Active people, on the other hand, like novelty and are apt to react to strong stimulation with impulsive and excited movements and emotions. When threatened, reflective people tend to defend themselves by intellectualization and isolation, while active people tend to get even more excited. What is most interesting is Korner's conclusion, reached after studying 2- to 4-day-old infants, that these personality differences are present at birth.

Character Disorders

Ever since the psychological "revolution," when sympathy, hospitals, therapy, and drugs replaced the chains of insane asylums, psychologists and lawyers alike have puzzled over what to do with people with **character disorders** (conditions like sexual deviation, drug addiction, and sociopathology). These conditions are related by the fact that they all involve socially unacceptable expressions of the individual's impulses (unlike neuroses, which involve suppression and denial of impulses and desires). Some years back psychologists began to argue that homosexuality may become an emotional problem, but that it is not a crime. Many people feel that addiction to alcohol and drugs has reached epidemic proportions in this country, and thousands of researchers are looking for cures. A few years ago the drunkard and the addict were considered criminals; this view is also changing rapidly. Sociopathic or antisocial behavior is even more difficult to classify. Is the chronic lawbreaker an unreformable criminal to be locked away or a disturbed person who needs help?

Sexual Deviation

Ideas about what is normal and what is abnormal in sex vary with the times—and with the individual. As Kinsey demonstrated years ago, most Americans enjoy sexual activities forbidden by laws that have not kept up with sexual mores. Most sex laws are based on the idea that the sole purpose of sex is procreation: any act that does not lead to conception is therefore unnatural. But today most people consider sex a primary source of pleasure, intimacy, and personal fulfillment and feel that good sexual relations are a sign of physical and mental health. (In fact, with the population explosion, some people *now* feel that sex *for* procreation can be immoral.)

Among psychologists today there are two schools of thought about what is normal and abnormal in sex. On the one hand are those who feel that any activity that does not culminate in heterosexual intercourse is deviant. On the other hand are those who prefer not to judge specific activities. Rather, they focus on the person's feelings about whatever he does. According to this view, if a person is compulsive or guilty about his sex life, or if he is unable to enjoy sex fully, he is sexually maladjusted.

For purposes of description, sexual deviations are divided into three categories: ineffectiveness, unconventional sex objects, and unconventional modes of sexual expression. Perhaps because all of these are deviations from the heterosexual norm, and some are illegal, most result in guilt and unhappiness for the individual.

The term *ineffectiveness* refers to **impotence**—the male's inability to have or maintain an erection—and **frigidity**—the female's inability to experience sexual excitation or orgasm. Many people may experience occasional impotence or frigidity in response to some unusual stress in their lives. This condition is temporary, and when the stress is resolved, normal function generally returns. Truly impotent men and frigid women do not readjust in this way. Psychologists feel both problems are based on fear of heterosexual intimacy. The impotent man may have been warned as a child about venereal disease or domineer-

Figure 14-8
In many cases, homosexuals may have problems, not because they are homosexual, but because society has trouble accepting them. As our ideas about sex roles and expectations about how each sex may behave continue to change, homosexuals should find less difficulty in living their lives as they choose.
(Top: Leonard Freed, Magnum Photos; bottom: Chie Nishio, Nancy Palmer Photo Agency)

ing females and may feel threatened by all women. Frigidity usually results from fear of pregnancy, fear of male domination, or an overall fear of letting go. At the opposite extreme is promiscuity: the compulsive need to have sex often and with a variety of partners. Promiscuity may be a way of proving one's potency, a way of getting back at parents who condemned sex, or a search for fulfillment (frigidity and promiscuity sometimes go together).

There are various forms of **unconventional sex objects.** Perhaps the most familiar is homosexuality. In the past, homosexual behavior and even homosexual fantasies were considered shameful and perverse—but so was all sex outside marriage. Today the controversy centers not on whether having intercourse with someone of the same sex is sinful but on whether it is a psychological problem. Many people feel that any activity between two consenting adults that brings them pleasure is normal. Others argue that homosexuality is biologically unnatural and neurotic.

The labels **homosexual** and **lesbian** cover a wide range of behavior, from occasional sexual encounters to long-term relationships (such as that between Gertrude Stein and Alice B. Toklas). Many children and adolescents have homosexual experiences, often because physical contact with the opposite sex is forbidden. The same is true in prisons and other institutions where the sexes are segregated. Some homosexuals enjoy relations with both sexes, and some are exclusively attracted to their own sex. As in heterosexual relationships, a homosexual may vary between passive and active roles.

Psychoanalysts consider homosexuality the result of unresolved Oedipal conflicts. The young boy who wants exclusive rights to his mother, they say, fears retribution from his father. Specifically, he fears castration. To win his father's affection and to convince his father that he is not a rival, he begins imitating his mother. His sexual identity becomes confused, and in later life he tries to repair the damage to his self-image in "magical unity" with other men. The dynamics are somewhat different with girls. In the usual course of development, the girl transfers her love for her mother to her father. (Boys do not make this switch.) Psychoanalysts explain lesbianism as fixation in the mother-attached stage. Both homosexuality and lesbianism seem to develop most often in homes where one parent seems domineering, the other passive and ineffectual.

Opponents of this view argue that sex roles are nothing more than a cultural veneer. Both men and women are locked into certain roles—girls are supposed to be docile and passive, boys strong and aggressive. These roles are also applied to sex. Homosexuals often do have neurotic problems, they say, but only because society persecutes them. There is a suggestion that lesbians may find their homosexuality less unsettling than male homosexuals do. This may be because, despite their homosexuality, lesbians can still conform to society's stereotype

THE ORIGINS OF HOMOSEXUALITY

There are numerous conflicting theories about the origins of homosexual behavior. Even among theories that place its roots in early parent-child relations, there are differing interpretations of the data. An influential research study by the psychiatrist Irving Bieber and his associates described a family pattern that presumably produces homosexual behavior in the male offspring (Bieber et al., 1962). The mother behaves seductively toward her son from his infancy onward, engaging in an unusual degree of intimacy with him. (This mother-son relationship is referred to as "close-binding.") But the mother's attitude toward her husband is domineering and derogatory. In turn, the father's attitude toward his son is indifferent and often hostile. The Bieber hypothesis is that any male child exposed to this pattern in his childhood, or to any one of several variations on it, is a likely candidate for subsequent homosexuality or homosexual conflicts.

The data of the Bieber group were drawn from homosexual persons undergoing psychotherapy. Immediate objections were raised about the risks of generalizing from people in therapy to wider populations. Evans (1969) studied a group of homosexuals who were not in therapy and compared them with a control group of heterosexuals, using the questionnaire devised by Bieber. The homosexual males more often reported they had been fearful of physical injury, had avoided physical conflicts, and had been loners who did not engage in competitive sports. The mothers of the homosexuals had encouraged feminine rather than masculine attitudes, allied with the son against the father, and behaved seductively toward the son. The homosexuals had spent less time with their fathers, were more hostile toward and fearful of them, and felt less accepted by and accepting of them than did the heterosexuals.

Evans, while confirming some of the results of the Bieber study, nonetheless rejects Bieber's interpretation of the cause-effect relationship. He points out that the father of a son who ultimately becomes homosexual may be withdrawn from and hostile to his son because of childhood signs of the son's homosexual tendency. He further notes that some homosexuals were raised in families without a male parent.

Gundlach (1969) raises further complications by reporting that the behavior of lesbians often has an emotional content quite different from that of male homosexuals. The lesbians seek warmth and affection from their partners, whereas males often search for domination and power. This significant difference, as well as the early family origins of female homosexuality, is hard to explain with the Bieber theory.

Hooker, a psychiatrist who has conducted many studies of homosexuals, concludes that "it can no longer be questioned that faulty, disturbed, or pathological parental relationships in early childhood are more commonly reported by male homosexual patients than by a comparable group of male heterosexuals" (Hooker, 1969). She goes on, however, to warn that the origins of homosexuality cannot be established from psychiatric samples alone and that no conclusive pattern of causal relationships between early childhood relationships with parents and subsequent homosexuality has been determined. White and Watt (1973) suggest that the most important factor may be the mother's attitude that sex is ugly, nasty, and degrading. This is generalized by the child to mean all intimate heterosexual relationships. But as the child grows up, his sexual needs must be satisfied. Because he has learned to avoid the opposite sex, he may become homosexual. Thus we have several suggestive hypotheses, but as yet no firmly established set of conclusions about the origins of either male or female homosexual behavior.

of female behavior. The tenderness and gentleness expected of a woman can be expressed toward another woman just as it would be toward a man. But a male homosexual may have a double burden based on accepting his homosexuality and admitting that society's stereotype of male behavior does not apply to him. If this is the case, the loosening of sex-role expectations in society at large may help to relieve at least part of the homosexual's problems as a member of society.

Other deviations in choice of a sex object are **pedophilia** (having relations with children) and **fetishism** (attachment to objects that symbolize another person, such as underwear). In both cases psychologists feel that the person is too threatened to engage in person-to-person sex with another adult. Pedophiliacs and fetishists are usually compulsive about their behavior and often suffer extreme anxiety and guilt.

The classification *unconventional modes of sexual expression* once included all forms of oral and anal sex. Today these are usually considered deviant only when they become a substitute for genital sex. This judgment is based on the assumption that people who engage exclusively in these activities are anxious about conventional sexual behavior. Other unconventional ways of enjoying sex are **voyeurism,** where watching others engage in sexual activities or spying on people who are nude becomes a substitute for direct sexual contact, and **exhibitionism,** the compulsion to expose one's genitals in inappropriate situations. Voyeurism is explained as a mixed attraction to and fear of females—the person enjoys forbidden encounters more than those that involve consent on the women's part. Exhibitionism is seen as a need to reassure oneself of one's sex. Within limits, both voyeurism and exhibitionism are accepted in our culture. They are considered deviations when the behavior is compulsive, and when they become substitutes for direct sexual relations.

Sado-masochism is the linking of sex with aggression. The sadist must humiliate or physically harm his sex partner; the masochist cannot enjoy sex without emotional or physical pain. As with the other behavior described here, psychologists feel this attitude signals fear of heterosexual intimacy. The sadist feels threatened by sexual encounters and must assert his dominance; the masochist feels guilty about sex and wants to be punished.

Alcoholism and Addiction

Like sexual deviations, **alcoholism** and **drug addiction** are both social and personal problems. Driving under the influence of alcohol and using drugs without a prescription are both illegal. In effect, the law asserts that people do not have the right to alter their own body chemistry, particularly when the change leads to behavior that may harm others.

Dependency on alcohol may occur in stages. A person starts drinking regularly to ward off anxiety—a few drinks at lunch or before dinner make him feel better. Then he begins to feel that he cannot cope without those few drinks. This dependency is sometimes followed by a phase in which he periodically goes on sprees, drinking to the point of un-

(Burk Uzzle, Magnum Photos)

consciousness for days or even weeks. Eventually, if he does not drink heavily he experiences withdrawal symptoms—depression, nausea, the shakes. An overuse of alcohol usually also results in severe physical deterioration, mainly in the brain and liver.

No one is sure whether alcoholism is a physical addiction or a psychological habituation. In *addiction,* the person's body chemistry changes, and his dependence on the drug becomes a biological need. He requires larger and larger amounts of the drug to get high, cannot feel normal without it, and becomes physically sick on withdrawal. Psychological *habituation,* on the other hand, is emotional dependence on a drug—the person feels he needs a drug and feels sick when he does not use it, but the need is psychological, not biological.

Heroin, opium, and other narcotics affect the central nervous system. They relieve pain (hence their use in medicine), cause drowsiness ("nodding out"), and produce feelings of euphoria and well-being. Narcotics are physically addictive. The body gradually builds up a tolerance to these drugs, and a person must take larger amounts to relieve pain or get high. Withdrawal is accompanied by severe muscle cramps, vomiting, hot and cold flashes, depression, and restlessness.

Narcotics themselves do not cause physical deterioration, but addicts usually lose interest in food, sex, work, and family. The chief danger is that a person will take too much or that he will accidentally let air into a vein. (An air bubble in the brain causes immediate death.) But the social costs of addiction are immense—from robbery and prostitution to support a habit to broken families and ruined lives.*

Peele and Brodsky (1974) suggest that drug users and alcoholics are not the only addicts in our society. Many other Americans also have severe problems coping with reality and also become addicted, though not to drugs or drink. Rainwater (1956) found that lower-class people are more likely to become attached to concrete objects than middle-class people, who are more apt to make emotional attachments to other people. Thus, while lower-class people may turn to drugs and alcohol to escape anxiety, middle-class people may try to avoid their problems by falling into dependent love relationships. These relationships bear quite a close resemblance to dependency on heroin or alcohol. According to Peele and Brodsky, "addicted" lovers cannot cope with the real demands and disappointments of life and become fixated on one relationship that they feel will satisfy all of their personal needs and solve all of their problems. Their horizons gradually shrink until the only thing that is important to them is the maintenance of their "habit." In this sense, Peele and Brodsky do not see heroin users and alcoholics as being a "race apart." Only their particular type of addiction separates them from other people.

---

*Alcohol, the various narcotics (heroin, cocaine, amphetamines, and barbiturates), and marijuana and the hallucinogens (LSD, peyote, and mescaline) and their effects are discussed in Chapter 9.

DRUGS IN SOCIETY

Today, most people believe that drugs such as heroin, LSD, and opium are harmful and dangerous, and that drugs such as alcohol, tobacco, and tea are less harmful, but this was not always so.

Actually, the history of drug use in various societies is somewhat surprising, given our current biases (Freedman, 1973). In 1634 the Tsar of Russia forbade the smoking of tobacco and decreed that persistent violators were to be executed. Tea was once believed to be a dangerous drug that would lead to the end of family life, among other evils. Its introduction in England, where it is now a national drink, was violently opposed.

In the United States, opium and morphine were widely used for medical and therapeutic purposes in the late 1800s. Each was sold widely in grocery stores and pharmacies. Many respectable, middle-class citizens became addicted to opium, yet this addiction did not lead to crime, since opium could be openly purchased.

These examples demonstrate that the evaluation of any particular drug is primarily determined by current social mores and taboos. Drugs that were once considered dangerous are now commonplace, while drugs that were once commonplace are now considered dangerous. Moreover, in our society, there is an increasing tendency to view drugs as the answer for many medical, social, and personal problems. Even children can easily come to believe, simply from watching enough television, that one bottle or another in the medicine cabinet holds the solution to any of their needs.

Freedman proposes that the reasons people take drugs are more important than whether the drugs they take are "good" or "bad." In his view, taking any drug is a person's attempt to deal with the ambiguities of modern life. For example, the atrocities committed during World War II and subsequent conflicts have made it impossible for many people to believe that man is innately good. At the same time, since the American and French Revolutions, we have come to think of all forms of social deprivation as injustice rather than as being the misfortune of birth. Freedman thus sees widespread drug use in our society as being a response to the feelings of anger, frustration, and powerlessness caused by these new ways of looking at ourselves and our society.

Sociopathic Behavior

With the help of popular books and movies, the term *psychopath* became a household word in the fifties and early sixties. Although the term has changed—delinquents and unrepentant criminals are now called **sociopaths**—the stereotype remains. The sociopath has no concern for other people, lacks emotional attachments, and completely disregards social conventions. He lies and cheats, steals and hurts without guilt. He has no loyalties and no sense of responsibility. Often he is charming, but he uses charm to manipulate others—not to establish friendships. Sometimes he seems oblivious to any code of right and wrong; sometimes he knows the rules and delights in breaking them. Unlike the homosexual, the alcoholic, and the addict, the sociopath feels no anxiety about his deviant behavior.

Some psychologists feel that sociopathic behavior is the result of emotional deprivation in early childhood. Respect for others—"Do unto others as you would have them do unto you"—is the basis of our social code. In order to understand why it is wrong to take a friend's toy, a child must be able to imagine that he is that friend. If he can see things from another person's point of view, rules about what he can and cannot do make sense. If he cannot, the rules seem to be nothing more than an assertion of adult power and the child begins to violate them as soon as he is able to get away with it. This failure to identify, to take the role of others, occurs in situations of emotional isolation. The child whom no one cares for, cares for no one.

Others feel sociopathic behavior results from a *confusing* childhood. The sociopath's parents were inconsistent. Sometimes they punished him for not making his bed, sometimes they did not; sometimes they worried over him and gave him lavish attention, other times they ignored him. The parents often push the child to become independent before he is really ready. Gradually the child begins to feel that the way he acts does not seem to influence the way people act toward him. He grows up unable to connect what he does with what happens to him.

The line between sexual abnormality and sexual normality, alcoholism and martinis at lunch, drug addiction and Miltown three times a day with a doctor's prescription, sociopathic behavior and alienation is thin. But all these problems can be the source of personal tragedy as well as social disapproval. This is why psychologists consider character disorders to be abnormal behavior.

Figure 14-9
Charles Manson. Because of his lack of remorse for his "family's" killing spree and the way he callously used people for his own purposes, psychologists would consider him to be a sociopath. This does not mean that he should be considered legally insane and thus not responsible for his actions. One of the characteristics of a sociopath is that he knows his actions go against the conventions of society—making him legally sane—but he doesn't care.
(*Wide World Photos*)

Psychoses

Psychoses are severe disturbances characterized by disordered thought, inappropriate emotions, and bizarre behavior. The psychotic is out of touch with reality. Usually he cannot function socially or professionally. Often he is unable or unwilling to communicate.

The most striking feature of psychosis is *autism*. The psychotic is motivated by internal events, rather than external situations. He may hear voices when no one is speaking, may see things that others cannot, may feel sensations that are not caused by physical stimulation. Delusions or false beliefs distort his relations with his environment. He may think the doctors want to kill him, or that radio waves from distant planets control his behavior and force him to perform certain rituals. Often psychotics feel that their own body—as well as the world around them—is alien and hostile. Because they are living in a world outsiders

Figure 14-10
A drawing made by an institutionalized psychotic patient. Such drawings are sometimes used as a diagnostic tool, for they may reveal thoughts or fantasies that the patient is reluctant to talk about. Painting is also used as therapy in many institutions.
(*Wide World Photos*)

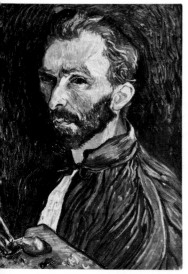

Figure 14-11
Vincent Van Gogh, *Self-Portrait.* Van Gogh suffered from extreme fluctuations in mood throughout his life and was hospitalized several times when he became severely psychotic and violent. He eventually committed suicide rather than live in constant terror of becoming insane again.
(*The Bettmann Archive*)

do not experience, their behavior seems bizarre and unreasonable. A psychotic may giggle when he or someone else is hurt, invent new words, repeat a nonsensical phrase over and over, echo word for word anything said to him, remain frozen in one position for hours, dance incessantly, or walk in a stiff, mechanical gait.

To organize information on the wide range of emotional, cognitive, and behavioral disorders found in psychoses, psychologists divide psychosis into three main categories—affective psychosis, schizophrenia, and organic psychosis—and associate certain behavior patterns with each. In real life, however, psychologists often disagree on a diagnosis and patients rarely conform to their label. Nevertheless, the classifications are useful as a starting point.

Affective Psychosis

Extreme and inappropriate moods and emotions are called **affective psychosis.** This term covers both deep **depression** (what was once called melancholia) and extreme elation, or **mania.** Sometimes manic and depressive behavior go together: the person rises on a tide of elation, then collapses into severe depression.

In the early stages of a depressive episode, the person is sad, apathetic, and self-recriminating. His sadness is inappropriate: nothing in his recent life situation explains his feelings. He moves and thinks slowly and is unable to sleep soundly or eat regularly. Later, unable to relax, he may become extremely agitated and restless. As the depression deepens, he begins to feel that his hopelessness is justified, that he deserves to suffer. Delusions about having treated other people badly or about lacking ability follow. At this point he may begin to think suicide is the only solution. In the acute stages, the person may become completely mute, unresponsive, and inactive.

A manic psychotic is the exact opposite. In the early stages of a manic episode, he is excited, talkative, outgoing, and confident—as most of us are when something good happens to us. But the manic's hopes are unlimited. He invents fabulous schemes, but has little interest in carrying them out. He speaks rapidly, rarely pausing to listen to comments from his audience, and is angry with anyone who lacks confidence in his plans and ability. In time he becomes increasingly aggressive and arrogant. His self-confidence becomes delusional—he loses the ability to evaluate things accurately. In the acute stage, manic psychotics may become wild, incomprehensible, or violent until they collapse from exhaustion. Most psychologists see manic behavior as a defense against depression: the person unconsciously senses deep despair and does everything possible to deny his feelings.

The term **involutional psychosis** is reserved for mood disturbances that occur in middle age, usually between the ages of 40 and 55 for women, 50 and 65 for men. The involutional psychotic is anxious, depressed, and irritable. His moods shift from one extreme to the other without apparent reason. He is unable to relax or sleep. For a long time doctors attributed this behavior to the biochemical changes that accompany menopause in women, aging in men. Today, however, they are more inclined to view involutional disorders as a social problem. Many people in our society spend their lives trying to be good providers and good parents, and some cannot make the transition to "senior citizen" and retirement. When a person feels that he has not lived up to his expectations and no longer has the opportunity to do so, serious adjustment problems may result.

Figure 14-12
Francisco Goya, *Self-Portrait*. Throughout his life Goya suffered periods of severe depression, which became even more intense after he lost his hearing when he was 53. Some have speculated that Goya's problems were organically caused—that the titanium-based white paint the artist used resulted in deterioration of his nervous system.
(*The Bettmann Archive*)

Schizophrenia

The term **schizophrenia** refers not to multiple personality, as many people think, but to disordered thought, emotions, and behavior. Unlike manic-depressive psychotics, who are deeply concerned about their relations with other people, schizophrenics are absorbed in fantasies and hallucinations that prevent their making contacts with the outside world. Schizophrenia is what most of us have in mind when we use the word "crazy." Schizophrenia may develop suddenly or gradually over the years. If it is sudden, psychologists refer to it as *reactive schizophrenia*, because, in general, the individual is reacting to a severe and very real stress in his life. *Process schizophrenia*, on the other hand, develops slowly over time and is likely to be genetically

(Jesse Miller, Nancy Palmer Photo Agency)

influenced. Within these two dimensions, psychologists distinguish four main types of schizophrenia.

The **simple schizophrenic** is withdrawn and apathetic. He is isolated from other people and shows little or no emotional response to the world around him. This withdrawal is accompanied by intellectual decline: he performs poorly in jobs and on tests. Simple schizophrenics are not retarded or "slow," just indifferent. Absorbed in daydreams, they have little interest in their environments. Their detachment from reality may be so gradual that family and friends fail to notice. Simple schizophrenics can manage to get by on the fringes of society, passively accepting whatever happens to them. They may never get help unless they drift into socially disapproved behavior.

In contrast, **catatonic schizophrenics** cannot function on any level in everyday life. The catatonic is not only detached, he is unable to *act* in any meaningful way. When psychologists are able to communicate with such patients, they find the catatonic has vivid hallucinations and delusions that promise destruction at every turn. This is not to say that the catatonic is unaware of what is going on—on the contrary, the catatonic is actually quite observant and alert. But he chooses not to react. The person has immobilized himself in order to survive. The "stuporous catatonic" may remain frozen in a single position for hours at a time, apparently oblivious to pain. His body may be completely limp or tight and rigid. Usually he is mute. Some catatonics obey commands to move from one place to another like robots. Some allow a doctor to mold them into a strange and uncomfortable position, with their arms in the air, and will hold the position indefinitely. Others are extremely belligerent and do the exact opposite of what they are told. Sometimes, however, catatonics release suppressed energy in violent frenzy, which may be dangerous to themselves and others.

The most striking feature of **hebephrenic schizophrenia** is regression: the hebephrenic is silly and childish, giggles when serious reflection would be appropriate, eats with his hands, repeats nonsense rhymes, forgets to use the toilet. But his hallucinations are quite different from the average child's daydreams. Most often the hebephrenic's delusions center around his identity and his body. He may believe that he is 1,000 years old, or invisible, or a member of an alien race transplanted to earth through a cosmic error. Hebephrenics deal with their worlds in magical, ritualistic ways, using words and behaving in ways that outsiders find incomprehensible.

Paranoid schizophrenics are much easier for other people to understand. They are coherent, alert, and responsive. In fact, their thinking and behavior would be quite appropriate for a person whose life is threatened. But paranoid schizophrenics misread their environment, seeing danger where none exists. They believe they are being persecuted unmercifully—by family, friends, psychologists, other patients. Usually they "know" why. A paranoid might think that he has learned a top secret that others want to know or that he has special abilities

SOCIAL ISOLATION AND SCHIZOPHRENIA

One theory about the development of schizophrenia relates to increasing social isolation: the person becomes so cut off from other people that he develops the withdrawn, shut-in personality common among schizophrenics. The process begins when a child with low self-esteem withdraws from social relationships to avoid anxiety and stress. A vicious cycle ensues—the more he withdraws, the less feedback he gets from other people, the lower his social skills become, and the less able he is to orient himself successfully to his environment. This in turn further lowers his self-esteem and increases his anxiety.

Barthell and Holmes (1968) tested the social isolation theory of schizophrenia through an imaginative use of data from high school yearbooks. They hypothesized that adults hospitalized for schizophrenia had been more socially isolated as adolescents than their peers. Therefore they would have participated in fewer social activities, as recorded in their high school yearbooks. They selected twenty hospitalized schizophrenics and twenty hospitalized neurotics who had not been hospitalized for at least 2 years after their graduation and whose hospital stay had exceeded 3 months. Then they turned to the patients' high school yearbooks for information about their social participation. As a control, they recorded similar data about the student whose picture was next to each of the patients in the yearbook.

High school activities were divided into three categories. Social activities were those with a high level of social interaction, such as student government, school publications, and special interest clubs. Service activities were those involving a service for the school, for example, hall guard, teacher's aide, or office monitor. Athletic activities included both interschool and intramural sports.

They found no significant difference between the two groups in participation in service or sports activities, which involve relatively little social interaction. But in social activities the schizophrenics and neurotics showed significantly less participation than did the control group. The schizophrenics showed an even greater tendency toward withdrawal and isolation than did the neurotics.

The study is, of course, suggestive rather than conclusive. Some people who had been active in social activities in high school subsequently became schizophrenic and some who had been inactive did not. Nonetheless, the results do tend to support the viewpoint that schizophrenic behavior is rooted to some degree in a person's past history.

Figure 14-13
William Blake, *Self-Portrait.* Blake claimed to be "under the direction of messengers from Heaven," and his hallucinations provided much of the material for his poetry and engravings. Considered a mystic in his own time, Blake might well be classified as a paranoid schizophrenic today. (*The Bettmann Archive*)

that his enemies want to exploit. Delusions of grandeur—believing oneself to be Christ or Joan of Arc—support delusions of persecution. Gradually the paranoid becomes totally absorbed in the business of protecting himself. Often he is hostile and aggressive toward anyone who questions his thinking or offers evidence to contradict his delusions.*

* *Paranoia* is a disorder characterized by similar delusions of persecution, but without the extreme withdrawal from reality typical of paranoid schizophrenia.

Sometimes children are diagnosed as schizophrenic, although they do not develop the complex hallucinations and delusions found in adults. Regression and detachment characterize **childhood schizophrenia.** Many disturbed children appear normal and well adjusted until the age of 5 or 6, when, for some reason, they stop growing emotionally and socially. The child may revert to infantile behavior—wetting his bed, sucking his thumb, talking baby talk, refusing to feed or dress himself. Or he may continue to act like a 5-year-old year after year. Rejected by peers, he withdraws further and further from reality.

Other children seem detached and withdrawn from birth. They do not respond to smiles, hugs, and other expressions of affection. From an early age they avoid eye contact and ignore verbal communications. Their behavior is unpredictable. For example, they may sit on the floor and rock back and forth for hours or may tear around the house in an orgy of destruction. Such children often become strongly attached to inanimate objects, which they seem to find less threatening than people. Because such **infantile autism** appears so early in the child's development, many psychologists feel it must have a biological or genetic basis, but this has yet to be proved.

In summary, the term *schizophrenia* covers a wide range of behavioral and thought disorders—from the generalized detachment of the simple schizophrenic and the immobility of the catatonic to the distortions of hebephrenia and the complex delusions of paranoid schizophrenia. Schizophrenics see the world differently and behave in accordance with what they see.

Organic Psychosis

The behavior of an **organic psychotic** may resemble that of schizophrenics and affective psychotics, but his behavior can be explained biologically. His brain and/or nervous system are damaged; thus his ability to perceive reality, to control his emotions, and to think clearly is impaired. Aside from accidents that cause serious brain damage and varying levels of mental retardation, the most common sources of organic psychosis are disease, old age, and, in rare cases, alcoholism.

Syphilis once accounted for most of the admissions to mental hospitals and asylums. Today, of course, this disease can be cured quite easily with penicillin, but only if it is caught in the early stages. After a short period, syphilis *symptoms* disappear without treatment. The victim may feel quite healthy and normal for 10 to 30 years. But by this time the syphilis spirochete (a spiral-shaped bacterium) will have worked into the central nervous system. Paresis inevitably results. The person loses his coordination and sometimes is partially paralyzed. His memory and orientation are poor. Frequently people with advanced syphilis experience delusions, hallucinations, and affective disorders. At this stage, there is no cure.

Figure 14-14
Al Capone. In his heyday, his illegal operations brought him $2 million a day and he owned the city of Chicago. But somewhere along the line, he had contracted syphilis, and while lesser gangsters of the time were killed by machine-gun bullets, the great Capone was "rubbed out" by tiny bacteria.
(*Wide World Photos*)

Some degree of physical deterioration is inevitable with *old age*. At about 70, a person's body stops replacing cells that are damaged or destroyed. The heart and other muscles begin to shrink. In some people this process is accelerated by arteriosclerosis, a hardening of the arteries that reduces the supply of oxygen to the brain. Weakened, the brain functions poorly: the person's memory and judgment are impaired. Confused and disoriented, he may invent stories to fill gaps in his memory and mix up past and present, reality and fantasy. The emotional instability of senile people often makes them seem childish. It is as if the fears and impulses the person controlled throughout his life break loose and flood his consciousness.

Of course, not all old people become senile. For a time psychologists thought this was because physical deterioration proceeds more rapidly in some people than in others. But a number of studies have shown that some old people suffer extreme brain damage without losing coherence (Ullmann & Krasner, 1969). Apparently senility depends on the person's ability to accept losses in mental agility. The man who is upset by not being able to remember something becomes confused. The man who accepts the symptoms of age is better able to cope.

In some cases excessive drinking is directly responsible for acute, temporary psychosis—*delirium tremens*, the D.T.'s. Usually the symptoms begin after the person has stopped drinking. He begins to feel sick, restless, and unsteady on his feet. Delirium, in which the person cannot distinguish between reality and fantasy, sets in, bringing terrifying hallucinations that can last for as long as a week. Delirium tremens is rare—only a small percentage of alcoholics are affected.

The Causes of Psychosis

Ever since Fournier discovered a link between paresis and syphilis in the late nineteenth century, psychologists and doctors have looked for a biological explanation of psychotic behavior. Some researchers focus on genetics. A number of investigators have found that the incidence of psychosis is higher in children of psychotic parents than in the general population. In addition, if one of two identical twins is psychotic, the chances are quite high that the other will also be psychotic (see Chapter 2). But in most of these studies the twins were raised in the same home, making it impossible to rule out environmental factors.

One strong argument against a purely genetic theory of psychosis is the fact that autistic children, who often begin to show signs of extreme detachment and withdrawal at the age of 3 or 4 months, are almost always unique in their families. To account for this, many psychologists hypothesize that children inherit a predisposition for autism. Whether they in fact become psychotic depends on the environment. To date, this hypothesis has been neither proved nor disproved.

Other researchers look for a biochemical explanation. For example, Gjessing (1966) related periodic psychotic episodes to malfunction in the thyroid gland. Heath (1960) injected taraxein, a protein that affects the central nervous system, from schizophrenics into monkeys and found that their behavior and brain waves changed dramatically. Other researchers point to the similarities between mescaline and epinephrine (Hoffer & Osmond, 1959). Perhaps psychotics have some metabolic disorder that releases the hallucinogenic potential in epinephrine.

All these findings are hotly disputed. Critics point out that in most experiments the psychotic subjects have been hospitalized for an extended period. Perhaps hospitalization, institutional food, and in-activity change body chemistry. Moreover, even if we can demonstrate biochemical differences, we do not know whether these are the cause or the result of psychosis. For example, although it is known that the drugs that are most effective in relieving schizophrenic symptoms act to increase the amount of norepinephrine in the brain, Snyder (1974) cautions against assuming that a lack of norepinephrine caused the disorder in the first place. The search for a biological explanation and cure continues.

Although psychoanalytic clinicians may use drugs as an emergency measure in treating severely disturbed patients, they do not agree with the biological explanation. Rather they consider psychosis an emotional disorder resulting from childhood trauma. At some point in his early years, they say, the psychotic faced a crisis in family relations that he could not resolve—for example, the real or imagined loss of a parent. Terrified, he began erecting defenses. The child's maladjustment may not have been noticeable—his defenses worked. But later on (usually in late adolescence), new crises take him back to the early, unresolved conflict. His overstrained defenses collapse—impulses, fears, memories, and fantasies that most people repress flood his consciousness, making rational behavior impossible. According to this view, the psychotic is literally living in a nightmare from which he cannot awaken. The ego is overwhelmed and cannot function effectively.

Learning theorists disagree with this theory. They see psychosis as a severe learning problem. It may be that they are unable to discrim-inate between what is meaningful and what is not. The psychotic is overly sensitive—he is like someone standing in the middle of a large cocktail party who is unable to hear what the person in front of him is saying because he cannot shut off conversations two and three groups away. He hears everything and therefore understands nothing. Another possible explanation is that the person is listening to internal and external signals at once. Most of us can turn off daydreams to listen to a friend or to an interesting lecture. Perhaps the psychotic cannot.

Other learning theorists suggest that psychotics perceive reality correctly, but have learned to respond in bizarre ways. The *double-bind theory* is an interesting formulation of this view. It suggests that as a child the psychotic was taught to act in ways that contradicted his perception of reality and his own feelings. For example, his mother resents him and is stiff and remote when she holds him, but nevertheless demands that he act as if she were warm and loving. He knows that if he hugs her, she will pull away, but that if he does not, she will reproach him for lack of affection. This is the double bind: he is damned if he does and damned if he doesn't. The child grows up mistrusting others and distorting the expression of his own feelings.

Brown (1973), in an article on schizophrenia, is critical of the double-bind theory. He notes that "there are plenty of ways of responding to double binds without losing your grip on rationality" (p. 402). These include ignoring one part of the message, or responding with a double-bind reply, or avoiding the situation entirely. Brown denies that the existence of the bind in itself is the cause of mental illness. He sees the need for an explanation of why some people are overwhelmed by double-bind messages, while others are capable of reacting with more ordinary forms of behavior.

Sociological theorists, as you might imagine, consider psychosis a social as well as a personal problem. Society makes numerous demands on its citizens. Sometimes those demands are contradictory, and sometimes they exceed the person's abilities. Sociologists point out that psychosis usually occurs in late adolescence or middle age. Both are critical times, when the person faces major role changes. The 20-year-old in our culture is expected to go off on his own. He must abandon the role of a child for that of an adult. The middle-aged person, in contrast, can no longer think in terms of opportunity. He is at a point where people begin to look back over their lives and evaluate themselves, to exchange the role of father or mother for that of senior citizen, and to face the inevitability of death. Some people are not able to negotiate these crises. Why?

One explanation is that the person has learned behavior that makes him unsuited for a new role. The adolescent who has consulted his parents on every decision does not know how to act on his own; the woman who has devoted her life to her children is lost without them. A move from one culture to another, or a change in socioeconomic position, may create similar problems. A man who has worked his way up in business may not know how to behave at an exclusive country club and may find himself socially ostracized. Sociologists see crises that lead to extreme social isolation—that is, problems in living—as the major cause of psychotic breakdowns.

Although quite different in emphasis, the biological, psychoanalytic, learning, and sociological views of psychosis are not mutually exclusive. In actual practice, psychologists often use a combination of drugs and psychoanalytic or behaviorist therapy to treat psychosis. Psychoanalysts do not deny the possibility of physiological changes, although they feel these are the result and not the cause of psychological problems. Learning theorists reject the classical idea of an unconscious, but their explanation of psychosis frequently leads to descriptions of childhood problems identical with those uncovered in psychoanalysis. No psychologist denies the effect of social conditions on mental health. The truth is that psychosis is a disturbing and puzzling phenomenon that no one as yet has been able to explain fully.

Summary

1. There is no clear distinction between normal and abnormal behavior. What is considered "normal" varies from time to time and place to place. Psychologists attempt to evaluate a person's behavior in terms of his own life by applying *intrapersonal standards*. Distorted perception of reality, ineffectiveness, the discomfort of not being able to cope, and danger to oneself and others are four criteria for evaluating abnormal behavior.

2. The treatment of abnormal behavior has taken various forms. By the 1920s, three explanations of abnormal behavior had acquired substantial followings. The *organic model* holds that abnormal behavior has a biochemical or physiological basis. The *psychoanalytic model* says that irrational behavior and psychosomatic disorders are symbolic of internal, unconscious conflicts. The *medical model* suggests that the person who behaves abnormally is sick, and it has led to the classification of psychological symptoms and the naming of diseases. Learning theorists argue that abnormal behavior is learned. Others argue that our standards for normal behavior are too rigid, while others take the view that the so-called mentally ill have dared to step over the boundaries of the external world into the unknown and chaotic parts of the self. Most psychologists think partly in terms of the medical model and partly in terms of "problems in living."

3. *Neurosis* is characterized by inappropriate emotions and behavior. Psychoanalytic theorists feel that neurotic behavior is caused by a reaction to internal threats. Behavior theorists believe that a person who acts neurotically has learned to associate fear and anxiety with an apparently innocuous situation or object. Some psychologists see personality factors as influences on "choice" of neurosis. In any case, most psychologists agree that the person realizes his fears and actions are unreasonable, but finds it difficult or impossible to change.

4. *Anxiety neurosis* is a chronic state of apprehension without an identifiable source of danger. A person may be unable to sleep or relax for weeks on end, and anxiety attacks may be so severe that he is nearly paralyzed.

5. A *phobia* is an intense, paralyzing fear of something that most people find tolerable. Psychoanalytic theorists see phobias as a displacement of a person's fear of his own unconscious wishes. Other psychologists believe that phobias are learned in response to trauma. People sometimes deal with phobias by forcing themselves to confront the situation and conquer it, but more often they try to avoid the thing they fear.

6. *Dissociative neurosis* occurs when a part of the individual's personality is separated from the rest and he is unable to reassemble the pieces. *Amnesia* may occur as a reaction to intolerable experiences. A *fugue* state

involves temporary amnesia and an escape into a new, less confining, less responsible life a person dreamed of before but could not pursue without guilt. *Somnambulism* refers to anything a person does while asleep. Often a somnambulist's activities reflect emotions he cannot express during his waking hours. A person with a *multiple personality* possesses two or more separate personalities, representing conflicting values and desires.

7. *Conversion reaction,* or *hysteria,* is a transplantation of emotional problems to the body. It can take the form of paralysis, blindness, or deafness, without biological basis. *Hypochondria*—the belief that one is sick in the absence of symptoms—and *psychophysiological disorders*—very real biological problems resulting from prolonged anxiety and stress—are relatively more common today than hysteria.

8. The term *obsessive-compulsive neurosis* applies to a wide range of behavior. Obsessions are recurring thoughts and fantasies that are almost impossible to get rid of. Compulsions are strong, uncontrollable impulses that often go against a person's conscious intentions. The obsessive-compulsive neurotic is rigid, hyperactive, and meticulous and often engages in repeated thoughts and actions, which psychologists refer to as ritualistic behavior. Recent research indicates that it may be necessary to consider general personality characteristics in order to fully understand how these behaviors are learned.

9. In *neurotic depression,* people fully acknowledge and exaggerate their guilt and helplessness. Depression is characterized by sadness, feelings of worthlessness, and varying degrees of inactivity. Psychoanalytic theorists believe that depression is an expression of ambivalence—a person wants love, but is unable to believe that anyone loves him and resents the people on whom he has become dependent. Behavior theorists agree that mistrust causes depression, but believe that a depressed person has learned to expect loss and failure. Recently, psychologists have begun to investigate the effects of neurochemical imbalances in the body on depression.

10. There is a great deal of controversy about whether people with *character disorders*—sexual deviation, addiction, sociopathy—should be looked upon as having emotional problems and treated accordingly or should be viewed as criminals, as they are in several states.

11. Among psychologists, there are two schools of thought about what constitutes *sexual deviation.* Some feel any activity that does not culminate in heterosexual intercourse is deviant; others prefer to focus on the person's feelings about whatever he does. Sexual deviations are divided into three categories. *Ineffectiveness* refers to impotence—the male's inability to have or maintain an erection—and frigidity—the female's inability to experience sexual excitation or orgasm. *Unconventional sex objects* include homosexuality, lesbianism, pedophilia, and fetishism. *Unconventional modes of sexual expression* once included all forms of oral and anal sex, which are now considered deviant only when they become a substitute for genital sex. Others are *voyeurism*—spying on a nude person or watching others engage in sexual activities as a substitute for direct sexual contact—and *exhibitionism*—the compulsion to expose one's genitals in inappropriate situations. *Sado-masochism* is the linking of sex with aggression.

12. *Alcoholism* and *drug addiction* are both social and personal problems. In *addiction,* the person's body chemistry changes and his dependence on

the drug becomes a biological need. Psychological *habituation* is emotional dependence on a drug—the person feels he needs it and feels sick when he does not use it, but the need is psychological, not biological. Addiction and habituation are considered psychological problems because they can serve as escape mechanisms.

13. True *sociopaths* have no concern for other people, lack emotional attachments, and disregard social conventions. Unlike the homosexual, the alcoholic, and the addict, the sociopathic person feels no anxiety about his deviant behavior. Some psychologists feel that sociopathic behavior results from emotional deprivation in early childhood. Others believe that sociopathic behavior results from a confusing childhood, where parents' actions toward a child were inconsistent and the child grows up without learning to connect what he does with what happens to him.

14. *Psychoses* are severe disturbances characterized by disordered thought, inappropriate emotions, and bizarre behavior. The psychotic is out of touch with reality, living in a private world and behaving in ways other people find difficult or impossible to understand. The most striking characteristic of psychosis is *autism*—the psychotic is motivated by internal events rather than external situations.

15. *Affective psychosis* describes extreme and inappropriate moods and emotions—either deep depression or extreme elation, or mania. In some cases manic and depressive behavior alternate in the same person—he is first elated, then collapses into severe depression, and then starts the cycle over again. *Involutional psychosis* refers to mood disturbances that occur in middle age, when the person becomes anxious, depressed, and irritable, usually because of problems in adjusting to the new roles he must assume.

16. *Schizophrenia* refers to disordered thought, emotions, and behavior. Schizophrenics are absorbed in fantasies and hallucinations that prevent them from making contact with the outside world. Psychologists distinguish between *reactive schizophrenia,* which develops suddenly in response to some real crisis in the individual's life, and *process schizophrenia,* which develops slowly over time and may be genetically influenced. Within these dimensions, psychologists recognize four main types of schizophrenia. *Simple schizophrenics* are withdrawn and apathetic, showing little or no emotional response to the world around them, but often being able to function on the fringes of society, passively accepting whatever happens to them. *Catatonic schizophrenics* cannot function on any level in everyday life, being unable to act in any meaningful way, often immobilizing themselves to survive the destruction they see in their hallucinations and delusions. *Hebephrenic schizophrenics* are active and involved, but in worlds of their own making, with which they deal in magical, ritualistic ways, using words and behavior that outsiders find incomprehensible. *Paranoid schizophrenics* are coherent, alert, and responsive, exhibiting behavior that would be quite appropriate for a person whose life is threatened, but the danger they see is imaginary. *Infantile autism,* or childhood schizophrenia, appears so early in life that psychologists suspect that it may be genetically or biologically based. Such children are unresponsive and seem to live in their own world.

17. People suffering from *organic psychosis* exhibit behavior that may resem-

ble that of schizophrenics and affective psychotics, but the disorder has a biological base. The brain and/or nervous system are damaged and the ability to perceive reality, control emotions, and think clearly is impaired. Senility and delirium tremens are two examples.

18. Explanations of the causes of psychosis are varied and often hotly disputed. Some biological researchers focus on genetics; others on physiological disorders. Psychoanalytic clinicians consider psychosis an emotional disorder resulting from childhood trauma. Learning theorists see psychosis as a severe learning problem—some hold that psychotics do not respond to the stimuli other people find rewarding because they cannot identify them; others suggest that psychotics perceive reality correctly, but have learned to respond in bizarre ways. Sociological theorists consider psychosis a social as well as a personal problem, seeing crises that lead to extreme social isolation as the major cause of psychotic breakdowns. None of these views is mutually exclusive and psychologists often look for various combinations in treating psychotic patients.

Suggested Readings

Coleman, J. C., *Abnormal Psychology and Modern Life,* 4th ed. (Chicago: Scott, Foresman, 1972). A thorough and readable discussion of abnormal psychology.

Green, H., *I Never Promised You a Rose Garden* (New York: Holt, Rinehart & Winston, 1964). A dramatic fictionalized account of the internal struggles of a young schizophrenic torn between her desires to remain in her own personal world and to enter the world outside her.

Kaplan, B. (Ed.), *The Inner World of Mental Illness* (New York: Harper & Row, 1964). A moving collection of case histories, ranging from first-person clinical accounts to the words of famous writers.

Kleinmuntz, B., *Essentials of Abnormal Psychology* (New York: Harper & Row, 1974). A good introduction to the field that includes case histories.

Lindner, R. M., *The Fifty-Minute Hour: A Collection of True Psychoanalytic Tales* (New York: Holt, Rinehart & Winston, 1954). An engrossing collection of case histories from the author's psychoanalytic practice.

Parker, B., *A Mingled Yarn: Chronicle of a Troubled Family* (New Haven, Conn.: Yale University Press, 1972). An account of a family whose problems were such that all three of the children developed psychological difficulties, two becoming neurotic and the third, schizophrenic. Because the book combines the memories of the youngest child and the interpretations of a psychologist, it provides a personal, yet scientific, approach to the subject.

Szasz, T., *The Manufacture of Madness: A Comparative Study of the Inquisition and the Mental Health Movement* (New York: Harper & Row, 1970). A long-standing opponent of traditional definitions of mental illness attacks institutional psychiatry as comparable to the Inquisition's treatment of witches and heretics.

White, R. W., and Watt, N. F., *The Abnormal Personality,* 4th ed. (New York: Ronald Press, 1973). A psychoanalytic approach to abnormal psychology.

outline

INDIVIDUAL PSYCHOTHERAPIES 528

Psychoanalysis
Client-Centered Therapy
Existential Therapy
Rational Therapy
Reality Therapy

BEHAVIOR THERAPIES 535

Operant Conditioning
Aversive Conditioning
Desensitization
Reciprocal Inhibition

GROUP THERAPIES 539

PHYSICAL TREATMENT 544

Shock Treatments
Psychosurgery
Drug Therapy

INSTITUTIONALIZATION 546

Token Economies

COMMUNITY PSYCHOLOGY 550

SUMMARY 551

SUGGESTED READINGS 555

Therapies

Many Americans are voluntarily or involuntarily confined in mental hospitals, most diagnosed as psychotic. Others are hospitalized because of suicide attempts, violence, alcoholism, or drug addiction. Many of these patients will go back to their families and communities in 3 months or less; some will return to hospitals periodically. Only a small percentage of the people in mental hospitals spend their lives there, and this percentage seems to be declining.

Many other Americans are in private therapy, for a variety of reasons. Some are troubled by chronic problems—anxiety, tension, sexual difficulties. Some consult a psychologist in moments of crisis—when their family seems to be falling apart, or when they are having trouble at work or in school. Still others go into therapy because they want to learn more about themselves and to enjoy life more fully. In addition, thousands of Americans depend on tranquilizers, stimulants, or sleeping pills prescribed by family doctors.

Nonetheless, relatively few Americans know what psychotherapy is. Some families consider it a black mark on their record if one member decides to see a therapist. Others see psychotherapy as self-indul-

527

gence—people should work out problems on their own, they feel. Asking for help—and paying for it—are a sign of weak character. When it comes to severely disturbed people, however, family and friends are often quite willing to turn them over to doctors and to admit that their problem is mental illness.

Surprisingly, psychotherapy is as controversial within psychology as it is without. Many academic psychologists look down on therapy as a vague and poorly defined art. They point out that it is practically impossible to measure the effectiveness of one treatment over another. Confusion over the use and effectiveness of therapy made national headlines in the summer of 1972 when Democratic vice-presidential nominee Thomas Eagleton revealed that he had been treated for depression with shock therapy on three occasions. Reporters interviewed a number of prominent psychiatrists and found little agreement on when to use shock treatment, how the treatment works, and whether or not severe depression can be cured.

Most psychotherapies developed as professionals attempted to treat neurotic behavior, and so most therapies are problem-oriented. In recent years, however, new therapies have emerged that are designed to help individuals develop skills rather than solve problems. These therapies—for example, assertiveness training—are aimed at the individual who is basically well adjusted but who would like to improve his effectiveness in dealing with other people or in handling stress. Thus, these new therapies emphasize growth rather than cure.

This chapter surveys the various therapies in use in private practice and in institutions and describes some of the new directions being taken, particularly in community programs. Most therapists today do not adhere strictly to one technique, but will borrow from several to meet the needs of their patients. This is all to the good, as recent studies have indicated that no one form of therapy is "best." However, in any therapy, the more flexible the therapist is, the more likely that the therapy will be successful. Indeed the personal qualities of the therapist turn out to be more important to successful therapy than the particular technique used. And, in most cases, any therapy seems to be better than none at all (Di Loreto, 1971; Sloane et al., 1975).

Individual Psychotherapies

Psychoanalysis

Psychoanalysis, the classical approach to psychotherapy, is based on the belief that the anxiety and problems that cause a person to seek help are symptoms of feelings the person repressed in early childhood. Usually the repressed emotions are related to aggressive or sexual drives that the child perceived to be dangerous. Psychoanalysis is a method for reversing this process and bringing the repressed feelings

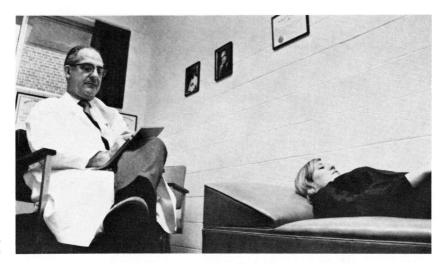

(Van Bucher, Photo Researchers)

Figure 15-1

An artist's conception of free association. You can see how each figure seems to grow out of the one before it.
(Courtesy Picture Collection, New York Public Library)

to consciousness so the person can deal with them in a more effective way.

Successful analysis depends on two conditions. First, the person must make an effort not to inhibit or control thoughts and fantasies. Slips of the tongue and associations between seemingly unrelated thoughts provide the analyst and the patient with clues to underlying problems. This procedure is called **free association.** Second, the analyst must remain completely neutral and, for the most part, silent. Usually the person lies on a couch and the analyst sits behind the person, so that he cannot be seen easily. The analyst's silence becomes a blank screen on which the person projects feelings he might otherwise suppress.

Analysis typically proceeds in stages. After the initial awkwardness wears off, most people begin to enjoy the opportunity to talk without interruption and the idea that someone is interested in their problems. After a few sessions they may begin to test the analyst, telling him about desires and fantasies they have never revealed to anyone else. When they find the analyst does not express shock or disgust, they feel reassured and begin to see him as a warm and accepting person. Many people feel they are getting better at this point and express confidence in the analyst's ability to help them. Good feelings for one's analyst, which psychoanalysts see as reflecting positive feelings toward one's parents, are called **positive transference.**

Gradually, however, this euphoria wears off. The person has exposed his innermost feelings and feels terribly vulnerable. He wants the analyst to reassure him and to return his affection, but the analyst remains silent. The person's anxiety builds. Threatened by the analyst's silence and by his own thoughts, he may feel more unhappy than he did when he entered therapy. He may feel cheated and accuse the analyst of being a money-grabber. Or he may feel that the analyst is really disgusted by his disclosures, or that the analyst laughs about him with his friends. This **negative transference** is a crucial step, for it reveals both the person's negative feelings about authority figures and his resistance to uncovering repressed emotions.

At this point the analyst will begin to interpret the person's feelings. The goal of interpretation is *insight:* the person must see why he feels and acts as he does, and how his present state of mind relates to childhood experiences. The analyst may encourage him to confront events he has mentioned only briefly and try to recall them fully. In this way the analyst helps the person to relive the traumas of his childhood and work through conflicts he was unable to solve in the past. *Working through* provides the person with a second chance, with the opportunity to revise the feelings and beliefs that underlie his problems.

The description above applies to traditional, or orthodox, psychoanalysis. But, only a handful of the many people who consult psychologists go into traditional analysis. For one thing, as Freud himself recognized, analysis depends on the person's being motivated to change and on his having the ability to deal rationally with whatever analysis uncovers. Schizophrenics may talk about their fantasies and unconscious wishes quite freely, but they often are not able to make effective use of the analyst's interpretations. Psychoanalysis is best suited to "potentially autonomous" people (Hersher, 1970)—neurotics, not psychotics. Moreover, analysis may take as long as 4 or 5 years or more, and most analysts feel that at least three and sometimes five sessions a week are essential. Thus few people can afford psychoanalysis, and many others may need immediate help for immediate problems.

In addition, some psychologists feel that orthodox psychoanalysis itself is outdated. Freud invented this technique in the late nineteenth century. He worked primarily with upper-class people who were struggling with the strict moral and social codes of a Victorian society. But society has changed. Today people are more likely to have trouble *finding* guidelines for behavior than breaking through them.

Other critics of psychoanalysis point out that little research has been done on the effects of the psychoanalytic process itself, how it works, and why it works. Many contemporary psychologists feel that this lack of scientific validity is a significant weakness and have turned away from psychoanalysis because of it.

Finally, as we saw in Chapter 12, the neo-Freudians—Alfred Adler, Otto Rank, and Karen Horney—proposed theories of personality that were somewhat different from Freud's, and these differences are reflected in their approaches to therapy. For example, although Freud felt that understanding the past was essential in understanding the present, most neo-Freudian therapists try to get their patients to focus on coping with current problems, rather than on trying to cope in the present with unresolvable past conflicts.

Adler, for example, felt that the therapist's job is to assure the patient

"Mr. Prentice is *not* your father. Alex Binster is *not* your brother. The anxiety you feel is *not* genuine. Dr. Froelich will return from vacation September 15th. Hang on."
(*Drawing by Lorenz;* © 1973 *The New Yorker Magazine, Inc.*)

that he is capable of taking charge of his life, that he is adequate and need not hide from life. Rank felt that classical analysis merely encourages a person to feel dependent, and that within the therapeutic relationship, the therapist should refuse the person's attempts to lean on him and encourage him to be strong. Karen Horney felt that the purpose of therapy is to teach a person to give up his illusions and to accept his real self. Once this is accomplished, the person does not have to make excuses for himself. Perhaps most important is the fact that neo-Freudians favor face-to-face discussions, and most take an active role—interpreting the patient's statements freely, suggesting areas he might want to discuss, role-playing to illustrate comments, and so on.

Some psychoanalysts feel that Freud did not give adequate attention to the workings of the ego. These ego psychologists—for example, Heinz Hartmann, Erik Erikson, and Anna Freud (Sigmund Freud's daughter)—emphasize the ego's effects on the personality and thus on behavior. Hartmann (1964) notes that the ego does function independently of the id at times, and thus ego psychology can lead to a more comprehensive understanding of how the different layers of human motivation interrelate. In addition, concentrating on the id implies concentrating on conflicts and problems, while concentration on the ego allows the analyst to more easily delve into the individual's successes as well as his difficulties.

In recent years several distinct schools of psychotherapy have developed from, and in addition to, these early rebellions against Freud: client-centered therapy, existential therapy, rational therapy, and reality therapy.

Client-Centered Therapy

Carl Rogers, the founder of **client-centered therapy,** took bits and pieces of the neo-Freudians' views, revised and rearranged them, and came up with a new theory of personality development and a radically different approach to therapy. Rogers agrees with Adler and Rank that infants often feel inadequate and dependent, but he does not feel that this is a necessary fact of the human condition. He agrees with Karen Horney that there is often a difference between who people actually are, who they think they are, and who they would like to be. But Rogers expands the concept of "ideal self" to include both positive and negative feelings. The gap between the real self and the ideal self, says Rogers, is the source of anxiety. The healthy or "fully functioning" person does not judge himself or others and therefore has no reason to act defensively. He knows himself, he is open to new experiences, and he possesses "unshakable self-esteem." The goal of therapy, in Rogers's view, is to help a person become fully functioning, to open him to all his experiences and to all of himself.

Rogers calls his approach to therapy "client-centered" because he does not feel the image of a patient seeking advice from an expert, the doctor, is appropriate. The best expert on a person is the person himself.

Rogers's ideas about therapy are quite specific. First, the therapist must offer the client *unconditional positive regard*. By this he means that the therapist must demonstrate that he genuinely likes and accepts the client—no matter what the client says or does. Rogers feels that the therapist's acceptance is the first step toward getting the client to accept himself. Instead of waiting silently for the client to reveal his life story or offering expert, objective interpretations, the Rogerian therapist tries to understand things from the client's viewpoint. Second, the Rogerian therapist is militantly *nondirective*. He does not suggest why a client feels as he does, how he might handle a difficult situation, or how he should interpret his dreams. Instead, he tries to reflect the client's statements, sometimes asking questions and sometimes hinting at feelings the client has not quite verbalized. Given this open atmosphere and the genuine respect of the therapist, Rogers feels, the client can find himself.

Existential Therapy

Existential therapists like Rollo May agree with Rogers that the goal of therapy is self-knowledge and self-actualization, but they approach the problem somewhat differently. Unlike Freudians, who felt that temperament and life style are largely determined by childhood experiences beyond the individual's control, existentialists see the individual as a free being, capable of determining for himself who he is and how he will live. But many people give up their freedom, defining their lives in terms of jobs, social position, financial success, and so on. The goal of psychotherapy, according to May, is to restore a person's desire to take charge of his life.

Existentialists are extremely flexible in techniques. They view therapy as part of life, not as a temporary retreat from it. The therapist and the client are two *real* people who have committed themselves to a relationship and are free to shape that relationship in any way they see fit. By asking the client to examine both his reasons for entering therapy and his immediate behavior, the therapist attempts to demonstrate a self-directed, active, here-and-now approach to life. He may also encourage the client to discard empty beliefs, to make decisions, and to risk himself in intimate relationships.

Rational Therapy

Unlike Rogerians and existentialists, **rational therapists** see themselves as experts and their clients as individuals who do not know how to help themselves. According to Ellis (1973a), the mistake most people

RATIONAL THERAPY: AN ILLUSTRATION

Patient: . . . I always doubt that I have what it takes intellectually. . . .

Therapist: Well, let's suppose you haven't. Let's just suppose for the sake of discussion that you really are inferior to some degree, and you're not up to your fellows—your old peers from childhood or your present peers. Now what's so catastrophic about that, if it were true?

P: Well, this is a fear, I'm not . . . if they found out, then . . . if I can't keep my job teaching then I . . . I couldn't support my family.

T: How long have you been teaching?

P: Seven years.

T: So, being inferior, you've done pretty well in keeping your job. You're not that concerned about your job.

P: I know my wife says this. She says that somebody would find me out, but I . . . I still feel that I . . . I'm kidding everybody, that I have to be very careful what I say and what I do, because if they should find out that I haven't got it, then I don't know what I would do. If I don't feel that I'm capable of being a teacher, then I shouldn't be a teacher.

T: Who said so?

P: I don't know.

T: I know. You said so. Don't you think there are lots of teachers in the school system who are not very good teachers?

P: Yes, I know there are a lot of them, and I don't respect them. I don't feel they should be teachers if they aren't qualified.

T: So you're saying you don't respect yourself, if you act ineffectively as a teacher. Right?

P: Yes, I wouldn't respect myself.

T: Why not?

P: Because if . . . well, it wouldn't be right to say that I'm teaching when . . . if I haven't got the qualifications, if I'm not capable to do the job.

T: Let's assume you're a lousy teacher. Now why are you tying up your performance? Lousy teacher, we're assuming now. You are a lousy teacher and may always be a lousy teacher. Why are you tying that aspect of you up with your total self? I am a slob because my teaching is slobbish. Now do you see any inconsistency with that conclusion?

P: No, but I agree that I would be . . . it would be a terrible thing if I were to teach, and it wouldn't . . . and I wouldn't be capable. That it wouldn't be right. That would be like I was a fraud.

T: But the terrible thing is that you would be a slob, a no-goodnik, a louse who couldn't respect you.

P: It would be dishonest of me.

T: Well, yes. What's terrible about that?

P: Well, it's terrible.

T: But according to you, about half or more of the teachers in the school system are not so hot teachers. Right?

P: Yes, and if I were administrator I would have to do something about that.

T: Meaning fire them?

P: Fire them.

T: And then who would teach the kids?

P: You mean, if I was the administrator I'd have to . . .

T: Tolerate.

P: To tolerate it . . . (Hersher, 1970, pp. 64–66).

make is rating themselves against other people and then labeling themselves. This prevents them from accepting their natural fallibility and almost always results in self-contempt or in a defensive pose of superiority. Regardless of what happened to the individual in the past, the therapist assumes that the person is solely responsible for the way he feels about himself and thus is responsible for his happiness or unhappiness. The goal of rational therapy is to show the client how his misinterpretations of events are causing his problems and to teach him to see things in a more rational manner.

Rational therapists feel that people seek help when they habitually act in self-defeating ways. For example, some people feel something is wrong if everyone they meet does not love and admire them. Others "beat their brains out" trying to solve a problem that is beyond their control. Still others simply refuse to examine obvious evidence and persist in thinking they are weak, sinful, or stupid. To correct these illogical and self-defeating goals and beliefs, rational therapists use a wide variety of techniques, including persuasion, confrontation, challenge, commands, even theoretical arguments. They do not "baby" their clients, and some people may find their toughness hard to accept. They may go so far as to give "homework" assignments, encouraging clients to risk arguing with their boss, asking the girl down the hall for a date, patting a dog that frightens them. In short, rational therapists are very directive.

Reality Therapy

Like rational therapy, **reality therapy,** developed by William Glasser (1965), also assumes that people bear a significant responsibility for their own problems, and the primary goal of this form of therapy is to help the individual develop responsible behavior. The reality therapist follows five basic principles:

1. He encourages the client to make a value judgment about his own behavior.
2. He encourages the client to make a plan aimed at some desired goal.
3. He asks him to commit himself to that plan.
4. He asks him to make no excuses if he fails to keep that commitment.
5. For his part, the therapist makes it clear he will inflict no punishment on his client, that is, he will never reject him (Barr, 1974, p. 64).

Reality therapy and rational therapy are both highly directive, and in each form of therapy the therapist is frank and occasionally brutal with patients. The main difference between the two is that reality therapy is more concerned with *behavior* than with *belief*. While the rational therapist encourages his client to *view events* in a more rational manner, the reality therapist prefers that his client *act* in a more responsible manner.

Behavior Therapies

Behaviorists reject the idea that behavior disorders are symptoms of hidden emotional conflicts that must be uncovered and resolved. Behaviorists argue that the behavior disorder *is* the problem, not a symptom of the problem. If a therapist can teach a person to respond more appropriately, they feel, he has "cured" him.

Behavior therapies are based on the belief that all behavior, normal and abnormal, is learned. The hypochondriac has learned that he gets attention when he is sick; the catatonic has learned that he is safe when he withdraws entirely. The therapist's job is to extinguish such inappropriate responses and to teach the person more satisfying ways of behaving. He does not need to know how or why the person learned to behave as he does. Behaviorists use a variety of techniques to build new habits.

Operant Conditioning

Operant conditioning techniques are based on the idea that a person will learn to behave in a different way if the new behavior is rewarded and the old behavior is ignored. Kennedy (1964), for example, had the staff in one hospital disregard all the irrational behavior of three chronic schizophrenics. When the patients said something rational and appropriate, they were rewarded with smiles and attention. When their communications were unintelligible or irrational, they were ignored. All three patients improved markedly within a few months.

Isaacs, Thomas, and Goldiamond (1960) used a similar approach with a mute patient. They noticed that the man was extremely fond of chewing gum. Using this as a reinforcer, they began to give him gum every time he moved his mouth. When the patient had mastered this, they withheld the gum until he made a sound. They gradually increased their demands to the point where the patient had to say words to get gum. In this way, they taught him to speak.

Operant conditioning works best in situations where the therapist can control rewards and punishments completely. If the mute patient had lived at home and his family gave him gum whenever he looked as though he wanted it, the therapy would not have worked.

Figure 15-2
Ivar Lovaas, a behavior therapist, is shown here with two autistic boys. They have been given ice cream as a reward for interacting with each other, and now Lovaas is encouraging them to feed each other.
(*Allan Grant*)

Aversive Conditioning

Aversive conditioning is a technique for eliminating specific behavior patterns. The therapist teaches the person to associate pain and discomfort with the response he wants to unlearn. This form of behavior therapy has been used successfully to treat alcoholism, homosexuality, obesity, and smoking.

Sometimes the therapist uses real physical pain. Dent (1954) treated alcoholics by giving them a drug that produces extreme nausea when

PARENTS AS THERAPISTS

Many forms of therapy restrict parental involvement in the treatment process. The primary work with the patient is done by a trained, experienced therapist. Yet recent research on the use of behavior therapy with autistic children suggests that parents can be an essential part of the treatment process and can make a significant contribution to the child's improvement (Schreibman & Kogel, 1975).

For example, 3-year-old Kristin was prone to terrible temper tantrums, endless crying, and occasional physical attacks on those who tried to comfort her. After working with the therapist, Kristin's parents learned to stop rewarding her antisocial behavior. If Kristin had a tantrum in a public place, her mother spanked her, instead of comforting her or accepting her demands. When Kristin behaved well, her parents rewarded her with love and praise. Her parents helped Kristin to make remarkable progress, and she is now able to attend a preschool with normal children.

Schreibman and Kogel note that the successful parent therapist must make a significant emotional investment in helping the child. Effective parent therapists work at increasing the child's frequency of approved behaviors and learn to avoid pitying the child or blaming themselves for the child's condition. When parents have been trained in behavior modification principles, they feel better able to cope with the child, which does much to improve the atmosphere at home. Moreover, they help the child to maintain gains made in professional therapy by providing continuous training and support. Parents' success in helping their autistic children has led Schreibman and Kogel to suggest that normal children might also benefit if their parents were trained in behavior modification techniques. One of the advantages of behavior therapy is that it is easy to teach and can be learned in a matter of hours. Learning what to reward and what to punish or ignore, how to shape behavior and phrase instructions, and what constitutes a proper response and how to most effectively reward it—becoming behavior therapists, in other words—can help many parents to better cope with their children's behavior.

Figure 15-3
Aversive conditioning to stop smoking. Every time this woman takes a puff of her cigarette, she gets a blast of stale cigarette smoke in her face.
(*Wide World Photos*)

mixed with alcohol in the stomach. The people were encouraged—in fact, instructed—to drink, and each time they did, they became violently sick. Gradually they began to feel sick every time they even saw a bottle of whiskey. Thorpe and his colleagues (1963) created an aversion to homosexual activity, and Lubin (1968) helped people stop smoking by similar means. Convicted child molesters have been cured by showing them pictures of naked children and giving them electric shocks (Knight, 1974). More recently, behaviorists have discovered that physical pain is not necessary. People can be taught to block behavior with unpleasant fantasies. For example, while undergoing shock therapy, the child molesters also learned to associate things they were afraid of with pictures of children and things they enjoyed with pictures of adults.

Figure 15-4
Desensitization has been used to treat people with phobias about snakes. People learn first to touch rubber snakes, then to look at live snakes in a cage, then to handle them while wearing rubber gloves, until finally they are able to hold and handle live snakes without fear. (From A. Bandura, E. B. Blanchard, and B. Ritter, "Relative Efficacy of Desensitization and Modeling Approaches for Inducing Behavioral, Affective, and Attitudinal Changes," *Journal of Personality and Social Psychology*, 1969, *13*, 173–199. Courtesy Albert Bandura; reprinted by permission of Dr. Bandura and the American Psychological Association.)

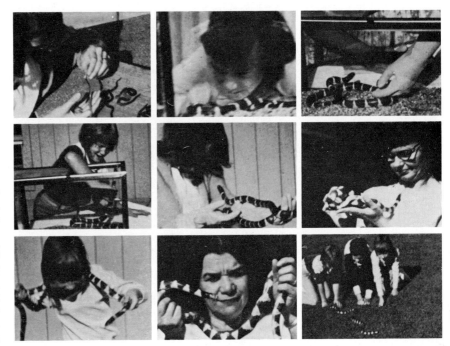

Desensitization

In some cases, aversive conditioning can be harmful. For example, if a child who is afraid of dogs were taken by the hand and forced to approach the dog that bit him, he might well be terrified the next time someone took his hand. In such cases, **desensitization,** a method for gradually reducing irrational fear, would be a more useful technique. A therapist might give the child cookies and milk if he will sit by a window and watch a dog chained outside. Once he seems calm in this situation, the therapist will give him cookies only if he goes out into the yard and plays 30 feet away from the chained dog. Waiting at each stage until the child seems relaxed, the therapist gradually moves the child closer to the dog. Behaviorists have used desensitization to cure phobias about snakes, heights, closed rooms, and sex.

Reciprocal Inhibition

The examples given so far indicate that behaviorists can be successful in treating specific problems and fears, from psychotic behavior to a child's fear of dogs. But many of the people who consult psychotherapists are vague about their problems—they feel anxious and unhappy most of the time. Can behaviorists treat diffuse anxiety?

Wolpe (1969*a*) believes they can. Chronically anxious people may not be able to say why they feel tense, but they are nearly always able

ANIMAL PSYCHOTHERAPY

One of the most interesting developments in psychotherapy in recent years has been the involvement of animals both as patients and as therapists. This completes a cycle in which experiments with animals led to the development of therapeutic techniques for humans, which are now being applied to animals.

Tuber, Hothersall, and Voith (1974) describe the case of Higgins, a 4-year-old Old English sheepdog, who was terribly frightened by thunderstorms. When he sensed that a storm was coming, Higgins would begin to pace and would pant and salivate heavily. But that was nothing compared with what happened when the storm actually arrived: Higgins weighed 110 pounds and in his desperate efforts to escape could cause an incredible amount of destruction. When a thunderstorm caught Higgins and his owner while they were driving in a little sports car, it was the last straw. He was brought in for therapy.

The therapists used a desensitization technique to cure Higgins. They played a record of a storm on a stereo phonograph, gradually increasing its loudness. At each level of loudness, Higgins was told to lie down and was rewarded with chocolate as long as he was able to stay still. He eventually learned to cope with thunderstorms, although he has not learned to enjoy them, and has become much more restrained and is more easily calmed down.

In Chapter 10, we discussed Harry Harlow's experiments with monkeys raised in isolation and the fact that these monkeys were later unable to establish normal sexual and maternal behavior patterns. Suomi, Harlow, and McKinney (1972) decided that they would try to cure these "neurotic monkeys." They put the monkeys in a cage with normal young monkeys and waited to see what would happen. At first, the neurotic monkeys sat passively in corners rocking back and forth, not interacting with each other or with the normal monkeys. But the normal monkeys would not allow the isolates to remain isolated. They forced them to interact by constantly clinging to them and by drawing them into play. After two years of "monkey psychiatry" the neurotic monkeys had been completely cured. As the researchers put it: "In conclusion, we are all aware of the existence of some therapists who seem inhuman. We find it refreshing to report the discovery of non-humans who can be therapists" (p. 932).

to distinguish different levels of anxiety. For example, in his first session a politician tells the therapist that he is very anxious about speaking to crowds. The therapist looks for more detail. He asks if the man is more threatened by an audience of 500 than by an audience of 50, more tense when he is addressing an all-male audience than when he is speaking to a women's group, and so on. Perhaps this politician feels most anxious talking to adolescents, least anxious talking to small children. In this way the therapist establishes a *hierarchy*, from the least to the most anxiety-provoking situations.

Next he teaches the person to clear his mind, release tense muscles, and relax. (In some cases he may use drugs or mild hypnosis to produce relaxation.) Once the client has mastered the technique of deep relaxation, they begin at the bottom of his anxiety hierarchy. The therapist asks the person to imagine the least threatening scene and to signal when he begins to feel tense. At the signal, the therapist tells him to forget the scene and concentrate on relaxing. After a short period, he instructs him to return to the scene. This process is repeated until the person feels completely relaxed. Gradually they move up the list until the client is able to imagine the situation he most feared without anxiety. Wolpe reports that most clients are able to transfer what they learn in his office to real-life situations. In effect, they learn to *inhibit* anxiety responses with incompatible, deep-muscle relaxation.

Some psychologists are critical of behavior therapies. They feel that, by concentrating only on behavior, behavior therapies present an oversimplified version of human psychology. These psychologists feel that an individual's mental behavior is just as important in therapy as his overt behavior. The chief opposition to behavior therapies comes from traditional psychoanalysts. Analysts, as noted earlier, believe that neurotic and psychotic behavior is a symptom of unconscious problems. They argue that if you teach a person to give up his symptoms without resolving the conflicts that caused them, new symptoms—perhaps even less desirable—will appear. Wolpe (1969b) defends his approach with follow-up studies: of 249 people he treated for neurotic problems, only 4 developed new symptoms.

This is not to say that behavior therapies are foolproof. Successful conditioning and retraining depend on the client and therapist establishing a valid hierarchy, on the therapist's discovering an adequate reinforcer (in operant conditioning), and on the lack of counterconditioning outside the therapy sessions.

Group Therapies

By definition, individual psychotherapy is limited to the interaction of two people, the client and the therapist. Many psychologists think this is less than ideal. A person may attach a great deal of importance to his therapist's real and imagined reactions. Therapists are human, so there is always some degree of **countertransference** (the therapist's projecting his emotions onto the client). Furthermore, therapy sessions bear little resemblance to everyday life. The chances are slim that a person will encounter the analyst's neutrality or the Rogerian's unconditional positive regard in his friends and family. He may find it difficult to transfer the insight and confidence he has gained in therapy to other relationships.

Group therapies allow both the therapist and the client to see how the person interacts with others. Therapy groups also give people a chance to shed inhibitions and practice self-expression in a safe atmosphere. Finally, groups are a source of reinforcement.

Traditional groups. Traditional therapy groups are an extension of individual psychotherapy. Usually the participants are also seeing the therapist individually. Such groups meet once or twice weekly, typically for an hour and a half. The emphasis in these sessions is often on uncovering ghosts from the past that haunt individuals' behavior in the present. John, an older man, is extremely hostile toward a young student, Tim. Is he projecting the image of a younger brother onto Tim? Acting out his frustrations with his son? When he attacks Tim's appearance, is he speaking for himself or echoing his father's values?

Gestalt groups. Gestalt therapy is largely an outgrowth of the work of Frederick (Fritz) Perls at the Esalen Institute in California. Perls began his career as a psychoanalyst, but later turned violently against Freud and psychoanalytic techniques. Perls felt that "Freud invented the couch because he could not look people in the eye" (cited in Gaines, 1974, p. 118). Gestalt therapy is quite similar to existential therapy—both emphasize the here-and-now, and both encourage face-to-face confrontations.

Gestalt therapy is designed to make people self-supporting. It can be used with individuals, but it is more frequently undertaken in a group setting. The therapist plays an active and directive role, usually concentrating on one person at a time. The emphasis in Gestalt therapy is on the *whole* person, and the therapist's role, as Perls describes it, is to "fill in the holes in the personality to make the person whole and complete again" (Perls, 1969, p. 2). The therapist attempts to make the person aware of his feelings, to awaken him to sensory information he may be ignoring. A variety of techniques may be used—the person is told to talk about himself in the first person ("I keep looking away" instead of "My eyes keep looking away"). By this, the therapist is reminding the person that he alone is responsible for everything he does. If he wants to discuss a third person, he must speak directly *to* that person or role-play a conversation if that person is not present. Gestalt therapy, like psychoanalysis, uses people's dreams to help uncover information. Often a person is asked to act out all parts in his dream—both people and objects.

Fritz Perls
(Courtesy Real People Press/ Deke Simon)

Encounter groups. These groups also stress the here-and-now. In part they are based on the realization that people who have been in therapy for a while become very good at analyzing their feelings and tend to hide behind psychological jargon. For example, John attacks Susan and she responds by saying, "You're projecting." This may be correct, but Susan is avoiding her own feelings about being attacked. How does *she* feel? Threatened? Hurt? Angry? By demanding that participants

GESTALT THERAPY: THE CASE OF LINDA

Linda: *I dreamed that I watch . . . a lake . . . drying up, and there is a small island in the middle of the lake, and a circle of . . . porpoises—they're like porpoises except that they can stand up, so they're like porpoises that are like people, and they're in a circle, sort of like a religious ceremony, and it's very sad—I feel very sad because they can breathe, they are sort of dancing around the circle, but the water, their element, is drying up. So it's like a dying—like watching a race of people, or a race of creatures, dying. And they are mostly females, but a few of them have a small male organ, so there are a few males there, but they won't live long enough to reproduce, and their element is drying up. And there is one that is sitting over here near me and I'm talking to this porpoise and he has prickles on his tummy, sort of like a porcupine, and they don't seem to be a part of him. And I think that there's one good point about the water drying up, I think—well, at least at the bottom, when all the water dries up, there will probably be some sort of treasure there, because at the bottom of the lake there should be things that have fallen in, like coins or something, but I look carefully and all that I can find is an old license plate. . . . That's the dream.*

Fritz: *Will you please play the license plate.*

L: *I am an old license plate, thrown in the bottom of a lake. I have no use because I'm no value— although I'm not rusted—I'm outdated, so I can't be used as a license plate . . . and I'm just thrown on the rubbish heap. That's what I did with a license plate, I threw it on a rubbish heap.*

F: *Well, how do you feel about this?*

L: *(quietly) I don't like it. I don't like being a license plate—useless.*

F: *Could you talk about this. That was such a long dream until you come to find the license plate, I'm sure this must be of great importance.*

L: *(sighs) Useless. Outdated. . . . The use of a license plate is to allow—give a car permission to go . . . and I can't give any more permission to do anything because I'm outdated. . . . In California, they just paste a little—you buy a sticker—and stick it on the car, on the old license plate. (faint attempt at humor) So maybe someone could put me on their car and stick this sticker on me, I don't know . . .*

F: *Okeh, now play the lake.*

L: *I'm a lake. . . . I'm drying up, and disappearing, soaking into the earth . . . (with a touch of surprise) dying. . . . But when I soak into the earth, I become a part of the earth—so maybe I water the surrounding area, so . . . even in the lake, even in my bed, flowers can grow (sighs). . . . New life can grow . . . from me (cries). . . .*

F: *You get the existential message?*

L: *Yes. (sadly, but with conviction) I can paint—I can create—I can create beauty. I can no longer reproduce, I'm like the porpoise . . . but I . . . I'm . . . I . . . keep wanting to say I'm food. . . . I . . . as water becomes . . . I water the earth, and give life—growing things, the water—they need both the earth and water, and the . . . and the air and the sun, but as the water from the lake, I can play a part in something, and producing—feeding.*

F: *You see the contrast: On the surface, you find something, some artifact—the license plate, the artificial you—but then when you go deeper, you find the apparent death of the lake is actually fertility. . . .*

L: *And I don't need a license plate, or a permission, a license in order to . . .*

F: *(gently) Nature doesn't need a license plate to grow. You don't have to be useless, if you are organismically creative, which means if you are involved.*

L: *And I don't need permission to be creative. . . . Thank you* (Perls, 1969, pp. 85–87).

respond to the immediate situation and express themselves directly, encounter groups try to strip away the social pretenses of everyday life on the assumption that if people give up such inhibitions and stop trying to act in the way they think others expect, they will feel better and less anxious.

Sensitivity groups. Therapy groups like those conducted at the Esalen Institute are designed to enhance individual awareness by focusing on nonverbal communication and the senses. Often the participants are well adjusted—in their minds, too well adjusted. They feel they have lost touch with simple things. Rushing around, how many people ever pause to look into a stranger's eyes or smell a spring day? How many people ever touch anyone except their lover, spouse, or children? Sensitivity groups provide exercises to reawaken the senses.

Many people who do not feel anxious enough to want to go into individual therapy participate in encounter and sensitivity groups because they want to grow. Sometimes these groups are conducted in **marathon sessions.** Participants meet all day, every day, for a weekend or more, either in the therapist's office or in a vacation retreat.

Figure 15-5
Many of the exercises used in sensitivity training groups are designed to reawaken the senses, to make people more aware of their own bodies, and to develop people's ability to trust in others.
(*Paul Fusco*)

Therapy groups enable psychologists to reach more people at a lower cost and, with marathons, in a shorter period of time. But are such short-term groups therapeutic? They seem to fulfill some people's need for openness, intimacy, and physical warmth. But there is considerable disagreement about other effects.

Goldenberg (1973) identifies several important criticisms of encounter and sensitivity groups:

- Their benefits may be only short-term. After the "high feeling passes, the individual may be no better off than he was before.
- Not all groups are run by trained psychotherapists. The number of untrained, self-styled group leaders is increasing, and this can be dangerous in view of the intensity of emotion in the group.
- Often group leaders are not careful enough about who to accept into the group. They should interview each applicant at length to ensure that he will have a positive influence on the rest of the group and is strong enough to stand the strain of intense, undefended interactions with other people.
- Some leaders have been criticized for not taking responsibility for the members of their groups. For example, most leaders of "weekend workshops" neglect to make follow-up studies to see how participation in the group has affected the group's members. As some people have become seriously disturbed by their experiences with such groups, the responsibility of the group leader should not end when the marathon is over.
- These groups emphasize emotions and play down the intellect. "Gut-level feelings are in, while head trips are out. . . . Yet lasting change probably requires some integration of the intellect with the senses" (Goldenberg, 1973, p. 407).

Transactional analysis. Originated by Eric Berne (1957, 1964), transactional analysis is based on the idea that humans are always acting out of any one of three ego states: the Child, the Parent, or the Adult. The *Child* represents the person's behavior and attitudes at an earlier stage of development; the *Parent* represents the attitudes, responses, and behavior absorbed from his own parents and other authority figures; and the *Adult* represents his abilities to act and think independently, without being influenced by the demands of the Child and the Parent. Berne does not suggest that a person should act as an Adult all the time, but that he should learn to recognize communication directed to his Adult and to respond appropriately. The primary goal of transactional analysis is to improve communication between people by making them more aware of what they are communicating.

Transactional analysis aims at understanding which ego states people are acting from by studying transactions between two or more people. Thus, although therapists can conduct transactional analysis with individuals, it is more effective in the context of group therapy. The analyst basically wishes to minimize "crossed transactions" (for example, when one person acts as Adult and the other responds as Child) and "ulterior transactions" (for example, when one person acts as Adult because he feels that is the best way to draw out the other person's Child) (Berne, 1968).

Family therapy. This form of therapy is based on the idea that if one person in the family has problems, it is often a signal that the entire family unit needs assistance. Family therapists feel that most psychotherapists treat the individual in a vacuum. Most never meet the person's parents, spouse, and children. The primary goals of family therapy include improving communication, encouraging family members to become more empathetic, getting them to share the responsibilities of leadership, and reducing conflict. To achieve this, all family members must see that they will benefit from changes in their behavior. The therapist must thoroughly understand the family relationships and must concentrate on changing the ways family members satisfy their needs rather than trying to change those needs or the people's personalities (Horn, 1975).

Family therapy is most obviously indicated when problems exist between husband and wife, parents and children, and other family members. It may also be indicated when a person's progress in individual therapy seems to be slowed by his family or when a member of the family seems to be having deep trouble adjusting to the person's improving condition. Goldenberg (1973) notes, however, that all families may not benefit from family therapy. Some problems may be too entrenched; in some families, important members may be absent or unwilling to cooperate, and in others one member of the family may so monopolize the session that the therapy becomes unworkable. In such cases, some other therapeutic approach might work better.

Physical Treatment

Sometimes therapists find they cannot "get through" to a person with any of the therapies we have described because the person is extremely agitated, disoriented, or depressed and totally unresponsive. In these cases, the therapist may decide to use **physical treatment** to change the person's behavior so that he can benefit from therapy. Physical treatment is also used to restrain patients who are dangerous to themselves and others, as well as in institutions where there are only a few therapists for large numbers of patients.

Shock Treatments

Shock is most often used to alleviate sudden and severe depression, especially in psychotics. In **electric shock therapy,** one electrode is placed on each side of the person's head and a mild current is turned on for a very short period. This produces a brief convulsion, followed by a temporary coma. **Insulin shock treatment** consists of an intramuscular injection of insulin, which lowers the level of sugar in the blood, producing a brief period of coma.

Shock is a stimulant. After treatment the person is happier, more responsive, and more active. No one knows exactly why shock treatment works as it does, but most researchers feel that convulsions produce both physiological and psychological changes (Ullmann & Krasner, 1969.

Because of negative side effects, insulin shock therapy is rarely used today. Muscle relaxants to prevent dislocations and fractures during the convulsion have made electric shock therapy more manageable, but its use is also declining. Both treatments can temporarily impair a person's memory, and both are risky with people who have other medical problems such as heart disease.

Psychosurgery

Brain surgery to change a person's behavior and emotional state is a drastic step, since the effects of **psychosurgery** are difficult to predict. One procedure may work with one person, but fail completely with another, perhaps producing undesirable side effects.

Techniques for **prefrontal lobotomies** were introduced in this country in 1942 by Freeman and Watts. By severing the nerves connecting the thalamus and the frontal areas of the cortex, tension and anxiety are often relieved and emotional activity decreased. But in most people the surgery is also followed by apathy, introversion, and some loss of memory. For these reasons, lobotomies are rarely performed today. As we noted in Chapter 2, new areas of the brain—particularly in the limbic system—are being tested as possible sites for psychosurgery.

Most of the more recent techniques are aimed at reducing aggressive, violent impulses. Doctors have been able to cure schizophrenia and to reduce the incidence of "homicidal rage" in many of their patients. However, all these researchers consider psychosurgery a "desperation measure," which literally kills a part of the individual's personality.

The debate on the effectiveness and ethical implications of psychosurgery continues today. Mark (1974) argues that psychosurgery is a worthwhile form of treatment to be used when other methods have clearly failed. But Chorover (1974) sees the claims of psychosurgeons as "grossly exaggerated" (p. 60). As part of his criticism of psychosurgery, he reexamines the case of "Thomas R.," which Mark and Ervin (1970) cite as an example of successful psychosurgery. Chorover claims that information available about Thomas R. from sources other than his psychosurgeons suggests quite the opposite. Since the operation, Thomas has been divorced, unable to work, arrested in a fight, and periodically rehospitalized. His mother claims that he has been "almost a vegetable" as a result of the surgery. In late 1973, a $2-million lawsuit was filed on behalf of Thomas R. against Vernon Mark, who performed the psychosurgery, and Frank Ervin, the consulting psychiatrist on the case. Such cases undoubtedly will be a forum for the continuing debate over the medical, legal, and ethical issues involved in psychosurgery.

Drug Therapy

Nearly all psychiatrists prefer drugs to either shock treatment or psychosurgery. Drugs produce only temporary changes in body chemistry, their effects are reversible, the dosage can be varied from one individual to another, and the side effects are easier to predict.

Until the mid-1950s drugs were not used widely—for the simple reason that the only sedatives available made people sleepy as well as calm. Then, *reserpine* and *phenothiazine* were introduced. Both of these drugs are antipsychotic tranquilizers. They reduce anxiety and aggressive behavior, and sometimes alleviate delusions and hallucinations. How do they work? Research with animals indicates that they inhibit the hypothalamus, which controls arousal. Brain wave studies suggest that this prevents internal arousal signals from reaching the higher portions of the brain (Sarason, 1972). In addition, psychiatrists sometimes prescribe antidepressants, which speed up all physiological processes and thus alleviate severe depression.

Of course, drugs do not cure psychological problems. If the medication is stopped, the person will return to his original condition. But they do calm agitated and depressed people, and in some cases enable people who might otherwise be confined to institutions to return to their communities and families.

Institutionalization

How and why are people committed to mental institutions? Most often, people are committed at the request of family members, either acting on their own or on the recommendation of a physician. Others enter hospitals voluntarily. Still others are committed by the courts, either because of violent behavior or because of a suicide attempt.

Most people are initially placed on a psychiatric ward in a general hospital. During the first few days in the hospital, the patient is interviewed and tested by staff psychologists. At the end of this period the staff meets to decide how to proceed. They ask, first, whether the patient is potentially dangerous to himself or others; second, whether he would benefit from hospitalization; third, whether he would be able to get along if they decided to release him.

In most states, two psychiatrists must certify that a person is "mentally ill" before he can be committed. The final decision rests with the courts (Lazarus, 1969). If he is to be institutionalized, the person is usually transferred to a state mental hospital. (There are private hospitals, but few people can afford them.)

Typically, state institutions are isolated from the community, either by walls or by location. The patient who has been committed loses his legal rights—he cannot come or go as he pleases, and he has only limited opportunities to petition for his freedom. Currently, mental

"ON BEING SANE IN INSANE PLACES"

D. L. Rosenhan (1973) wanted to study the quality of care in mental hospitals. Eight sane people—five men and three women; Rosenhan himself, three psychologists, a pediatrician, a psychiatrist, a painter, and a housewife—applied for admission at 12 different psychiatric hospitals. The hospitals were a mixed group—old and new, public and private, understaffed and adequately staffed. The "pseudopatients" all told the admitting doctor that they heard voices that seemed to say "empty," "hollow," and "thud." (These words were chosen because they suggest *existential psychosis*—a feeling that life is meaningless—no cases of which have ever been reported.) The voices were the only problem the pseudopatients said they had, and all gave their real life histories to the doctor. They all "passed" and were admitted. Seven of them were diagnosed as schizophrenic and the eighth was labeled manic-depressive.

Once they were in the hospitals, all behaved normally. They talked to the patients and openly took notes about what they saw on the wards. They told the staff they no longer heard voices and actively tried to get discharged. Many of the real patients knew right away that the pseudopatients were sane. One said, "You're not crazy. You're a journalist, or professor [referring to the constant note-taking]. You're checking up on the hospital." The staff, on the other hand, knew the pseudopatients were psychotic because the admitting diagnosis said so. One staff nurse described the note-taking—recognized by the patients as evidence of sanity—as "Patient engages in writing behavior."

The pseudopatients found the hospital atmosphere to be highly dehumanizing. They had no privacy, their direct questions were often ignored, and they were treated as though they did not really exist. In a men's ward, one nurse showed how little attention she gave to the patients by unbuttoning her blouse to adjust her bra. In over 3 months of hospitalization, six of the pseudopatients estimated that they talked with a doctor for about 7 minutes a day. They also noted that the doctors did not respond openly to their direct questions and avoided looking them in the eyes. Rosenhan concluded that "the consequences to patients hospitalized in such an environment—the powerlessness, depersonalization, segregation, mortification, and self-labeling—seem undoubtedly countertherapeutic" (p. 252).

This study caused a good deal of controversy among the psychiatric community. Rosenhan's critics said that his sample was too small and thus his judgment should not be generalized to all mental hospitals. However, most doctors did agree that the care in hospitals could be greatly improved if there were more qualified people available, as well as more money.

patients across the nation are fighting what they see as unfair restrictions on their freedom. They are suing doctors, government officials, and even judges to win basic rights—such as the right to humane treatment, to due process in commitment proceedings, and to fair pay for their labor in state institutions.

(Paul Fusco, Magnum Photos)

The legal plight of mental patients is perhaps best described by Offir (1974):

If you merely act a little strange and someone wants to lock you up in a mental hospital, you've got real problems. In many states you may be denied some or most of the legal rights usually guaranteed to criminals, including the automatic right to counsel; the right to a prompt hearing into the reasonableness of the seizure; the right to a jury trial; the right to call independent experts; the right to a trial that conforms to standard rules of evidence; the privilege against self-incrimination; and the requirement of proof "beyond a reasonable doubt." Once you are committed, you may also forfeit your right to enter into a contract, drive a car, vote, or even marry (p. 66).

The patient in a state institution has many other problems as well. Most large institutions are poorly funded and cannot afford enough staff to give all patients intensive therapy. In such cases, it is the patient who is judged to have the best chance to be cured, or at least to improve, who receives therapy. Others are given only custodial care—the staff looks after them, sees that they are washed, dressed, and fed, and that they take their medicine; these patients may see a psychologist for only a few minutes a week. Some hospitals have good recreational and vocational facilities; others have only a television set. Not surprisingly, the patients on many wards are apathetic and indifferent.

(Burk Uzzle, Magnum Photos)

In recent years a number of psychologists have begun to feel that such institutions are not only inadequate, but that they have a negative effect on patients. Some argue that all the hospitals do is to teach people how to be "good patients," thus promoting the behavior they are supposed to cure. In the last decade, the emphasis has moved away from custodial care toward returning the person to his family and community as rapidly as possible. This requires preserving the patient's community ties while he is in the hospital. As a result, many hospitals have become more therapeutic and less custodial. **Halfway houses,** which are run by the hospital but located within the community, help the person to make a transition between institutionalization and self-support.

Within the institutional framework, some psychologists are looking for alternative ways to promote healthy behavior. Of all the experiments in on-the-ward therapy, the token economies program is the most interesting.

Token Economies

As we noted in Chapter 4, **token economies** are based on the behaviorist approach to therapy—if you consistently reward a person for desirable behavior, he will begin to respond appropriately. In everyday life the chief medium for reinforcement is money. People work and are re-

Figure 15-6

This patient is holding her job card, which lists the chores she is to perform each day. When the chores are finished, she receives tokens as a reward, which she can use to purchase meals, excursions, or small items from the shop on her ward.
(*State of California Department of Mental Hygiene*)

warded with money. This money enables them to buy things they want. If their work improves, their salary increases.

Psychologists Teodoro Ayllon and Nathan Azrin (1968) decided to re-create this incentive system on a ward for chronic psychotic patients. All the patients were women, and all had been in the hospital a long time. Ayllon and Azrin's chief objective was to encourage the patients to behave in a way that might eventually enable them to return to society—to care for themselves and their rooms, to relate to other people in an appropriate way, and to work at jobs around the hospital. Each time a patient on their ward behaved in a desirable way, she was given tokens that could be exchanged for candy and cigarettes, extra TV time, the right to choose a dinner table, a chance to see the psychologist or chaplain, a pass to go out on the grounds, and so on.

Ayllon and Azrin chose the token system of reinforcement for two reasons. First, tokens resemble money and thus create a bridge back to society. (Some of the patients they worked with had been hospitalized as long as 20 years and had forgotten what life was like "on the outside.") Second, tokens are a concrete form of reward. On the average ward a patient may strive for such rewards as smiles and attention. But these rewards are ambiguous, particularly to disturbed people who have difficulty interpreting other people's signals. Tokens enabled the staff to establish a definite, reliable scale for rewards. The patients could see and touch evidence of "good social behavior."

Patients in this program improved dramatically. Some who had spent years sitting off by themselves began to take an interest in hospital activities. Many performed useful jobs and some even began to "pay" for their rooms with the tokens they had earned. In addition, staff morale increased throughout the hospital. In the past, doctors and attendants alike had been pessimistic about the possibility of ever helping their patients. Now they had a workable method. However, as we noted in Chapter 4, many psychologists have reservations about token economies. They feel that people learn how to earn tokens rather than actually learning a new behavior, and that when the tokens stop, the learning does too. Thus, although token economies may be valuable in an institution to encourage patients to change their behavior, these psychologists caution against generally applying such a program to other situations.

Repucci and Saunders (1974), who have been particularly outspoken about the limitations of behaviorist methods, write that "even minimal conditions necessary for behavior change are difficult to obtain" (p. 659). They describe eight types of problems or constraints that face the behavior modifier when he attempts to work in less than ideal settings. Among these are *institutional constraints* (such as bureaucratic stalling and "red tape"); *external pressure* (such as newspapers and police insisting on tight security in a school); and *limited resources* (in one school, it took a year and a half to build desired sleeping alcoves for boys, primarily because of the lack of cooperation from the campus maintenance people). Such problems have led Repucci and Saunders to caution against accepting the more extravagant claims of behavior modification.

Community Psychology

In recent years, the rate of institutionalization has decreased. One reason is that drugs enable many psychotics to return to their families. Another is that the public is more sophisticated about emotional problems and mental health care than it was 10 or 15 years ago. As a result, people are seeking treatment for themselves and for family members *before* hospitalization becomes necessary (Satloff & Worby, 1970). In addition, psychologists are reaching out—looking for people in difficulty instead of waiting for people to come to them. This new approach is largely the result of a developing school of research and practice— **community psychology.**

The goals of applied community psychology are to *prevent* mental illness and to *educate* the public—particularly those segments of the public that have had only limited access to psychotherapy. How can psychologists prevent mental illness? By establishing closer links with the community so that teachers, clergymen, and neighbors recognize the signs of psychological crisis. Education has two purposes: to inform people that help for emotional problems exists (that there is someplace they can go), and to teach people how they themselves can cope with psychological problems.

One of the pilot studies in community approaches to mental health was conducted in Susanville, a small town in northern California. Until the late 1960s, Susanville had depended on visiting professionals who were called in whenever local officials discovered an individual with psychological problems. (About 12 people a year were committed to state mental hospitals from this town.) Then a number of concerned citizens got together to look for a better plan. They decided that instead of hiring outsiders whenever someone needed help, they would hire professionals to teach local people how to deal with individual and family problems. The group was primarily concerned with deviant behavior, "school phobias," and family breakdowns.

Eighteen adults, most of whom worked in the community's social agencies, and 14 high school students were selected as trainees. All attended lectures on the basic principles of behavior therapy and practice sessions in which some trainees would role-play families in crisis. Then "problem families" were selected from a list of those whose children were often in trouble at school.

The lay therapists met with individuals and entire families about once a week. The purpose of these sessions was to show the clients how they interacted with each other, and to impress on them the idea that if they behaved differently they might eliminate interpersonal problems. All the participating families reported that their home life was improved during the 8 weeks of the program. Nearly half the lay therapists planned to continue seeing "their" families after the program ended (Beier, Robinson, & Micheletti, 1971).

The community can involve itself in several areas. Two of the most important types of community action that can be taken are:

1. *Prevention of mental illness.* The final report of the Joint Commission on Mental Health of Children in 1970 called for a new focus for mental health work. The Commission found a need for *prevention* of mental disorders rather than *treatment* after the disorders were already obvious (Hamm, 1974). But vigorous community action may be necessary to promote relevant research efforts and appropriate and innovative programs aimed at the prevention of mental illness in children. A crucial step in such an approach may involve use of school systems to monitor the physical and mental health of children.

2. *Crisis intervention.* Goldenberg (1973) characterizes this psychotherapeutic approach as "prompt, brief, here-and-now, and action-oriented" (p. 344). The clients of crisis intervention programs can include adults with suicidal tendencies, adolescents with serious drug problems, and young children who are nervous about entering school. Crisis intervention is an important element in a community approach to mental illness, because "crisis centers" tend to become involved in the most pressing social problems of the population.

Iscoe (1974) stresses that the goal of community psychology should be to create the *competent community.* In such a community, members would be able to make sound and rational decisions about critical issues, after carefully weighing all available alternatives. They would not be problem-free, but they would be better able to cope with the problems of their community. The competent community would fully develop all of its resources—especially the untapped human resources of its members. Ideally, it would become as self-sufficient as possible and would be able to function well without help from community psychologists. According to Iscoe, the goals of the competent community might not be the goals of the mental health professionals; the community's goals might not conform to white, middle-class standards. But the community's goals would spring from the members of the community and would be relevant and realistic, given the needs of the community.

Summary

1. Psychotherapy is a highly controversial, often misunderstood, means of helping people with behavior disorders. It is a general term that covers a wide variety of different therapies used in private practice, in institutions, and in community programs. In recent years, psychotherapy has become

less problem-oriented, and new therapies have been designed to help people develop skills, rather than solve problems.

2. *Psychoanalysis,* as developed by Freud, is based on the belief that the anxiety and problems that cause a person to seek help are symptoms of feelings the person repressed in early childhood. Psychoanalysis is a method for achieving *insight*—for bringing these repressed feelings to consciousness so that the person can deal with them directly by *working through* them. Successful analysis depends on the person's making an effort not to inhibit or control his thoughts and fantasies, but to describe them in *free association*. The analyst remains neutral and, for the most part, silent. Early in the course of analysis, the patient begins to have good feelings toward the analyst, a process known as *positive transference*. Later he may feel more dissatisfied or uneasy, as he experiences *negative transference*.

3. Many psychologists disagree with Freud's approach to psychotherapy. Alfred Adler felt that the therapist's job is to assure the patient that he is capable of taking charge of his life. Otto Rank felt that the therapist should refuse the patient's attempts to become dependent on him and encourage him to be strong. Karen Horney felt that the purpose of therapy is to teach a person to give up his illusions about himself so that he will no longer have to make excuses for himself. All these neo-Freudians favor face-to-face discussions and feel that therapists should take an active role. Also, most neo-Freudian therapists try to get their patients to focus on coping with current problems rather than on resolving past conflicts. Ego psychologists focus on the workings of the ego rather than the id. In therapy this allows the therapist to delve into the person's successes as well as his problems.

4. *Client-centered therapy* was developed by Carl Rogers, who believes that the gap between the real self and the ideal self is the source of anxiety. The goal of client-centered therapy is to help a person become fully functioning, to open him to all his experiences and to all of himself so that he has no reason to act defensively. The client-centered therapist offers the client *unconditional positive regard,* by demonstrating that he genuinely likes and accepts the client and by trying to understand things from the client's viewpoint. He is also *nondirective* and tries only to reflect the client's statements.

5. *Existential therapy* is based on the belief that man is a free being, capable of determining for himself who he is and how he will live. The goal of existential therapy is to restore a person's desire to take charge of his own life. Existentialists are extremely flexible in techniques, viewing therapy as part of life and concentrating on the here-and-now situation.

6. *Rational therapy* is based on the idea that all people are goal-seeking and that if they cannot achieve their goals, it is because they are making some logical mistake. Rational therapists see themselves as experts and their clients as individuals who do not know how to help themselves, so they play a very directive role in showing the client where his mistakes lie and in teaching him more reasonable beliefs.

7. *Reality therapy* assumes that people are responsible for their own problems, and the primary goal of therapy is to get people to accept this responsibility. Reality therapists are very directive and attempt to help the

person develop better ways of dealing with current problems rather than worrying about what happened in the past. While rational therapy is concerned with the individual's beliefs, reality therapy emphasizes the development of more satisfying behavior.

8. Behaviorists reject the idea that behavior disorders are symptoms of hidden emotional conflicts and argue that the behavior disorder is the problem, not a symptom of the problem. *Behavior therapies* are based on the belief that behavior is learned and that the therapist's job is to extinguish inappropriate responses and to teach the person more satisfying behavior.

9. *Operant conditioning* is based on the idea that a person will learn to behave in a different way if the new behavior is rewarded and the old behavior is ignored. It works best in situations where the therapist can control rewards and punishments completely.

10. *Aversive conditioning* is a technique for eliminating specific behavior patterns by teaching the client to associate pain and discomfort with the response he wants to unlearn. In cases where aversive conditioning might be harmful, *desensitization*, a method for gradually reducing irrational fear, can be more useful.

11. *Reciprocal inhibition*, an approach developed by Wolpe to treat diffuse anxiety, is based on the idea that chronically anxious people may not be able to say why they feel tense, but they are nearly always able to distinguish different levels of anxiety. The therapist establishes a *hierarchy* from the least to the most anxiety-producing situations and then teaches the person to relax, beginning with the least threatening scene and working up to the most threatening. The client learns to inhibit anxiety responses with incompatible, deep-muscle relaxation.

12. Individual psychotherapy, since it is limited to the interaction of two people, bears little resemblance to everyday life and usually produces some degree of *countertransference* (the therapist's projecting his emotions onto the client). A person may find it difficult to transfer the insight and confidence he has gained in therapy to other relationships. *Group therapy* may provide some solutions to these problems by allowing both the therapist and the client to see how the person interacts with others, by giving a person a chance to shed inhibitions and practice self-expression in a safe atmosphere, and by providing a source of reinforcement.

13. *Traditional therapy groups* are an extension of individual psychotherapy and emphasize uncovering repressed feelings and conflicts. *Gestalt groups* emphasize the wholeness of the personality and attempt to reawaken people to their feelings and sensory experiences, with the therapist taking an active directive role and encouraging face-to-face confrontations. *Encounter groups* stress the here-and-now by demanding that participants respond to the immediate situation and by trying to strip away the social pretenses of everyday life. *Sensitivity groups* are designed to enhance individual awareness by focusing on nonverbal communication and providing exercises to reawaken the senses. Some psychologists question whether short-term group therapy is really therapeutic. They suggest that the intensity of the group situation may cause people to feel that more has been accomplished than is actually the case.

14. New trends in group therapy include transactional analysis and family therapy. *Transactional analysis* is based on the assumption that people

have three ego states: the Child, the Parent, and the Adult. By studying communication between two or more people, the transactional analyst can determine which ego state the person is operating from and can help the person to communicate with and relate to others more effectively. *Family therapy* is based on the assumption that often when one member of the family has problems, the whole family may need assistance either because the gains an individual may make in therapy can be undermined by problems at home, or because one family member may be having trouble adjusting to the individual's improving condition. Family therapy may also be indicated when problems exist between husband and wife, parents and children, and other family members.

15. When therapists find they cannot get through to a person who is extremely agitated, disoriented, or depressed, they may use *physical treatment* to change the person's behavior so that he can benefit from therapy.

16. *Electric shock therapy* and *insulin shock treatment* are most often used to alleviate sudden and severe depression, especially in psychotics. After shock treatment the person is happier, more responsive, and more active, but shock can be harmful and its use is declining. *Psychosurgery* is a drastic step, which changes a person's behavior and emotional state. *Prefrontal lobotomies* are rarely performed today, and more recent techniques aimed at reducing aggressive, violent impulses are only used as desperation measures. Almost all therapists prefer *drug therapy* to either shock treatment or psychosurgery. Drugs do not cure psychological problems, but they do calm agitated and depressed people, helping them to function more easily on a day-to-day basis and sometimes enabling them to benefit from other forms of therapy.

17. People may be institutionalized at the request of family members, voluntarily, or by court order. State institutions are usually isolated from the community, the patient loses his legal rights, and he may or may not receive therapy. Due to lack of funds, many institutions are poorly staffed and can provide only custodial care. Recently, some social scientists have begun to argue that institutions can have a negative effect on patients by depriving them of personal identity and merely teaching them how to be good patients. In response to such criticisms, some institutions have begun to concentrate on returning the person to the community as soon as possible, rather than providing him indefinitely with custodial care. *Halfway houses* enable ex-patients to work their way back into society gradually. The patient pays for his room, helps around the house, and gradually gets used to living in the real world again.

18. A new approach to on-the-ward therapy is *token economies,* which derive from the behaviorist approach to therapy. The chief objective is to encourage patients to behave in ways that may eventually enable them to return to society. In everyday life the chief means of reinforcement is money, so psychologists re-create this incentive system by rewarding patients for desirable behavior by giving them tokens that can be exchanged for various items or privileges. Patients in token economy programs often improve dramatically.

19. A developing school of research and practice, called *community psychology*, is aimed at reaching people for treatment before hospitalization becomes necessary and at looking for people in difficulty instead of waiting

for people to come for help. The goals of community psychology are to *prevent* mental illness, to *educate* the public by informing people that help for emotional problems exists and by teaching them how to cope with problems, and to encourage the community to establish *crisis intervention* programs.

Suggested Readings

Axline, V., *Dibs: In Search of Self* (Boston: Houghton Mifflin, 1964). A gripping narrative of the changes in a young boy's life as a result of client-centered play therapy.

Ayllon, T., and Azrin, N., *The Token Economy: A Motivational System for Therapy and Rehabilitation* (New York: Appleton-Century-Crofts, 1968). An account of the development and operation of a token economy program for psychotic patients in a state mental institution.

Bandura, A., *Principles of Behavior Modification* (New York: Holt, Rinehart & Winston, 1969). A comprehensive description of the use of learning principles to modify human behavior.

Brand, M., *Savage Sleep* (New York: Crown, 1968). An engrossing novel about the insensitivity of mental hospitals and the rigidity of their hierarchies.

Goldenberg, H., *Contemporary Clinical Psychology* (Belmont, Calif.: Brooks/ Cole, 1973). A well-written overview of recent research and practice in clinical psychology.

Hersher, L., *Four Psychotherapies* (New York: Holt, Rinehart & Winston, 1970). Several therapists compare their ways of treating behavior problems and illustrate their approaches with hypothetical clinical interviews.

Jefferson, L., *These Are My Sisters* (Garden City, N.Y.: Anchor Books, 1974). A woman's account of time spent in a mental hospital in the Midwest.

Perls, F. S., *Gestalt Therapy Verbatim* (Lafayette, Calif.: Real People Press, 1964). A clear account by the originator of Gestalt therapy of the ideas behind this form of therapy and its applications.

Rotter, J. B., *Clinical Psychology,* 2nd ed. (Englewood Cliffs, N.J.: Prentice-Hall, 1971). A concise, nontechnical introduction to the interests and approaches of clinical psychologists.

SIX

Psychology and Society

outline

INTERPERSONAL RELATIONS 560

Person Perception
Attribution Theory
Attraction and Liking
Interpersonal Influence

GROUP DYNAMICS 574

Leadership
Patterns of Communication
Problem Solving

ATTITUDES AND ATTITUDE CHANGE 577

The Development of Attitudes
Attitude Change

POSTSCRIPT: ENVIRONMENTAL PSYCHOLOGY 587

Effects of the Social Structure on the Individual
Personal Space and Crowding

SUMMARY 590

SUGGESTED READINGS 593

Social Psychology

It is almost impossible to imagine what life would be like without other people—with no families, with no friends, with no one to talk to or fight with or fall in love with. Although there are moments when each of us wants to "get away from it all" and be alone for a while, it's a good bet that the thought of living a lifetime in complete isolation appeals to nobody. That is why solitary confinement is one of the most severe punishments in our society.

Our relationships with other people perform many functions. Different relationships provide us with testing grounds for our own ideas, with new ideas and attitudes, and with models of behavior. They also give us a sense of well-being and a sense of belonging, for the support we get from friends is one of the most important determinants of the way we feel about ourselves.

Social psychology is the study of how people relate to other people. Groups are any collection of two or more people who have some influence on one another, and they play such an important role in day-to-day life that it's impossible to study a person without studying the groups he belongs to. How do we relate to other people? How do we perceive them? What are the grounds for our liking or disliking other people? How are we influenced by the groups we belong to? What are the patterns of communication and leadership in groups? These are some of the questions social psychologists are concerned with.

Interpersonal Relations

Life in groups is almost synonymous with human life. We are continually meeting people, sizing them up, being sized up by them, liking or disliking them, being liked or disliked by them, and influencing their attitudes and behavior as they influence ours. Even people who have never met before, when thrust together, manage to sort themselves out amazingly rapidly.

Person Perception

How do we form our first impressions of people? What sorts of cues do we use in this process? How accurate and reliable an enterprise is it?

(Joel Gordon)

(Joel Gordon)

Whenever two strangers meet for the first time, they look at each other's way of dressing, gestures, manner of speaking, tone of voice, and other easily observable cues and use these cues to make assumptions about each other. We often make crucial judgments about people based on the sketchy information we get from the look in their eyes, the firmness of their handshake, their style of dress, and so forth. No matter how little information we have, no matter how contradictory the information, no matter how many times we have been wrong in the past, the tendency to classify and categorize people persists.

When we form our first impressions of a person, we use those external cues to fit him into a particular category. Then, based on this category, we draw inferences about the person we have just met and we adjust our own behavior accordingly. Our culture and the social groups to which we belong provide us with a wide range of "ready-made" inferences to be drawn from particular external cues. Fat people are supposed to be jolly; people with long, thin fingers are said to be sensitive; a person who is always carefully dressed and meticulously groomed is thought to have an orderly mind, and so on. The perception of another person's emotions is also part of forming an impression of him. As we noted in Chapter 11, we find clues to emotions in facial expressions, posture, gestures, and tone of voice. In most situations, the judgments we make on the basis of first impressions are reasonably accurate. But several processes can lead to inaccuracy and error in first impressions.

(Judy Gurovitz, Photo Researchers)

Insufficient information. This is perhaps the most common cause of error in our first impressions of others. We often do not have enough time to form a reliable impression. At a large party, for example, there may be so many other people present, so much noise and smoke and general distraction, that the minimal cues we perceive through the social and atmospheric haze are inadequate. If we categorize people in circumstances like these, we often do so reluctantly, adding qualifications like "I didn't really have a chance to get to know her," or "It's hard to say what I think of him." Since we typically categorize people rapidly and readily, these reactions indicate that even the minimal cues we customarily employ were probably lacking.

False cues. Sometimes we are misled by **false cues.** The effusively friendly automobile salesman who sells us the prize lemon on his lot at an inflated figure may deliberately attempt to mislead us by posing as "the smiling, friendly, honest used-car salesman."

Stereotyping. In other cases, we may mislead ourselves by using crude categories that do not take sufficient account of the variations among individuals. **Stereotyping** is the general process of rigidly categorizing people on the basis of a single characteristic and then assuming that they possess a whole bundle of associated traits and behavior patterns. A trim, attractive young woman hardly fits our stereotype of a Wall Street tax specialist, for example. Many stereotypes are based on prejudice and can be harmful to those they categorize, as well as misleading for those who consistently employ them. Stereotypes often have a kernel of truth, surrounded by a complex set of distortions and fantasies. Stereotypes learned in childhood are amazingly persistent.

Figure 16-1
When we stereotype a person, he ceases to be a person and becomes a symbol, like this hissable villain. When we see him, we automatically assume that he kicks beggars, cheats old ladies, and takes advantage of orphans.
(Culver Pictures)

Errors in logic. Another source of incorrect inferences is the **logical error.** When a person displays one trait, we often assume that he also has the other traits customarily associated with it. Because someone appears carefree in one situation, we may tend to assume that he is also irresponsible, demanding, and illogical. Or we may assume that someone who seems serious is also pompous and unemotional. We often associate high intelligence, for example, with wit, originality, cleverness, and competence. In reality, an intelligent person may be dull, humorless, plodding, and incompetent.

Asch (1946) attempted to discover whether there were some traits that were more important than others in determining our inferences about other people. He found that traits do differ in their influence and that the traits "warm" and "cold" are particularly important. Kelley (1950) followed up Asch's study of "central traits" by giving undergraduates in a psychology course descriptions of a guest lecturer before he spoke. The descriptions were identical, except that half the students were told the lecturer was "warm"; the other half that he was "cold."

All the students heard the same lecturer, but those who had been told he was "warm" had more favorable perceptions of him, asked more questions, and were friendlier and more relaxed with him.

The halo and devil effects. Related to the logical error are the **halo** and **devil effects.** If we like someone, we tend to view everything he does in a favorable light and to attribute positive characteristics to him. If we dislike him, the reverse is true—we view his behavior in a negative light and attribute unfavorable traits to him. We may like the person because of external cues that impress us favorably (perhaps his bearing, voice, or manner seem to us to be "warm") or because we expect to interact with him more frequently in the future.

Even though person perception can often be inaccurate, inconsistent, and incorrect, for the most part we get by without major difficulties. One reason is that most of the time, in all but our most intimate and sustained interpersonal relationships, we interact with others mainly on the basis of our assigned social roles. For example, there are certain broad patterns of mutual expectations that define the student-instructor relationship. Once we correctly identify the situation and determine the proper roles, the bulk of our interaction is determined. Although personal preferences and predilections may shape and color perform-ances of a given role, so long as the basic obligations are met, the relationship is accepted as satisfactory.

Indeed, in playing roles, it is sometimes wiser *not* to behave accord-ing to accurate perceptions of the personal qualities of those with whom we have to interact. The private in the army who perceives correctly that his platoon sergeant is stupid would be well advised not to let his accurate perception influence his behavior. The relationship be-tween them is defined by the military institution, and those who want to get along will go with the institutional prescriptions. The same is true of almost every large group, be it a school, a hospital, a corporation, or a government agency. Most of the social relationships in these groups do not depend on accurate perception of personal qualities.

Attribution Theory

Just as we make judgments about people's personalities, we also make decisions about the causes of their actions. As we noted in Chapter 11, these inferences about people's internal states are based on very limited external cues such as facial expressions, posture, and gestures. How do we use these cues to make decisions about people's actions?

The judgments we make about why people do things are different from those we make about the actions of inanimate objects. If your automobile won't start, you will look for some *external* cause: the weather is too cold or damp, or the battery is dead, or there's no gas.

In looking for causes behind other people's behavior, however, most people tend to assume that the actions of others have *internal* causes (Jones et al., 1972; Nisbett & Valins, 1971). For example, if your mother loses her temper, your judgments about causality are liable to include such things as "She can't take pressure," "She's a nervous person," or "She is feeling poorly." Interestingly, we see more external causes for our own actions.

Attribution theory attempts to define this process by which people make judgments about other people's behavior more exactly. For example, according to Kelley (1973) we use four different criteria, more or less automatically and simultaneously, to judge other people's behavior: *the entity causing that person's response; the consensus of other people's responses; the consistency of the individual's response over time;* and *the modalities of interaction with the entity.*

To illustrate, we can use the example of your mother's losing her temper. Our first question involves the entity that caused her response. In this case, it was her discovery of a dozen empty beer cans in the back of your car. To judge how seriously we should take her anger, we must first know if the entity that caused her response was a unique one, or if she gets angry at almost any little thing. Second, the question of consensus. Was your father angry too, and did your parents' friends also consider your drinking excessive? What was the reaction of your friends? The third question involves consistency over time. Had your mother always been opposed to drinking, or had she just read an article about alcoholism that temporarily made her upset at the thought of your drinking? And fourth is the question of modality of interaction with the entity. Does your mother always respond to the thought of your drinking by becoming upset? Or was this an unusually strong

(*Burk Uzzle, Magnum Photos*)

response? The answers to these questions determine whether you are likely to attribute her behavior to internal or external causes.

This process goes on when we evaluate the behavior of individuals, but it also occurs when we make judgments about social groups. Are the causes of deliquency internal—do some young people just have trouble adjusting to the world? Or are they external—the result of social deprivation or frustration or lack of good models? Do children in the ghetto often grow up to be poor as adults because they're not very smart? Or are they the product of a subculture that starts them off with two strikes against them (Ashmore & McConahay, 1975)? Because our tendency to find external or internal causes for people's actions colors many of our political opinions and social attitudes, the question of attribution of causality is recognized as a highly significant issue and has attracted a good deal of research attention in recent years.

Attraction and Liking

When people meet, what determines whether they will like or dislike each other? These are subjects of much speculation and not a little mystification, with popular explanations running the gamut from Fate to compatible astrological signs. It may refresh our romantic souls to feel that ineluctable forces of the universe will propel us toward an inevitable meeting with our beloved, but the people who run computer dating services, for example, take a more hardheaded view of the matter. Their criteria are **proximity, similarity of interests, complementary expectations,** and **rewardingness.**

Proximity. Sheer proximity is perhaps the most decisive factor in determining who will become friends. Our friends are likely to live nearby. Although it is said that absence makes the heart grow fonder, it also causes friendships to fade. While relationships may be maintained in absentia by correspondence, they usually have to be reinforced by periodic visits, or they dissolve.

(Ron Sherman, Nancy Palmer Photo Agency)

Festinger, Schachter, and Back (1950) decided to investigate the effects of proximity on friendships. They chose an apartment complex, made up of two-story buildings with five apartments to a floor. People moved into the project at random, so previous social attachments did not influence the results of the study. In interviewing the residents of the apartment complex, the researchers found that 44 percent said they were most friendly with their next-door neighbors, 22 percent saw the people who lived two doors away the most often socially, and only 10 percent said that their best friends lived as far away as down the hall. People were even less likely to be friendly with those who lived upstairs or downstairs from them (see Figure 16-2).

One way of explaining the effects of proximity is to say that the more often people see each other, the more they tend to like each other. This has been demonstrated with photographs as well (Zajonc, 1968). People

Figure 16-2
The relationship between proximity and liking. "Units of approximate physical distance" means how many doors apart the people lived—2S means 2 doors and a stairway apart. As you can see, the closer together people lived, the more likely that they would become friends. (Reprinted from *Social Pressures in Informal Groups,* by Leon Festinger, Stanley Schachter, and Kurt Back, with the permission of the publisher, Stanford University Press. © 1950 by Leon Festinger, Stanley Schachter, and Kurt Back.)

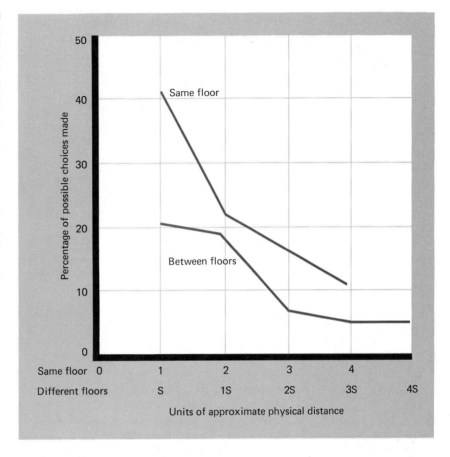

Figure 16-2
The relationship between proximity and liking. "Units of approximate physical distance" means how many doors apart the people lived—2S means 2 doors and a stairway apart. As you can see, the closer together people lived, the more likely that they would become friends. (Reprinted from *Social Pressures in Informal Groups,* by Leon Festinger, Stanley Schachter, and Kurt Back, with the permission of the publisher, Stanford University Press. © 1950 by Leon Festinger, Stanley Schachter, and Kurt Back.)

were shown groups of photographs of other people. Some of the photographs were repeated at random. The more often people saw these particular faces, the more they came to like them. Familiarity, it seems, does not always breed contempt. Sometimes it leads to liking.

Similarity. Similarity of interests is the basis for most friendships, once proximity is established. When we meet people who share our interests, attitudes, and values, we are more likely to want to develop a deeper relationship. The more the areas of common interest, the greater the chance of our getting to know and to like another person. When a person knows that someone shares his attitudes, he tends to have more positive feelings toward him and to be more complimentary when evaluating him (Byrne, 1961). The weight and the subject of the issue of agreement do not seem to matter as much as the proportion of shared attitudes (Byrne & Nelson, 1964).

Sometimes perceived similarity may be more important than actual similarity (Marsden, 1966). We often think or assume that we have attitudes in common with people who attract us in other ways. Some

Figure 16-3

Like attracts like—people who share similar interests, attitudes, or values tend to like one another.

(From left to right: Ron Sherman, Nancy Palmer Photo Agency; Rohn Engh, Photo Researchers; David Krasner, Photo Researchers)

recent findings (Rosenblood & Goldstein, 1969) indicate that similarity in intelligence may be more important in determining how well people will like each other than shared attitudes or opinions. And agreement following prior disagreement leads to greater attraction bonds than does agreement from the start (Sigall & Aronson, 1967).

Complementarity. Opposites do sometimes attract. These relationships are based on complementarity, rather than similarity. It is generally true that quiet people are more comfortable in the presence of others who are subdued, but often a pair of friends or a couple seems to be made up of one extravert and one introvert. One person's need to talk is met by the other person's need to listen. Perhaps this is one reason why we sometimes like a person in one role but dislike him in another. If you are used to your friend's playing straight man to your jokes, you may not like him as much if he starts telling his own jokes.

Rewardingness. We all tend to like people who are kind and who say nice things about us more than people who are cruel and who we feel do not accept or like us. Hearing favorable comments about oneself is rewarding and we like the person who praises us.

Flattery, however, will not get you everywhere. We are all suspicious of ingratiating behavior and tend to have little respect for a person who seems to be deliberately trying to get on our good side by excessive compliments. We wonder about his motives—what he wants from us and why he is "buttering" us up. But when we believe the nice things we hear, we tend to look more positively on the person.

Interpersonal Influence

Just knowing that other people are present can affect our behavior and our attitudes. We continually compare our ideas and feelings with those

PEOPLE DO JUDGE BOOKS (AND PEOPLE) BY THEIR COVERS
A lot of people think that looking pretty leads to happiness and popularity. One recent busy Saturday, the cosmetics department at a large store in New York City grossed over $10,000! What do psychologists say? Do we really tend to like beautiful people more than less attractive people?

Some research shows that there is more truth to this than most of us care to admit. Although we maintain that we choose our friends and partners on the basis of their sincerity, or warmth, or "goodness," research that asked college students how they liked the blind dates they had spent an evening with showed that physical appearance was by far the most important determinant of the attraction they felt (Berscheid & Walster, 1972; Berscheid et al., 1971).

A person's looks affect more than just his social life in young adulthood: its influence starts even in nursery and grade school (Dion, 1970; Rosenthal & Jacobson, 1968), and it continues through middle age. Teachers tend to be more lenient in judging an exceptionally cute youngster's naughtiness; they also tend to have higher expectations for physically attractive children's intellectual abilities and performance. In later years, too, good looks add to a person's attractiveness. There is reason to believe that John Kennedy's dashing demeanor was at least a minor factor in his victory over Richard Nixon in 1960. But the fading of beauty in middle age may also cause problems for once-attractive people, especially women. Often the more attractive women were in young adulthood, the less satisfied and less well adjusted they were 25 years later (Berscheid & Walster, 1972).

of others, rate our performance against others, conform with or resist their attitudes and expectations, and behave differently when other people are present than when we are alone.

Social comparison. The theory of social comparison, first elaborated by Leon Festinger (1954), proposes that people have a need to evaluate themselves. In the absence of objective scales to rate themselves against, they compare themselves with other people. When a person wants to know where he stands or how he stacks up against the competition, he will usually pick someone he feels is close to him in attitudes or skills and compare himself with that person. For example, a graduate student in physics will rate his performance against that of his fellow students, rather than against a liberal arts major who is floundering through elementary physics or against Albert Einstein.

Conformity. Some conformity to group standards is essential for getting along in society. But the degree of conformity varies from one person to another and from one situation to another. An individual's strong commitment to a deviant belief or practice, his confidence in the correctness of a different position, his disdain for the group, or his feeling of security within the group's leadership will increase the likelihood that he will "dare to be different." Commitment to the contrary beliefs of another group provides a very strong basis for resistance to group pressure, too, as the long history of religious martyrs illustrates.

Situational factors influence conformity, too. If the group is working on a complicated task where nobody feels very sure-footed, conformity will probably be high. Also, if the group seems to know more about what it's doing than the person does (Hollander & Willis, 1967), or if the rest of the group is in unanimous agreement on a subject, then the individual feels more pressure to conform. We look to other people for information when we're not sure of something ourselves. Another factor influencing conformity is publicity: if the individual's judgments are made known to the rest of the group, there is greater risk of embarrassment, punishment, or ostracism, and so there is greater pressure to conform (Deutsch & Gerard, 1955).

In a series of interesting experiments, Asch (1951) demonstrated the importance of group pressures to conform, even where this resulted in denial of physical evidence. The study was ostensibly a test of visual judgment. A group of people were assembled around a table and were requested to select from a card with several lines of differing lengths, the line most similar to the line on a comparison card (see Figure 16-4). Deliberately, the lines were drawn so the comparison was obvious and the correct choice was clear. All but one of the people at the table were confederates of the experimenter. On certain trials, the experimenter's

Figure 16-4

In Asch's experiment on conformity, subjects were shown a comparison card, like the one on the left, and were asked to indicate which of the three lines on the card on the right was the most similar.

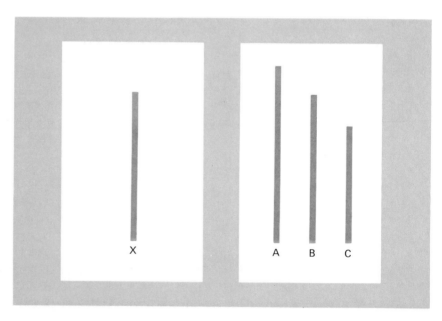

Figure 16-5
One of the subjects in
Asch's experiment becomes
more and more perplexed as
he listens to Asch's stooges
announce their incorrect
choices. Finally, he says
with a shrug, "I have to call
them as I see them," and
gives the correct choice.
(*William Vandivert*)

confederates deliberately gave the same incorrect answer. When the subject's turn came to announce his choice, he was faced with a dilemma: should he conform to what he knew to be an incorrect decision and agree with the group, thereby denying the evidence of his own senses, or should he disagree with the group and not conform?

Over many trials and with numerous subjects, conforming responses were given about 35 percent of the time. Some subjects never conformed, others conformed most of the time. A variety of experiments using different stimuli have confirmed this significant result.

Obedience to authority. Just as people tend to look to others in a group for cues on how to behave or what decisions to make, they also seek out the judgments of authority figures. We saw in Chapter 1 that Milgram's studies showed how far many people will go in obeying the directions of someone in authority (Milgram, 1963). When "teachers" were told to give "learners" an electric shock for each wrong answer, almost two-thirds of them did what they were told to do to the point of administering what they thought was a near-lethal shock. Other research supports Milgram's findings: a survey showed that 67 percent of Americans felt most people would act as William Calley did when he carried out an order to shoot women and children in the Vietnamese hamlet of My Lai (Kelman & Lawrence, 1972).

What factors influence the degree to which people will do what they're told? Studies in which people were asked to put a dime in a parking meter by people wearing uniforms showed that one important factor is the amount of power vested in the person who's giving the orders (Bickman, 1974). A guard whose uniform looked like a policeman's got far more obedient responses than either a man dressed as a milkman or a civilian. Another factor is surveillance. If someone is ordered to do something, then left alone to do it on his own, he may not be as likely to carry out the command as when he is being supervised. This seems to be more true when the order involves an unethical act. Most of Bickman's subjects still put a dime in the meter when the policeman-impersonator was out of sight, but Milgram found that his "teachers" were much less willing to administer severe shocks when the experimenter left the room.

Milgram's experiments showed other factors that influence a person's ability to follow orders. When the victim was in the same room as the teacher, obedience dropped sharply. When another "teacher" was present who refused to administer shocks, obedience dropped again. But when there is a shared responsibility for an unethical act, so that the subject is only an accessory to a crime, obedience is much greater. Executions by firing squad are an illustration of this principle.

What makes people so willing to obey an authority figure, even when it means doing something completely contrary to their principles? Milgram (1974) thinks that people feel obliged to the person in power—

(Ken Regan/Camera 5)

(Norris McNamara, Nancy Palmer Photo Agency)

(Norris McNamara, Nancy Palmer Photo Agency)

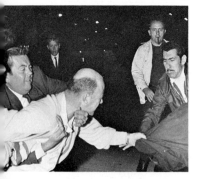

first, because they respect his credentials and assume he knows what he's doing; and second, because often they have already established a relationship of trust with the person in authority, by making a prior agreement to do whatever he asks. Once this happens, the subject may experience conflict about what he's doing, but by a process of rationalization he is able to forget what he's doing and so reduce the internal conflict to a minimum.

These experiments show people's willingness to obey a person in authority. But obedience doesn't just extend to specific authority figures: we are also so socialized to following the norms of our culture that sometimes it is almost impossible to go against its customs. Try singing at the top of your lungs on a crowded bus, for example, or asking a total stranger for his subway seat, without giving any excuse like feeling faint or having a twisted ankle. Milgram had his own students try this (Tavris, 1974), and they found out something interesting about themselves. While they could easily envision themselves doing such things, it was virtually impossible to actually do them. The words stuck in their throats when they came face to face with a seated subway passenger or when they settled into their seat in the bus. It's not easy to go against authority, be it in the form of a person or a custom.

Social conflict. What is social conflict? A good working definition is that it is any situation where two or more parties must divide the available resources so that the more one party gets, the less the others get (Brickman, 1974).

There are many kinds of social conflict, and Brickman (1974) suggests that they can be divided into four major categories along a continuum of social control or superimposed structure. In an **unstructured conflict** almost anything can happen. There are virtually no social controls to regulate the situation.

In a **partially structured conflict,** there are some rules or expectations governing the relationship. If two people simultaneously see a bank teller opening a new window in a crowded bank, they will both walk quickly toward it, each one hoping to be first in line. Even though their competition is very real, their competitive behavior will be quite regulated. There will be no fistfights or shouting matches; in fact, neither person is even likely to break his calm demeanor enough to run. The competition will be carried out in the reserved, quiet manner dictated by the atmosphere of a bank.

In a **fully structured** (or **normative**) **conflict,** the behavior of each participant is completely prescribed by the norms of the society or situation. The resources at stake are completely specified; so is the way these resources will be allocated. In most normative situations, the conflict is often not even recognized as a conflict. Most athletic contests are ideal examples of this. Another relationship, which Brickman calls a **revolutionary conflict,** occurs when the rule structure is chal-

(Michael C. Hayman, Photo Researchers)

(Ken Regan/Camera 5)

lenged—for example, when an army private points his firearm at his sergeant instead of carrying out an order.

While we usually think of conflict as something to be avoided, conflicts can serve important functions (Brickman, 1974; Coser, 1956). First, conflict often produces group solidarity and cohesiveness, as when a group unites in the face of an antagonist. Second, competition can be a source of innovation and change. And third, a conflict situation may give individuals caught between the opposing forces more freedom. In Western societies where Protestants and Catholics profess opposing beliefs, neither one can enforce its theology on the society, so people are able to choose their religion for themselves.

But conflict situations are not always beneficial, and we usually try to find resolutions for them. There are many ways of doing this (Brickman, 1974). If opposing parties are given a common goal to work toward, they may lose sight of their original conflict (Sherif, 1958). Role-playing, where each party acts out the opposing position, also serves to increase understanding and reduce conflict (Rapoport, 1962). Another method involves sublimating the conflict into a more controlled, less destructive way of playing out the opposing positions—for instance, sports or chess games, instead of wars.

These methods of conflict resolution work mostly for fully structured situations. Other conflicts require other types of resolutions. The nonviolent protests used by Mahatma Gandhi and Martin Luther King, Jr., can be seen as methods of resolving unstructured conflict situations that otherwise could have gotten totally out of hand (Frank, 1968). In another kind of unstructured situation, like the panic in a crowded theater where someone has just yelled "Fire!" the answer may lie in the introduction of a structure. If lines of communication are established so that people will take turns going out the exit, or in a less urgent

MOB BEHAVIOR

The very idea of a fire in a crowded building is enough to frighten most people. And with good reason: all too often, the cry of "Fire!" causes people to stampede to the nearest exit, trampling each other on the way. Fear seems to break down normal rational behavior. The result is unnecessary injury.

Research studies have duplicated this panic behavior. In one experiment (Mintz, 1951), several people were given strings to hold, each of which was attached to a spool placed inside a bottle. The bottle neck was only large enough for one spool at a time to be removed. Told to get the spools out before the bottle filled with water, everyone tried to remove his spool at the same time. The resulting traffic jam kept everyone from getting his spool out in time. Even worse jams were produced by Kelley and his colleagues (1965), when they threatened their subjects with electric shocks if they did not get their spools out before the bottle filled.

case, draw lots to resolve the conflict, then the result is likely to be a more satisfactory resolution (Kelley et al., 1965; Mintz, 1951). Third parties, such as an authority figure or moderator or a coalition, are often important agents in establishing legitimate avenues of behavior and resolutions to both panic situations and other kinds of conflict.

Social facilitation. How does the presence of other people affect performance? Does it make a difference? And if so, what sort of difference and under what conditions? Research has shown that on many tasks subjects do work faster in groups than alone, even when the tasks are explicitly defined as noncompetitive and results are not compared. Energy output seems to be increased and, for relatively simple tasks, productivity also goes up. Interestingly, in some cases it doesn't seem to matter whether the other people in the group are working along with the subject or just observing him—their simple presence is enough to stimulate him to perform better (Zajonc, 1965, 1966).

But the effects of competition and the presence of an audience vary with the circumstances. Often a simple task goes slower (Cottrell, Rittle, & Wack, 1967). Too high a motivation level can interfere with performance. Competition can produce anxiety and an overly high motivation level. In some experiments women performed better when they worked alone than when they worked in a group that included men. The presence of other people is generally distracting and can also interfere, especially when new learning is taking place. Although the presence of others can improve performance if you know the material well, it may interfere when you are trying to learn something new.

Risk-taking. When are we most likely to take risks—when we are alone or when we are a part of a group? Will a gambler bet higher when he is alone contemplating calling his bookie or when he is with four others in a poker game? Research shows groups are often willing to take bigger risks than the members of the group would take individually. This increase in risk-taking in a group is known as the **risky shift.** Take a gang of young boys—they will taunt and dare each other to jump from a high fence. When in the group, they will make ridiculously dangerous leaps that they would not attempt if they were alone. Reasons include pressure from the group and the lessened feeling of individual responsibility. It is demeaning for most American males to be called "chicken," to "back down from a fair fight," or to not "stand up for their rights." According to Roger Brown (1965), people in our society greatly admire risk-taking ability. In one experiment, he asked people to rate themselves on their riskiness. Then he told them how high another group of people had been rated. A significant number of Brown's subjects then revised their own ratings to show even more risk-taking than before. Brown thus suggests that competition within the group may contribute to this risky shift.

BYSTANDER APATHY

The killing of Kitty Genovese has become a symbol for bystander apathy:

> Kitty Genovese is set upon by a maniac as she returns from work at 3 a.m. Thirty-eight of her neighbors in Kew Gardens come to their windows when she cries out in terror; none come to her assistance even though her stalker takes over half an hour to murder her. No one even so much as calls the police. She dies (Latané & Darley, 1970).

Alarmed by human indifference, many attribute it to modern urban living. But good Samaritans were rare even in Biblical times. Moreover, Latané and Darley found that Kitty Genovese's neighbors were not really indifferent. The problem seemed more complicated, and the two psychologists set out to study it experimentally.

First, they discovered that strangers are often willing to help others. Most will give the time, directions, or change. Thirty-four percent of those interviewed would give a stranger a dime.

Emergencies, however, seem to increase reluctance to help. Perhaps, Latané and Darley point out, our social rules against staring prevent us from seeing emergencies until it is too late.

More seriously, however, people who see emergencies sometimes refuse to help. Several experiments showed that failure to help was greatly increased by the presence of others who were passive. In one experiment, subjects completing a questionnaire heard a taped "emergency" in the next room, complete with a crash and screams. Seventy percent of those who were alone offered help, but only 7 percent offered help if they were with an experimenter who did nothing (Latané & Rodin, 1969).

In staged liquor store robberies, customers were more likely to report the "robberies" when alone than when another customer was present. Fear of reprisal was a frequent explanation of refusal to help, though familiarity with one's surroundings makes helping somewhat more likely.

Failure to give aid may stem from confusion. Latané and Darley questioned people who did not help one of their fellows who staged a "fit" during an experiment. Nonhelpers were nervous and emotional, not apathetic. Most seemed to doubt whether the emergency had been real. Conflict between the costs of helping (especially if there is no real emergency) and the guilt of not helping causes anxiety. Unfortunately for the victims, guilt is not enough to make most people risk making fools of themselves.

Being an anonymous part of the crowd also offers protection from punishment. If you do not have to worry about being caught, you may be tempted to do things that you would not otherwise do. Strikes, walkouts, protests, riots, lynch mobs—all involve actions of people in groups that probably would not occur if the members were acting as individuals. When a person feels himself part of a group, his individual responsibility is downplayed and diffused by his feeling of being part of the mass. He feels more anonymous—a feeling known as **deindividuation.** Singer and his colleagues (1965) compared the behavior of people in a discussion who were easily identifiable and called by name with people dressed uniformly whose names were not revealed. The anonymous subjects were much looser, used more obscene language, and revealed more of themselves.

Group Dynamics

We have been examining groups and their effects on individual performance and behavior. Now we turn to the structure and processes of groups themselves: how leadership is exerted, how members of a group communicate with one another, and how groups go about solving problems.

Leadership

Group leadership may be formal, perhaps residing in a board of directors and other officers, or informal. It may be self-perpetuating or it may change at fixed intervals. The group may welcome new leaders or it may fiercely resist them as intruders. Whatever the case, leadership always exists and shapes the behavior of the group.

Physical strength, beauty, skill at hunting, intelligence, superior knowledge, access to scarce resources, ability to manipulate people—all these may serve as means for achieving leadership in various groups. Many groups have several leaders, sometimes informal and unacknowledged. In a number of American Indian tribes, the most skillful hunter was selected as the leader when foraging for food. But social skills, age, and inherited status became the criteria in determining who led the entire tribe. On a committee, there may be a formally appointed group leader, but actual leadership may be a shared responsibility. Leadership may change over time as topics change, with the most knowledgeable member being most influential when the topic on which he is especially competent is under discussion. There may also be a sort of emotional or cathartic leader, who by his display of appropriate social skills, such as humor, resolves conflicts and relieves tensions, thus ensuring effective group performance and continuity.

The leader is usually an outgoing, outspoken person. He must make himself heard and also facilitate the communication of others' ideas. Because people tend to appoint a person they look up to, the leader is often of higher status than the other group members.

The extent to which the leader's status influences the group is shown in a study by Torrance (1955) of problem-solving effectiveness. He studied a number of three-man airplane crews composed of a pilot, a navigator, and a gunner. The pilot had the highest status and the

"Yes, he's definitely assuming leadership. A case of the right ant in the right place at the right time, evidently."

(Drawing by Richter; © 1971 The New Yorker Magazine, Inc.)

(The Bettmann Archive)

(UPI)

gunner the lowest. When the pilot was correct, his ideas were accepted by the crew 100 percent of the time. But when the gunner was correct, his ideas were accepted only 40 percent of the time. Often, the pilot's ideas triumphed even when he was wrong. The rest of the crew expected him to be right because they perceived him as the authority.

The leader must also be "one of the gang"—not too different from the other members of the group. Someone who is a well-known nonconformist is not likely to be selected as a leader. The leader is more often an outstanding representative of the group, someone who typifies the status quo and how the group members like to think of themselves.

Other less important leadership characteristics are such personal qualities as intelligence, sensitivity, and flexibility. The leader is likely to be well adjusted, to know where he stands in relation to the power structure, to be able to accommodate himself to the wishes of those around him without harm to himself, and to be able to compromise.

Patterns of Communication

No group can exist without communication: the exchange of information, feelings, and attitudes among its members. The effectiveness of the group often depends on the adequacy of its communication network. Different groups have worked out a variety of mechanisms so that the leaders and the members are reciprocally informed about what is happening in the group and between the group and its external environment.

In an authoritarian system, communications are directed from the leader to the members. A democratic system emphasizes discussion and wide agreement on decisions. In almost any group, leaders talk more than other members. Some members may be consulted extensively in their areas of expertise, but otherwise not enter into the communication system. Still others may specialize in communicating feelings and emotions, serving, as we noted earlier, to assist the group in relieving tensions.

Psychologists have identified a variety of communication patterns or networks and have explored their consequences for group effectiveness and member satisfaction. Among the common patterns, illustrated in Figure 16-6, are the **circle,** the **chain,** the **Y-shape,** and the **wheel.**

These communication networks are studied by arranging people so that they can communicate, using written notes or an intercom, only in the pattern under investigation. The group is then assigned a task and, as they work, the observers are able to study the operation of the communication network. The results clearly show that the structure of the communication network has significant effects on the effectiveness in problem solving and the satisfaction of group members.

In the circle arrangement, the leader is not set apart, but is an equal member of the group. In the wheel arrangement, only the leader, the

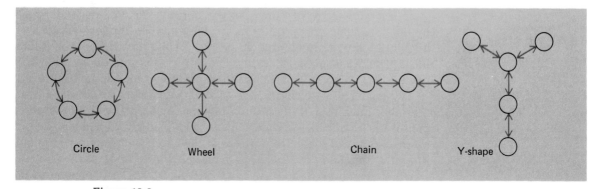

Circle   Wheel   Chain   Y-shape

Figure 16-6

Common communication networks. Arrows indicate who can talk to whom and the overall flow of discussion.

person at the center, can talk to everyone else. The others can communicate only through him. In the chain network, the persons at the end have access to only one other person. In a five-person Y-shape arrangement, the persons in the center positions have greater access than those at the ends.

In general, those at the centers of the communication networks are named most often as leaders by the members of the group. The more a position in a network allows its occupant to communicate, the greater satisfaction he expresses. The decentralized circle network seems to be best at solving complex problems. The tightly centralized wheel is more effective in solving simple problems that can be easily directed by the person at the center.

Communication networks seem to become less rigid as the members get to know each other better. Less formal patterns of communication (and hence of influence and leadership) develop over time. Even where, as in many large organizations, the communication system is defined by a formal organizational chart, there are often informal systems of communication that bypass the formal pattern. In almost every academic department, the chairman's secretary has more to say about what goes on than do most of the instructors. She is at the center of the network of communication and controls access to her boss. Whether she exercises it or not, she is in a position of considerable informal power by virtue of her strategic position in the communication network.

Problem Solving

When we discussed group influence on behavior earlier, we noted the phenomenon of the **risky shift,** the tendency of persons acting together in groups to make decisions entailing greater risks than they would as separate individuals.

When trying to solve a problem, is it better to work at it alone or with others in a group? One study compared people working alone and people working with others to produce creative ideas in response to open-ended questions (Taylor, Berry, & Block, 1958). Each group of five was measured against five single persons. Individuals got 68.1 ideas in all, compared with 37.5 for the group. Those working alone had 19.8 creative ideas versus 10.8 from the group. When alone, people let themselves go more, worried less about competition, were freer of criticism. When people were able to express their own ideas and follow their own impulses, the result was higher productivity and creativity, as well as higher concentration.

Janis (1972) shares this negative view of group decision making. Strong group pressure to conform, he feels, may prevent people from expressing critical ideas. Amiability and morale take precedence over judgment. As group cohesiveness increases, self-criticism decreases, and members seem more willing to act at the expense of nonmembers. Members with real doubts may hesitate to express them. The result may be bad decisions—a Bay of Pigs or a Watergate cover-up.

But often a group has resources that an individual does not have. In trying to devise ways to stop airplane hijackings, a group composed of an engineer, a pilot, a stewardess, a passenger, and a bomb expert will come up with more ideas than any one of these people could. Also, groups are better than individuals at solving certain kinds of problems. A group's members can check each other for correctness of a solution, can divide up the work of solving a complex problem so that each person performs specific operations, and can avoid repeating work.

Where different skills and a division of labor are useful, mixed groups do better than homogeneous groups. When members of a group are of different sexes, different ages, and different backgrounds, the group is usually more effective. Groups also seem to be more efficient when the people know each other well. Each member's specific strengths and weaknesses are known to the group. Abilities can thus be used effectively and shortcomings compensated for.

Attitudes and Attitude Change

Attitudes are a focus of both popular and professional interest. "I don't like his attitude" is an all too common phrase in our everyday language. People are frequently instructed to develop "the proper attitude" or to adopt "a better attitude." An important part of how we perceive other people has to do with what we think their attitudes are. But just what are attitudes? How are they formed? How do they change? And how susceptible are they to being changed?

An attitude toward something has three major components—**beliefs** about the object, **feelings** about the object, and a **tendency to behave** in certain ways toward the object. Beliefs include facts, opinions, and the general knowledge we have about the object. Feelings include love, hate, like, dislike, and similar sentiments. The tendency to behave implies the likelihood (though not the certainty) that certain actions toward the object will occur.

THE MEASUREMENT OF ATTITUDES

Almost everyone knows about public opinion polls, especially in election years. Polls attempt to uncover what a great many people think of a candidate, incumbent, or policy. Merchants, manufacturers, and social scientists vie with politicians in their concern with how people feel about things. Some other ways they can measure attitudes include surveys, attitude scales, and projective techniques.

Surveys use questionnaires to measure attitudes of a large segment of the population. *Descriptive surveys* show how many people share a characteristic or count the incidence of some event. Public opinion polls and market surveys are descriptive—they can tell politicians and manufacturers how to conduct a campaign or whether that flip-top box will sell. *Relational surveys,* in contrast, focus on relationships among variables and attempt to answer questions like "How does income affect parents' attitudes toward busing?" Careful questionnaire design and control of the sample are essential.

Surveys frequently include *attitude scales*—lists of items with which people must agree or disagree. Their main purpose is to divide people into broad categories, not to provide a full picture of one person's feelings. Attitude scale design is tricky, for several reasons. Attitudes do not necessarily form a smooth continuum from positive to negative. Moreover, extreme positive or negative attitudes are usually strongly held, but neutral attitudes are less intense. Some beliefs are stable, some subject to change.

To tap hidden or irrational, possibly embarrassing, attitudes, researchers may use *projective techniques.* The Thematic Apperception Test is a familiar one: people make up stories about ambiguous pictures. To measure a specific attitude, researchers use the most relevant pictures. Advertisers can even use card sorting to find out how people feel about different brands of toothpaste, dog food, or soap.

(*Constantine Manos, Magnum Photos*)

For example, let us look at attitudes toward the women's movement. Suppose a person believes that the members of the movement are a bunch of wild-eyed, radical fanatics who seek to overturn the social order. This set of beliefs may be supported by a string of "facts" and "reasons" derived from what the person has determined about the women's movement from newspapers, magazines, and television. This person is likely also to have strong feelings about the movement— probably dislike and fear. Finally, this person may be inclined to avoid ardent members of the movement and to ridicule it in conversation. In this example, there is general consistency among the components of the attitude: the beliefs, feelings, and behavior tendency are all negative. There is a common tendency to strive for consistency among the parts of an attitude.

But it is not safe to infer from a person's attitude what his behavior will be. The person described above might be a reporter for a major network. When covering a women's rally, he would probably not display his attitude and he would inhibit his tendency to behave negatively because of his professional commitment to objectivity.

Even attitudes that have a strong emotional component and are persistent and deeply rooted may not always be manifested in behavior. A famous study by R. T. LaPiere (1934) demonstrated this clearly. Traveling through the United States with a Chinese couple in 1934, when prejudice against Orientals was still quite strong, LaPiere discovered they were refused service only once out of 66 hotels and motels and 184 restaurants they stopped at. Subsequently, LaPiere wrote to the establishments they had visited and asked if they would provide service for Chinese persons. Ninety-two percent of those replying indicated they would refuse to accept Chinese guests. Similar results have been obtained in studies of service to blacks.

These cases show that inconsistencies or apparent inconsistencies between attitudes and behavior can be the result of the method of the study. The social constraints present in an actual situation—like LaPiere's travels—may be totally lacking in a survey that asks the subject to talk, not to act. When research studies are planned so that the study itself places realistic constraints on the subject, the findings are much more likely to show that behavior is consistent with attitudes (Schofield, 1972; Warner & DeFleur, 1969).

The Development of Attitudes

How do we acquire our attitudes? Where do they come from? A major part of socialization involves acquiring the attitudes considered to be appropriate by our family, peer groups, and other groups. Some attitudes are taught formally as part of the educational process, while others are learned informally by identification and modeling.

The learning techniques described in Chapter 4 apply here—we are

(Wayne Miller, Magnum Photos)

reinforced when we express the proper attitudes, and inappropriate or disapproved attitudes are often grounds for punishment. For example, love of parents, respect for elders, and love of country are taught at an early age and reinforced repeatedly. For younger children, the feeling component of attitudes is probably the most important—they feel strongly about things, liking what they have been taught is good and disliking what is bad. Appropriate beliefs are added to and expanded later, often through schooling. Along with attitude learning through reinforcement, attitudes are learned by modeling. Children observe the way their family and friends behave and shape their own attitudes and behavior accordingly.

Reference groups, groups that we value and identify with, are an important source of attitudes. They reinforce us for expressing appropriate attitudes, and they provide us with models of correct attitudes that we may imitate. If a young man wants to join a fraternity, for example, he may begin to model his behavior and attitudes on those of the members.

Our previous discussion of social comparison theory suggested that when we evaluate our own actions we look around for a person to compare ourselves with. We do the same thing with our attitudes: once

Figure 16-7

The changes in political attitudes during the college years in five classes at Bennington College. The lower the score, the more liberal the attitudes. (Based on data in T. M. Newcomb, *Personality and Social Change.* New York: Holt, Rinehart & Winston, 1943.)

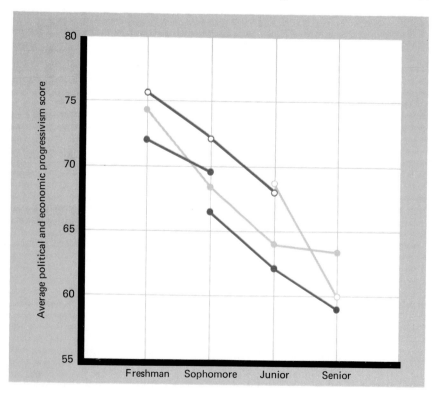

they are formed, they don't remain unchanged for the rest of our lives. Instead, we constantly reevaluate them as we come into contact with new ideas and information. A man who comes from a small, midwestern town with a predominantly white, Protestant population may have learned negative attitudes toward Jews. But if he then goes off to college in a large, urban university with many Jewish students, his stereotyped attitude may undergo alterations. First, groups that he aspires to join may not share his attitude. Then, direct experience with Jewish people may show him that his beliefs are incorrect. He may find that the people he wants to emulate and model himself on are Jews. Under these circumstances, his attitude is likely to change.

In 1943, Theodore Newcomb published the results of a study he had conducted at Bennington College, a small college in Vermont, which at that time was exclusively for women. His results illustrate how important reference groups can be in the development of attitudes. The Bennington students, largely from upper-class, conservative families, generally arrived at the start of their freshman year with conservative values. By the time they graduated, however, their attitudes had been greatly liberalized (see Figure 16-7). The liberal faculty had become their new reference group, and the stimulating environment of new ideas, new opinions, and new beliefs caused a period of emotional and intellectual ferment.

(Burt Glinn, Magnum Photos)

The liberal attitudes persisted 20 years later. The attitudes developed during college, not the attitudes the women had been brought up with, were the ones they held throughout adult life (Newcomb, 1963). This tendency for basic political attitudes to persist in adult life still exists. A survey 5 years later of some of the radical students arrested for participating in sit-ins at the University of California during the Free Speech Movement of the late 1960s shows that most of them retained their radical attitudes, although they were much less active politically (Melville, 1972).

Attitude Change

During the Korean War, the Chinese and North Korean Communists took great pains to try to convert American prisoners to their cause (Schein, 1956). The prisoners were obviously in a high stress situation. Their captors tried to manipulate their beliefs by rewarding compliant behavior with food and freedom to move around and punishing resistance and noncompliance with deprivation of food, loss of freedom to move around, and various forms of harassment. Group structure was also manipulated in an effort to secure compliance. Prisoners were segregated by rank, race, and nationality. Collective punishments were administered to whole groups of prisoners if one member did not conform to the captors' demands. Officers were ordered to report to enlisted men. Models for behavior were provided—prisoners who had

PREJUDICE

No one likes to be called prejudiced. Even Archie Bunker believes that his dislike of blacks, hippies, and just about everybody else is justified by their real defects. Nevertheless, prejudice does exist, and some people seem more prone to it than others. How do we recognize prejudice, and where does it come from?

If prejudice simply means a tendency to prejudge, then everyone is prejudiced to some degree. Without the ability to classify individual objects, events, and people, we would find life hopelessly confusing. However, prejudice normally refers to a specific attitude, a combination of hostile feelings toward others and actual hostile behavior. The prejudiced person tends to think in stereotypes. Prejudiced behavior ranges from negative comments ("Men! They're all alike!") through mild forms of discriminatory behavior (separate black and white tables in the high school cafeteria) to outright violence (pogroms, lynching).

Some people consistently display more prejudice than others. Thus psychologists must ask how prejudice develops in the first place. Some favor the "scapegoat theory"—frustration produces aggression, which must find a target. When the real source of the frustration cannot be attacked—because it is unknown or unapproachable—aggression is vented on a scapegoat. Others feel that hostility is inborn, waiting to be aroused by the example of others, or by the mere strangeness of a new person or object.

Two basic personality types are common among prejudiced people. One is the so-called *authoritarian personality* identified by Adorno and his colleagues (1950). The authoritarian is rigid, lacking insight into his own and others' feelings. He projects his aggressive feelings onto others. His parents probably discouraged emotion and demanded unquestioning obedience. About one-fifth of Americans seem to fall into this category, and these people are unlikely to change.

About another fifth of us are reasonably free of prejudice, and the remaining three-fifths fall into the category of the *conforming personality*. These people may simply be conforming to group norms when they display bigotry. They can change, however, if they are placed in non-prejudiced groups. In effect, they shift their behavior and attitudes to conform to those of the new group. Karlins, Coffman, and Walters (1969) found that the prejudices of college undergraduates have changed substantially since 1933. In 1969, Jews, blacks, and Chinese were all seen much more positively than they were in 1933. Perhaps "you can't legislate morality," as defenders of segregation used to maintain. But it seems clear that a society's norms can modify the prejudices of its members.

"converted" were cited as examples of desirable attitudes and behavior.

Some of the prisoners became confused, some became ill or died under the stress, but most complied only enough to ensure their survival, maintaining sufficient mental reservations so that on release they returned to their previous attitudes. Only a handful of men became genuine "converts" to the Communist cause. We may derive comfort from the relative intractability of the human spirit under such conditions of extreme stress, but we must also note that the Chinese and North Koreans used relatively unsophisticated techniques.

What makes one attempt to change attitudes fail and another succeed? More generally, just how and why do attitudes change? Under what circumstances do we resist change? How successful is our resistance likely to be?

We mentioned earlier that we have a tendency to strive for consistency among the three aspects of an attitude—the belief (or cognitive) component, the feeling component, and the behavior tendency. Whenever one of the three is out of line, the discrepancy causes a degree of tension, and we seek to reduce or resolve the discrepancy in order to escape the tension. One of the ways we can reduce the discrepancy is to change our attitude. It follows, then, that attitudes can be changed in three ways. We can change a person's beliefs, perhaps by presenting him with new facts or additional information. Or, as we saw in Chapter 11, we can change the emotional component and hope that the beliefs and behavior will change to fall more closely in line with the new emotions. The third alternative is to change the person's behavior, in the hope that his underlying beliefs and feelings will change to correspond to the changed behavior.

The informational approach. Attempts to change attitudes by changing the belief component of an attitude are most often discussed in terms of a source-message-audience model. The **source** may be a television program, a billboard, a newspaper editorial, a teacher, a friend, a group—in short, anyone or anything that produces a **message,** new or additional information about an object or event. The **audience,** of course, is the person or persons whose attitudes the source is attempting to change. The most obvious example is the television commercial.

Several different factors influence the effectiveness of attitude change. Some of these factors have to do with the source of the new information. One such factor is the **credibility** of the source. We are less likely to change our attitude toward the oil industry's antipollution efforts if the president of a major refining company tells us how much he and his colleagues are doing than if we hear the same information from an impartial commission appointed to study the situation. Another factor is the **prestige** of the source. A source that is high in prestige is likely to effect more change in attitudes than one with lower prestige. In one experiment, for example, a group of people were asked to evaluate nine stanzas of modern poetry (Aronson, Turner, & Carlsmith, 1963). After they had rated the stanzas, they were given another person's favorable evaluation of one of the stanzas they had criticized severely. Some were told that the evaluation had been written by T. S. Eliot, others that it was by a student at a state teachers college. Not surprisingly, when asked to reevaluate the stanzas, those who thought they

IS SOCIAL PSYCHOLOGY DOING ITS JOB?

Social psychology helps to explain how people interact. With his specialized knowledge of human nature, human attitudes, and interpersonal needs, the social psychologist is in a unique position to apply his learning to improve people's relationships and to make the world a better place. Chris Argyris (1975) thinks that this opportunity has not been fully used.

According to Argyris, we can look at the world in two ways: the way it is—cut-throat, manipulative, competitive (he calls this Model 1); or the way it *could* be—cooperative, harmonious, and trusting (Model 2). Because they are scientists first, social psychologists describe the world realistically, and any attempts they make to apply their knowledge are made within the framework of the Model 1 world. They study the conditions under which people are most likely to conform to group norms and to obey authority; they know what conditions let people think more for themselves; they know what situations are most likely to cause people to broaden their attitudes or change their minds. But according to Argyris, this understanding has been used only to maintain and to exploit the *status quo*—not to make people more independent, or cooperative, or broad-minded. An example he gives is work by Abelson and Zimbardo (1970; Zimbardo, 1972) that gives explicit advice for peace advocates on the most effective tactics of political persuasion. Here, the social psychologists tell would-be proselytizers how to impress an audience, how to make a potential convert feel that his ideas are respected, how to disguise manipulative intent, and so forth: ploys that Argyris thinks are almost Machiavellian.

Argyris thinks that social psychologists should start asking themselves some ethical questions. Should experiments and their applications be designed to reinforce the Model 1 world we live in? Should social psychologists restrict their knowledge to descriptive functions only, without trying to improve the world? Or can social psychology be applied to give mankind a better culture, like the Model 2 world he envisions, where people's interactions can be made to bring out the best in everyone?

had read a favorable evaluation by T. S. Eliot changed their own evaluations more than those who thought they had read an essay by a college student. The **intentions** of a source can also help to determine the effectiveness of attitude change. If we can tell from the outset that someone is out to change our attitudes—if he comes on with a "hard sell"—we may be more likely to resist or dismiss his message. In addition, how well we know a person, how attractive he is to us, how similar he is can all affect the degree to which we will change our attitudes in response to his message.

Another set of factors has to do with the message itself—how the material is presented and how much discrepancy it arouses. Up to a point, it appears that the higher the **discrepancy** between a message and our attitude, the greater the likelihood and magnitude of attitude change. We say "up to a point" because if the discrepancy is too great, there is a good chance that the person will reject the new information altogether. Usually, a **two-sided message** is more effective than one that presents only one side of the issue. Other evidence indicates that a message is more effective if it presents the pleasant part of the information first (McGuire, 1957).

Perhaps the most important factors in the attitude-change situation are those that have to do with the audience. These factors are often the most difficult to control, because of the immense variations among individuals—one housewife may be convinced by a television commercial to buy Super Clean laundry detergent, while another changes her attitude very little; one voter may be persuaded by a political speech to vote for John Hamilton for mayor, while another stands firm in his intention to vote for the opposition. Nonetheless, certain general conclusions can be drawn about the ways different attributes of an audience affect the likelihood that their attitudes will be changed. One is the **commitment** of the person to his present attitudes. Someone who has just completed a speaking tour advocating liberalized abortion laws is less likely to change his attitudes toward the subject than someone who has never openly expressed an opinion one way or the other and is thus not "on the record." If a person has had an attitude imposed on him or has merely adopted the attitudes of his parents or friends, he is more susceptible to change than someone who has considered a number of alternatives and made a **free choice** among them. McGuire (1964) has identified a number of what he calls "cultural truisms"— attitudes that are so universal in our society that they are almost never challenged. These cultural truisms—like "Democracy is good" or "You should brush your teeth after each meal"—are, he feels, highly susceptible to change, because the person has never been "inoculated" against persuasive attempts. An attitude that is **interwoven** with many of a person's other attitudes is more difficult to change, because it would be necessary for the person to alter or adjust a whole complex of attitudes. Someone who is given **advance warning** that another person is going to try to change his attitudes is less likely to change—forewarned, it seems, *is* forearmed. Another personal characteristic that can affect attitude change is the level of a person's **self-esteem.** Someone who is highly self-confident is more resistant to change than someone who doubts his own worth or adequacy.

Theoretically, our attitudes are dynamic: as we continue to interact with people, objects, and ideas, we have the opportunity to test and reevaluate our original attitudes. But, in fact, we seldom change our attitudes easily, for our very biases limit the ways we interact with the objects of our attitudes (Kelman, 1974). A person may have concluded from his reading and from what others tell him that all the effects of drugs are harmful. This very opinion may prevent him from ever being exposed to a situation that lets him try out drugs and test his attitudes for himself.

Faced with a message, a person can resist changing his attitude in several different ways. He can downgrade the source of the message ("What does he know about it anyway?"). He can draw on other facts or beliefs to refute the message. He can reject the message altogether. Or he can distort the message and perceive it as being less different than it really is. All these alternatives can serve to reduce the amount of discrepancy, without the person's having to change his attitude very much or at all.

The cognitive consistency approach. Another approach to changing attitudes derives from the theory of **cognitive dissonance.** As proposed by Leon Festinger (1957), this theory holds that any kind of cognitive inconsistency is uncomfortable and thus motivates us to do something to relieve the discomfort. With respect to attitudes, then, dissonance can occur when we are faced with two incompatible beliefs ("Powder-blue shirts are effeminate," "The quarterback for the Houston Oilers wears powder-blue shirts"); when our beliefs and feelings are discrepant ("I know carrot juice is healthy," "I dislike carrot juice intensely"); or when we behave in some way that is out of line with what we believe or feel (such as when we visit the dentist, even when we don't want to go).

This last situation presents some very interesting implications for the process of attitude change. Is it necessary to change the "hearts and minds" of men before you can alter their behavior? Or can we change overt behavior first, perhaps by legislation, on the assumption that the hearts and minds will follow along in the wake? Much of the effort to desegregate public facilities takes as its premise, for example, that once overt behavior is changed, attitudinal changes will follow. There is some evidence that this can be an effective way to change attitudes, in certain circumstances.

After performing some act that is discrepant with his attitudes, a person can choose one of several alternate ways of reducing the dissonance. He can add more consonant elements to outweigh the dissonant one. For example, in order to stay alive, the survivors of a recent plane crash in the Andes Mountains had to eat the flesh of the people who had died. Although all of the survivors initially were revolted by the idea of cannibalism, they were able to change their attitudes in the face of their strong desire to survive. One of the survivors later described how he justified his act: "It's like Holy Communion. My friend has given us his body so that we can have . . . life" (Read, 1974, p. 83). In this case, we can see how the three parts of an attitude system become consistent: the new *belief* that cannibalism in some cases can be a moral act; the *feeling* of wanting to live; and the *behavior*—the actual eating of human flesh.

Another way to reduce dissonance is for the individual to tell himself that the dissonant behavior is really not so important after all. A person who disapproves of multiple-choice exams, but is taking a course in which they are used, can tell himself that the kind of test does not matter so much after all, as long as he can pick the right answers and get a decent grade on his final. Still another alternative is to alter or minimize the dissonant element so that it no longer is discordant with his attitudes. When the dissonance is the result of two incompatible beliefs or feelings, this is a less difficult alternative than when dissonance has been aroused by an action that has already been taken. In those situations, a person often has no other way to reduce the dissonance than to change his attitude. He has already performed the act—there is no way he can deny or change that fact. And the more discrepant the act is, the more dissonance will be aroused and the more the attitude will have to change to reduce it.

Several factors can affect the amount of attitude change that results from cognitive dissonance. They determine how much dissonance is aroused and how many alternative ways there are to reduce the dissonance. One factor is **choice**—if people feel personally responsible for a dissonant action, they are more susceptible to attitude change than if they feel they were coerced or compelled to act in a way that is discrepant with their beliefs (Cooper, 1971; Kelman, 1974). Another factor is **reward**—people who are paid to behave in ways that go against their attitudes experience less dissonance than those who are not, and thus are less likely to change their attitudes. (Note that the opposite situation can occur when people are rewarded for behaving in ways that are consistent with their beliefs and feelings. As we noted in Chapter 4, such rewards can make people value the behavior *less* than they did before.) A third important factor is **justification**—if a person is convinced that there is a good reason why he should perform a discrepant act, he will experience little dissonance and his attitudes are not likely to change.

Postscript: Environmental Psychology

In this chapter, we've been looking at the interactions of people—their relationships with each other, and their relationships with groups. In an age in which our world is becoming so crowded that we often tend to become overpowered by our surroundings, a third dimension of human interaction becomes crucial to the social psychologist's study. That dimension is our relationship to our environment.

Effects of the Social Structure on the Individual

Environments, just like people, have their own personalities, and we are influenced by our environment just as we are influenced by other people (Insel & Moos, 1974). Some social psychologists have looked into the way that man reacts to the social structure of his environment, and their findings show that the structure in which man operates has quite

(Joel Gordon)

(Camera 5)

an important effect on the way he functions, on his sense of satisfaction, and even on his physical health.

Competitive, hurried environments with heavy work loads, high pressure, and high rates of change seem to increase the likelihood of stress and disease (Kiritz & Moos, 1974). These environments have even been tentatively linked to higher probabilities of heart disease (Caffrey, 1969; Sales, 1968). In contrast, atmospheres of support, cohesion, and affiliation appear to have quite positive effects, such as high morale, personal growth, and even shorter recovery time from illness (Cumming & Cumming, 1962; Kiritz & Moos, 1974). Of these two kinds of environments, there is no question that the one that comes closest to the world we live in is the former. What does this mean to us as individuals? We will look at a few specific examples to see what social psychologists have been able to discover about how man is relating to his modern, increasingly urban environment.

Personal Space and Crowding

In crowded urban areas like New York City, as many as 70,000 people coexist in a single square mile. One of New York City's larger apartment complexes could house the entire population of the city of Peoria, Illinois. Sidewalks are so crowded during certain hours of the day that the simple act of walking from one place to another becomes a skillful art of dodging and sidestepping. Even in the suburbs, houses and apartments are often jammed together, so it's easy to hear what the neighbors are arguing about and to smell what they're having for supper. What ever happened to the old American concept of "elbow room," and what effect does its disappearance have on the vast majority of Americans who live in crowded urban and suburban areas?

E. T. Hall (1959) coined the term "personal space" to identify the amount of physical space between people, the way they relate to this space, and the way they use this space to relate to each other.

The etiquette of personal space is dictated in large part by our culture. Americans, for instance, stand much farther apart than almost any other nationality. What happens when two people with different preferences of personal space talk is illustrative of how important this subconscious force is. When a Brazilian talks to an American, the Brazilian will try to get close to the American, while the American will try to maintain what he considers a proper distance. The result will be that during their conversation, the American will constantly edge backward in response to the Brazilian's advances. By the time they've finished talking, the American will probably be backed against the wall (Hall, 1959).

Thus, the space around us is sort of a safety zone, and we don't like it to be violated except by certain people. How strongly do we react to the constant impingement on personal space in highly crowded urban areas?

The effects of crowding on animals. Studies of many different kinds of animals show that high population density often has sharp negative effects. In a classic study by Calhoun (1962), rats were raised under *almost* ideal conditions. They had all the food and water they needed, and their living quarters were kept clean. The only thing lacking was room for expansion. As their numbers grew—and they did rapidly in this setting—they became more and more crowded within their enclosed space until a strange thing happened. Calhoun noted that at a certain point, the population declined sharply. In addition, the rats developed quite bizarre behavior: mothers would eat their babies, homosexuality increased, and some rats became severely depressed and withdrawn. This same reaction to overcrowding has been observed in many other species, from deer to mice to lemmings, who march into the sea when their population cycle reaches an untenable peak.

Man in an urban environment. Does man have any population safety valve like animals, which lets him control for an environment that has become too crowded to be livable? Both naturalistic observation and experimental studies, so far, show that man, unlike most animals, seems able to adapt quite well to any stress caused by overcrowding.

We are used to linking high crime rates to urban areas, and with good reason. But studies of city life that have tried to link high crime with overcrowding alone find that these two are not correlated significantly when controls are made for income and other social factors (Freedman, Heshka, & Levy, 1973; Galle, Gove, & McPherson, 1972;

(Marilyn Silverstone, Magnum Photos)

Winsborough, 1965). The same is true of mental illness and other kinds of pathologies we often connect with urban life. It seems that all of these elements have much more complicated origins than merely high population density.

High density does seem to exaggerate an individual's natural behavioral tendencies (Freedman, Carlsmith, & Sears, 1974; Stokols et al., 1973). Under high-density conditions, men tend to react more aggressively than in normal situations, while women tend to react more positively, by being more cooperative. Other studies (Hutt & Vaizey, 1966) have noted that children who are brain-damaged or autistic tend to become more withdrawn or aggressive in crowded conditions, again magnifying personality characteristics that already exist.

All of these studies only begin to tell us some of the ways that man might respond to the world he lives in. Other important studies have been made on the effects of noise, for example, which in urban centers can become so overpowering as to interfere with people's ability to hear each other talk. Other research in environmental psychology is starting to tell us how our own buildings can affect our behavior.

In all of these areas, we are finding out that man is indeed more adaptable than many other animals. He seems quite able to adjust to environmental stress, whether it be caused by crowding or by noise or by other factors. But we still don't know exactly what the cost of this adjustment is. And we don't know where the breaking point of too much crowding, or too much noise, is—if indeed any breaking point exists. There have still been relatively few studies about the way man interacts with his environment, and there is a lot more to be learned. Environmental psychology is sure to become an increasingly important area of study in the coming years.

Summary

1. Most of man's life is spent in groups, from the family into which he is born to the increasingly widening, overlapping, and complex groups with which he interacts in modern society. *Social psychology* is the study of groups—their structure, their interactions, and their influence on the individual.
2. The first impressions we form of people are often based on the sketchy information we get from such external cues as dress, gestures, and manner of speaking. We use these cues to categorize people. Then, based on these categories, we draw inferences about people and adjust our own behavior accordingly. *Person perception* is influenced by our culture and the groups we belong to.
3. In most situations our first impressions of people are reasonably accurate, but several processes can lead to inaccuracy and error. Among the most common causes of error are *insufficient information, false or misleading*

cues, and *stereotyping.* Another source of incorrect judgments is the *logical error*—when a person displays one trait, we often assume that he also has the other traits customarily associated with it. Related to the logical error are the *halo effect*—attributing positive characteristics to a person we like—and the *devil effect*—attributing negative characteristics to a person we dislike.

4. Just as we make judgments about people's personalities, we also make decisions about the causes behind their actions. *Attribution theory* looks at whether people are more likely to blame internal causes or external causes for their own and others' behavior. Research indicates that most people tend to assume internal causes for other people's behavior and external causes for their own.

5. The major factors contributing to the way people meet and whether they will like one another are *proximity, similarity of interests, complementarity,* and *rewardingness.*

6. The presence of other people influences our behavior and our attitudes. The theory of *social comparison* proposes that people have a need to rate their performance against others. Interaction with others requires us to conform to or resist their attitudes and expectations. A certain amount of *conformity* to group standards and norms is essential for getting along in society, but the degree of conformity varies with the individual. We also seem to behave differently when other people are present than when we are alone. In addition our society socializes us to be *obedient to authority.* This may not be such a good thing when taken to extremes.

7. *Social conflict* is inevitable. Conflicts may be resolved by giving the two parties a common goal or by having them role-play each other's positions. Third-party mediators, respected authority figures, and coalitions of interested people can also be effective.

8. The theory of *social facilitation* holds that people usually perform better when they are in direct competition with others than when they are competing against themselves. However, competition can produce anxiety and interfere with performance, especially on difficult tasks or when new learning is taking place. *Risk-taking* seems to be greater in groups. Because of group pressure, sharing of responsibility, and deindividuation, people will take larger risks when acting as a group than when acting alone.

9. Psychologists who study *group dynamics* look at leadership, communication networks, and group problem solving.

10. Group *leadership* may be informal or formal, but all groups have leaders who shape the behavior of the group. The leader is usually an outgoing, outspoken person who must make himself heard and also facilitate the communication of others. He is usually a person people look up to and who typifies the way group members like to think of themselves.

11. The exchange of information, feelings, and attitudes among members is essential to the effectiveness of a group. Among the most common *communication networks* are the circle, the chain, the Y-shape, and the wheel. Each has different effects on the group's ability to solve various kinds of problems and on the satisfaction of the members. Generally, communication networks become less rigid as the members get better acquainted.

12. In some kinds of *problem solving,* people tend to do better alone than in groups, because they need not worry about competition and are freed from pressure to conform. In some cases, though, groups may be better equipped

to solve problems than the individual. Often a group has resources that an individual does not have. A group's members can check each other for correctness of a solution, can divide up the work of solving a complex problem, and can avoid repeating work. Mixed groups tend to do better than homogeneous groups when different skills and a division of labor are needed, and groups seem to be more effective when the members know each other well.

13. An important part of how we perceive other people is what we think of their *attitudes* about the world in general and about us in particular. An attitude is made up of three components—*beliefs, feelings,* and a *tendency to behave* in certain ways. We have a tendency to strive for consistency among these three components, but it is not always safe to infer from a person's attitude what his behavior will be.

14. Attitudes are acquired through our associations with family, peer groups, and other groups, especially *reference groups.* Some are formally taught as part of the educational process and others are learned informally by identification and modeling.

15. Attitudes can be changed in three ways—by changing the belief, the emotional, or the behavioral component of the attitude. The *informational approach* attempts to change a person's beliefs by presenting him with new facts or additional information. The *credibility, prestige,* and *intentions* of the source influence its effectiveness in changing attitudes. The amount of *discrepancy* a message arouses and how the message is presented are very important in determining the effect of the message. A *two-sided message* is often more effective than a one-sided message. The most important factors in the attitude-change situation relate to the audience. *Commitment* to present attitudes, whether attitudes are acquired by *free choice* or by force, whether the attitude in question is *interwoven* with other attitudes, whether there is *advance warning* that someone is going to try to change one's attitudes, and level of *self-esteem* all affect a person's susceptibility to attitude change.

16. A person can resist changing his attitude about something by downgrading the source of the message, by drawing on other facts or beliefs to refute the message, by rejecting the message altogether, or by distorting the message and perceiving it as being less discrepant than it really is.

17. The *cognitive consistency approach* to changing attitudes is based on the theory of *cognitive dissonance,* which holds that any kind of cognitive inconsistency is uncomfortable and thus motivates us to do something to relieve the discomfort. Dissonance can occur when we are faced with two incompatible beliefs, when our beliefs and feelings are discrepant, or when we behave in some way that is not in accord with what we believe or feel. There are several ways of reducing dissonance, including adding more consonant elements to outweigh the dissonant ones, downplaying the importance of the dissonant behavior, altering or minimizing the dissonant element so that it is no longer discordant with existing attitudes, or changing attitudes. Whether a person acts by *choice,* whether he is *rewarded* for a discrepant act, and whether he can provide a *justification* for his actions all affect how much attitude change will result from cognitive dissonance.

18. We are influenced by our environment as well as by other people. One

important area that *environmental psychologists* have studied is the effects of overcrowding. Man, so far, seems to have been able to adapt to increasingly high population densities. High crime rates in urban areas appear to be related more to income level and other social factors than to population density alone. High density does seem to exaggerate personality characteristics already present in the individual. This area of psychology is quite new, and much remains to be learned.

Suggested Readings

Allport, G., *The Nature of Prejudice* (New York: Anchor Books, 1958). An examination of the psychology of prejudice and different ways it can be studied.

Aronson, E., *The Social Animal* (San Francisco: Freeman, 1972). An interesting brief overview of social psychology, with some real-world applications.

Bem, D., *Beliefs, Attitudes, and Human Affairs* (Belmont, Calif.: Brooks/Cole, 1970). A concise and very readable discussion of attitudes and their social implications.

Berscheid, E., and Walster, E., *Interpersonal Attraction* (Reading, Mass.: Addison-Wesley, 1969). A thorough review of research and theories in the field of interpersonal attraction.

Davis, J. H., *Group Performance* (Reading, Mass.: Addison-Wesley, 1969). A good discussion of research on problem solving and decision making in groups and the various factors that enhance or diminish effectiveness.

Freedman, J. L., Carlsmith, J. M., and Sears, D. O., *Social Psychology*, 2nd ed. (Englewood Cliffs, N.J.: Prentice-Hall, 1974). An excellent textbook that covers all the major topics in social psychology.

Ittleson, W. H., *Introduction to Environmental Psychology* (New York: Holt, Rinehart & Winston, 1974). A good introduction to the new and rapidly growing field of environmental psychology.

Kiesler, C. A., and Kiesler, S. B., *Conformity* (Reading, Mass.: Addison-Wesley, 1969). A concise analysis of the nature of conformity, when it occurs, and the effects of interpersonal relations and intergroup communication.

Malec, M. A. (Ed.), *Attitude Change* (Chicago: Rand McNally, 1971). A collection of important articles in the field of attitude change.

Mann, R. D., et al., *The College Classroom: Conflict, Change and Learning* (New York: Wiley, 1970). An interesting examination of interpersonal relations in the college classroom.

Rubin, Z. (Ed.), *Doing unto Others: Joining, Molding, Conforming, Helping, Loving* (Englewood Cliffs, N.J.: Prentice-Hall, 1974). A stimulating collection of articles by well-known social psychologists including Stanley Schachter, Solomon Asch, Stanley Milgram, Elaine Walster, and Zick Rubin.

Triandis, H. D., *Attitude and Attitude Change* (New York: Wiley, 1971). A thorough analysis of the cognitive, affective, and behavioral aspects of attitudes in our own and other cultures.

Wheeler, L., *Interpersonal Influence* (Boston: Allyn and Bacon, 1970). A short, enjoyable discussion of the major theories and research in the area of interpersonal influence.

Appendix: Measurement and Statistical Methods

Nearly all the experiments described in this book involve measuring one or more variables and then analyzing the data statistically. The design and scoring of all the tests we have discussed are also based on statistical methods. **Statistics** is a branch of mathematics. It provides techniques for sorting and talking about quantitative facts and ways of drawing conclusions from them. Statistics let us organize and describe a set of data quickly, then guide the conclusions we can draw from any set of data and help to tell us what inferences we are and are not justified in making.

Statistical analysis is essential to the psychologist who is conducting an experiment or designing a test, but statistics can only handle numbers—groups of them. To avail himself of the help of statistics, the psychologist has to begin by measuring things—counting them and expressing them in some sort of quantities.

Scales of Measurement

No matter what it is we are measuring—height, loudness, intelligence, attitudes, or whatever—we have to use some sort of scale. The kind of data we want to collect determines what kind of scale we will use and, in turn, the scale we use will help to determine what kind of conclusions we can draw from our data.

Nominal Scales

If we decide to classify a group of people by the color of their eyes, we are using a **nominal scale.** We can count how many people have blue eyes, how many have green eyes, how many have brown eyes, and so on, but we cannot say that one group has more or less eye color than another. The colors are simply different.

A nominal scale is just a set of categories, arbitrarily named or numbered. If we look up how many Republican, Democratic, and Independent voters registered in a certain congressional district in the last election year, we are using a nominal scale. Since a nominal scale is more a way of classifying than of measuring, it is the least informative kind of scale. If we want a way of comparing our data more precisely, we will have to use a scale that tells us more.

Ordinal Scales

If we make up a list of horses in the order in which they finish a race, we are using an **ordinal scale.** On an ordinal scale, data are ranked from first to last according to some criterion. An ordinal scale tells us about order, but it does not tell us anything about the distances between what is ranked first and second or ninth and tenth. It does not tell us how much faster the winning horse ran than the horse that came in second or the horse that finished last. If a person ranks his preferences for various kinds of soup—pea soup first, then tomato soup, then chicken noodle, and so on—we know what soup he likes most and what soup he likes least, but we have no idea how much better he likes tomato than chicken noodle, or whether those two are actually quite close, while pea soup is far more favored than either of them.

Since we do not know the distances between the items ranked on an ordinal scale, we cannot add or subtract ordinal data. If mathematical operations are going to be necessary, we will have to use a still more informative scale.

Interval Scales

An **interval scale** is often compared to a ruler that has been broken off at the bottom—it only goes from, say, $5\frac{1}{2}$ to 12. The intervals between 6 and 7, 7 and 8, 8 and 9, and so forth, are equal, but there is no zero. A thermometer is an interval scale—even though a certain degree registered on a Fahrenheit or Centigrade thermometer specifies a certain state of cold or heat, there is no such thing as no temperature at all. We can never say that one day was twice as hot as another, only that it was so many equal degrees hotter.

An interval scale tells us how many equal-sized units one thing lies above or below another thing of the same kind, but it does not tell us how many times bigger, smaller, taller, or fatter one thing is than another. An intelligence test cannot tell us that one person is three times as intelligent as another, only that he scored so many points above or below someone else.

Ratio Scales

The only time we can say that a measurement is twice as long as another or three times as high is when we use a **ratio scale,** one that has a true zero. For instance, if we measure the amount of snowfall in a certain area over several winters, we can say that 6 times as much snow fell during a winter in which we measured a total of 12 feet as during a winter in which only 2 feet fell. This scale has a zero—there is such a thing as no snowfall at all.

Measures of Central Tendency

Usually when we measure a number of instances of anything—from popularity ratings of daytime TV shows to weight of 8-year-old boys to the number of times a guinea pig's optic nerve fires in response to electrical stimulation—we get a distribution of measurements that range from smallest to largest or lowest to highest. More often than not, the measurements will cluster around some value near the middle. This value is the **central tendency** of the distribution of the measurements.

Suppose, for example, you have ten children on your hands one rainy day and decide to keep them busy tossing rings around a bottle. You give them three rings to toss each turn, the game has 6 rounds, and each player scores 1 point every time he gets the ring around the neck of the bottle. The highest possible score is 18. The distribution of scores might end up like this: 11, 8, 13, 6, 12, 10, 16, 9, 12, 3.

What could you say quickly about the ring-tossing talent of the group? To begin with, you could arrange the scores in order from lowest to highest: 3, 6, 8, 9, 10, 11, 12, 12, 13, 16.

In this order, the central tendency of the distribution of scores begins to become clear. A relatively large number of scores seems to cluster around the values between 10 and 12. There are three ways of describing the central tendency of a distribution. In everyday language, we usually refer to all three as the *average*.

The Mean

The arithmetical average is called the **mean**—the sum of all the scores in the group, divided by the number of scores. If you add up all the scores and divide by 10, the total number of scores in this group, you find that the mean for this group is 10.

The Median

The **median** is the point that divides a distribution in half—50 percent of the scores fall above the median and 50 percent fall below. In the ring-tossing scores, five scores fall at 10 or below, five at 11 or above. The median is thus halfway between 10 and 11—10.5.

The Mode

The point at which the largest number of scores occurs is called the **mode.** In this distribution, the mode is 12. More people achieved a score of 12 than any other.

If we take a large number of measurements of just about anything, we are likely to get a distribution of scores in which the mean, median, and mode are all approximately the same—the score that occurs the most frequently (the mode) will also be the point that half the scores are below and half above (the median). And the same point will represent the arithmetical average (the mean). This is not universally true of all characteristics, of course, and small samples rarely come out so symmetrically. In these cases, we often have to decide which of the three measures of central tendency—the mean, median, or mode—will be the most likely to tell us what we want to know.

For example, suppose a shopkeeper wants to know the general income level of the people who walk by his store during their lunch hours so he can stock an appropriate kind of merchandise. He might conduct a rough survey by standing outside for a few days from 12:00 to 2:00 and asking every tenth person who walks by to check a card indicating the general range of his income. Suppose a great majority of the people checked the ranges between $4,000 and $6,000 a year. However, a couple of the people made a great deal of money—one checked $100,000–$150,000, one checked the $200,000-or-above box. The mean for the set of income figures would be pushed higher by those two large figures and would not really tell the shopkeeper what he wants to know about the majority of his potential customers. In this case, he would be wiser to use the median or the mode.

Suppose instead of meeting two people whose incomes were so great, he noticed that people from two distinct income groups walked by his store—several people checked the box for $5,000–$6,000, several others checked $10,000–$11,000. The shopkeeper would find that his distribution was bimodal. It has two modes—$5,500 and $10,500. This information might be more useful to him than the mean, which could lead him to think his customers were a homogeneous group with an average income of about $8,000.

Frequency Distributions

Another way of approaching a set of scores is to arrange them into a **frequency distribution**—to select a set of intervals and count how many scores fall into each interval. A frequency distribution is a useful way of dealing with large groups of numbers—it reduces the number of individual scores into more manageable groups.

Suppose a psychologist conducts an experiment on memory. He asks 50 college students to learn a list of 18 nonsense syllables, then records the number of syllables each student can recall 2 hours later. He arranges his raw scores from lowest to highest in a rank distribution:

2	6	8	10	11	14
3	7	9	10	12	14
4	7	9	10	12	15
4	7	9	10	12	16
5	7	9	10	13	17
5	7	9	11	13	
6	8	9	11	13	
6	8	9	11	13	
6	8	10	11	13	

He can see quite easily that the scores range from 2 to 17, but decides that a mass of 50 individual scores is too cumbersome to work with. So he chooses a set of 2-point intervals and tallies the number of scores in each interval:

Interval	Tally	Frequency (f)
1–2	|	1
3–4	|||	3
5–6	ⱶⱵ |	6
7–8	ⱶⱵ ||||	9
9–10	ⱶⱵ ⱶⱵ |||	13
11–12	ⱶⱵ |||	8
13–14	ⱶⱵ ||	7
15–16	||	2
17–18	|	1

Now he can tell at a glance what the results of his experiment were—most of the students had scores near the middle of the range, very few had scores in the high or low intervals.

He can see these results even more dramatically if he uses the frequency distribution to construct a bar graph—a **frequency histogram.** Marking the intervals along the horizontal axis and the frequencies along the vertical axis would give him the graph shown in Figure 1. Another way of presenting the data from the frequency distribution graphically is to construct a **frequency polygon,** a line graph. A frequency polygon drawn from the same set of data is shown in Figure 2. Note that the figure is not a smooth curve, since the points are connected by straight lines. With a very large number of scores, however, and with small intervals, the angles would seem to smooth out and the figure would begin to resemble a rounded curve.

The Normal Curve

Ordinarily, if we take a large enough number of measurements of almost any characteristic or event, we come up with a *normal distri-*

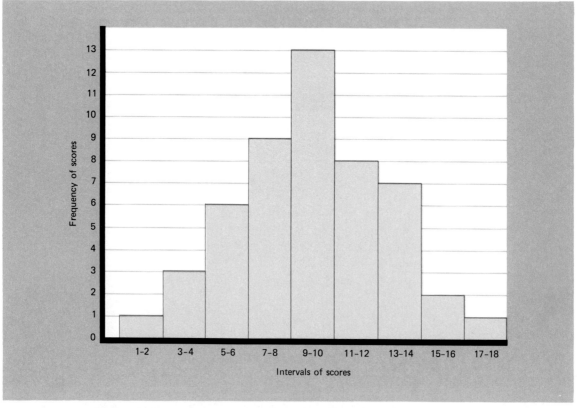

Figure 1

A frequency histogram for a memory experiment. The bars indicate the frequency of scores within each interval.

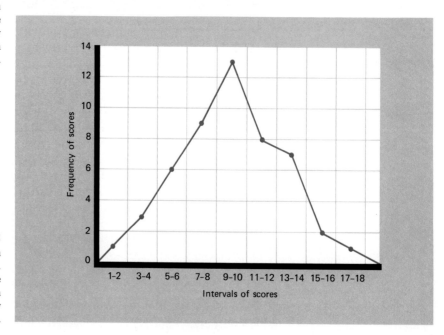

Figure 2

A frequency polygon drawn from data used in Figure 1. The dots, representing the frequency of scores in each interval, are connected by straight lines.

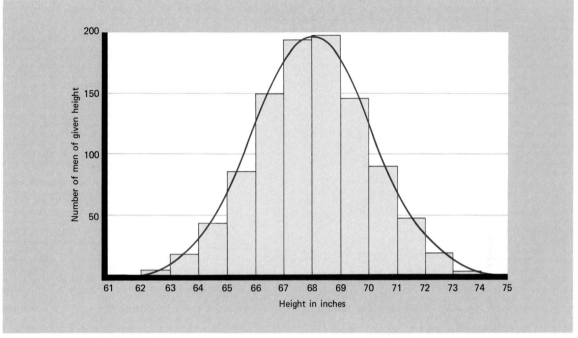

Figure 3
A normal curve, based on measurements of the heights of 1,000 adult males. (From A. B. Hill, *Principles of Medical Statistics*, 8th ed. London: Oxford University Press, 1966.)

bution. Tossing coins is a favorite example of statisticians. If you were to take 10 coins, toss them into the air 1,000 times, and record the various combinations of head and tails on each toss, your tabulations would reveal a normal distribution. The combination of 5 heads and 5 tails would occur most frequently, 6 heads/4 tails and 4 heads/6 tails would be the next most frequent, and so on down to the very infrequent combinations of all heads or all tails.

Plotting a normal distribution on a graph yields a particular kind of frequency polygon called a **normal curve.** A normal curve for the heights of 1,000 men is shown in Figure 3. Note that the curve is absolutely symmetrical—the left slope parallels the right slope exactly. Another significant characteristic of the normal curve is that the mean, median, and mode all fall on the same point—the highest point on the curve.

Actually, the normal curve is a hypothetical entity. No set of real measurements shows such a smooth gradation from one interval to the next or so purely symmetrical a shape. But, because so many things in nature, when they are measured, do approximate the normal curve so closely, the curve provides a useful model for dealing with many of the characteristics we measure.

Skewed Distributions

If a frequency distribution is asymmetrical—if most of the scores are gathered at either the high end or the low end—the frequency polygon

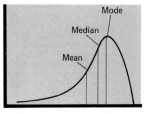

Figure 4
A skewed distribution. Most of the scores are gathered at the high end of the distribution, causing the hump to shift to the right. Since the tail on the left is longer, we say that the curve is skewed to the left. Note that the mean, median, and mode are different.

will be *skewed*. The hump will sit to one side or the other and one of the curve's tails will be disproportionately long.

If a high school mathematics instructor, for example, gives his students a sixth-grade arithmetic test, we would expect nearly all the scores to be quite high. The frequency polygon would probably look like the one in Figure 4. But if the sixth-grade class (whose arithmetic test is missing) is asked to solve a series of advanced algebra problems, their scores would probably be quite low. The frequency polygon would be very similar to the one shown in Figure 5.

Note too that the mean, median, and mode fall at different points in a skewed distribution, unlike in the normal curve, where they coincide. Usually, if you know that the mean is greater than the median of a distribution, you can predict that the frequency polygon will be skewed to the right. If the median is greater than the mean, the curve will be skewed to the left.

Bimodal Distributions

We have already mentioned a bimodal distribution in our description of the shopkeeper's survey of his customers' incomes. The frequency polygon for a bimodal distribution has two humps—one for each mode. The mean and the median may be the same, as in Figure 6, or different, as in Figure 7.

Measures of Variation

Sometimes it is not enough to know the distribution of a set of data and what their mean, median, and mode are. Suppose an automotive safety expert feels that too much damage occurs in tail-end accidents because automobile bumpers are not all the same height. It is not enough for him to know what the average height of an automobile bumper is. He also wants to know something about the variation in bumper heights—how much higher is the highest bumper than the mean? How do the bumpers of all the cars on the road vary from the mean? Are the bumpers on the latest models coming closer to the same height?

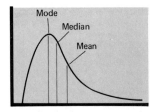

Figure 5
In this distribution, most of the scores are gathered at the low end, so the curve is skewed to the right. The mean, median, and mode do not coincide.

Range

The simplest measure of variation is the **range**—the difference between the largest and smallest measurements. Perhaps the safety expert measured the bumpers of 1,000 cars 2 years ago and found that the highest bumper was 18 inches from the ground, the lowest only 12 inches from the ground. The range was thus 6 inches—18 minus 12. This year he measures the bumpers on another 1,000 cars and finds that the highest bumper is still 18 inches high, the lowest still 12 inches from the ground. The range is still 6 inches. Moreover, he finds that

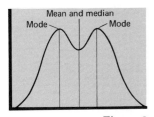

Figure 6

A bimodal distribution in which the mean and the median are the same.

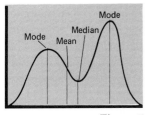

Figure 7

In this bimodal distribution, the mean and median are different.

the means of the two distributions are the same—15 inches off the ground. But look at the two frequency polygons in Figure 8—obviously there is still something he needs to know, since the way the measurements are clustered around the mean is so drastically different. To find out how the measurements are distributed around the mean, our safety expert has to turn to a slightly more complicated measure of variation—the standard deviation.

The Standard Deviation

The **standard deviation,** in a single number, tells us a great deal about how the scores in any frequency distribution are dispersed around the mean. Calculating the standard deviation takes a bit more time than the other statistical operations we have described so far, but it is one of the must useful and widely used tools the statistician has at his command.

To find the standard deviation of a set of scores, we first find the mean. Then we take the first score in the distribution, subtract it from the mean, square the difference, and jot it down in a column to be added up later. We then go on to the next score and do the same thing, then to the third, and so on until we have used up all the scores in the distribution. Then we add up the column of squared differences, divide the total by the number of scores in the distribution, and find the square root of that number. Figure 9 shows the calculation of the standard deviation for a small distribution of scores.

In a normal distribution, however peaked or flattened the curve may be, approximately 68 percent of the scores fall between 1 standard deviation above the mean and 1 standard deviation below the mean (see Figure 10). Another 27 percent fall between 1 standard deviation

Figure 8

Frequency polygons for two sets of measurements of automobile bumper heights. Both are normal curves and in each distribution the mean, median, and mode are 15. But the variation from the mean is different, causing the first curve to be flattened, the second much more sharply peaked.

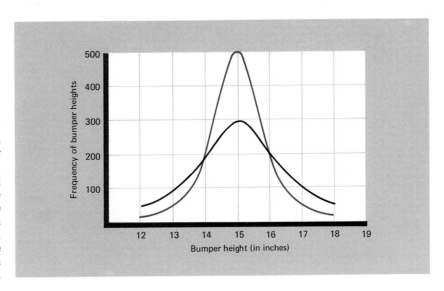

Figure 9

Step-by-step calculation of
the standard deviation for a
group of 10 scores with a
mean of 7.

Number of scores = 10   Mean = 7

Scores	Difference from mean	Difference squared
4	$7 - 4 = 3$	$3^2 = 9$
5	$7 - 5 = 2$	$2^2 = 4$
6	$7 - 6 = 1$	$1^2 = 1$
6	$7 - 6 = 1$	$1^2 = 1$
7	$7 - 7 = 0$	$0^2 = 0$
7	$7 - 7 = 0$	$0^2 = 0$
8	$7 - 8 = -1$	$-1^2 = 1$
8	$7 - 8 = -1$	$-1^2 = 1$
9	$7 - 9 = -2$	$-2^2 = 4$
10	$7 - 10 = -3$	$-3^2 = 9$

Sum of squares = 30
$\div$
Number of scores = 10
Variance = 3
Standard deviation = $\sqrt{3}$ = 1.73

and 2 standard deviations on either side of the mean, 4 percent more
between the second and third standard deviations on either side. Altogether, more than 99 percent of the scores fall between 3 standard
deviations above and 3 standard deviations below the mean. It is this
information that makes the standard deviation useful for comparing
two different normal distributions.

Now let us return to our automotive safety expert and see what the
standard deviation can tell him about the variations from the mean
in his two sets of data. The standard deviation for the cars he measured
2 years ago, he finds, is about 1.4. A car with a bumper height of 16.4

Figure 10

A normal curve, divided to
show the percentage of
scores that fall within each
standard deviation from
the mean.

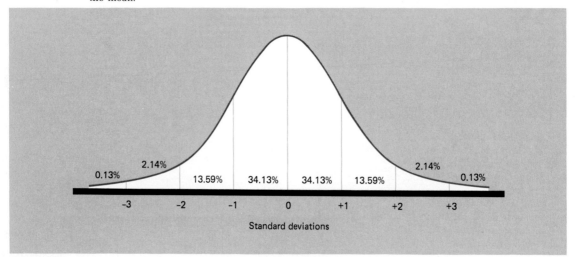

is 1 standard deviation above the mean of 15; one with a bumper height of 13.6 is 1 standard deviation below the mean. Since he knows that his data fall into a normal distribution, he can figure that approximately 68 percent of the 1,000 cars he measured will fall somewhere between these two heights—680 cars will have bumpers between 13.6 and 16.4 inches high. For his more recent set of data, the standard deviation is just slightly less than 1. A car with a bumper height of about 14 inches is 1 standard deviation below the mean; one with a bumper height of about 16 inches is 1 standard deviation above the mean. Thus in this distribution 680 cars have bumpers between 14 and 16 inches high. This information tells the safety expert that car bumpers are indeed coming more into line with one another, even though the range of heights is still the same (6 inches) and even though the mean height of bumpers is still 15.

Measures of Correlation

Measures of central tendency and measures of variation are used to describe a single set of measurements (like the children's ring-tossing scores) or to compare two or more sets of measurements (like the two sets of bumper heights). Sometimes, however, we are interested in finding out whether two sets of measurements are in any way associated with one another—whether they are correlated. Is smoking related to lung cancer? Is IQ associated with sex? Does the way a person votes have anything to do with his income?

One way to determine quickly whether two variables are correlated is to draw a **scatter plot.** We assign one variable (X) to the horizontal axis of a graph, the other (Y) to the vertical axis. Then we plot a person's score on one characteristic along the horizontal axis and his score on the second characteristic along the vertical axis. At the point where the two scores intersect we draw a dot. When a group of people's scores have been plotted in this way we can tell from the pattern of dots whether the two characteristics are in any way correlated with each other.

If the dots on a scatter plot form a straight line running between the lower left-hand corner and the upper right-hand corner, as they do in Figure 11a, we have a perfect *positive correlation*—a high score on one of the characteristics is always associated with a high score on the other one. A straight line running between the upper left-hand corner and the lower right-hand corner, as in Figure 11b, is the sign of a perfect *negative correlation*—a high score on one of the characteristics is invariably associated with a low score on the other one. If the pattern formed by the dots is cigar-shaped in either of these directions, as in Figure 11c, we have a modest correlation—the two characteristics are related to some extent, but not highly correlated. If the dots spread out over the whole graph, forming a circle or a random

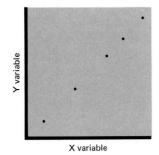

Y variable

X variable

Figure 11a

Scatter plots can be used to give a rough idea of the strength and direction of correlation. Here, plot *a* shows a perfect positive correlation.

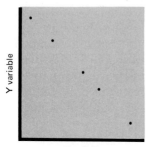

X variable

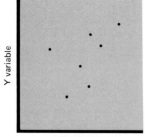

X variable

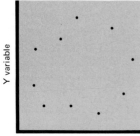

X variable

Figure 11b, c, d
In these three scatter plots, plot *b* shows a perfect negative correlation, plot *c* indicates a moderate positive correlation, but in plot *d* there is no correlation at all.

pattern, as they do in Figure 11d, we can usually assume that there is no correlation between the two characteristics.

A scatter plot can give us a general idea of whether or not a correlation exists and how strong it is. To describe the relation between two variables more precisely, it is necessary to use a **correlation coefficient**—a statistical measure of the degree to which two variables are associated. The correlation coefficient tells us the degree of association between two sets of matched scores—that is, to what extent high or low scores on one variable tend to be associated with high or low scores on another variable. It also provides an estimate of how well we would be able to predict from a person's score on one characteristic how high he will score on another characteristic. If we know, for example, that a particular test of mechanical ability is highly correlated with success in engineering courses, we could predict that a person who did well on the test would also do well as an engineering major.

Correlation coefficients can run from +1.0 to −1.0. The highest possible value (+1.0) indicates a perfect positive correlation—high scores on one variable are invariably and systematically related to high scores on a second variable. The lowest possible value (−1.0) means a perfect negative correlation—high scores on one variable are invariably and regularly related to low scores on the second variable. In life most things are far from perfect, of course, so most correlation coefficients fall somewhere between +1.0 and −1.0. Generally, a correlation below ±.20 is considered insignificant, from ±.20 to ±.40 is low, from ±.40 to ±.60 is moderate, from ±.60 to ±.80 is high, and from ±.80 to ±1.0 is very high. A correlation of zero is an indication that there is no correlation between two sets of scores—no regular relation between them at all.

Correlation indicates only that two sets of scores are somehow related. It does not tell us anything about causality. If we found a very high correlation between voting preferences and income levels, for example, we still could not say that being poor made people vote Democratic or that voting for Republican candidates made people become wealthy. We would still have no idea which came first, or whether some third variable accounted for both income levels and voting patterns. All correlation tells us is that we have found a certain degree of association (perhaps none) between scores on two specified characteristics.

Using Statistics to Make Predictions

Underlying many uses of statistics is the hope that we can generalize from our results and use them to predict behavior. We hope, for example, that we can record how well a group of rats run through a maze today and use that information to predict how another group of rats will perform in the same maze tomorrow, that we can use a person's scores on a sales aptitude test to predict how well he will do in a job selling life insurance, that we can measure the attitudes of a relatively small group of people about pollution control and use that information as an indication of what the attitudes of the whole country are. But first we have to determine whether our measurements are representative and whether we can have confidence in them.

Sampling

In many situations it is impossible, or at least impractical, to measure every single occurrence of a characteristic. No one could expect to measure the memory of every human being, or test all the rats or pigeons in the world in Skinner boxes, or record the maternal behavior of all female monkeys, or study every separate individual in almost any population.

When a population is large, we usually study a **sample** of cases of some reasonable, practical size and then generalize our results to the population as a whole. One way to guarantee that the results of our measurements are accurate for the whole population is to make sure that the sample is gathered in a truly random fashion.

When a neighborhood association sells chances on door prizes, then puts all the stubs into a big drum and churns it around, and a blindfolded person reaches into the drum and pulls out the winning numbers, the prizewinners constitute a **random sample.** In theory, every single stub in that drum is equally likely to be picked—chance determines which numbers are selected.

A **biased sample** is one that is not truly representative of the population in question. If we want to find out whether a town's garbage pick-up service is being performed adequately, we could not just stand outside the best department store in town at 3:00 in the afternoon and ask everyone who happened by how many times his garbage had been collected that week and at what time. The people who saunter in to shop at that department store in the middle of the afternoon on an ordinary day are unlikely to be totally representative of the town's population. We would have to figure out a way to make sure that all the town's neighborhoods will be represented proportionally in our sample.

Making generalizations based on biased samples can lead to some very erroneous conclusions. If the advertising manager of a bank wanted to test out a few potential campaigns designed to persuade middle-aged men with incomes over $100,000 to set up trust funds for their children, he would not be very wise to base his decisions on a set of interviews with migrant workers. The classic sampling story involves a national magazine that predicted the election of a certain candidate, who then lost the election. The magazine had based its prediction on a telephone survey. They forgot, however, that a large number of voters did not have telephones, and many of the people without phones voted for the other candidate.

"Young man, I am no random sample."
(© Punch, London—Rothco)

ROTHCO

Probability

Errors based on inadequate sampling procedures are somebody's fault. Other kinds of errors occur randomly. In the simplest kind of experiment, a psychologist will gather a representative sample, split it randomly into two groups, and then apply some experimental manipulation to one of the groups. Afterward he will measure both groups and determine whether the experimental group's score is now different from the score of the control group. But, even if there is a relatively large difference between the scores of the two groups, the psychologist may still be wrong to attribute the difference to his manipulation. Any number of random effects might be influencing his results and introducing error.

Statistics provide the psychologist with a number of ways to determine precisely how likely it is that the difference between the two groups is really significant and that something other than chance produced the results, and how likely it is that he would get the same results if he were to repeat the experiment with a different group of subjects. These probabilities are expressed as measures of **significance.** If the psychologist computes the significance level for his results as .05, he knows that there are 19 chances out of 20 that his results are not due to chance. But there is still 1 chance in 20 (or a .05 likelihood) that his results are due to chance. A .01 significance level would mean that there is only 1 chance in 100 that his results are due to chance.

In any experiment or test or survey using statistical methods, after the characteristics in question have been measured and analyzed statistically, we still face the problem of *interpretation*—in English, not algebra. Many conflicting theories can be offered to explain just about every set of quantitative facts ever gathered. Statistics are a useful and necessary tool, but unfortunately they do not think for us, either before or after we use them.

Glossary

A **absolute refractory period** period just after nerve cell discharge, during which the cell cannot be excited.

absolute threshold the least amount of energy that can produce a sensation 50 percent of the time.

accommodation adjustment of the eye to focus on objects at different distances.

acetylcholine a chemical that transmits nerve impulses across synapses.

achievement test test designed to measure what a person has learned.

activation theory of emotion theory that emotion is a state of general excitation.

activity theory contends that the more active and productive people are in old age, the more satisfied they will be.

addiction strong physical need for a substance, such as some drugs.

adjustment attempts to adapt to the demands of the environment.

adolescence the developmental period between the ages of 12 and 17, marked by dramatic physiological changes and psychological preparation for and adjustment to the challenges of adulthood.

adrenal glands endocrine glands located above the kidneys that secrete epinephrine, norepinephrine, and steroids; these glands affect nerve and muscle function and the ability of the body to react to stress.

adreno-corticotropic hormone (ACTH) pituitary hormone that stimulates the adrenal cortex.

adulthood the stage of development usually beginning in the early twenties and lasting approximately 40 to 45 years in which the individual comes to accept himself and devotes himself mainly to work and family.

aerial perspective a cue to distance perception based on the relative blurriness of objects in the environment.

affective psychosis severe behavior disorder characterized by inappropriate emotional responses, disordered thought, and maladaptive behavior.

afferent neuron neuron that carries messages to the brain or spinal cord from internal organs or sense receptors; also called *sensory neuron*.

affiliation motive need to be with others.

afterimage sense experience that occurs after the stimulus has ceased.

aggression hostile feelings or behavior aimed at doing harm to others.

aldosterone adrenal hormone that regulates the body's sodium-potassium balance and carbohydrate metabolism.

altered states of consciousness (ASCs) any state of awareness that the individual or an observer would recognize as a substantial deviation from normal functioning.

amnesia loss of memory as a result of brain injury or psychological trauma.

amplitude the magnitude of a sound wave; primary determinant of loudness.

ampulla enlarged sac at the base of the semicircular canals in the vestibular organ of the inner ear; sense organ for equilibrium.

anal stage second stage in Freud's theory of personality development, when a child's erotic feelings center on the anus and on elimination.

androgen hormone that promotes and maintains secondary sex characteristics in males; also secreted in small amounts by females.

anxiety feelings resembling fear, but without an identifiable source.

anxiety neurosis behavior disorder characterized by chronic fear or anxiety, sometimes with physical symptoms, but not centered on a specific object.

applied psychology utilizes psychological research in concrete, practical ways to solve, or investigate, social problems.

approach-approach conflict situation in which a person is simultaneously attracted to two incompatible goals.

approach-avoidance conflict situation in which a person is simultaneously attracted to and repelled by the same goal.

aptitude test test designed to measure a person's ability to learn.

archetype in Jung's theory of personality, a thought form common to all men, carried in the collective unconscious.

association area area of the cortex responsible for integrating incoming and outgoing messages; believed to be involved in learning, memory, speech, and thinking.

association neuron small neuron that connects afferent and efferent neurons; also called *interneuron*.

associative thinking relatively undirected forms of thinking, such as daydreaming, dreaming, and creativity.

attachment infantile reactions, like clinging, that gain the mother's attention.

attention focusing of awareness.

attitude beliefs, feelings, and behavior tendencies toward an object.

autistic thinking thinking that consists entirely of personal associations.

autokinetic illusion illusion that a stationary spot of light in a darkened room is moving.

autonomic conditioning learning to voluntarily control involuntary responses.

autonomic nervous system part of the peripheral nervous system that controls the largely involuntary functions of internal muscles and glands.

autonomy a sense of one's own abilities and powers.

avoidance-avoidance conflict situation in which a person is simultaneously repelled by two undesirable possibilities and cannot escape.

avoidance training teaching a learner how to prevent an unpleasant condition.

axon nerve fiber that carries impulses from one cell body to other nerve cells or to a muscle or gland.

axon terminal knob at the end of an axon; also called *synaptic knob*.

B   **basilar membrane** vibrating membrane in the cochlea of the inner ear that contains sense receptors for sound.

basket nerve ending nerve ending wrapped around the base of a hair; receptor for the pressure sense.

behavior chain a sequence in which each event acts as a cue for the next.

behavior genetics a field of psychological study concerned with determining the influence of heredity on behavior.

behavior modification attempts to change people's behavior by operant conditioning used in therapy as well as in schools and businesses.

behaviorism school of psychology devoted to the objective study of behavior.

bimodal distribution concentration of scores at two points on a scale.

Binet-Simon scale original intelligence test designed by Binet to use with children.

binocular parallax slight difference in the position of objects as seen by one eye or the other; seen by both eyes at once, the two images come together.

binocular vision vision through both eyes at once.

biofeedback used in research on autonomic conditioning to let the person measure his own responses.

blind spot small spot in the retina with no light-sensitive cells, where the optic nerve leaves the retina.

brain waves measure of electrical activity of the brain.

brainstem lower part of the brain, an enlargement of the spinal cord.

branching program a type of learning program in which a student is free to follow any of several paths as long as he continues giving correct answers.

brightness constancy perception of brightness as the same, even though the amount of light reaching the retina changes.

C   **Cannon-Bard theory of emotion** theory that the experience of emotion occurs simultaneously with biological changes.

castration complex in Freud's theory of personality development, the child's unconscious fear of losing his genitals.

catatonic schizophrenia type of schizophrenia generally characterized by immobility and unresponsiveness.

categories groupings based on similarities among items.

central nervous system the brain and spinal cord.

central tendency area near the center of a frequency distribution where scores tend to congregate; measures of central tendency are the mean, median, and mode.

cerebellum area of the hindbrain that controls movement, posture, and balance.

cerebral cortex gray matter that forms the outer layer of the cerebrum.

cerebrotonic in Sheldon's theory of personality, a type of temperament characterized by intellectual faculties; usually associated with ectomorphy.

cerebrum largest part of the brain, composed of the two cerebral hemispheres and covered by the cerebral cortex.

character disorder behavior disorder often marked by inability to live within the norms of society.

chemical inhibitory substance chemical at synapses that counteracts the effects of the chemical transmitters.

chemical transmitter substance chemical that carries neural impulses across synapses.

chromosome threadlike body in the cell nucleus that contains genes.

chunking grouping associated bits of material into one unit for processing by memory.

classical conditioning a type of learning in which an organism learns to transfer a response from one stimulus to a previously neutral stimulus.

client-centered therapy nondirective form of treatment for behavior disorders characterized by unconditional positive regard on the part of the therapist.

clinical psychology branch of psychology concerned with diagnosis and treatment of psychological problems.

closure in perception, the tendency to perceive an incomplete stimulus pattern as a whole.

cochlea part of the ear containing fluid that vibrates, which in turn causes the basilar membrane to vibrate.

coding processing of material in short-term memory to fit into the categories in long-term memory.

cognition the process of acquiring, storing, retrieving, and revising knowledge.

cognitive dissonance perceived inconsistency between beliefs or knowledge or between a belief and a behavioral tendency.

cognitive map according to Tolman, a spatial representation, comparable to a road map, of routes to a goal.

cognitive psychology school of psychology devoted to the study of thought processes generally.

cognitive style a person's characteristic way of perceiving and dealing with his environment.

cognitive theory of emotion idea that emotion stems from one's interpretation of a physiological state occurring under specific circumstances.

cognitive theory of learning holds that the result of learning is a bonded conceptual unit that has sufficient boundary strength to resist interference from other conceptual units.

collective unconscious in Jung's theory of personality, the part of the unconscious that is inherited and common to all members of a species.

color an experience combining hue, saturation, and brightness of a visual stimulus.

color blindness partial or total inability to perceive colors.

color mixture presentation of two or more colors at the same time, to find out how the combination is perceived.

common fate in perception, the tendency to see objects moving in the same direction as a whole pattern.

community psychology branch of psychology that attempts to prevent behavior disorders by educating members of a community about mental health and by diagnosing and treating problems early.

comparative psychology the study of the behavior of different animal species, including man.

computer-assisted instruction a more modern version of the teaching machine used as a tool in programmed instruction.

concept an idea that includes objects that share some characteristic.

concrete operations third stage in Piaget's theory of cognitive development (7–11 years), during which the child learns to retrace his thoughts and to look at objects or problems in several different ways.

conditioned response the response an organism learns to produce when a conditioned stimulus is presented.

conditioned stimulus an originally neutral stimulus that is paired with an unconditioned stimulus and eventually produces a response when presented alone.

cones receptor cells in the retina responsible for color vision.

conflict state of tension caused by opposing demands, opportunities, needs, or goals.

conformity behavior in accordance with prevailing standards or the standards of one's group.

conjunctive concept concept that includes only objects that have a feature in common.

conscience standards by which we judge behavior to be right or wrong.

construct validity refers to the ideas on which a test is based; the constructs must be valid for the test to be valid.

continuity in perception, the tendency to perceive objects that continue an established pattern as parts of the whole.

control group group used for comparison with the experimental group.

convergence movement of the eyes to focus light from a single source on the foveas of both eyes.

convergent thinking Guilford's term for thought that aims at finding a single, logical solution.

conversion reaction behavior disorder characterized by bodily symptoms, such as paralysis or blindness, with no organic cause; also called hysterical neurosis.

cornea the transparent protective coating over the front part of the eye through which light enters the eyes.

corpus callosum mass of white matter that connects the hemispheres of the cerebrum to each other and to other parts of the nervous system.

correlation degree of association between variables, reflecting the extent to which one changes when the other does.

correlation coefficient statistical measure of the strength of association between two variables.

corticosterone adrenal hormone that regulates the body's sodium-potassium level and carbohydrate metabolism.

cortisol adrenal hormone that regulates the body's sodium-potassium balance and carbohydrate metabolism.

countertransference a term used to denote a therapist's projecting his own emotions onto the patient.

creativity capacity to discover; a mixture of realistic and imaginative thinking, often resulting in novel solutions.

cretinism mental and physical retardation caused by thyroid deficiency in childhood.

crystallized general ability Cattell's term for a kind of general intelligence employed in applying prior knowledge to new information.

cueing in memory, checking each of a number of categories in turn until one finds the desired information.

culture-fair test intelligence test designed to eliminate cultural bias.

D **dark adaptation** increasing ability to see after being in the dark for a time.

daydreaming a type of autistic thinking, based on one's private thoughts and wishes.

death instincts in Freud's theory of personality, the group of instincts that lead toward destruction and death.

decibel unit of measurement for the loudness of sounds.

defense mechanism technique for avoiding anxiety or awareness of something unpleasant through self-deception.

deindividuation loss or diminution of identity among members of a group.

delta sleep the fourth and deepest stage of sleep, characterized by slow, even brain waves; decreases with age but is always the first sleep to be made up after sleep has been lost.

dendrite short nerve fiber that receives stimuli and conducts them to the cell body.

dependent variable in an experiment, the variable that changes when the independent variable is manipulated.

depression a state of sadness or futility. Neurotic depression is characterized by feelings of helplessness and worthlessness and varying degrees of inactivity. In psychotic depression, these reactions are more extreme.

desensitization behavior therapy technique designed to gradually reduce anxiety about a particular object or situation.

development psychological and physical changes in an organism over time.

developmental norms ages when an average individual is expected to reach the various milestones of development.

developmental psychology study of the psychological and physical changes that take place as a person ages.

diabetes mellitus condition caused by lack of insulin in the body, which results in a too-high blood-sugar level.

dichotic listening simultaneous aural stimulation, whereby separate and different messages are presented to each ear.

dichromat person who can perceive only two of the three primary colors.

difference threshold the difference between two stimuli that is required to produce a just noticeable difference 50 percent of the time.

dimensional concept a type of concept that sees relevant properties as being a continuum.

directed thinking thinking aimed at reaching a certain goal or solving a particular problem.

discrimination distinguishing among many stimuli and responding to only one.

disengagement theory contends that old age is characterized by a decline in an individual's involvement with society.

disjunctive concept concept that includes objects that share one of several possible attributes on an either/or basis.

displacement defense mechanism involving redirection of unrealizable motives to another outlet.

dissociative neurosis behavior disorder characterized by the separating of certain thoughts or experiences from the other parts of the personality.

divergent thinking Guilford's term for a type of thinking characteristic of creativity, aimed at finding several correct answers to a problem.

DNA deoxyribonucleic acid, found in the chromosomes; controls heredity and protein synthesis.

dominant gene a gene that takes precedence over the other gene in a pair in determining inherited characteristics.

dopamine a chemical that transmits nerve impulses across synapses.

Down's syndrome type of mental retardation resulting from extra chromosome-21 material; also called *mongolism*.

drive unlearned physiological motive, such as hunger or thirst.

E   **eardrum** membrane separating the middle ear from the outer ear.

ectomorphic in Sheldon's theory of personality, a body type that is thin and has a large amount of skin surface in relation to body weight.

educational psychology branch of psychology concerned with the application of learning and educational methods.

effector responding organ (muscle or gland).

efferent neuron neuron that conducts impulses from the central nervous system to a muscle or gland.

ego according to Freud, the part of the personality that mediates between environmental demands, conscience, and instinctual needs; now often used as a synonym for "self."

ego ideal part of the superego, consisting of standards of what one would like to be.

eidetic image image of unusual clarity and vividness; a person with eidetic imagery is sometimes said to have a "photographic memory."

Electra complex equivalent in girls of the boy's Oedipal complex; persistent erotic attachment to the father and hostile feelings toward the mother.

electrical stimulation of the brain (ESB) stimulating part of the brain with electrical current to produce "counterfeit" nerve impulses.

electroshock therapy a physical therapy where a mild electrical current is passed through the brain and into a person's nervous system for a short period, often producing convulsions and temporary coma; used to alleviate sudden and severe depression.

elevation in perception, the principle that the higher on the horizontal plane an object is, the farther away it appears; the lower the horizontal plane, the nearer it seems.

emotion a complex, conscious affective experience involving physiological changes and overt behavior.

enactive representation first stage in Bruner's theory of cognitive development, during which the child represents objects and past events in terms of appropriate motor responses.

encapsulated end organ sense receptor in the skin, consisting of a nerve ending enclosed in a shell or capsule.

encounter group therapy group emphasizing sensory experiences and interpersonal communication.

endocrine gland ductless gland that secretes hormones directly into the bloodstream.

endocrine system the internal network of glands that secrete hormones directly into the bloodstream to regulate the activity of other bodily systems.

endomorphic in Sheldon's theory of personality, a body type characterized by a rounded, fat body.

engram chemical or structural change that accompanies learning.

epinephrine adrenal hormone that is released mainly in response to fear and increases heart rate; also called *adrenalin*.

equilibrium ability to stand upright; also, balance of body processes (see **homeostasis**).

equipotentiality in general learning theory, the view that any response an animal is capable of making can be arbitrarily paired with any stimulus or reinforcement with no effect on acquisition or extinction of learning.

escape training teaching a learner how to end an unpleasant condition once it has started.

estrogen hormone that promotes and maintains secondary sex characteristics in females.

estrus cycle female fertility cycle.

eugenics a term referring to the science of improving species through restrictive or selective breeding.

exhibitionism a character disorder in which there is a compulsion to expose one's genitals in inappropriate situations.

existential psychology school of psychology that emphasizes identity, freedom, and responsibility for one's actions.

existential therapy form of psychotherapy designed to enable people to take responsibility for their actions.

experiment controlled condition in which an independent variable is manipulated and changes in a dependent variable are studied.

experimental group in a controlled experiment, the group subjected to a change in an independent variable.

experimental neurosis reactions produced in laboratory animals when they are subjected to certain kinds of stress or conflict.

experimental psychology branch of psychology that studies behavior by means of controlled experiments, most often in a laboratory.

experimenter bias problem that arises when an experimenter's values or expectations influence his interpretation of experimental data.

explanatory concept helps us to understand and predict events and behavior by pointing out relationships between concepts.

external inhibition disappearance of a conditioned response because of a change in a learner's surroundings.

extravert person who usually focuses on social life and the external world instead of his internal experience.

F **face validity** the appearance of validity to the people taking a test.

family therapy a therapeutic approach that sees the family as a unit and as part of the problem in an individual's treatment.

fetishism an attachment to objects that symbolize another person or sex object; considered deviant only when it becomes a substitute for genital sex.

figure-ground two parts of a visual stimulus; the figure is perceived as a unit standing apart from a background.

fixation according to Freud, binding of energy to an unresolved childhood crisis.

fixed-interval schedule reinforcement of a response after a given length of time.

fixed-ratio schedule reinforcement after a specified number of correct responses.

fluid general ability Cattell's term for the kind of general intelligence employed in adapting to new situations.

follicle-stimulating hormone (FSH) pituitary hormone that stimulates production of ova and sperm.

forebrain top part of the brain, including the cerebrum, thalamus, and hypothalamus.

forgetting inability to remember learned material.

formal operations the fourth stage in Piaget's theory of cognitive development (11–15 years), characterized by development of abstract thinking.

fovea area of the retina where cones are concentrated.

fraternal twins two offspring developed from two ova fertilized at the same time; also called *dizygotic twins*.

free association in psychoanalysis, the uninhibited relation of thoughts and fantasies as they occur to the patient.

free nerve endings finely branched nerve endings in the skin that serve as receptors for pressure, pain, and temperature.

free recall the recall of learned material in any order.

frequency in sound, the number of cycles per second; primary determinant of pitch.

frequency distribution the frequency of occurrences at various levels of a variable or variables.

frequency histogram type of bar graph showing frequency distributions.

frequency polygon figure constructed by plotting frequencies and connecting the points representing them.

frequency theory of hearing theory that pitch is determined by receptors in the ear, which fire as rapidly as the frequency of sound waves being received.

frigidity in the female, an inability to experience sexual excitation or orgasm.

frontal lobe large section of the cerebrum, containing the motor projection areas and centers for speech, problem solving, and reasoning.

frustration psychological state resulting when an obstacle prevents one from attaining a goal.

frustration-aggression hypothesis idea that aggression is the product of frustration aroused by the nonfulfillment of other motives.

fugue state type of dissociative neurosis characterized by a relatively long period of amnesia, during which a person may leave home and begin a new, and often radically different, life.

functional disorder behavior disorder for which no organic causes can be found.

functional fixedness the tendency to perceive only a limited number of uses for an object.

functionalism school of psychology that studies the purposes underlying behaviors.

G **gamete** reproductive cell (ovum or sperm).

gate-control theory of pain holds that the pain-signaling system contains a gatelike mechanism that, depending on the level of activity of the sensory fibers, may be open, partially open, or closed, thus affecting the degree to which the receptors can transmit pain messages from injured tissues to the brain.

gene DNA molecule, contained on a chromosome, that determines inheritance of traits.

genetics study of heredity.

genital stage in Freud's theory of personality development, the stage of normal adult sexual behavior.

genotype an organism's underlying genetic make-up.

gestalt pattern or whole.

Gestalt psychology school of psychology stressing patterns or wholes in perception, behavior, and so on.

Gestalt therapy form of therapy, either individual or group, that emphasizes the wholeness of the personality and attempts to reawaken people to their emotions and sensations in the here-and-now.

***g* factor** Spearman's term for general intelligence, a kind of fund of mental energy allowing a person to perform well in many areas.

global dementia amnesia a form of amnesia found among older people, in which the individual becomes consistently absent-minded about the present but can remember the past.

glucagon hormone secreted by the pancreas that regulates blood-sugar level.

glucose simple sugar; main source of body energy.

gonads reproductive glands (testes and ovaries).

gray matter nervous tissue composed of cell bodies and fibers lacking myelin sheaths.

group dynamics study of group structures and processes.

group test intelligence test designed for administration to a group by one examiner.

group therapy form of psychological treatment in which interaction of patients helps to modify the behavior of individual members.

H **habituation** strong psychological need for a substance, without biological addiction.

hallucinogenic drug drug that distorts perception, such as mescaline and LSD.

halo effect tendency for positive ratings on some traits to result in positive ratings on other traits.

hammer, anvil, stirrup the three small bones in the middle ear that, when vibrated from a received sound, hit each other in sequence and carry the vibrations into the inner ear.

hebephrenic schizophrenia form of schizophrenia marked by giggling, childish behavior, delusions, and incomprehensible speech.

hemophilia disorder that prevents the blood from clotting; a sex-linked characteristic that appears only in males.

heredity transmission of traits from parents to offspring through the genes.

heritability extent to which a characteristic is inherited, rather than produced by the environment.

Hertz (Hz) unit of measurement for the frequency of waves (light, sound, and so on); cycles per second.

higher-order conditioning conditioning based on previous learning; a new conditioned stimulus is presented with the original conditioned stimulus, which now serves as an unconditioned stimulus.

hindbrain brain region containing the medulla, pons, and cerebellum.

hippocampus part of the limbic system of the brain that plays a part in memory.

homeostasis the body's tendency to maintain physiological balance.

homosexuality an exclusive preference for sexual relations with people of the same sex; a female homosexual is referred to as a lesbian.

hormone chemical secreted by the endocrine glands that produces physical or psychological changes.

humanistic psychology school of psychology focusing on achieving identity through nonverbal experience and altered states of consciousness.

hunger one of the basic drives; a psychological state produced by lack of food.

Huntington's chorea incurable hereditary disease that appears in adulthood; symptoms include loss of muscle control and mental deterioration.

hypnagogic state state between waking and sleeping that is half dream, half daydream or fantasy.

hypnosis production of a trance state, in which the hypnotized person responds readily to suggestions.

hypochondria an individual's consistent belief that he is sick in the absence of any organic symptoms.

hypoglycemia condition caused by oversecretion of insulin and resulting low blood sugar.

hypothalamus forebrain region that plays a critical role in motivation and emotional responses.

hypothesis idea that is tested experimentally.

hysterical amnesia forgetting brought on by extreme repression of an individual's personal history.

hysterical neurosis behavior disorder characterized by bodily symptoms, such as paralysis or blindness, with no organic cause.

I   **iconic representation** second stage in Bruner's theory of cognitive development (infancy to age 6), during which the child pictures things to himself.

id in Freud's theory of personality, the source of instincts; the unconscious.

identical twins two offspring that develop from a single fertilized ovum; also called *monozygotic twins*.

identification unconsciously taking on the characteristics of another.

identity an individual's intellectual and emotional integration (usually during adolescence), of the various life styles, concepts, examples, and so on, which becomes his unique self-concept.

image recollection or reconstruction of a sense experience, often visual.

imageless thought thinking that occurs without the use of images.

imitation consciously behaving the way another does.

impotence in the male, an inability to have or maintain an erection.

imprinting very rapid learning that occurs upon presentation of a stimulus with specific characteristics.

independent variable variable that is manipulated in an experiment, while all others are held constant.

individual differences characteristics that distinguish one person from another, they appear shortly after birth and are influenced by the combined effects of heredity, prenatal environment, and the circumstances at birth.

industrial psychology branch of psychology concerned with the application of psychological knowledge to problems of industry.

infantile autism a condition occurring in early childhood where an infant, perhaps from birth, does not respond to eye contact, touch, or verbal communication and may often become strongly attached to inanimate objects; a form of childhood schizophrenia.

infantile sexuality in psychoanalytic theory, the idea that very young children have sexual drives.

information processing a research model based on computer technology currently used to study human cognitive processes, including memory and perception.

inhibition in classical conditioning, the process that counters the conditioned response and results in extinction.

innate grammar according to Chomsky, an inborn capacity to structure language.

insight sudden grasp of a situation or problem.

instinct unlearned drive that leads an organism to behave in specific ways; the unlearned behavior itself.

insulin hormone secreted by the pancreas that regulates blood-sugar level.

insulin shock therapy a physical therapy consisting of intramuscular injections of insulin, which lowers the level of blood sugar, producing a brief coma; rarely used today.

intellectualization defense mechanism in which abstract thinking is used as a means of avoiding emotion.

intelligence a general term covering all intellectual abilities, defined in various ways by different investigators.

intelligence quotient (IQ) comparison of a person's chronological age with his mental age, as measured by an intelligence test.

intelligence test test designed to measure scholastic aptitude.

interactionism the prevailing viewpoint of personality psychologists, which states that consistencies in the individual's physical and psychological environments are responsible for consistencies in personality and behavior.

interference decreased learning as a result of other learning.

interference theory of forgetting the theory that we forget things because other knowledge gets in the way; there are two types of interference, proactive and retroactive inhibition.

interstimulus interval time lapse between the presentation of a conditioned stimulus and presentation of an unconditioned stimulus.

interval scale scale with equal differences between the points or values.

introvert person who usually focuses on his own thoughts and feelings instead of the outside world.

involutional psychosis mood disturbances primarily found in middle-aged people, characterized by anxiety, depression, irritability, and the inability to relax or sleep; once thought to be biochemical in nature, now inclined to be viewed as a social problem of middle age.

iodopsin chemical substance in cones, which decomposes in response to light.

iris colored part of the eye.

J   **James-Lange theory of emotion** theory that physical reactions precede experienced emotions.

just noticeable difference (j.n.d.) the smallest change or difference in stimulation that a person can detect.

K   **kinesthesis** feedback from one's body about position or movement.

Klinefelter's syndrome genetic abnormality in which males receive an extra X chromosome; XXY males develop breasts, lack sperm, and are slightly retarded.

L   **language** complex system of signs, composed of letters and sounds that represent concepts, experiences, and objects.

latency stage fourth stage in Freud's theory of personality development, when the child appears to have no interest in sex.

learning the process by which experience or practice results in a relatively permanent change in behavior.

learning set the learning of a specific approach that can be used in solving similar problems.

learning theory model of abnormal behavior suggests that abnormal behavior, like all other behaviors, is a result of learning.

lens transparent part of the eye that focuses light onto the retina.

leveling tendency to minimize real differences between objects or events.

libido according to Freud, instinctual (primarily sexual) energy.

life instincts in Freud's theory of personality, the group of instincts that lead toward construction and integration and away from death.

light adaptation adjustment of the eye to bright light.

limbic system system of nerve cells including parts of the thalamus, the hypothalamus, and parts of the cerebrum; among other things, the limbic system plays a role in memory and emotion.

linear perspective a cue to the estimation of depth and distance based on the fact that two parallel lines seem to converge at the horizon.

linear program a type of programmed instruction in which the material to be learned is organized sequentially.

linguistic relativity hypothesis Whorf's idea that thinking is patterned by the specific language one speaks.

localization division of labor in the brain, with different areas responsible for different functions.

logic use of formal rules of reasoning.

logical error in person perception, inferring from the existence of one trait the presence of other traits presumed to be associated with it.

longitudinal method a type of psychological research used to investigate behavior in a single individual over a long period of time.

long-term memory third level in memory; a relatively permanent and highly organized storage.

luteinizing hormone (LH) pituitary hormone that stimulates the production of androgen (in males) or estrogen (in females).

M **mandala** round figure, found in children's art and folk art the world over, thought by Jung to represent the unity of the self.

mania abnormal state of excitement; a psychosis characterized by agitation.

manic-depressive psychosis psychosis marked by extreme mood cycles, depression alternating with elation.

masochism need to suffer pain.

maternal drive urge to protect and care for one's young.

maturation physical development of an organism as it grows.

mean statistical average calculated by dividing a sum of values by the number of cases.

median a statistical average, a value below which half the cases fall.

medical model of abnormal behavior holds that a person who behaves abnormally is physiologically or psychologically sick; also called the mental illness model.

medulla part of the hindbrain that regulates breathing, heartbeat, and blood pressure.

memory process by which learned material is retained.

memory trace a fragile, highly perishable neural response, produced by sensory experience, which can become an actual change in the nervous system if it is repeated often enough.

mesomorphic according to Sheldon, a body type with well-developed bones and muscles.

metabolism chemical conversion of food into energy in the body.

midbrain region of the brain above the pons and cerebellum that is important in vision, hearing, and other responses.

Minnesota Multiphasic Personality Inventory (MMPI) objective personality test orginally used for psychiatric diagnosis.

mnemonics techniques to make material easier to remember.

mode statistical average that represents the value having the largest number of cases.

monochromat person who can perceive only one of the three primary colors.

monocular vision vision through one eye.

morpheme a combination of sound units (phonemes) to make the smallest unit of meaning in a language.

motivation something that propels action, originating from within the person who acts.

motive a specific instance of motivation, such as hunger, thirst, achievement, and so on.

motor nerve bundle of efferent neurons that carries messages from the central nervous system to the muscles and glands.

motor projection area area of the cortex where messages to the muscles and glands originate.

multiple personality a form of dissociative neurosis involving amnesia combined with the fugue state in which an individual's personality is split into two or more distinct personalities.

myelin sheath fatty covering found on some axons.

N **nAch** need for achievement; general motive to succeed and gain excellence for its own sake.

naturalistic observation a research method for the systematic study of animal or human behavior in natural settings, rather than under laboratory or artificially imposed conditions.

need state of deprivation or tension caused by a lack of something necessary to survival or comfort.

negative reinforcement reducing or terminating a stimulus that is unpleasant for the learner.

negative transfer process wherein learning one task makes it harder to learn another.

negative transference displacement of hostility felt for a parent or other authority figure to one's therapist.

nerve bundle of nerve fibers or axons.

nervous system the brain, spinal cord, and all the nerves throughout the body.

neural impulse electrochemical discharge of a nerve cell.

neuron individual nerve cell.

neurosis functional disorder, less severe than psychosis.

nominal scale a set of categories for classifying objects.

norepinephrine adrenal hormone, released mainly in states of anger, that raises blood pressure; also acts as a transmitter of nerve impulses across synapses; also called *noradrenalin*.

norm standard against which individual scores are measured.

normal curve symmetrical, bell-shaped distribution curve that reflects the natural occurrence of many events.

NREM sleep non-rapid eye movement sleep; the first four stages of sleep, which alternate with REM sleep during the sleep cycle.

O **object constancy** in perception, the tendency for objects to look the same despite changes in position, lighting, and other conditions.

objective test personality test that can be scored in a routine fashion, thereby eliminating bias on the part of the scorer.

observational learning a major emphasis of social learning theory that states that we are able to learn by watching other people's behavior.

obsessive-compulsive neurosis behavior disorder characterized by ritualistic behavior (compulsions) and persistent unpleasant thoughts (obsessions).

occipital lobe region at back of the cortex, where visual projection areas are located.

Oedipal complex according to Freud, the boy's persistent sexual attachment to his mother and jealousy toward his father.

old age the last stage of human development marked by a physiological decline as well as psychosocial readjustments.

olfactory bulb smell center in the cerebrum.

olfactory epithelium nasal membranes containing receptor cells sensitive to odors.

operant conditioning type of learning in which desired voluntary behavior is rewarded and incorrect responses are ignored or punished.

opponent-process theory theory of color vision that holds that three sets of cones respond in an either/or fashion to each of three primary color pairs.

optic chiasma crossing point of optic nerves from the retina, near the base of the brain.

oral stage first stage in Freud's theory of personality development, in which the infant's erotic feelings center on feeding and the mouth.

ordinal scale scale indicating order or relative position of items, thus permitting ranking.

organ of Corti spiral structure in the cochlea that contains the receptor cells for hearing.

organic amnesia memory loss caused by physiological factors such as disease, injury, alcoholism, nutritional deficiencies, or brain damage.

organic disorder behavior disorder attributable to disease or malfunction of body tissues.

organic model of abnormal behavior the theory that abnormal behavior has a biochemical or physiological basis; particularly related to research on schizophrenia and depression.

otoliths small crystals in the vestibular organ of the inner ear that activate receptor cells to send messages about balance and head position.

oval window membrane across the opening between the middle ear and inner ear that conducts vibrations to the cochlea.

ovaries female sex glands that produce egg cells and sex hormones.

overlearning extra practice after learning has produced one successful performance.

overtones partial tones that combine with a fundamental tone to produce a compound tone; primary determinant of timbre.

ovum female gamete, or sex cell.

oxytocin hormone secreted by the posterior pituitary that signals the uterus to start contractions during childbirth and the mammary glands to produce milk.

P **pancreas** gland located near the stomach that helps in digesting proteins and also regulates blood-sugar level by secreting the hormones insulin and glucagon.

paranoid schizophrenia common type of schizophrenia, in which personality is dominated by hostility and delusions of persecution or grandeur.

parasympathetic division branch of the autonomic nervous system that leads to relaxation of internal organs and muscles after stress.

parathormone hormone secreted by the parathyroid glands that regulates the body's calcium-phosphorus ratio.

parathyroid glands endocrine glands located on the thyroid gland that secrete parathormone.

parietal lobe region of the cerebrum behind the central fissure, controlling discrimination learning.

pedophilia a disorder characterized by desire for sexual relations with children.

peer group one's associates, by whom one is treated as an equal.

penis envy according to Freud, the female's unconscious desire to have a penis, expressed in adulthood as desire to achieve or have a child.

perception the process of creating meaningful patterns from jumbled sensory stimuli.

perceptual set suggestions or preconceived ideas or expectations that can affect perception.

performance test intelligence test that does not involve words.

peripheral nervous system any nerves not contained in the brain or spinal cord.

personal unconscious according to Jung, one of the two levels of the unconscious; the personal unconscious contains the individual's repressed thoughts, forgotten experiences, and undeveloped ideas.

personality a person's own characteristic pattern of behavior, emotions, motives, thoughts, and attitudes.

phallic stage third stage in Freud's theory of personality development, when the child is strongly interested in the genitals.

phenotype an organism's measurable characteristics.

phi phenomenon illusory movement caused by flashing lights in sequence.

phobia intense or morbid fear of, for example, enclosed spaces, animals, high places.

phoneme simplest unit of language, a basic speech sound.

phrenology study of head measurements, in an attempt to link head shape to intelligence and other attributes.

physical treatment a therapeutic approach that includes such methods as electric shock therapy, insulin shock treatment, psychosurgery, drug therapy, and physical restraint.

physiological motive motive stemming from a bodily need, for example, thirst; also called *primary drive.*

physiological psychology branch of psychology concerned with the relationship between physiological states and behavior.

pitch auditory experience corresponding to frequency of sound vibrations, resulting in a higher or lower tone.

pituitary gland endocrine gland located near the hypothalamus that regulates growth; often called the "master gland" because it controls a wide range of behavior by activating other endocrine glands.

place theory of hearing theory that different places on the basilar membrane vibrate in response to sounds of different frequencies.

pleasure principle according to Freud, the idea that human behavior is dominated by seeking gratification of instinctual needs.

polarization the condition of a neuron before it fires, when positive ions are on the outside and negative ions are on the inside of the cell membrane.

polygenic inheritance determination of a single trait by the interaction of several genes.

pons hindbrain nerve center connecting the cerebellum to the cortex; helps regulate breathing and produces rapid eye movements during sleep.

positive reinforcement following an action or response with something that is pleasant for the learner.

positive transfer process in which skills learned in one task make another task easier to learn.

positive transference development of warm feelings toward one's therapist.

predictive validity the degree to which a test can correctly measure an individual's potential ability in a specific area.

prefrontal lobotomy an early psychosurgical technique whereby the nerves connecting the thalamus and the frontal areas of the cortex are severed; tension, anxiety, and emotional activity are decreased, but there are generally unpleasant side effects such as deterioration of intellectual ability and diminished self-control.

prejudice an attitude composed of stereotyped beliefs, hostile feelings, and a tendency to behave in discriminatory ways.

preoperational thought second stage in Piaget's theory in cognitive development (2–7 years), when the child develops systematic methods for representing the world internally.

preparedness the view of comparative psychology that holds that, because of the unique biological and evolutionary history of its species, an animal may be more prepared to learn some responses than others.

pressure a form of psychological stress in which an individual feels that he must live up to a particular standard of behavior or adapt to rapid change.

primacy effect the principle that the first items in a series tend to be remembered better than later items.

primary drive a physiologically based drive, for example, the hunger drive.

primary mental abilities according to Thurstone, independent basic abilities that underlie any intelligent activity: spatial ability, perceptual speed, numerical ability, verbal meaning, memory, word fluency, and reasoning.

primary process thinking in Freud's theory of personality, the process by which the id achieves immediate satisfaction of an instinct, either through conscious activity or through wish fulfillment.

primary reinforcer reinforcer that is rewarding in itself, such as food, water, sex, and termination of pain.

proactive inhibition process in which previous learning interferes with memory of new learning.

probability statistical likelihood that something will occur.

progestin sex hormone that prepares the female's body for pregnancy, nursing, and childbirth.

programmed instruction an application of learning principles to education; the material to be learned is broken down into frames, composed of statements and questions; the student goes through the program a frame at a time and receives feedback by finding out immediately whether or not his answer is correct.

projection defense mechanism characterized by attributing one's own wishes and feelings to others.

projective test unstructured personality test not limiting the response to be given, such as the Rorschach inkblot test and the Thematic Apperception Test (TAT).

prolactin pituitary hormone that stimulates milk production and secretion of progesterone.

proximity in perception, grouping of separate stimuli that are near to one another and perceiving them as a whole.

psychiatrist a medical doctor trained in psychotherapeutic techniques.

psychoanalysis therapeutic technique created by Freud, based on uncovering people's unconscious motives.

psychoanalytic model of abnormal behavior a Freudian theory that behavior disorders are symbolic expressions of internal, unconscious conflicts, usually originating in infancy and childhood.

psycholinguistics discipline combining psychology and linguistics, devoted to studying the connections between language and thought.

psychopharmacology study of the effects of drugs on behavior.

psychophysics study of the attributes of physical stimuli and the sensations they produce.

psychosexual stages Freud's theory of developmental stages characterized by the place where erotic feelings are centered.

psychosis a severe mental disorder.

psychosocial stages eight stages in Erikson's theory of personality development, from the infant's basic trust (or mistrust) to the old person's integrity (or despair).

psychosomatic illness a physical disorder having an emotional origin.

psychosurgery brain surgery designed to change behavior based on the assumption that psychological functions are localized in specific areas in the brain.

psychotherapist person usually holding a doctorate in psychology, who treats people with behavior disorders.

psychotherapy a general term referring to the use of psychological techniques to treat behavior disorders.

punishment an unpleasant stimulus that can inhibit an undesirable response.

pupil opening in the iris through which light enters the eye.

pure research research for its own sake usually growing out of a theory or other research and rarely conducted to solve practical social problems.

R **random sample** sample chosen in such a way that each potential subject has an equal chance of being selected.

range distance between the lowest and highest scores in a distribution.

ratio scale scale that has a true zero.

rational therapy a therapeutic approach based on the idea that an individual's problems have been caused by his misinterpretations of events and goals.

reaction formation defense mechanism characterized by development of behavior exactly opposite to unconscious wishes.

reality principle according to Freud, action of the ego in mediating between the demands of the environment and the demands of the id.

reality therapy a therapeutic approach that attempts to help the individual to develop more responsible behavior.

reasoning logical thinking, including ability to perceive symbolic relationships.

recall measure of retention in which a person reproduces or reconstructs learned material.

recency effect principle that items at the end of a series will be remembered better than those that come earlier.

receptor specialized cell that responds to stimuli.

recessive gene gene whose hereditary potential is not expressed when it is paired with a dominant gene.

reciprocal inhibition behavior therapy technique that aims at eliminating maladaptive behaviors by teaching the person to associate them with painful or unpleasant thoughts.

recoding a term used in information processing to describe the cataloging of information into chunks or codes for short- or long-term storage in memory.

recognition measure of retention in which a person identifies learned material when presented with it.

reference group a group with which a person identifies or compares himself.

reflex involuntary, unlearned, immediate response to a stimulus.

regression returning to the habit patterns and desires of childhood or infancy.

rehearsal process of repetition in short-term memory that results in material's being transferred into long-term memory.

reinforcement strengthening a response, making it more likely to recur; in classical conditioning refers to the unconditioned stimulus.

relational concept concept based on a characteristic that is relative, such as "fullness" or "east."

relative refractory period period after nerve cell discharge when the cell will not discharge again without a stronger than normal stimulus.

relearning learning a previously learned task under the same conditions; the savings in time is a measure of retention.

reliability ability of a test to produce similar scores for an individual on separate occasions.

REM sleep rapid eye movement sleep, characterized by saw-toothed brain wave activity, greater muscle relaxation, and a rapid movement of the eyes; REM sleep alternates with NREM sleep during the sleep cycle and is the period of sleep during which most dreams occur.

repression defense mechanism that involves excluding uncomfortable thoughts and feelings from consciousness.

response any behavior of an organism that can be identified and measured.

response generalization giving a response that is slightly different from the response originally learned to the stimulus.

retention storage of material in memory.

reticular activating system bundle of nerve fibers running through the hindbrain and midbrain to the hypothalamus; responsible for general arousal of the organism.

retina layer of the eye containing receptor cells that are sensitive to light.

retinal disparity the difference between the images cast on the two retinas when both eyes are focused on the same object.

retrieval recovery of memories.

retroactive inhibition interference with memory of previous learning by more recent learning.

retrograde amnesia inability to recall events that took place immediately before a critical event, even though there is no loss of earlier or later memory.

reversible figure in perceptual organization, when the figure and ground of a pattern do not have enough contrast, or cues, to be readily perceived and distinguished.

reward positive or negative reinforcer.

rhodopsin chemical substance in rods, which decomposes in response to light.

risky shift greater willingness to take decision-making risks in a group than as an individual.

RNA ribonucleic acid, a molecule manufactured by DNA that plays a role in protein production and possibly in memory.

rods retinal cells responsible for night vision and not specialized to receive color.

role expected behavior for a person occupying a certain position.

role-playing conscious assuming of role behavior, often used as a therapeutic technique.

rooting behavior reflex movements a newborn baby makes when its cheek is touched, including head turning and attempts to suck.

Rorschach Test a projective test composed of ambiguous inkblots; the way a person interprets the blots will reveal his unconscious thoughts.

round window membrane between the middle ear and inner ear that absorbs the changes in pressure when sound vibrations reach the oval window above it.

S **saccule** small sac at the base of the semicircular canals in the vestibular organ of the inner ear; sense organ for equilibrium.

sadism need to inflict mental or physical pain on someone else.

sampling selecting part of a population to use in an experiment.

savings the difference between the number of trials needed to learn something originally and the number needed to relearn it; a measure of retention.

scapegoat person or group chosen as an object of displaced aggression.

scatter plot diagram showing the association between scores on two variables.

schedule of reinforcement program for choosing which responses to reinforce.

schemata Piaget's term for the frameworks one uses to organize experience, which change as one develops.

schizophrenia psychosis involving withdrawal from reality, lack of emotion, and other disturbances.

scientific method formulation and experimental testing of hypotheses about natural events and relationships.

secondary process thinking in Freud's theory of personality, activity within the limits of objective reality.

secondary reinforcer reinforcer whose value is learned through association with primary reinforcers.

secondary sex characteristics sex differences such as facial hair in men, not directly involved in reproduction.

self-actualization the highest motive in Maslow's hierarchy; the motive to realize one's potential.

self-reinforcement in social learning theory, the view that personal assessment such as pride or guilt can affect an individual's behavior.

semantics study of meaning in a language, both its structure and its inflection.

semicircular canals bony structures in the inner ear, important to the sense of equilibrium.

senile psychosis pyschotic symptoms caused by changes in the brain as a result of age.

sensation awareness of sense stimulation.

sense organ specialized organ receptive to sensory stimuli.

sensitivity group group that meets over a period of time to share feelings and help members gain insight into their own emotional reactions.

sensory adaptation changes in the responsiveness of receptors that result either in increased sensitivity (when the level of stimulation is consistently low) or reduced sensitivity (when the level of stimulation is consistently high).

sensory coding a process that occurs during transduction in which the initially diffuse neural impulse received from a sensory receptor is coded so that when the message is received by the brain it is precise and detailed.

sensory deprivation total or near-total removal of normal sensory stimuli.

sensory gating process by which only selected sensory messages reach the higher brain centers.

sensory-motor stage first stage in Piaget's theory of cognitive development (birth–2 years) when a child learns to organize his perceptions and to explore and experiment with objects.

sensory nerve bundle of afferent neurons that carries messages from the sense organs to the central nervous system.

sensory projection area cerebral cortex area where messages from the sense organs register.

sensory store first level in memory; processes information from the senses.

serial recall the recall of learned material in a specific order, most often in the order in which it was learned.

serotonin a chemical that transmits neural impulses across synapses.

set readiness to react in a certain way to a problem or situation or to perceive a situation in a certain way; as applied to altered states of consciousness, the expectations and feelings the person brings with him to the experience.

setting in drug-induced experiences, the physical, social, and emotional atmosphere in which the drug is taken.

sex chromosomes X and Y chromosomes, the twenty-third chromosome pair in humans, containing genes that determine sex.

sex drive primary drive that gives rise to reproductive behavior.

sex hormones hormones, such as androgen in males and estrogen in females, that produce, maintain, and regulate sexual characteristics and behaviors.

sex-linked characteristics inherited characteristics carried by the X or Y chromosomes.

sex role learned behavior appropriate to one's sex.

s **factors** Spearman's term for different manifestations of general intelligence in specific activities.

shape constancy tendency to see an object as the same shape no matter what angle it is seen from.

shaping teaching complex behavior by rewarding each successive approximation to the behavior and building up to a complete response.

sharpening tendency to maximize the differences between events or objects.

shock therapy electrical shocks to the brain, used in the treatment of mental illness.

short-term memory second level of memory; can retain information for a brief period of time after which it is either discarded or transferred to long-term memory.

significance probability that a statistic would not occur by chance.

simple schizophrenia type of schizophrenia characterized by withdrawal from the world and other people.

singular concept involves the understanding of a single object or event, including all the associations we have with it.

situationism a perspective on personality theory that holds it is the particular situation, not the internal personality variables, which determines behavior.

size constancy perception of an object as the same size regardless of the distance from which it is viewed.

skewed distribution frequency curve with the greatest concentration of scores toward one end.

Skinner box box equipped with a bar, in which an animal is placed during operant conditioning; pressing the bar releases food, which reinforces the bar-pressing behavior.

social comparison tendency to compare oneself with others, especially when one is uncertain or uneasy about one's attitudes or performance.

social facilitation effects on an individual's behavior due to the presence of other people.

social learning theory a learning theory that combines elements of traditional operant conditioning and cognitive theory, with particular emphasis placed on observational learning.

social motive learned motive associated with relationships among people, such as affiliation, achievement, and so on.

social psychology branch of psychology that studies interpersonal relations and behavior of individuals in groups.

socialization process by which a child learns the behavior appropriate to his family and culture.

sociopath person who suffers from any of a broad range of disorders in his relationship with the society in which he lives, such as a failure to internalize moral values.

somatic nervous system part of the peripheral nervous system that carries sensory information to the central nervous system and information from the central nervous system to the muscles and glands.

somatotonic in Sheldon's theory of personality, a type of temperament characterized by vigorous muscular activity and usually associated with mesomorphy.

somatotropic hormone (STH) growth hormone secreted by the anterior pituitary.

somnambulism sleepwalking; also any other complex activities performed while in a sleeplike state; often associated with dissociative neurosis.

specific hunger desire for certain foods (as opposed to hunger drive in general).

specific theory of pain the theory that states that an individual is expected to feel pain at the precise point of injury and that the pain receptors have a one-to-one signaling relationship to the brain.

spectrum full range of light waves of varying lengths; when refracted through a prism, these show up as colors.

sperm male gamete contained in semen.

spinal cord bundle of nerve fibers running through the spinal column, connecting the brain to the rest of the nervous system.

split-half reliability a method of determining test reliability by comparing a person's scores on odd-numbered items with his scores on the even-numbered items of the same test.

spontaneous recovery reappearance of an extinguished response after the passage of time, without further training.

S-R psychology school of psychology based on the stimulus-response relationship and theories of learning.

standard deviation statistical measure of variability in a group of scores or other values.

standardization administration of a test to a group representative of the people for whom the test is designed, to establish norms.

standardization group group to whom a test is given for the purpose of establishing norms.

statistics use of numbers to represent data and numerical treatment of these values.

stereoscopic vision the coalescence of two retinal images to achieve more accuracy in depth and distance perception; possible only for animals whose eyes are set in front of their heads.

stereotypes beliefs presumed to apply to all members of a given group.

stimulus an event that produces a response.

stimulus generalization reaction to a stimulus with the same response one has learned to give to another, similar stimulus.

stress physical or psychological threat to an organism or system and the reaction to that threat.

stroboscopic motion illusory movement that results from flashing a series of still pictures in rapid succession.

structuralism school of psychology emphasizing the basic units of experiences and their combination.

structured interview a technique of personal interview in which the interviewer follows a predetermined plan of questioning.

subject person or animal studied in an experiment.

sublimation defense mechanism characterized by the redirection of sexual energy (libido) into socially acceptable channels.

superego according to Freud, the part of the psyche that represents the social and parental standards the individual has internalized (the conscience) and the ego-ideal.

syllogism in logic, a sequence of sentences in which a major premise and a minor premise lead to a conclusion.

symbolic reinforcement in social learning theory, the view that reinforcement, such as attention or approval, can affect an individual's behavior, and that this reinforcement is distinct from secondary reinforcement.

symbolic representation third stage in Bruner's theory of cognitive development, during which the child gains the ability to picture or represent rules to himself and to use symbols in an abstract way.

sympathetic division branch of the autonomic nervous system that arouses the body in stress reactions.

synapse area where an axon of one nerve cell meets a dendrite of another.

synaptic vesicles tiny sacs on an axon terminal, which release a chemical that crosses the area between two neurons and may cause the second to fire.

synesthesia form of imagery in which a person experiences one sense in terms of another.

syntax study of grammar, or the rules for combining words and morphemes into phrases and sentences.

T **taste buds** structures on the tongue that contain the receptor cells for taste.

temporal lobe an association area in the cerebral cortex.

testes male sex glands, which produce sperm and sex hormones.

testosterone hormone that promotes and maintains secondary sex characteristics in males; one of the androgens.

test-retest reliability a method of determining the reliability of a test by giving the same test to the same subject twice, with a short interval in between.

texture gradient appearance of increasing smoothness as an object is seen at greater and greater distances.

thalamus part of the forebrain that relays impulses from sense receptors, regulates electrical activity in the brain, and controls autonomic reactions.

Thematic Apperception Test (TAT) a projective test composed of ambiguous pictures; the stories a person writes about the pictures will reveal his unconscious thoughts and motives.

thirst state caused by a lack of water; a primary drive.

threshold level of stimulus intensity required for a neuron to fire or a receptor cell to respond (see also **absolute threshold** and **difference threshold**).

thyroid gland endocrine gland located below the larynx that secretes thyroxin, which controls metabolism.

thyrotropic hormone (TTH) pituitary hormone that activates the thyroid gland.

thyroxin hormone secreted by the thyroid gland; regulates metabolism.

timbre tone quality, produced by a sound's overtones.

token economy therapeutic technique used in some institutions, schools, and businesses to encourage changes in behavior; people are reinforced for adaptive behavior by being given tokens, which may be exchanged for privileges or something they want.

trace decay theory of forgetting states that unless the memory trace is strengthened through repetition and practice, it will fade; applies only to forgetting of material in short-term memory.

trait in genetics, any physical characteristic that can be observed; in personality, a measurable characteristic.

transactional analysis a technique of group therapy that aims at understanding people by studying communication between two or more persons.

transduction conversion of stimulus energy into a neural impulse.

transfer of learning process in which the learning of one skill affects the ability to learn another, either positively or negatively.

traveling wave theory of hearing a recent version of the place theory of hearing, which holds that sound waves traveling through the cochlear fluid of the ear move the different places on the basilar membrane in direct proportion to the pitch of the sound wave.

trichromat person who is able to detect all three primary colors and thus has normal color vision.

trichromatic theory theory of color vision that holds that all color perception is a combination of three basic hues.

Turner's syndrome genetic abnormality in which females inherit only 45 chromosomes; causes retarded sexual development.

U **unconditioned response** the reaction that takes place whenever an unconditioned stimulus occurs.

unconditioned stimulus a stimulus that invariably causes an organism to react in a specific way.

unconscious in Freud's theory, all the ideas, thoughts, and feelings of which we are not aware.

unstructured interview a technique of personal interview that allows the interviewer freedom to develop the conversation along any lines.

utricle one of two sacs in the inner ear, source of information about balance and stationary posture.

V **validity** ability of a test to measure what it sets out to measure.

variable aspect of a person, environment, or object that can be changed or held constant in an experiment.

variable-interval schedule reinforcement schedule in which the first correct response after various lengths of time is reinforced.

variable-ratio schedule reinforcement schedule in which a varying number of correct responses must occur before reinforcement is presented.

variation extent of differences among scores in a sample.

vasopressin hormone secreted by the posterior pituitary that helps prevent dehydration of nerve cells by controlling kidney functions.

verbal ability skill in using language; one of the basic abilities measured by most intelligence tests.

vestibular organ structure in the inner ear that is the sense organ for equilibrium, the vestibular sense.

vestibular sense sense of equilibrium; source of information about the position of the body in relation to gravity.

vicarious reinforcement in social learning theory, the view that seeing others rewarded or punished can encourage an individual to change his behavior.

viscerotonic in Sheldon's theory of personality, a type of temperament characterized by sociability and love of comfort.

visible light the small part of the spectrum of electromagnetic energy to which the human eye is sensitive.

visual acuity the ability to distinguish fine details and spatial separations.

volley principle theory that receptors in the ear respond in volley, with one group responding, then a second, then a third, and so on, so that the complete pattern of firing corresponds to the frequency of the sound wave.

voyeurism watching others engage in sexual activities or spying on nude people; considered deviant only when it takes the place of genital sex.

W **Weber's law** mathematical expression of the relationship between the intensity of an original stimulus and the amount of change required before a difference can be detected.

white matter nervous tissue composed of axons with myelin sheaths.

whole-part perception seeing a picture either as a whole, or as a group of parts; young children tend to see wholes and ignore parts.

X **X chromosome** X-shaped sex chromosome; males have one, females two.

Y **Y chromosome** Y-shaped sex chromosome, found only in males.

Z **Zeigarnik effect** name given to the observation that an interrupted task is usually remembered better than a task that is completed.

zygote a fertilized ovum.

References

Abelson, R. B., & Zimbardo, P. G. *Canvassing for peace.* Ann Arbor, Mich.: Society for the Study of Social Issues, 1970.

Adorno, T. W., et al. *The authoritarian personality.* New York: Harper & Row, 1950.

Allport, G. W. *Personality: A psychological interpretation.* New York: Holt, Rinehart & Winston, 1937.

Allport, G. W. *Becoming: Basic considerations for a psychology of personality.* New Haven, Conn.: Yale University Press, 1955.

Allport, G. W. *Pattern and growth in personality.* New York: Holt, Rinehart & Winston, 1961.

Allport, G. W. Traits revisited. *American Psychologist,* 1966, *21,* 1-10.

Allport, G. W., & Odbert. H. S. Trait-names: A psycholexical study. *Psychological Monographs,* 1936, *47* (1, Whole No. 211).

Allport, G. W., Vernon, P. E., & Lindzey, G. *A study of values.* Boston: Houghton Mifflin, 1960.

American Psychological Association. *Ethical Standards of Psychologists.* Washington, D.C.: Author, 1953.

Amoore, J. E., Johnston, J. W., Jr., & Rubin, M. The stereochemical theory of odor. *Scientific American,* February 1964, 42-49.

Argyris, C. Dangers in applying results from experimental social psychology. *American Psychologist,* April 1975, 469-485.

Arnold, M. B. *Emotion and personality* (2 vols.). New York: Columbia University Press, 1960.

Aronfreed, J. *Conduct and consciousness: The socialization of internalized control over behavior.* New York: Academic Press, 1968.

Aronson, E., Turner, J., & Carlsmith, J. M. Communicator credibility and communication discrepancy. *Journal of Abnormal and Social Psychology,* 1963, *67,* 31-36.

Asch, S. E. Forming impressions of personality. *Journal of Abnormal and Social Psychology,* 1946, *41,* 258-290.

Asch, S. E. Effects of group pressure upon the modification and distortion of judgments. In H. Guetzkow (Ed.), *Groups, leadership and men.* Pittsburgh: Carnegie Press, 1951. Pp. 177-190.

Ashmore, R. D., & McConahay, J. *Psychology and America's urban dilemmas.* New York: McGraw-Hill, 1975.

Ayllon T., & Azrin, N. *The token economy: A motivational system for therapy and rehabilitation.* New York: Appleton-Century-Crofts, 1968.

Bahrick, H. P., Bahrick, P. O., & Wittlinger, R. P. Those unforgettable highschool days. *Psychology Today,* December 1974, pp. 50-56.

Balagura, S. *Hunger: A biopsychological analysis.* New York: Basic Books, 1973.

Baltes, P. B., & Schaie, K. W. The myth of the twilight years. *Psychology Today,* March 1973, pp. 35-40.

Bandura, A. Social learning through imitation. In M. R. Jones (Ed.), *Nebraska Symposium on Motivation.* Lincoln: University of Nebraska Press, 1962. Pp. 211-269.

Bandura, A. *Aggression: A social learning analysis.* Englewood Cliffs, N.J.: Prentice-Hall, 1973.

Bandura, A., Ross, D., & Ross, S. A. Imitation of film-mediated aggressive models. *Journal of Abnormal and Social Psychology,* 1963, *66,* 3-11.

Barr, N. I. The responsible world of reality therapy. *Psychology Today,* February 1974, pp. 64-68.

Barron, F. *Creativity and psychological health.* Princeton, N.J.: Van Nostrand, 1963.

Barron, F., Jarvik, M., & Bunnell, S., Jr. The hallucinogenic drugs. *Scientific American,* April 1964.

Barthell, C. N., & Holmes, D. S. High school yearbooks: A nonreactive measure of social isolation in graduates who later became schizophrenic. *Journal of Abnormal and Social Psychology,* 1968, *73,* 313-316.

Bartlett, F. C. *Remembering: A study in experimental and social psychology.* Cambridge: University Press, 1932.

Bass, B. M. The substance and the shadow. *American Psychologist,* December 1974, 870-876.

Bastock, M. A gene mutation which changes a behavior pattern. *Evolution,* 1956, *10,* 421-439.

Baur, S. First message from the planet of the apes. *New York,* February 24, 1975, pp. 30-37.

Baxter, D. W., & Olszewski, J. Congenital insensitivity to pain. *Brain,* 1960, *83,* 381.

Beauvoir, Simone de. *The coming of age* (Patrick O'Brian, trans.) New York: Putnam's, 1972.

Beier, E. G. Nonverbal communication: How we send emotional messages. *Psychology Today,* October 1974, pp. 53-56.

Beier, E. G., Robinson, P., & Micheletti, G. Susanville: A community helps itself in mobilization of community resources for self-help in mental health. *Journal of Consulting and Clinical Psychology,* 1971, *36,* 142-150.

Békésy, G. von. The ear. *Scientific American,* August 1957, 66-78.

Bell, R. Q. A reinterpretation of the direction of efforts in studies of socialization. *Psychological Review,* 1968, *75,* 81–95.

Belmont, L. & Marolla, F. A. Birth order, family size, and intelligence. *Science,* December 14, 1973, *182* (4117), 1096–1101.

Beloff, H. The structure and origin of the anal character. *Genetic Psychology Monographs,* 1957, *55,* 141–172.

Berkowitz, L. The case for bottling up rage. *Psychology Today,* July 1973, pp. 24–32.

Berne, E. Ego states in psychotherapy. *American Journal of Psychotherapy,* 1957, *11,* 293–309.

Berne, E. *Games people play.* New York: Grove Press, 1964.

Berne, E. *Principles of group treatment.* New York: Grove Press, 1968.

Berscheid, E., et al. Physical attractiveness and dating choice: A test of the matching hypothesis. *Journal of Experimental Social Psychology,* March 1971, *7* (2), 173–189.

Berscheid, E., & Walster, E. Beauty and the beast. *Psychology Today,* March 1972, pp. 42–46; 72.

Bettelheim, B. Individual and mass behavior in extreme situations. *Journal of Abnormal and Social Psychology,* 1943, *38,* 417–452.

Bettelheim, B. *The informed heart.* New York: Free Press, 1960.

Bexton, W. H., Heron, W., & Scott, T. H. Effects of decreased variation in the sensory environment. *Canadian Journal of Psychology,* 1954, *8,* 70–76.

Bickman, L. Social roles and uniforms: Clothes make the person. *Psychology Today,* April 1974, pp. 49–51.

Bieber, I., et al. *Homosexuality: A psychoanalytic study.* New York: Basic Books, 1962.

Birdwhistell, R. L. *Introduction to kinesics.* Louisville, Ky.: University of Louisville Press, 1952.

Birdwhistell, R. L. Toward analyzing American movement. In S. Weitz (Ed.), *Nonverbal communication: Readings with commentary.* New York: Oxford University Press, 1974. Pp. 134–143.

Blodgett, H. S. The effect of the introduction of reward upon the maze performance of rats. *University of California Publications in Psychology,* 1929, *4,* 117.

Botwinick, J. *Cognitive processes in maturity and old age.* New York: Springer, 1967.

Bouchard, T. J., Jr. Current conceptions of intelligence and their implications for assessment. In P. McReynolds (Ed.), *Advances in psychological assessment* (Vol. I). Palo Alto, Calif.: Science and Behavior Books, 1968. Pp. 14–33.

Bower, G. H. How to . . . un . . . remember. *Psychology Today,* October 1973. pp. 63–70.

Bower, T. G. R. The object in the world of the infant. *Scientific American,* October 1971, 30–38.

Brady, J. V., et al. Avoidance behavior and the development of gastroduodenal ulcers. *Journal of the Experimental Analysis of Behavior,* 1958, *1,* 69–72.

Bramel, D. A dissonance theory approach to defensive projection. *Journal of Abnormal and Social Psychology,* 1962, *64,* 121–129.

Breland, K., & Breland, M. The misbehavior of organisms. In M. E. P. Seligman & J. L. Hager, *Biological boundaries of learning.* Englewood Cliffs, N.J.: Prentice-Hall, 1972. Pp. 181–186.

Brener, J., Kleinman, R. A. & Goesling, W. J. The effects of different exposures to augmented sensory feedback on the control of heart rate. *Psychophysiology,* 1969, *5,* 510–516.

Brickman, P. (Ed.). *Social conflict.* New York: Heath, 1974.

Bridges, K. M. B. Emotional development in early infancy. *Child Development,* 1932, *3,* 324–334; 340.

Brody, N. *Personality: Research and theory.* New York: Academic Press, 1972.

Brown, B. B. New mind, new body. *Psychology Today,* August 1974, pp. 48–56; 74–96; 102–112.

Brown, P. K., & Wald, G. Visual pigments in single rods and cones of the human retina. *Science,* 1964, *144,* 45–52.

Brown, R. Development of the first language in the human species. *American Psychologist,* February 1973, 97–106.

Brown, R. Schizophrenia, language, and reality. *American Psychologist,* May 1973, 395–403.

Brown, R. W. *Social psychology.* New York: Free Press, 1965.

Brown, R. W., & Berko, J. Word association and the acquisition of grammar. *Child Development,* 1960, *31,* 1–14.

Brown, R. W., & McNeill, D. The tip-of-the-tongue phenomenon. *Journal of Verbal Learning and Verbal Behavior,* 1966, *5,* 325–337.

Bruner, J. S. The course of cognitive growth. *American Psychologist,* 1964, *19,* 1–15.

Burt, C. The genetic determination of differences in intelligence: A study of monozygotic twins reared together and apart. *British Journal of Psychology,* 1966, *57,* 137–153.

Burtt, H. E. An experimental study of early childhood memory. *Journal of Genetic Psychology,* 1941, *58,* 435–439.

Butler, R. N. The life review: An interpretation of reminiscence in the aged. *Psychiatry,* January 1963, *26,* 63–76.

Byrne, D. Interpersonal attraction and attitude similarity. *Journal of Abnormal and Social Psychology,* 1961, *62,* 713–715.

Byrne, D. *An introduction to personality* (2nd ed.). Englewood Cliffs, N.J.: Prentice-Hall, 1974.

Byrne, D., & Nelson, D. Attraction as a function of attitude similarity-dissimilarity: The effect of topic importance. *Psychonomic Science,* 1964, *1,* 93–94.

Calhoun, J. B. Population density and social pathology. *Scientific American,* 1962, *206,* 139–148.

Cameron, P. The generation gap: Time orientation. *Gerontologist,* February 1972, *12,* 117–119.

Campos, J. L., Langer, A., & Krowitz, A. Cardiac responses on the visual cliff in prelocomotor human infants. *Science,* 1970, *170,* 196–197.

Cannon, W. B. The James-Lange theory of emotion: A critical examination and an alternative theory. *American Journal of Psychology,* 1927, *39,* 106–124.

Carr, A. T. Compulsive neuroses: A review of the literature. *Psychological Bulletin,* May 1974, *81* (5), 311–318.

Cattell, R. B. *The scientific analysis of personality.* Baltimore: Penguin, 1965.

Cermak, L. S. *Human memory: Research and theory.* New York: Ronald Press, 1972.

Chance, P. Race and IQ: A family affair. *Psychology Today,* January 1975, p. 40.

Chomsky, N. *Aspects of the theory of syntax.* Cambridge, Mass.: M.I.T. Press, 1965.

Chorover, S. L. The pacification of the brain. *Psychology Today,* May 1974, pp. 59–70.

Cohen, D. B. Repression is not the demon who conceals and

hoards our forgotten dreams. *Psychology Today*, May 1974a, pp. 50–54.

Cohen, D. B. Toward a theory of dream recall. *Psychological Bulletin*, February 1974b, *81*, 138–154.

Colavita, F. B. *Interspecies differences in sensory dominance.* Paper presented at the Twelfth Annual Meeting of the Psychonomic Society, St. Louis, November 1971.

Coleman, J. C., & Hammen, C. L. *Contemporary psychology and effective behavior.* Glenview, Ill.: Scott, Foresman, 1974.

Coleman, J. S. President's Science Advisory Committee. *Youth: Transition to adulthood.* Chicago: University of Chicago Press, 1974.

Committee on Ethical Standards. Ethical standards for psychological research: Proposed ethical principles submitted on the APA membership for criticism and modification. *APA Monitor*, 1971, *2* (7), pp. 9–28. Revised in *APA Monitor*, 1972, *3* (5), pp. i–xix.

Cooper, J. Personal responsibility and dissonance. *Journal of Personality and Social Psychology*, 1971, *18*, 354–363.

Cooper, R., & Zubek, J. Effects of enriched and restricted early environments on the learning ability of bright and dull rats. *Canadian Journal of Psychology*, 1958, *12*, 159–164.

Coser, L. *The functions of social conflict.* New York: Free Press, 1956.

Cottrell, N. B., Rittle, R. H., & Wack, D. L. Presence of an audience and list type (competitional and noncompetitional) as joint determinants of performance in paired-associates learning. *Journal of Personality*, 1967, *35*, 217–226.

Cummings, E., & Henry, W. E. *Growing old: The process of disengagement.* New York: Basic Books, 1961.

Dalal, A. S., & Barber, T. X. Yoga and hypnotism. In T. X. Barber (Ed.), *LSD, marijuana, yoga and hypnosis.* Chicago: Aldine, 1970.

D'Amato, M. R. Derived motives. *Annual Review of Psychology*, 1974, *25*, 83–106.

Davis, C. M. Results of self-selection of diets by young children. *Canadian Medical Association Journal*, 1939, *41*, 257–261.

Davis, J. D., Gallagher, R. L., & Ladove, R. Food intake controlled by a blood factor. *Science*, 1967, *156*, 1247–1248.

Davitz, J. R. *The language of emotion.* New York: Academic Press, 1969.

Davitz, J. R. A dictionary and grammar of emotion. In M. B. Arnold (Ed.), *Feelings and emotions.* New York: Academic Press, 1970. Pp. 251–258.

Deese, J., & Hulse, S. H. *The psychology of learning* (3rd ed.). New York: McGraw-Hill, 1967.

Deikman, A. J. Deautomatization and the mystic experience. In R. E. Ornstein (Ed.), *The nature of human consciousness.* San Francisco: Freeman, 1973b. Pp. 216–233.

Dekker, E., Pelser, H. E., & Groen, J. Conditioning as a cause of asthmatic attacks. *Journal of Psychosomatic Research*, 1957, *2*, 97–108.

Delgado, J. M. R. *Physical control of the mind: Toward a psycho-civilized society.* New York: Harper & Row, 1969.

Dember, W. N. The new look in motivation. *American Scientist*, 1965, *53*, 409–427.

Dember, W. N., Earl, R. W., & Paradise, N. Response by rats to differential stimulus complexity. *Journal of Comparative and Physiological Psychology*, 1957, *50*, 514–518.

Dement, W. C. The effect of dream deprivation. *Science*, 1960, *131*, 1705–1707.

Dement, W. C. An essay on dreams: The role of physiology in understanding their nature. In F. Barron et al., *New directions in psychology II.* New York: Holt, Rinehart & Winston, 1965.

Dement, W. C. *Some must watch while some must sleep.* San Francisco: Freeman, 1974.

Dement, W. C., & Wolpert, E. Relation of eye movements, body motility, and external stimuli to dream content. *Journal of Experimental Psychology*, 1958, *55*, 543–553.

Dennis, W. The performance of Hopi children on the Goodenough Draw-a-Man test. *Journal of Comparative Psychology*, 1942, *34*, 341–348.

Dennis, W., & Dennis, M. G. The effect of cradling practices upon the onset of walking in Hopi children. *Journal of Genetic Psychology*, 1940, *56*, 77–86.

Dent, J. Y. Dealing with the alcoholic at home. *Medical World of London*, 1954, *81*, 245.

Deutsch, J. A. (Ed.). *The physiological basis of memory.* New York: Academic Press, 1973.

Deutsch, M., & Gerard, H. B. A study of normative and informational social influences upon individual judgment. *Journal of Abnormal and Social Psychology*, 1955, *51*, 629–636.

Di Loreto, A. O. *Comparative psychotherapy: An experimental analysis.* Chicago: Aldine, 1971.

Dimond, E. G. Acupuncture anaesthesia. *Journal of the American Medical Association*, 1971, *218*, 1558.

Dion, K. *Social desirability and the evaluation of harmdoers.* Unpublished doctoral dissertation, University of Minnesota, 1970.

Dobzhansky, T. Differences are not deficits. *Psychology Today*, December 1973, pp. 97–101.

Dollard, J., & Miller, N. E. *Personality and psychotherapy.* New York: McGraw-Hill, 1950.

Doty, R. W., The brain. In F. Leukel (Ed.), *Issues in physiological psychology.* St. Louis: Mosby, 1974. Pp. 3–12.

Drag, R. M., & Shaw, M. E. Factors influencing the communication of emotional intent by facial expressions. *Psychonomic Science*, 1967, *8* (4), 137–138.

Dublin, L. I., Lotka, A. J., & Spiegelman, M. *Length of life: A study of the life table.* New York: Ronald Press, 1949.

Duffy, E. An explanation of "emotional" phenomena without the use of the concept "emotion." *Journal of General Psychology*, 1941, *25*, 283–293.

Dworkin, G. Open minds and ideology. *American Psychologist*, December 1974, 920–921.

Ebbinghaus, H. *Memory: A contribution to experimental psychology.* (H. A. Ruger & C. E. Bussenius, trans.). New York: Teacher's College, Columbia University, 1913. (Originally published Leipzig: Altenberg, 1885.)

Ehrhardt, A. A., & Money, J. Progestin-induced hermaphroditism: IQ and psychosexual identity in a study of ten girls. *The Journal of Sex Research*, 1967, *3*, 83–100.

Elkind, D. Egocentrism in adolescence. In R. E. Grinder (Ed.), *Studies in adolescence* (2nd ed.). New York: Macmillan, 1969. Pp. 497–506.

Elkind, D., Koegler, R. R., & Go, E. Studies in perceptual development: II. Part-whole perception. *Child Development*, 1964, *35*, 81–90.

Ellis, A. *Humanistic psychotherapy: The rational emotive approach.* New York: Julian Press: 1973a.

Engen, T. The sense of smell. *Annual Review of Psychology,* 1973, *24,* 187–206.

Englund, S. "Birth without violence." *New York Times Magazine,* December 8, 1974, pp. 113–120.

Epstein, A. N., Fitzsimmons, J. T., & Simons, B. Drinking caused by the intracranial injection of angiotensin into the rat. *Journal of Physiology* (London), 1969, *200,* 98–100.

Epstein, S. The measurement of drive and conflict in humans: Theory and experiment. In M. R. Jones (Ed.), *Nebraska Symposium on Motivation.* Lincoln: University of Nebraska Press, 1962. Pp. 127–209.

Erikson, E. H. Identity and the life cycle. *Psychological Issues,* 1959, *1,* 1–165.

Erikson, E. H. *Childhood and society* (2nd ed.). New York: Norton, 1963.

Erikson, E. H. *Identity: Youth in crisis.* New York: Norton, 1968.

Estes, W. K. Learning theory and intelligence. *American Psychologist,* October 1974, 740–749.

Etzioni, A. *The genetic fix.* New York: Macmillan, 1973.

Evans, R. B. Childhood parental relationships of homosexual men. *Journal of Consulting and Clinical Psychology,* 1969, *33,* 129–135.

Eysenck, H. J. *The structure of human personality* (3rd ed.). London: Methuen, 1970.

Fantz, R. L. The origin of form perception. *Scientific American,* May 1961, 450–463.

Fantz, R. L. Patterns of vision in newborn infants. *Science,* 1963, *140,* 296–297.

Farb, P. *Word play.* New York: Knopf, 1974.

Fast, J. *Body language.* New York: M. Evans, 1970.

Festinger, L. A theory of social comparison processes. *Human Relations,* 1954, 2 (2), 117–140.

Festinger, L. *A theory of cognitive dissonance.* Evanston, Ill.: Row, Peterson, 1957.

Festinger, L., Schachter, S., & Back, K. *Social pressures in informal groups: A study of human factors in housing.* New York: Harper & Row, 1950.

Flynn, J. P., et al. Neural mechanisms involved in a cat's attack on a rat. In R. E. Whalen, et al. (Eds.), *The neural control of behavior.* New York: Academic Press, 1970. Pp. 135–173.

Frank J. D. *Sanity and survival: Psychological aspects of war and peace.* New York: Vintage Books, 1968.

Freedman, A. M. Drugs and society. In J. O. Cole, A. M. Freedman, & A. J. Friedhoff (Eds.), *Psychopathology and psychopharmacology.* Baltimore: Johns Hopkins University Press, 1973. Pp. 275–286.

Freedman, J. L., Carlsmith, J. M., & Sears, D. O. *Social psychology* (2nd ed.). Englewood Cliffs, N.J.: Prentice-Hall, 1974.

Freedman, J. L., Heshka, S., & Levy, A. *Population density and pathology: Is there a relationship?* Unpublished manuscript, 1973.

Freud, S. The analysis of a phobia in a five-year-old boy. (1909). In *Collected papers* (Vol. 3). London: Hogarth, 1950.

Freud, S. *Collected Papers* (Vol. 2). London: Hogarth, 1924.

The basic writings of Sigmund Freud (A. A. Brill, Trans. & ed.). New York: Random House, 1928.

Freud, S. *An outline of psychoanalysis.* New York: Norton, 1949.

Freud, S. *The complete introductory lectures on psychoanalysis* (J. Strachey, Trans. & ed.). New York: Norton, 1966.

Fromm, E. *The sane society.* New York: Fawcett, 1955.

Funkenstein, D. H., King, S. H., & Drolette, M. The experimental evocation of stress. In *Symposium on Stress.* Division of Medical Sciences of the National Research Council and Army Medical Services Graduate School of Walter Reed Army Medical Center. Washington, D.C.: Government Printing Office, 1953.

Funkenstein, D. H., King, S. H., & Drolette, M. E. *Mastery of stress.* Cambridge, Mass.: Harvard University Press, 1957.

Gaines, J. The founder of Gestalt therapy: A sketch of Fritz Perls. *Psychology Today,* November 1974, pp. 117–118.

Galle, O. R., Gove, W. R., & McPherson, J. M. Population density and pathology: What are the relationships for man? *Science,* 1972, *176,* 23–30.

Gardner, R. A., & Gardner, B. T. Teaching sign language to a chimpanzee. *Science,* 1969, *165,* 664–672.

Gardner, R. A., & Gardner, B. T. Early signs of language in child and chimpanzee. *Science,* February 28, 1975, *187,* 752–753.

Gergen, K. F. *The concept of self.* New York: Holt, Rinehart & Winston, 1971.

Gergen, K. F., & Morse, S. J. Social comparison, self-consistency, and the concept of self. *Journal of Personality and Social Psychology,* 1970, *16,* 148–156.

Gergen, K. F., & Taylor, M. G. Social expectancy and self-presentation in a status hierarchy. *Journal of Experimental Social Psychology,* 1969, *5,* 79–92.

Gergen, K. J. The codification of research ethics—Views of a Doubting Thomas. *American Psychologist,* October 1973, 907–912.

Getzels, J. W., & Jackson, P. W. *Creativity and intelligence.* New York: Wiley, 1962.

Gewirtz, J. L., & Gewirtz, H. B. Stimulus conditions, infant behaviors and social learning in four Israeli child-rearing environments: A preliminary report illustrating differences in environment and behavior between the "only" and the "youngest" child. In B. M. Foss (Ed.), *Determinants of infant behavior III.* New York: Wiley, 1965. Pp. 161–184.

Giambera, L. Daydreams: The backburner of the mind. *Psychology Today,* December 1974, pp. 66–68.

Gilinsky, A. S. Comment: Adaptation level, contrast, and the moon illusion. In M. H. Appley (Ed.), *Adaptation-level theory.* New York: Academic Press, 1971. Pp. 71–79.

Gjessing, L. R. A review of the biochemistry of periodic catatonia. *Excerpta Medica, International Congress Series,* 1966 (150).

Glasser, W. *Reality therapy.* New York: Harper & Row, 1965.

Glucksburg, S., & King, L. J. Motivated forgetting mediated by implicit verbal chaining: A laboratory analog of repression. *Science,* 1967, *158,* 517–519.

Goldenberg, H. *Contemporary clinical psychology.* Monterey, Calif.: Brooks/Cole, 1973.

Goldiamond, I. A diary of self-modification. *Psychology Today,* November 1973. pp. 95–102.

Gray, F., Graubord, P. S., & Rosenberg, R. Little brother is changing you. *Psychology Today,* March 1974, pp. 42–46.

Greenberg, D. J., & O'Donnell, W. J. Infancy and the optional level of stimulation. *Child Development,* 1972, *43,* 639–645.

Greene, D., & Lepper, M. R. How to turn play into work. *Psychology Today*, September 1974, pp. 49–54.

Greenspoon, J. The reinforcing effect of two spoken sounds on the frequency of two responses. *American Journal of Psychology*, 1955, *68*, 409–416.

Gregory, R. L. *Eye and brain: The psychology of seeing.* New York: McGraw-Hill, 1966.

Grinker, R. R., & Spiegel, J. P. *War neurosis.* Philadelphia: Blakiston, 1945.

Grinspoon, L. Marihuana. *Scientific American*, December 1969.

Guilford, J. P. Traits of creativity. In H. H. Anderson (Ed.), *Creativity and its cultivation.* New York: Harper & Row, 1959. Pp. 142–161.

Guilford, J. P. Factorial angles to psychology. *Psychological Review*, 1961, *68*, 1–20.

Gundlach, R. H. Childhood parental relationships and the establishment of gender roles of homosexuals. *Journal of Consulting and Clinical Psychology*, 1969, *33*, 136–139.

Gutmann, D. L. An explanation of ego configurations in middle and late life. In. B. L. Neugarten et al. (Eds.), *Personality in middle and late life.* New York: Atherton, 1964.

Haber, R. H., & Hershenson, M. *The psychology of visual perception.* New York: Holt, Rinehart & Winston, 1973.

Haber, R. N. Eidetic images. *Scientific American*, April 1969, 36–44.

Hahn, J. F. Somethesis. *Annual Review of Psychology*, 1974, *25*, 233–246.

Hall, C. S., & Lindzey, G. *Theories of personality* (2nd ed.). New York: Wiley, 1970.

Hall, E. T. *The silent language.* Garden City, N.Y.: Doubleday, 1959.

Hamm, N. H. The politics of empiricism. *American Psychologist*, January 1974, 9–13.

Hansel, C. E. M. *ESP: A scientific evaluation.* New York: Scribner, 1966.

Harlow, H. F. The formation of learning sets. *Psychological Review*, 1949, *56*, 51–65.

Harlow, H. F. Learning and satiation of responses in intrinsically motivated complex puzzle performance by monkeys. *Journal of Comparative and Physiological Psychology*, 1950, *43*, 289–294.

Harlow, H. F. The nature of love. *American Psychologist*, 1958, *13*, 673–685.

Harlow, H. F. Learning set and error factor theory. In S. Koch (Ed.), *Psychology: A study of a science.* New York: McGraw-Hill, 1959. Pp. 492–537.

Harlow, H. F. The heterosexual affectional system in monkeys. *American Psychologist*, 1962, *17*, 1–9.

Harlow, H. F., & Zimmerman, R. R. Affectional responses in the infant monkey. *Science*, 1959, *130*, 421–432.

Harlow, M. K., & Harlow, H. F. Affection in primates. *Discovery*, 1966, *27*, 11–17.

Harrell, R. F., Woodyard, E., & Gates, A. I. *The effect of mother's diet on the intelligence of the offspring.* New York: Teachers College, Columbia Bureau of Publications, 1955.

Harrell, T. W., & Harrell, M. S. Army General Classification Test scores for civilian occupations. *Education and Psychological Measurement*, 1945, *5*, 229–239.

Harris, A. H., et al. Instrumental conditioning of large-magnitude, daily 12-hour blood pressure elevations in the baboon. *Science*, 1973, *182*, 175–177.

Harris, F. R., Wolf, M. M., & Baer, D. M. Effects of adult social reinforcement of child behavior. *Young Children*, 1964, *20*, 8–17.

Harris, I. D. *The promised seed: A complete study of eminent first and later sons.* New York: Free Press, 1964.

Hartmann, H. *Essays on ego psychology: Selected problems in psychoanalytic theory.* New York: International Universities Press, 1964.

Hathaway, S. R., & McKinley, J. C. *The Minnesota Multiphasic Personality Inventory.* Minneapolis: University of Minnesota Press. 1942.

Havighurst, R. J., Neugarten, B. L., & Tobin, S. S. *Disengagement and patterns of aging.* Paper presented at the meeting of the International Association of Gerontology, Copenhagen, August 1973.

Hayakawa, S. I. *Language in thought and action.* New York: Harcourt Brace Jovanovich, 1949.

Heath, R. G. A biochemical hypothesis on the etiology of schizophrenia. In D. D. Jackson (Ed.), *The etiology of schizophrenia.* New York: Basic Books, 1960. Pp. 146–156.

Hebb, D. O. *The organization of behavior.* New York: Wiley, 1949.

Henry, W. E. *The analysis of fantasy.* New York: Wiley, 1956.

Hernandez-Péon, R., Scherrer, H., & Jouvet, N. Modification of electric activity in the cochlear nucleus during "attention" in unanesthetized cats. *Science*, 1956, *123*, 331–332.

Heron, W. The pathology of boredom. *Scientific American*, January 1957.

Hersher, L. (Ed.). *Four psychotherapies.* New York: Appleton-Century-Crofts, 1970.

Hess, E. H. Imprinting: An effect of early experience, imprinting determines later social experience in animals. *Science*, 1959, *130*, 133–141.

Heston, L. L. Psychiatric disorders in foster-home-reared children of schizophrenic mothers. *British Journal of Psychiatry*. 1966, *112*, 819–825.

Hilgard, E. R. Pain as a muzzle for psychology and physiology. *American Psychologist*, 1969, *24*, 103–113.

Hilgard, E. R. Hypnosis is no mirage. *Psychology Today*, November 1974, pp. 121–128.

Hilgard, E. R. Hypnosis. *Annual Review of Psychology*, 1975, *26*, 19–44.

Hilgard, E. R., & Bower, G. H. *Theories of learning* (4th ed.). Englewood Cliffs, N.J.: Prentice-Hall, 1975.

Hill, W. F. Activity as an autonomous drive. *Journal of Comparative and Physiological Psychology*, 1956, *49*, 15–19.

Hilton, I. Differences in the behavior of mothers toward first and later born children. *Journal of Personality and Social Psychology*, 1967, *7*, 282–290.

Hoebel, B. G., & Teitelbaum, P. Hypothalamic control of feeding and self-stimulation. *Science*, 1962, *135*, 375–377.

Hoffer, A., & Osmond, H. The adrenochrome model and schizophrenia. *Journal of Nervous and Mental Diseases*, 1959, *128*, 18–35.

Hofstatter, L., & Girgis, M. *Depth electrode investigations of the limbic system of the brain by radiostimulation, electrolytic lesion and histochemical studies.* Paper presented at the Third International Congress of Psychosurgery, Cambridge, August 15–18, 1972.

Hollander, E. P., & Willis, R. H. Some current issues in the psychology of conformity and nonconformity. *Psycholog-*

ical Bulletin, 1967, 68, 62–76.

Holmes, D. S. Investigations of repression. *Psychological Bulletin*, October 1974, *81*, 632–653.

Holmes, T. H., and Rahe, R. H. The social readjustment rating scale. *Journal of psychosomatic research*, *11*, 1967, 213.

Holzman, P. S. Personality. *Annual Review of Psychology*, 1974, *25*, 247–276.

Hooker, E. Parental relations and male homosexuality in patient and nonpatient samples. *Journal of Consulting and Clinical Psychology*, 1969, *33*, 140–142.

Horn, J. Family therapy—A quick fix for juvenile delinquency. *Psychology Today*, March 1975, pp. 80–81.

Horner, M. A bright woman is caught in a double bind. *Psychology Today*, November 1969, pp. 36–38; 62.

Howes, D., & Solomon, R. L. A note on McGinnies "Emotionality and perceptual defense." *Psychological Review*, 1950, *57*, 235–240.

Hulse, S. H., Deese, J., & Egeth, H. *The psychology of learning* (4th ed.). New York: McGraw-Hill, 1975.

Hunter, W. S. The delayed reaction in animals and children. *Behavior Monographs*, 1913 (2).

Hunter, W. S. The behavior of raccoons in a double alternation temporal maze. *Journal of Genetic Psychology*, 1928, *35*, 374–388.

Hurwich, L. M., & Jameson, D. Opponent processes as a model of neural organization. *American Psychologist*, February 1974, 88–102.

Hutt, C., & Vaizey, M. J. Differential effects of group density and social behavior. *Nature*, 1966, *209*, 1371–1372.

Huxley, A. *Brave new world*. New York: Harper & Row, 1939.

Inhelder, B., & Piaget, J. *The growth of logical thinking from childhood to adolescence* (A. Parson & S. Milgram, trans.). New York: Basic Books, 1958.

Insel, P. M., & Moos, R. H. Psychological environments. *American Psychologist*, March 1974, 179–188.

Isaacs, W., Thomas, J., & Goldiamond, I. Application of operant conditioning to reinstate verbal behavior in psychotics. *Journal of Speech and Hearing Disabilities*, 1960, *25*, 8–12.

Iscoe, I. Community psychology and the competent community. *American Psychologist*, August 1974, 607–613.

Izard, C. E. *The face of emotion*. New York: Appleton-Century-Crofts, 1971.

James, W. What is an emotion? *Mind*, 1884, *9*, 188–205.

James, W. *The principles of psychology* (2 vols.). New York: Holt, 1890.

Janis, I. L. *Victims of groupthink: A psychological study of foreign-policy decisions and fiascos*. Boston: Houghton Mifflin, 1972.

Jenkins, J. G., & Dallenbach, K. M. Oblivescence during sleep and waking. *American Journal of Psychology*, 1924, *35*, 605–612.

Jensen, A. R. How much can we boost IQ and scholastic achievement? *Harvard Educational Review*, 1969, *39*, 1–123.

Jensen, A. R. The strange case of Dr. Jensen and Mr. Hyde? *American Psychologist*, June 1974, *29* (6), 467–468.

Jessor, R. The problem of reductionism in psychology. *Psychological Review*, 1958, *65*, 170–178.

Johnson, D. M. *Systematic introduction to the psychology of thinking*. New York: Harper & Row, 1972.

Johnson-Laird, P. N. Experimental psycholinguistics. *Annual Review of Psychology*, 1974, *25*, 135–160.

Jones, E. E., et al. *Attribution: Perceiving the causes of behavior*. New York: General Learning Press, 1972.

Kagan, J. Learning, attention and the issue of discovery. In L. S. Shulman & E. R. Keislar (Eds.). *Learning by discovery: A critical appraisal*. Chicago: Rand McNally, 1966. Pp. 151–161.

Kahneman, D. *Attention and effort*. Englewood Cliffs, N.J.: Prentice-Hall, 1973.

Kallman, F. J. *Heredity in health and mental disorder*. New York: Norton, 1953.

Karlins, M., Coffman, T. L., & Walters, G. On the fading of social stereotypes: Studies of three generations of college students. *Journal of Personality and Social Psychology*, 1969, *13*, 1–16.

Katz, I. Review of evidence relating to effects of desegregation on the intellectual performance of Negroes. *American Psychologist*, 1964, *19*, 381–399.

Kaufman, L., & Rock, I. The moon illusion. *Scientific American*. July 1962, 120–130.

Keele, S. W. *Attention and human performance*. Pacific Palisades, Calif.: Goodyear, 1973.

Kelley, H. H. The warm-cold variable in the first impressions of persons. *Journal of Personality*, 1950, *18*, 431–439.

Kelley, H. H. The processes of causal attribution. *American Psychologist*, February 1973, 107–128.

Kelley, H. H., et al. Collective behavior in a simulated panic situation. *Journal of Experimental Social Psychology*, 1965, *1*, 20–54.

Kelly, G. A. Man's construction of his alternatives, In G. Lindzey (Ed.), *Assessment of human motives*. New York: Rinehart, 1958. Pp. 33–64.

Kelman, H. C. Attitudes are alive and well and gainfully employed in the sphere of action. *American Psychologist*, May 1974, 310–324.

Kelman, H. C., & Lawrence, L. H. Violent man: American response to the trial of Lt. William L. Calley. *Psychology Today*, June 1972, pp. 41–45; 78–81.

Keniston, K. *Young radicals: Notes on committed youth*. New York: Harcourt Brace Jovanovich, 1968.

Kennedy, G. C. The role of depot fat in the hypothalamic control of food intake in the rat. *Proceedings of the Royal Society*, 1953, *B140*, 578–592.

Kennedy, T. Treatment of chronic schizophrenia by behavior therapy: Case reports. *Behavior Research Therapy*, 1964, *2*, 1–7.

Kennedy, W. A., & Lindner, R. S. A normative sample of intelligence and achievement of Negro elementary school children in the Southeastern United States. *Monographs of the Society for Research on Child Development*, 1963 (28).

Kimmel, D. C. *Adulthood and aging*. New York: Wiley, 1974.

Kiritz, S., & Moos, R. H. Physiological effects of social environments. *Psychosomatic Medicine*, 1974.

Klein, G. S. The personal world through perception. In R. R. Blake & G. V. Ramsey, *Perception: An approach to personality*. New York: Ronald Press, 1951.

Kleitman, N. *Sleep and wakefulness* (rev. ed.). Chicago: University of Chicago Press, 1963.

Klineberg, O. Emotional expression in Chinese literature.

Journal of Abnormal and Social Psychology, 1938, *33,* 517–520.

Knight, M. Child molesters try "shock" cure. *New York Times,* May 21, 1974, pp. 43; 83.

Koch, K. *Wishes, lies and dreams.* New York: Vintage Books, 1970.

Kohlberg, L. Moral education in the schools: A developmental view. *School Review,* 1966, *74,* 1–30.

Kohn, R. R. Human aging and disease. *Journal of Chronic Disease,* 1963, *16,* 5–21.

Kopanev, V. Man and outer space: An international symposium in Yerevan. *Space World,* January 1972, 48.

Korner, A. F. Individual differences at birth. Implications for early experience and later development. *American Journal of Orthopsychiatry,* 1971, *41,* 608–619.

Kübler-Ross, E. *On death and dying.* New York: Macmillan, 1969.

Lambert, W. W., Solomon, R. L., & Watson, P. D. Reinforcement and extinction as factors in size estimation. *Journal of Experimental Psychology,* 1949, *39,* 637–641.

Lange, C. G. *The emotions.* Baltimore: Williams & Wilkins, 1922. (Originally published, 1885.)

LaPiere, R. T. Attitudes versus actions. *Social Forces,* 1934, *13,* 230–237.

Lashley, K. S. In search of the engram. In *Symposia of the Society for Experimental Biology,* 1950, *4,* 454–482.

Latané, B., & Darley, J. M. *The Unresponsive bystander: Why doesn't he help?* New York: Appleton-Century-Crofts, 1970.

Latané, B., & Rodin, J. A lady in distress: Inhibiting effects of friends and strangers on bystander intervention. *Journal of Experimental Social Psychology,* 1969, *5,* 189–202.

Laughlin, H. P. *Mental mechanisms.* New York: Appleton-Century-Crofts, 1963.

Laughlin, H. P. *The ego and its defenses.* New York: Appleton-Century-Crofts, 1970.

Lazarus, R. S. *Psychological stress and the coping process.* New York: McGraw-Hill, 1966.

Lazarus, R. S. Emotions and adaptation: Conceptual and empirical relations. In W. J. Arnold (Ed.), *Nebraska Symposium on Motivation.* Lincoln: University of Nebraska Press, 1968.

Lazarus, R. S. *Patterns of adjustment and human effectiveness.* New York: McGraw-Hill, 1969.

Lazarus, R. S. *The riddle of man.* Englewood Cliffs, N.J.: Prentice-Hall, 1974.

Lazarus, R. S., Averill, J. R., & Opton, E. M., Jr. Toward a greater cognitive theory of emotion. In M. B. Arnold (Ed.), *Feelings and emotions.* New York: Academic Press, 1970. Pp. 207–232.

Lazarus, R. S., & Erickson, C. W. Effects of failure stress upon skilled performance. *Journal of Experimental Psychology,* 1952, *43,* 100–105.

Leboyer, F. *Birth without violence.* New York: Knopf, 1975.

Leeper, R. W. A motivational theory of emotion to replace "emotion as disorganized response." *Psychological Review,* 1948, *55,* 5–21.

Lefcourt, H. M. The function of the illusions of control and freedom. *American Psychologist,* May 1973, 417–425.

Lefkowitz, M., et al. Television violence and child aggression: A follow-up study. In G. A. Comstock & E. A. Rubinstein (Eds.), *Television and social behavior* (Vol. 3).

Television and adolescent aggression. Washington, D.C.: U.S. Government Printing Office, 1972.

Lehman, H. C. *Age and achievement.* Princeton, N.J.: Princeton University Press, 1953.

LeMasters, E. E. Parenthood as crisis. *Marriage and Family Living,* April 1957, *19,* 352–355.

Levine, F. M., & Fasnacht, G. Token rewards may lead to token learning. *American Psychologist,* November 1974, 816–820.

Lewin, K. A. *A dynamic theory of personality* (K. E. Zener & D. K. Adams, trans.). New York: McGraw-Hill, 1935.

Liddell, H. S. *Emotional Hazards in animals and men.* Springfield, Ill.: Charles C Thomas, 1956.

Lieberman, M. A., & Coplan, A. S. Distance from death as a variable in the study of aging. *Developmental Psychology.* January 1969, *2,* 71–84.

Liebert, R. M., & Baron, R. A. Short-term effects of televised aggression on children's aggressive behavior. In J. P. Murray, E. A. Rubinstein, & G. A. Comstock (Eds.), *Television and social behavior* (Vol. 2). *Television and Social Learning.* Washington, D.C.: U.S. Government Printing Office, 1972.

Lindsley, D. B. Emotion. In S. S. Stevens (Ed.), *Handbook of experimental psychology.* New York: Wiley, 1951. Pp. 499–510.

Lindsley, D. B. The role of nonspecific reticulo-thalamo-cortical systems in emotion. In P. Black (Ed.), *Physiological correlates of emotion.* New York: Academic Press, 1970. Pp. 147–188.

Lipsey, M. W. Research and relevance. *American Psychologist,* July 1974, 541–553.

Lipsitt, L. P. Babies: They're a lot smarter than they look. *Psychology Today,* December 1971, pp. 70–72; 88–89.

Lubin, I. *Aversive conditioning of cigarette addiction.* Paper presented at the 76th meeting of tle American Psychological Association, San Francisco, 1968.

Ludwig, A. M. Altered states of consciousness. In C. T. Tart (Ed.), *Altered states of consciousness.* New York: Wiley, 1969. Pp. 9–22.

Lundin, R. W. *Personality: A behavioral analysis* (2nd ed.). New York: Macmillan, 1974.

Lykken, D. T. Guilty knowledge test: The right way to use a lie detector. *Psychology Today,* March 1975, pp. 56–60.

McClearns, G. E., & DeFries, J. C. *Introduction to behavior genetics.* San Francisco, Freeman, 1973.

McClelland, D. C. Methods of measuring human motivation. In J. W. Atkinson (Ed.), *Motives in fantasy, action and society: A method of assessment and study.* New York: Van Nostrand, 1958. Pp. 7–42.

McClelland, D. C., & Atkinson, J. W. The projective expression of needs: I. The effect of different intensities of the hunger drive on perception. *Journal of Psychology,* 1948, *25,* 205–222.

McClelland, D. C., et al. *The achievement motive.* New York: Appleton-Century-Crofts, 1953.

McConnell, J. V. Memory transfer through cannibalism in planaria. *Journal of Neuropsychiatry,* 1962, *3,* 45.

McConnell, J. V., Jacobson, A. L., & Kimble, D. P. The effects of regeneration upon retention of a conditioned response in the planarian. *Journal of Comparative and Physiological Psychology,* 1959, *52,* 1–5.

McConnell, R. A. ESP and credibility in science. *American Psychologist,* 1969, *24,* 531–538.

McElheny, V. K. World biologists tighten rules on "genetic engineering" work. *New York Times*, February 28, 1975, pp. 1; 38.

McGaugh, J. L. Facilitation of memory storage processes. In F. Leukel (Ed.), *Issues in physiological psychology.* St. Louis: Mosby, 1974. Pp. 171–178.

McGinnies, E. Emotionality and perceptual defense. *Psychological Review*, 1949, 56, 244–251.

McGuire, W. J. Order of presentation as a factor in "conditioning" persuasiveness. In C. I. Hovland et al. (Eds.), *The order of presentation in persuasion.* New Haven, Conn.: Yale University Press, 1957. Pp. 98–114.

McGuire, W. J. Inducing resistance to persuasion. In L. Berkowitz (Ed.), *Advances in experimental social psychology* (Vol. I). New York: Academic Press, 1964. Pp. 192–229.

Macmillan, D. L. *Behavior modification and education.* New York: Macmillan, 1973.

McMurray, G. A. Experimental study of a case of insensitivity to pain. *Archives of Neurology and Psychiatry.* 1950, 64, 650.

Maddox, G. L. Activity and morale: A longitudinal study of selected elderly subjects. *Social Forces*, February 1963, 42, 196–204.

Maddox, G. L. Persistence of life styles among the elderly: A longitudinal study of patterns of social activity in relation to life satisfaction. *Proceedings of the 7th International Congress of Gerontology*, Vienna, 1966, 6, 309–311.

Maddox, G. L. Themes and issues in sociological theories of human aging. *Human Development*, 1970, 13, 17–27.

Maehr, M. L. Culture and achievement motivation. *American Psychologist*, December 1974, 887–896.

Maier, N. R. F. Reasoning in humans: I. On direction. *Journal of Comparative Psychology*, 1930, 10, 115–143.

Mandler, G. Verbal learning. In T. M. Newcomb (Ed.), *New directions in psychology: I.* New York: Holt, Rinehart & Winston, 1967. Pp. 1–50.

Marcia, J. E. *Determination and construct validity of ego identity status.* Unpublished doctoral dissertation, Ohio State University, 1964.

Mark, V. H. A psychosurgeon's case for psychosurgery. *Psychology Today*, July 1974, pp. 28–33; 84–86.

Mark, V. H., & Ervin, F. R. *Violence and the brain.* New York: Harper & Row, 1970.

Marks, W. B., Dobelle, W. H., & MacNichol, E. R. Visual pigments in single primate cones. *Science*, 1964, 143, 1181–1183.

Marrow, A. J. Goal tensions and recall: I. *Journal of General Psychology*, 1938, 19, 3–36.

Marsden, E. N. Values as determinants of friendship choice. *Connecticut College Psychological Journal*, 1966, 3, 3–13.

Maslow, A. H. *Motivation and personality.* New York: Harper & Row, 1954.

Masserman, J. H. *Principles of dynamic psychiatry.* Philadelphia: Saunders, 1946.

Mednick, S. A. The associative basis of creativity. *Psychological Review*, 1962, 69 (3), 220–232.

Melton, A. W. Implication of short-term memory for a general theory of memory. *Journal of Verbal Language and Verbal Behavior*, 1963, 2, 1–121.

Melville, K. *Communes in the counter culture.* New York: Morrow, 1972.

Melzack, R. *The puzzle of pain.* New York: Basic Books, 1973b.

Melzack, R., & Scott, T. H. The effects of early experience on the response to pain. *Journal of Comparative and Physiological Psychology*, 1957, 50, 155–161.

Melzack, R., & Wall, P. D. Pain mechanisms: A new theory. *Science*, 1965, 150, 971.

Mendel, G. Letter to Carl Nagele (1867). In M. Gabriel & S. Fogel (Eds.), *Great experiments in biology.* Englewood Cliffs, N. J.: Prentice-Hall, 1955. Pp. 228–233.

Milgram, S. Behavioral study of obedience. *Journal of Abnormal and Social Psychology*, 1963, 67, 371–378.

Milgram, S. Issue in the study of obedience. *American Psychology*, 1964, 19, 848–852.

Milgram, S. *Obedience to authority.* New York: Harper & Row, 1974.

Miller, G. A. The magical number seven, plus or minus two: Some limits on our capacity for processing information. *Psychological Review*, 1956, 63, 81–96.

Miller, N. E. Studies of fear as an acquirable drive. I: Fear as motivation and fear-reduction as reinforcement in the learning of new responses. *Journal of Experimental Psychology*, 1948, 38, 89–101.

Miller, N. E., & DiCara, L. Instrumental learning of heart rate changes in curarized rats: Shaping and specificity to discriminative stimulus. *Journal of Comparative and Physiological Psychology*, 1967, 63, 12–19.

Mintz, A. Non-adaptive group behavior. *Journal of Abnormal and Social Psychology*, 1951, 46, 150–159.

Mischel, W. *Personality and assessment.* New York: Wiley, 1968.

Mischel, W. *Introduction to personality.* New York: Holt, Rinehart & Winston, 1971.

Mitchell, G., Redican, W. K., & Gomber, J. Males can raise babies. *Psychology Today*, April 1974, pp. 63–68.

Moyer, K. E. The physiology of violence. *Psychology Today*, July 1973, pp. 35–38.

Murdock, B. B., Jr. The retention of individual items. *Journal of Experimental Psychology*, 1961, 62, 618–625.

Muuss, R. E. *Theories of adolescence* (2nd ed.). New York: Random House, 1968.

Myers, G. C., & Pitts, A. M. *The demographic effects of mortality reduction on the aged population of the U.S.: Some Baseline Projections.* Paper presented at the meeting of the Gerontological Society, San Juan, Puerto Rico, December 1972.

Nashold, B. S., Jr. Foreword. In R. Melzack, *The puzzle of pain.* New York: Basic Books, 1973. P. vii.

National Commission on Marihuana and Drug Abuse. *Drug use in America: Problem in perspective.* Washington, D.C.: U.S. Government Printing Office, 1973a.

National Commission on Marihuana and Drug Abuse. *Drug use in America: Problem in perspective. Technical papers —Appendix.* Washington, D.C.: U.S. Government Printing Office, 1973b.

Neugarten, B. L. The awareness of middle age. In R. Owen (Ed.), *Middle age.* London: British Broadcasting Corporation, 1967.

Neugarten, B. L. Adult personality: Toward a psychology of the life cycle. In E. Vinacke (Ed.), *Readings in general psychology.* New York: American Book, 1968a.

Neugarten, B. L. (Ed.). *Middle age and aging.* Chicago: University of Chicago Press, 1968b.

Neugarten, B. L., & Gutmann, D. L. Age-sex roles and personality in middle age: A thematic apperception study. *Psychological Monographs*, 1958, *72* (17, Whole No. 470).

Neugarten, B. L., Havighurst, R. J., & Tobin, S. S. Personality and patterns of aging. *Gawein: Tijschrift vande Psychologische Kring aan de Nijmessgse Universiteit Jrg.* May 1965, *13*, 249–256.

Neugarten, B. L., Moore, J. W., & Lowe, J. C. Age norms, age constraints, and adult socialization. *American Journal of Sociology*, June 1965, *70*, 710–717.

Newcomb, T. M. *Personality and social change.* New York: Holt, Rinehart & Winston, 1943.

Newcomb, T. M. Persistence and regression of changed attitudes: Long range studies. *Journal of Social Issues*, 1963, *19*, 3–14.

Newell, A., Shaw, J. C., & Simon, H. A. Report on a general problem-solving program. In *Proceedings of the International Conference on Information Processing*. Paris: UNESCO, 1960, 256–264.

Nisbett, R. E., & Valins, S. *Perceiving the causes of one's own behavior.* New York: General Learning Press, 1971.

Norman, D. A. *Memory and attention.* New York: Wiley, 1969.

O'Connor, N., & Franks, C. M. Childhood upbringing and other environmental factors. In H. J. Eysenck (Ed.), *Handbook of abnormal psychology.* London: Pitman, 1960.

Offir, C. W. Field report. *Psychology Today*, October 1974, pp. 61–72.

Olds, J. Pleasure centers in the brain. *Scientific American*, October 1956, 105–116.

Olds, J., & Milner, P. Positive reinforcement produced by electrical stimulation of septal area and other regions of rat brain. *Journal of Comparative and Physiological Psychology*, 1954, *47*, 419–427.

Orlofsky, J. L., Marcia, J. E., & Lesser, I. M. Ego identity status and the intimacy versus isolation crisis of young adulthood. *Journal of Personality and Social Psychology*, February 1973, *27* (2), 211–219.

Pahnke, W. N., & Richards, W. A. Implications of LSD and experimental mysticism. In C. T. Tart (Ed.), *Altered states of consciousness.* New York: Wiley, 1969. Pp. 399–432.

Paivio, A. *Imagery and verbal processes.* New York: Holt, Rinehart & Winston, 1971.

Pavlov, I. P. *Conditioned reflexes* (G. V. Anrep, trans.). London: Oxford University Press, 1927.

Peele, S., & Brodsky, A. Love can be an addiction. *Psychology Today*, August 1974, pp. 22–26.

Penfield, W. The interpretive cortex. *Science*, 1959, *129*, 1719–1725.

Perls, F. S. *Gestalt therapy verbatim.* Lafayette, Calif.: Real People Press, 1969.

Peterson, L. R. *Learning.* Glenview, Ill.: Scott, Foresman, 1975.

Phillips, J. L., Jr. *The origins of the intellect: Piaget's theory.* San Francisco: Freeman, 1969.

Piaget, J., & Inhelder, B. *The child's conception of space* (F. S. Langdon & J. L. Lunzer, trans.). London: Routledge & Kegan Paul, 1956. (Original French edition, 1948.)

Piaget, J., & Szeminska, A. *The child's conception of number* (C. Gattegno & F. M. Hodgson, trans.). New York: Humanities Press, 1952. (Original French edition, 1941.)

Pierrel, R., & Sherman, J. G. Train your pet the Barnabus

way. *Brown Alumni Monthly*, February 1963, 8–14.

Pines, M. Infants are smarter than anybody thinks. *New York Times Magazine*, November 29, 1970, pp. 32–33; 110; 114–120.

Pines, M. We are left-brained or right-brained. *New York Times Magazine*, September 9, 1973, pp. 32–33; 121–127; 132; 136.

Plutchik, R. *The emotions: Facts, theories, and a new model.* New York: Random House, 1962.

Poincaré, H. *The foundations of science* (G. B. Halstead, trans.). London: Science Press, 1924.

Pollio, H. R. *The psychology of symbolic activity.* Reading, Mass.: Addison-Wesley, 1974.

Porter, R. W., et al. Some experimental observations on gastrointestinal ulcers in behaviorally conditioned monkeys. *Psychosomatic Medicine*, 1958, *20*, 379–394.

Postman, L. Verbal learning and memory. *Annual Review of Psychology*, 1975, *26*, 291–335.

Premack, D. The education of S*A*R*A*H*. *Psychology Today*, September 1970, pp. 54–58.

Pulaski, M. A. S. The rich rewards of make believe. *Psychology Today*, January 1974, pp. 68–74.

Rainwater, L. A study of personality differences between middle and lower class adolescents. *Genetic Psychology Monographs*, 1956, *54*, 3–86.

Rapoport, A. Rules for debate. In Q. Wright, W. M. Evan, & M. Deutsch (Eds.), *Preventing World War III: Some proposals.* New York: Simon & Schuster, 1962.

Read, P. P. *Alive.* New York: Avon, 1974.

Reese, H. W. Perceptual set in young children. *Child Development*, 1963, *34*, 151–159.

Repucci, N. D., & Saunders, J. T. Social psychology of behavior modification: Problems of implementation in natural settings. *American Psychologist*, September 1974, 649–660.

Richter, C. P., Holt, L. E., Jr., & Barelare, B., Jr. Nutritional requirements for normal growth and reproduction in rats studied by the self-selection method. *American Journal of Physiology*, 1938, *122*, 734–744.

Roe, A. A. Study of imagery in research scientists. *Journal of Personality*, 1951, *19*, 459–470.

Rogers, C. R. A theory of therapy, personality, and interpersonal relationships, as developed in the client-centered framework. In S. Koch (Ed.), *Psychology: A study of a science* (Vol. 3). *Formulations of the person and the social context.* New York: McGraw-Hill, 1959. Pp. 184–256.

Rosen, J. L., & Neugarten, B. L. Ego functions in the middle and late years: A thematic apperception study. In B. L. Neugarten et al. (Eds.), *Personality in middle and late life.* New York: Atherton, 1964.

Rosenberg, M. J. An analysis of affective cognitive consistency. In M. J. Rosenberg & C. I. Hovland (Eds.), *Attitude organization and change.* New Haven, Conn.: Yale University Press, 1960. Pp. 15–64.

Rosenberg, S., & Jarvella, R. J. Semantic integration and sentence perception. *Journal of Verbal Learning and Verbal Behavior*, 1970, *9*, 548–553.

Rosenblood, L. K., & Goldstein, J. H. Similarity, intelligence, and affiliation. *Proceedings of the 77th Annual Convention of the American Psychological Association*, 1969, *4*, 341–342.

Rosenhan, D. L. On being sane in insane places. *Science*,

1973, *179*, 250–258.

Rosenthal, R. The Pygmalion effect lives. *Psychology Today*, September 1973, pp. 56–63.

Rosenthal, R., & Jacobson, L. Pygmalion in the classroom. New York: Holt, Rinehart & Winston, 1968.

Rosenthal, R., et al. Body talk and tone of voice: The language without words. *Psychology Today*, September 1974, pp. 64–68.

Rothenbuhler, W. C. Genetics of a behavioral difference in honey bees. *Proceedings of the 10th International Congress on Genetics*, Montreal, 1958, *2*, 242.

Rothenbuhler, W. C. Behaviour genetics of nest cleaning in honey bees: I. Response of four inbred lines to disease-killed brood. *Animal Behaviour*, 1964a, *12*, 578–583.

Rothenbuhler, W. C. Behaviour genetics of nest cleaning in honey bees: IV. Response of F_1 and backcross generations to disease-killed brood. *American Zoologist*, 1964b, *4*, 111–123.

Rothenbuhler, W. C. Genetics and evolutionary considerations of social behavior of honey bees and some related insects. In J. Hirsch (Ed.), *Behavior genetic analysis*. New York: McGraw-Hill, 1967.

Ryan, B. A. *PSI, Keller's personalized system of instruction: An appraisal*. Washington, D.C.: American Psychological Association, 1974.

Saltz, E. *The cognitive bases of human learning*. Homewood, Ill.: Dorsey Press, 1971.

Saltz, E., & Wickey, J. Resolutions of the liberal dilemma in the assassination of President Kennedy. *Journal of Personality*, 1965, *33*, 636–648.

Sanford, R. N. The effects of abstinence from food upon imaginal processes: A further experiment. *Journal of Psychology*, 1937, *3*, 145–159.

Sarason, I. G. The effects of anxiety and threat on the solution of a difficult task. *Journal of Abnormal and Social Psychology*, 1961, *62*, 165–168.

Sarason, I. G. *Abnormal psychology: The problem of maladaptive behavior*. New York: Appleton-Century-Crofts, 1972.

Sarnoff, I., & Zimbardo, P. G. Anxiety, fear and social affiliation. *Journal of Abnormal and Social Psychology*, 1961, *62*, 356–363.

Satloff, A., & Worby, C. M. The psychiatric emergency service: Mirror of change. *American Journal of Psychiatry*, 1970, *126*, 11.

Scarf, M. He and she: Sex hormones and behavior. *New York Times Magazine*, May 7, 1972, pp. 31; 101–107.

Schachter, S. *The psychology of affiliation: Experimental studies of the sources of gregariousness*. Stanford, Calif.: Stanford University Press, 1959.

Schachter, S. The assumption of identity and peripheralist and centralist controversies in motivation and emotion. In M. B. Arnold (Ed.), *Feelings and emotions*. New York: Academic Press, 1970.

Schachter, S. Eat, eat. *Psychology Today*, April 1971a, pp. 44–47; 78–79.

Schachter, S. Some extraordinary facts about obese humans and rats. *American Psychologist*, February 1971b, 129–144.

Schachter, S., Goldman, R., & Gordon, A. Effects of fear, food deprivation, and obesity on eating. *Journal of Personality and Social Psychology*, 1968, *10*, 98–106.

Schachter, S., & Singer, J. E. Cognitive, social and physiological determinants of emotional state. *Psychological Review*, 1962, *69*, 379–399.

Schein, E. H. The Chinese indoctrination program for prisoners of war: A study of attempted "brainwashing." *Psychiatry*, 1956, *19*, 149–172.

Schildkraut, J. J., & Kety, S. S. Biogenic amines and emotion. *Science*, April 7, 1967, *156*, 21–30.

Schofield, J. W. *A framework for viewing the relation between attitudes and actions*. Unpublished doctoral dissertation, Howard University, 1972.

Schneirla, T. C. An evolutionary and developmental theory of biphasic processes underlying approach and withdrawal. In M. R. Jones (Ed.), *Nebraska Symposium on Motivation*. Lincoln: University of Nebraska Press, 1959. Pp. 1–42.

Schulman, J. L., et al. Effect of glucagon on food intake and body weight in man. *Journal of Applied Psychology*, 1957, *11*, 419–421.

Schulman, M. Backstage behaviorism. *Psychology Today*, June 1973, pp. 51–54; 88.

Schutte, R. C., & Hopkins, B. L. The effects of teacher attention on following instructions in a kindergarten class. *Journal of Applied Behavior Analysis*, 1970, *3*, 117–122.

Schwartz, G. E. Biofeedback as therapy. *American Psychologist*, August 1973, 666–673.

Schwartz, G. E. TM relaxes some people and makes them feel better. *Psychology Today*, April 1974, pp. 39–44.

Sears, R. R., Maccoby, E. E., & Levin, H. *Patterns of child rearing*. New York: Harper & Row, 1957.

Seligman, M. E. P. Phobias and preparedness. In M. E. P. Seligman & J. L. Hager, *Biological boundaries of learning*. Englewood Cliffs, N.J.: Prentice-Hall, 1972. Pp. 451–462.

Seligman, M. E. P. Fall into helplessness. *Psychology Today*, June 1973, pp. 43–48.

Seligman, M. E. P., & Hagar, J. L. *Biological boundaries of learning*. Englewood, Cliffs, N. J.: Prentice-hall, 1972.

Sewell, W. H., Mussen, P. H., & Harris, C. W. Relationships among child-training practices. *American Sociological Review*, 1955, *20*, 137–148.

Sheldon, W. H. *The varieties of temperament*. New York: Harper & Row, 1942.

Sherif, M. Superordinate goals in the reduction of intergroup conflict. *American Journal of Sociology*, 1958, *13*, 349–356.

Siegler, M., & Osmond, H. Models of madness: Mental illness is not romantic. *Psychology Today*, November 1974, pp. 71–78.

Sigall, H., & Aronson, E. Opinion change and the gain-loss model of interpersonal attraction. *Journal of Experimental Social Psychology*, 1967, *3*, 178–188.

Siipola, E. M. A study of some effects of preparatory set. *Psychological Monographs*, 1935, *46* (210).

Singer, J. E., Brush, C., & Lubin, S. D. Some aspects of deindividuation: Identification and conformity. *Journal of Experimental Psychology*, 1965, *1*, 356–378.

Singh, D. Preference for bar pressing to obtain reward over freeloading in rats and children. *Journal of Comparative and Physiological Psychology*, 1970, *73*, 320–327.

Singh, D., & Query, W. T. Preference for work over "freeloading" in children. *Psychonometric Science*, 1971, *24*, 77–79.

Sinnott, E. W., Dunn, L. C., & Dobzhansky, T. F. *Principles of genetics* (5th ed.). New York: McGraw-Hill, 1958.

Skeels, H. M. Mental development of children in foster homes. *Journal of Consulting Psychology*, 1938, *2*, 33–43.

Skeels, H. M. The study of the effects of differential stimulation on mentally retarded children: A follow-up report. *American Journal of Mental Deficiencies*, 1942, *46*, 340–350.

Skeels, H. M. Adult status of children with contrasting early life experiences. *Monographs of the Society for Research in Child Development*, 1966, *31* (3), 1–65.

Skinner, B. F. Drive and reflex strength: II. *Journal of General Psychology*, 1932, *6*, 38–48.

Skinner, B. F. "Superstition" in pigeons. *Journal of Experimental Psychology*, 1948, *38*, 168–172.

Skinner, B. F. *The technology of teaching.* Englewood Cliffs, N.J.: Prentice-Hall, 1968.

Sloane, R. B., et al. *Short-term analytically oriented therapy vs. behavior therapy.* Cambridge, Mass.: Harvard University Press, 1975.

Smith, R. K., & Noble, C. E. Effects on a mnemonic technique applied to verbal learning and memory. *Perceptual and Motor Skills*, 1965, *21*, 123–134.

Snyder, S. H. *Madness and the brain.* New York: McGraw-Hill, 1974.

Solomon, R. L., & Corbit, J. D. An opponent-process theory of motivation: II. Cigarette addiction. *Journal of Abnormal Psychology*, 1973, *81*, 158–171.

Spearman, C. E. "General intelligence" objectively determined and measured. *American Journal of Psychology*, 1904, *15*, 72–101.

Spiesman, J. C. Autonomic monitoring of ego defense process. In N. S. Greenfield & W. C. Lewis (Eds.), *Psychoanalysis and current biological thought.* Madison: University of Wisconsin Press, 1965. Pp. 227–244.

Spranger, E. *Types of men: The psychology and ethics of personality.* New York: Johnson Reprint Corp., 1928.

Stein, A., & Friedrich, L. K. Television content and young children's behavior. In J. P. Murray, E. A. Rubinstein, & G. A. Comstock (Eds.), *Television and social behavior* (Vol. 2). *Television and social learning.* Washington, D. C.: U.S. Government Printing Office, 1972.

Steiner, J. A. A questionnaire study of risk-taking in psychiatric patients. *British Journal of Medical Psychology*, 1972, *45*, 365–374.

Stekel, W. *Conditions of nervous anxiety and their treatment* (R. Gabler, trans.). New York: Liveright, 1950.

Stendler, C. B. Critical periods in socialization and overdependency. *Child Development*, 1952, *23*, 1–2.

Stock, M. B., & Smythe, P. M. Does undernutrition during infancy inhibit brain growth and subsequent intellectual development? *Archives of Disorders in Childhood*, 1963, *38*, 546–552.

Stokols, D., et al. Physical, social, and personality determinants of the perception of crowding. *Environment and Behavior*, 1973, *5*, 87–115.

Stolz, S. B., & Lott, D. F. Establishment in rats of a persistent response producing a net loss of reinforcement. *Journal of Comparative and Physiological Psychology*, 1964, *57*, 147–149.

Stone, L. J., & Church, J. *Childhood and adolescence: A psychology of the growing person* (2nd ed.). New York: Random House, 1968.

Strongman, K. T. *The psychology of emotion.* New York: Wiley, 1973.

Stroop, J. R. Studies of interference in serial verbal reactions. *Journal of Experimental Psychology*, 1935, *18*, 643–662.

Suedfeld, P. The benefits of boredom: Sensory deprivation reconsidered. *American Scientist*, January-February 1975, 60–69.

Suomi, S. J., Harlow, H. F., & McKinney, W. T. Monkey psychiatrists. *American Journal of Psychiatry*, 1972, *128*, 927–932.

Szasz, T. Our despotic laws destroy the right to self-control. *Psychology Today*, December 1974, pp. 20–29; 127.

Tavris, C. The frozen world of the familiar stranger. *Psychology Today*, June 1974, pp. 71–80.

Taylor, D. W., Berry, P. C., & Block, C. H. Does group participation when using brainstorming facilitate or inhibit creative thinking? *Administrative Science Quarterly*, 1958, *2*, 23–47.

Thomas, A., Chess, S., & Birch, H. G. The origin of personality. *Scientific American*, August 1970, 102–109.

Thomas, A., et al. *Behavioral individuality in early childhood.* New York: New York University Press, 1963.

Thomas, D. W., & Mayer, J. The search for the secret of fat. *Psychology Today*, September 1973, pp. 74–79.

Thompson, D. F., & Meltzer, L. Communication of emotional intent by facial expression. *Journal of Abnormal and Social Psychology*, 1964, *68*, 129–135.

Thorpe, J. G., Schmidt, E., & Castell, D. A comparison of positive and negative (aversive) conditioning in the treatment of homosexuality. *Behavior Research Therapy*, 1963, *1*, 357–362.

Thurstone, L. L. Primary mental abilities. *Psychometric Monographs*, 1938 (1).

Toffler, A. *Future Shock.* New York: Random House, 1970.

Tolman, E. C. Cognitive maps in rats and men. *Psychological Review*, 1948, *55*, 189–208.

Tomkins, S. S., & McCarter, R. What and where are the primary affects? Some evidence for a theory. *Perceptual and Motor Skills*, 1964, *18*, 119–158.

Torrance, E. P. Some consequences of power differences on decision making in permanent and temporary three-man groups. In A. P. Borgatta & R. F. Bales (Eds.), *Small groups: Studies in social interaction.* New York: Knopf, 1955. Pp. 482–491.

Treisman, A. M. Verbal cues, language, and meaning in selective attention. *American Journal of Psychology*, 1964, *77*, 206–219.

Tresemer, D. Fear of success: Popular, but unpopular. *Psychology Today*, March 1974, pp. 82–85.

Truffaut, Francois. *Hitchcock.* New York: Simon & Schuster, 1967.

Tryk, H. E. Assessment in the study of creativity. In P. McReynolds (Ed.), *Advances in psychological assessment* (Vol. I). Palo Alto, Calif.: Science and Behavior Books, 1968. Pp. 34–54.

Tryon, R. C. Genetic differences in maze-learning abilities in rats. In *39th Yearbook, Part I.* National Society for the Study of Education. Chicago: University of Chicago Press, 1940. Pp. 111–119.

Tuber, D. S., Hothersall, D., & Voith, V. L. Animal clinical psychology. *American Psychologist*, October 1974, 762–766.

Tulving, E., & Psotka, J. Retroactive inhibition in free recall: In accessability of information available in the memory store. *Journal of Experimental Psychology*, 1971, *87*, 1–8.

Turnbull, C. M. Observations. *American Journal of Psychology*, 1961, *1*, 304–308.

Ullmann, L. P., & Krasner, L. *A psychological approach to abnormal behavior*. Englewood Cliffs, N.J.: Prentice-Hall, 1969.

Underwood, B. J. Interference and forgetting. *Psychological Review*, 1957, *64*, 49–60.

Uttal, W. R. *The psychobiology of sensory coding*. New York: Harper & Row, 1973.

Valins, S. Cognitive effects of false heart-rate feedback. *Journal of Personality and Social Psychology*, 1966, *4*, 400–408.

Valenstein, E. S. *Brain control*. New York: Wiley, 1973.

Van Lawick-Goodall, J. *In the shadow of man*. Boston: Houghton Mifflin, 1971.

Verhave, T. The pigeon as a quality-control inspector. *American Psychologist*, 1966, *21*, 109–115.

Vernon, P. E. *Intelligence and cultural environment*. London: Methuen, 1969.

Vinacke, E. A. *The psychology of thinking* (2nd ed.). New York: McGraw-Hill, 1974.

Walk, R. D., & Gibson, E. J. A comparative and analytical study of visual depth perception. *Psychological Monographs*, 1961, no. 75.

Walker, P. C., & Johnson, R. F. Q. The influence of presleep suggestions on dream content: Evidence and methodological problems. *Psychological Bulletin*, 1974, *81* (6), 362–370.

Wallace, R. K., & Benson H. The physiology of meditation. *Scientific American*, February 1972.

Wallach, M. A., & Kogan, N. *Modes of thinking in young children*. New York: Holt, Rinehart & Winston, 1965.

Wallach, M. A., & Wing, C. W., Jr. *The talented student*. New York: Holt, Rinehart & Winston, 1969.

Warner, L. G., & De Fleur, M. L. Attitudes as an interaction concept: Social constraint and social distance as intervening variables between attitudes and action. *American Sociological Review*, 1969, *34*, 153–169.

Watson, J. B. Psychology as the behaviorist views it. *Psychological Review*, 1913, *20*, 158–177.

Watson, J. B., & Raynor, R. Conditioned emotional reactions. *Journal of Experimental Psychology*, 1920, *3*, 1–14.

Weil, A. The open mind. *Psychology Today*, October 1972, pp. 51–66.

Weintraub, D. J. Perception. *Annual Review of Psychology*, 1975, *26*, 263–289.

Weiss, J. M. Effects of coping behavior in different warning signal conditions on stress pathology in rats. *Journal of Comparative and Physiological Psychology*, 1971, *1*, 1–14.

Weiss, J. M., Glazer, H. I., & Pohorecky, L. A. Neurotransmitters and helplessness: A chemical bridge to depression? *Psychology Today*, December 1974, pp. 58–62.

Wheatley, M. D. The hypothalamus and affective behavior in cats. *Archives of Neurological Psychiatry*, 1944, *52*, 298–316.

White, B., & Held, R. Plasticity of sensorimotor development in the human infant. In J. F. Rosenblith & W. Allinsmith (Eds.), *The causes of behavior: Readings in child development and educational psychology*. Boston: Allyn & Bacon, 1966. Pp. 60–70.

White, R. W. *Lives in progress* (2nd ed.). New York: Holt, Rinehart & Winston, 1966.

White, R. W., & Watt, N. F. *The abnormal personality* (4th ed.). New York: Ronald Press, 1973.

Whorf, B. L. *Language, thought, and reality*. New York: M.I.T. Press–Wiley, 1956.

Whyte, W. H. *The organization man*. New York: Simon & Schuster, 1956.

Wiener, S., & Sutherland, G. A normal XYY man. *Lancet* (London), 1968, *ii*; 1352.

Wiesel, T. N., & Hubel, D. H. Effects of visual deprivation on morphology and physiology of cells in the cat's geniculate body. *Journal of Neurophysiology*, 1963, *26*, 978–993.

Willerman, L., & Churchill, J. A. Intelligence and birthweight in identical twins. *Child Development*, 1967, *38*, 623–629.

Williams, D. R., & Williams, H. Auto-maintenance in the pigeon: Sustained pecking despite contingent non-reinforcement. In M. E. P. Seligman & J. L. Hager (Eds.), *Biological boundaries of learning*. Englewood Cliffs, N.J.: Prentice-Hall, 1972. Pp. 158–173.

Winsborough, H. H. The social consequences of high population density. *Law and Contemporary Problems*, 1965, *30*, 120–126.

Winter, D. G. *The power motive*. New York: Free Press, 1973.

Witkin, H. A., et al. *Psychological differentiation*. New York: Wiley, 1962.

Wolf, M., Mees, H., & Risley, T. Application of operant conditioning procedures to the behavior problems of an autistic child. *Behavior Research Therapy*, 1964, *1*, 305–312.

Wolff, C. T., Friedman, S. B., Hofer, M. A., & Mason, J. W. Relationship between psychological defenses and mean urinary 17-hydroxycorticosteroid excretion rates: I. A study of parents of fatally ill children. *Psychosomatic Medicine*, 1964, *26*, 576–591.

Wolitzky, D. L., & Wachtel, P. L. Personality and perception. In B. B. Wolman (Ed.), *Handbook of general psychology*. Englewood Cliffs, N.J.: Prentice-Hall, 1973. Pp. 826–857.

Wolpe, J. *The practice of behavior therapy*. New York: Pergamon Press, 1969a.

Wolpe, J. For phobia: A hair of the hound. *Psychology Today*, June 1969b, pp. 34–37.

Wolpe, J., & Rachman, S. Psychoanalytic evidence: A critique of Freud's case of Little Hans. *Journal of Nervous and Mental Diseases*, 1960, *130*, 198–220.

Woodworth, R. S. *Dynamic psychology*. New York: Columbia University Press, 1918a.

Woodworth, R. S. *Personal data sheet*. Chicago: Stoelting, 1918b.

Woodworth, R. S., & Schlosberg, H. *Experimental psychology* (rev. ed.). New York: Holt, Rinehart & Winston, 1954.

Wundt, W. *Principles of physiological psychology* (E. B. Titchener, trans.). New York: Macmillan, 1904. (Originally published in German in 1874.)

Yarmey, A. D. I recognize your face but I can't remember your name: Further evidence on the tip-of-the-tongue phenomenon. *Memory and Cognition*, 1973, *1*, 287–290.

Young, M. N., & Gibson, W. B. *How to develop an exceptional memory*. Philadelphia: Chilton, 1962.

Zajonc, R. B. Social facilitation. *Science*, 1965, *149*, 269–274.

Zajonc, R. B. *Social psychology: An experimental approach*. Belmont, Calif.: Wadsworth, 1966.

Zajonc, R. B. Attitudinal effects of mere exposure. *Journal of Personality and Social Psychology,* 1968, *8,* 1–29.

Zajonc, R. B. Dumber by the dozen. *Psychology Today,* January 1975, pp. 37–43.

Zajonc, R. B., & Markus, G. B. Birth order and intellectual development. *Psychological Review,* 1975, *82* (1), 74–88.

Zeigarnik, B. Ueber das Behalten von Erledigten und unerledigten Handlungen. *Psychologische Forschung,* 1927, *9,* 1–85.

Zeigler, P. H., & Leibowitz, H. Apparent visual size as a function of distance for children and adults. *American Journal of Psychology,* 1957, *70;* 106–109.

Zelazo, P., Zelazo, N. A., & Kolb, S. "Walking" in the newborn. *Science,* April 1972, *176,* 314–315.

Zimbardo, P. G. The tactics and ethnics of persuasion. In B. T. King & E. McGinniss (Eds.), *Attitudes, conflict and social change.* New York: Academic Press, 1972.

Zubek, J. P. Review of effects of prolonged deprivation. In J. E. Rasmussen (Ed.), *Man in isolation and confinement.* Chicago: Aldine, 1973, 13–67.

Name Index

Adler, Alfred, 14, 432–434, 530–531
Allport, Gordon, 381, 441–442, 446, 453
American Psychological Association (APA), 23
Amoore, John E., 297
Angell, James R., 10
Aquinas, Thomas, 6
Argyris, Chris, 584
Arnold, Magda, 400–401
Asch, S. E., 561–562, 568, 569
Ayllon, Teodoro, 549
Azrin, Nathan, 549

Bandura, Albert, 101–102, 151, 153
Bard, L. L., 394–395
Bartlett, Frederic C., 177, 184
Beethoven, Ludwig von, 101, 229
Békésy, Georg von, 294
Bellugi-Klima, Ursula, 217
Berkowitz, Leonard, 409
Berne, Eric, 543
Bettelheim, Bruno, 480, 482, 485
Bieber, Irving, 509
Binet, Alfred, 250
Birdwhistell, Ray, 412–413
Blake, William, 517
Bogart, Humphrey, 502
Bonaparte, Napoleon, 187
Bower, T. G. R., 86, 158, 164, 306
Bramel, Dana, 482–483
Breuer, Dr. Josef, 425–426
Broz, Barbara, 158–159
Brown, Roger, 217, 572
Bruner, Jerome, 74, 95–96
Buckley, William F., Jr., 235
Bunker, Archie, 582
Butler, Robert, 114

Caesar, Julius, 101
Calley, William, 569
Cameron, Paul, 114
Cannon, W. B., 394–395
Capone, Al, 518
Cavett, Dick, 235
Cermak, L. S., 179, 191, 194
Charcot, Jean-Martin, 425, 495
Chichester, Sir Francis, 113
Chomsky, Noam, 90, 216
Cohen, D. B., 182, 201
Coleman, J. S., 100, 103
Committee on Ethical Standards, 24
Cottell, Raymond, 253, 257, 443

Darrow, Clarence, 483
Darwin, Charles, 7, 35, 412

Davitz, Joel, 411–412
deBeauvoir, Simone, 114
Deese, J., 175, 183, 195
DeFries, J. C., 40, 44
Deikman, A. J., 345, 350
Delgado, José, 66–67
Dennis, M. G., 77
Dennis, W., 77, 258
Descartes, René, 228
Dewey, John, 10
Dietrich, Marlene, 113
Dix, Dorothea, 495
Dobzhansky, T., 41, 268
Dollard, John, 433

Eagleton, Thomas, 528
Ebbinghaus, Herman, 175, 195
Edison, Thomas Alva, 31
Egeth, H., 175, 183, 195
Einstein, Albert, 78, 101, 200, 442, 567
Eliot, T. S., 583–584
Epstein, Seymour, 468
Erikson, Erik, 104–106, 109, 114, 435–438, 531
Ervin, Frank, 545
Estes, W. K., 243
Etziani, Amatai, 44

Fantz, Robert L., 83–84
Farb, P., 213, 216
Festinger, Leon, 567, 586
Fischer, Bobby, 470
Freud, Anna, 531
Freud, Sigmund, 13–14, 97, 101, 155, 201, 229, 343, 373, 381–382, 425–430, 445–446, 479, 484–485, 495–496, 501, 503, 530–531, 540
Fromm, Erich, 435

Galton, Sir Francis, 8–9, 35
Gandhi, Mahatma, 571
Gardner, Beatrice, 216, 218
Gardner, Robert, 216, 218
Genovese, Kitty, 573
Gergen, Kenneth, 24, 440
Glasser, William, 534
Glucksberg, S., 199–200
Gogh, Vincent van, 514
Goya, Francisco, 515
Guilford, J. P., 238–240

Hall, E. T., 588
Hansel, C. E. M., 326
Harlow, Harry, 149, 189, 538
Hartmann, Heinz, 531

Hathaway, S. R., 451–453
Hayakawa, S. I., 212
Heidbreder, E., 210–211
Helmholtz, Hermann von, 287–289, 294
Hering, Ewald, 287–289
Hilgard, E. R., 158, 164, 306
Holmes, Justice Oliver Wendell, 44
Hopkins, Johns, 10
Horner, Matina, 377–378
Horney, Karen, 434, 530–531
Hulse, S. H., 175, 183, 195
Humphrey, Hubert, 578
Huxley, Aldous, 128

Jagger, Mick, 471–473
James, William, 9–10, 12–13, 83, 394, 401
Jarvik, L. F., 114, 349
Jensen, A. R., 266–268
Joint Commission on Mental Health of Children, 551
Jost, Alfred, 49
Jung, Carl, 13, 431–432

Kafka, Franz, 228
Kant, Emanuel, 101
Karpov, Anatoly, 470
Keele, S. W., 180
Kelly, George, 444
Keniston, Kenneth, 106
Kennedy, John F., 567
Kimmel, D. C., 108–109. 111–112, 114
King, Billie Jean, 378
King, J. L., 199–200
King, Martin Luther, Jr., 571
Klineberg, Otto, 415
Koch, Kenneth, 136–137
Koffka, Kurt, 11–12
Köhler, Wolfgang, 11–12
Kübler-Ross, Elisabeth, 115

Laing, R. D., 14–15, 496–497
Lange, Carl, 394, 401
LaPiere, R. T., 579
Lawrence, Mary Wells, 378
Lazarus, Richard, 401–402
Leboyer, Frederick, 75
LeMasters, E. E., 108
Lenneberg, Eric, 217
Lesser, Ira, 436
Lewin, Kurt, 181
Lorenz, Konrad, 99, 373
Lovaas, Ivar, 535
Lykken, David, 159

McCarthy, Eugene, 476

McClearns, G. E., 40, 44
McClelland, David, 243
McConnell, J. V., 192
McConnell, R. A., 326
McGough, J. L., 191
McKinley, J. C., 451–453
Manson, Charles, 513
Marcia, James, 436
Mark, Vernon, 545
Marrow, A. J., 181
Maslow, Abraham, 15, 382–383
Masserman, Jules, 481
May, Rollo, 14, 532
Mayer, Jean, 362
Mead, Margaret, 378
Mednick, S. A., 240, 259
Melzack, Ronald, 60–61, 305–306
Mendel, Gregor, 32, 35, 40
Mesmer, Franz Anton, 343, 495
Milgram, Stanley, 22–24, 569–570
Miller, G. A., 180
Miller, Neal E., 157, 433
Mischel, Walter, 446–447
Mozart, Wolfgang Amadeus, 229
Müller, Johannes, 177, 279
Murray, H. A., 457–458

Neugarten, B. L., 107, 113–114
Newcomb, Theodore, 581
Nixon, Richard, 567
Norman, D. A., 185

Orlofsky, Jacob, 436

Pavlov, Ivan, 124–134, 165

Perls, Frederick (Fritz), 540
Peterson, L. R., 134
Piaget, Jean, 14, 91–95, 97
Pinel, Philippe, 494–495
Pines, M., 63, 74
Poincaré, Henri, 225
Pollio, H. R., 206
Premack, David, 218
Pressey, S. L., 161–164

Rank, Otto, 530–531
Reese, H. W., 86–87
Rogers, Carl, 438–439, 531–532
Rosen, B. C., 101
Rosen, J. L., 107
Rosenhan, D. L., 547

Saltz, E., 151, 211
Sartre, Jean-Paul, 14
Schachter, Stanley, 361–362, 399–402
Sheldon, William, 424–425
Simon, Theodore, 250
Skeels, H. M., 265–266
Skinner, B. F., 12–13, 135–136, 138, 146,
    156, 161–164, 445
Spearman, Charles, 237
Spender, Stephen, 229
Sperry, Roger, 63
Spiesman, Joseph C., 403
Spranger, Eduard, 453–454
Strasberg, Lee, 165
Strongman, K. T., 390
Szasz, Thomas, 496

Terman, L. M., 249–250

Terrace, Herbert, 218–219
Thomas, Alexander, 447
Thomas, Donald, 362
Thurstone, L. L., 237–238
Titchener, Edward Bradford, 6–9
Toffler, Alvin, 470
Tolman, Edward C., 14, 208
Treisman, Anne, 315
Turnbull, Colin, 337–338
Tyron, R. C., 260–262, 264

Underwood, B. J., 196

Valenstein, Elliot, 66–67
Valins, Stuart, 400
Verhave, Thom, 145

Wall, Patrick, 60–61, 305–306
Watson, John B., 10–13, 132
Wechsler, David, 254
Weil, A., 339, 345
Wertheimer, Max, 11–12
White, Robert, 105–106
Whorf, Benjamin, 212–214, 216
Whyte, W. H., 18–19
Wolff, C. T., 480
Woodworth, R. S., 381, 451
Wundt, Wilhelm, 6–7

Young, Thomas, 287–289

Zeigarnik, Bluma, 181
Zubek, J. P., 36, 264, 340

Subject Index

abnormal behavior
  current views of, 496–497
  defined, 491–493
  historical views of, 493–495
  mental illness models, 496–497
  see also character disorders, genetics,
    neuroses, psychoses
absolute refractory period, 52
absolute threshold, of sensation, 280–281
accommodation, of eye lens, 325
acetylcholine, 53–54
achievement
  alienated, 436
  need for (nAch), 375–376
achievement tests, 244–245
ACTH, see andrenocorticotrophic hormone
activation theory, of emotion, 405–406
activity, as motivator, 367
activity theory, 113
acupuncture, 305
adaptation
  sensory, 281
  in vision, 286
adaptive emotions, 408–409
adjustment
  defined, 465–466
  factors requiring, 466–467
  ways of, 476–486
  well-adjusted individual, 486–487
Adler theory of personality, 432–434
adolescence, physical changes in, 78–80
adrenal glands, 47–48
adrenalin, see epinephrine
adults
  development, 106–111
  family, 108–109
  milestones, 107–111
  personality development, 106–107
  transition, from child, 104–106
  work cycle, 109–111
  young, 105
affectional systems, 396
affective psychosis, 514–515
  see also specific psychoses
afferent nerve fibers, 57
afferent neuron, 51
affiliation, as motivator, 378–379
afterimages, 288
aggression
  behavioral inhibition of, 66
  as direct coping, 477
  frustration-aggression hypothesis, 374
  innate drive theory of, 373
  as motivator, 373–374
  therapy for, 409

aging, 111–114
  cognitive changes, 112–113
  physical changes, 111–112
  "successful," 113–114
alcohol, affecting perception, 346
alcoholism
  as character disorder, 510–512
  delirium tremens, 519
alienation
  in achievement, 436
  vs. individuation, 106
  in personality, 436
altered states of consciousness, 338–350
  defined, 338
  major kinds of, 339–350
American Sign Language (Ameslan),
    216–219
amnesia
  as dissociative neurosis, 500
  global demential, 200
  hysterical, 199
  organic, 200
  retrograde, 183
amphetamines, 54
  affecting perception, 347
  and barbiturates, 347
amplitude, of sound waves, 290
ampulla, 301
amygdala, 393
anal stage, of psychosexual development,
    430
andrenocorticotrophic hormone (ACTH),
    47–48
androgens, 48
animals
  psychotherapy for, 538
  use of, in research, 25–26
anvil, in ear, 291
anxiety
  adjustment to, 471
  aggression and, 374
  as motivating force, 434
  neurosis, a case history, 498–499
apathy, bystander, 573
applied psychology, 24–25
approach
  cognitive consistency, to attitude
    change, 586–587
  cognitive dissonance, to attitude change,
    586–587
  emotions and, 404–405
  informational, in attitude change, 583–
    586
approach/approach conflict, 473–474
approach/avoidance conflict, 404–405, 475

aptitude tests, 244–245
archetypes, 431
ASCs, see altered states of consciousness
association areas, of cerebral cortex, 61
association neuron, 51, 57
associative thinking, 225–231
attachment theory, 98
attention, 312–317
  focus of, 312–313
  marginal, 313–314
  selective, 314–315
attitudes, 577–587
  change, 577–587
  components, 577–579
  development, 579–581
  measurement of, 578
  vs. traits, 441
attraction, in interpersonal relations,
    564–566
attribution theory, 562–564
authority, obedience to, 569–570
autism, 513–514
  child, 536
  infantile, 518
autistic thinking, 227
autonomic nervous system, 55–56
  conditioning and, 156–158
  parasympathetic, 55–56, 59
  sympathetic, 55–56, 59
autonomy
  in personality development, 98–99
  vs. shame, 437
aversive conditioning, 535–536
avoidance/avoidance conflict, 474
avoidance, emotions and, 404–405
avoidance training, 139, 146
axon, 51
axon terminal, 53–54

babies, see infants
balance, 106
barbiturates
  affecting perception, 347
  amphetamines, 347
basket nerve ending, in skin, 303
basilar membrane, in ear, 292–293
behavior
  abnormal, 491–522
  aggressive, 374
  chains, 147
  classroom, 158–161
  elicited, 135–136
  emitted, 135
  forcing, 137
  functional autonomy, 381

Behavior (continued)
  genetics, 35–44
  infant, 74–76
  inhibition of aggressive drive, 66
  maternal, 366–367
  mob, 571
  modification, 158–161
  physical environment and, 446–448
  psychological environment and, 446–448
  reinforcement of, 135–136
  self-modification of, 164–166
  shaping, in operant conditioning, 146–147
  sociopathic, 512–513
  space, 446
  stimulus-seeking, 367
  tendency, as attitude component, 577–579
  see also classical conditioning, operant conditioning, personality development
behaviorism, 10–11
behavior therapy
  aversive conditioning, 535–536
  desensitization, 537
  operant conditioning, 535
  reciprocal inhibition, 537–539
belief, as attitude component, 577–579
Bennington College, 580–581
bias, experimenter, 21
  see also prejudice
Binet-Simon Scale, 250–252, 255–258
binocular cues, in vision, 322, 325–327
biofeedback, 156–158
biological clocks, 364
biological preparedness, 154–156
birth order, intelligence and, 261
Birth Without Violence (Leboyer), 75
Black English, 215
blind spot, 284–285
body language, 413–415
body senses, 299–302
  see also specific senses
brain, 58–60
  development of, 78
  in nervous system, 54–55
  see also brainstem, cerebral cortex, forebrain, hindbrain, hypothalamus, medulla, memory, midbrain, psychosurgery, thalamus
brainstem, 58–59, 64
Brave New World (Huxley), 128
bystander apathy, 573

Cannon-Bard theory of emotions, 394–395, 401
cardinal traits, 442
catatonic schizophrenia, 516
categories, in memory storage, 187–189
cells, sex, 32–33
centering, 92
central nervous system, 54–60
  see also brain
central tendency, measures of, 597–598
central traits, 442
cerebellum, 58–59
cerebral cortex, 59–61, 63–65
  sex and, 365
cerebrotonia, 424–425
cerebrum, 58
chain, as communication pattern, 575–576

character disorders, 506–513
  alcoholism, 510–512
  drug addiction, 510–512
  sexual deviation, 507–510
  sociopathic behavior, 512–513
  see also abnormal behavior, neuroses, psychoses, specific disorders
chemical messages, of nervous system, 45
chemical senses, 295–299; see also specific senses
childhood schizophrenia, 518
children, developmental norms, 78; see also development; infants
chimpanzees, language learning in, 216–219
Christensen-Guilford Test, 259
chromosomes, 32–33, 38
  and criminality, 40
  and mental deficiency, 40
  X, 36–37
  Y, 36–37
chunking, 180
circle, as communication pattern, 574–576
classical conditioning, 126–134, 136
  discrimination, 133
  extinction, 129–130
  generalization, 133
  higher-order, 133–134
  inhibition, 130
  Pavlov's experiments, 124–134
  spontaneous recovery, 129–130
  see also behavior
client-centered therapy, 531–532
clinical psychology, 16–18
closure, in perception, 319
cocaine, affecting perception, 348–349
cochlea, in ear, 292–293
coding
  in hearing, 294
  in memory, 183
  neural impulse, 278
cognition, 91–96; see also cognitive development; thinking
cognitive consistency approach
  attitude change and, 586–587
cognitive development, 91–96
  adolescent thought, 94
  sensory-motor stage, 91–93
cognitive dissonance, 211, 380–381
  attitude change and, 586–587
cognitive map, 208
cognitive psychology, 14
cognitive revolution, in learning, 150–151
cognitive style, perception affected, 336–337
cognitive theory of emotions, 399–403
cold sensation, see temperature sensation
collective unconscious, 431
color blindness, 288
  genetics and, 37
color vision, 287–290
  opponent-process theory, 287–290
  trichromatic theory, 287–289
Columbia University, 147
common fate principle, in perception, 321
common traits, 442
communication, patterns of, 575–576
community psychology, 550–551
comparative psychology, 154–156
complementary expectations, in interpersonal relations, 564, 566
compromise, as direct coping, 477, 478

computer-assisted instruction, 164
concepts, and thought, 206, 209–211
concrete operations, in stage theory, 93–94
conditioned response (CR), 126–127, 129–130, 133–134
conditioned stimulus (CS), 126–127, 129, 131, 133
conditioning, 11, 123
  classical, see classical conditioning
  higher-order, 133–134
  operant, see operant conditioning
cones, in retina, 283–284
  adaptation, 286
  neural connections, 284–285
conflict
  adjustment to, 473–476
  approach/approach, 473–474
  approach/avoidance, 475
  avoidance/avoidance, 474–475
  double approach/avoidance, 475–476
  social, 570–572
conformity, 567–569
conjunctive concept, in thought, 209
conscience, growth of, 97; see also superego
consciousness, altered states of, 338–350
consistency, as motivator, 380–381
constitutional theory of personality, 424–425
construct validity, 247
contact, as motivator, 371–372
continuity, in perception, 320
continuous reinforcement, 141
control group, 21
convergence, of eyes, 327
conversion reaction, see hysteria
convolutions, 61
coping
  defensive, 476, 478–487
  direct, 476–478
cornea, 282
corpus callosum, 59, 63
correlation
  coefficients, in testing, 246
  in measurement, 605–606
correlational method, 21–23
countertransference, 539
CR, see conditioned response
creativity
  associative thinking and, 225–231
  autistic thinking and, 227
  capacity to discover, 228–229
  Christensen-Guilford Test, 259
  convergent thinking, 240–241
  daydreaming, 226–227
  dreams, 227–228
  illumination, 225
  incubation, 225
  and intelligence, 241–242
  and logic, 231
  measuring, 242–245
  nature of, 239–242
  preparation for, 225
  in problem solving, 224–225
  process of, 240–241
  Remote Associates Test, 259
  tests for, 259–260
  Torrance Test of, 259
  verification of, 225
cretinism, 46
criminality, and Y chromosome, 40
crowd behavior, see mob behavior

crowding, 588–590
  effects on animals, 589
crystallized general ability, 257
CS, see conditioned stimulus
cued-recall tests, in interference theory, 198
cueing, in memory retrieval, 186, 190
cues, false, 561
cultural differences, affecting perception, 337–338
cultural patterns
  emotional expression and, 415–416
Culture-Fair Intelligence Test, 256–258
curiosity, as motivator, 369–370
cytoplasm, 34–35

daydreams, 226–227
death, preparation for, 114–115
decibels, of sound, 290
decreasing restraint, in operant conditioning, 136
defense mechanisms, 479–487
defensive coping, 476, 478–487
  denial, 479–480
  displacement, 481–482
  identification, 483–485
  intellectualization, 480
  projection, 482–483
  reaction formation. 480–481
  regression, 485–486
  repression, 480–481
  sublimation, 482
deindividuation, 574
delirium tremens (D.T.'s), 519
delta sleep, 342
dendrite, 51, 54
denial, as defense mechanism, 479–480
deoxyribonucleic acid (DNA), 34–35, 192
dependent variable, 20–21
depression, 54
  neurotic, 504–506
  psychotic, 514–515
depth perception, 84–85, 88, 322–327
desensitization, 537
despair, vs. integrity, 114, 438
development
  adolescent, 78–80
  adulthood, 104–111
  aging, 111–114
  child, 78–104
  cognitive, 91–96
  genetics and, 41–43
  language, 88–91
  maturation in, 77–78
  moral, 97
  motor, 80–83
  neural system, 78–79
  newborn baby, 74–76
  norms for, 78
  perceptual, 83–88
  personality, 96–104
  physical, 78–80
  prehensile, 82
  sexual characteristics, 78–79
  see also infants, personality development
developmental norms, 78
developmental psychology, 15, 17
devil effects, in person perception, 562
diabetes mellitus, 47
dichotic listening, 315
dichromat, 289

difference threshold, in sensation, 280–281
Digit Span Test, 243
Digit Symbol Test, 243
dimensional concept, in thought, 209, 211
direct coping, 476–478
discrimination
  in classical conditioning, 133
  in learning, 149–150
  in operant conditioning, 143–144
  visual, 83–84
  see also prejudice
disengagement theory, 113
disjunctive concept, in thought, 209
displacement
  as defense mechanism, 482
  of instinct, 429
disruptive emotions, 408–409
distance
  as body communication, 415
  perception of, 322–327
DNA, see deoxyribonucleic acid
dominant gene, 33–34
dopamine, 53–54
double approach/avoidance conflict, 475–476
Down's syndrome, 38–39
dreams
  creativity and, 227–228
  need for, 363
  sleep and, 340–343, 363–364
drugs
  addiction as character disorder, 510–512
  experiences with, 345–350
  in society, 512
  in therapy, 546
dying, psychological changes when, 115
dynamic forces, 429–430
dynamics, group, 574–577
dynamic traits, 442

ear
  neural connections, 293
  structure, 291–292
  see also hearing; sound waves; specific parts of ear
ectomorphy, 424–425
educational psychology, 15–18
effectors, in nervous system, 55
efferent nerve fibers, 57
efferent neurons, 51
ego, 426–431, 435
eidetic imagery, 207
Electra complex, 430
electrical messages
  of the nervous system, 45
electrical stimulation of brain, 66–67
electric shock therapy, 544–545
Ellis Island, 43
emitted behavior, 135
emotional experiences, basic, 402–407
emotional expression, cultural patterns of, 415–416
emotion
  adaptive vs. disruptive, 408
  attitudes and, 407–408
  Cannon-Bard theory of, 394–395
  cognitive theory of, 399–403
  communication of, 410–416
  development of, 395–399
  dimensions of, 404–406
  function of, 407–410
  intensity of, 405–406

James-Lange theory of, 394
  as motives, 409–410
  nature of, 390–407
  physiology of, 390–395
  pro and con, 410
  psychology of, 395–402
  Yerkes-Dodson law, 408–409
enactive representation, 95
encapsulated end organs, in skin, 303
encounter groups, 540, 542
endocrine glands, 45–48, 59
endocrine system, 31–32, 44–50
endomorphy, 424–425
engram, 191
environment
  crowding, 588–590
  effects on individual, 587–590
  intelligence and, 263–266
  personal space, 588
  urban, 589–590
environmental psychology, 15, 26, 587–590
epinephrine, 48, 391, 399–400
equipotentiality, 154
Esalen Institute, 15
ESB, see electrical stimulation of brain
ESP, see extrasensory perception
estrogens, 48, 365
estrus cycle, 365
ethics, in psychology, 23–24
ethnocentrism, 376–377
eugenics, 43
exhibitionism, 510
existential psychology, 14
existential therapy, 532
expectations
  complementary, in interpersonal relations, 564, 566
  and perception, 336
experience, in perceptual development, 87–88
experimental method, 20–21
experimental neurosis, 134
experimental psychology, 16
experimenter bias, 21
explanatory concepts, in thought, 211
exploration, as motivator, 369–370
external inhibition, 132
extinction
  in classical conditioning, 129–130
  in operant conditioning, 144–146
extrasensory perception (ESP), 7, 326
extraverted personality, 431
eye
  accommodation of lens, 325
  adaptation, 286
  brief visual storage, 316
  color, see color vision
  neural connections, 284–285
  rods and cones, 283–284
  see also specific parts of eye; vision

facial expressions, emotions and, 412–413
false cues, in person perception, 561
family
  in adult development, 108–109
  intelligence and, 261
  therapy, 544
fear
  as motivator, 372–373
  of success (FOS), 378
fetishism, 510

firstborn children, 101
fixed-interval schedule, of reinforcement, 141
fixed-ratio schedule, of reinforcement, 142
fluid general ability, 257
forcing behavior, in operant conditioning, 137
forebrain, 59, 62, 64
forgetting, 192–201
    motivated, 198–200
    theories about, 193–198
    see also memory; retention
formal operations, in stage theory, 93–94
FOS, see fear of success
fovea, 283
frames, in programmed instruction, 162
free association, in psychoanalysis, 529
free nerve endings, 302–303
free recall, 175
Free Speech Movement, 581
frequency, of sound waves, 290
frequency distributions, in measurement, 598–602
frequency theory, of hearing, 294
Freudian slips, 13, 426–427
Freud theory of personality, 425–430
frigidity, 507–508
Fromm theory of personality, 435
frustration
    adjustment to, 471–473
    five sources of, 472–473
frustration-aggression hypothesis, 374
fugue states, 500–501
fully structured conflict, 570–572
functional autonomy, 318
functional fixedness,
    in problem solving, 221, 223–224
functionalism, 9–10

galvanic skin response (GSR), 165
gametes, 32–33, 38
gate-control theory of pain, 60–61, 305–306
generalization
    in classical conditioning, 132–133
    in operant conditioning, 143
generativity
    in personality development, 106
    vs. stagnation, 438
genes, 32
    biochemical basis, 34–35
    dominant, 33
    phenotype, 33–34
    polygenic system, 41
    recessive, 33, 37–38
    see also genetics
genetics, 31–32
    abnormalities, 37–40
    behavior, 35–44
    and development, 41–43
    polygenic inheritance, 40–41
    sex-linked characteristics, 36–37
    social implications of, 43–44
genital stage, of psychosexual development, 430
Gesell Developmental Schedules, 253
Gestalt group therapy, 540
Gestalt psychology, 11–14, 317, 335
gestures, emotion and, 416
g factor, in intelligence, 237
glands, see specific glands
global demential amnesia, 200

glucagon, 47
gonads, 47–48
Goodenough Draw-a-Person Test, 257–258
gray matter
    in cerebral cortex, 59–60
    in spinal cord, 56–58
group
    control, 21
    experimental, 21
    reference, as attitude source, 580–581
group dynamics, 574–577
    leadership and, 574–575
    patterns of communication in, 575–576
    problem solving and, 576–577
group psychotherapies
    encounter groups, 540, 542
    family, 544
    Gestalt, 540–541
    sensitivity, 542
    traditional, 540
    transactional, 543
GSR, see galvanic skin response
Guilford's Structure of the Intellect, 238–239
guilt vs. initiative, 437

habit vs. trait, 441
halfway houses, 548
hallucinogens
    affecting perception, 349–350
halo effects, in person perception, 562
hammer, in ear, 291
hearing
    neural connections, 293
    sound waves, 290–291
    theories of, 293–295
    see also ear; sound waves; specific parts of ear
hebephrenic schizophrenia, 516
hemophilia, genetics and, 37–38
heredity
    cell mechanisms in, 32–34
    intelligence and, 260–263
heroin, affecting perception, 348
higher-order conditioning, 133–134
hindbrain, 58, 61–62
hippocampus, 64
homeostasis, 45
homosexuality, 508–510
    origins of, 509
hormones, 45
Horney theory of personality, 434
human development, see adolescence; adulthood; development; dying; infants
humanistic psychology, 14
hunger
    learning, 361
    physiological mechanisms, 359–360
    specific, 360–361
Huntington's chorea, and genetics, 41
hypnosis, 343–345
hypochondria, 502
hypoglycemia, 47
hypothalamus, 47, 49, 59, 62, 64, 66, 363, 365, 392
hypothesis, 20–21
hysteria neurosis, 501–502
hysterical amnesia, 199

iconic representation, 95
id, 426–431

identification
    as defense mechanism, 483–485
    personality development and, 100–101
identity
    achievement, 436
    development of, 103–104
    diffusion, 436
    personality and, 440, 435
    vs. role confusion, 436–437
    stabilization of ego, 105–106
images
    eidetic, 207
    in thought, 206–209
imitation, personality development and, 100–101
impotence, 507–508
imprinting, 99
impulse, neural, 51
independent variable, 20–21
individual psychotherapies
    client-centered, 531–532
    existential, 532
    psychoanalysis, 528–531
    rational, 532–534
    reality, 534
individual traits, 442
individuation vs. alienation, 106
industrial psychology, 15–16
industry vs. inferiority, 437
infantile autism, 518
Infant Intelligence Scale, 253
infants
    cognitive development, 91–96
    firstborns, 101
    individual differences, 76
    language development, 88–91
    motor development, 80–83
    newborn, 74–76
    perceptual development, 83–88
    personality development, 96–104
    rights of, 75
    see also development
inferiority
    drive, 432–434
    vs. industry, 437
inhibition
    in classical conditioning, 130–132
    in forgetting, 194–198
initiative vs. guilt, 437
insight
    in problem solving, 224–226
    in psychoanalysis, 530
    see also creativity
instincts
    death, 429
    life, 429
    sex, see libido
institutionalization, see mental institutions
insufficient information, in person perception, 561
insulin, 47
insulin shock treatment, 544–545
integration, language development and, 96
integrity vs. despair, 114, 438
intellectualization, as defense mechanism, 480
intelligence
    birth order and, 261
    and creativity, 241–242
    determinants of, 260–271
    environment and, 263–266
    family size and, 261

g factor, 237
  heredity and, 260–263
  measuring, 242–245
  nature of, 236–239
  race differences, 266–269
  sex differences and, 270
  tests, 247–259
intelligence quotient (IQ), 38–39, 243,
    248–249, 253, 255–256, 258, 261–
    263, 265–266, 268
  and creativity, 241–242
  meaning of, 251
  and occupation, 264
  older people and, 112–113
  sex differences and, 270
  teacher expectations and, 269
  tests, 112–113
  verbal, 447
  see also intelligence
interactionism theory, of personality de-
    velopment, 446–448
interest similarity, in interpersonal rela-
    tions, 564–566
interference theory, in forgetting, 194–198
interneuron, 51
interpersonal influence, 566–574
interpersonal relations, 560–574
  attraction in, 564–566
  attribution theory, 562–564
  interpersonal influence in, 566–574
  liking in, 564–566
  person perception, 560–562
interstimulus interval, 127
interview, in personality testing
  structured, 449–450
  unstructured, 449–450
intimacy vs. isolation, 105, 436–437
introverted personality, 431
involuntary psychosis, 515
involuntary responses, 156; see also classi-
    cal conditioning
ions, 51
IQ, see intelligence quotient
iris, eye, 282
irrational personality, 431–432
isolation vs. intimacy, 105, 436–437

James-Lange theory of emotion, 394, 401
Jung theory of personality, 431–432
just noticeable difference (j.n.d.), in sensa-
    tion, 280–281

kinesics, 413–415
kinesthesis, 299, 301
Klinefelter's syndrome, 39

language
  Black English, 215
  body, 413–415
  chimpanzees, teaching to, 216–219
  phonetics, 214
  psycholinguistics, 214
  semantics, 216
  signs, 211–212
  syntax, 214
  and thoughts, 206, 211–219
language development
  chronology of, 88–89
  in infants, 88–91
  integration and, 95
  theories of, 89–91
latency stage, of psychosexual develop-
    ment, 430

lateral hypothalamus, 360
LCUs, 469
leadership, in groups, 574–575
learned motivation, 372–380
learning, 124–166
  applications of principles, 156–166
  biological factors in, 154–156
  branching program, 163
  cognitive factor in, 150–151
  computer-assisted, 164
  discrimination in, 133, 143–144, 149–
    150
  hunger and, 361
  to learn, 147
  linear program, 163
  to love, 396
  neurosis, as response, 433
  new viewpoints, 150–156
  observational, 152
  paired-associate, 175–177
  programmed instruction, 161–164
  serial, 177
  social theory of, 151–154
  theorists, 445–446, 503–504
  transfer of, 148–150
  see also classical conditioning; condi-
    tioning; operant conditioning
learning curves, 130
learning set, 149–150
learning theory, in mental illness, 496
lens, of eye, 282
lesbian, 508–510
libido, 429, 431
lie detector, 159
life change units (LCUs), 469
limbic system, 64–65
linguistic relativity hypothesis, 212–214,
    216
logic
  errors, in person perception, 561–562
  in thinking, 219–220
longitudinal method, 22
longitudinal studies, of personality, 449
long-term memory, 179–183, 185–192,
    194, 197–198, 200
love, learning to, 396

manic psychotic, 514–515
manipulation, as motivator, 370–371
marijuana, 400
  and perception, 346–347
maternal drive, 366–367
maturation, 77
measurement
  of attitudes, 578
  of central tendency, 597–598
  of correlation, 605–606
  frequency distributions, 598–602
  of life stress, 469
medical model, in mental illness, 496
meditation, and hypnosis, 343–345
medulla, 58–59, 61
memory
  biological bases, 189–192
  categories, 187–189
  chunking, 180
  coding, 183
  cues, 186, 190
  halographic theory, 190
  hippocampus and, 190
  levels of, 178–189, 316–317
  limbic system, 190

location of, 189–190
  long-term, 179–183, 185–190, 194,
    197–198, 200, 316–317
  photographic, 207
  primary, 178–179
  rehearsal, 182
  repression, 198–200
  retrieval process, 185
  secondary, 179
  sensory store, 179–180, 183, 190–191
  serial reproduction, 184
  short-term, 179–183, 190, 193, 316–317
  storage unit, 190–192
memory trace, 191
  decay of, 193
mental abilities, 238–239
mental deficiency
  genetics and, 40
mental institutions
  halfway houses, 548
  history of, 546–548
  legal plight of patients, 548
  token economies, 548–550
mesomorphy, 424–425
message, in attitude change, 583–585
  discrepancy, 584–585
  two-sided, 585
messenger-RNA, 35
metabolism, 46
metaphor, 206
Method acting, 165
midbrain, 59, 62
Minnesota Multiphasic Personality Inven-
    tory (MMPI), 451–453
mistrust vs. trust, 437
mnemonic device, 186, 188
mob behavior, 571
modeling, in operant conditioning, 137
models
  influence, in observational learning,
    152–154
  organic, in mental illness, 496
mongolism, see Down's syndrome
monochromat, 289
monocular cues, 322–325
moon illusion, 334
moratorium, in identity crisis, 436
morphemes, 214
motivation
  to avoid success, 377–378
  in operant conditioning, 136
  defined, 357–358
  hierarchy, 382–383
  learned, 372–380
  perception affected by, 335–336
  physiological, 359–366
  sex, 365–366
  stimulus, 367–369
  unconscious, 381–382
motor development, 80–83
motor nerves, 55
motor neuron, 51
motor projection areas, 61
movement
  illusory, 327–329
  perception of, 325, 327–329
  real, 327
multiple aptitude batteries, 244
multiple personality, 501
muscular dystrophy, genetics and, 37
myelinated axon fibers, 59–60
myelin sheath, 51, 56

nAch, 375–376
naturalistic observation, 18–19
need for achievement (nAch), 375–376
negative reinforcement, 138–139
negative transfer
    of learning, 148–149
    in psychoanalysis, 530
nerves, 51
    motor, 55
    sensory, 55
    in skin, 302–304
    specific nerve energy doctrine, 279
nervous system, 31, 45, 50–67
    autonomic, see autonomic nervous system
    central, 54–60; see also brain
    divisions of, 54–55
    electrical messages, 45
    and emotion, 392–393
    parts, 50–54
    peripheral, 54–60
neural connections
    ear, 293
    in skin, 302–304
    vision, 284–285
neural impulse, 51, 53
    coded, 278
neural system, development of, 78–79
neuron, 50
neurosis, 497–506
    anxiety, 498–499
    conversion reaction, 501–502
    depression, 504–506
    dissociative, 500–501
    hysteria, 501–502
    individual differences in, 506
    as learned response, 433
    obsessive/compulsive, 502–504
    phobias, 498–499
neurotic behavior
    individual differences and, 506
neurotic depression, 504–506
nonverbal communication, 412–416
nonverbal cues, 414
norepinephrine (noradrenalin), 48, 53–54, 391, 399, 505
normative conflict, 570–572
norms, developmental, for children, 78
NREM sleep, 342–344

obedience, to authority, 569–570
obesity, theories of, 362
objective personality tests, 451–453
object perception, 85–86, 88
observation, in personality testing, 450
observational learning, 152
obsessive/compulsive neurosis, 502–504
Oedipus complex, 155, 430
old age, see aging
olfactory epithelium, 295–296
operant conditioning, 134–150, 535
    behavior chains, 147
    discrimination, 143–144
    extinction, 144–146
    generalization, 143
    methods, 136–137
    reinforcement in, 135–136, 138–143
    shaping in, 146–147
    spontaneous recovery, 144–146
    transfer of learning, 148–150
Operation Head Start, 266–268
opponent-process theory, of vision, 287–290

optic chiasma, 285
optic nerve, 284–285
oral stage, of psychosexual development, 430
organ of Corti, in ear, 292–293
organic amnesia, 200
organic model, in mental illness, 496
organic psychosis, 518–519
otoliths, 302
output process, 316–317
oval window, of ear, 291
ovaries, 47, 49
overtones, in sound, 290–291
ovum, 33, 38
oxytocin, 47

pain centers, in brain
    gate-control theory, 60–61, 305–306
    physiological, 60–61
    psychological, 60–61
    specificity theory, 60
pain, sensation of, 302, 304–306
    acupuncture, 305
    as motivation, 364–365
    theories of, 305–306
paired-associate learning, 175–177
pancreas, 47
paradoxical heat, 304
paranoia, 517
paranoid schizophrenia, 516–517
parasympathetic division, of autonomic
    nervous system, 55–56, 59
parathormone, 46–47
parathyroid glands, 46–47
parenthood, 108
parents, as therapists, 536
partially structured conflict, 570
partial reinforcement, 141
pattern theory of pain, 60
peak experiences, 384
pedophilia, 510
peer groups
    personality development and, 103
perception, 311–350
    altered states of consciousness and, 338–350
    attention and, 312–317
    of brightness, 332–334
    of color, 334–335
    constancy of, 329–335
    cultural differences and, 337–338
    defined, 311
    depth, 84–85, 88
    of distance and depth, 322–327
    and drugs, 345–350
    expectations and, 336
    factors affecting, 335–338
    information-processing model of, 315–317
    through intuition, 432
    of movement, 327–329
    object, 85–86, 88, 329–331
    organization of, 317–322
    perceptual set, 86–87
    person, 560–562
    personality and, 336–337
    selective, 335
    through sensation, 431–432
    of shape, 332
    of size, 329, 332
    whole-part, 86–87
perceptual development, 83–88
perceptual hypothesis, 331

perceptual set, 86–87
performance tests, 248–254
peripheral nervous system, 54–60
personality
    alienated, 436
    assessment of, 448–458
    constitutional theory, 424–425
    cyclothymic, 505
    extraverted, 431
    introverted, 431
    irrational, 431–432
    origin of, 438–439
    psychoanalytic theories of, 425–438
    rational, 431–432
    self theory of, 438–439
    testing, see personality tests
    trait theory of, 439–448
    see also personality development; specific entries
personality development, 96–104
    adulthood in, 106–107
    child, 100–104
    genetic factors in, 447
    infant, 96–99
    interactionism, theory of, 446–448
    psychosexual stages of, 430
    of the self, 439
    see also personality
personality tests
    by interview, 449–450
    measuring values, 453–454
    objective, 451–453
    by observation, 450
    projective, 454–458
    Rorschach Test, 455–457
personal relationships, freeing of, 105–106
personal unconscious, 431
person perception, 560–562
perspective, 323
phallic period, of psychosexual development, 430
phenotype, 33–34
phobias, 155, 498–499
phoneme, 214
phonetics, 214
phrenology, 189, 236
physical changes, aging and, 111–112
physical treatment, 544–546
    drugs, 546
    psychosurgery, 545
    shock, 544–545
physiological motivation, 359–366
    primary drives, 359
physiological pain, 60–61
physiological psychology, 15, 17
Piaget's approach, 91–95
pitch, of sound waves, 290, 293
pituitary gland, 47, 59
place theory, of hearing, 294
pleasant/unpleasant conflict, 406
pleasure principle, 427
polarization, in neurons, 52
polygenic inheritance, 40–41, 260
polygraph tests, 159
pons, 58–59
Porteus Maze, 251
positive reinforcement, 138
positive transfer, 148–149
    in psychoanalysis, 529
power motive, 375
predictive validity, 247
prefrontal lobotomies, 545
prehensile development, 82–83

prejudice, 582
preoperational thought, in stage theory, 92–93
pressure
  adjustment to, 470–471
  sensation, 302, 304
primacy effect, in interference theory, 197–198
primary drives, 359, 433
primary mental abilities, 237–238
primary process thinking, 427
primary reinforcer, 140, 153, 161
proactive inhibition, in interference theory, 194–198
problem solving
  creative, 224–225; see also creativity
  factors affecting, 221–224
  group, 576–577
  insight and, see creativity
  steps in, 220–221
  see also logic, thinking
Profile of Nonverbal Sensitivity (PONS), 414
progestins, 48
projection, as defense mechanism, 479–487
  case history, 484
projective personality tests, 454–458
  Rorschach Test, 455–457
  Thematic Apperception, 457–458
prolactin, 366
proximity, in interpersonal relations, 564–565
psychoanalysis, 13–14, 528–531
psychoanalytic model, in mental illness, 496
psychoanalytic psychology, 13
psychoanalytic theories, of personality, 425–438
psycholinguistics, 214, 217
psychological pain, 60–61
psychological research
  use of animals, 25–26
psychology
  behavioral sciences and, 4–6
  clinical, 16–18
  cognitive, 14
  community, 550–551
  control in, 4–5
  developmental, 15, 17
  educational, 15–18
  environmental, 15, 26
  ethics, 23–24
  existential, 14–15
  experimental, 16, 19
  Gestalt, 12
  goals of, 4–6
  growth of, 6–15
  humanistic, 15
  industrial, 15–16
  methods of, 18–24
  and natural science, 10
  new directions in, 26
  physiological, 15, 17
  to predict behavior, 4–6
  psychoanalytic, 13
  pure vs. applied, 24–25
  scientific, 19
  social, 15, 18
  social relevance of, 24–26
psychophysics, 280
psychophysiological disorders, in neurosis, 502

psychosexual stages, of personality development, 430
psychosis, 513–522
  affective, 514–515
  causes of, 519–522
  depression, 514–515
  involuntary, 515
  mania, 514–515
  organic, 518–519
  schizophrenia, 515–518
psychosomatic illness, 242
  in neurosis, 502
psychosurgery, 65, 67, 545
psychotherapy, 14
  animal, 538
  behavior, 535–539
  foundation for, 14
  group, 539–544
  individual, 528–534
punishment, in operant conditioning, 139–140
pupil, eye, 282
"Pygmalion effect," 269

race differences
  intelligence and, 266–269
RAS, see reticular activating system
RAT, see Remote Associates Test
rational personality, 431–432
rational therapy, 532–534
reaction formation, as defense mechanism, 480–481
reality principle, 427
reality therapy, 534
reasoning, in thinking, 219–220
recall, 175, 201
recency effect, in interference theory, 197–198
receptors, 55
  in skin, 302–304
recessive gene, 33–34
reciprocal inhibition, 537–539
recoding, 316
recognition, 175–176
reconstruction, of memory, 175
redundancy, in perception, 317
reference groups, as attitude source, 580–581
reflex movement, 57
regression, 242
  as defense mechanism, 485–486
rehearsal, for memory, 182
reinforcement, 13, 14
  continuous, 141, 145
  fixed-interval, 141
  fixed-ratio, 142
  in observational learning, 152
  in operant conditioning, 135–137, 140–143
  partial, 141, 145
  primary, 140
  schedules, 141–143, 160
  secondary, 140
  self-, 153
  symbolic, 153
  token economies, 548–550
  variable-interval, 141–142
  variable-ratio, 142–143
reinforcers
  amphetamines, 347
  cocaine, 348–349
relatedness, personality and, 435
relational concept, in thought, 209

relative refractory phase, 52
REM sleep, 342–344
Remote Associates Test (RAT), 259
renin, 363
repression
  as defense mechanism, 480–481
  Freudian, 201
  of memory, 198–200
research, use of animals in, 25–26
response, to stimulus, 11; see also conditioned response
response generalization
  in classical conditioning, 133
  in operant conditioning, 143
restraints, operant conditioning and, 137
retention
  improving, 195
  measuring, 174–178
  see also memory; forgetting
reticular activating system (RAS), 61–64
retina
  neural connections, 284–286
  structure, 283–284
retinal disparity, 326
retrieval
  cueing, 186, 190
  from memory, 185–186
retroactive inhibition, in interference theory, 194, 196–198
retrograde amnesia, 183
reversible figure, in perception, 319
revolutionary conflict, 570–571
reward, in attitude change, 587
rewardingness, in interpersonal relations, 564, 566
ribonucleic acid (RNA), 35, 192
  messenger-RNA, 35
  transfer-RNA, 35
risk-taking, groups and, 572–574
risky shift, 572–574, 576–577
RNA (see ribonucleic acid)
rods, in retina, 283–284
  adaptation, 286
  neural connections, 284–285
role confusion, 104
  vs. identity, 436–437
rootedness, personality and, 435
rooting behavior, 74
Rorschach Test, 455–457
round window, of ear, 291

saccule, 301–302
sado-masochism, 510
SAT, see Scholastic Aptitude Test
savings, in retention, 175–178
scales, of measurement, 595–597
schemata, in cognitive development, 92
schizophrenia, 36, 54, 515–518
  catatonic, 516
  childhood, 518
  and genetics, 42–43
  hebephrenic, 516
  paranoid, 516–517
  simple, 516
  social isolation and, 516
scientific psychology, 19
secondary drives, 433
secondary memory, 179
secondary process thinking, 428
secondary reinforcement, 140, 153
secondary traits, 442
selective perception, 335
self-actualization, as motivator, 382–384

self-actualizing person, characteristics of, 383
self-reinforcement, in operant conditioning, 153
self theory, of personality development, 438–439
semantic memory, 177
semantics, 216
semicircular canals, 301
sensation
    general characteristics, 278–279
    measurements of, 279
    nature of, 278–281
    perception through, 431–432
    sensory adaptation, 281; see also adaptation
    specific nerve energy doctrine, 279
    see also perception; specific sensations
senses
    body, 299–302
    chemical, 295–299
    skin, 302–306
    see also specific senses
sensory adaptation, 281; see also adaptation
sensory deprivation, 339–340
sensory gating, 314–315
sensory messages, 61
sensory-motor stage, of cognitive development, 91–93
sensory nerves, 55
sensory neuron, 51
sensory projection areas, of cerebral cortex, 61
sensory store, in memory, 179–180, 183, 190–191
Sequin Form Board, 251
serial learning, 177
serial recall, 175
serial reproduction, 184
serotonin, 53
set, in problem solving, 221–223
sex
    cells, 32–33
    cerebral cortex and, 365
    motivation and, 365–366
sex differences, intelligence and, 270
sexual characteristics
    development of, 78–79
    genetics and, 36–37
sexual deviation, 507–510
shadowing, in perception, 324
shame vs. autonomy, 437
short-term memory, 179–183, 190, 193
signs, in language, 211–212
similarity
    of interests, in interpersonal relations, 564–566
    in perception, 321
simple schizophrenia, 515–518
singular concepts, in thought, 211
situationism, in personality development vs. trait theory, 444–446
Sixteen Personality Factor Questionnaire (16 PF), 443
Skinner box, 13, 135–138, 146, 162, 392
skin senses, 302–306
sleep
    and dreaming, 340–343, 363–364
    REM, 342–344
    stages of, 341–343
smell, 295–296
    stereochemical theory of odor, 297

social comparison, theory of, 567
social conflict, 570–572
social facilitation, performance and, 572
social implications, of genetics, 37–40
social isolation, schizophrenia and, 516
social learning theory, 151–154
social motives, 374–375
social psychology, 15–17, 559; see also attitudes; group dynamics; interpersonal relations
Social Readjustment Rating Scale (SRRS), 469
social self, in personality development, 107
sociopaths, 512–513
somatotonia, 424–425
somatotrophic hormone (STH), 47
somnambulism, 501
sound waves, 290–293
    amplitude, 290
    decibels, 290
    frequency, 290
    loudness, 290, 293
    overtones, 290–291
    pitch, 290, 293
    timbre, 291, 293
source, in attitude change
    credibility, 583
    intentions of, 584
    prestige of, 583
source traits, 443
space, personal, 588
    crowding, 588
Spearman's g factor theory, 237
special aptitude tests, 244
specific hungers, 360–361
specificity theory, of pain, 60, 305–306
speech, see language
sperm, 33, 38, 44
spinal cord, 56–58
split-half reliability, 246
spontaneous recovery
    in classical conditioning, 129–130
    in operant conditioning, 144–146
S-R learning theory, 13–14, 156
stagnation
    vs. generativity, 438
    in personality development, 106
standardization, of tests, 247
Stanford Achievement Test, 244
Stanford-Binet Scales, 247–248
statistical methods
    of measurement, 595–606
    using, to predict, 606–608
    see also tests
stereochemical theory of odor, 297
stereoscopic vision, 326
stereotyping, 561
STH, see somatotrophic hormone
stimulus
    in motivation, 367–371
    -seeking behavior, 367
    of work, 368
stimulus generalization
    in classical conditioning, 132–133
    in operant conditioning, 143
stimulus motivation, 367–371
stimulus-response formula, 11, 13
stimulus-response (S-R) theory, 433
stimulus-seeking behavior, 367
stirrup, in ear, 291
stress
    adjustment to, 466–470
    measuring, in life, 469

    see also anxiety; frustration
structuralism, 6–9, 11–12
structured interview, 449–450
stylistic traits, 442
subject, in experimental method, 20–21
sublimation
    case history, 483
    as defense mechanism, 482
    of instinct, 429
sucking, infant, 74
success, avoiding, 377–378
"successful" aging, 113–114
successive approximation method, in operant conditioning, 146–147
superego, 426–430
superiority drive, 432–434
superposition, in perception, 323
syllogism, 220
symbolic reinforcement, in operant conditioning, 153
symbolic representation, 95–96
sympathetic division, of autonomic nervous system, 55–56, 59
synapse, 53–54
synaptic vesicles, 53–54
synesthesia, 206
syntax, 214, 216
syphilis, 518

talking, see language
"talking cure," 14
taste, 296–299
TAT, see Thematic Apperception Test
temperature sensation, 302, 304
tests
    achievement, 244–245
    alternate forms, 245
    aptitude, 244–245
    Binet-Simon Scale, 250–252, 255–258
    Christensen-Guilford, 259
    Culture-Fair Intelligence, 256–258
    Digit Span Test, 243
    Digit Symbol Test, 243
    Gesell Developmental Studies, 253
    Goodenough Draw-A-Person, 257–258
    group, 258–260
    Infant Intelligence Scale, 253
    IQ, see intelligence quotient
    performance, 248–254
    personality, see personality tests
    Porteus Maze, 251
    reliability of, 245–246
    Remote Associates Test (RAT), 259
    retest reliability, 245
    School and College Ability Tests, 258
    Sequin Form Board, 251
    Social Readjustment Rating Scale (SRRS), 469
    standardized, 247
    Stanford Achievement Test, 244
    Stanford-Binet Scales, 247–248
    Torrance, of Creative Thinking, 259
    validity of, 246–247
    vocabulary, 243
    Wechsler Adult Intelligence Scale (WAIS), 254–256
    word-naming, 243
testes, 47
testosterone, 49, 365
texture gradient, in perception, 323
thalamus, 59, 64
Thematic Apperception Test (TAT), 376, 457–458, 578

theory
    of attribution, 562–564
    of social comparison, 567
therapists, parents as, 536
therapy, see behavior therapy; group
        therapy; psychotherapy
thinking
    adolescent, 94
    associative, 225–231
    autistic, 227
    centering, 92
    changes in old age, 112–113
    concepts and, 206, 209–211
    contents of, 238–239
    convergent, 240–241
    directed, 219–225
    divergent, 240–241
    images and, 206–209
    irreversible, 92–93
    language and, 206, 211–219
    logic and, 219–220
    by machines, 222
    operations of, 238–239
    preoperational, 92–93
    problem-solving, see problem solving
    products of, 238–239
    reasoning and, 219–220
    representational, in animals, 208
    units of, 206–219
    see also cognitive development
thirst, 361–363
Thurstone's Primary Mental Abilities
        theory, 237–238, 244
thyroid gland, 46
thyrotropic hormone (TTH), 47
thyroxin, 46
timbre, of sound, 291, 293
"tip-of-the-tongue" phenomenon (TOT),
        187
TM, see transcendental meditation
token economies, 160–161, 548–550
Torrance Test of Creative Thinking, 259
TOT, see "tip-of-the-tongue" phenomenon
trace decay theory of forgetting, 193
traits
    cardinal, 442
    central, 442
    classification of, 441–442
    common, 442
    defined, 440–441
    development of, 441–442
    dynamic, 442
    heritability, 41–43
    individual, 442

measurement of, 442–443
    secondary, 442
    source, 443
    stylistic, 442
tranquilizers, 546
transactional analysis, 543
transcendence, personality and, 435
transcendental meditation (TM), 345
transduction, 278
transfer of learning, 148–150
    negative, 148–149
    positive, 148–149
transfer-RNA, 35
traveling wave theory, of hearing, 294
trial and error, in operant conditioning,
        136
trichromatic theory, of vision, 287–289
trichromatism, 288–289
trust vs. mistrust, 437
TTH, see thyrotropic hormone
Turner's syndrome, 39

unconditioned response (UR), 125–127,
        129, 133
    and conditioned response (CR), 126–
        127, 129–130, 133–134
unconditioned stimulus (US), 125–126,
        129, 131, 133
    and conditioned stimulus (CS), 126–127,
        129, 131, 133
unconscious
    archetypes, of collective, 431
    collective, 431
    personal, 431
unconscious motivation, 381–382
unconventional sex objects, 508
unmyelinated axons, 59
unpleasant emotions, 406
unstructured conflict, 570
unstructured interview, 449–450
UR, see unconditioned response
urban environment, 588–590
US, see unconditioned stimulus
utricle, 301–302

validity test, 246–247
values
    humanizing of, 106
    measuring, 453–454
variable-interval schedule, of reinforce-
        ment, 141–142
variable-ratio schedule, of reinforcement,
        142–143
variables
    dependent, 20–21

independent, 20–21
variation, in measurement, 602–605
vasopressin, 47
verbal communication, 411–412
verbal instruction, in operant conditioning,
        137
vestibular organ, 301
vestibular sacs, 301–302
vestibular sense, 299–302
violence, physiology of, 393
viscerotonia, 424–425
visible light, 281
vision, 281–290
    adaptation, 286
    color, see color vision
    neural connections, 284–285
    stereoscopic, 326
    see also eye; specific parts of eye
visual acuity, 283
visual discrimination, 83–84
volley principle, of hearing, 294–295
voluntary responses, in operant condition-
        ing, 156
voyeurism, 510

WAIS, see Wechsler Adult Intelligence
        Scale
warmth sensation, see temperature sensa-
        tion
Wechsler Adult Intelligence Scale, 254–
        256, 258
weightlessness, effects of, 301
wheel, as communication pattern, 575–576
white matter
    in cerebral cortex, 59–60
    in spinal cord, 56–58
whole-part perception, 86–87
withdrawal, as direct coping, 478
work
    cycle, 109–111
    as stimulus motive, 368

X chromosome, 36–37
    genetic abnormalities, 39–40
XY genetic makeup, 49

Y chromosome, 36–37
    and criminality, 40
Yerkes-Dodson law, of emotion, 408–409
Y-shape, as communication pattern, 575–
        576

Zeigarnik effect, 181
zygote, 33–34

150
M875p

Please remember that this is a library book,
and that it belongs only temporarily to each
person who uses it. Be considerate. Do
not write in this, or any, library book.

WITHDRAWN